"I Could Not Speak My Heart"

"I Could Not Speak My Heart"

Education and Social Justice for Gay and Lesbian Youth

Edited by James McNinch and Mary Cronin

2004

UNIVERSITY OF
REGINA

CANADIAN PLAINS
RESEARCH CENTER

Canadian Plains Research Center
University of Regina
Regina, Saskatchewan S4S 0A2
Canada
Tel: (306) 585-4758
Fax: (306) 585-4699
e-mail: canadian.plains@uregina.ca
http://www.cprc.uregina.ca

National Library of Canada Cataloguing in Publication Data
I could not speak my heart : education and social justice for gay and lesbian youth / edited by James McNinch and Mary Cronin.

(University of Regina publications ; 12)
Includes bibliographical references and index.
ISBN 0-88977-178-2

1. Gay youth—Prairie Provinces. 2. Bisexual youth—Prairie Provinces. 3. Transsexual youth—Prairie Provinces. 4. Homophobia—Prairie Provinces. 5. Homosexuality and education—Prairie Provinces. I. McNinch, James, 1947– II. Cronin, Mary III. University of Regina. Canadian Plains Research Center IV. Series.

HQ76.3.C3I2 2004   306.76'6'09712   C2004-902526-0

Printed and bound in Canada by: Houghton Boston, Saskatoon
Cover image courtesy Michael W. Hamann
Cover design by Brian Danchuk, Regina
Index prepared by Patricia Furdek (www.userfriendlyindexes.com)

We acknowledge the financial support of the Government of Canada through the Book Publishing Industry Development Program (BPIDP) for our publishing activities. Further funding support for this project was provided by the President's Fund, the Faculty of Education, the Faculty of Social Work, and the Humanities Research Institute, all at the University of Regina.

Contents

Preface
David L. McIntyre vii

Introduction
Mary Cronin and James McNinch ix

Part I: Hearing the Voices

Chapter 1: This Little Light of Mine: Growing Up Gay in the Lutheran Church
Michael W. Hamann 3

Chapter 2: Safe in My Heart: Found Poetry as Narrative Inquiry
Kristopher Wells 7

Chapter 3: Growing Up Outside the Gender Construct
Darrin Hagen 19

Chapter 4: Gay and Out in Secondary School: One Youth's Story
John Guiney Yallop 29

Chapter 5: A Mother's Story: Critical Consciousness, Conscience and Homophobia
Marilyn Totten 43

Chapter 6: Everyday Acts of Survival and Unorganized Resistance: Gay, Lesbian and
Bisexual Youth Respond to Oppression
Cheryl Dobinson 49

Chapter 7: Gender Ambiguity and Heteronormativity: The Case of Two Alberta Youth
Gloria Filax and Debra Shogan 81

Part II: Understanding the Context

Chapter 8: The Regulation of First Nations Sexuality
Martin Cannon 95

Chapter 9: Activism = Public Education: The History of Public Discourses of
Homosexuality in Saskatchewan, 1971–93
Valerie J. Korinek 109

Chapter 10: Queer Youth and Strange Representations in the Province
of the "Severely Normal": Alberta in the 1990s
Gloria Filax 139

Chapter 11: Christian Opposition to Homosexuality
Donald Cochrane 163

Chapter 12: A Queer Reading of the Swift Current Hockey Scandal Through
Representations of Family Dysfunction and Youth Innocence
Debra Shogan 181

Chapter 13: Teaching Tolerance, Mirroring Diversity, Understanding Difference:
The Effect and Implications of the Chamberlain Case
Bruce MacDougall and Paul T. Clarke 193

Part III: Implications for Practice

Chapter 14: Playing by the Rules: Building a Rationale to Offer a Course on Schooling
   and Sexual Identities in a Faculty of Education
   James McNinch 223

Chapter 15: Disrupting Binaries of Self and Other: Anti-homophobic Pedagogies
   for Student Teachers
   Carol Schick 243

Chapter 16: Performing and Culture: Homophobia in Canadian Theatre
   Wes D. Pearce 255

Chapter 17: Operation "Special": Interrogating the Queer Production of Everyday
   Myths in Special Education
   Scott Anthony Thompson 273

Chapter 18: Engaging Sex-and-Gender Differences: Educational and Cultural Change
   Initiatives in Alberta
   André P. Grace and Kristopher Wells 289

Chapter 19: From Naïveté to Advocacy: Student-Teachers Reflect on a Course
   on Schooling and Sexual Identities
   James McNinch 309

Index 333

Contributors 361

Acknowledgements 365

Preface

David L. McIntyre

I T IS WITH GREAT PLEASURE THAT I LEND THE TITLE OF one of my compositions to be the title of this important and timely book. "I Did Not Speak My Heart" is the third song in Watershed Stories I. It comes directly after "Taunts," a song which represents the shutting-down response to the cruelty so many of us experience in our school years. The dark period which follows may last a few years or the better part of a lifetime. "I could not speak my heart ... afraid that knowing me, you'd turn away..."

I grew up in a home and church environment where transparency was encouraged. I came to value the healthy aspects of confession, of being honest about one's strengths, and accountable for one's weaknesses. Therefore it was with increasing alarm and fear that I gradually discovered the truth about my own minority sexual orientation, a "weakness" I felt I would never be able to disclose. I could never envision speaking my heart about that. Not in the community I had been nurtured in. As a result a great sadness grew in me. It was not until my early 40s that circumstances allowed, prodded me towards the disclosure which quite literally saved my life.

Reclaiming joy, and the lightness of a transparent life has become something of a mission for me. A huge part of that is realized in my work as artistic director of the Prairie Pride Chorus, the gay, lesbian, bisexual and transgendered choir in Regina. The publication of this book demonstrates just how much has changed since I grew up. I would suggest that, on a public level, this volume will help others to reclaim the joy of a transparent life that they deserve.

I applaud the appearance of *"I Could Not Speak My Heart": Education and Social Justice for Gay and Lesbian Youth*. It is a book that uncovers experience, reveals insights, fosters understanding and spreads hope that gay and lesbian youth can indeed be transparent, and live joyfully and without fear.

"Herein [we] speak [our] hearts."

I did not speak my heart

I did not speak my heart,
I passed in silence, relentless silence,
And watched my spirit ebb,
And cease to flow.

I could not speak my heart,
Alone and fearful, in isolation,
Afraid that knowing me,
You'd turn a way.

I would not speak my heart,
The inner striving, relentless striving,
To live the truth,
Yet not give truth a voice.

Herein I speak my heart.

David L. McIntyre
© 2002

Introduction

Mary Cronin & James McNinch

Only in an open, nonjudgemental space can we acknowledge what we are feeling.
Only in an open space where we're not all caught up in our own version of reality
can we see and hear and feel what others really are, which allows us to be with
them and communicate with them properly.

Pema Chodron, 2001 (p. 78)

This book is the result of a co-operative undertaking between two people who teach in the Faculty of Education at the University of Regina. Mary, who is not a student of Gay and Lesbian Studies or Queer Theory, was moved, by the many stories of struggles for recognition told her by gay and lesbian students and friends, to help create a space for public dialogue on the mistreatment of gay, lesbian, bisexual and transgendered youth (GLBT) and the prejudice directed against them.[1] Initiating an edited book with this end in view seemed like an obvious first step for two colleagues concerned with equity and social justice in education. James, the co-editor, has been an enthusiastic colleague in the venture from start to finish; in working together on this book the two of them have formed a straight-gay partnership. Mary is straight and lives with her husband Doug, James is gay and lives with his partner Michael. And apart from the obvious difference of their respective sexual orientations both couples live remarkably similar lives! This mix of sexual orientation is reflected in the contributors as well.

In a small but significant way our main hope in bringing out this collection is for a "better," i.e., a more caring and understanding, world in which Canadian gay and lesbian youth can grow up with the same expectations of all young people, not feeling ashamed of who they find themselves to be, and being fully respected as human beings. This ideal, of course, cannot be achieved as long as homophobic attitudes remain socially acceptable in Canada. Homophobia is a strong and pernicious force that causes great harm. It is embodied in feelings that range from unease to fear to outright disgust. It crosses generational, cultural and socio-economic lines affecting the lives of gay and lesbian youth at almost every turn.

Despite considerable progress in recent years, the struggle for equity and social justice for gay and lesbian youth is far from over. The most recent visit of the Dalai Lama to Canada in May 2004 has helped to focus our attention on the need for greater compassion in the world and on the importance of the education of the heart. A compassionate heart comes from being able to nurture a deeper understanding of the lives and suffering of others by listening to them and hearing them without the filter of prejudice. Understanding of the causes of injustice, including our own role in it, is necessary for change to occur through "compassionate social action" (Dalai Lama, 2000).

Change occurs because people change. Although certain changes to laws and professional training and practice have improved life somewhat for gay youth, there has been almost no impact on school curricula or practice, particularly on the prairies. Significant gains will not be achieved until there is a transformation in the hearts and minds of individual Canadians. That change occurs "at the margins," and not at the centre or from "on high," was the conviction of Reverend Ted Scott, former head of the Anglican Church in Canada who recently died in a tragic car accident. Scott believed that it is oppressed people themselves and those who band together with them in common cause who force institutional change (McCullum, 2004; Valpy, 2004). Only as more Canadians become aware of their own overt or latent homophobia, and the suffering caused by it, will they understand the urgency of taking action to help GLBT youth live open and fulfilled lives.

The aspirations of gay youth are reasonable: like the majority of young people, they simply want to be part of the accepted life of their families, schools, churches and communities. GLBT youth, generally speaking, do not want to draw attention to themselves. They would rather be accepted and be included as a "normal" part of the social environment. It, therefore, behooves us as parents, and professionals involved in helping others, to broaden our worldview to include gay youth, not as the exception that needs special consideration, but simply as part of the normal range of young people that we should expect to encounter. We trust that educators in many fields might find this collection useful so that their students preparing for professions in education, social work, human justice, and health and environmental and cultural studies will better understand the need to combat homophobia, and be more willing to embrace and celebrate sexual differences.

The title of this collection, "I Could Not Speak My Heart," is from an original cycle of songs entitled "Watershed Stories," by Regina composer David McIntyre. The cycle is based on the lives and experiences of gay and lesbian members of the city of Regina's Prairie Pride Chorus. A watershed, normally a line of separation between waters flowing in different directions, can also be regarded as a turning point. Similar to McIntyre's composition, we, the editors of this collection, see it as a turning: a significant watershed in the development of a better understanding of queer issues in Canadian society and more compassionate education for social justice for gay and lesbian youth. The anthology documents the pain and misunderstanding that GLBT youth typically confront as well as the progress being made.

Readers will find much diversity in this collection of 19 articles: difference in genres including autobiography, testament, memoir, and found poetry as well as the more traditional personal and analytic essays; and intellectual perspectives including human rights, social reform and human justice, feminist, liberationist, critical and queer theories. Divided into three parts, this collection contributes to theory and practice in cultural studies. Part I, "Hearing the Voices," invites us to read and hear directly the experiences of gays and lesbians (including the mother of a young lesbian) in Canadian society. Part II, "Understanding the Context," contains articles which explore historical, political, religious, judicial, journalistic, and social constructs and contexts in which homosexuality has been misrepresented and misunderstood. In the articles that form Part III, "Implications for Practice," educators share their research and explorations of, and teaching students about, homophobia and heterosexism.

Part I: Hearing the Voices

In Chapter 1, "Growing Up Gay in the Lutheran Church," Michael Hamann helps the reader to appreciate the damage that exclusion, through the construction of homosexuality as a sin, can do. Originally spoken and sung to a convention of Saskatchewan Lutherans in 2001, the chapter begins with memories of hymns sung joyously in the car with his family on the way to church. This soon dissolves into a growing sense of guilt and fear when he hears from the pulpit that his difference, that is, his sexual orientation, is evil. Closeted and "damned," the author's identity is conflicted, but running away from the authority of the church only compounds the problem of his relationship with his family. This story is representative of the lives of many queer youth from small towns on the prairies.

In Chapter 2, Kris Wells investigates the experiences of queer youth as they struggle to become visible and vocal in their schools, families, and communities. "Safe in My Heart" uses found poetry as a narrative strategy to explore important and difficult questions and themes. Found poetry takes the words of others and edits them into "living biographies." These "poems" answer such questions as: What is it like for queer youth who are in the process of coming out? How are adult, community, family, and public education spaces sites of structural, symbolic, and actual violence towards queer youth? What do queer youth do to survive (and sometimes even thrive in) this marginalization? Where to queer youth turn to find support and acceptance as they come out and come to terms with their marginalized identities?

For Chapter 3, Darrin Hagen, well known writer, drag queen, and community activist from Edmonton, has contributed two connected pieces—part memoir, part testimonial—entitled "Growing Up Outside the Gender Construct." The narratives of "The Cult of Masculinity" and "Why Do You Talk Like a Girl?" switch from the past to the present to follow the chain of fear and humiliation that many queer youth have to break if they are to take their rightfully proud place in Canadian society: "In my family, 'different' became the word that was whispered whenever I was referred to... [but] 'Listen up guys: the man they want you to be: doesn't exist. He has to be created'."

In Chapter 4, "Gay and Out in Secondary School," John Guiney Yallop relates the story of a gay secondary school student and what it took for him to come out of the closet. The chapter documents the various stages of this journey and the impact of home, school and peers on the formation of the identity of one individual. This narrative enquiry will encourage heterosexual and homosexual readers alike to make comparisons and contrasts to their own emerging sexual and gendered identity.

In Chapter 5, Marilyn Totten, a secondary school English teacher and guidance counselor, tells "A Mother's Story" where growing critical consciousness provides insights into her own homophobia after her daughter tells her of being attracted to members of the same sex. From this honest and engaging reflection, anyone involved in education or in the public limelight will understand why they need to "out themselves" as allies of GLBT people in order to confront internal and external sources of homophobia and heterosexism.

"Everyday Acts of Survival and Unorganized Resistance" is the title of Chapter 6 by Cheryl Dobinson. First Dobinson explains the nature of oppression and domination that queer youth are subject to. Then she explores the range of strategies, from survival to resistance, that queer youth use in their everyday lives. This chapter is based on autobiographical narratives and personal knowledge of the experiences of GLBT youth in Alberta and Ontario where Dobson was a peer support at the Lesbian Gay Bi Youth Line.

In the final chapter of this first section, "Gender Ambiguity and Hetero-normativity," Gloria Filax and Debra Shogan point out that it should come as no surprise that psychological notions of gender normalcy and gender deviance have permeated educational discourse and practice since education emerged alongside psychiatry and psychology as one of the human sciences in the latter part of the 19th century. Maturation theory and education theory are heavily implicated in the gender normalization of children and youth. Listening to the voices of two queerly gendered youth, who happen to be Albertans of Aboriginal ancestry, this chapter posits a new definition of normal beyond the binaries of the merely masculine or feminine.

Part II: Understanding the Context

The ancestry of the two queer youth in the previous chapter offers an interesting segue to the second section of the book. Filax and Shogan suggest that the Aboriginal ancestry of the youth does not play a role in the perceptions and constructions of their gendered identity. Martin Cannon argues in Chapter 8, "The Regulation of First Nations Sexuality," that race, gender, and sexuality are not separate categories of experience and analysis, but rather "dynamic sets of social constructions which, as they interconnect, impact upon individuals and their (re)productive activities in distinctive, historically specific ways." Cannon shows that a broad range of gender and erotic relationships existed among Aboriginal populations at the time of first contact with Europeans, but that it is problematic to impose contemporary constructs such as "gay and "lesbian" on historic First Nations sexuality. In the second part of this chapter Cannon documents how racism, sexism, and heterosexism worked together through the Indian Act to legislate gendered roles and identities for First Nations peoples. Cannon gives us much to think about the intersections of class, sexuality, racism, and patriarchy in historical and contemporary cultures.

Chapter 9, "Activism = Public Education," by Valerie Korinek, provides a useful and insightful historical overview of the public discourses of homosexuality in Saskatchewan between 1971 and 1993. This article explains what caused the 20-year delay between the first call by the Saskatchewan Human Rights Commission to extend basic rights protection to gays and lesbians and the passing of such legislation in 1993. Using the framework of human-rights activism, Korinek demonstrates the importance of gay and lesbian activists and their public education campaigns—both with elected government officials and with the general public: "emphasizing the routine discrimination that could be meted out, [was] fundamental to changing provincial perceptions of homosexuality."

Chapter 10 looks to Saskatchewan's neighbour, Alberta, for an analysis of a notorious media representation of homosexuality. "Queer Youth and Strange Representations in the Province of the 'Severely Normal'" by Gloria Filax examines the homophobic agenda in the 1990s of the newsmagazine, *Alberta Report*. "Severely normal" was a phrase used by the premier, Ralph Klein, to describe fundamental Christian Albertans. "While curriculum, pedagogy, policy, and practice related to issues for queer and questioning youth were mostly absent in Alberta schools, the *Alberta Report*, with its [obsession with] 'homosexuality' was available in schools and often used as a teaching tool." Filax vividly proves how "paying attention to the *Alberta Report* provides a unique understanding of both mainstream and queer Alberta culture and politics during this time."

In Chapter 11 Donald Cochrane looks behind media rhetoric to examine the nature and logic of the "Christian Opposition to Homosexuality." As he says, "Organized religion continues to be a powerful factor in society's evaluation of behaviour... In Canada, religious institutions remain the one major social force that openly supports discrimination against gay and lesbian citizens." Cochrane discusses the basic tenets of religious opposition to homosexuality, scriptural and theological bases for moral disapproval, the constructs of sexual orientation as a "choice" and as a "lifestyle," and concludes by asking: "What can account for the vehemence of the religious right in condemning homosexuality?" Readers are encouraged to answer this question from their own background and understanding of Christianity.

In Chapter 12, "A Queer Reading of the Swift Current Hockey Scandal," Debra Shogan takes us into the bungalows and ice-rinks of the Canadian plains to reveal how the popular media covered the scandal of Graham James, former coach of the Swift Current Broncos Junior Hockey Team. Shogan's analysis highlights the media's reliance on dominant cultural stories about sexual abuse and the presumed innocence of children and youth. Shogan then uses her own experiences as a youth growing up in Swift Current to do a "queer" reading of the constructs of family and innocence. The value of such a "disruptive" reading is that it helps us understand that sexual orientation and sexual behaviour are not just issues of personal identity; they are embedded in the very heart of our cultural understanding of who we think we are as a people and as a society.

Chapter 13, "Teaching Tolerance, Mirroring Diversity, Understanding Difference," shifts the discussion of sexual orientation into the courtroom where adversarial legal battles ensued following what the media called the "Surrey Book Banning Case." James Chamberlain, a primary teacher in British Columbia, used books in his classroom which depicted children in same-sex families, which the Surrey School Board attempted to prevent. Bruce MacDougall and Paul Clarke scrutinize what they regard as "one of the most important cases on educational administration." The authors conclude that, while courts are designed to be reactive and educators' roles are proactive, "it is important to remember that the law and education are normative forces ... [and] both of these social institutions help shape and mould human conduct. Each is concerned with inculcating values and norms, which govern human behaviour."

Part III: Implications for Practice

The third section begins with Chapter 14, "Playing by the Rules: Building a Rationale to Offer a Course on Schooling and Sexual Identities in a Faculty of Education." Explaining why such a course is necessary in, as well as congruent with, existing teacher education objectives, this chapter also documents the changing identity of the author, James McNinch, as an advocate for curricular change. The rationale for the course appeals to several foundational assumptions found in most teacher education programs: a largely feminist-driven concern for equity and social justice and small "l" liberalism reflected in the concepts of ethics, citizenship, and an ideology of inclusiveness. Further, it is suggested that these foundational arguments contribute effectively to the construction of the identity of teachers and teacher educators on the basis of notions of authenticity and integrity.

Carol Schick, in Chapter 15, describes her approach to teaching about the construction of oppression in education, particularly with respect to homophobia. "Disrupting Binaries of Self and Other: Anti-homophobic Pedagogies for Student Teachers" offers a thoughtful examination of the role and power of the teacher in the classroom. Schick herself explains that her discourse with students comes directly from how she is positioned with respect to GLBT issues, as a white, straight woman, as well as from her stand as a feminist and anti-racist educator. Challenging student teachers to come to terms with the roles they might play in unwittingly enforcing heteronormativity in schools, she invites them to consider how they might instead become the allies of all students whose schooling is diminished and compromised by homophobia.

First as a student in university drama departments and now as a theatre designer and a university educator himself, Wes Pearce in Chapter 16, "Performing and Culture: Homophobia in Canadian Theatre," challenges stereotypes about the world of theatre as either a sanctuary and safe haven for gay men or a dumping ground for deviants. This chapter examines the subtle and not-so-subtle homophobia that exists in the world of theatre. Citing many of his colleagues across Canada, Pearce critiques theatre as a place of art, as a form of community, and as an academic experience. Pearce explains why the received canon of the theatrical repertoire needs revision, as does the curriculum of theatre schools, if only so that heterosexual and homosexual youth in schools, "in or out," can come to better know who they really are.

S. Anthony Thompson's field of expertise is "special" education and "special" needs. Chapter 17, "Especially Queer Myths in Special Education," "que(e)ries" the institutional spaces where ableism and heternormativity conspire to produce certain kinds of "acceptable" students with "acceptable" special needs. This chapter is based on research into the identity of Canadian queer men with disabilities and their educators and caregivers. Insights about what we regard as "normal" behaviour and identity across institutions and communities come from the fictive myths, Thompson argues, that are constructed around disability. When homosexuality is regarded in itself as a disability, and intersects with other disabling identities, we are confronted by harsh and sometimes ugly truths of denial, repression, exploitation, and invalidation that affect us all.

In Chapter 18, "Engaging Sex-and-Gender Differences," André Grace and Kris Wells discuss community and university initiatives in Edmonton that profile queer issues of equity, social justice, safety, and inclusion in education and the larger culture. These initiatives are seen as cultural practices that they use to transgress spaces where queer persons have historically been dismissed, defiled, and silenced. Four initiatives are discussed: Diversity Conferences of Alberta, Youth Understanding Youth, the Alberta Teachers' Association's Safe and Caring Schools Project, and a University of Alberta project called AGAPE. In these diverse spaces, Grace and Wells emphasized the importance of "seeing queer, knowing queer" in order to disrupt cultural dynamics where ignorance dominoes into fear, and fear dominoes into symbolic and real violence against queer persons in schools and in the community. The lessons learned from these projects will inform and motivate educators across the country.

The primary purpose of Chapter 19, the last chapter of the book, "From Naïveté to Advocacy: Student-Teachers Reflect on a Course on Schooling and Sexual Identities," is to share the feelings and thoughts of pre-service teachers engaged in the course on schooling and sexual identities (discussed earlier in Chapter 14) when it was first offered in 2003. The secondary purpose is a form of pedagogical enquiry into the author's own teaching practice and assessment of student learning. James McNinch tracks his students as they move from naïveté, ignorance and misconceptions, through sensitivity, awareness, and apprehension and, finally, to a sense of advocacy and activism. The chapter concludes with several examples of lesson plans proposed by the students that show how sexual difference can be included in today's classrooms at all levels.

Society and culture may be viewed as a series of interconnected "texts" that members of a culture learn how to read and interpret; at the same time, these "texts" give individuals a "read" or "take" on themselves and an account of how they are valued. In a similar fashion, curriculum theory represents materials used in classrooms as "windows and mirrors" that reflect images of who they are back to children and youth; these materials, however, may also open up vistas to the wider world for students. It is our intention, as editors of this collection, to help create such new spaces for interpretation and reflection. We would like to thank all the contributors to this book and particularly commend Brian Mlazgar, Publications Coordinator at the Canadian Plains Research Center, for championing the publication of this volume and guiding it through the many stages of production.

By continuing to "break the silence" on the complex issues of inequity faced by GLBT youth and their struggles with opposition to sexual difference, this collection will break the homophobic cycle of "knowing by not knowing" referred to by Eve Sedgewick and other queer theorists. This timely collection of Western Canadian writing on queer theory, educational practice, and the voices of gay and lesbian youth themselves, will contribute to a healthier, safer, and more open environment where sexual differences can be understood, appreciated, and celebrated as part of truly inclusive education. We, the editors of this book, want to situate it along the watershed of change helping readers to come to terms with the past and pointing them in the direction of a more "straight" forward future. As the following concluding quotation illustrates, such a turning point is possible:

> *The bishops who resisted every new idea were overtly negative about this subject. I did not want to be identified with that negativity and yet I was not ready either intellectually or emotionally to embrace homosexuality as anything other than an aberration, a distortion of normal behavior, or perhaps even a mental illness... I knew that I had work to do and that the ancient prejudices of my background would have to be examined... Then I focused on the one prejudice still considered socially acceptable, namely, the prejudice against homosexual people. Examining it, I made simple points: No one chooses their sexual orientation; gay and lesbian people are not strangers from a distant planet, but our sons and daughters, our brothers and sisters, our aunts and uncles, our friends and neighbors.*

John Spong, 2000 (pp. 279, 280, 335)

Note

1. Like the naming of Aboriginal peoples, the changing nomenclature of gendered and sexual difference offers insight into the movement for self-representation across several generations of sexual minorities. The word "homosexual" is still narrowly accurate but tainted for some by its medical and judicial misuse during the 1950s and 1960s. Separate categories for gays and lesbians left bisexuals calling for equal representation. The rather clumsy acronym LGB (or BGL or GLB depending on those using the initials) soon grew a "T" to include transsexual and transgendered individuals who were marginalized by not being identified in the acronym. Another "T" has more recently been added to ensure that the Aboriginal concept of two-spiritedness is included, although not all First Peoples use this phrase to identify sexual difference. Since the 1990s the word "queer" has been reclaimed to celebrate difference, to critique so-called normality, and to embrace sexual minority differences. Social conservatives continue to use the word "gay" to mean insidious or unnatural, as in any reference to a "gay" agenda or a "gay" lifestyle. Authors in this anthology represent the fluidity inherent in a constructed, and often highly contested, field of study.

References

Chodron, P. 2000. *When Things Fall Apart: Heart Advice for Difficult Times*. Boston: Shambala.

The Dalai Lama, 2001. *An Open Heart: Practicing Compassion in Everyday Life*. New York: Little Brown.

McCullum, H. 2004. *Radical Compassion: The Life and Times of Archbishop Ted Scott, Tenth Primate of the Anglican Church*. Toronto: ABC Publishing.

Sedgwick, E. 1990. *Epistemology of the Closet*. Berkeley, CA: University of California Press.

Spong, J.S. 2000. *Here I Stand: My Struggle for a Christianity of Integrity, Love, and Equity*. San Francisco: Harper.

Valpy, M. 2004. "A Man of Radical Compassion." In *Globe and Mail*, June 20, p. F10.

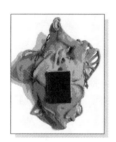

Part I
Hearing the Voices

1

This Little Light of Mine:
GROWING UP GAY IN THE LUTHERAN CHURCH

Michael W. Hamann

This little light of mine

Until I was six, my family had to drive for half an hour every Sunday, from the village of Goodwater where my parents ran the general store and post office, to go to church in Weyburn, a small city of about 10,000 people in southeastern Saskatchewan.

I'm gonna let it shine.

Whatever songs we sang—and they were always church songs—my brother and sister and I would sing the melody, and our mother and eldest sister would come in with the harmonies.

This was the same story to all our family outings. Singing to pass the miles away.

This little light of mine. I'm gonna let it shine.
Let it shine...

Of course, once we would get to church and down to Sunday School, I could only sing with half a voice, and there was no way I could get the courage to do any of the actions to the songs. I was so scared that my eyes would start to water. Everyone thought it was because I was "shy." But it was because even at that young age, I knew I was different, and I didn't want to draw any attention to myself.

Jesus loves me, this I know.
For the Bible tells me so.

Early Sunday School years were a wonderful time for me, even though I was "shy."

All the stories of Jesus and his miracles, and the beautiful wonders of God's creation! Most important though was learning about the everlasting Grace of God, and his unending love for all of us, his creations, his children.

Jesus loves the little children.
All the children of the world.

Who could ask for anything more: to be in a close loving family, and to be a part of the Family of God. Through the sacrament of Holy Baptism, we have all become God's Children, and God loves each and every one of us. Yes, I had a happy early childhood. And my feelings of being different didn't matter because I was surrounded by love.

Then the cruellest thing that can happen to a child happened to me. I was sent to school: the name-calling, the bullying, and getting pushed around on a daily basis. By the time I was in Grade 3, I wanted to die. I couldn't live with myself and I was full of self-loathing. I was always playing sick so I wouldn't have to go to school because I couldn't bear the thought of the taunting and teasing. All I ever wanted was to be liked. Instead, all I ever got was hatred from the other kids. I did learn something though: I finally had a name for my being different. I was a homosexual or as the kids in the schoolyard preferred to call me—faggot, homo, queer, sissy boy, freak.

Sticks and stones may break my bones.
But names forever scar me.

Normally, when you begin school, you start to learn "ABCDEFG, 1+1=2, HIJKLMNOP, 2+2=4." I learned, without knowing the actual word for it: "paranoia," how to lie and hide. And I was so caught up in being the best liar and hider that I didn't have much time to learn anything else. I was a poor student because my little paranoid mind couldn't concentrate on anything other than the fact that I had to hide and lie. I lied to my peers, my teachers, my ministers, and the worst was lying to my parents.

I learned through the church that Jesus didn't love people like me. I was taught that God knows our every thought, word, and deed, and I couldn't stop my thoughts no matter how hard I tried. I was also taught and made to memorize John 3:16: "For God so loved the world that he gave his only begotten son, Jesus Christ, to suffer and die, for the forgiveness of our sins, so that we too, may have everlasting Life." Except for you, you little sissy boy. Faggot. You're destined to burn in Hell for your unspeakable sins, your evils thoughts, words, and deeds.

Jesus loves you, so I'm told.
As for me, the church says no.

Every night I would pray to God. Why me Lord, why am I so evil. I didn't ask to be different. I've tried to be a loving, caring person and to live by Jesus' example. Why do I feel this way? I DIDN'T CHOOSE THIS!

Through the years, I never had many friends, because I was scared to get close to anyone, lest they find out my horrible secret. Better not to have any friends rather than to have them reject you when they found out. One of the best things about being alone, is that you can cry all you want, and nobody will be there to call you names because of it.

Faggot, Homo, Queer, Freak

One of my favourite winter pastimes was tunnelling into huge snow banks and then lie there talking to God. "Well Lord, here's your chance. Please end this lonely existence of mine. I've tried to change Lord. I don't want to be different. I can't live like this anymore. I've already lost your love; I can't lose my family's too. It would be better for everyone if I were dead. I couldn't take having my parents hate me too."

I guess one thing I was good at was digging snow tunnels, because none of them ever collapsed on me, so I would just lie there crying in the snow, trying to freeze myself to death.

One of the leading causes of teen suicide is guilt and fear about their sexual difference. When you grow up in a society like ours, that is Christian-based, and from an early age you know you're headed straight to Hell just for being who you are, it is no wonder so many kids kill themselves. I was no different. I never actually had the guts to do the dirty deed, but if I had a dime for every time I wished myself dead…

I was one of those rare types of people. I actually continued to attend church after confirmation. And since I was tired of being lonely, I created a facade for myself. Everyone loves a clown, so that's what I became. I'd always be the one to say something goofy or do something stupid to make people laugh. It was great; I was making friends, and people actually seemed to like me. Of course, I couldn't let anyone get to know the real me, because then they would all hate me.

Faggot, Homo, Queer, Freak

At Bible Camps and National Youth Conferences, I became a wild and crazy guy. I made lots of friends; it was wonderful. And at the end of camp, or conference week, when it was time to depart, there were always lots of tears. It was good to be able to cry openly. My new friends would be crying because they didn't want to go, and they would miss me. I cried because I knew that the whole time I was with them, I was lying to them. I wasn't a wild and crazy guy. I was a scared, lost, little boy, and knew that nobody would ever love me, the real me, the gay me.

We're all sinners. Why? Because we are human; it is in our natures to sin.

Let they who are without sin cast the first stone.

Now I've done some things in my life that I am greatly ashamed of and wish I could take back, but it is the lies that I feel I was forced to tell since the age of five that turned me into a guilt-ridden, suicidal, manic depressive, substance abuser. And, did I mention how much I hated myself.

After graduation, I immediately left home to discover myself and the world. I found that I wasn't the only gay person out there. I found out that there are millions of gays and lesbians around the world. For the first time in my life, I felt accepted for whom I really was. As long as my parents never found out, I'd be okay. Right?

It turned out that everything wasn't all right, because now I had to start lying to my parents about my new gay life, my new gay friends and why I hadn't found a new church yet.

How could I tell my parents that I was gay, and risk losing their love? How could I tell them that I had no intention of looking for a new church, because the church hates fags?

So in my newfound happiness, I was miserable, I was depressed, and I was still alone.

This little light of mine, I'm gonna let it shine.

Something had to change in my life or I really might try something more danger-ous than waiting to freeze to death or have my snow tunnel collapse on me. I wasn't 10 anymore, and knew of quicker more efficient ways of killing myself.

This little light of mine, I'm gonna let it shine, let it shine...

The church had always been the centre of my life. My life with my family and with God. I needed to feel a part of that again and yet knowing, who and what I was, that the church would never accept me. It was in the depths of my depression, that I started talking to God again.

So began my personal journey with Christ. I had to look back at my childhood, remember the songs from Sunday School, Bible Camp, and family trips, and recap-ture the joy I felt knowing that God loved me, and sent his only son to die for me, for my sins.

I realized that I'm not an evil being. I am one of God's beautiful creations, I am a child of God, and nobody can take that away from me.

Jesus Loves the Little Children, all the children of the world.
Aboriginal and Asian.
Gay or Lesbian persuasion.
Jesus loves that Little Children of the world.

I know that I'm not alone in this. I know that we are all scarred by life-experi-ences. Emotional scars cannot heal over if they are kept hidden inside of us. As Christians we should be able to open our hearts and arms to all people.

In 1992, at 30 years of age, I finally came out to my parents, and I learned that they still loved me, and will always love me. The lies and the hiding were over.

For years, I always thought that *"This Little Light of Mine"* was about the light of the Holy Spirit, and as Christians, we should always show that light in everything we do. We should live in Jesus' example and be loving, and understanding, and not to judge others. For me now, that childhood song has so much more meaning. This lit-tle light of mine is the light of my spirit infused with God's spirit, and as a Christian, I can't hide that light, as a Gay Christian, as a loving being, as a child of God, I can't hide it anymore.

Hide it under a bush, oh no.
I'm gonna let it shine.
Hide it under a bush, oh no.
I'm gonna let it shine.
Let it shine. Let it shine. Let it shine.

Safe in My Heart:

FOUND POETRY AS NARRATIVE INQUIRY

Kristopher Wells

HISTORICALLY, QUEER (LESBIAN, GAY, BISEXUAL, AND TRANSGENDER) youth have been marginalized in adult, community, and school educational environments (Baker, 2002; Grace and Wells, 2001; Lipkin, 1999; Ryan and Futterman, 1998; Schneider, 1997). Contemporary educational research increasingly demonstrates that heterosexism and homophobia, in conjunction with other forms of discrimination, function to reinforce and reproduce specific forms of power and privilege that define and regulate the status quo in schools (Epstein and Johnson, 1998; Friend, 1998). In Alberta, this marginalization continues to be pervasive. As recently as 1998, Queer persons were not even considered worthy of basic human rights protections in Alberta. In the 1998 *Vriend* decision, the Supreme Court of Canada legislated that sexual orientation be read in as a protected ground against discrimination in the Alberta Human Rights, Citizenship, and Multiculturalism Act (Lahey, 1999; MacDougall, 2000). Five short years later, Queer youth in Alberta are still struggling to be accepted as full and valued citizens in their school, family, and community environments.

This chapter uses found poetry[1] (Ely, et. al, 1997; Butler-Kisber, 2000; Richardson, 1992, 1998) as a narrative strategy (Clandinin and Connelly, 2000) to investigate the experiences of Queer youth as they struggle to become visible and vocal in their school, family and community environments. These found poems explore the following questions and themes: What is life like for Queer youth who are in the process of coming out and coming to terms with their sex-and-gender differences in Canada? How does heterosexism and homophobia impact the personal, political, social, and cultural lives of Queer youth? In what ways are Queer youth simultaneously included and excluded in their educational, family and community contexts? What impact does this inclusion/exclusion have on their mental, physical, and emotional well-being? How are adult, community, family, and public education-al spaces sites of structural, symbolic and actual violence towards Queer youth? What do Queer youth do to survive (and in some cases thrive) amidst this marginal-ization? Where do Queer youth turn to find support and acceptance as they come out and come to terms with their marginalized identities?

To explore these questions I engaged four Queer youth, variously positioned in terms of ethnicity and sex-and-gender differences, in an arts-based relational inquiry that focused on their lived and learned educational experiences in Alberta schools, families and communities (Wells, 2003). In this narrative inquiry we used found poetry techniques to evocatively explore and convey some of the essences, experi-ences, and emotions of the research participants' storied lives. By using poetic tran-scription we are attempting to collectively create a counterhegemonic discourse that strives to rub up against the grand narratives of culture and schooling that celebrate and maintain the heteronormative status quo. These poetic narratives seek to strug-gle to "reclaim and rewrite untold histories, to subvert what counts as knowledge and truth, and to challenge those who claim to have the authority to speak for [or about Queer youth]" (St. Pierre and Pillow, 2000, p. 5). These found poems serve as a map that explores the ways in which Queer youth navigate, resist, reclaim, and make use of the available discourses that surround them to construct and challenge represen-tations of their everyday realities within their formal and non-formal learning envi-ronments. We hope that these found poems will speak to readers on a personal, tem-poral and evocative level as they portray what life is like for many Queer youth as they seek to live, learn, love and work in their everyday lives.

Seventeen and Gay

(Kevin, age 17)

I was twelve when I finally had a word for it
I told my mom when I was fourteen
She was fine with it, but there was crying
Was it sadness or just shock?

My mother doesn't want to see me hurt
She has images of Matthew Shepard burned deeply in her mind
She doesn't want to see that happen to me

It changes the relationship between me and my father
He asked if I was sure
There were always indicators
I was very effeminate when I was younger
I never had a girlfriend
I only displayed interest, because I wanted to be like everyone else
Ya, I'm sure

My dad doesn't want his family to know
I guess it must be something to be ashamed of

I remember thinking that I've got to change this
I just tried ignoring it
I tried to be interested in girls
It didn't work

It's something that you just learn to live with
Even now I don't really want to be gay
I don't think that it's something you want to be
It's just something you are

I decided to go to the youth group
I was tired of being someone I didn't think I was
I wanted to meet other gay people
I wanted to share a part of myself that I wasn't able to share

At the youth group you don't have to worry about looking at someone the wrong way
Or saying the wrong thing
You can just let it all hang out
You can be yourself
You get to see that you are not the only person out there
Wow, it's not so bad when we can go through it together
I don't have shame for what I am, at least not anymore
I realize that this is just me
Take it or leave it

If I choose to feel bad about it, then life is just going to suck
I know some people who think that way and it's terrible
I don't understand why it's such a big deal
It's better to come to terms with what you are than to fight it

Well I didn't choose to be gay
I'm choosing to be happy

Lucky People

(Kevin, age 17)

A few people at school know
I feel safer on the Internet
I can be whoever I want to be
You don't have to worry about homophobia
They can't kill you through the Internet

I don't feel safe at home
I don't flaunt it in front of my dad

What is gay?
Is gay the way I act?
Or is gay the fact that I like guys?
I struggle with it

The locker room
Guys walking around half naked
I'm seventeen
I've got eyes
Sometimes they wander
Afraid that someone might see
People know you are gay
They threaten you

Ignore it

I don't want to be singled out

Name calling

Shoving

I don't really remember much
It's something that I've blocked out

No one likes to be the black sheep

I've been hit
I've been kicked
I've been spat on

I don't think there is a gay person who hasn't
If they haven't they are not out or they are very lucky
I don't think that there are very many lucky people out there

Invisible Alliances

(Kevin, age 17)

Schools have faltered
I feel invisible
Teachers need to be trained
People are more accepting of colour, ethnic, and religious backgrounds than they are of
sexuality
Sexuality is the last form of acceptable discrimination

I tried to start a gay-straight alliance at my school
An atmosphere where you could be safe
A place where people could meet at lunch and say
"OK, I'm gay"
Strength in numbers

The teacher pulled out
She was afraid
Afraid of the impact that it would have on her career

At first I understood
Now, I'm not so understanding

She's a counselor
That's her job
She should have found someone else
When you're kicked down once
It's hard to get back up
If she wasn't going to do it
Then no one would

There was a boy who went to my school
He would have been my age
He killed himself because he was gay
When that happens there is something wrong

A gay-straight alliance could make a difference
Even if the person doesn't attend the meetings
The resources will be there if they want them or if they ever need them
That youth never got the chance

Always on the Outside

(Jamie, age 22)

Excluded from certain rights
Just because I'm gay

I'm different
I think it's in a good way

They think I'm different in a bad way

I'm always on the outside

Angry
Frustrated
Confused

I dated boys
I learned to disguise it
I was in denial

I'm always on the outside

Then I came out

It has really strained the relationship with my dad
There's always this weird tension in the air
He feels like he had a part in it

He never says the word gay
I've never heard him use the word lesbian

It's the same with my mom
She used the word lesbian for the first time today
And she whispered it

I'm always on the outside

Teaching It Wrong

(Jamie, age 22)

There's that other box that never seems to exist on any form
Schools really aren't giving me an option to talk about it

I wasn't learning the words
I never learned about gay history or culture
They just left me on my own to figure it out

Missed opportunities

It doesn't take very many positive comments
It just takes one
If I had just one suggestion that lesbians actually exist
It would have changed my whole life

On the other hand
The negative comments just hit you in the gut

There are no gays in this school

I'm sitting right here!
Apparently I don't exist

I've seen this teacher as a mentor
In one moment everything changes
I can no longer respect them

Wow, that's really offensive, bye

Truth and Fear

(Jamie, age 22)

The world isn't a perfect place
At least I have my integrity

I have people who love me for who I am

I started to be myself when I came out at eighteen
That was the point in my life when things really started to fit together

I actually feel like I can be myself now

It's easier to live in truth than to hide in fear

At first I was shy and reclusive
I was unsure of who I was
I was unsure of where I was going

We are driven into the dark corners of the night
People are so angry and hateful towards us when we are out in the light

When I walk down main street holding my partner's hand
I don't get a lot of smiles

Now I see myself as an activist

The gay community has given me so much
I have the strength and power to find happiness in being who I am

I owe it to every gay person out there that's fighting
I owe it to every gay person living in the closet
I owe it to them all to put myself forward and speak OUT

It's easier to live in truth than to hide in fear

Normal is Boring

(Jamie, age 22)

I didn't choose to be gay
But I wouldn't change it

I want to utilize my difference in a positive way
That's the exciting thing for me

I'm counter-balancing the dominant culture that doesn't ask enough why questions
They just blindly follow traditions, rules, and norms
It doesn't leave a lot of room to just be who you are
Do what you need to do
And love who you need to love

I'm proud that I know I'm being myself

Because I'm a lesbian
I know that I am being myself

It's by no means easy

For any out gay and lesbian person
Simply existing is a courageous act

It's that element of pride
It's the one thing that I will always hold onto

I will fight to the bitter end for that rainbow flag

Who am I?

(Alex, age 18)

Eighteen, Christian, Chinese, and gay

My mom is in denial
She doesn't like it

I can't really be gay at home

My Godfather provides for our financial support
He told my mom that if *"your son is gay, I will not support you"*

I can't really be gay at home

It's a cultural thing
It's like family honour

If one person knows, then ever person knows

I've grown accustomed to hiding it

Dreams

(Alex, age 18)

In Grade five or six I remember looking…
I couldn't find the word gay

I got the Internet in grade seven
I found a site for Queer youth
I read the articles
I found people who were in the same situation as me
I wasn't alone
That site was very important.
It helped me to feel comfortable with myself
It showed me that it wasn't my own special situation

I didn't get any support from my school
It was all very heterosexual, even in health class

For Queer youth the only place they can find information about themselves is on the Internet

Before the Internet I was really homophobic
I hated myself
I would always stay away from other Queer people

I ended up in a deep depression
I got into this sex addiction
washrooms
parks
peep shows

Six months
Over twenty people

I didn't feel loved
So I had sex with people

I thought that even if it was just for a moment
I was at least wanted by someone

So I kept going to those places

I thought that maybe it was because I was Chinese that I couldn't find anyone to love me
I thought I was ugly

The more I did it
The more I felt terrible for doing it
And the more I felt unloved
It was an endless cycle

I looked at myself one day
I had ended up in the middle of the park looking for sex
That's when I went to get help
I needed help before I got myself killed
Or got an STD or something

I should go get help

I went to Youth Understanding Youth for the first time
I started healing
We had a session on self-esteem at a youth group retreat
I realized that I wasn't the only one who thought like this

I became more comfortable
I went to gay pride week

I've come to peace with myself
I know why I am here...
To help people

I have dreams to help people with my music
I see the future as a place where everybody is equal and accepted

I feel like I've been called by God to help the gay community
To help connect the two together

I want to be a teacher and change young minds so that we can have a better future

When I went back to school to pick up my yearbook
One of the teachers saw my rainbow
She said, "good for you"

I have dreams

The Scars Remind Me

(Jordana, age 19)

The Ellen Show
My mom, dad, and I used to watch that show
Then on that one day, during that one episode, Ellen was coming out
My parents refused to watch it

I realized that they thought that she was gross for being gay
It was my first clue that my parents didn't like homosexuals

I kept quiet for a long time after that
I thought that maybe I was bad or wrong
I journaled to myself
I talked to myself
I researched
I started feeling like I was alone

When I figured out that my parents didn't know that I was gay
It was really disappointing
I didn't know that I had to come out
I've known that I'm gay all along

I've been slashing myself since grade eight
Slashing became an escape for me
Whenever I got depressed or when something went wrong
I slashed more
These aren't fancy scars or tattoos
These are horrific scars
You can tell it's from madness

It's nothing to be ashamed of
The scars remind me of all the hard days that I had to go through just to come out

Every single scar has a meaning
They remind me of different events

The very recent scars will probably be the last ones ever
I really blacked out after those ones
I had to get stitches
I walked from my home to the lesbian bar
So many people helped me there
I realized that I wasn't alone
I don't need to do things like this

It's over

I feel like there is support and hope
There are people who will listen to me
I have support now
I just have to learn to use it in a positive way
Until eventually I become a support for myself

Pride

(Jordana, age 19)

Pride pins on my backpack as I walk down the hallway
No body bashes me for that
Lesbian and gay magazines in class
Other kids take a peek

Wearing pride colors
I like those colors
It's a part of who I am

There is no formula
Or definition for what it means to be a lesbian
We are like everyone else
We are no different
I'm just like other students

I'm a girl who is nineteen
I happen to be a lesbian
I happen to be of a darker skin color

When it comes down to it, it just doesn't matter

What really matters is what I have been through…

suicide
anorexia
depression
family problems
relationship issues
self-discovery

This is what makes me different
Not my sexual orientation

Safe in My Heart

(Jordana, age 19)

I was feeling doubt
I was worried
I wasn't out to my parents

I had no support
I had no understanding

You can be your worst enemy
You can be your worst critic

You are the one who can take your own life
I almost did three or four times

I have control over my life

I can be comfortable within myself whether I'm gay, lesbian, bisexual or transgender

If I'm not comfortable
I will never feel safe in my heart

If I'm not comfortable with who I am
I will have trouble everywhere else
I will be scared

It's a fact that I'm a lesbian
I've faced it
I was created like this
I know that in my heart
I don't have to prove myself to anyone

I don't know what it feels like to be straight
I don't know what it feels like to be a gay man
I only know what it feels like to be a lesbian

I like what I have right now

I feel a lot of independence
I don't have to fit into a stereotype of what a female should be
I don't have to look like Barbie to be liked
I don't feel the pressure to compete

I feel stronger
I have more self-confidence
I'm out
I'm not ashamed of who I am

I feel safe in my heart

Note

1. Found poetry or poetic transcription is the process in which the researcher works with interview transcripts to create poems or "living biographies" of a research participant's experiences (Pink,

2001). The found poems are created by using only the research participant's words and the researcher's lens to create a new "third voice" that emerges from a collaborative research process (Glsene, 1997). For methodological approaches to found poetry see Butler-Kisber, 2000; Glsene, 1997; Richardson, 1992.

References

Baker, J.M. 2002. *How Homophobia Hurts Children: Nurturing Diversity at Home, at School, and in the Community*. Binghampton, NY: Harrington Park Press.

Butler-Kisber, L. 2000. "Whispering Angels: Revisiting Dissertation Data With a New Lens." *Journal of Critical Inquiry into Curriculum and Instruction* 2, no. 3: 34–37.

Clandinin, D.J. and F.M. Connelly. 2000. *Narrative Inquiry: Experience and Story in Qualitative Research*. San Francisco: Jossey-Bass.

Ely, M., R. Vinz, M. Downing and M. Anzul. 1997. *On Writing Qualitative Research: Living by Words*. Washington, DC: Falmer Press.

Epstein, D. and R. Johnson (eds.). 1998. *Schooling Sexualities*. Bristol, PA: Open University Press.

Friend, R.A. 1998. "Heterosexism, Homophobia, and the Culture of Schooling," in S. Books (ed.), *Invisible Children in the Society and Its Schools*, 137–66. Mahwah, NJ: Lawrence Erlbaum Associates.

Glesne, C. 1997. "That Rare Feeling: Re-presenting Research Through Poetic Transcription." *Qualitative Inquiry* 3, no. 2: 202–13.

Grace, A.P. and K. Wells. 2001. "Getting an Education in Edmonton, Alberta: The Case of Queer Youth." *Torquere, Journal of the Canadian Lesbian and Gay Studies Association* 3: 137–51.

Lahey, K. 1999. *Are We Persons Yet? Law and Sexuality in Canada*. Toronto: University of Toronto Press.

Lipkin, A. 1999. *Understanding Homosexuality, Changing Schools*. Boulder, CO: Westveiw Press.

MacDougall, B. 2000. *Queer Judgments: Homosexuality, Expression and the Courts in Canada*. Toronto: University of Toronto Press.

Pink, S. 2001. *Visual Ethnography: Images, Media and Representation in Research*. Thousand Oaks, CA: Sage Publications.

Richardson, L. 1992. "The Consequences of Poetic Representation: Writing the Other, Rewriting the Self," in C. Ellis and M.G. Flaherty (eds.), *Investigating Subjectivity: Research on Lived Experience*, 125-37. Newbury Park, CA: Sage.

——. 1998. "Writing: A Method of Inquiry," in N.K. Denzin and Y.S. Lincoln (eds.), *Collecting and Interpreting Qualitative Materials*, 345–71. Thousand Oaks, CA: Sage.

Ryan, C. and D. Futterman. 1998. *Lesbian & Gay Youth: Care & Counseling*. New York: Columbia University Press.

Schneider, M.S. (ed.). 1997. *Pride & Prejudice: Working with Lesbian, Gay and Bisexual Youth*. Toronto: Central Toronto Youth Services.

St. Pierre, E.A. and W.S. Pillow (eds.). 2000. *Working the Ruins: Feminist Poststructural Theory and Methods in Research*. New York: Routledge.

Wells, K. 2003. *Understanding Difference Differently: Sex-and-Gender OUTlaws in Alberta Schools* (Master's thesis, University of Alberta).

3

Growing Up Outside the Gender Construct

Darrin Hagen

The Cult of Masculinity

It's just a hallway, nothing more. To get to the other end is all I have to do.

The coast is clear, as far as I can tell. My shoes squeak with every step. It's hard to be invisible with squeaky shoes. I try to lift my feet higher so they don't make any noise, but the hard shiny tile is persistent, loudly announcing my every move.

On this day, the hallway is empty. The sunlight bounces off the polished tiles. I squint as if I'm outside.

But here there is no breeze in the hallway. And the only sound today is a hollow ringing, silence echoed upon silence until the quiet is a deafening roar, punctuated by the squeak of my running shoes.

I get to the other end. My heart is racing. I say to myself that it doesn't matter, stop being so scared all the time. I tell myself this knowing that it DOES matter.

— • —

On the day Columbine became a household word, I got in a huge argument.

The straight guys in the smoking room were all talking about the tragedy when I got to work. Rumours were already running rampant as to how and who and why it happened. But already, students had reported that the guys who did the shooting had been bullied. After being excluded, ostracized and mocked for much of their teen school careers, the boys had snapped.

This happens all the time in North America. The big difference is, this time the boys that snapped had some major access to some major artillery.

The straight guys in the smoking room all work in various departments in the media. It's one of the few things I have I common with most of the guys at work. Not because they're straight, but because we have very different views of how the world should work.

When I said, "When are they finally going to do something about bullying?," they all stared at me like I was crazy.

"Bullying isn't the problem here," one of them said. "Kids today are just fucked up."

When you're in the smoking room of the place you work and the place you work is the media, some of these headlines take on a dark subtext. Hours after the shooting, the media was already being blamed for twisting the minds of the boys who attacked their school that day. The merciless repetition of the images of violence and anger that the media claims falls under the "right to know" clause was being cited as inciting the youths to use their schoolmates for target practice. The media, defending itself, looked to the availability of deadly info on the internet as a possible scapegoat.

Everyone ignored the most obvious catalyst. You see, there are still people who view bullying as a rite of passage, a necessary evil, a phase young people go through before the laws of propriety begin applying to them. Children and young teens are expected to torment each other. The only question is what determines whether you're the attacker or the attacked.

In my hometown, it came down to this: you can't be a man until you defend yourself. And the word that should incite you to violence in your own defense is "Faggot." If that word didn't send you flying into a rage, then chances are, you were one.

I first heard it in kindergarten. For the next 13 years, I heard it daily. Most of those days, it was directed at me. That's because I'm a faggot.

Or is that really the only reason? All through my life, I've known young men who were driven through that route of humiliation over and over and over. Many of them weren't gay. Most of them were just … not willing to resort to violence to prove themselves. Over and over. And over.

— • —

It's just a hallway, nothing more. To get to the other end is all I have to do.

The coast is clear, as far as I can tell. My shoes squeak with every step. It's hard to be invisible with squeaky shoes. I try to lift my feet higher so they don't make any noise, but the hard shiny tile is persistent, loudly announcing my every move.

On this day, the hallway is not empty. I can see them hanging out where they always hang out, staking out their territory, guarding empty space.

I have to pass right by them. This is the only way. We all know that.

I quicken my pace a bit, to appear confident, but also to make it last even just one second less. I approach their territory. I avoid eye contact. I pray for invisibility.

Today it seems to work. I pass, never looking back, the squeak of my shoes marking my progress down the hallway.

I feel their stares burning into my spine. My shoulders ache from the heat.

— • —

Back to my fight in the smokeroom at the TV station. Here's my favourite quote from the conversation: "Survival of the fittest. There are the weak, and there are the strong who attack them. It's the way nature works. It's how the unworthy are weeded out of the clan. It's how the strength of the pack is maintained."

The head wolf who was saying this obviously spent his formative years helping to maintain the strength of his pack. He freely admits to being a bully in school, but fails to see how it's relevant to the way he conducts his adult life today. He's a man.

He doesn't really ever have to worry about the ramifications of the abuse he shelled out back then.

The strong attack the weak. That's the way of the world.

So that's what was happening when my Grade 10 Physics teacher kicked me out of class permanently because I was effeminate. That's what caused the tough guys to prey on guys like me. That's what caused guys like me to prey on guys even weaker than us. That's what was happening when my Drama teacher forbid us to create any plays that had gay characters in them. That's what caused my Grade 8 Social Studies teacher to turn beet red and say "Don't tell your parents I told you this," every time he was forced to mention homosexuality because some male leader had the audacity to turn up Queer hundreds of years ago.

In their eyes, that wasn't homophobia … it was the strong protecting their own.

— • —

It's just a hallway, nothing more. To get to the other end is all I have to do.

The coast is clear, as far as I can tell. My shoes squeak with every step. It's hard to be invisible with squeaky shoes. I try to lift my feet higher so they don't make any noise, but the hard shiny tile is persistent, loudly announcing my every move.

On this day, the hallway is not empty. I can see them hanging out where they always hang out, staking out their territory, guarding empty space.

I have to pass right by them. This is the only way. We all know that.

Today I can tell by the way they stand, pelvis forward, hands in pockets, that I won't be allowed to simply pass by. Today there is a toll to pay.

The short one starts walking towards me. He is the cruel one. His smile, his sneer, comes from knowing that cruelty gets results.

"Saw you looking at me in the shower, faggot."

For a short guy, he was well hung.

"You love it in there, don't ya? Checking out our cocks. Fuckin' faggot."

He was always the one who paraded, who enjoyed being naked in the locker room more than anyone else. He always got dressed slowly, giving me lots of time to see his back, his ass, then a flash of his cock as he tucked it into his white underwear. He was always the one who laughed when someone complained about the stink of that many teenage men/boys in one room.

"That's what MEN smell like," he would say proudly, referring, of course, to his own smell, which he reveled in. Then he would snap some unsuspecting bare ass with his wet towel, the angry snap of contact ricocheting through the steam.

"You want my cock, don't you?"

I do but I don't tell him that.

The tall one with the moustache steps forward. "He wants to suck you off, dude." This is the same tall one who made everyone marvel at his hard dick when we were at camp last month. Even the short guy was impressed enough to take his buddy's cock in his hand.

But of course, that's just male bonding.

I keep walking. I could stop and tell them that if they had the guts that I didn't need them, that assholes who want to get their cocks sucked are, frankly, a dime a dozen.

But I keep walking.

I get to the end of the hallway, where it turns sharply to the right. Ten more steps and I'm out of range. Seven. Three. Two. One. I turn right. It's over. For now.

— • —

There's a crisis of masculinity happening right now. Men have been taught how to be men. Now they're being told that's not good enough.

For centuries, men thought they knew what was expected of them. Be a hero, be a warrior, be a provider, be strong, big boys don't cry.

But now we live in a time that refutes many of those assumptions. What is the next phase of manliness? Does that word even belong in our lexicon anymore?

I've never had much use for masculinity. Most of the problems I faced growing up stemmed from the oh-so-narrow view of what appropriate male behaviour was. You see, I just couldn't act like the rest of the boys. Actually, I could … but I didn't. It felt unnatural to me.

I paid dearly for my decision. The price for opting out of the Boys' Club is high. Guys have a way of letting you know that you're not one of them anymore. And I feel there is a special venom reserved for "traitors" to the Cause. Suddenly, ostracization, verbal abuse and violence are allowed. Because if a guy won't play the Guy Game, he needs to be punished.

I thought when I became an adult that all of that would fall away, that maturity would teach the boys I grew up with to let the façade fall away, to blaze a new path in the world, to shed the shackles of masculine assumption and find their own way.

Most of them just continued to buy in. The only world order they knew was not something to be abandoned, but reinforced with every butch breath, with every macho gesture and suppressed cry of anguish.

If I had known that the harrassment and bullying I experienced were, in fact, the first signs of my freedom from the Boys' Club, from the Guy Game, I probably would have viewed them with a sense of relief. But at the time, I didn't even know that opting out was a choice.

Listen up, guys: the man they want you to be: doesn't exist. He has to be created.

If you have to go to all the trouble of creating a man, why not build yourself one who is resilient and flexible, able to adapt and cope without checking in the Rulebook to determine whether or not your choices are manly enough?

Aah … but to do that, you have to let go of the prize. This is the point where Men start to pay.

— • —

I keep walking.

It's just a hallway, nothing more. To get to the other end is all I have to do.

I get to the other end. My heart is racing. I say to myself that it doesn't matter, stop being so scared all the time. I tell myself this knowing that it DOES matter.

That's when a rotten apple from one of their lunches hits the wall right beside my head. It explodes against the industrial green-painted cinderblock wall, rank and sweet and messy, spraying on the floor and my shoulder and my shoes. I can hear them laughing.

I keep walking.

Why Do You Talk Like a Girl?

I've always been different.

But even the word "different" is one of those terms that doesn't quite fit in … it's one of those words that had come to represent something which has no proper adjective. It's a word my Mom would use to describe something she wasn't sure about:

"How was the play, Mom?"

"Oh, you know … different."

Different is the word some of my relatives use to describe my book once they've read it. One cousin even went so far as to use the superlative form:

"So … what did you think of the book?"

"Oh, you know…pretty different…"

It's not really a compliment…it's more like a recognition that they don't, nor will they ever, really understand what makes something tick. It's outside their realm of experience.

In my family, "different" became the word that was whispered whenever I was referred to. I presented challenges because I was "different." Now, looking back on the world I grew up in, "different" could have meant that I cared what my hair looked like. Or that I was a boy who actually got good marks at school. Or that I was polite to my elders. Or that I hadn't been arrested for drunk driving.

But when the word "different" was used in reference to me, it meant one thing and one thing only: I didn't act like the rest of the boys. I was the mama's boy, the girly-boy, the nancy-boy, the sissy-boy. I was, and sometimes still am, the boy who acted more like a girl.

From age 0–6, being different didn't cost me too much. It made me precocious and noticeable, which at the time I thought were good things. It made me stand out, which I hadn't learned to be ashamed of yet.

But from age 6–12, I gradually learned the cost of not fitting in.

School is where most children learn who they are. They see themselves reflected in the eyes of a mini-society, with its own laws and pecking orders and status seekers and criminals. For children growing up outside the gender construct, it's generally their first real experience with exclusion.

If the place where you spent 8 hours a day was a place of verbal harassment, psychological torture, with an omnipresent threat of physical violence at any moment, you wouldn't stay. Now imagine you have no choice but to go to that place. Daily. Imagine knowing that you are expected to simply and quietly endure. Imagine the authorities turning away when you brought your concerns to them.

The only thing lacking in this social microcosm is an effective source of law. Or justice. Or accountability. These qualities, which every adult in Alberta takes for granted, are all missing in the pre-adult world.

There are many in this room today who know what those politics of exclusion feel like. Women know what it feels like to be on the receiving end of misogyny. Non-whites know what it feels like to be on the receiving end of racism. For many, the only real hope is that someday, adulthood would vanquish those experiences. The laws of the majority would eventually kick in and start protecting.

But what if that never happens? What if adulthood just brings more of the same?

Queer children don't know they're queer. They may realize they're "different," but have no idea why or what that difference represents to their future. We're talking about pre-sexual human beings ... the word "queer" has no meaning until the gradual dawning of a sexual identity kicks in.

"Gay" has no meaning until you know what "straight" means. "Straight" has no meaning until you know what "sex" means.

The first time I was called a fairy, I could tell right away they weren't talking about mystical creatures with wings that cast spells. I was 4. I had never had sex. I had barely figured out that boys and girls were different. I didn't know what gay meant, or what fag meant. Neither did the boys calling me fairy ... but that didn't stop them from identifying me as an outcast. My crime? I talked like a girl.

Never mind that until a boy's voice changes, we all sound pretty feminine. It had nothing to do with how high or low my voice was.

It had more to do with what I said, the words I chose, the way I used my hands to punctuate my speech. It had to do with the fact that I had not yet learned the rural Alberta masculine monotone, the voice that hides all emotional connection, the manner of speaking that states, without ever stating, its naturally understood supremacy.

One day I walked through the trailer court with a towel over my head. I wasn't hiding ... it was just that I desperately wanted long hair ... but back then, boys didn't have long hair unless they were juvenile delinquents or their parents were hippies. My mother, seeing this feminine transgression, called me back into the house. She ripped my long hair off my head, folded it expertly and put it back in the linen closet, saying, "That's enough of that."

Once puberty loomed, the "need" to guide me towards fitting in began. Suddenly, all my girlfriends were not allowed to play house or Barbie or anything with me. I was encouraged to play with boys ... apparently nobody caught the irony inherent in that mission. Their efforts were hampered by the fact that I didn't really like the way boys acted; it seemed alien to me. I viewed them in a similar fashion to how they viewed girls: confusing, complicated and kinda cute.

But playing with the boys underlined, rather than erased, those "differences." Being the last to be chosen for the team, reacting to a ball hurtling towards my face with a scream instead of a lunge, not knowing how football worked ... being a boy was hard work. It was hard work because it just wasn't natural for me.

The first time I was called a fag ... there have been so many times I don't really remember the first time. They all blur together. I do remember the first time I realized that the word "fag" applied to me. I caught myself writing a boy's name on the inside of my binder over and over ... when I realized what I had done, I took a Jiffy marker and blacked the whole thing out. Don't let anyone see. Don't let anyone know.

In retrospect, that's what every queer child must do. Erase themselves. Block it out. Don't let anyone see what you're really thinking; who you really are. Thus, at the early age of 12, I learned self-censorship.

But it would take one mighty censor to erase all the traces of gay in a boy like me.

The more I suppressed who I was, the more despondent I became. Around the same time as I started dating girls (proving once and for all that denying yourself hurts EVERYONE involved), the anti-gay bullying started. So ... pretending to be straight wasn't going to change the way they treated me, either.

I've had people ask me, "Was it really that bad? Were you beat up every day?" The answer is, no, I didn't get beat up every day ... and yes, it really was that bad.

Because I never knew when it would happen, whether it would happen, what form it would take. I never knew if someone would step in and defend me. I never knew if I could walk down that hallway safely. I never knew who was going to be hanging around that corner, waiting to prove what a man he was. It's the not knowing that ultimately destroys a soul ... as we know from watching cultures subjugated by colonialism, it's not just through the violence, but through the simple threat of violence, that a population is kept afraid.

I had been a straight-A student ... my marks started to drop. I couldn't concentrate at school ... class became purgatory; a pause between navigating the hateful hallways again. And some of the teachers just reinforced the shame ... my Social Studies teacher would turn beet-red if homosexuality came up in an anthropological text, and say, "Don't tell your parents we talked about that." My Drama teacher wouldn't allow any gay characters onstage. My Physics teacher kicked me out of class because ... well, I made him sick. Don't ask me how I know. I just do. It's all in the sneer.

Wanna hear a teacher update? My Drama teacher got raked over the coals for teaching evolution, my Physics teacher later became a client of mine at the phone sex company where I was an operator, and my Social Studies teacher had a gay brother that I met at a gay dinner party a few years later. And guess who got the good hair and the nice body in the family? No wonder Mr. Thompson was so bitter. These were the men who guided us through our teens. Good thing I wasn't taught by a fag or something.

I craved being accepted, included, but as the years went on I realized there was one major roadblock that was preventing me from ever gaining entry into their world: Men despised me. And the only men who didn't were like me. And finally, in Red Deer one summer, I found one. And then I found more.

I started using drugs, thinking that if I was bad like my abusers, they would respect me. I started vandalizing, shoplifting, skipping school. It was when I got caught shoplifting gay porn from the billiard hall that I came out to my parents: a combination "desperate-cry-for-help" and "change-the-subject-quick" tactic. It worked. Their anger became a real concern. But the concern was for who I became in their eyes in that moment:

One of Them.

Some counseling, which I lied all the way through (I couldn't tell my Dad that yes, I had had sex with a man); some tense months of getting to know each other all over again, and a sort of uneasy peace returned. And I, who loved my parents, started counting the seconds until I could finally be free. I grew up, came out to some of my friends, graduated (I avoided the party afterwards ... good thing, because I heard later some of the guys were looking for me: "Last chance to beat up the fag.")

I packed a suitcase. I said goodbye. I left.

Within a year I was performing in full drag for a living.

Why do I talk like a girl? Because I can. Because I have to. Because I'm not a liar. Because it's who and what I am.

What did I miss growing up queer?

I missed feeling safe in school. I missed seeing myself in every TV show, every movie, every newspaper, every magazine. I missed imagining a future for me and my partner. Dating. Teen romance. School spirit. My grad party. Inclusion in the community. A life free from the effects of bigotry. Promotions. Jobs. Walking down the street at night without looking over my shoulder. Kissing my lover on the street. Getting married. Having a family. Going to my in-laws for Thanksgiving. Cards that come to the house at Christmas addressed to the two people who live together in harmony as they have for damn near two decades, instead of just one "bachelor" son.

Look into a child's eyes. Does anyone have the right to take all of that away from them?

— • —

When we allow homophobia to dictate how these issues are treated, it's not just the queer kids that suffer. We also hold straight kids hostage to a way of thinking that can only hold them back. When people write letters to the editor bitching about gay marriage or gay pride day, it sends a powerful message to the gay community: you're not good enough. Act as straight as you want, but you're a second-class citizen.

Acting straight never helped me. Here I can speak from personal experience. I wear a dress because I have to. Because there is something inside me that needs that experience. I can't fully explain why I need it, but that need was there on day one. The moment I realized that men and women were viewed as polar opposites, I struggled to become one or the other. I knew that in a world of men and women, I was neither. And both. And a world that had no place for me had to be challenged, because I believed—I HAD to believe—that I had the right to exist, just the way I was.

Although I didn't realize the implications at the time, I became a gender warrior. The battle is fought in people's minds. Their own stereotypes are my weapons.

And victory for me means freedom for all.

In reality, we all have a choice. Are you masculine or feminine? And how does that manifest? Leave the city and go to a farming community, and you'll see all the women wearing jeans, cowboy boots, their husband's company bomber jackets, short no-nonsense hair and no makeup. These women choose to be less feminine ... maybe for practical reasons, maybe to blend in with the macho surroundings.

Yet a man in a dress can inspire violence. A man wearing makeup is called "faggot." A man who is feminine is automatically the enemy.

The future is a place where equality is taken literally. It doesn't ask this of us ... rather, it demands it. The future calls for an end to the devaluing of all that is feminine. The future holds the potential for freedom from sexism and homophobia.

The future is a place where advantage isn't affected by gender. I have seen the future, but never the whole picture. So far, it emerges only in fragments, like shards of the mirror I use to transform myself from him to her. The future holds the possibility of a social construct built on entitlement: not of a select few, but of all, regardless of what exists between our legs; the entitlement that is our right as human beings, without exception.

Don't be intimidated by the fact that laws will be re-written, that our social structure will have to change, that some will lose the status they now take for granted. All of these have outlived their usefulness anyway. Don't be afraid of the future, because it will come with or without cooperation from us. We can't stop it. The future is fearless.

λ

4

Gay and Out
in Secondary School:
ONE YOUTH'S STORY

John Guiney Yallop

You made me believe that I could do anything that I set my mind to, and you made me self-confident. That certainly came in handy when I came out to all my friends and family over a year ago...

(Donnee, an out gay secondary school student, in a letter to one of his elementary school teachers. Quoted in Guiney, 2002, p. 114)

A Personal Journey

My Master of Education Research Project, "School Life for Gays: A Critical Study Through Story" (Guiney, 2002) used narrative inquiry to take a critical look at how gays experience school. "Narrative as research method ... is less a matter of application of a scholarly technique to understanding phenomena than it is a matter of 'entering into' the phenomena and partaking of them" (Clandinin and Connelly, 1991, p. 260). The research became a personal journey for me as I reflected back on my own life in school as a closeted gay student and later as an out gay educator, a school life that spanned four decades. One participant was Donnee (a pseudonym), a 17-year-old gay male secondary school student who was out at school as well as in other areas of his life. This chapter focuses on Donnee's story as an out gay youth attending secondary school. In the original writing up of my research, I used **bold italics** to identify when I was quoting Donnee directly from the interview transcripts.[1] I have continued a similar practice in this chapter, using *italics* when quoting Donnee. In this way I hope to both honour Donnee's voice and allow the reader to share in Donnee's journey through his own words.

Why Stories?

Clandinin and Connelly (2000) explain that people "live stories, reaffirm them, modify them, and create new ones. Stories lived and told educate the self and others" (p. xxvi). This education happens through a process of engagement and identification with the stories. While the reader may not have had similar experiences in terms of detail to those presented in this chapter, the *qualities* of the experiences are still there to engage with, to identify with, and to be transformed by: "One of the purposes of narrative research is to have other readers raise questions about their practices, their ways of knowing... The intent is to foster reflection, storying, and restorying for readers" (Clandinin and Connelly, 1991, p. 277). Dewey (1938) refers to this purpose when he says that the "most important attitude that can be formed is that of the desire to go on learning" (p. 48).[2] What this makes clear is that doing research or reading research texts, like life, is not neatly packaged and does not neatly unfold according to predetermined procedures. Reflection allows each of us to see patterns in our storied lives. Reflection also enables us to engage with and identify with the stories of others. Donnee's stories can teach us about ourselves, how we live, and how we know. Reflection is essential in the educative process: "One learns about education from thinking about life, and one learns about life from thinking about education" (Clandinin and Connelly, 1991, p. 261).

Methods

I contacted Donnee directly to request his participation.[3] While the methodologies for my research were narrative and critical inquiry, I used two specific methods to gather information: the interview and a *letter unsent*.[4]

Limitations

The story presented here is from one out gay male secondary school student. This chapter is not intended to be representative of any population, including out gay male secondary school students. This study is one contribution to the telling of stories and the living of lives. Others may, however, find in the stories resonances with their own lived storied lives.[5]

Awareness

The school years are often a time when young gay males become aware of their sexual orientation and form an identity based on that awareness. D'Augelli (1998) states that the process of evolution of a same-sex sexual orientation may follow the same path as gender development. Because of societal attitudes toward sexuality, however, the former becomes repressed in childhood and does not fully assert itself until later, usually at puberty. The development from self-awareness to self-identity varies across individuals, societies, and time (Savin-Williams, 1995). Citing the two Masters' theses of Eric Dube and Lisa Diamond at Cornell University, Savin-Williams (1998) noted that younger groups of white gay males did not follow the same developmental path from self-awareness to self-identity that older, white gay males followed. Savin-Williams proposes "differential developmental trajectories" to help us understand the development of a sexual identity. This focus enables us to be more aware of the diversity of gay youth. A gay youth's family and social setting affect this development, as does the youth himself. This approach invites us away from simply looking at averages to looking at the life of each individual. The question, "Are you gay or straight?," for Savin-Williams, does not capture the complexities of sexuality.

An exclusive focus on mean ages may obscure (Savin-Williams, 1998), because some gay youth report never remembering a time when they were not aware of their same-sex attractions. Such statistics do refute some beliefs, such as the one that homosexuals do not exist in elementary school, a sentiment I frequently heard expressed throughout my career. D'Augelli (1996) points out that while no representative samples have focused on sexual orientation before puberty, the most recent studies indicate that erotic feelings occur before puberty and are later crystallized at or following puberty. Some studies found that the average age of awareness of their sexual orientation for gay youth was 10 years (D'Augelli and Hershberger, 1993; D'Augelli, Hershberger and Pilkington, 1998). Another study puts the age even lower (Savin-Williams, 1998). D'Augelli and Hershberger reported that over 90% of sexual minority youth were aware of their sexual orientation by age 15.

Donnee recalled no early memories of being gay:

> *I really didn't think about being gay that young ... to be completely truthful the thoughts or ideas never crossed in my head. I was just a regular, everyday kid. Woke up and went to school, had lunch, went outside and played in the playground for the lunch hour, then came in and did a few more classes. It was completely average for the 6 years I was there.*

The response of youth to the realization that they have same-sex erotic attractions are varied from relief (that the issue is finally resolved) and joy to depression and self-destructive thoughts and actions (Savin-Williams, 1995). Anderson (1995) states that the realization is sudden because the cognitive development that happens at puberty enables a young person to make the connections that they previously could not. Others view it as a gradual progression. While the responses are diverse, many experience reactions of denial and internalized homophobia before they cross what Adnan (1998) calls the zone of half-denials and half-truths about oneself and one's affections. Lowenthal (1998) recalls being petrified as an adolescent by the vision of his future. Russell (1998) recalls himself from photos as looking like a kid destined to be a pervert. Mabry (1998) recalls the "sick urges." Many gay youth begin dating girls to prove to themselves and others that they are heterosexual (Savin-Williams, 1998). Some even engage in harassment of other gays (Anderson, 1995; Savin-Williams, 1998). The denial and self-hatred intensify at puberty (Chase, 1998; D'Augelli, 1996) and continue until the self reveals itself so strong that resistance becomes impossible (D'Augelli, 1996; Savin-Williams, 1998). It is a particularly painful time, a time when the feeling of difference becomes more acute because the reason becomes more obvious. This feeling of being different is very common among sexual minority youth (Isay, 1989, 1996; Savin-Williams, 1995, 1998). The realization that one will not be traveling the same life path as one's peers is so sad (Holleran, 1998) that some can only talk or write about it in retrospect, as do many of those in Chase's (1998) collection of writers who recall their years in junior high or middle school.

Awareness of same-sex attraction is not the same as adopting a gay identity. Self-identifying or self-labeling usually happens some time, even many years, after becoming aware of same-sex attractions. Particularly noteworthy, however, is that the age at which such milestones as first awareness of same-sex attractions, self-labeling, and coming out or disclosure to others, happen has been steadily declining since the 1970s. Savin-Williams (1998) presents the results of eight other studies, besides his own, which demonstrate this.

Identifying as Gay

Some studies report gay youth self-identifying four years after self-awareness (D'Augelli and Hershberger, 1993; D'Augelli et al., 1998). Savin-Williams (1998) provides a range of experiences in his study of gay and bisexual male youth from self-identifying simultaneously with self-awareness to postponing self-labeling until later in adult life. Youth in Savin-Williams's study reported self-identifying as young as third or fourth grade up to being in graduate school when they reached this milestone.

The catalysts that lead to self-identification as gay vary. D'Augelli (1996) states that solitary and social sexual behaviours impact on how soon a same-sex sexual orientation is concretized. The youth in Savin-Williams's study reported that their first sexual experience with another male was not as significant a factor as falling in love with another male (Savin-Williams, 1998). Isay (1996) makes the same observation.

The belief that one has to be sexually active in order to credibly self-identify as gay is a double standard. This same measure is not used for heterosexuals because heterosexuality is assumed. In one study, adolescents who experienced same-sex attraction waited an average of four to five years after awareness before acting on that attraction (D'Augelli and Hershberger, 1993). Males waited longer than females. Another study revealed that half of the male participants acted on their same-sex attractions prior to puberty (Savin-Williams, 1998). Many youths, however, realize a same-sex identity without same-sex activity (Savin-Williams, 1995). As well, homosexual sex is not the sole domain of sexual minority individuals and, as noted above, heterosexual sexual activity is often engaged in by those of us who are not heterosexuals as *proof* of heterosexuality.

Whenever it happens, self-labeling as gay is a breaking away from heterosexual socialization (D'Augelli, 1996) and the creation of a new self. This journey brings its own challenges. If the individual has knowledge only of fragments of gay life, which is usually the case, he may not be able to identify with that life. Given some of the attitudes toward homosexuals, a youth may even fear identifying as gay (Lipkin, 1995). Once again, this process is not the same for everyone, and statistics may lead us away from individual realities.

Racial minority gay youth have more than one stigmatized identity to explore and claim (Savin-Williams, 1995). There may be a tension because the racial minority and sexual minority youth may feel more attached to, or more supported in, one community than the other. The youth may feel pulled in opposite directions by both communities. Savin-Williams also indicates that this can happen with gay youth who are members of religious communities. Religious restrictions can play a role in delaying self-identifying as gay.

While diverse in *when* they self-identify, gays seem to have similar feelings following their self-identification as gay. Many describe it as a relief (Savin-Williams, 1998). Looking back on his coming out, Chin (1998) said that it gave him back a sense of self and that it was an end to his feeling of worthlessness. Savin-Willliams (1995) found a positive link between self-identification as gay and self-esteem. D'Augelli (1996) points out that for today's gay youth, unlike the experiences of many gay adults, coming out happens in a context of gay pride and greater social acceptance.

Donnee's Awareness and Self-identification

Awareness requires language if one is to articulate that awareness to self and others, and claim an identity. Donnee recalls finding a language in elementary school:

> It was probably in grade 8. I can even remember the exact class. It was in health class actually, because we did health all the way up until grade 9. But … in health class there was a chapter in our book on homosexuality, and I can even remember the teacher being extremely tactful in how she taught that chapter, because she didn't want to impress the students to decide one way or the other… I can remember her talking about that you might grow up and find that some of your friends are gay and that's okay. I guess that's when the idea of the possibility was put into my head. I guess somewhere deep down I always knew, but when we went through that chapter it kind of struck me. Then I started seriously thinking about it in the right terminology. I may have thought about it in grade 7 but just didn't have a word for it or a way to describe what I was thinking or feeling. But in grade 8 I was given that terminology, and I thought about it then right through grade 8 to grade 9, as well as in grade 10 in high school, and then I finally came out at the end of grade 10 because I had finally managed to make a decision.

Donnee also remembered this first experience of finding a language as being one where he encountered homophobia in school. In talking about the tact that his elementary school teacher exhibited when she spoke about the topic of homosexuality, Donnee recalled that "she even tried to make an effort to kill some of the homophobia that might have been in the room." Donnee added, "there were kids that laughed when that chapter was read and that kind of turned me off talking about it to anyone."

Coming Out

Donnee related his experience of coming out to someone he knew:

> The first person I ever came out to was my best friend at the time. We were up at his cabin. The entire day I kind of danced around it, and I think a lot of people were starting to question whether or not I was, at school. They kind of thought I was but weren't sure… I kind of hinted towards it and I asked him how he felt, trying to feel him out, to see how he would react. He kind of looked at me strangely and then he answered in a positive fashion, and so that was good enough. I kind of left it. I had almost gotten up the guts to tell him then and there on the dock, but I let it go and kind of went through the rest of the day and the afternoon… . That night I decided that I was going to tell him, and I did tell him that night, and it went extremely well and he was extremely supportive. He thought it was completely fine that I was gay and he didn't have an issue with it and our friendship would never change. Subsequently he has pulled away a little bit in the past 2 years, and the friendship has kind of fizzled out. Now whether or not that's because he knows I'm gay now, I have no idea.

Out in School

Donnee has not waited until adulthood to come out. After coming out to his best friend, Donnee began a very deliberate process of coming out to his peers:

> I had originally decided that I would tell my direct circle of friends, that I would do it in a very paced-out manner and that I would do it in a very quiet manner, and I really had no intention of telling my … mom right away. And so I worked on that

for the next little while, for the next month or so... We'd be in school and I'd pull someone aside and say to them... Actually, to go back even further, when I first start-ed coming out I came out as a bisexual, not as a gay man, because I think it was easier for me, and I think in my mind I thought if I came out as a bisexual, people would be less shocked because there are still girls involved at times and it wouldn't have been a complete reversal. So, I think that's how I thought. And then eventual-ly, after a while, I got so comfortable saying that I was, I thought about it even more, and I thought this is absolutely ridiculous... I should just tell people that I'm gay because that's what I really am. So I went back and I changed it, and I talked to people, and that's how it went.

Donnee talks about his coming out experiences in very positive terms:

I never got a negative reaction when I came out to people, so I think that kind of helped me stepping forward and telling more people, and by the time 2 or 3 months had passed it had almost become general knowledge at school without me even try-ing hard, because it became so natural for me to say, and I think it was because of all of the positive reactions that I got that allowed me to do that. And at this point I still hadn't planned on telling ... my mom.

When asked what he thought school was like for a gay person, Donnee spoke about his own reality:

I can really only talk from my perspective, because everybody is different. But I know I started thinking about it at the end of grade 7 and 8 ... the summer between 7 and 8 ... so 7, 8, 9, and 10, there was a 4-year span from the time I started to think about it until I definitely came out. Two and a half of those years it wasn't that big of an issue because I was only thinking about it. I could brush it off when I want-ed to. But for the last year and a half to 2 years, personally it was very difficult for me and frustrating that I basically decided who I was and knew who I was and wanted to date people and wanted to talk about it but I couldn't because I was ter-rified of the reaction that my friends might have. You shouldn't be terrified like that. You shouldn't be terrified about the dating process. It's supposed to be a fun thing to do. The main feelings and sentiments are those of terror, confusion, and frustration. I think that's the main three feelings that people have. Because not only is there the worry about your friends' reactions ... of dating and that kind of thing, but I mean there is also the bullying aspect. As much as we don't want to admit it, there is still mean people out there like that. I've been fortunate enough never really to have encountered any of it, but they are still out there and I know that at schools, even in my city, I wouldn't be able to be as out as I am.

Coming Out: The Other Research

Schneider (1997) points out that while the heterosexual assumption, the assumption that everyone is heterosexual, works well for heterosexuals, it injects considerable complication into the lives of sexual minority youth because, in order to live authen-tically, they must challenge this assumption. This coming out, Schneider emphasizes, is a developmental process that happens alongside other developmental processes of adolescence.

Coming out is both a personal and a political act (Henderson, 1998). Disclosing one's sexual orientation to others means an exiting from the assumed heterosexual identity and the lifelong expectations that come with it (D'Augelli, 1998). The new gay identity needs to be developed in a gay context (D'Augelli and Garnets, 1995). This cannot be done if the individual remains in the closet and cut off from gay life.

Young gay people come out at different time lapses following their self-awareness and self-identity. In some cases all three happen simultaneously, or the person is *outed*, meaning that their sexual orientation, or perceived sexual orientation, is disclosed by someone else. Sometimes this revelation is also a revelation to the youth. In those cases, the youth is most often a gender nonconforming youth. An average age of disclosure reported by some researchers is 16 years (D'Augelli and Hershberger, 1993; D'Augelli et al., 1998). This first disclosure to another person may be several years after becoming aware of one's sexual orientation and self-identifying as gay (D'Augelli, 1996). D'Augelli and Hershberger found that the average length of time between awareness and coming out to at least one other person was six years. Savin-Williams (1995) found that the most popular time for disclosing to another person was during the first year of college or university. The college experience is an opportunity for prolonged adolescence, which allows a gay person more time to work through internalized homophobia and come out to self and others (Anderson, 1995). The statistics, however, do not reveal the whole story. One youth in the Savin-Williams study disclosed to his parents when he entered junior high school. On the other end are those who are aware of their sexual orientation for many years before coming out. For some, their sexual orientation remains a lifelong secret.

While there is considerable diversity in when gays first disclose their sexual orientation, there is much similarity in whom they come out to. D'Augelli and Hershberger (1993) and D'Augelli et al. (1998) reported that over 75% of gay youth had told a friend first about their sexual orientation. In most cases, this friend is a female (Savin-Williams, 1995). Savin-Williams reported that a considerably smaller percentage, 20%, first came out to a family member. This was usually a sibling rather than an extended family member.

It is significant to note that very few youth disclose first to the professionals in their lives, such as teachers or counselors (5%) and clergy (2%) (D'Augelli and Hershberger, 1993). Despite the fact that I have been an out gay and gay-positive elementary educator for many years, I have never had a student come out to me while they were in the school where I was teaching. Donnee did not come out to any of his elementary school teachers or even mention to them that he was considering that he was gay:

> Things changed when I got to high school. I didn't tell any teachers in grade 10, because it was only that year that I had started to come out to my friends, and then I came out to friends, and then my mom, and then to family friends, and then my teachers. They were the last people that I came out to.

Donnee reported coming out to three of his teachers, and he feels that other teachers in the school know that he is gay: "No teachers have treated me any differently since I've told them."

The majority of gay youth do not come out in school. Those who do usually face the most difficult challenges (D'Augelli, 1996). D'Augelli points out that there will probably be more youths facing this experience, and professionals, including, or especially, teachers, need to be prepared to provide them with protection and support.

Two apparently opposing views summarize researchers' opinions about youth disclosing to others their same-sex sexual orientation. Savin-Williams (1998) holds that

> *adolescents who disclose to others are generally assumed to experience a diverse array of positive mental-health outcomes that are associated with openness, including identity synthesis and integration, healthy psychological adjustment, decreased feelings of loneliness and guilt, and positive self-esteem. Disclosure is thus assumed to reduce the stress that accrues to adolescents who actively hide or suppress their sexual orientation.* (p. 142)

D'Augelli (1998), however, cautions that identifying earlier and coming out sooner may make today's gay youth "vulnerable to psychological risks unknown to earlier cohorts" (pp. 188–89). I do not believe D'Augelli (1998) is suggesting that youth stay in the closet, but that the responsibility for the supports those young people will need is a responsibility that belongs to the adults in their lives. Among those significant adults are educators.

Donnee speculated about why coming out seemed more of a possibility for him in his current educational environment:

> *I don't know if it's because of the school that I'm in, because of the people that are there now, or what it is. But I know that based on other schools' reputations ... if I came out and was as out as I am in the community, I would be uncomfortable with other people in the school. I would be more afraid. Because there definitely are bullies in those schools that would probably take some form of action.*

The action that Donnee was talking about he clarified as "physical, violent action." He said that he would be worried about "making it home in the same condition" that he went to school in.

Coming Out to Parents

Home and *school* are considered *partners* in education. This can be a dilemma for the gay child who may experience both places as sites of homophobia and heterosexism. Even when the youth has a safe space at school, homophobic parents can jeopardize a young gay person, even at school. Disclosure to parents is a very emotionally charged stage of the coming out process, and can put the youth at considerable risk, especially if they are still living at home and going to school (D'Augelli and Hershberger, 1993; D'Augelli et al., 1998; Henderson, 1998; Savin-Williams, 1998). D'Augelli et al. reported that the average age of first disclosure to a parent was 17 years. Mothers (65%) were preferred over fathers (9%) for coming out to. In that study, more males than females had disclosed to parents. Mothers (93%) were much more likely to have known or suspected in the case of their gay sons. Mothers were more accepting than fathers, but they were also reported to have been the most verbally abusive. Brothers of gay males were the most likely to be physically threatening and physically abusive. It is abuse, both verbal and physical, as well as the loss of emotional and financial support, up to complete ejection from the family home, that some sexual minority youth experience, and many fear, if they come out.

Pilkington and D'Augelli (1995) found that more persons of colour than white respondents described the prospect of family disclosure as extremely troubling (29% versus 20%). This highlights a major difference between members of other minority groups and individuals who identify as part of a sexual minority. The parents of gays are most often heterosexual, whatever their race, ethnicity, or religion. Heterosexuality is assumed within the family, and families are unprepared to deal with any reality other than heterosexuality. Racial, ethnic, or religious minorities, however, can usually find, within their families, solace and safety from the harassment and discrimination they may experience elsewhere. When gays come out to their families, however, that solace and safety are not always there.

Coming Out to Mom: First Steps

Donnee's story of coming out to his mother is a poignant story of trust, support, and love. It is also a story that contains pain and loss for both:

> *One night ... I thought, well, maybe I should start or I should tell her something. The night I told my mom I remember it like it was last night... She was in her room lying in bed ... doing a crossword ... and she was eating a tuna sandwich... I remember walking into her room and sitting down on the corner of her bed by her feet... At that point I knew that I was gay and I had been telling people that I was gay for the past 3 months, but I thought that I'd use the same tactic with her as I used with them... I decided that I would tell her that I was bi if I was going to tell her anything... I knew that when I told her, her immediate thought would be, "Oh my God, I'm not going to have any grandchildren." I knew that would be the first thought that she would have in her head... I had actually done research on coming out to your parents prior to telling her. I had gone on the net, and I had read books and I had asked people about it... I wanted to be able to answer those questions when she asked them... I wanted to be able to defend my thinking. Not to say that I would have to defend myself against my mother, but that I just wanted to make sure that I had the knowledge to tell her. I told her ... the exact words that I used were... "I think I'm bisexual."*

> *She kind of laid down her sandwich and her mouth gaped open and that was kind of to be expected, and I wasn't shocked by the reaction I got. And all things considered I think that I have the greatest mom on earth, for the type of reception she gave me. We didn't talk about it much that night. She told me that, you know, if it was something I was thinking about, then I had to be sure, that she would love me either way, no matter what I decided, but she thought I had to give it some time before I made my final decision. And she also told me that she thought I would have to experience both sides before I was able to make my decision. And by experiencing both sides, I mean have sex with a member of each sex. And of course, she promoted safe sex all the way through, as a mother would. And that was about it... I gave her a big hug and a kiss and left the room, and she went back to her crossword puzzle.*

Coming Out to Mom as Gay

Three or four months after coming out to his mother as bisexual, Donnee came home one night later than expected. The van belonging to the friend he was with had broken down. His mother had been extremely worried. As he walked in the door he met her anger, her joy, and her tears:

> *I asked her what's on the go, and she said that she was worried that I had gone out and gotten picked up by some guy and something, anything, could have happened to me and she was worried. And so that's when it all came out. I told her that, look, I would never do something like that, not without you knowing and without setting up safety guards. I wouldn't meet anyone off the internet unless I knew enough about that person to feel comfortable and unless I had safety nets put in place to know that if something did go wrong that I would be able to get out of the situation.*

Donnee did eventually go on a date with someone he met on the internet. This date was with his mother's permission and with safety nets in place:

It had obviously been weighing on her mind. We stayed up the next hour and a half talking about college, my career, the family, absolutely everything under the sun, and I appreciate that. I appreciate that so much because I know that there are not a lot of kids out there who have mothers that would care that much or would be that supportive. We also talked about dating, and we talked about bringing other guys home. We talked about sex. I was surprised about the amount she knew. She told me about gay friends that she had had in her 20s and she blew my mind by the amount of information she knew as well, because she went quite into depth. We also had a talk about safe sex.

Donnee related one painful part for him of his experience coming out to his mother. He also talked about what he believed his mother was facing:

The only bad feeling that I was left with that night was that one of the sentences that Mom told me that night, and I remember the sentence word for word exactly as she told me, "You realize that the family bloodline will end with you?" And hearing that line killed me. I didn't know what to think at first, and then the fact that she had said that in the open and the facial expression she had ... when she told me that, and the tears that were streaming down her cheeks when she told me that, the only way to describe it was that it killed me, because although she was right... I could certainly adopt... I do have other relatives that will carry on. It just meant that my particular bloodline would probably end, and that's depressing to an extent. But at the same time, I don't believe that I should live my life in a lie for that one reason. I don't think that's enough.

She didn't say [this] to hurt me, and I know she didn't say the line to hurt me. I think she more or less said it to bring it out in the open and make sure that I realized, and I also think she said it because she was shocked as well. Her thoughts, her questioning of whether or not she had a gay son, had been confirmed that night, and she knew for sure, for 100% sure, that night that she was never going to have any grandchildren. And I think she said it for that reason. And it's fine, because we were both shocked that night... Since then she has been completely supportive. I don't think I'd be wrong in saying that she is probably one of the most supportive parents I've ever encountered, and she's amazing for that reason. Since telling her that night that I was gay for sure was probably the most liberating experience that I had ever gone through in my life. While it was extremely difficult to go through emotionally, it completely changed my life, because I knew then that I would be able to date... It felt like there was 20 tons coming off my shoulders, that I didn't have to hide anymore, and that I didn't have to not be who I was.

When Donnee's mother told him that she didn't want to see him "bringing home a guy next week" Donnee understood. "I understood that because I had a year and a half to think about this by now and she's had 3 months. So I understood that, and I didn't [bring home a guy the next week]." Subsequently, Donnee's mother has met some of his dates:

Since I've come out I've probably seriously dated seven other guys and the one I was with for 6 months and Mom knew him well... She's met at least four of them... One of them slept over one night, actually. She made the stipulation, when I asked her if he could sleep over, that he had to sleep in another room, but I was fine with that. I can respect that. Even parents of straight kids don't let their children sleep with the person they are seeing right off the bat.

Donnee's mother has also met members of the various gay community groups he is involved in.

The Internet

Certain realities highlight the generational differences between some of Donnee's and my own experiences. The internet is one of them. When I was Donnee's age, the manner in which he now uses the internet as a gay youth, was the stuff of my science fantasy. Donnee used the internet as a first avenue to explore gay culture. The use of the internet for this purpose began as research around grade 9:

> I went to different sites about coming out and about being young and gay and this kind of thing... Towards the middle of grade 9 and getting closer to the end, I started looking for visuals and looking at guys and saying to myself, "Well, he's good looking," and being able to say it to myself. And that's when I started to pin things down for sure. And then it was the summer between grade 9 and 10 ... when I started chatting ... and I have been chatting for 2 years.

The year before telling his mother that he was bisexual, Donnee had been chatting with other gay and bisexual males on the internet. Donnee said that there was danger with chatting on the internet, but he also felt that it was positive

> because it gave me kind of a support group and people to fall back on... I had been going there for quite some time and I had developed friendships. I had developed really strong friendships from the room, and there were people that I had wanted to meet, and mom probably knew that, but I continuously said no to them for the simple safety factor. For an entire year of my life I was going online, I was going to this room, and every time I got off my computer I was deleting the cache. I was deleting the history and I was doing computer cleanup and I was covering my tracks, for a year. And I think that's what finally pushed me to tell people and to tell Mom. It was because I got fed up with covering who I was, that I was covering my tracks, like I felt like I was a criminal in my own house and like I couldn't even do the things I wanted to do even on my own computer.

Out, and an Activist at School

While many students still do not feel safe enough at school to come out, and many educators, whether queer or heterosexual, are oppressed into silence by homophobia and heterosexism, Donnee has found that he has a voice and he uses it to make a difference:

> Health Canada put out a booklet for teenagers who are young and confused and trying to decide if they are gay or what their sexual orientation is... I took one of them to school and I passed it to my guidance counselor and I told her that I felt our school should have some literature on that subject because there was nothing there for any student who was thinking about it, and she has taken the booklet and she has ordered a box of one thousand of them from Health Canada. So there's support within my school.

The Future

My sexual orientation became an issue for me as I was looking at career choices. While working as an educational assistant I became very attracted to teaching. I felt that it was a natural fit for me, but one day I recall saying to someone from whom I was seeking advice as I made my decision, "I want to find a career where I will not experience homophobia." His response was that my choices would be very limited. He encouraged me to not limit my choices and to do what I wanted to do. Once I figured out what that was, I did. Despite the homophobia and heterosexism that I have encountered in the education community, I have remained grateful to him for that advice.

Donnee seems to have no such concerns about his future:

> Well, career-wise, when I finish high school I am planning on going to our universi-ty here in the province and doing a Bachelor of Arts in English, and then I will be moving to Toronto when that's done and over with ... and I'll be doing a Bachelor of Journalism. As to how that relates to me being gay, I don't think it really changes much. I don't think the fact that I'm gay is going to change the career that I want to get into or how I go through the career. The other career choice that I'm planning on making is to go into politics for political office. Being gay may have a bit more impact there, but I don't plan on letting it... You know, I wake up every morning and I put my pants on one leg at a time just like everybody else in the city, province and country. So the fact that I'm gay, I don't think it should make a difference and I won't let it make a difference in the career that I choose. That's how it relates to my career, that's how I've decided to let it relate to my career. I'm going to live my life, and if I run for a position or whatever, they bring their wives up on the stage, if I've got a husband he's coming up there with me. It's not something that I'm going to hide or make an effort to hide, but it's not something I'm going to flaunt either. The same way as I live my life.

A Final Word of Thanks

When I asked Donnee to write a *letter unsent* to one of his elementary school teach-ers, he responded with a touching letter to a teacher who had made a difference in his life. His letter, I feel, contains a message for all educators:

> I wanted to write to you to tell you that I think I have become successful and part of it can be attributed to you and all the help that you gave me when I was going to school... It makes a lot of difference when the teacher actually cares enough to sit down and get to know the students... My life was probably drastically changed and my self-esteem boosted by all the encouragement and support that you gave me. You made me believe that I could do anything that I set my mind to, and you made me self-confident. That certainly came in handy when I came out to all my friends and family over a year ago... That is definitely something I wouldn't have been able to do if you hadn't been there to make me feel like I was important... I wanted you to know that you did make a difference in someone's life, and that is probably what makes teaching so worthwhile. Thanks a lot.

Notes

1. This manner of honouring voice was used by Shields (1997) in her PhD thesis.
2. According to Packwood and Sikes (1996, p. 343) narrative also "attempts to recognize and cap-ture the fragmentary, fractured, and chaotic reality of the research process for all of the individ-uals concerned. It embeds that process within the textual product. The voice of the researcher telling the story/stories of the research becomes part of the polyphony through which the text evolves. The dilemmas and tension are made explicit as a counterpoint to the harmony."

3. This contact was made following approval of my research by the Brock University Senate Research Ethics Board. An Information Letter and a copy of the Informed Consent form were given. Donnee selected his own pseudonym. As Donnee was under 18 years of age at the time of the study, it was necessary that his mother also agree to his participation in the study and sign the Informed Consent form. Parental consent was received once Donnee had decided that he wanted to be a participant in the study.

4. Qualitative research interviews, unlike quantitative interviews, do not have as a goal the collection of *hard data* such as statistics or percentages. Qualitative interviews are open and do not have set techniques or rules (Kvale, 1996). Kvale calls the qualitative research interview "a construction site of knowledge" (p. 42). Both the researcher and the interviewee are engaged in that construction of knowledge. The reader of the final research text also constructs knowledge by engaging with the stories told. "The qualitative interview is theme oriented" (p. 29). The themes of the interview that I conducted with Donnee were themes from his experiences in school as a gay student. Oakley (1981) says that "the goal of finding out about people is best achieved when the relationship of interviewer and interviewee is non-hierarchical and when the interviewer is prepared to invest his or her own personal identity in the relationship" (p. 41). In the Information Letter I identified as an "out gay elementary school teacher." I felt that it was important for Donnee to know that he was talking with another person who identified as gay. As well, prior to the interview, Donnee became familiar with some details of my life. The interview with Donnee was carried out by telephone from his home. Donnee lives in a Canadian city with a population of less than 200,000. The interview was tape recorded and transcribed. Donnee received a copy of the transcript of his interview for review and approval prior to the contents of the transcript being used for the study. The purpose of this exercise is to give the participant an opportunity to produce a reflective piece of writing subsequent to the interview. It was anticipated that the thoughts and feelings generated during the interview would need a vehicle for further exploration and expression. Donnee was asked to write a letter to one of his former elementary school teachers. This letter was given to me and formed part of the data for this study. Donnee's *letter unsent* was cited at the opening of this chapter. More about that letter later.

5. Finally, the interview with Donnee was conducted at a specific time and place, and I write from a time and a place in my own life. If the times and the places were different, how Donnee would tell his stories might be different. Which stories I would write from those he told might also be different. Lives and the telling of stories of lives are not static. We change, and how we view our lives changes as we experience new events and situations across our lifespan (Dewey, 1938).

References

Adnan, E. 1998. "First Passion." In C. Chase (ed.), *Queer 13: Lesbian and Gay Writers Recall Seventh Grade*. New York: Rob Weisbach Books.

Anderson, D.A. 1995. "Lesbian and Gay Adolescents: Social and Developmental Considerations." In G. Unks (ed.), *The Gay Teen: Educational Practice and Theory for Lesbian, Gay, and Bisexual Adolescents*. New York: Routledge.

Chase, C. 1998. "Introduction." In Chase (ed.), *Queer 13*.

Chin, J. 1998. "The Beginning of My Worthlessness." In Chase (ed.), *Queer 13*.

Clandinin, D.J. and F.M. Connelly. 1991. "Narrative and Story in Practice and Research." In D. Schon (ed.), *The Reflective Turn: Case Studies in and on Educational Practice*. New York: Teachers College Press.

——. 2000. *Narrative Inquiry: Experience and Story in Qualitative Research*. San Francisco: Jossey-Bass.

D'Augelli, A.R. 1996. "Lesbian, Gay, and Bisexual Development During Adolescence and Young Adulthood." In R.P. Cabaj and T.S. Stein (eds.), *Textbook of Homosexuality and Mental Health*. Washington, DC: American Psychiatric Press.

D'Augelli, A.R. 1998. "Developmental Implications of Victimization of Lesbian, Gay, and Bisexual Youths." In. G.M. Herek (ed.), *Stigma and Sexual Orientation: Understanding Prejudice Against Lesbians, Gay Men, and Bisexuals*. Thousand Oaks, CA: Sage.

D'Augelli, A.R. and L.D. Garnets. 1995. Lesbian, Gay, and Bisexual Communities. In A.R. D'Augelli and C.J. Patterson (eds.), *Lesbian, Gay, and Bisexual Identities Over the Lifespan: Psychological Perspectives*. New York: Oxford University Press.

D'Augelli, A.R. and S.L. Hershberger. 1993. "Lesbian, Gay, and Bisexual Youth in Community Settings: Personal Challenges and Mental Health Problems." *American Journal of Community Psychology* 21, no. 4: 421–48.

D'Augelli, A.R., S.L. Hershberger and N.W. Pilkington. 1998. "Lesbian, Gay, and Bisexual Youth and Their Families: Disclosure of Sexual Orientation and Its Consequences." *American Journal of Orthopsychiatry* 68, no. 3: 361–71.

Dewey, J. 1938. *Experience and Education*. New York: Macmillan.

Guiney, J.J. 2002. "School Life for Gays: A Critical Study Through Story" (Master of Education Research Project, Brock University).

Henderson, M.G. (1998). "Disclosure of Sexual Orientation: Comments from a Parental Perspective." *American Journal of Orthopsychiatry* 68, no. 3: 372–75.

Holleran, A. 1998. "The Wind in the Louvers. In Chase (ed.), *Queer 13*.

Isay, R.A. 1989. *Being Homosexual: Gay Men and Their Development*. New York: Avon Books.

——. 1996. *Becoming Gay: The Journey to Self-acceptance*. New York: Henry Holt.

Kvale, S. 1996. *Interviews: An Introduction to Qualitative Research Interviewing*. Thousand Oaks, CA: Sage.

Lipkin, A. 1995. "The Case of a Gay and Lesbian Curriculum." In Unks (ed.), *The Gay Teen*.

Lowenthal, M. 1998. "Lost in Translation." In Chase (ed.), *Queer 13*.

Mabry, M. 1998. "Mud Pies and Medusa." In Chase (ed.), *Queer 13*.

Oakley, A. 1981. "Interviewing Women: A Contradiction in Terms." In H. Roberts (ed.), *Doing Feminist Research*. London: Routledge and Kegan Paul.

Packwood, A. and P. Sikes. 1996. "Adopting a Postmodern Approach to Research." *Qualitative Studies in Education* 9, no. 3: 335–45.

Pilkington, N.W. and A.R. D'Augelli. 1995. "Victimization of Lesbian, Gay, and Bisexual Youth in Community Settings." *Journal of Community Psychology* 23: 34–56.

Russell, P. 1998. "Underwater." In Chase (ed.), *Queer 13*.

Savin-Williams, R.C. 1995. "Lesbian, Gay Male, and Bisexual Adolescents." In D'Augelli and Patterson (eds.), *Lesbian, Gay, and Bisexual Identities*.

——. 1998. *And Then I Became Gay: Young Men's Stories*. New York: Routledge.

Schneider, M.S. 1997. "Pride, Prejudice and Lesbian, Gay and Bisexual Youth." In M.S. Schneider (ed.), *Pride & Prejudice: Working with Lesbian, Gay and Bisexual Youth*. Toronto: Central Toronto Youth Services.

Shields, C. 1997. "Behind Objective Description: Special Education and the Reality of Lived Experience" (PhD dissertation, University of Toronto).

5

A Mother's Story:
CRITICAL CONSCIOUSNESS,
CONSCIENCE AND HOMOPHOBIA

Marilyn Totten

ALMOST AS SOON AS I FINISHED TAKING CLASSES toward a Master's degree in educational psychology, I was anxiety ridden over the choice of a topic for the thesis that would complete my degree. After finally choosing a topic I found, much to my dismay, that many people questioned it. When extended family, friends and colleagues inquired as to the topic of my thesis, I would tell them I had chosen to write about homophobia in schools and how teachers might better support sexual minority youth. Frequently the response I got was, "Why did you choose *that* topic?" Although the question itself did not bother me, the emphasis on the word "that" made me automatically defensive. The emphasis, along with the tone of voice, implied that the topic I had chosen was somehow inappropriate, distasteful— perhaps even offensive. I stuck with it, however, and over the course of my research and writing, I discovered that I had much to learn about my relationship with the topic, as well as my relationship with my lesbian daughter. What follows is the story of how I discovered not only my thesis topic, but my own unconscious homophobia.

A significant part of my story comes from the discovery of critical theory as a basis for my thesis. Critical theory involves understanding the constructed nature of our consciousness, that is, we all are shaped by our past experiences and influences, and therefore each person has a unique understanding of each situation he/she encounters (Hinchey, 1998). Our past experiences and influences (parents, church, media, etc.) shape our beliefs and attitudes. Should we desire to transcend merely accepting our beliefs and attitudes, and achieve a critical consciousness, we must explore why we believe what we believe, and question the same. Hinchey (1998, pp. 122–23) explains this task as follows:

> When some experience causes us to question our firmest beliefs about the world, there is a domino-like effect which can change our entire perspective both on who and

> *where we are... . Such chains of questioning, such probing of our assumptions, are*
> *elementary examples of a process Paulo Freire calls conscientization. Critical theo-*
> *rists often name the state of mind that is nurtured by this process "critical conscious-*
> *ness." Critical consciousness is the mental habit of asking ourselves what assump-*
> *tions are guiding our actions; why we believe what we believe; who gains and who*
> *loses from the assumptions we endorse; whether things might be otherwise, and pos-*
> *sibly better; and how we might effect change if we think it desirable.*

My growing awareness of this process began slowly but surely, as I worked my way through the literature review, and the interviewing and writing process for my thesis, and continues to the present. Since I believe it is important for the reader to understand my own cultural standpoint, or where I come from, I offer a synopsis of my growth in critical consciousness as it pertains to homophobia.

I grew up in the 1950s and 1960s in rural Saskatchewan. I think one could safely say that I was naïve about many things. I was 12 before I even knew that homosexuality existed. In Grade 7, a church group (sponsored by what I would now describe as a fundamentalist Christian church) distributed pamphlets to the students in our school. Not only did the content of the pamphlets explain the dangers of alcohol and drug use in graphic detail, but it also addressed the sin of homosexuality. I had no idea what homosexuality was, but because it contained the word "sex" I was not about to ask my fellow classmates or teacher. However, as soon as I could without anyone noticing, I looked up the meaning of the word in the source I trusted to be honest and uncensored—my *Thorndike-Barnhart High School Dictionary*. The definition I found was: "*adj.* Having to do with or manifesting sexual feelings for one of the same sex.—*n.* a homosexual person." I was confused on two counts. First of all, I did not really understand why two people of the same sex would have "sexual feelings" for each other or how they would manifest those feelings. Secondly, I did not understand why it was a sin. My concept of sin, having grown up attending the United Church of Canada, included breaking the Ten Commandments, or not following Jesus's dictum to love thy neighbour as thyself, which I interpreted to mean not hurting other people. I could not understand how it was a sin for a person to have sex with someone who happened to be of the same sex. Some religions had some strange ideas I thought. Clearly, their beliefs about what constituted a sin did not mesh with mine. Since homosexuality did not really concern me in any significant way, and I really did not understand much about it, I quickly tucked the issue away.

For more than a decade homosexuality was a non-issue in my life. Aside from feeling somewhat smug over the "decriminalization" of homosexuality enacted in 1969 by Pierre Trudeau (clearly homosexuality was not as bad as the pamphlet I had received in Grade 7 made out), homosexuality was off my "radar screen." Although I understand now that I undoubtedly knew many people who were homosexual and were just not willing to make it public knowledge, I was not aware at the time of knowing anyone who was homosexual, and neither was I really aware of homophobia in any significant way. The next occasion I had to think much about homosexuality occurred in the mid-1970s when my husband asked me if I wanted to go to the local press club to listen to a presentation by two men who were seeking signatures on a petition. While I do not remember exactly how the petition read, I believe its purpose was to lobby to have gay marriage legalized. (They were obviously three decades ahead of our legal system!) I do not remember the specifics of the talk the two men gave, but I do remember feeling a great sense of outrage at the unjust persecution and gross inequalities these men faced just because of their sexual orientation. I signed the petition with absolutely no qualms about what other people might think. It was the right thing to do in my mind, so I did it. It would be more than two decades later before I had occasion to think much about homosexuality again.

On Thanksgiving weekend 1999, I was in Edmonton visiting my middle daughter who had been married for two years. Over the course of the weekend she informed me that she and her husband were going to get a divorce, and eventually it came out in our conversation that she had significant feelings for other women. Strangely enough I had somehow intuited this, and it came as less of a shock than the news of her divorce. There were many tears and all I could think of was how much I loved her and how much I wanted to protect her. I let her know I would support her however I could in whatever manner she needed. The weekend was soon over and I was back to teaching high school.

Before that weekend I had certainly heard the words *gay*, *fag* and *dyke* used at school as terms of derision. Up until the time I found out my daughter was gay, however, I had for the most part ignored them. Now when I heard those slang insults a slow rage burned within me. I could imagine my daughter being at the receiving end. How dare those young people use terms that stood for the people others chose to love—to hurt other children? I had no idea, however, how to deal with either my rage or the young people who were using the hateful language.

Fortuitously, I was enrolled in a group counselling course in my quest to obtain a Master's degree in educational psychology. One of the assignments was to come up with a rationale and a plan for running a counselling group for adolescents who might be in need of group support, such as students with addictions or eating disorders. I decided to check out the need for group support for lesbian, gay and bisexual youth. While researching the issues that sexual minority youth encounter, I was appalled at the statistics I found. Gay youth were two to three times more likely to become addicted to alcohol or drugs (Sears as cited in Muller and Hartman, 1998) and/or commit suicide (Gibson, 1994) than teens who were "straight." In addition to the statistics I was haunted by the stories told of youth who were harassed mercilessly at school and even asked to leave their own homes—solely because they were gay. I also became familiar with the term *homophobia* as a name for the prejudice and hate directed toward homosexuals. My heart went out to these children and as a matter of conscience I became determined to do something to help better their situation. It became a social justice issue for me, as I believe "in a society in which the distribution of resources is equitable and all members are physically and psychologically safe and secure" (Adams, Bell and Griffin, 1997, p. 3).

I had no idea where to start and aside from challenging the use of *gay* to mean "something stupid or not cool" and banning the use of *fag* and *dyke* when used as words meant to hurt, my teaching practice did not really change. On one occasion, however, a student had brought a tape of the local Christmas carol festival to watch so we could see the kids in the class perform. After our high school choir was done, a gay pride choir was up next and the students laughed and snickered and made several homophobic remarks. It was just before the end of class and I was fuming. I thought I had best think about it overnight before I acted. After phone calls to my daughter (who now lived in Toronto) and a trusted colleague, I decided to show a video called *One of Them*, which tackles the issue of discrimination based on sexual orientation. Before I showed the video, I explained to the class that I had been angry with their behaviour the previous day because it was based on prejudice, and prejudice leads to discrimination and hate. We had a brief discussion about the prejudices surrounding homosexuality and homophobia. I told them I wanted them to watch the video about discrimination based on sexual orientation. After the video I asked them to tell me in a written response if it had changed their opinion about discriminating against people who had a different sexual orientation. I encountered a great deal of homophobia during the initial discussion, but found that after the video the written responses were much more positive and a few minds had been opened. This gave me a glimmer of hope that I could do something positive with regard to fighting homophobia, but I still did not know exactly what.

In the meantime, I had managed to finish my required classes for my Master's and I had chosen the thesis route to complete my degree. I was struggling with what to write about and changed my mind several times. One day I ran into a colleague of mine who was also doing his Master's. However, he was doing the class route and he was fast-tracking it through the program. After he had gone, I thought to myself that I did not want to just take classes, because for me, part of achieving my Master's was the idea that by writing a thesis I could produce something that could make a positive difference for someone—anyone—in the education system. My thesis had to be a meaningful topic and my conversation with my colleague helped bring that home to me. Then suddenly, as if I had an epiphany, the idea came to me of writing about homophobia in schools, and how teachers could better support lesbian, gay, bisexual, transgendered, transsexual, two-spirited and questioning students. Writing about this issue was something I could do to help, in some small way, the sexual minority youth who suffered in schools.

I began the process by refining my topic and continued by writing a proposal and designing research. In the meantime I joined a local group that had been formed to help educate people about sexual minorities. As I did more literature research and interviewed the youth who had been courageous enough to agree to participate in my research, my empathy for sexual minority youth continued to grow. Indeed, I found what Roman and Apple (as cited in Bogdan and Biklen, 1998, p. 31) had to say about critical theorists as researchers was true: "'the prior theoretic and political commitments' of the researcher are 'informed and transformed by the lived experiences of the group she or he researches'." Overall, I was excited about at last being able to do something that might help these students. The writing process, however, slowed me down considerably and it was during this phase that I truly became conscious that I was not as enlightened as I thought I was.

From the time I first discovered that homosexuality existed at the age of 12, I believed that I was someone who supported homosexual people. Didn't I sign a petition in support of gay marriage? And hadn't I accepted my daughter's coming out with great sympathy and concern? And, of course, I was writing a whole thesis on the topic of homophobia—surely that proved I was not a homophobe. One night when the writing process was becoming particularly burdensome and I was in need of inspiration, I decided to watch *The Matthew Shepard Story*, a movie about the brutal gay bashing/murder of a young man in the United States. Something that one of the characters said in the movie started me thinking and when it was over, I was hit with another realization, much more painful than any I'd had previously. My journal entry from that night perhaps explains it best:

> I have a lesbian daughter and only a handful of people know about it. I have not told any close family member aside from one brother. I have not told my best friend. I have only told one colleague at work, and that was someone who I trust complete- ly not to blab. So if I don't tell people about my gay daughter, if I keep her gayness a big dark secret—which is easy to do because she lives in Toronto with her part- ner who can easily be referred to as her roommate—how am I any better than the people who avoid gay people or who tell gay jokes or even those who physically harm gay people just for being gay? If I am willing to be silent about my own daughter's gayness—and it's more than that—I am afraid to tell people about it—because I am not sure how they will react—how am I any better than the worst homophobe? I used to tell myself it was because I didn't want people to think any less of her and I would be mad and react badly if anyone said something mean or nasty about her. But really—she is out to almost everyone she knows—and if they can't accept her for what she is—well then too bad. So I can't really use that as an excuse—not really— it's lying—it's lying to myself and I call myself on that lie. I realize that I am guilty of being afraid of what people will think of me. I am afraid that I can't handle what they might say to me. I am just afraid. And fear is an ugly thing and it is the emo- tion that hate is based on and it is at the root of homophobia. I am so ashamed and I am so sorry. I love my daughter—my God I would give my life to save hers—so why don't I have the courage to step up to the plate and be "out" about her gayness? (Personal Journal, March 21, 2004)

Undoubtedly that journal entry marks the lowest point in my thesis-writing process. However, it was a huge step on my journey toward critical consciousness. I had dis- cussed this fear with people before and written it off as a phobia about homophobes, but I came to see it was, in fact, internalized homophobia. Overtly I was not homo- phobic; covertly I definitely was. I realized that even though I meant to be progres- sive and change the system for the better, I needed to confront my own homopho- bia before I could ask the same of others.

Since then, I have participated in action research in my classroom around the issue of homophobia. I have also "come out" as a mother of a gay daughter to a class I teach, and I struggle to be more willing to address homophobia in colleagues, friends and family, and not just in students. I am convinced that I am still en route to critical consciousness with regard to homosexuality and homophobia, but happy that I have made significant progress on my journey.

So the short answer to the question—why *that* topic?—is mainly because I believe that prejudice and discrimination lead to hate which causes only pain and suf- fering, and homophobia is one of the last bastions of prejudice and discrimination in North American society. I have my daughter to thank for bringing the issue into focus for me. Love can be a strong motivator and I love not only my daughter but all chil- dren, and it is my hope that one day all children will feel safe and secure in our edu- cation system, regardless of their abilities, their sex, their race, their economic sta- tus or their sexual orientation.

References

Adams, M., L. Bell and P. Griffin. 1997. *Teaching for Diversity and Social Justice: A Sourcebook.* New York: Routledge.

Bogdan, R. and S. Biklen. 1998. *Qualitative Research for Education: An Introduction to Theory and Methods.* Toronto: Allyn and Bacon.

Gibson, Paul. 1994. "Gay Male and Lesbian Youth Suicide." Pp. 15–68 in Gary Remafedi (ed.), *Death by Denial: Studies of Suicide in Gay and Lesbian Teenagers.* Boston: Alyson Publications.

Hinchey, Patricia. 1998. *Finding Freedom in the Classroom: A Practical Introduction to Critical Theory.* New York: Peter Lang.

Muller, Lynne and Joyce Hartman. 1998. "*Group Counseling for LGBT Youth.*" *Professional School Counseling* 1, no. 3: 38–41.

Everyday Acts of Survival and Unorganized Resistance:
GAY, LESBIAN AND BISEXUAL YOUTH RESPOND TO OPPRESSION[1]

Cheryl Dobinson

Most of the political life of subordinate groups is to be found neither in overt collective defiance of powerholders nor in complete hegemonic compliance, but in the vast territory between these two polar opposites (Scott, 1990, p. 136).

THIS "VAST TERRITORY" OF POLITICAL LIFE IS LARGELY UNMAPPED, especially in the area of gay, lesbian and bisexual (GLB) youth,[2] as much work on queer politics focuses only on the organized efforts of social movements and activists (cf. Vaid, 1995; Cruikshank, 1992; Adam, 1987), and there are "very few gay youth activists" (Brent Calderwood, in Due, 1995, p. 225). Rick Aguirre, who founded a U.S. national magazine for GLB youth in 1991 at age 19, comments that "the youth movement is happening on an individual basis… There is some organization, but the organized part is a very small part of the actual movement" (Chandler, 1995, pp. 336–37). Thus, studies of organized resistance would not tell the full story of queer[3] youth struggles. The key reason for this is that the more severe the conditions of powerlessness and dependency, the less likely the members of an oppressed group will utilize organized forms of public resistance (Scott, 1990, p. 17). This chapter takes the position that GLB youth in Canada and the U.S. are subject to extreme conditions of oppression at the intersection of sexuality and age, and that therefore the best way to understand their struggle is through an exploration of the specific ways they experience oppression and their everyday acts of survival and unorganized individual resistance.

The time is right for an examination of GLB youth survival and resistance. Numerous authors point to the fact that GLB youth are coming out progressively younger than ever before (Signorile, 1994, p. 88; Chandler, 1995, p. 101; Faye, 1997, p. 8; Newman and Muzzonigro, 1993, p. 214) and the current generation of queer youth is the youngest and largest yet. Thus, their experiences of oppression, survival and resistance in such large numbers is a new phenomenon. Existing research on GLB youth tends to focus on negative or problem responses by youth such as drug and alcohol abuse, dropping out of school, running away from home, and sex work (Unks, 1995; Anderson, 1995; Reynolds and Koski, 1995; Remafedi, 1994; Travers and Schneider, 1997; Hetrick and Martin, 1987), rather than considering how some of these responses (and a wealth of others *not* examined in the scholarly literature) might be (re)conceptualized as positive strategies oriented towards surviving and resisting the oppression these youth experience. There is enormous value in the existing research with respect to raising awareness of the tragic consequences of the oppression of GLB youth, particularly work on GLB youth and suicide such as Bagley and Tremblay (1997) and Remafedi (1994, 1999), and the need to take action to support this highly vulnerable population. However there is also a need for work which includes a more positive consideration of the ways in which GLB youth respond actively to mitigate the effects of oppression.

Researchers and writers studying the oppressive conditions faced by GLB youth *are* discovering and acknowledging the resiliency, strength, and ability to survive and resist oppression that these youth demonstrate (Unks, 1995, p. 8; Harbeck, 1995, p. 126; Hetrick and Martin, 1987, p. 41; Chandler, 1995, p. 305). Plummer (1989, p. 209) notes that:

> Throughout all the studies there are clear signs that gay youth do not passively accept this suffering and condemnation, but instead make very active paths to construct a gay identity, to enter a gay world, to work for acceptance, and even challenge the heterosexual assumption.

However, to my knowledge, there are currently no academic works which focus on this aspect of GLB youth experience. The only type of survival responses which are the subject of academic discourse are psychological coping mechanisms (Sullivan and Schneider, 1987; Hetrick and Martin, 1987; Newman and Muzzonigro, 1993; Durby, 1994). This is the gap in research which this chapter addresses.

I begin with a literature review in which I establish that GLB[4] youth are subject to severe and unique conditions of oppression in the areas of family, work, law, education, health and social services, religion, media and adult GLB communities. Understanding the nature of the oppression that queer youth are subject to is key in that it provides the context for exploring their strategies of survival and resistance. This first section utilizes the theoretical work of Frye (1983) on oppression, and Hill Collins (1990) and Anderson and Hill Collins (1995) on the matrix of domination, which is based on the importance of understanding connections between systems of domination.

I then take up the idea that GLB youth respond actively to their experiences of oppression, revealing a continuum of responses, ranging from survival to individual resistance, necessitated by the existence of the particularly extreme conditions of oppression outlined. Information used for this section has been gathered from autobiographical narratives, biographical accounts, academic literature,[5] and personal knowledge of the experiences of GLB youth (in Alberta, from personal contacts, and in Ontario, from my peer support work at the Lesbian Gay Bi Youth Line.[6] Theoretically, this section is framed by the assumption that the matrix of domination is responsive to human agency (Hill Collins, 1990, p. 626), and that those most severely oppressed by systems of structural inequality will respond with individualized, practical, and low-profile forms of daily resistance and survival, rather than organized resistance (Scott, 1990, p. 17).

Oppression Experienced by Gay, Lesbian, and Bisexual Youth

Gay, lesbian, and bisexual youth experience specific forms of inequality and oppression based not only on their sexuality, but also on their age. Frye's conceptualization of oppression is being employed here, as she describes very eloquently the macroscopic and structural nature of oppression, and how it is more than just suffering:

> *The experience of oppressed people is that the living of one's life is confined and shaped by forces and barriers which are not accidental or occasional and hence avoidable, but are systematically related to each other in such a way as to catch one between and among them and restrict or penalize motion in any direction* (Frye, 1983, p. 39).

This captures the essence of what Frye calls the "double bind" (p. 38), where the oppressed have few options afforded to them by the very structure of society and each one entails some negative consequences, a situation that GLB youth face in many, if not all, aspects of their daily lives.

Accounting for oppression on multiple bases is also key to an understanding of queer youth experiences. The theoretical model applied in this chapter is "the matrix of domination" perspective (Hill Collins, 1990, p. 617), which differs from an additive model[7] in that it acknowledges important social structural connections between systems of inequality, in this case, heterosexism and age-based oppression. The matrix of domination approach recognizes the interlocking nature of systems of oppression, the ways they interact with each other and need each other in order to operate successfully (Hill Collins, 1990, p. 616). This perspective also points to social institutions as the fundamental conduits for oppression, as they are structured based on particular power relations.

Thus, I will focus on understanding GLB youth oppression through an analysis of the intersection of the systems of oppression based on age and sexuality as manifest structurally in the major social institutions of family, work, law, education, health and social services, religion, and media. Adult GLB communities will also be examined, as a place where queer youth might expect to find some comfort and assistance, but where in reality the effects of heterosexism and ageism are still apparent. The reader will soon see that there is significant overlap between these areas; all are connected and mutually reinforcing, forming the systematically related barriers described by Frye (1983).

Family

Our understanding of family is often coloured by what Myra Marx Ferree refers to as the "solidarity myth, according to which the family is a unitary whole in which everyone shares a standard of living, class position, and set of interests" (Eshelman, 1997, p. 70). The reality is that there are underlying conflicts which are often hidden or ignored (Thorne, in Anderson and Hill Collins, 1995, p. 196), and families are organized around structures of power and generational struggles (Ferree, in Eshelman, 1997, pp. 70–71). Parents have tremendous control over the lives of their children, who are usually dependent on them for survival needs, such as food, shelter, money, and emotional support (Travers and Monahan, 1997, p. 184). Legally, in both Canada and the U.S., anyone under 18 is still a child, thus parents have the right to determine their residence, give consent for medical treatment, and make decisions regarding their education (Abinati, 1994, p. 149; Taylor, 1994, p. 62; Khayatt, 1994, p. 51).

It is within this relationship of legalized dependence that parents and other family members put enormous pressure on youth to be heterosexual, assuming that they have developed or will develop interest in the opposite sex and that they will eventually marry and produce children (Rubin, 1984, p. 22; Durby, 1994, p. 5; Leck, 1995, p. 199). Within some cultural groups, sexuality is even more subject to parental control, as in the case of parents' negotiating arranged marriages (Schneider, 1997b, p. 108). This legally and socially enforced relationship of dependency allows parents enormous power over GLB youth. Unlike the situation experienced by many other marginalized groups, the family of a queer youth is unlikely to have a similarity of experience upon which to base any understanding or support (O'Conor, 1995, p. 98; Chandler, 1995, p. 41).[8]

In this context, youth who come out or who are found out may be faced with a wide range of inequalities based on the inherent power imbalance in the contemporary institution of family. Although not all families react negatively, the extent of such experiences may be roughly gauged by the results of a study done by Telljohann and Price in 1993 on adolescent gay and lesbian life experiences, in which only one-third of the youth had experienced *any* support from their family (p. 41), and even this was often only after the passage of time. Parental emotional responses to finding out their child is gay, lesbian or bisexual often include denial, sadness, anger, guilt, and shame (Gover, 1996, p. 174; Travers and Monahan, 1997, p. 189; Strommen, 1989, p. 42). Some parents attempt to change their gay, lesbian or bisexual child's sexual orientation through prayer, religious counselling, conversion groups, unwanted psychiatric intervention, or forced institutionalization (Travers and Monahan, 1997, p. 192; Signorile, 1994, p. 90; Strommen, 1989, p. 41). GLB youth may suffer from mistreatment, ranging from withdrawal of affection and financial support (Rivers, 1997, p. 39; Newman and Muzzonigro, 1993, p. 223) to emotional and physical abuse (Travers and Monahan, 1997, p. 184; Blumenfeld, 1995, p. 216; Hetrick and Martin, 1987, p. 33) to complete rejection and expulsion from the home (Ricketts and Achtenberg, 1989, p. 93; Uribe, 1995, p. 206; Travers and Schneider, 1997, p. 51). Such reactions from family are closely tied to the negative social value of homosexuality or bisexuality being attached now to their child, as well as the child's homosexuality or bisexuality being interpreted as somehow negating their previous family roles, causing them to be seen as a stranger in their own family (Strommen, 1989, p. 37). Other parental responses that contribute to queer youth inequality include increased monitoring and restrictions on activity (such as prohibiting dating or the attending of GLB groups, and setting an earlier curfew), and an ongoing, back and forth pattern of support and then its withdrawal (Travers and Monahan, 1997, pp. 191–93).

Given the wide range of negative and unsupportive parental responses coupled with a structural relationship of dependency, it is no wonder that for many youth, telling their parents (or having them find out) that they are gay, lesbian or bisexual, is the beginning of one of the most traumatic periods of their lives (Heron, 1994). Youth from small and/or close-knit ethnocultural groups may additionally experience a dramatic change in the relationship to their entire ethnocultural community once they come out to their family (Herdt and Boxer, 1996, p. 217). For those youth who are not out, living in the fear of such potential parental reactions as those described is also an oppressive experience, involving lying, secrecy, and lack of opportunity for intimacy with family members (Goodman et al., 1983, p. 17). GLB youth, both out and closeted, suffer from a lack of the support that families are expected to provide with regard to adolescent development.

It is also worthwhile to add that even gay-positive parents and GLB parents may deny the validity of a queer adolescent's sexual knowledge due to their age (Kleinerman, 1996, p. 183–84), and that GLB parents are further plagued by the pressure of wanting to disprove anti-gay rhetoric arguing that gay parents make their children gay (Signorile, 1994, p. 150). Thus societal heterosexism and ageism can still have an impact on the experiences of GLB youth in families that would be expected to be supportive.

Work

Because of official and unofficial discrimination in hiring and firing, being out on the job remains impossible for many GLB persons, including youth (Herdt and Boxer, 1996, p. 227). Those who are out may face harassment by co-workers in addition to employer discrimination,[9] while those who are not out must adamantly work at keeping their identity a secret (Goodman et al., 1983, p. 10). Youth are further at a disadvantage, having little bargaining power due to lower educational levels and fewer job skills and experiences than adults (Hunter and Haymes, 1997, p. 139). They are highly disposable in the labour force and have less access to legal recourse due to lack of information and resources. Thus, GLB youth may experience partic-ular difficulty getting and keeping work (Hetrick and Martin, 1987, p. 34). This is extremely problematic given that employment is one of the few ways youth can achieve any independence from their families. A source of income is crucial to par-ticipation in many activities in queer communities, and even more so for a young per-son who is forced out of home or for whom home life is so difficult that leaving is the best option.

Runaway and throwaway street youth have few employment options, as they tend to lack marketable skills (due to both their age and often having dropped out of school) and have no fixed address at which employers can contact them (Tremble, 1993, p. 40; Boyer, 1989, p. 156). These youth may find it difficult to get any legiti-mate work, or to live off of the income of a part-time and/or low-paying job (Tremble, 1993, p. 40; Chandler, 1995, p., 197; Boyer, 1989, p. 178). They may therefore turn to illegal activities such as theft, selling drugs, or sex work (Hunter and Haymes, 1997, p. 139).[10] For many young gay and bisexual men on the street, selling sex becomes their job, especially since police and courts go lighter on prostitution than on theft or drug trafficking (Tremble, 1993, p. 42; Coleman, 1989, p. 139).

Legal

Although a 1995 Supreme Court decision in Canada has read sexual orientation into the Canadian Charter of Rights and Freedoms (Caragata, 1995, p. 31), and a 1998 ruling brought sexual orientation under the protection of provincial human rights legislation (Laghi and Makin, 1998), the Canadian legal system continues to perpetuate inequalities for GLB people, and youth in particular, in other ways. The situation in the U.S. is even worse, as discrimination based on sexual orientation is still legal in most states (Walling, 1996, p. 1).

A major area of legal discrimination against GLB youth is in sex law. The existence of age of consent laws limits the sexual activity of all youth, and often GLB youth even more so (Rubin, 1984, p. 20). In Canada, the age of consent for anal sex is 18, while for vaginal sex it is 14, although both the Ontario Court of Appeal and the Quebec Court of Appeal have struck down the relevant section of the Criminal Code, meaning that in Ontario and Quebec the age of consent is effectively 14 for both, as long as the anal sex is practised in private (Pilon, 1999). In many parts of the U.S., age of consent for same-sex sex or anal sex is irrelevant, as the acts themselves are still considered illegal (Schneider, 1997a, p. 19). Concern with the legal regulation of anal sex is particularly relevant to gay and bisexual men, for whom this is a common form of sexual expression.

Laws regarding pornography and access to explicit sexual expression also contribute to GLB youth inequality. Child pornography laws[11] mean that representations of youth sexuality are legally unavailable, while persons under 18 in both Canada and the U.S. are denied access to *any* explicit representations of sexuality that do exist (Rubin, 1984, p.20). Further, obscenity and censorship laws continue to be exercised with a heterosexist bias, meaning that gays, lesbians, and bisexuals are regularly denied images of self-defined sexual expression similar to those that heterosexuals are permitted (Kinsman, 1987, p. 210; Bergman, 1994, p. 28; Rubin, 1984, pp. 18–19). Thus, even youth who circumvent age-based regulations regarding access to sexually explicit material will still find it hard to locate gay, lesbian or bisexual sexual representations and especially depictions of queer youth sexuality.

GLB youth who run away from abusive or unaccepting homes may come in contact with the legal system in a number of ways. They may end up involved in illegal activity in order to survive, and even youth who do not violate criminal codes can end up in conflict with the legal system as "status offenders," based on the legal right of parents to control their children's activities (Abinati, 1994, p. 163).

Queer youth who experience violence may have particular difficulty gaining police support (Durby, 1994, p. 25; Heron, 1994, p. 96). Many feel hesitant about contacting police when crimes related to their sexuality are committed against them; they fear ridicule, abuse, not being taken seriously, and the possibility of being outed to parents. Thus, the police both directly victimize young gays, lesbians and bisexuals and contribute to their indirect victimization by seeming (and being) inaccessible to members of the GLB community.

Education

Unks (1995) has described the educational system as one of the most heterosexist institutions in society (p. 5), yet GLB youth in Canada and the U.S. are legally required to attend this institution which largely ignores, stigmatizes, or abuses them (Monahan, 1997, p. 203; Abinati, 1994, p. 155).

The most overt forms of homophobic abuse take place most often in schools

(Travers and Schneider, 1997, p.51), including violence, threats of violence, intimidation, verbal abuse, and homophobic slurs (Durby, 1994, p. 14; Rivers, 1997, p. 32; Khayatt, 1994, p. 53; Monahan, 1997, pp. 204–05). Bass and Kaufman (1996, p. xix) indicate that one-quarter of gay and bisexual males drop out of school in the U.S. due to harassment. Not only peers, but staff as well may contribute to this abuse, either directly, by permitting it to continue (Bass and Kaufman, 1996, pp. 202–03), or by expelling or suspending the victimized gay, lesbian or bisexual student as the cause of the problems with other students (Khayatt, 1994, p. 58).

Uribe (1994) tells us that homosexuality is "overlooked, denied [and] abused" (p. 203) in schools. Students are usually faced with silence on GLB existence in curriculum (Monahan, 1997, p. 201; Epstein and Johnson, 1994, p. 198; O'Conor, 1995, p. 99); the topic is avoided and relevant persons/issues/contributions are not mentioned (Unks, 1995, p. 5). In the few instances where homosexuality is discussed in the classroom, it is usually distorted and inaccurate (Khayatt, 1994, p. 56; Anderson, 1995, p. 21) or described as a problem, phase, or perversion (Epstein and Johnson, 1994, p. 223; Telljohann and Price, 1993, p. 41). It is often noted that boards will not permit GLB-positive endeavours, and thus such initiatives (ie. anti-homophobia workshops) can only be brought in through the back door by concerned individual teachers (Other Young Lives II, 1996). With regards to sexual education, material on same-sex sex and safer sex is often omitted (Monahan, 1997, p. 210). If GLB sexuality is mentioned, it may be medicalized or viewed only in relation to AIDS (Monahan, 1997, p. 210). Counselling services, such as support groups for queer students and information on appropriate referrals, are also lacking, along with GLB-positive library and resource materials (Monahan, 1997, pp. 216–17; Khayatt, 1994, p. 53). This educational agenda of heterosexism is exacerbated by the hidden or informal curriculum as well, which actively reinforces a purely heterosexual ideology in all areas of school life such as the prom and heterosexual dating rituals (Unks, 1995, p. 5; Leck, 1995, pp. 96–97).

Educators also often reflect societal heterosexism through their attitudes and actions. Many claim that they have no gay, lesbian or bisexual students, and therefore GLB issues are not a concern in their classroom (Other Young Lives II, 1996). When queer students are obviously present, teachers may believe it is a phase, think that the students need psychiatric help, tell parents without the student's consent, or turn a blind eye to harassment and abuse (Bass and Kaufman, 1996, pp. 202–03; Hunter and Schaecher, 1992, p. 306; Lesbian Gay Bi Youth Line, 1996–97). GLB teachers may hide their sexual orientation for fear of dismissal, thus youth are denied positive role models (Anderson, 1995, p. 21; Reynolds and Koski, 1995, p. 89).

There exists little governmental or policy support for GLB-inclusive schooling in most parts of North America (DeCrescenzo, 1994, p. xx). Even in Ontario, in spite of the fact that the Common Curriculum, the Violence Free Schools Policy and the sexual harassment provisions of the Ontario Human Rights Code all require Ontario school boards to take action against homophobia, many boards, administrators, and staff are doing nothing (The Rainbow Classroom, 1996, p. 1). Catholic and rural schools tend to be the most lax in enforcing the above policies (Other Young Lives II, 1996), and Catholic schools in particular may take the Church's prohibition of homosexuality as an excuse to not deal with GLB student issues (Kutz, 1996, p. 27).

In addition, anti-gay initiatives continue to take place in the educational policy arena. For example, school boards in Surrey and other parts of BC have implemented specific policies against GLB-positive curriculum, including the banning of resource materials prepared by GLB groups, while right-wing groups such as Parents' Response in Calgary have attempted to block policy changes which would allow for queer-positive literature in schools and for school counsellors to refer GLB youth to queer-positive counselling services without parental consent (Woodward, 1997; Sillars, 1997). Similar initiatives take place across Canada and the U.S.

In summary, when it comes to homosexuality and queer student concerns, schools are lacking in the areas of ensuring safety, developing and implementing inclusive curriculum, providing counselling services, resource materials, and professional development for teachers, and creating and enforcing inclusive policies (Monahan, 1997, pp. 204, 211–19). Thus, GLB youth remain the most underserved students in education systems (Uribe, 1995, p. 209), lacking the educational structures needed to support their emerging identities (Blumenfeld, 1995, p. 215). Further, due to high drop-out rates and low achievement, which are responses to the conditions described, the future educational and career choices of GLB youth may also be profoundly affected (Schneider, 1997a, p. 22).

Health and Social Services

Gays, lesbians, and bisexuals continue to face a variety of problems with the medical, psychiatric, and social service professions. In the medical sphere, doctors remain largely uninformed about GLB health concerns, uncomfortable with queer patients, or inclined to attribute any and all health problems to their sexuality (Ryan, Brotman and Rowe, 2000; CLGRO, 1997). There is the assumption that all patients are heterosexual, which can make it difficult or uncomfortable for GLB persons to bring up the topic of their sexuality where it is relevant. Youth experience additional barriers to quality health care, such as the fear that their sexuality will be disclosed to their parents if they come out to their doctor (Durby, 1994, p. 17, Ryan, Brotman and Rowe, 2000).

Although homosexuality was removed from the *Diagnostic and Statistical Manual III* in 1973, some psychiatric practitioners and institutions continue to treat homosexuality as a mental illness (Schneider, 1997a, p. 20). As a result, it is not difficult for concerned parents to locate mental health services that will treat their child's sexuality as a sickness requiring a cure (Schneider, 1997a, p. 20; Bass and Kaufman, 1996, p. 316). GLB youth are often subjected to unwanted psychiatric treatment, sometimes in the context of forced institutionalization, which focuses on changing their sexual orientation through a variety of means; the extremes include the use of drugs, isolation rooms, and electroshock treatment (Plummer, 1989, p. 205; Signorile, 1994, p. 90; Travers and Monahan, 1997, p. 192; Bass and Kaufman, 1996, pp. 316–17). Because of parental rights to determine children's medical treatment, including psychiatric commitment, a GLB youth may have no choice about participating in these treatments (Abinati, 1994, p. 149; Bass and Kaufman, 1996, p. 316).

In the area of social services, many service providers are homophobic and uninterested in changing their attitudes or becoming informed (Mallon, 1997, p. 225;

Ricketts and Achtenberg, 1989, p. 95; Sheridan, 1997, p. 70). Even those who are not actively homophobic are usually lacking in the ability to serve GLB youth adequately; they may lack accurate information on queer youth issues, community resources, and GLB youth development (Sheridan, 1997, p. 70; Travers and Schneider, 1997, p. 52; Mallon, 1997, pp. 226, 233), an understanding of how heterosexual assumptions influence counselling and interventions (Sheridan, 1997, p. 70), and relevant education and training (Sheridan, 1997, p. 77; ferren, 1997, p. 247; Mallon, 1997, p. 232). They may attribute GLB youth problems too readily to their sexuality or, conversely, fail to see where such issues are relevant (Sheridan, 1997, p. 76). Another problem is the fear of being seen as encouraging or promoting homosexuality if they provide support for queer youth sexual identities (Mallon, 1997, p. 226). Thus, there exists a pressing need to educate social service providers, along with creating conditions that will make it possible for them to use the knowledge (Sullivan, 1994, p. 302).

Services in the areas of HIV/AIDS, substance abuse and suicide prevention fail to adequately meet the needs of GLB youth. HIV/AIDS education and prevention programs usually do not address GLB youth issues or reasons that these youth may ignore prevention practices (Feldman, 1989, p. 185), and often fail to consider lesbians to be at any risk (Hunter and Haymes, 1997, p. 150, 157–58). Cranston (1992) argues that the high risk behaviour of young gay and bisexual males is related to HIV/AIDS education programs not addressing their unique concerns (p. 247). In addition, for those youth who are infected, there are minimal services available (Durby, 1994, p. 20). Similarly, substance abuse programs and preventions do not deal with the issues of queer youth in particular, often missing major causes of their behaviour and failing to make recovery programs inclusive (Hunter and Haymes, 1997, p. 97; Durby, 1994, p. 21). Suicide prevention research, programs, and education tend to miss GLB youth by overlooking sexuality as a potential risk factor and neglecting the specific experiences of young queer lives (Remafedi, 1994, pp. 9–10; Hunter and Schaecher, 1992).

GLB youth also face difficulties in finding supportive temporary shelters or foster care if they are homeless or need to be removed from abusive homes (Sullivan, 1994). This is especially troubling considering that GLB youth make up a high percentage of the youth requiring shelter services and foster care (Ricketts and Achtenberg, 1989, p. 93), partially due to the estimated 25–40% of street kids who are gay, lesbian or bisexual (Durby, 1994, p. 16; The Rainbow Classroom, 1996). Many foster care and group home settings are homophobic, and there is a lack of funding for queer-positive programs (Rivers, 1997, p. 44), thus GLB youth may be ridiculed, ignored, punished or rejected in these settings (Ricketts and Achtenberg, 1989, p. 94; Mallon, 1997, pp. 227, 230; Sullivan, 1994, p. 295). Shelters may have age limits which deny youth access, and even if a young person is accepted, they often face homophobic abuse from staff and other clients (Gretchel, 1997, p. 169; Mallon, 1997, p. 231).

Many of the programs and services just described lack the awareness that they are serving GLB youth or actively deny it in order to justify inaction on inclusivity (Mallon, 1997, p. 228). In general, there is a "lack of incorporation of current research and knowledge in policies and practices that affect sexual minority youth" (Sullivan, 1994, p. 295). GLB youth are neglected in medical, mental health, and social service provision through a lack of appropriate programming and personnel who are willing and able to meet their needs (ferren, 1997, p. 248). It should be noted that youth in rural areas are likely to be the most severely affected by these systemic inequalities (Langen, 1994, p. 26).

Religion

Most religious establishments explicitly condemn homosexuality (Schneider, 1997a, p. 19; Durby, 1994, p. 5), with some religious leaders claiming that it is a "danger not only to the family but to civilization as well" (Hunter and Schaecher, 1992, p. 300). This means ostracism of GLB members by their religious communities (Travers and Schneider, 1997, p. 52), as well as extreme feelings of guilt for queer people who were raised in a religious environment (Goodman et al., 1983, p. 22). Bass and Kaufman (1996, p. 259) state that:

> For many lesbian, gay, and bisexual youth, religious institutions have not been a source of support or nurturance. Instead they have been places of condemnation, rejection, and hatred.

GLB believers of all ages are faced with either denying who they are for the sake of their religion, or seeking a place of worship which is more accepting—a daunting task, especially in smaller communities. Youth in particular may not have any choice about whether they attend religious services at all, or which place of worship they attend.

By far the most serious effect of religion (in North America, Christianity in particular) is its profound influence on politics and on social and moral values (Green, 1983, pp. 146–54, 157). The powerful place of religion in North America is regularly used (or conveniently appropriated) to justify and support oppressive political actions towards gays, and youth in particular. This is the case where efforts to change school policy to provide GLB-inclusive counselling or curriculum materials are defeated by right-wing religious groups. Religious-based resistance to accepting the existence of GLB youth is rampant in individual families and in social services, such as the Catholic Children Aid Society in Ontario. Further, many nonbelievers are nonetheless influenced in their moral stance by Christian ideology, which reinforces anti-gay attitudes.

Media

Mainstream media remains lacking in terms of representation of GLB persons. Kielwasser and Wolf (1992), in their study of mainstream television and adolescent homosexuality, argue that this contributes to a specific form of invisibility termed "symbolic annihilation," which reinforces the sense of isolation felt by many GLB youth (p. 352).

When interrupted, this pattern of silence is largely broken by stereotyped or heterosexually defined images (Kielwasser and Wolf, 1992, p. 362; Fejes and Petrich, 1993, p. 412; Gross, 1994; Hantzis and Lehr, 1994). Dominant images include the "confused teen, the situational homosexual and the assimilated gay" (Kielwasser and Wolf, 1992, p.362), while heterosexually defined representations of homosexuality exclude any of its aspects which are incompatible with or directly challenging to the heterosexual regime (Fejes and Petrich, 1993, p. 412). In my research with lesbians about their film viewing experiences, the respondents indicated that they found little representation of lesbians in film, and that the few images which did exist were irritating, unrealistic, and stereotypical—showing lesbians as lonely and asexual, as dangerous, as male fantasy creations, or as going through a phase (Dobinson and Young, 2000, p. 106). Youth tend to be particularly affected by such misrepresentation, as media may provide the only images of homosexuality available to them (Kielwasser and Wolf, 1992, p. 352).

It is also worth noting that realistic, sensitive media representation of GLB youth has caused enormous public controversy, such as the case of the "For Better or For Worse" comic strip by Canadian Lynn Johnson, which dealt with the coming out of a teenage character in a 1993 series. The publication of this series of the comic strip resulted in a great deal of public uproar and debate, including threats to the author and cancellations by newspapers and subscribers (Walling, 1996, pp. 145–46).

Adult Gay, Lesbian, and Bisexual Communities

The existence of adult GLB communities does not necessarily mitigate the difficulties faced by queer youth, as these communities may be inaccessible in practical terms or simply unwelcoming to youth (Other Young Lives II, 1996, Sullivan and Schneider, 1987, p. 21). Youth are excluded from many activities central to adult GLB communities as a result of legal, financial, political, and social barriers which prevent legitimate involvement (Unks, 1995, p. 4). Legal barriers keep youth out of bar scenes (legally at least), which are a major hub of adult GLB communities, and age restrictions on driving mean that rural and small town youth may have little access to the queer communities in cities (Singerline, 1995, p. 229). Lack of financial resources also prevents youth from participating in numerous community activities which may be costly. Politically and socially, GLB communities are adult-focused in their activities (Schneider, 1989, p. 127; Unks, 1995, p. 4; Taylor, 1994, p. 43), having few youth venues (Schneider, 1997a, p. 25) and often not addressing youth issues in programs or services (Signorile, 1994, p. 89).[12] Underlying the lack of inclusivity efforts on behalf of adult GLB communities are very real fears—of social and/or legal reprisal based on accusations of "recruiting" (Durby, 1994, p. 25; Schneider, 1989, p. 124), encouraging homosexuality among youth (Taylor, 1994, p. 46), exploitation, and pedophilia (Travers and Schneider, 1997, p. 66; Bass and Kaufman, 1996, p. 358). Thus, wider societal age restrictions and the impact of heterosexist beliefs about the dangers of GLB persons interacting with youth can prevent adult queer communities from actively including GLB youth.

It is clear that GLB youth are subject to specific forms of institutionalized oppression, and that the most useful way of viewing their experiences of inequality is through an examination of the intersection of societal configurations of sexuality and age relations. Although some level of understanding could be achieved by trying to understand this oppression using an additive model—exploring heterosexism and age-based oppression separately and then arguing that queer youth experience both—all the significant interactions between the two systems which constitute the specific, unique ways that GLB youth are oppressed which cannot be reduced to age or sexuality alone would be missed. Our analysis does not stop at this point however, as the matrix of domination model conceptualized by Hill Collins (1990) is responsive to human agency (p. 626), allowing for creative acts of survival and resistance in the face of oppressive conditions.

Everyday Acts of Survival and Individual Resistance

If, as previously argued, severe conditions of inequality and dependency mean that members of an oppressed group will be unlikely to utilize organized public resistance (Scott, 1990, p. 17), how then do the members of these groups actually respond to their oppression? As mentioned in the introduction, Scott (1990) answers this question in part by arguing that most of the struggle of oppressed groups takes place between the two extremes of "overt collective defiance" and "complete hegemonic compliance" (p. 136). In this section I take up the task of proving this argument by documenting the range of strategies of survival and individual resistance[13] (as opposed to passive acquiescence or organized collective action) used by gay, lesbian, and bisexual youth in response to the severe conditions of oppression they face.

Given the assumption that systems of domination are never absolute (Hill Collins, 1990, p. 626; McClaren, 1985, p. 93), my approach is based on the general idea that people "respond creatively to their social and economic conditions through various daily and cultural practices" (Beal, 1995, p. 265). There exists the possibility of a whole range of responses (Martinez, 1997, p. 269; Harbeck, 1995, p. 127), in which oppressed people can enact individualized strategies of survival and resistance in their everyday experiences (Anderson and Hill Collins, 1995, p. 488; Hill Collins, 1990, p. 619; Beal, 1995, pp. 245, 253). Anderson and Hill Collins (1995) encourage the recognition of these forms of power as used by marginalized groups (p. 490).

Because of the extreme nature of the oppression GLB youth face, most of the strategies that were uncovered in my research relate to survival or invisible/low-profile forms of resistance (Scott, 1990, p. 19), although there are two sections which include more direct, yet still individualized, challenges to dominant culture and practices. In all areas, the strategies are intensely practical; queer youth make "choices born of a prudent awareness of the balance of power" (Scott, 1990, p. 183). I first examine and critique the scholarly literature on the use of psychological coping mechanisms by GLB youth, before moving into a contextual analysis of survival and resistance. The following three sections, on staying in the closet, escape, and prostitution, are broadly concerned with survival, and the ways in which behaviour patterns which are often viewed as problems can in reality be interpreted as solutions to problems (Rodman, in Hutter, 1998, p. 154) or strategic poses (Scott, 1990, p. xii). Then, in the section on reaching out, I explore youth strategies for surviving and resisting by seeking information or like others, which can often be done "offstage" (Scott, 1990, p. 20), or at least without coming out in any non-supportive contexts. The next section, on coming out, is divided into two parts, the first looks at resistance through expressing a gay, lesbian or bisexual identity in ways which are partial, disguised, or anonymous (Scott, 1990, p.17, 139) and the second deals with openly coming out as defiance, in the "declared refusal to comply" in maintaining hegemonic appearances (Scott, 1990, p.203) of, in this case, heterosexuality. The final section describes the resistance inherent in individual, unorganized challenges to dominant relations, drawing on the theoretical work of Clarke (in Martinez, 1997), Beal (1995), Donnelly (1988), Donnelly and Young (1985) and King (1982).

Psychological Coping Mechanisms

The only academic literature that systematically deals with the survival-oriented responses of GLB youth is that on psychological coping mechanisms. These mechanisms are most often conceptualized as corresponding to particular stages of various identity development models, and thus occurring in a developmental sequence (Sullivan and Schneider, 1987; Newman and Muzzonigro, 1993; Durby, 1994).

Sullivan and Schneider (1987) describe three solutions to the pre-homosexual adolescent's identity crisis stage, as conceptualized by Malyon—repression of same-sex desires, attempts to be heterosexual through denial, compensation and compartmentalization of same-sex desires, and finally, coming out (pp. 20–21). Newman and Muzzonigro (1993) also link coping strategies to stages of coming out, specifically what they call the identity confusion stage, arguing that the strategies which are used during this time include denial, repression, and heterosexual activity (p. 215). The outcome of this stage is either a life of denial or acceptance and pride in one's sexual identity, the latter being viewed as the "highest level of development" (pp. 215–16). In Hetrick and Martin's (1987) work on GLB youth development, they describe responses including learning to hide through self-monitoring after accepting a gay, lesbian or bisexual sexual identity (p. 35), denial of membership (identification with the dominant group and interpretation of same-sex acts or desires as phases or isolated incidents) in the dissociation and signification stage (p. 37), and gender deviance, which does not belong to any one particular stage (p. 38).

The most fully elaborated account of psychological coping mechanisms is found in Durby (1994). He describes in detail various ways of coping corresponding with three key stages of identity development. During the identity confusion stage, youth may respond with repair (attempting to "fix" their sexuality), avoidance, redefinition, denial, and finally acceptance of same-sex feelings before proceeding to the next stage (p. 7). While undertaking identity assumption, capitulation (avoiding homosexual activity), minstrelization (acting out popular stereotypes), passing (leading a double life), or group alignment (joining GLB groups) are ways that queer youth cope (pp. 8–11). Finally, during the commitment stage, available responses include covering (being gay, lesbian or bisexual but respectable), blending (neither publicly confirming nor denying a queer identity), and conversion (a feeling of personal destigmatization).

I agree that all of the above responses are possible psychological coping mechanisms employed by GLB youth as they come to terms with their sexuality, however I take issue with some of the underlying assumptions of this literature. I find the idea that coping mechanisms are attached to context-independent developmental stages, and thus occur in a linear progression, to be very problematic.

Even if we grant that GLB youth go through identity development in stages (which could also be contested), it would be erroneous to think that all queer youth fit existing developmental models. Some may not go through all the stages of a model (for example, proceeding directly to the commitment stage from identity confusion, skipping over identity assumption), others may experience the stages in differing orders, or may be at different points in relation to different contexts of their lives (for example, out at school, but passing as straight at home). This undermines the usefulness of viewing psychological coping mechanisms as following a corresponding linear progression.

Further, although psychological factors such as stage of identity development can certainly influence the strategies used by GLB youth, my position is that it is social context more than the internal characteristics of a person which affects strategy choices. For example, Durby's (1994) model cannot explain how it is that young persons could be engaging in group alignment by joining a GLB group at their school (a coping mechanism of identity assumption), while blending by acting straight and neither denying or announcing their identity at home or work (a coping mechanism of the commitment stage), because these responses are likely due to the characteristics of the contexts in which they take place. This point will become even more apparent in the following sections of this chapter, as the same gay, lesbian or bisexual youth can be seen using multiple strategies of survival and resistance based on the practical requirements of different situations, rather than on stages of identity development.

Although problematic for the above reasons, I nonetheless find that a number of the particular strategies outlined by the literature on psychological coping mechanisms are very much present in the lives of the youth considered in this chapter, but not always in the ways this body of literature suggests. Thus I will be referring to some key concepts and distinctions made by authors cited here, while outlining my own more contextually focused analysis of GLB youth strategies for survival and resistance.

The Safety of the Closet

> There are two kinds of closets, the closet where you hide your sexuality from the world, and the closet where you hide your sexuality from yourself (entry from my journal during my coming out, 1994).

I wrote the above passage when I first came out at age 21, realizing that there was more than one way of keeping one's sexuality a secret, and certainly numerous motivations. In this section I will consider youth experiences of both types of closets, and the reasons for using secrecy and denial to survive.

Sometimes GLB youth adopt a policy of self-denial in order to survive emotionally and psychologically in the face of the stigma of homosexuality and the cognitive dissonance that may be the result of beginning to identify with a reviled minority group. This is often exacerbated by a keen understanding of what the negative consequences of being queer will be in their particular circumstances, combined with a lack of ability to identify with any GLB persons, as a result of the silence, stereotypes, and misinformation perpetuated by schools, media and other social institutions. Many specific strategies for self-denial were outlined in the section on coping mechanisms, but without a full consideration of the social context for such psychological responses.

Two of the primary ways that denial is manifest are in seeking alternative explanations for actions or desires and trying to change or repress same-sex attractions (Durby, 1994, p. 7; Sullivan and Schneider, 1987, pp. 20–21; Bass and Kaufman, 1996, p. 17; Newman and Muzzonigro, 1993, p. 215; Hetrick and Martin, 1987, p. 37). With regard to the former, Deborah, of Los Angeles, at age 16 knew she had strong feelings for an older married woman, but when asked if she was gay, responded honestly, "Who me? I'm too young to be gay. I'm sure it's only a stage" (in Heron, 1994, p. 101). I have talked to numerous callers at the Lesbian Gay Bi Youth Line who explained their same-sex attractions or experiences as isolated, situational, or the result of not yet having had the opportunity for opposite-sex sexual experiences (1996–97).

Other youth took the second approach, trying to change or repress same-sex desire, often consciously acknowledging the influence of external factors on their choice of strategy:

> I thought I'll do anything for this not to be me. I decided I just won't have sex with men. I'll just have sex with women and get married and live a normal life. That was my attitude for a long time. I didn't know anyone gay, not anyone. So I tried all this different stuff to make myself be straight, like going to dances with girls. (Matt, in Bass and Kaufman, 1996, pp. 17–18)

> If my "naturalness" wasn't going to come by itself, then I was ready to force it upon myself... I did some really drastic things—all of which I hoped would make me do a complete turnaround and become a heterosexual. (Brandon, New Mexico, 17 years old, in Heron, 1994, p. 123)

The influence of religion and the fear of condemnation due to homosexuality acts as a strong motivator in youth for whom religion is important, often resulting in praying to be straight (Bass and Kaufman, 1996, p. 262). Mickie, a young woman, recounts:

> I used to kneel down in my room and pray to God to make these feelings go away. I used to cry and cry—make this go away or show me that it's not wrong (in Bass and Kaufman, 1996, p. 263).

Self-denial is the only strategy that I will be addressing in this chapter that actually does tend to correspond with a particular stage of identity development, the stage prior to coming out to oneself.

Even after GLB youth have come out to themselves, they may continue to conceal their sexuality from others or in certain settings—a tactic broadly referred to as "passing" (Monahan, 1997, p. 207; Uribe, 1995, p. 206). This type of response can be explained by Scott's (1990) argument that "the powerless are often obliged to adopt a strategic pose in the presence of the powerful" (p. xii) or to use deception in order to survive (p. 17). Travers and Monahan (1997) list some of the reasons that youth do not come out, including financial and emotional dependence, fear of rejection, harassment and abuse, familial and community religious beliefs, and cultural factors, such as to avoid shaming their family in the eyes of their ethnic community (184–85). Chandler (1995) points to the major factor being the problem of not being able to support themselves if thrown out by their parents (p. 130). In the words of Jaime Barber, an 18-year-old lesbian from Seattle, "Sometimes it's just not safe to come out until you are independent and out of school and out of the house" (in Chandler, 1995, p. 328).

GLB youth may hide their sexuality through social withdrawal, isolating themselves in order to conceal the part of their identity that is to be kept secret (Anderson, 1995, p. 25). Several of the youth who tell their stories in Heron's (1994) book describe withdrawal as a strategy they used at some point. Aaron Fricke, of Rhode Island, related that in seventh grade, "I became withdrawn. I had no means of expression" (p. 138). While Kenneth, of Mississippi, recounts that for two years, between the ages of 14 and 16, "I stopped doing everything and going anywhere. I lived in my bedroom, coming out only when my family was gone or asleep" (p. 116).

Another way that lesbian youth in particular disguise their sexuality is through continuing heterosexual dating (Schneider, 1989, p. 117; Due, 1995, p. xiv). Although some young gay men may do this as well (Hunter and Schaecher, 1992, p. 305), it is a strategy primarily used by lesbian youth because of the gender-specific effects of compulsory heterosexuality, which allow women less leeway to acceptably opt out of heterosexual dating and sexual activities (Khayatt, 1994, p. 49). Lesbian youth may have sex with men and become pregnant in order to avoid suspicion (Hunter and Schaecher, 1992, p. 305; Newman and Muzzonigro, 1993, p. 218). Neely Boudier, a 16-year-old lesbian from Louisiana, has a fiancé "to contribute to the heterosexual assumption" (Due, 1995, p. 169). Lisa, of Massachusetts, acknowledged, "I found myself having sex with boys to prove I wasn't gay" (age 18, in Heron, 1994, p. 151).

Many GLB youth find it necessary for their own self-preservation to lie about their sexuality or to explicitly deny it. They describe similar situations: "The name-calling [at school] really does hurt sometimes… A few people have even asked me right out, 'Are you gay?' and I've denied it" (Gary, Pennsylvania, age 17, in Heron, 1994, p. 166), and "It's been real bad with my parents… I just lie to them more and more" (John Swenson, Sante Fe, New Mexico, age 16, in Due, 1995, p. 78). Liza, of Los Angeles, explained:

> [F]or my own reasons, I had to lie about my being gay. I told [my mother] that I was probably just going through a phase. This, you must understand, was to ease the hostility around me (age 17, in Heron, 1994, p. 76).

Other GLB youth do not lie, explicitly deny their sexuality or pretend to be straight, but nonetheless do not come out of the closet. As Allyson, of Massachusetts, explained, "There are plenty of reasons to hide … and not many to come out" (age 18, in Due, 1995, p. 57). Reasons include not being willing to face the isolation, harassment, or violence which would result at school (Due, 1995, p. 85; Herdt and Boxer, 1996, p. 122): "I knew, for basic survival, that it wasn't a good idea to let anyone in school or my parents know" (Derek, a black youth from St. Paul, Minnesota, in Chandler, 1995, p. 12), and "I knew that my family would disown me" (Vicky, age 17, in Chandler, 1995, p. 91). Dan related "I never said I was heterosexual. I couldn't do that to myself… So it was a badly kept secret. But it was still a secret" (in Bass and Kaufman, 1996, p. 196). Daphne said the following about not coming out in some school settings:

> If your high school is anything like the high school I went to in Louisiana, you just don't come out at all. To do so would probably mean certain death, very literally (in Bass and Kaufman, 1996, p. 197).

Denial of their own sexuality through seeking alternate explanations or trying to repress or change their sexuality, and hiding it from others through withdrawal, heterosexual dating, lies, denial, or simply not coming out are all ways that queer youth attempt to solve the problems related to surviving in a heterosexist society and in their relationships of familial dependence. Even though not coming out is often viewed as a weakness within GLB communities (Rivers, 1997, p. 42; Herdt and Boxer, 1996, p. 122), in some cases it is a necessary response for youth. Self-denial is often employed for temporary psychological survival, while concealment from others is intended to preserve the physical and material aspects of existence until GLB youth are independent from families or finished school.

Escaping Oppressive Situations

As has been discussed in detail earlier in this chapter, GLB youth face severe conditions of oppression in the institutions which they are most dependent on (family or social services) or are legally required to attend (school). Given their relative powerlessness to effect change in these settings, which are characterized by high levels of inequality based on legally and socially constructed systems of sexuality and age relations, some youth find that their only recourse is to escape.

Many GLB youth run away from where they live or move out at an early age (Gretchel, 1997, p. 168; Travers and Monahan, 1996, p. 194; Unks, 1995, p. 7; Khayatt, 1994, p. 55). The literature reviewed points to two different but related reasons for leaving—fleeing specific problems, such as violence, harassment, or attempts to change the young person's sexual orientation (Gretchel, 1997, p. 175), and a more general hope of finding something better, such as acceptance in adult GLB communities (Sullivan and Schneider, 1987, p. 21; Tremble, 1993, p. 39). The latter is especially resonant for youth in rural areas or small towns, who run to cities because there are no GLB communities near them (DeCrescenzo, 1994, p. 7; Rivers, 1997, p. 40).

There are numerous accounts of youth running away, mostly for the former reason, "leaving out of fear," as Derek Johnson, a young black gay man from St. Paul, Minnesota, puts it (in Chandler, 1995, p. 187). Lyn Duff, who was placed into forced institutionalization by her parents, faked a medical reason to leave the institution in her mother's care, then she described, "once back in L.A., while we were in a store, I ran out the back door and ran away to San Francisco, where I lived on the streets for awhile" (in Signorile, 1994, p. 91). Renee McGaughy, a black lesbian from Minneapolis, explained "my mom was very abusive, so I decided to leave when I was 14," at which point she went to stay with her grandmother, but then ran away from her and ended up on the streets as well (in Signorile, 1994, p. 91). Another young woman fled a violent father:

> Nancy hit the road wearing a T-shirt, a pair of shorts, loafers and no socks ... the 17 year old honors student was running away from her Milwaukee home—specifically from her father. He had turned abusive since he found out she was gay (Chandler, 1995, p. 227).

Young gay and bisexual men also ran away from their families or group homes (Chandler, 1995, p. 226; Due, 1995, p. 17).

GLB youth who run away may end up homeless and living on the streets (Hunter and Schaecher, 1992, p. 306). This may nonetheless be a better living situation than staying with their families (Gretchel, 1997, p. 168), a sentiment shared by numerous homeless runaways who I spoke to at the Lesbian Gay Bi Youth Line (1996–97). Rather than seeing these responses as problematic, we can see them as Chandler (1995) does, as "desperate act[s] of survival" (p. 197).

GLB youth may also have difficulties at school which cause them to drop out or skip classes, especially when teachers and administrators do nothing to ameliorate the problems these students face (Khayatt, 1994, p. 59; Monahan, 1997, p. 207; Unks, 1995, p. 7; Anderson, 1995, p. 25; Lesbian Gay Bi Youth Line, 1996–97). Chandler (1995) describes Marcus's (a black bisexual male) experience: "He felt estranged and unsupported. School seemed pointless. So he dropped out" (p. 226).

Tommy, a young gay man interviewed by O'Conor (1995) dropped out because of harassment at school (p. 97) and Alex has dropped out of school repeatedly because of verbal and physical abuse (Lesbian Gay Bi Youth Line, 1996–97). D.B., a 15-year-old male from New York also dropped out, stating that:

> I could never get along with the students, and some of them thought I was gay. This really bothered me, and it was too much to handle at the time (in Heron, 1994, p. 81).

Brent Calderwood, a 16-year-old gay man from California, also faced harassment at school. In retrospect he remarked:

> I realize I've made choices, but when I first started cutting I felt I was making the only choice. It was for simple survival. I wasn't choosing to fuck up, I was choosing to not kill myself... I decided I didn't feel pride in graduating from a school that had treated me in this way (in Due, 1995, pp. 223, 228).

Unlike most of the literature, which characterizes these types of responses as problematic, Bass and Kaufman (1996) state that they are understandable, and Monahan (1997, p. 206) argues they are "legitimate responses to school systems which have failed" GLB youth.

Another way that queer youth escape the heterosexism in a particular school is to transfer to a different school (Herdt and Boxer, 1996, p.126; Travers and Schneider, 1997, p. 58; Chandler, 1995, p. 88). In North America there are two alternative high schools—the Harvey Milk High School in New York and the Triangle Program in Toronto—that exist as transitional schools for youth "whose needs will be better met in a lesbian, gay, and bisexual-positive environment" (Toronto Board of Education, 1996, p. 1). William transferred to the Harvey Milk School at age 15 because he was failing and withdrawn. He explained: "I was isolating myself from the rest of the students. I knew if I came out there would be consequences" (in Due, 1995, p. 187). Outside of the areas served by the above two programs there may still be some schools that are more responsive to the needs of queer students than others. For example, Amy Grahn, of Minneapolis, changed to a school with a GLB support group (Chandler, 1995, p. 158) and Brooke also took the initiative to switch to a more supportive school:

> I wanted to just forget about the teasing. I thought, it'll just go away, but it didn't. It definitely affected my actions. I started ditching school... That was when I decided to switch schools ... to the public high school in the city next to mine, which has a liberal reputation (in Bass and Kaufman, 1996, p. 209).

Although changing schools may seem like a preferable solution to skipping or dropping out, obviously not all GLB youth have access to an alternative or supportive school. Many youth live in rural areas or small towns where there is only one school available to them, and even youth in cities where changing schools might be an option may not be able to secure parental approval for a transfer, especially if they are not out to their parents or if their parents are not supportive.

It is apparent then, that for many GLB youth who are unable to handle the homophobia and heterosexism manifest in their situation at school or at home, removing themselves from these settings is the only route available for their survival. Thus their responses can more accurately be understood as solutions to the problems faced rather than as problems themselves (as per Rodman, in Hutter, 1998, p. 154).

Sex Work—Sex for Survival

For runaway or throwaway GLB youth living on the street or on their own at a young age, learning to survive independently can be difficult due to social and financial disadvantages. These youth have few legitimate options available to them, and many young men in particular turn to selling sex or exchanging it for survival needs (Hunter and Haymes, 1997, p. 139; Durby, 1994, p. 3; Hunter and Schaecher, 1992, p. 307; Coleman, 1989, p. 138; Tremble, 1993, p. 39). Young men themselves explained:

> Hustling is quick money. The majority of them [other hustlers] do it because they've been kicked out of their parents' house or they lost a job (Jeremy, in Chandler, 1995, p. 229).

> I got involved in prostitution for awhile. You know, you do what you have to [on the street] (Devon, in Bass and Kaufman, 1996, p. 45).

Tangerine, a 15-year-old male who left an abusive home, lived with his much older lover because he could not afford his own place on his income working at a fast-food restaurant, even after dropping out of school to work more hours (Bass and Kaufman, 1996, p. 314). His situation involved exchanging sex for survival needs:

> Robert [the older lover] passed me on to his friends as a toy... If you're under 18 and you live with someone, sex is the only thing you can give... You have to do it. What choice do you have? (p. 314)

Although less documented, possibly because these women are less identifiable as lesbian or bisexual due to the fact that their commercial sex activity is more likely with men, young lesbian or bisexual woman may also engage in sex work or survival sex. Jessica, who was living on the street after been thrown out of her home by her abusive mother, related that "sometimes I had sex with someone just to have a place to sleep" (in Bass and Kaufman, 1996, p. 314).

Although some writers characterize sex work or survival sex as a problem (Reynolds and Koski, 1995, p. 86), others recognize that it is an adaptation geared towards meeting basic survival needs (Sullivan and Schneider, 1987, p. 21; Chandler, 1995, p. 198), as it is relatively easy to find clients and the legal system is more lenient on sex work than on theft or drug trafficking (Tremble, 1993, p. 42; Coleman, 1989, p. 139). When working at the Lesbian Gay Bi Youth Line, I spoke to many young male callers who were very aware of these facts, taking them into consideration when trying to solve the problem of surviving outside of the family home (1996–97).

Young gay and bisexual males who work as sex workers may feel a sense of power and control over their own lives, perhaps for the first time (Coleman, 1989, p. 138; Chandler, 1995, p. 198). Although financial need is the primary motivation, these young men sometimes also find sex work to be a way to explore their sexuality or become involved in gay life, through clients and other sex workers (Boyer, 1989, pp. 173–76; Tremble, 1993, p. 42; Chandler, 1995, p. 199; Coleman, 1989, p. 138). For example, Blake, at age 16, commented, "I started hustling to see what sex was about and to get money for a room" (in Durby, 1994, p. 4) and Paul Johnson, of Portland, started at age 16 because he could not get into bars and did not know how else to explore sex or meet gay people (Due, 1995, p. 18).

Although efforts to make connections to the adult GLB communities are not always successful, as older gay male clients often fail to treat these younger men like anything other than sex objects (Due, 1995, p. 18), for many young gay and bisexual men, sex work is their first step towards taking control of their lives outside of their parents' home, coming to terms with their sexuality, and reaching out to find like others.

Reaching Out—Breaking Isolation

> [GLB] teenagers manage to make contact—through pen-pal programs, computer bulletin boards, personal ads, telephone datelines, or simply by word of mouth (Chandler, 1995, p. 235).

The isolation resulting from the oppression faced by queer youth can be overwhelming, and they may find that they cannot go on feeling so alone, that they need to break their isolation as a means to survive and resist the forces of oppression they face. This process of reaching out can involve either seeking information on GLB lives or searching for a community or like-minded individuals. Many youth use these strategies while remaining closeted, or at least without coming out in a non-queer setting. The main motivation for this is that by reaching out "offstage" (Scott, 1990, p. 20), they are better able to ensure continuing survival in their daily life surroundings; keeping their sexuality hidden in most contexts is a necessary survival strategy as described in detail in the previous section on the safety of the closet.

The least risky ways to reach out are the least visible ones, such as seeking information or making contact from home through the Internet, telephone services, or penpals. On the topic of looking for information, youth said:

> I wrote the Hetrick Martin Institute in New York asking for some information... I stayed up all night in my room reading every word... I became a vacuum, gathering every scrap of information I could (Roy, San Diego, age 17, in Heron, 1994, p. 64).

> I've begun to educate myself on homosexuality. I'm reading books on gay and lesbian teens... I found lesbian romance books... I've been reading feminist books and lesbian poetry (Robin, Ohio, age 16, in Heron, 1994, pp. 130–31).

The internet has become a primary way for youth who have private access to a computer and modem to break their isolation. Chandler (1995) argues that the widespread availability of internet access has had a profound effect on the lives of the current generation of GLB youth, especially those in rural areas or who have few or no other sources of information or contact (p. 277). Some of the main benefits of the internet include anonymity, being able to just "listen in" or actively participate, access to current information which may not be available where a young person lives, and avoiding the risk of having books or letters around which parents could find. Tim Dee commented that:

> The Internet let me listen in on discussions relevant to identifying with my sexuality, information that I couldn't find elsewhere (age 16, Washington, in Chandler, 1995, pp. 277–78).

Many youth find refuge in the peer support available online (Chandler, 1995, p. 281; Lesbian Gay Bi Youth Line, 1996–97). For example, David from Indiana stated, "I would have committed suicide if it wasn't for the support I got online" (age 16, in Chandler, 1995, p. 282) and John Swenson, of Santa Fe, New Mexico, uses the internet "so he can talk to *someone*" (age 16, in Due, 1995, p. xxxv). Many youth in rural areas and small towns feel that their online contact with other GLB youth is one of the most important ways they keep sane (Lesbian Gay Bi Youth Line, 1996–97).

Through my experiences as a volunteer at the Lesbian Gay Bi Youth Line I became aware of the full extent to which a service such as the Youth Line provides a lifeline to many youth who are suffering and alone, with no one to turn to in their daily lives. Many callers with no other source of support phoned on a daily or week-ly basis, including some who were struggling with repeated suicidal feelings (1996–97). In many cases, I have no doubt that being able to reach out over the phone and talk to another gay, lesbian or bisexual young person contributes directly to saving lives. Youth may also find that being able to talk to someone who has sim-ilar experiences helps give them strength to resist the oppression they face and per-haps stand up for their rights at home or at school (Lesbian Gay Bi Youth Line, 1996–97). Quong, a young Asian gay man, suggested that calling a help line can be a "very empowering step" for GLB youth (in Bass and Kaufman, 1996, p. 38).

Having penpals is another way that GLB youth reach out to each other (Youth Voices, 1996, p. 189; Due, 1995, p. 165). Many of the youth whose stories make up Heron's (1994) book write to other queer youth across North America. They may find penpals through organized services, such as Alyson Publications penpal exchange program (Youth Voices, 1996, p. 189), or by their own initiative, as in Gary's case:

> Once there was a gay 17 year old on a talk show... I contacted the show to find out if there was any way I could get in touch with this kid. I didn't expect anything, but to my surprise, I got a letter from him a month later. We've been corresponding ever since (age 17, Pennsylvania, in Heron, 1994, p. 164).

A benefit of all of the low visibility strategies just described for seeking informa-tion or making contact is that youth do not require access to a major urban centre with an active GLB community to use them. However, the corresponding limitation for queer youth in rural areas or small towns is that these may be the only ways avail-able for them to reach out.

In addition to the less visible ways of seeking like others, GLB youth (primarily those who live in or have access to larger centres) may reach out to physically meet other GLB people or find a queer community (Khayatt, 1994, p. 59; Hunter and Schaecher, 1992, p. 303). With regard to how this meets survival needs, Aaron Fricke from Rhode Island related that finding other GLB youth kept him "out of the coffin" (in Heron, 1994, p. 140). GLB youth may still keep their sexuality a secret in other settings, although there is a higher risk of being discovered when using more visible strategies. However, some youth may be using more visible approaches because they have come out or been found out by parents and are now homeless or simply desperate for support from somewhere in order to meet basic survival needs.

Locating and attending GLB youth groups is very common where such groups are available (Heron, 1994; Due, 1995). Meeting others and sharing experiences in this context can have a tremendous impact on the quality of life for queer youth. Chris recounted how he felt after an initial visit to a GLB youth group:

> For the first time I wasn't alone. I didn't have to bottle everything up. I could laugh about the hard times ... after my first meeting, I went home and for the first time I went to bed happy (in Bass and Kaufman, 1996, p. 30).

GLB youth may go to gay bars, even when they are underage. Lesbian youth in

Schneider (1989) explained that fake ID or wearing make-up can allow them entry (p. 124), and Gretchen Anthony from New Hampshire advised, "Even if you're underage, you can still get in. All it takes is brains and plans" (age 17, in Heron, 1994, p. 22). Sex work is another way that some young gay or bisexual men try to gain entry into the GLB world. Additional ways that youth try to meet others include going to GLB bookstores, music festivals, or Pride Day celebrations (Heron, 1994; Chandler, 1995, p. 114) and joining social or recreational groups that are not specifically youth-focused (Heron, 1994, p. 39).

For many queer youth, breaking the isolation they face through seeking information or like others can be critical to supporting their survival and their resistance against the oppressive influence of their circumstances. That this reaching out most often occurs "offstage" with youth remaining closeted in most areas of their lives, demonstrates the use of strategies which are necessarily low-profile, practical, and motivated by self-preservation (Scott, 1990, pp. 19–20).

Coming Out of the Closet

As has been touched on earlier, there is more than one kind of closet; correspondingly there is more than one kind of coming out. Previously in this chapter I have addressed the matter of coming out to oneself, and in this section I will examine two more ways of coming out which can be conceptualized as resistant. The first is the strategy of expressing a gay, lesbian or bisexual identity in partial, disguised, or anonymous ways. Scott (1990) describes the ways in which resistance of the severely oppressed may take the form of such "hidden transcripts," where disguise of either the message or the messenger (ie. anonymity) is employed in order to communicate discreetly with like others in the presence of the powerful, or to enact resistance without being traceable (pp. 139–40). The second type of coming out which will be considered is that of openly coming out and declaring through words or other overt signs that one is gay, lesbian or bisexual. This can be seen as an "act of defiance" in that it goes beyond just being queer, to publicly stating that one is queer, embodying a "declared refusal to comply" in the maintenance of hegemonic appearances of heterosexuality (Scott, 1990, p. 203).

Through subtle signs and clues that are primarily recognizable to other GLB persons, youth can disguise their attempts to communicate their sexual orientation to others "in-the-know" while avoiding alerting members of the dominant group. For example, Becky explained that she wears a pink triangle pin to school because it is "unlikely that anyone other than someone who is gay or lesbian, or gay and lesbian positive would recognize the pin and understand its significance" (in Schneider, 1997b, p. 107). Similarly, Angela wore rainbow pins and an earring with a double women's sign to her Calgary high school (age 17, personal contact) and John Erwin, of California, related that at age 15, "I wore a pink triangle to school for like a month, and no one said anything" (in Signorile, 1994, p. 88). Even though there is not always a response, it is the attempt to communicate in this way in the midst of the heterosexual world which is significant as resistance, and it should be noted that communication could nonetheless take place.

Anonymous revelations regarding GLB sexuality are another way of getting a message out, a strategy which leaves the messenger's identity safely disguised. This tactic was used by Alex, where he placed an ad reading: "It's OK to be gay. Jesus loves you" (Lesbian Gay Bi Youth Line, 1996–97) in his small town paper. Other examples include Kirsten, age 17, who wrote an anonymous letter to her high school principal in Calgary on the need for GLB inclusive schooling, letting him know that there was indeed at least one lesbian student in the school (personal contact), and Lenin, a Hispanic youth from New York City, who had a teacher read to his class-mates an anonymous personal statement he had written about how a homophobic class discussion had made him feel (Kuklin, 1993, p. 103).

Overt coming out is a way of resisting the tyranny of heterosexuality used by some youth who are in situations where it is possible to do so without facing certain harm, significant loss, or withdrawal of the physical means of survival. With regard to coming out in school, Sara Marckx, of Seattle, commented that "everyone at my school knows—literally everyone" (age 18, in Signorile, 1994, p. 148), while Jamie Stuart Nabozny from St. Paul, Minnesota, related that at age 15, "I was coming out in school, wearing T-shirts saying that I was gay" (Signorile, 1994, p. 148), and Allyson came out to her whole school during a presentation for Diversity Day (age 18, Massachusetts, in Due, 1995, p. 59). Many GLB youth are out to their parents or other family members (Heron, 1994; Due, 1995; Chandler, 1995; Lesbian Gay Bi Youth Line, 1996–97). Some youth are out more publicly, notably through same-sex expressions of affection, such as Sue, who noted, "Probably my favorite part of being gay is being open enough to tell my friends, and to walk out in public with Diane holding hands or kissing (age 17, Chicago, in Heron, 1994, p. 59). Coming out may also occur in conjunction with explicitly demanding rights or recognition. For exam-ple, Daphne described the following remarkable incident at her high school:

> There was a big blowup at the school board meeting with some parents protesting because the number of the Billie De Frank Gay and Lesbian Community Centre was put on the back of student ID cards along with other community organizations. Two or three people came out that night and said, "I'm who you're talking about. I'm a straight A student. I'm on the school paper. And you're putting me down" (in Bass and Kaufman, 1996, pp. 353–54).

Coming out can contribute to survival when it is accompanied by increased sup-port or provides a form of support for other GLB youth (Travers and Monahan, 1997, p. 186). This played into Daphne and her girlfriend deciding to come out: "As a way of supporting other gay kids [we] decided in our senior high school year to be out" (in Bass and Kaufman, 1996, p. 20). But it is not without its costs, even in the best of circumstances. Brent Calderwood describes the decision to come out as a sort of trade-off:

> I knew my coming out wouldn't allow me to have the same everyday existence het-erosexuals did. I knew I'd have more people treating me badly. But at least I would-n't be treating myself badly. I'd rather be bashed by other people than by myself (age 16, California, in Due, 1995, p. 225).

Whether through the subtle signs or anonymity of hidden transcripts or overt declaration through words and/or actions, the current generation of queer youth is using coming out as a means of resisting oppression. These methods of coming out can be viewed as challenges to dominant culture, in either their subversive commu-nication efforts or their declared refusal to comply with heterosexual norms.

Challenges to Relations of Domination

GLB youth challenge the social relations of domination in four key ways—first, in the transformation and re-creation of the activities of dominant culture into newly meaningful ones (Clarke, in Martinez, 1997, p. 270; Donnelly, 1988, p. 72; Donnelly and Young, 1985, p. 33); second, through personal efforts to educate others, represent GLB lives, or defend queer rights; third, in the subversive continuation of activities which have been prohibited by authorities (Donnelly, 1988, p. 72); and fourth, through involvement in new cultural practices (Beal, 1995, p. 265; Donnelly, 1988, p. 74; Donnelly and Young, 1985, p. 74). These types of resistance are the most widely theorized of the different approaches to survival and resistance which are dealt with in this paper, as they are overt and thus available for use by members of other marginalized groups who may not be subject to the same level of severity of oppression and dependency that GLB youth experience.

Queer youth often transform or re-create the activities of dominant school culture. For Jamie Stuart Nabozny, of St. Paul, Minnesota, this meant:

> I decided to make up posters from gay magazines of men together and women together, and I put them up on my locker, just like the straight kids put up pictures of people they liked on their lockers (age 15, in Signorile, 1994, p. 148).

One of the pinnacles of heterosexual celebration in schools is the prom, which makes it a prime target for transformation into an event relevant for GLB youth. For example, Tom Winters, of Portland, subverted the gender normativity of his prom by attending in drag (Due, 1995, p. 42). A second, and more common, way that the occasion is re-created and the dominance of heterosexual relations is challenged is through GLB youth taking same-sex dates to the prom. Daphne and Marsha attended their prom together, and even though their friends urged them to be subtle by both wearing dresses, Marsha wore a tux and Daphne wore a dress (Bass and Kaufman, 1996, p. 192), while Jessica also took a same-sex date to the prom, knowing it would be political (Blumenfeld, 1995, p. 220). A widely publicized example of this in Ontario is that of Marc Hall, a student who took the Durham Catholic District School Board to court in order to win permission to take his boyfriend to the prom in 2002 (CBC News).

There are a variety of approaches to educating others, depicting GLB lives, and supporting queer rights which are taken up by GLB youth. In their schools, they may challenge homophobia and heterosexism in class discussions or do papers/projects on GLB topics (Heron, 1994; Due, 1995, p. 98; Signorile, 1994, p. 148; Khayatt, 1994, p. 55; Kuklin, 1993, p. 84; Lesbian Gay Bi Youth Line, 1996–97). Youth related the following specific accounts:

> I have begun to speak up for homosexual rights in my private Catholic school and will soon deal with gay issues in my photography (Rachel Corbett, age 16, Wisconsin, in Heron, 1994, p. 15).

> I do find myself defending gays when I hear us attacked in school. [Other students] are very close-minded about homosexuals, and I'm trying to rid them of the stereotypes they fell prey to (Robin, age 16, Ohio, in Heron, 1994, p.132).

Speaking out on GLB issues can go beyond individual classrooms. Dan Birkholz was on his Minnesota high school's drama team and at the regional tournament he performed a segment of *Torch Song Trilogy*, by Harvey Fierstein, dealing with a confrontation between a gay man and his mother (Chandler, 1995, p. 111). Kathryn Zamora Benson gave a speech at a school assembly on Diversity Day, in which she addressed homophobia and her own questioning of her sexuality; she reflected, "My speech was a plea for change, a request for tolerance, and an offer of myself" (age 16, Albuquerque, in Youth Voices, 1996, p. 178). GLB youth also educate others through providing queer positive resources to parents, teachers, or peers, or through producing "queer zines" for distribution (Lesbian Gay Bi Youth Line, 1996–97).

GLB youth may undermine systems of authority by continuing banned activities or subverting rules, particularly in relation to parental control. This is the case for Joanne from Pennsylvania, who explained the following situation from early in her high school years, after her parents found out she was a lesbian:

> [My parents] forbade me to socialize with anyone out of high school. Since I knew no lesbians in school, the restriction was extremely unpleasant. Obviously, the limitation included my lover, so I had to do a lot of sneaking around in order to see her (in Heron, 1994, p. 40).

Dan Birkholz, of Minnesota, also snuck out of the house to meet lovers (Chandler, 1995, p. 33). When working at the Lesbian Gay Bi Youth Line (1996–97) I spoke to many youth whose parents had placed restrictions on their activity due to their sexuality—subversive responses included sneaking out at night or skipping school to meet lovers and lying in order to attend GLB youth groups or dates.

Finally, some young gay and bisexual men in certain large cities, such as New York, involve themselves in the new cultural practice of drag balls or the house scene, which although not originating from youth themselves, is a marginalized practice created by gay male subculture. Young gay and bisexual men may experience this involvement in drag primarily as a form of escape; Evann Hayes of New York expressed, "It's such a fantasy!" and Paul Johnson of Portland stated:

> I don't think I would have been able to hold myself together if it wouldn't have been for drag. Sometimes life got too hard for me to deal with, and so I'd have to escape into what I like to call a fantasyland (in Due, 1995, p. 21).

However, King's (1982) work on play as resistance provides an additional layer of meaning to these experiences. She explains that although escaping limitations through forms of play or fantasy may seem trivial, such acts can actually be conceptualized as resistant in that they provide alternatives to and a critique of dominant culture (p. 321).

Thus we can see that some GLB youth are able to challenge the normativity of heterosexual culture in schools, subvert the authority of their parents, and participate in gay cultural forms. These are the most obviously resistant actions described in this chapter, as they clearly challenge systems of domination. Nonetheless, these strategies remain largely individualized, as we would expect based on Scott's (1990) conception of the types of responses available to severely oppressed and dependent groups; only being used when circumstances permit such actions without evoking serious negative repercussions related to survival.

Many of the strategies described above are used by the same young person at different times and in different contexts, depending on what a situation demands or permits. I have not tried to delineate a hierarchy of types or stages of survival and resistance through which GLB youth progress in a linear fashion (as I critiqued the psychological literature on coping strategies for doing). Rather, my aim is to show, through an analysis of the available material on queer youth, the broad scope of approaches taken to creatively ensuring survival and individually resisting oppression, in the numerous contexts of oppression in which GLB youth live their daily lives.

Conclusion

Understanding the context of oppression faced by a particular marginalized group is the key to an accurate and thoughtful investigation of the various means of survival and resistance that will be used by the members of that group, as responses are chosen based on characteristics of actual situations rather than internal psychological factors. Gay, lesbian, and bisexual youth are subject to severe conditions of oppression based on the intersection of societal configurations of age and sexuality relations, and thus their responses to this particular experience of oppression take practical and often low-profile forms in everyday acts of survival and unorganized individual resistance. Numerous specific strategies of survival and individual resistance were uncovered, all intimately informed by the particular nature of the oppression GLB youth face; these were broadly conceptualized as staying in the closet, escape, sex work, reaching out to break isolation, coming out, and challenging the dominant culture.

The matrix of domination model (Hill Collins, 1990) effectively framed the examination of the extreme oppression of queer youth through recognition of the connections between multiple systems of oppression. Scott's (1990) theoretical work has also proven invaluable, as his argument regarding the limited responses available to members of the most severely oppressed and dependent groups in society explains both (1) why most of the picture of GLB youth political struggle would be missed if we were to focus only on organized public resistance and (2) that a thorough understanding of the specificity and severity of conditions of oppression is critical to interpreting GLB youth responses to these conditions.

However, there still exists the pressing need for *empirical* studies of GLB youth, focusing on the ways they respond to the lived experiences of oppression they face. Future research in this area should take issues of race, class, gender, ability, and geographic location into account, as survival and resistance strategies will necessarily be affected by such factors, due to their influence on the conditions of oppression experienced and the options available for response. It was not always possible to consider these differences in this paper, due to the absence of the requisite information in the sources used. Gender was the only information consistently provided, and thus I was able to address some gender differences in the use of strategies such as staying in the closet, sex work, and involvement in a drag scene. I also made some logical assertions about how geographic location would affect a youth person's options, as living in or near an urban centre is a prerequisite for strategies such as changing schools, prostitution, reaching out to an actual physical GLB community, or participating in a drag scene. With regard to race, class, and ability, this information was very rarely (if at all) supplied, and thus I do not feel well-informed enough to comment on how these factors affect GLB youth responses. Another suggestion for future research would be on bisexual youth, in terms of both specific experiences of and responses to oppression, as these youth are not consistently included in studies of gay and/or lesbian youth, and are even more rarely considered in their own right.

Overall, scholars and researchers need to take steps to try and understand more fully what Alisa Gayle-Deutsch (1993), a young lesbian from Toronto, refers to as the "many aspects of resistance" and to "deconstruct our myth that simply because we are lesbian [gay] and bisexual youth, we are [only] powerless and persecuted" (pp. 103–04).

Notes

1. This chapter is based on the Research Review Paper I completed for my Master's Degree in Sociology at York University in 1998. I'd like to thank my supervisors, Tania Das Gupta and Livy Visano, for all their feedback, advice and support.

2. There is no consensus in the literature on what the upper age limit is for defining youth. For the purposes of this chapter, I have not set an absolute age limit. Rather, I have considered such factors as dependence on parents, still being in school (not post-secondary), and being under the legal drinking age as determining youth status, which puts the upper age limit between 18 and 21 years of age.

3. In this chapter I will use the term "queer" interchangeably with "gay, lesbian and bisexual." Neither is more correct than the other and using both reflects the diversity of ways of identifying, and the limits and challenges of the language used to describe, sexual identity.

4. It is worth noting that much of the literature informing this section focuses on gay and lesbian youth. Thus, the specific experiences of bisexual youth remain largely unexplored, and my application of such literature to this group is based on their commonalities with gay and lesbian youth rather than their unique experiences as bisexual youth.

5. In utilizing existing academic literature I will most often be reconceptualizing responses considered negative or problematic as solutions or strategies of survival/resistance.

6. "The Lesbian Gay Bi Youth Line is a service provided for youth, by youth that affirms the experiences and aspirations of lesbian, gay, bisexual, transgendered, two-spirited and questioning youth in Ontario." www.youthline.ca 1-800-268-YOUTH

7. An additive model is one in which the independent effects of factors such as race, class, gender, age, or sexuality are studied and then "added up" when considering groups of people who are oppressed on more than one basis (Anderson and Hill Collins, 1995).

8. This is due to the lack of reproductive continuity which characterizes many other forms of oppression (Warner, 1993, p. xvii).

9. Little is known about sexuality-based harassment of GLB youth in the workplace, as it is rarely reported due to fear that disclosure would potentially make things worse, especially if the young person is not out to family or at school (Rivers, 1997, p. 38).

10. This may be even more likely in the U.S., where there is less public assistance than in Canada, and what does exist is largely unavailable to runaway youth (Abinati, 1994, p. 164).

11. An example is Bill C-138, passed in Canada in 1993, which prohibits visual representation of any explicit sexual act involving those under 18 or depicted as under 18 (Canadian Press Newswire, October 3, 1994).

12. The recognition of this problem in Toronto led to the 1998 development of a project called "Supporting Our Youth" which aims to establish more links between youth and adult gays, lesbians, and bisexuals.

13. In delineating different strategies of resistance, I take the advice of King (1982), who cautions against an overly general use of the term, arguing for a focus on particular types of resistance (p. 327).

References

Abinati, Abby. 1994. "Legal Challenges Facing Lesbian and GayYouth." Pp. 149–70 in *Helping Gay and Lesbian Youth: New Policies, New Programs, New Practice*, edited by Teresa DeCrescenzo. New York: Harrington Park Press.

Adam, Barry. 1987. *The Making of a Gay and Lesbian Movement*. Boston: Twayne Publishers.

Anderson, Dennis A. 1995. "Lesbian and Gay Adolescents: Social and Developmental Considerations." Pp. 17–30 in *The Gay Teen: Educational Practice and Theory for Lesbian, Gay, and Bisexual Adolescents*, edited by Gerald Unks. New York: Routledge.

Anderson, Margaret L. and Patricia Hill Collins, eds. 1995. *Race,Class, and Gender: An Anthology*. Belmont CA: Wadsworth Publishing.

Bagley, C. and P. Tremblay. 1997. "Suicidality Problems of Gay and Bisexual Males: Evidence From a Random Community Survey of 750 Men Aged 18-27." Pp.169–86 in *Suicidal Behaviors in Adolescents and Adults: Research, Taxonomy and Prevention*, edited by C. Bagley and R. Ramsey. Brookfield VT: Avebury.

Bass, Ellen and Kate Kaufman. 1996. *Free Your Mind: The Book for Gay, Lesbian and Bisexual Youth and Their Allies*. New York: HarperPerennial.

Beal, Becky. 1995. "Disqualifying the Official: An Exploration of Social Resistance Through the Subculture of Skateboarding." *Sociology of Sport* Journal 12: 252–67.

Bergman, Brian. 1994. "The Battle Over Censorship." *Maclean's*, October 24: 26–29.

Blumenfeld, Warren J. 1995. "'Gay/Straight' Alliances: Transforming Pain to Pride." Pp. 211–24 in *The Gay Teen: Educational Practice and Theory for Lesbian, Gay, and Bisexual Adolescents*, edited by Gerald Unks. New York: Routledge.

Boyer, Debra. 1989. "Male Prostitution and Homosexual Identity." *Journal of Homosexuality* 17: 151–84.

Canadian Press Newswire. 1994. "Hearing Will Decide if Art is Child Porn." *Canadian Press Newswire*, October 3.

Caragata, Warren. 1995. "Mixed Messages on Pensions and Payments." *Maclean's*, June 5: 30–31.

CBC News. 2002. "Prom over, but not gay student's court fight." http://www.cbc.ca/ stories/2002/05/11/hall_020511

Chandler, Kurt. 1995. *Passages of Pride: True Stories and Lesbian and Gay Teenagers*. Los Angeles: Alyson Books.

Coalition for Gay Rights in Ontario (CLGRO). 1981. *The Ontario Human Rights Omission: A Brief to Members of the Ontario Legislature*. Toronto: Kitchener-Waterloo Gay Media Collective.

——. 1997. *Systems Failure: A Report on the Experiences of Sexual Minorities in Ontario's Health-Care and Social-Services Systems*. Toronto: Coalition for Lesbian and Gay Rights in Ontario.

Coleman, Eli. 1989. "The Development of Male Prostitution Activity Among Gay and Bisexual Adolescents." *Journal of Homosexuality* 17: 131–49.

Cranston, Kevin. 1992. "HIV Education for Gay, Lesbian and Bisexual Youth: Personal Risk, Personal Power, and the Community of Conscience." Pp. 247–59 in *Coming Out of the Classroom Closet: Gay and Lesbian Students, Teachers and Curricula*, edited by Karen Harbeck. New York: Harrington Park Press.

Cruikshank, Margaret. 1992. *The Gay and Lesbian Liberation Movement*. New York: Routledge.

DeCrescenzo, Teresa, ed. 1994. *Helping Gay and Lesbian Youth: New Policies, New Programs, New Practice*. New York: Harrington Park Press.

Dobinson, Cheryl and Kevin Young. 2000. "Popular Cinema and Lesbian Interpretive Strategies." *Journal of Homosexuality* 40, no. 2: 97–122.

Donnelly, Peter. 1988. "Sport as a Site for 'Popular' Resistance." Pp. 69–82 in *Popular Cultures and Political Practices*, edited by Richard B. Gruneau. Toronto: Garamond Press.

Donnelly, Peter and Kevin Young. 1985. "Reproduction and Transformation of Cultural Forms in Sport: A Contextual Analysis of Rugby." *International Review for Sociology of Sport* 20: 19–38.

Durby, Dennis. 1994. "Gay, Lesbian and Bisexual Youth." Pp.1–38 in *Helping Gay and Lesbian Youth: New Policies, New Programs, New Practice*, edited by Teresa DeCrescenzo. New York: Harrington Park Press.

Due, Linnea. 1995. *Joining the Tribe: Growing up Gay and Lesbian in the 90's*. New York: Anchor Books.

Epstein, Debbie and Richard Johnson. 1994. "On the Straight and the Narrow: The Heterosexual Presumption, Homophobia and Schools." Pp. 197–230 in *Challenging Lesbian and Gay Inequalities in Education*, edited by Debbie Epstein. Buckingham: Open University Press.

Eshelman, J. Ross. 1997. *The Family*, 8th edition. Boston: Allyn and Bacon.

Faye, Mike. 1997 "Foreword." Pp. 7–8 in *Pride and Prejudice: Working With Lesbian, Gay and Bisexual Youth*, edited by Margaret S. Schneider. Toronto: Central Toronto Youth Services.

Fejes, Fred and Kevin Petrich. 1993. "Invisibility, Homophobia and Heterosexism: Lesbians, Gays and the Media." *Critical Studies in Mass Communication* 10: 396–422.

Feldman, Douglas A. 1989. "Gay Youth and AIDS." *Journal of Homosexuality* 17: 185–93.

ferren, don. 1997. "Making Services Accessible to Lesbian, Gay and Bisexual Youth." Pp. 239–58 in *Pride and Prejudice: Working With Lesbian, Gay and Bisexual Youth*, edited by Margaret S. Schneider. Toronto: Central Toronto Youth Services.

Fricke, Aaron. 1981. *Confessions of a Rock Lobster: A Story About Growing Up Gay*. Boston: Alyson.

Frye, Marilyn. [1983] 1995. "Oppression." Pp. 37–41 in *Race, Class, and Gender: An Anthology*, 2nd ed, edited by Margaret L. Anderson and Patricia Hill Collins. Belmont CA: Wadsworth Publishing.

Gayle-Deutsch, Alisa. 1993. "Challenging Fragmentation: White Privilege, Jewish Oppression and Lesbian Identity." Pp. 70–93 in *Resist! Essays Against a Homophobic Culture*, edited by Mona Oikawa. Toronto: Women's Press.

Goodman, Gerre et al. 1983. *No Turning Back: Lesbian and Gay Liberation for the 80's*. Philadelphia: New Society Publishers.

Gover, Jill. 1996. "Gay Youth in the Family." Pp. 173–82 in *Open Lives Safe Schools: Addressing Gay and Lesbian Issues in Education*, edited by Donovan R. Walling. Bloomington: Phi Delta Kappa Educational Foundation.

Green, Robin. 1983. "The Church." Pp. 139–64 in *Prejudice and Pride: Discrimination Against Gay People in Modern Britain*, edited by Bruce Galloway. London: Routledge and Kegan Paul.

Gretchel, Michele M. 1997. "Homeless Lesbian and Gay Youth: Assessment and Intervention." Pp. 165–82 in *Pride and Prejudice: Working With Lesbian, Gay and Bisexual Youth*, edited by Margaret S. Schneider. Toronto: Central Toronto Youth Services.

Gross, Larry. 1994. "What is Wrong with This Picture? Lesbian Women and Gay Men on Television." Pp. 143–56 in *Queer Words, Queer Images: Communication and the Construction of Homosexuality*, edited by R. Jeffrey Ringer. New York: New York University Press.

Hantzis, Darlene M. and Valerie Lehr. 1994. "Whose Desire? Lesbian (Non) Sexuality and Television's Perpetuation of Hetero/Sexism." Pp. 107–21 in *Queer Words, Queer Images:Communication and the Construction of Homosexuality*, edited by R. Jeffrey Ringer. New York: New York University Press.

Harbeck, Karen. 1995. "Invisible No More: Addressing the Needs of Lesbian, Gay and Bisexual Youth and Their Advocates." Pp. 125–34 in *The Gay Teen: Educational Practice and Theory for Lesbian, Gay, and Bisexual Adolescents*, edited by Gerald Unks. New York: Routledge.

Herdt, Gilbert and Andrew Boxer. 1996. *Children of Horizons: How Gay and Lesbian Teens are Leading a New Way Out of the Closet*. Boston: Beacon Press.

Heron, Ann, ed. 1994. *Two Teenagers in Twenty: Writings by Gay and Lesbian Youth*. Los Angeles: Alyson Publications.

Hetrick, Emery S. and A. Damien Martin. 1987. "Developmental Issues and Their Resolution for Gay and Lesbian Adolescents." *Journal of Homosexuality* 14: 25–43.

Hill Collins, Patricia. [1990] 1993. "Black Feminist Thought in the Matrix of Domination." Pp. 615–26 in *Social Theory: The Multicultural and Classic Readings*, edited by Charles Lemert. Boulder: Westview Press.

Hunter, Joyce and Richard Haymes. 1997. "It's Beginning to Rain: Gay/Lesbian/Bisexual Adolescents and AIDS." Pp. 137–64 in *Pride and Prejudice: Working With Lesbian, Gay and Bisexual Youth*, edited by Margaret S. Schneider. Toronto: Central Toronto Youth Services.

Hunter, Joyce and Robert Schaecher. 1992 "Lesbian and Gay Youth." Pp. 297–316 in *Learning to Live: Evaluating and Treating Suicidal Teens in Community Settings*. Oklahoma City: University of Oklahoma Press.

Hutter, Mark. 1998. *The Changing Family*. Toronto: Allyn and Bacon.

Kielwasser, Alfred P. and Michelle A. Wolf. 1992. "Mainstream Television, Adolescent Homosexuality, and Significant Silence." *Critical Studies in Mass Communication* 9: 350–73.

King, Nancy R. 1982. "Children's Play as a Form of Resistance in the Classroom." *Journal of Education* 164: 320–29.

Kinsman, Gary. 1987. *The Regulation of Desire: Sexuality in Canada*. Montreal: Black Rose Books.

Kleinerman, Shulamit. 1996. "Old Enough to Know." Pp. 183–86 in *Open Lives Safe Schools: Addressing Gay and Lesbian Issues in Education*, edited by Donovan R. Walling. Bloomington: Phi Delta Kappa Educational Foundation.

Khayatt, Didi. 1994. "Surviving School as a Lesbian Student." *Gender and Education* 6: 47–61.

Kuklin, Susan. 1993. *Speaking Out: Teenagers Take on Race, Sex, and Identity*. New York: G.P. Putnam's Sons.

Kutz, Stan. 1996. "Sexual Orientation, Homophobia, and the Catholic School." *The Reporter* (February): 27–28.

Laghi, Brian and Kirk Makin. 1998. "Court Protects Gays." *Globe and Mail*, April 3.

Langen, Scott. 1994. "Calling for Help." *This Magazine* 28: 26.

Leck, Glorianne M. 1995. "The Politics of Adolescent Sexuality and Queer Responses." Pp. 189–200 in *The Gay Teen: Educational Practice and Theory for Lesbian, Gay, and Bisexual Adolescents*, edited by Gerald Unks. New York: Routledge.

Lesbian Gay Bi Youth Line. 1996. Training Manual and Sessions. October.

———. 1996–97. Information gathered from peer support work with youth callers.

Mallon, Gary. 1997. "The Delivery of Child Welfare Services to Gay and Lesbian Adolescents." Pp. 223–38 in *Pride and Prejudice: Working With Lesbian, Gay and Bisexual Youth*, edited by Margaret S. Schneider. Toronto: Central Toronto Youth Services.

Martinez, Theresa A. 1997. "Popular Culture as Oppositional Culture: Rap as Resistance." *Sociological Perspectives* 40: 265–86.

McClaren, Peter. 1985. "The Ritual Dimensions of Resistance: Clowning and Symbolic Inversion." *Journal of Education* 167: 84–97.

Monahan, Nicki. 1997. "Making the Grade: Responding to Lesbian, Gay and Bisexual Youth in Schools." Pp. 203–22 in *Pride and Prejudice: Working With Lesbian, Gay and Bisexual Youth*, edited by Margaret S. Schneider. Toronto: Central Toronto Youth Services.

Newman, Bernie Sue and Peter Gerard Muzzonigro. 1993. "The Effects of Traditional Family Values on the Coming Out Process of Gay Male Adolescents." *Adolescence* 28: 213–26.

O'Conor, Andi. 1995. "Who Gets Called Queer in School: Lesbian, Gay and Bisexual Teenagers, Homophobia, and High School." Pp.95–104 in *The Gay Teen: Educational Practice and Theory for Lesbian, Gay, and Bisexual Adolescents*, edited by Gerald Unks. New York: Routledge.

Other Young Lives II. 1996. Conference in Toronto, October 18–20.

Pilon, Marilyn. 1999. Canada's Legal Age of Consent to Sexual Activity. http://www.parl.gc.ca/information/library/PRBpubs/prb993-e.htm

Plummer, Ken. 1989. "Lesbian and Gay Youth in England." *Journal of Homosexuality* 17: 195–223.

Remafedi, Gary. 1994. *Death by Denial: Studies of Suicide in Gay and Lesbian Teenagers.* Boston: Alyson Publications.

Remafedi, Gary. 1999. "Sexual Orientation and Youth Suicide." *Journal of the American Medical Association* 282 (13): 1291–92.

Reynolds, Amy L. and Michael J. Koski. 1995. "Lesbian, Gay and Bisexual Teens and the School Counsellor: Building Alliances." Pp. 85–94 in *The Gay Teen: Educational Practice and Theory for Lesbian, Gay, and Bisexual Adolescents*, edited by Gerald Unks. New York: Routledge.

Ricketts, Wendell and Roberta Achtenberg. 1989. "Adoption and Foster Parenting for Lesbians and Gay Men." *Marriage and Family Review* 14: 83–118.

Rivers, Ian. 1997. "Violence Against Lesbian and Gay Youth and its Impact." Pp. 31–48 in *Pride and Prejudice: Working With Lesbian, Gay and Bisexual Youth*, edited by Margaret S. Schneider. Toronto: Central Toronto Youth Services.

Rubin, Gayle S. [1984] 1993. "Thinking Sex: Notes for a Radical Theory of the Politics of Sexuality." Pp. 3–44 in *The Lesbian and Gay Studies Reader*, edited by Henry Abelove, Michele Aina Barale and David M. Halperin. New York: Routledge.

Ryan, Bill, Shari Brotman and Bill Rowe. 2000. *Access to Care: Exploring the Health and Well-being of Gay, Lesbian, Bisexual and Two-Spirit People in Canada.* Montreal: McGill Centre for Applied Family Studies.

Schneider, Margaret. 1989. "Sappho Was a Right-On Adolescent: Growing Up Lesbian." *Journal of Homosexuality* 17: 111–30.

Schneider, Margaret. 1997a. "Pride, Prejudice and Lesbian, Gay and Bisexual Youth." Pp. 11–30 in *Pride and Prejudice: Working With Lesbian, Gay and Bisexual Youth*, edited by Margaret S. Schneider. Toronto: Central Toronto Youth Services.

Schneider, Margaret. 1997b. "The Significance of Relationships in the Lives of Young Lesbians." Pp. 97–116 in *Pride and Prejudice: Working With Lesbian, Gay and Bisexual Youth*, edited by Margaret S. Schneider. Toronto: Central Toronto Youth Services.

Scott, James C. 1990. *Domination and the Arts of Resistance: Hidden Transcripts.* New Haven: Yale University Press.

Sheridan, Peter M. 1997. "Preparing to Work with Lesbian, Gay and Bisexual Youth." Pp. 69–82 in *Pride and Prejudice: Working With Lesbian, Gay and Bisexual Youth*, edited by Margaret S. Schneider. Toronto: Central Toronto Youth Services.

Signorile, Michelangelo. 1994. "The Post-Stonewall Generation." *OUT*, July/August: 86–93, 148–50.

Sillars, Les. 1997. "Calgary Classrooms Get Gay-Friendly: The City's Public School Board Wants Homosexual Activists to Counsel Students." *British Columbia Report* 8: 18–19.

Singerline, Hugh. 1995. "OutRight! Reflections on an Out-Of-School Gay Youth Group." Pp. 225–32 in *The Gay Teen: Educational Practice and Theory for Lesbian, Gay, and Bisexual Adolescents*, edited by Gerald Unks. New York: Routledge.

Strommen, Erik F. 1989. "'You're a What?': Family Member Reaction to the Disclosure of Homosexuality." *Journal of Homosexuality* 18: 37–57.

Sullivan, T. Richard. 1994. "Obstacles to Effective Child Welfare Service with Gay and Lesbian Youths." *Child Welfare* 73: 291–304.

Sullivan, Terrence and Margaret Schneider. 1987. "Development and Identity Issues in Adolescent Homosexuality." *Child and Adolescent Social Work* 4: 13–24.

Taylor, Nancy. 1994. "Gay and Lesbian Youth: Challenging the Policy of Denial." Pp. 39–73 in *Helping Gay and Lesbian Youth: New Policies, New Programs, New Practice*, edited by Teresa DeCrescenzo. New York: Harrington Park Press.

Telljohann, Susan K. and James H. Price. 1993. "A Qualitative Examination of Adolescent Homosexuals' Life Experiences: Ramifications for Secondary School Personnel." *Journal of Homosexuality* 26: 41–56.

The Rainbow Classroom. 1996. "Welcome to the Rainbow Classroom." *The Rainbow Classroom,* Newsletter of the Sexual Orientation and Education Project, Toronto 1: 1.

Toronto Board of Education. 1996. "Challenging Homophobia at the Toronto Board of Education." (pamphlet).

Travers, Robb and Carol Anne O'Brien. 1997. "The Complexities of Bisexual Youth Identities." Pp. 117–36 in *Pride and Prejudice: Working With Lesbian, Gay and Bisexual Youth*, edited by Margaret S. Schneider. Toronto: Central Toronto Youth Services.

Travers, Robb and Nicki Monahan. 1997. "Dear Mom, Dad and Bradley... When Lesbian and Gay Youth Come Out to Their Families." Pp. 183–201 in *Pride and Prejudice: Working With Lesbian, Gay and Bisexual Youth*, edited by Margaret S. Schneider. Toronto: Central Toronto Youth Services.

Travers, Robb and Margaret Schneider. 1997. "A Multifaceted Approach to Reduce Risk Factors for Lesbian, Gay and Bisexual Youth." Pp. 49–68 in *Pride and Prejudice: Working With Lesbian, Gay and Bisexual Youth*, edited by Margaret S. Schneider. Toronto: Central Toronto Youth Services.

Tremble, Bob. 1993. "Prostitution and Survival: Interviews with Gay Street Youth." *The Canadian Journal of Human Sexuality* 21: 39–45.

Unks, Gerald. 1995. "Thinking About the Gay Teen." Pp. 3–12 in *The Gay Teen: Educational Practice and Theory for Lesbian, Gay, and Bisexual Adolescents*, edited by Gerald Unks. New York: Routledge.

Uribe, Virginia. 1995. "Project 10: A School-Based Outreach to Gay and Lesbian Youth." Pp. 203–10 in *The Gay Teen: Educational Practice and Theory for Lesbian, Gay, and Bisexual Adolescents*, edited by Gerald Unks. New York: Routledge.

Vaid, Urvashi. 1995. *Virtual Equality: The Mainstreaming of Gay and Lesbian Liberation.* New York: Anchor Books.

Walling, Donovan, ed. 1996. *Open Lives Safe Schools: Addressing Gay and Lesbian Issues in Education.* Bloomington: Phi Delta Kappa Educational Foundation.

Warner, Michael, ed. 1993. *Fear of a Queer Planet.* Minneapolis:University of Minnesota Press.

Woodward, Joe. 1997. "Geek-Butt Gets His Revenge: A Calgary Teenager is Expelled for Gross Ridicule of Homosexuals." *Alberta Report* 24: 40.

"Youth Voices". 1996. *Harvard Educational Review* 66: 173–97.

Gender Ambiguity and Heteronormativity:

THE CASE OF TWO ALBERTA YOUTH

Gloria Filax & Debra Shogan

IN THIS CHAPTER WE OFFER TWO NARRATIVES FROM RESEARCH conducted with queer youth in the province of Alberta during the 1990s. The two accounts presented here are from interviews with two gender ambiguous Aboriginal youth. By surfacing these narratives we raise questions about what counts as gender, particularly in education and families, as well as how notions of gender are confounded by ancestry and class. Gender is often understood in education and family literature as signifying "a set of relations between the sexes" (Houston, 1996a, p. 61) and, therefore, as signifying social rather than biological "differences between the sexes" (Houston, 1996b, p. 84). This assumption that there are two sexes to which the social adheres, in turn, leads to the assertion that "we have only two genders" (Houston, 1996c, p. 146).

We are interested in shifting the margins of what counts as gender by opening up gender to other significations and thus expanding alternatives to questions related to gender. Questions such as, "'Is gender operative here?' 'How is gender operative?' and 'What ... effects do our strategies for eliminating gender bias have?'" (Houston, 1996a, p. 61) are resignified when the notion of gender is open to "a reusage or redeployment that previously has not been authorized" (Butler, 1992, p. 15). In opening up alternatives for gender, we question the presumed coherence between and among sexed bodies, gendered behavior, and sexuality. This permits the possibility, for example, that a female sexed child might "know" something about her/his gender not contained by the categories "boy" or "girl." Gender does not disappear, but it is polymorphous and unpredictable.

In a culture in which gender is arbitrarily tied to sex and in which "we are socially and communicatively helpless if we do not know the sex of everybody we have anything to do with" (Frye, 1983, p. 22), it is appropriate to worry about those who disrupt the assumption that sexed bodies, gender, and sexuality cohere because there are real punishing effects for those who confuse others about their gender or sexuality. But, if the alternative is conformity to a dishonest gender rigidity, it is as necessary to worry about ways in which all children, but particularly nonconforming children, are forced into normalizing their bodies, gender, and sexuality within an arbitrary two-sex, two-gender, one-sexuality system.

Let us explain by way of examples. In her literally shocking book, *Gender Shock: Exploding the Myths of Male & Female*, Phyllis Burke (1996) tells the stories of children forced by parents and teachers to conform to gender standards. One of the children, seven year old Becky, was identified by experts as having "female sexual identity disturbance" (Burke, 1996, p. 5). What did Becky do to be pathologized in this way? Burke writes:

> *Becky liked to stomp around with her pants tucked into her cowboy boots, and she refused to wear dresses. She liked basketball and climbing... . She likes to play with her toy walkie-talkies, rifle, dart game and marbles. She stood with her hands on her hips, fingers facing forward. She swung her arms, and took big, surefooted strides when she walked.* (1996, p. 5)

Gender Identity Disorder (GID) of Childhood is regarded as a "pathology involving the Core Gender Identity ... consistent with one's biological sex" (Sedgwick, 1993, p. 158). Clinics to "cure" gender identity disorder are often as near as the local university hospital where psychiatrists rely on an assumption of the 'realness' of a core gender identity to pathologize children. Nearer still, are schools in which the normalization of a two-sex, two-gender, one-sexual orientation system is fixed through educational theory regimented daily through a range of social practices.

In this chapter, we provide two accounts of youth who have been subjected to these normalizing practices in Alberta schools and communities. Their stories emerged from ethnographic interviews, a process which acknowledges that those interviewed are knowledgeable about their own lives. During the interview process, each was engaged in constructing a story of what he or she thought was important to his or her life. Without exception, the youth in this and the larger study found talking about their experiences to be a highly cathartic. Few adults had shown interest in or compassion for what they had experienced. Many of the youth wanted their stories to help put pressure on educational institutions and governments to change things they felt should never have happened to them. It is important to note, as well, that Jack and Jill's stories, while traumatic, are not just "painful stories of subjection and pathos" (Britzman, 1995, p. 68). Despite heterosexist desire for tales of the psychopathology of queer lives, these stories are representative of lives of considerable pleasure, even if exchanged for costs that are high.

The Case of the "Queer Young Dyke"

The early years of Jill's life were spent on a First Nations' reserve close to a large city. Jill was the eldest of six children and she often spent time taking care of her younger siblings, making sure they were cared for when her parents were not available. Frequently, Jill had to defend herself and her siblings, and by age six she was a highly skilled fighter as a result of fist-fights with other kids she described as bullies. Jill started school on the reserve and recalled liking school. However, she missed most of grade one because she took care of her younger siblings. Sometimes her "uncle" would look after them as well. On one of these occasions, her uncle raped her. Jill's father died in hospital when she was seven years old. Her mother died about two years later. Jill and her siblings were separated in foster care, with Jill and one of her younger brothers going to the same foster home far away from their birth home and extended family.

Jill's foster family was a boisterous and engaging group and both she and her brother quickly fit in. However, Jill was stigmatized in school as a "Native" in foster care. School professionals labelled her as incapable of learning and tried to place her in classes far below her achievement level throughout her school years. She was also labelled as difficult and disruptive. Her foster and later adoptive mother was a strong advocate on Jill's behalf and challenged the assessment of Jill's learning abilities. However, she was unable to overcome her own and the school's assessment of Jill's "unfeminine" behaviour. Jill's love of "rough and tumble play" which, "in psychological terminology, is the hallmark of the male child" (Burke 1996, p. 5), identified Jill as a gender nonconformist. Jill reported that teachers were all … weird about me … they did not really like me and were afraid of my behaviours especially when I did not act like a proper girl. I didn't even know how to act like a proper girl! When asked how she knew the teachers were uneasy about her non-feminine behaviour, she said that they told her to act more like a girl.

Meanwhile, Jill's adoptive mother admonished her to act like a girl, keep herself clean and tidy, and wear dresses more often. She also counselled Jill to talk "like a girl." As Jill demonstrated during the interview, this was to be accomplished by raising the pitch of one's voice, something she still had to work at years later. Jill reported that she had reasoned with her foster/adoptive mother that she could not do the activities she loved while wearing dresses. These activities included, "basketball, soccer, and climbing trees and, oh yes, I loved fighting."

Jill felt she had to fight as she and her brother were constantly teased because they were in foster care, they were "Native" and their last name was the name of an animal. Jill won all of the fights because she was not afraid, was highly skilled, and was a big kid compared to those she fought. Not only were some of her teachers "weird" about her, Jill stated

> some of them were afraid of me, I think because of my fighting but also because I was too big and they thought I was stupid. Some of the kids called me a stupid squaw but I think some of the teachers felt the same way.

When she turned nine years old, her foster parents adopted Jill and her last name changed. Jill said, "I was thrilled because no one could make fun of my last name anymore but I still had to fight all the time about other things." Still, life was secure and Jill loved her adoptive mother because she fought teachers and counsellors, even a principal, on behalf of Jill and the other children in the foster home. Through her adoptive mother's influence, Jill worked hard at school and, while never an outstanding student, progressed through grade school. Her adoptive mother provided Jill with love, care, security and the protection that Jill needed. The only point of contention between Jill and her foster mother was over her tomboyism as

> she was always on my case about being more like a girl and staying clean, wearing these dresses she bought, stop playing ball … but she really liked me, she adopted me and loved me; that's all that mattered.

Jill's adoptive mother worried that Jill's behaviours would get Jill into trouble at school and later on in life because, she advised Jill, Jill would not know her proper place. Jill's adoptive father did not figure in her narrative.

At one point, two 14-year old boys and a 15-year old girl were placed as foster children in her home. Jill, age thirteen, was drawn into a mini-gang formed by these three and her. For about six months, they did everything together. One night, one of the boys went into Jill's room and raped her. Jill tried to tell her adoptive mother who told her "to please not tell her this thing, she could not bear hearing this stuff." However, the boy was quickly removed from the home and the gang fell apart, with everyone blaming Jill. Around this time, Jill's adoptive mother was becoming very religious in what Jill described as a "very Christian church, not one of your regular ones but one of those alliance ones or something." Increasingly, Jill's adoptive mother put pressure on all the kids in her care to attend church. She became more fervent in trying to get Jill to act like a girl and started telling Jill that she would never tolerate her if she was bad and wanted to be with other girls.

Around age 12 or so, over a two-year period, Jill became increasingly aware of her attraction to other girls. She still preferred to play and fight with the boys but "I wanted to kiss and hug with the girls, especially the really cute ones." The cute girls, for Jill, were the ones who were physically active and smart. She tried to tell her adoptive mother about this attraction on many occasions but, as with the rape, her adoptive mother said she could not bear to hear what Jill wanted to tell her. Jill became increasingly agitated about this. "I love my mother," Jill said, "I wanted her to know about who I really am and I did not want to lie to her or mislead her because she saved me." Jill knew this was a highly contentious issue but also knew that this is "who I am."

Jill was fourteen and a half when she came out to her adoptive mother. Her adoptive mother packed Jill's bags when she went to school the next day and put them on the doorstep. Jill was not allowed in the house after that. Jill was forced into state care where " I had to fend for myself, I was alone again … I had lost my second mother." Not only was Jill refused entry into what had been her home, her adoptive mother refused to see her and would not let her make contact with her younger brother because "she said I was a bad influence."

Over the next few years Jill became increasingly alienated at school. She was constantly in fights and flunked out. Her social workers and counsellors at school did not know what to do with her. Teachers and students were either indifferent, afraid, or actively harassed her. Some teachers refused to have her in their classes, while students called her "queer," "a bull-dyke," or "a lezzie." Others gave her a wide berth in the hallways or refused to sit close to her in class. Jill hated school and quit attending on a regular basis. She was transferred from one school to another as a problem student. An incident in one high school stands out in relief against the constant harassment and marginalization she felt at the others. Some kids ganged up on Jill after school and wanted to beat her up. Jill got away and reported the incident and perpetrators to a school counsellor. The school counsellor advocated on Jill's behalf and ensured that the perpetrators were disciplined. Jill could not remember any other positive incidents from the years after she was kicked out of her adoptive home.

She attempted suicide several times and landed in a psychiatric ward. The attending psychiatrist referred Jill to another psychiatrist who was in charge of a programme specializing in individuals whose troubles were perceived to arise from confusion about gender identity. During counselling, over a period of several months, the psychiatrist convinced Jill that she had "a male brain stuck in a female body" and that, through a process of surgery and hormone treatments, this disjunction could be fixed. The psychiatrist told Jill, "that all of my problems were because of this male brain thing." At first Jill went along with the psychiatrist, but in a feat of bravery she was able to reject the starched white authority of scientia sexualis (Foucault, 1980) that, in addition to schools and family, have such a central place in the production of gender appropriate bodies. At the ninth hour, Jill refused to begin hormone treatments and instead insisted she was not confused about her gender. Rather, as she said, she was a "queer dyke." Jill was released from this programme back into alternative state care.

From the time she was kicked out of home until the time of this interview, Jill increasingly experienced great personal turmoil. State care was in the form of residential group homes but, with her suicide attempts and other misdemeanours like fighting and theft, Jill was in and out of lock-up facilities. In one facility, Jill was playing basketball with other girls in the gym and one girl accused Jill of feeling her up during a physically close moment, yelling that Jill "was nothing but a stupid dyke, keep your hands off me." Jill punched the girl in the face, breaking her nose and knocking out one of her teeth. Jill was disciplined for fighting. The other girl did not receive any censuring and, thus, Jill was effectively disciplined for inappropriate gender and sexual behaviour as well, even though Jill denied any sexual intention in her actions:

> I was just playing basketball and sometimes you touch the other players during intense play ... there was nothing sexual about it, as a matter of fact I hated her guts before that and loved pasting her in the face.

Jill did not complete high school. She reported that she has been raped at least once a year since her uncle raped her and had come to expect this would happen at some time or another every year. She was matter of fact about this. Jill also reported that she was beaten up regularly because she is so "butch" looking. She fought back and gave as good as she got, according to Jill. She also confessed to attempting suicide on at least nine separate occasions. Several of these attempts occurred in the lock-up facility where she received counselling and after one attempt was referred to the psychiatrist knowledgeable in Gender Identity Disorder.

At the time of our interviews, Jill worked in security for a small local company. She was in a committed relationship with Ellen, another young woman her age who had dropped out of school. Ellen was estranged from her birth family and did not work. Ellen took care of Jill emotionally, as both agreed in a joint interview that Jill was fragile. Ellen had pulled Jill out of her suicide attempts on several occasions and these were unreported.

Jill missed her siblings and tried reconnecting with her extended birth family and visited her father's grave on the reserve. She was angry at her birth mother for dying but dreamed about her constantly. She missed her adoptive mother "dreadfully" and tried to reconcile with her repeatedly, with no success. The last time Jill phoned, her adoptive mother did not recognize her voice. This devastated Jill. Her adoptive mother told Jill that she did not want to see her until Jill gave up her "lifestyle" and started acting like a girl. In Jill's words,

> I still don't know how to act like a girl, I can't do it, acting like a girl is not who I am, I can't wear a dress or talk differently. Yet, I am a girl.

The Case of Jack, The "Sissy-Fag Queer"

Jack remembered his schooling and growing-up years as a continuous struggle to hide from others the knowledge that he was different. Jack passed as white, although he is Métis from a two-parent, middle-class family. He had one older sister whom he adored with all his heart. "She was so perfect, so beautiful, so much my very most favourite person … next to my mother of course." Jack loved "My Little Ponies" and his younger girl cousins. He had a large stuffed animal collection that his mother and aunt indulged him in. Jack knew to hide his toy preferences during his first year of school. He was physically quite active and thin and wiry at this time. Although he preferred girls and girls' toys, he also loved to play games outside and ride his bike.

But Jack's first year of school was traumatic. During the fall, his beloved older sister was killed in a car accident on her sixteenth birthday. For Jack and his mother, the ensuing two years were extremely difficult as they tried to live without his sister. Jack still mourns her loss and finds the fall, with its smell of decaying leaves, a very emotionally difficult time of year. Jack's father has work that keeps him away from home for long stretches of time and Jack rarely mentions him.

Jack missed a significant amount of school during grade one as a result of his sister's death. Jack and his mother slept in on school days and his mother would not make him go late. She seemed tired and distant during this time and spent most of her time in his sister's bedroom. The result was that Jack's grade one marks were poor and he was held back while his cohort group of friends moved onto grade two. Jack felt like he never fit in after that. He recalled that he was not invited to birthday parties or other after school events. His former classmates made fun of him because he was "stupid." From grade two to the end of grade five, Jack became a bully. He was given two- and three-day detentions for hitting other kids. He hit one kid over the head with a bicycle chain. The other kid required five stitches. Jack also put on weight at this time. He did not want to go anywhere and withdrew into his house with his mother. He continued to gain weight and beat on other kids. None of his teachers asked him why he hit other kids but, if they had, Jack would have said that it was because they teased him about his weight. As well, Jack did not tell anyone that he was called names like "faggot" from a very young age and would beat up other kids for this as well. The name-calling puzzled Jack because he worked hard to keep his love of what he calls "girls' toys" a secret.

Over the years Jack and his mother kept his sister's room intact, a shrine to her. When Jack was stressed, he went to her room and played with and looked at her belongings, wishing she were alive. He also took his stuffed animals and little ponies into her room and played with them there. Jack felt safe in her room. His mother, as Jack recalls, remained withdrawn and depressed throughout his grade school. She did defend him from neighbours and teachers when he was accused of being a bully. Towards the end of grade five, Jack ended his bully stage and decided that he was going to excel at school. He had gained even more weight and described himself as "a fatso, that was me. I ate and ate and ate all the time, no one stopped me."

Since his sister's death, he spent increasing amounts of time alone in a more and more sedentary way and spent long hours studying. Jack was able to excel because he had few friends and once school was out, "I spent little time with any of my peers, oh I would walk part way home with some of them." His alienation from friends was related to being left behind in grade one, feeling older than his new cohort group, and the name-calling and other harassment he experienced. He liked things that most of his male cohorts would not approve of, so he kept "that part of me silent, out of the picture," yet Jack was harassed for being different. By the end of grade six Jack was the top honour student in his class and had taken on all kinds of extracurricular activities as well because "I wanted all the awards, it was not enough to just be the honour student, I wanted to be the best in everything."

Jack knew that most of his teachers were uncomfortable with him. At first, he related this to the fact he was a bully and that his sister had died. Then Jack thought teacher discomfort was related to the fact he was "a fat kid." Since he kept his like of playing with girls and girl's toys secret, he did not think the teachers knew about this difference. It was not until grade six that he became aware of another dimension to his difference, a "really serious" difference. At this point, Jack determined that teacher discomfort was because he was fat and because he was "showing." Showing for Jack meant that others could tell he was different because he liked boys "that way." "That way," for Jack, included kissing boys and living with them in the same house. Yet, Jack played mostly, when he did play, with his girl cousins. Showing was also related to the way he walked and talked, which Jack thought were very feminine. By feminine, Jack meant that he kept his arms tucked close to his sides; he used his hands to emphasize what he was saying; and he would "mince along" in smallish steps. His voice was too feminine, "girlie like," as well. Jack demonstrated a "girlie like" voice.

During grade six, Jack fell in love with his music teacher, an attractive 30-year-old man. Jack stared at this teacher whenever the opportunity arose but was increasingly afraid that his difference was showing more because of this action. Jack said he knew to keep this difference a secret because no one would approve. Even so, he believed the teachers did not approve of him, in spite of his academic achievements, because they knew his secret. While he worked at not showing, other students knew because they called him names.

One teacher stood out for Jack. In grade seven, Jack discovered that he liked dancing and the teacher, a woman, encouraged him and complimented him on his grace as a dancer. Jack was thrilled and worked hard at dancing. Unfortunately, Jack was made fun of by the other students because boys were supposed to hate dancing. Nevertheless, the teacher's approval was a high point in Jack's school years and interactions with teachers. The following year, grade seven, a group of boys pulled Jack's pants down to his ankles while he was getting his books from his locker and they whispered "faggot" at him. Up until this time, Jack wore jogging pants because they fit. Jack made his mother go out with him and buy two pair of jeans and he never wore jogging pants again. This incident was a horrific one for Jack and, as he talked about it, the shame and anger surfaced again:

> *I was so ashamed because I was so fat... I felt myself turning bright red as I pulled my pants up and looked around to see if anyone else noticed. Afterwards, I was*

enraged at not being able to say or do anything back. I am still emotional about this incident five years later.

Jack worked harder at "not showing" and losing weight as he now knew what faggot meant and that others would make him miserable because "I realized I was one" and that others despised him because of this.

Jack was a top honour student in his class up until grade eleven, yet mostly his teachers avoided him. A grade nine teacher physically moved back whenever Jack approached him leaving Jack feeling "unwanted and repulsive." As Jack says, "he made it clear that he had to acknowledge that I was at the top of the class but that he didn't have to do anything beyond that even though he made a big deal of inviting and including other students into his inner circle. Oh, he made it clear that he did not like me."

The lowest point in Jack's school years came in grade ten. Jack had to take physical education and found himself in a class with most of the members of the high school football team. They all seemed to hang around together and gave him funny looks. He was "terrified of showing. I did not want those guys to know about me." Also Jack was working hard at losing weight but was still overweight and out of shape. Being in the gym with the football team made Jack so nervous that "I broke into a sweat just thinking about phys ed and, in the class, I sweated buckets ... so much that I was constantly mopping my face, and my armpits were soaked down to my waist ... it was embarrassing!"

One day, several weeks into the term, Jack found himself in the boys' washroom with the football captain, a particularly scary person for Jack. Jack says this guy

> *talked in a gruff voice and gave me looks that made me feel small and foolish and very afraid like he was going to smash me in the face if I said or did anything ... .*
> *I was scared, I just kept thinking oh oh, oh, oh ... I'm in trouble now.*

Jack hurried into the bathroom stall, as using the urinal was not an option, and slammed the door shut. When Jack came out of the bathroom stall, he quickly ran his hands under the tap water in the sink and smoothed his hair back so he could make a quick escape. Jack reported that, as he was retreating, the football captain roared out, "What do you think you're doing?" Jack replied, "Me-ee? What do you mean?" The football captain roared again, "You haven't washed your hands properly!" Jack responded, "Oh, whatever," and raced out of the washroom.

The next gym class involved learning the rules for and playing basketball and, when Jack passed the ball to his classmates, several of them could not seem to catch the ball. It was subtle at first, but over the course of several classes more and more of his classmates would not catch the ball and whispered when game play stopped. Jack heard them saying they would not catch the ball because Jack's unwashed hands "contaminated" the ball. With each class, Jack felt that everyone was focussed more and more on him and he began sweating profusely. Some of the young men made a point of staring at Jack's armpits and most of them began to avoid standing anywhere close to Jack. Comments about his profuse sweating, the contaminated ball, and "one of those" circulated in whispers loud enough for Jack to hear.

Jack was devastated because he had worked hard to ensure that no one knew his secret and he worked against his own "inclinations" to prevent "showing." Inclinations for Jack meant the way he walked, gestured, talked, and sat. By this time, Jack was desperate to get out of the phys ed class and went to the school counsellor, who advised him to talk to his mother because it was not a good idea to drop any course given his outstanding academic record. His mother said that whatever he wanted was fine with her. Jack was not out to his mother, he thought, or to anyone else. Jack went back to the counsellor, who wanted to know why Jack wished to drop the class. Jack was increasingly desperate and refused to answer that question with more than a "because" and quit attending classes.

Finally the counsellor contacted the gym teacher, who was also the coach for the football team. The gym teacher/coach went back to the class and chastised the students for discriminating against "someone like Jack." The gym teacher contacted Jack and told him what he had done. Jack was even more devastated for being singled out in this way and because the gym teacher did not ask him if this was appropriate. Jack felt he had been "outed" with no input as to if, how, or when this would happen. To top this, the gym teacher's advice to him was "don't let them get you down and get back to class and face them like a man ... otherwise you will be a wimp for the rest of your life." Jack refused to go back to this class and negotiated a reduced mark instead. He spent the following high school years avoiding members of the football team, his former classmates. His high school was large enough that ducking into rooms and turning his head away seemed to accomplish this.

Jack spent a huge amount of time and energy being vigilant because he never felt safe:

> There were some ten of them in the class and chances of me coming across at least one of them everyday were enormous and besides, they were always together, so no matter what the counsellor or teacher said, I did not trust them and always felt afraid they would do something else to embarrass me or try to make me fight. I never felt safe.

In grade eleven, Jack found a friend, a young woman who he came out to. She was respectful and encouraging. He came out to his mother next who told him that she already knew and was okay with this as she loved him "just the way I am." Because Jack had found a friend, he did not put as much into his schoolwork; his time was spent elsewhere. "I was thrilled; this was my first real friend ever and I could tell her anything. I was afraid of losing her friendship but now I have lots of friends, many of them girls because they seem to be more understanding." Jack began volunteering at the local HIV/AIDS centre as well and found that community took him further away from school-work. School just began to feel so irrelevant to my life. I was teased and harassed. I was afraid most of the time. Teachers did not like or respect me even when I had great marks. I never learned anything about myself that was useful. When I found my best friend, even getting good marks was not important. I contemplated dropping out of school. Schooling was a constant struggle for Jack as he worked hard to control showing as well as keeping himself safe. Even though he became a model student through his marks and other good student activities, little at school alleviated his sense of alienation and isolation until he found a friend in grade eleven. He remembered observing the ways in which other boys were teased because they did not fit in and looked for reasons for his difference in the loss of his sister and his weight, because he was afraid to be like other boys who were teased. Yet he was one of those boys as the constant teasing he received attested. Jack's knowledge of himself as a "sissy" became more apparent with time as he came to know this was the "absolutely wrong thing to be in school if you were a boy. I knew I was not a normal boy, but I could not help myself... most of the time for being a sissy-fag, hey that's what I am ... that's what I was, even if school, teachers, other kids, whoever ... made sure I knew this was wrong, wrong, wrong."

Effects of Gender Normalization

The number of girls vulnerable to diagnosis of Gender Identity Disorder has dramatically increased as girls become more assertive and as they engage in "rough-and-tumble play." Ruckers, Becky's psychiatrist, has stated that gender identity disorder can be determined by comparing a child with same-sex, same-aged peers in athletic skills such as throwing a ball and percentage of baskets made from the free throw line. As Burke, sardonically comments, "I ... hate to think that a child's diagnosis of mental health ... depend[s] on basketball shots made, or not made, from the free thrown line" (1996, p. 205). That uncoordinated boys and coordinated girls are vulnerable to a gender identity disorder diagnosis or, at the very least regarded as gender nonconformists, has quite profound implications for a gender sensitive physical education. When two-gender categories are taken seriously, physical education for boys functions to normalize them through rough and tumble play while physical education for girls must stay away from physically challenging activity in order to avoid the perception of "gender deviance" (Burke, 1996, p. 204).

The "cure" for Becky's gender identity disorder consisted of 102 sessions of behaviour modification in the clinic and 96 sessions in her bedroom. She was rewarded for playing with "feminine sex-typed" toys and behaviour and rejecting "masculine sex-typed" toys and behaviour. Lest it is thought that Becky's story is an example of a 1950s overkill, these interventions are recommended to doctors in Ruckers's *Handbook of Child and Adolescent Sexual Problems* published in 1995 (Burke, 1996, p. 19). Jill's psychiatric treatment and prescribed body altering occurred in 1997.

As Burke indicates, "rather than being 'cured,' Becky's self-esteem was destroyed" by constant monitoring. "Her ... desires and feelings had been worn down, split off from her everyday world, only to become hidden within a secret and shamed place inside her. Becky valiantly strove for acceptance and to do what was necessary in the face of overwhelming odds. She wanted to earn back love, and if that meant choosing the pots and pans over the soft-ball mitt, so be it" (1996, p. 19). A desire to cooperate, a sanctioned, normalized 'feminine' behaviour, overrode Becky's desire to play with male sex-typed toys. Rather than recognize that gender identity is multiple and complex, Becky, like the rest of us, was forced into one of two manifestations of gender.

Jill was older than Becky when punishments designed to achieve gender conformity began. But the effects have been enormous for Jill as well. Jill's suicide attempt was the first of many that have taken place over the years. Her adoptive mother has yet to accept Jill's sexual orientation. Jill agrees that it is her gender nonconformity that gets her into trouble. She has been punished for her "masculinity" on a number of occasions including being raped by males intent on putting her in her proper place. That she is now actively pursuing education in spite of her experiences and was able to resist genital altering surgery is testimony to Jill's strength.

Jack too has suffered because of his gender ambiguity. Indifference and active denial of gender variation by school authorities sent strong messages to others that Jack was fair game to be ill-treated. The imperative to conform to gender norms provided a tacit permission for the treatment Jack received.

Implications for Engendering Education

It is our contention that gender theories and educational and family practices that focus on gender inequalities and/or differences, where gender is understood to include strictly configured notions of what it means to be a girl or boy or a woman or man, miss noticing and accepting variation in gender performances. What might it mean for theory and practice if the notion of gender is opened to other configurations? How might we address differently the questions, Is gender operative here? How is gender operative? and, What other effects do our strategies for understanding or eliminating gender have? We can only partially address these questions here but from what we have said it should be clear that we think that opening up gender and gender-sensitive education and family life would not only make it possible to recognize sexist distinctions between boys and girls, it would permit a sensitivity to the rigidity of these categories and alert us to heterosexist and homophobic effects—a sensitivity and awareness which are still so absent from home and school, theory and practice. In some instances gender-sensitivity might not even foreground gender; that is it wouldn't foreground equality or relations between two genders. In the cases of Jack and Jill, being sensitive to their needs as gender nonconformists may have less to do with their relationships to what is regarded as the "opposite" gender and more to do with their race, class, embodiment, and sexuality.

Expanding the limitations of gender in both theory and practice would take seriously the insight of second wave feminism: gender is entirely social and what is understood as femininity and masculinity can adhere to both male and female bodies. Recognizing gender as multiple would allow theory and practice to take seriously insights of more recent feminist musings as well: that what comes to count as sexed bodies has everything to do with the limits that have been placed on gender (Butler, 1992). Opening up the limits of gender to other significations would eliminate the dualistic notions of gender conformity and nonconformity. Most importantly, however, extending the limits of gender would make it possible to free children and youth like Becky, Jill, and Jack from normalizing, punishing social practices, including those that occur in homes and schools, that seek to make us all into "good" or gender conforming boys and girls.

References

Britzman, D. 1995. "What is This Thing Called Love?" *Taboo: The Journal of Culture and Education* 1: 65–93.

Burke, P. 1996. *Gender Shock: Exploding the Myths of Male & Female.* New York, London, Toronto, Sydney, Auckland: Anchorage Books.

Butler, J. 1992. "Contingent Foundations: Feminism and the question of 'postmodernism.'" In J.

Butler and J. Scott (eds.), *Feminists Theorize the Political*. New York and London: Routledge, pp. 3–21.

———. 1992. *Bodies That Matter: On the Discursive Limits of "Sex."* New York and London: Routledge.

———. 1997. "Melancholy Gender/Refused Indentification." In J. Butler (ed.), *The Psychic Life of Power*. Stanford, CA: Stanford University Press, pp.132–50.

Foucault, M. 1980. *The History of Sexuality. Vol I: An Introduction*. New York: Vintage Books.

Frye, M. 1983. *The Politics of Reality*. Freedom, CA: The Crossing Press.

Houston, B. 1996a. "Gender Freedom and the Subtleties of Sexist Education." In A. Diller, B. Houston, K. Morgan and M. Ayim (eds.), *The Gender Question in Education*. Boulder, CO: Westview Press.

———. (1996b). "Theorizing Gender: How Much of It do We Need?" In Diller, Houston, Morgan and Ayim, *The Gender Question in Education*.

———. (1996c). "Role Models: Help or Hindrance in the Pursuit of Autonomy." In Diller, Houston, Morgan and Ayim, *The Gender Question in Education*.

Sedgwick, E. 1993. *Tendencies*. Durham: University Press.

Part II
Understanding the
Context

The Regulation of
First Nations Sexuality

Martin Cannon

Introduction

Several aspects of Canadian political reality have led historical sociologists to maintain that race, gender and sexuality are not separate categories of experience and analysis but dynamic sets of social constructions which, as they interconnect, impact upon individuals and their (re)productive activities in distinctive, historically specific ways (Ng, 1993: 50; Pair, 1995: 356–60; McClintock, 1995). Informed by this understanding, any comprehensive analysis of Canada's Indian Act and early Indian policy should examine how configurations of racist, sexist and heterosexist knowledges were manifested in the process(es) of colonization. Such an analysis would seek to document the endeavours toward making (European) heterosexuality compulsory within status Indian communities (Rich, 1993). Such an analysis, in its most ambitious sense, would illuminate the convergent discriminations, directed toward those preferring same-sex intimacies, and make a contribution toward an integrated theory of race, gender and sexuality. Such an endeavour, though far from exhaustive, is the primary focus of this paper.

The first part of the paper will provide a critical review of the literature which suggests that a broad range of gender and erotic relationships existed among Aboriginal populations at early contact. Part of this exercise will be to specify homosexuality as an analytic category describing in turn the difficulty with using terms such as "gay" and "lesbian" to describe historic First Nations sexual categories (Sun, 1988: 35; Whitehead, 1993). The second part of the paper will then document how racist sexism and heterosexism worked together to legislate and define First Nations political reality. Upon illustrating the interactive relationship among these systems of domination, I will conclude that none of the development of class relations, the regulation of sexuality, racism or patriarchy can be explained as mutually exclusive.

Sexuality and Gender in Native North America

Even prior to Confederation and the emergence of the first statute entitled the Indian Act in 1876, the colonial enterprise in Canada had virtually enforced a system of Eurocentric policies, beliefs and value systems upon First Nations. The earliest missionaries, for example, were determined to "civilize" the Indian populations by attempting to indoctrinate a Christian ethos and patriarchal familial structure (Brodribb, 1984). It was within the context of such a conversion mission that same-sex erotic and sexual diversity was negatively evaluated and often condemned (Kinsman, 1987: 71; Katz, 1983: 28). This mission was a project fueled by heterosexism.[1]

One of the often-quoted passages related to the views of the early missionaries is that of the Jesuit, Joseph Francois Lafitau. Speaking of the erotic and gender relations which he observed among Native North Americans from 1711–1717, he noted:

> If there were women with manly courage who prided themselves upon the profession of warrior, which seems to become men alone, there were also men cowardly enough to live as women ... they believe they are honoured by debasing themselves to all of women's occupations; they never marry... (Joseph Francois Lafitau, quoted in Katz, 1976: 288)

The later diaries of the Jesuit, Pedro Font, resonated with the observations made by Lafitau. Only Pedro Font also identified an impending need to eradicate all such erotic or sexual relations and in their place establish a system of Christian morality. Making an assessment based on his observations taken from the expedition of Juan Bautista de Anza from 1775–76, he noted:

> Among the women I saw men dressed like women, with whom they go about regularly, never joining the men... From this I inferred they must be hermaphrodites, but from what I learned later I understood that they were sodomites, dedicated to nefarious practices. From all the foregoing I conclude that in this matter of incontinence there will be much to do when the Holy Faith and the Christian religion are established among them. (Pedro Font, quoted in Katz, 1976: 291)

Missionary accounts of sodomy were not always so subtly expressed. Jean Bernard Bossu, whose translated journals from the interior of North America between 1751 and 1762 spoke of "perverse" addictions among the Aboriginal nations he observed, expressed it thusly:

> The people of this nation are generally of a brutal and coarse nature. You can talk to them as much as you want about the mysteries of our religion; they always reply that it is beyond their comprehension. They are morally quite perverted, and most of them are addicted to sodomy. These corrupt men, who have long hair and wear short skirts like women, are held in great contempt. (Jean Bernard Bossu, quoted in Katz, 1976: 291)

The spectrum of erotic and gender diversity recorded in times of early contact suggests that same-sex relations were considered to be of some moral and political consequence.[2] Labelled as "nefarious," the relations that did exist were seen as illegitimate. Clearly, there is no superior foundation for such "common sense" forms of paternalistic judgement, but we can explain the claims to Euro-Christian preeminence as grounded in the ethos of the historical period.[3] Informed by notions of supremacy, ideologies of racial inferiority and of "civilized" (hetero)sexual behaviour, the early Europeans saw First Nations (indeed all non-Europeans) as subordinate and underdeveloped entities (Miles, 1989; Said, 1978).[4] Of pertinent interest in the aforementioned passages is also the way they reveal the interrelated nature of all systems of oppression.

Configurations of racist, patriarchal and heterosexist knowledges worked together to influence the views of the missionaries. Being a "nefarious sodomite," for example, not only meant "debasing" oneself by "cowardly" appropriating the gender and assumed sexual roles of a devalued (in this case) female class, it was an "unproductive" realm that, as I will describe in further detail, required complete refashioning. Salvation (sexual and otherwise) was to rest under the auspices of a religiously superior race of Europeans: a motive that was clearly racist. Salvation was something that required the regulation of a "savage" sexuality thought antithetical to Christian decorum, gendered domestic relations, and moral rationality. There may be reason to suggest, however, that the view toward individuals referred to as "nefarious" by the missionaries was an unshared sentiment among some of the original inhabitants of North America. It has been suggested that the *berdache* enjoyed an esteemed role within certain communities prior to contact.[5]

Among the Bella Coola Nation located in what is now called British Columbia, Franz Boas noted the special status accorded to the *berdache*, a status that was central to an origin myth on food (Boas, reprinted in Roscoe, 1988: 81–84). Toleration of the *berdache* and even "institutionalized homosexuality" is suggested in more contemporary anthropological literature and Native testimonials (Benedict, quoted in Roscoe, 1988: 16–17; Mead, quoted in Roscoe, 1988: 19; Owlfeather, 1988: 100; Kenny, 1988: 153). Sharing a similar perspective, Kenny (1988: 26) has noted that:

> Some tribes, such as the Minois, actually trained young men to become homosexuals and concubines of men. The Cheyenne and Sioux of the plains may not have purposely trained young men to become berdaches but certainly accepted homosexuals more readily than perhaps other tribes.

In short, some have been inclined toward emphasizing the *berdache* as a recognized and legitimate social institution. Nonetheless, is it necessary to look upon this claim with some scepticism.

First, there is some difficulty in making cross-cultural comparisons like the one made by Kenny (1988) in the above-noted excerpt. In his postulation, the tradition of *berdache* gets conflated with "homosexual," leaving little or no recognition of Native sex/gender systems. Such an interpretation is limited, for as Harriet Whitehead has argued, "sexual practices and beliefs must be understood within the context of the specific gender-meaning system of the culture in question" (Whitehead, 1993: 523; Rubin, 1975: 159). If we take a brief look at Native North American cultures, we grow increasingly familiar with the weaknesses of "homosexual" as an analytic category (Sun, 1988: 35).

The evidence to substantiate the claim that the Native North American *berdache* was an equivalent to the modern-day "homosexual" is limited. As Harriet Whitehead explains, such cross-cultural investigations tend to posit *a shared sexual identity* between the gender-crossing *berdache* and modern "homosexual": the very place where contradictions start to emerge (1993: 498). Alluding to the importance of sex/gender systems, Whitehead explains:

> *Western society foregrounds erotic orientation as the basis for dividing people into socially significant categories, but for Native North Americans, occupational pursuits and dress/demeanour were the important determinants of an individual's social classification, and sexual object choice was its trailing rather than leading edge.* (1993: 498)

Whitehead does not suggest that the role of the *berdache* excluded same-sex sexual behaviour (1993: 514). She illuminates instead a sex/gender system that renders one's chosen occupational behaviour of much greater importance than sexual object choice when it comes to social (re)classification (Whitehead, 1993: 511, 513). The role of *berdache*, according to Whitehead, was more about gender-crossing than it was about sexual relations. In making this point, she alerts anthropologist and social historian alike to the weaknesses of "homosexual" as an analytic category. In an historic or cross-cultural interpretation, modern-day Western categories may be unknown to the culture or past under study. The categories' applicability is subsequently limited. This is a position that is broadened by constructionist theorists who are interested in the history of sexuality. Foucault is exemplary.

For Foucault, sexuality is not a natural given, but the name that is granted to a historical construct (1990: 105, 127). Sexuality, in other words, is never more than a set of ever-varying developments tied to the mode of production and prevailing social/political realities (Foucault, 1990: 5–6; Padgug, 1989: 58). In short, sexuality and subsequently related behaviour is socially constructed. Failing to recognize this category as such presents the social historian with conceptual and interpretive difficulties. Kenny's postulation in the above-noted excerpt on Native "homosexuals" is again problematic.

The inclination to extract some *modern-day notion* of "homosexual," "gay" or even "lesbian" Native identity from the missionary statements on "sodomy" cannot be clearly substantiated. Nor can references to Indigenous sexualities be referred to as "homosexual" as this is known in the historical present. There are at least two reasons for this. First and foremost, the history of sexuality does not permit a conclusion such as the second. Foucault, for example, reminded us that the concept of "homosexuality" did not even emerge in western discourse until the 19th century (1990: 43). To be sure, and this is my second point, the missionaries were speaking of "sodomy" and "nefarious practices" as a set of sex related acts. The missionary statements, though they may speak of "morally perverse" behaviour and the outwardly physical attributes of the *berdache*, make no explicit mention of a specific personality type, sexual sensibility or sexual identity. It is not possible to make such an inference on that basis.

It is necessary to distinguish between behaviour and identity when we apply an analytic category such as "homosexual" to the historic past. We cannot take the sexual acts reported to have been witnessed by the missionaries and convert them to a history of personality or contemporary "gay" identity. For on this question of identity, Robert Padgug insists:

> *These identities are not inherent in the individual. In order to be gay... more than individual inclinations (however we might conceive of those) or homosexual activity is required; entire ranges of social attitudes and the construction of particular cultures, subcultures, and social relations are first necessary.* (1989: 60)

In sum, while it may be true that *homosexual behaviour* existed in history, we cannot call those whose behaviour was so inclined either "gay," "lesbian" or homo-sexual as these are known in the historic present.[6]

The third problem with postulating on and about "Native homosexuality" is in alluding to its prevalence as "institutionalized." This suggestion, as noted by Kenny and others, tends to overshadow any critical understanding of the practice from a culturally informed point of view. This characterization of homosexuality threatens to foreground the homosexual sex act over and above gender-crossing, occupational choice and the distribution of (cross-gendered) tasks. The effect of this characteri-zation is to suggest that sexual object choice was more important than gender-crossed behaviour in Native social classification systems. A mistaken conse-quence is thereby afforded to the homosexual or even heterosexual sex act since some *berdaches* "lapsed into anatomic heterosexuality and on occasion even marriage without any loss of their cross-sex status" (Whitehead, 1993: 512; also see Schnarch, 1992: 115). In sum, it is important to recognize when we speak of "institutionalized homosexuality" that:

> [H]omosexual acts were not in any way immediately suggestive of an enduring dis-position such as that which characterized the gender-crosser (or the "homosexual" in our culture), and such acts were not confused with gender-crossing in the Native mind. (Whitehead, 1990: 511)

This brief investigation on sexuality and cross-gendered behaviour in Native North America provides some insight into the diversity of erotic and gender relations that existed among a selection of Aboriginal populations at early contact. Through the use of secondary documents provided by Katz (1976), this investigation also illustrates the missionary response to such interactions. By no means exhaustive, what I have sought to illuminate is merely the care required when using "homosex-uality" to describe or interpret the historic past. To that extent, the preceding dis-cussion permits at least three conclusions.

First, missionary statements confirm the existence of "sodomy" following (and likely even prior to) contact and nothing more. While it may be tempting to trans-form the Jesuit accounts to reveal a history of homosexual *identity*, we can deduce only that homosexual *behaviour* existed in a selection of Native communities. Neither homosexual nor heterosexual behaviour was definitive to the (re)classifica-tion of social identity under Native sex/gender systems (Whitehead, 1993). On that account, the history of First Nations sexuality may be better thought a history of cross-gendered behaviour.

A second conclusion is that heterosexual behaviour could not have been as "mandatory" for Native North Americans as it was for the Euro-Jesuit newcomers since sexual behaviour did not set into motion an entire process of gender reclassifi-cation (see Schnarch, 1992: 111). Contrary to a European sex/gender system that characterized or equated the homosexual sex act with some enduring (cross)gendered disposition, the Native North American could engage in same-sex sexual conduct without necessarily acquiring the recognized status of (gender-crossing) *berdache*. Later colonial policy would work to alter this system through institutionalizing a structure of power and kinship relations that were both patriarchal and heterosexist. In the next section of this paper, this proposition will be further elaborated.

A third and more central conclusion based on the preceding analysis and evidence is the way that racism, patriarchy and heterosexism are witnessed to have developed in relation to one another. In the selected descriptions, the sexuality of Native North Americans was quite simply racialized and engendered. "Sodomy," for example, was viewed as a practice engaged in by a "morally perverted" and "coarse natured" race of people. By extension, the cross-gendered effeminacy and homosexual behaviour of the male *berdache* was socially constructed as "cowardly" or effeminate. In short, the dynamic interplay between "racial," sexual and gendered types of knowledge both produced and organized missionary recordings. A similar set of ethnocentric understandings would later translate into a set of policy objectives. These colonial knowledges would influence the contemporary circumstances of Native "gays" and "lesbians," some of whom continue to identify as "two-spirited" people. In the following section I explore the interactive relationship between racism, patriarchy and heterosexism in early "Indian" policy and the Indian Act.

Racism, Patriarchy and Heterosexism in the Indian Act

In this section I will highlight the way in which the Indian Act, in the assumptions that it made about the kinship and social organization of First Nations, assumed homosexual behaviour out of existence. Further research is needed to illustrate more precisely the actual impact, or causal effect that government initiatives and legislation had on the suppression of homosexual behaviour and same-sex intimacies. For an initial analysis of how the *berdache* tradition is no longer as recognized an institution as it once was in Native communities, see Williams (1986: 183–92), Roscoe (1988, Part II), and Brown (1997).

For well over 100 years, the Indian Act has been the central legislation governing the affairs of First Nations in Canada. Since its inception in 1876, the Act consolidated earlier policy and appointed the federal government in control of all aspects of "Indian" life including education, social services, health care and lands administration. For the purposes of this paper I will concentrate largely upon those sections of the Indian Act that deal with "Indian" status and citizenship. These were the sections that fundamentally reorganized kinship relations and delineated who was, and who was not, eligible to be registered as an "Indian" under the jurisdiction of the Indian Act.[7] While the historical development of these sections is most blatantly patriarchal, I will also illustrate how they combine to reveal an interactive relationship between racism, patriarchy and heterosexism. It is necessary, in other words, to understand patriarchal discrimination *in relation to* racism and heterosexism. Moreover, these systems of domination cannot be understood outside of the formation of capitalist relations.

The implementation of the reserve system in 1830s Upper Canada was among the earliest of statutory policies to affect First Nations prior to Confederation. This was a policy intended to resocialize First Nations into recognized "British-agricultural-Christian patterns of behaviour" (Frideres, 1983: 22). To that extent, the agricultural policy of the reserve system revealed underlying ideologies of racism and ethnocentrism. The reserve system was intended to "civilize" the "Indian" who, in the eyes of the European, would be otherwise susceptible to nomadism and societal decline.

The agricultural component of the reserve system was also among the earliest of policies to commence with the social construction of gendered tasks. Commenting on the sexual division of labour associated with this policy, Ng has observed that "men were taught farming skills such as how to clear land and hold a plow, [and] women, under the tutelage of the missionaries' wives and daughters were taught "civilized" domestic skills" (1993: 54). The reserve system policy thus represented a further endeavour toward the re-construction of gender relations among Aboriginal populations. These "common-sense" assumptions about the gendered division of tasks likely impacted upon First Nations women. At the same time, these assumptions likely influenced the position of the *berdache* discussed earlier in the paper. Had systems that recognized and affirmed an engagement in cross-gendered occupations existed prior to European contact, they would not have been possible during the 1830s.

A continued emphasis toward gender hierarchicalization continued well into the late 1800s. Most notably, it emerged in the status and citizenship sections of "Indian" policy. These were the sections that defined who was, and who was not, entitled to "Indian" status. In the tradition of earlier statutes, these initiatives made invidious distinctions between male and female "Indians."

The status and citizenship sections of the Indian Act have historically excluded Aboriginal women from recognition as status "Indians." As early as 1869, for example, Native women marrying non-Native men lost status, along with their children, as defined under section 6 of An Act for the Gradual Enfranchisement of Indians ([S.C. 1869, c. 6 (32–33 Vict.)], reprinted in Venne, 1981: 11–15).[8] This same loss of status did not apply to Native men or their children. In law, Native men retained their entitlement to status along with an ability to bestow it regardless of whom they married.

The exact motive for making invidious distinctions between Native men and women is not immediately discernable, but as one author has put it: "[T]he 1869 legislation ... was intended to reduce the number of Indians and 'half-breeds' living on reserves" (Jamieson, 1986: 113). The surface motivation behind the 1869 Act, then, was doubtlessly assimilationist. It may also have been about protecting "Indians" from White male encroachment onto reserve lands (Sanders, 1972: 98). To be sure, the mandate of the 1869 Act was to institutionalize a system of patrilineal descent and heterosexual marriage.

The status and citizenship sections of the 1869 policy carried connotations that were simultaneously racist, patriarchal and heterosexist. As Jamieson (1986: 118) has asserted, "the statute of 1869, especially section 6 ... embodied the principle that, like other women, Indian women should be subject to their husbands." At the level of "common sense," in other words, it went unstated that all Native women (and children) take on the "racial" status of their husbands at marriage. It also went unstated that Native women and men ought to be inclined toward the Euro-Christian institution of heterosexual marriage. Had there ever been a time where heterosexual behaviour was not judged "mandatory" in First Nations communities, it was unlikely to have been during the mid to late nineteenth century. By making marriage the only possible avenue through which to convey "Indian" status and rights, the 1869 Act simply legislated European forms of heterosexuality compulsory in First Nations communities.[9] Later legislation would only perpetuate such institutionalized domination.

In 1876, for example, the federal government passed the first legislation entitled the Indian Act. Like preceding legislation, this Act imposed patriarchal definitions of "Indian" by again emphasizing patrilineal descent. Section 6 of the 1869 statute became section 3(c) of the Indian Act, only later to become section 12(I)(b) in the revised 1951 Indian Act.[10]

Similar to previous legislation, the 1876 legislation did not require a loss of status for Native men. Native men retained their legal "Indian" status and, under section 3, were able to bestow it onto the non-Native women they married. Section 3 of the Indian Act would later become section 11(I)(f) in the revised 1951 Act.[11] Historically, these legislated changes institutionalized descent through the male line and simply "naturalized" the heterosexual nuclear family within First Nations communities.

Major changes to the Indian Act were common following 1876 and several systems of domination were upheld. In 1956, for example, an amendment to section 12(2) of the 1952 Act strengthened patriarchal definitions of "Indian" by enabling individual band members to contest the status and band membership of Native children thought to be "illegitimate." If an individual band member could prove that the father of a child was not an "Indian," then the child would not be entitled to statutory registration or band membership.[12] "Indian" women's status, henceforth from 1956, ceased to be of any official legal significance in and of itself since only men could bestow legitimacy (Department of Indian and Northern Affairs, 1991: 14). It was by entrenching this system of relations that a discourse of patrilineage was offered to First Nations. At the same time, notions of "illegitimacy" in the 1952 Act privileged heterosexual unions by emphasizing the importance of paternity to the exclusion of non-male partners. In this way, the existence—even possibility—of same-sex relationships in First Nations communities went unacknowledged.

This chronological selection of legislation provides some insight into the early provisions of the Indian Act. What I have sought to illustrate are the colonial assumptions made with respect to gender and sexuality. But in many ways, this brief explication requires further engagement. At least two considerations might guide this analysis. First, how can the Indian Act be considered a tool through which "Indians" were being "re-socialized" to become "productive" members of an emerging nation? Second, why did racism and (hetero)sexism interrelate as they did within "common-sense" attitudes about kinship organization? To what larger project, or sets of knowledges, was the interrelationship between these systems of domination tied? In short, what is so unique about the regulation of First Nations sexuality?

The historical development of the Indian Act and other "Indian" policy was a process coincident with the building of Canada as a nation. Between 1830 and 1950, for example, most of the Act's central prescriptions were being created. These were the years when Canada was moving toward an urbanized industrial economy. On that account, it is reasonable to speculate that the Indian Act and other "Indian" policies were informed by ideologies congruent with the impending processes of social and economic change. The Indian Act may be (re)interpreted as a mechanism fashioning the human infrastructure necessary for the growth of capitalism. Informed by that understanding, the reserve system of the 1830s may be revisited.

The agricultural policy of the 1830s not only placed emphasis on the state's motivation toward socializing "Indians" into economically viable entities, it also made some fundamental distinctions between the male and female genders. Policy makers of this new legislation, as mentioned, simply presupposed that "Indian" men would learn agricultural skills; and women, domestic chores. In this way, policy makers made "common-sense" assumptions about the gendered distribution of tasks. These assumptions were informed by ideologies of the sexual division of labour and the private and public spheres. It was within the broader context of these knowledges that the state mandated the regulation of gendered behaviour among First Nations. The imperative to divide tasks on the basis of gender must certainly have impacted upon women and also those inclined toward cross-gendered activity.

For women, capitalist and patriarchal knowledges combined to require that their labour be restricted to the private sphere. The implication of capitalist and patriarchal knowledges was to relegate women to the lower strata of the institutionalized gender hierarchy.[13] For those inclined to cross-gendered behaviour, capitalist and patriarchal knowledges relating to the sexual division of labour combined to mandate, even if unintentionally, the loss of gender flexibility. The effect of these knowledges was likely to have intensified gender classification systems making cross-gendered behaviour of considerable consequence. Seen in the 1880s an an *implicit* threat to the very project of nation building and economic prosperity, the cross-gendered individual was seemingly confronting legislative regulation if not vigilant policing. A similar concern over discordant individuals inhered within the "Indian" status sections of 1869 and 1876.

The status and citizenship sections of the Indian Act were as much about extending a project of invidious gender distinctions into First Nations communities as they were about the regulation of sexuality. The formulation of these sections were shaped through an historical context that ideologically prescribed the types of sexual behaviour thought most compatible with the mode of production. Capitalist and patriarchal knowledge relating to the (re)productive modes of sexuality combined in the 1800s to require the disavowal of same-sex relationships. Since only heterosexual marriage ensured a form of reproductive sexuality, these would become the only recognized unions through which to convey status in the Indian Act. Later Indian Act prescriptions on "illegitimacy" would reveal a similar influence from the historical period.

The "legitimacy" sections of the Indian Act were just as much inspired by the patriarchal emphasis on paternity as they were by the emerging productive relations of the late 19th century. The imperative of "legitimacy," for example, was tied intimately to capitalist notions of private property. Those status provisions that upheld notions of "illegitimacy" simply reflected a legal and social system which tried to ensure that only men could bequeath wealth onto their own children (Engels, 1942: 76; O'Brien, 1981: 54). The way that wealth was bequeathed was to declare that wives were the sole and exclusive property of their husbands and that subsequently, a man's children were those that his wife bore. It was in the broader context of wealth and the transference of property that the state endeavoured toward the regulation of women's sexuality. The imperative of paternity was largely to bring all First Nations into further congruence with a patriarchal system of private property.

To sum up, the historical development of the Indian Act was a process that coincided with the building of Canada as a nation. With that in mind, it is not possible to consider the Indian Act's development outside of the pervasive ideologies of that period. Engrained within the Act itself are "common-sense" assumptions about the gendered distribution of tasks, the forms of reproductive sexuality and capitalist notions of private property. All of these knowledges were contained within early "Indian" policy.

Conclusion

A central conclusion of this paper is that the regulation of First Nations sexuality cannot be explained apart from, or without reference to, racist and patriarchal configurations as those emerged in the Euro-Christian and subsequent colonial contexts.

For the early missionaries, descriptions of sexuality were informed by both "racial" and "gendered" knowledges. "Sodomy," for example, was a practice engaged in by a "coarse-natured" "race" of people. The cross-gendered behaviour of the *berdache* was further constructed as effeminate. Informed by knowledges that linked sexuality with "racial" difference, along with ideas that linked gender with masculinity and femininity, the Euro-Christian missions made the first attempt toward a "civilizing" agenda. In any attempt to reconsider that agenda, the dynamic interrelationship among all systems of domination needs to be recounted.

Racist and patriarchal configurations also influenced the later agenda of nation building. Capitalist and patriarchal knowledges relating to the (re)productive modes of sexuality, for example, combined to require the disavowal of same-sex relationships in the status and citizenship sections of the Indian Act. By extension, the sexual division of labour intensified gender classification systems in turn requiring the regulation of cross-gendered behaviour. All of these systems combined to deeply affect First Nations.

In short, the dynamic interplay between racist, patriarchal and capitalist knowledges all influenced the regulation of First Nations sexuality. Any account of the history of this regulation, or theory of state formation, needs to illuminate that interrelationship.

Notes

This chapter was first published in *The Canadian Journal of Native Studies* 18, no. 1 (1998): 1–18. It is reprinted with the permission of the author and the journal. Their willingness to allow its reprinting is acknowledged and appreciated.

1. By the term "heterosexism," I mean the system of knowledges or "political institution" through which heterosexuality is either implicitly or explicitly assumed to be the only acceptable or viable life option and/or sexual aim (Rich, 1993: 232; Blumenfeld and Raymond, 1988: 244–45).

2. The actual depth of missionary observation, comment and sentiment about "sodomic practices" cannot be thoroughly discussed in a paper of this size. Testimonies can be analyzed more closely, however, in Katz (1983) and Williams (1986). Goldberg (1992) provides further analysis of the evidence in both Katz and Williams, along with an overview of the sexual practices of Indians from the vantage point of Spanish explorers.

3. I borrow the term "common sense" from Himani Bannerji (1987), who draws attention to the

way that systems of discrimination "disappear from the social surface" and become ordinary ways of doing things of which we rarely have consciousness.

4. For a scholarly analysis of the genealogies of imperialist knowledge, see Anne McClintock (1995: 21–74).

5. As Burns has noted (1988: 1), *berdache* is the word used by early French explorers to describe male Indians who "specialized in the work of women and formed emotional and sexual relationships with other men" (also see Kinsman, 1987: 71).

6. It is worth noting—without delving too far into an analysis of "essentialist" versus "constructionist" theories of sexuality—that the (in)stability of analytic categories such as "gay," "lesbian" or "homosexual" are of some political urgency for communities interested in recounting "minority history" and validating an immemorial existence (Boswell, 1989: 20; also see Sharpe, 1992: 31, 38). This may represent one explanation as to why modern-day notions of "homosexuality" are sometimes conflated with the role of the *berdache*.

7. The very first attempt to define the term "Indian" and thereby racialize a heterogeneous and diverse group of people was made in 1850 under legislation entitled An Act for the Protection of the Indians in Upper Canada from Imposition, and the Property Occupied or Enjoyed by Them from Trespass and Injury (Indian and Northern Affairs Canada, 1991: 7).

8. As section 6 read: "Provided always that any Indian woman marrying any other than an Indian, shall cease to be an Indian within the meaning of this Act, nor shall the children issue of such marriage be considered as Indians within the meaning of this Act…" (An Act for the Gradual Enfranchisement of Indians… [S.C. 1869, c.6. (32–33 Vict.)] reprinted in Venne, 1981: 11).

9. Resistance to heterosexist status sections may have been possible by securing some alternate arrangement whereby the children of "two-spirited" people could obtain Indian status. However, this did not alter the fundamental effect of the legislation which was to privilege heterosexual over same-sex relationships. Had same-sex relationships ever been recognized and affirmed in First Nations communities—and it seems more than reasonable to suggest they were—the Indian Act would work toward ensuring that the legal and structural means with which to regain such systems were lost.

10. As section 3(c) of the 1876 Act read: "Provided that any Indian woman marrying any other than an Indian or a non-treaty Indian shall cease to be an Indian in any respect within the meaning of this Act… " (Indian Act [S.C. 1876, c. 18], reprinted in Venne, 1981: 25). In 1951, this section was amended to read: "The following persons are not entitled to be registered, namely… (b) a woman who is married to a person who is not an Indian" (Indian Act [S.C. 1951, c. 29], reprinted in Venne, 1981: 319).

11. As section 3 of the 1876 Act read: "The term "Indian" means, First. Any male person of Indian blood reputed to belong to a particular band; Secondly. Any child of such person; Thirdly. Any woman who is or was lawfully married to such person" (Indian Act [S.C. 1876, c. 18], reprinted in Venne, 1981: 24). In 1951, this section was amended to read: "Subject to section twelve, a person is entitled to be registered if that person … (f) is the wife or widow of a person who is entitled to be registered by virtue of paragraph (a), (b), (c), (d) or (e)" (Indian Act [S.C. 1951, c. 29], reprinted in Venne, 1981: 318–19).

12. As section 12(2) of the 1952 Act read: "The addition to a Band List of the name of an illegitimate child described in paragraph (e) of section 11 may be protested at any time within twelve months after the addition, and if upon the protest it is decided that the father of the child was not an Indian, the child is not entitled to be registered under paragraph (e) of section 11" (Indian Act [R.S.C. 1952, c. 149], reprinted in Venne, 1981: 360).

13. For many settlements, this meant a fundamental reconstruction of gender relations as some communities are said to have been egalitarian and matriarchal prior to contact. For a discussion of the matriarchal kinship organization and egalitarian relations among the Iroquoian Nations see Druke (1986: esp. 305). Also see Native Women's Association of Canada (1992) and Kirkness (1987: 410–13).

References

Bannerji, Himani. 1987. "Introducing Racism: Notes Toward an Anti-Racist Feminism." *Resources for Feminist Research* 16, no. 1: 10–12.

Blumenfeld, Warren J. and Diane Raymond 1988. *Looking at Gay and Lesbian Life*. Boston: Beacon Press.

Boswell, John. 1989. "Revolutions, Universals, and Sexual Categories." In Martin Duberman, Martha Vicinus and George Chauncey Jr. (eds.), *Hidden from History: Reclaiming the Gay and Lesbian Past*. New York: Meridian.

Brodribb, Somer. 1984. "The Traditional Roles of Native Women in Canada and the Impact of Colonization." *The Canadian Journal of Native Studies* 4, no. 1: 85–103.

Druke, Mary. 1986. "Iroquois and Iroquoian in Canada." In R. Bruce Morrison and C. Roderick Wilson (eds.), *Native Peoples: The Canadian Experience*. Toronto: McClelland & Stewart.

Engels, Frederic. 1942. *The Origin of the Family, Private Property and the State*. New York: International Publishers.

Foucault, Michel. 1978. *The History of Sexuality. Volume One: An Introduction*. New York: Vintage Books.

Frideres, James S. 1991. *Indian and Northern Affairs Canada The Indian Act Past and Present: A Manual on Registration and Entitlement Legislation*. Ottawa: Indian Registration and Band Lists Directorate.

——. 1983. *Native People in Canada: Contemporary Conflicts*. Scarborough: Prentice-Hall.

Jamieson, Kathleen. 1986. "Sex Discrimination and the Indian Act." In J. Rick Ponting (ed.), *Arduous Journey: Canadian Indians and Decolonization*. Toronto: McClelland & Stewart.

Katz, Jonathan. 1983. *Gay/Lesbian Almanac*. New York: Harper and Row.

——. 1976. *Gay American History*. New York: Thomas Y. Crowall.

Kinsman, Gary. 1987. "Sexual Colonization of the Native Peoples." In Gary Kinsman (ed.), *The Regulation of Desire: Sexuality in Canada*. Black Rose Books.

Kirkness, Verna. 1987–88. "Emerging Native Women." *Canadian Journal of Women and the Law*: 2,408–15.

McClintock, Anne. 1995. *Imperial Leather Race, Gender and Sexuality in the Colonial Contest*. New York Routledge.

Miles, Robert. 1989. *Racism*. London. Routledge.

Native Women's Association of Canada. 1992. *Matriarchy and the Canadian Charter: A Discussion Paper*. Native Women's Association of Canada.

Ng, Roxana. 1993. "Racism, Sexism, and Nation Building in Canada." In Cameron McCarthy and Warren Crichlow (eds.), *Race, Identity and Representation in Education*. New York: Routledge.

O'Brien, Mary. 1981. *The Politics of Reproduction*. London: Routledge.

Padgug, Robert. 1989. "Sexual Matters: Rethinking Sexuality in History." In Marlin Duberman, Martha Vicinus and George Chauncey Jr. (eds.), *Hidden From History Reclaiming the Gay and Lesbian Past*. New York Meridian.

Pair, Joy. 1995. "Gender, History and Historical Practice." *Canadian Historical Review*: 354–76.

Rich, Adrienne. 1993. "Compulsory Heterosexuality and Lesbian Existence." In Henry Abelove, Michele Aina Barale and David Halperin (eds.), *The Lesbian and Gay Studies Reader*. New York: Routledge.

Roscoe, Will. 1988. *Living the Spirit: A Gay American Indian Anthology*. New York: St. Martin's Press

Rubin, Gayle. 1975. "The Traffic in Women: Notes on the Political Economy of Sex." In Reyna R. Reiter (ed.), *Toward an Anthropology of Women*. New York: Monthly Review.

Said, Edward. 1979. *Orientalism*. New York: Vintage Books.

Sanders, Douglas. 1972. "The Bill of Rights and Indian Status." *University of British Columbia Law Review* 7, no. 1: 81–105.

Schnarch, Brian. 1992. "Neither Man nor Woman: Berdache—A Case for Non-Dichotomous Gender Construction." *Anthropologica* 34, no. 1.

Sharpe, Jim. 1992. "History from Below." In Peter Burke (ed.), *New Perspectives on Historical Writing*. Pennsylvania State University Press.

Venne, Sharon Helen. 1981. *Indian Acts and Amendments 1868–1975. An Indexed Collection.* Saskatoon: University of Saskatchewan Native Law Centre.

Whitehead, Harriet. 1993. "The Bow and the Burden Strap: A New Look at Institutionalized Homosexuality in Native North America." In Henry Abelove, Michele Aina Barale and David Halperin (eds.), *The Lesbian and Gay Studies Reader*. New York: Routledge.

9

Activism = Public Education:

THE HISTORY OF PUBLIC DISCOURSES OF HOMOSEXUALITY IN SASKATCHEWAN, 1971–93

Valerie J. Korinek

IN JUNE 1993, THE SASKATCHEWAN HUMAN RIGHTS CODE ACT, or Bill 38 as it was officially known, was passed by a vote of 31–10 in the Saskatchewan Legislature. With the passage of what proved to be controversial legislation, gays and lesbians were officially recognized within the province's human rights legislation and accorded protection in the areas of employment and housing. As the seventh province to include sexual orientation under the human rights code, Saskatchewan's record was far from progressive. Instead, it was a pragmatic response to the new Canadian political climate, in which the federal government and the majority of the other provinces were recognizing and grappling with equity rights for gays and lesbians. In many respects, Saskatchewan's legislation was purely derivative, an attempt to harmonize its human rights legislation with the standards elsewhere. However, at one time, in the mid-1970s, it appeared that the prairie province would lead the way for gay and lesbian human rights. In 1973 the Saskatchewan Human Rights Commission urged the government to extend coverage to gays and lesbians and the NDP government appeared in favour of such a move. Because of Saskatchewan's late entry into the extension of human rights for gays and lesbians, and due to the lack of emphasis accorded histories of sexuality outside of Ontario or British Columbia, it has meant that studies of gay activism or gay communities on the prairies are virtually unknown.[1] This chapter aims to reverse some of this historiographical neglect, and to point to ways in which the Saskatchewan chronology of rights extension, and the public educational campaigns towards that goal, were often distinctive.

It is a truism of Canadian history that the political culture of Saskatchewan is more progressive—thanks to the twin legacies of the first election of a socialist government in North America, and as the birthplace of Canadian medicare. More pertinently, it was Tommy Douglas's CCF government that implemented Canada's first human rights legislation when, in 1947, it introduced the Saskatchewan Bill of Rights. Yet this stereotype is worth closer analysis, and in this chapter the province's "progressive" nature is analyzed in light of its treatment of gays and lesbians. To do so is to challenge some of the provincial myths and omissions of "gay life" in the prairie provinces. First, not all Saskatchewan queers fled for greener pastures. Those who did leave left for much the same reasons that their heterosexual peers did—in search of better employment prospects. However, many often spent their formative, coming-out years in the province and a large number of those who left continued to make annual visits to family and friends. In this way, those "who went down the road" joined those who stayed in creating gay and lesbian community space. Thus it was that a relatively small number of tenacious individuals were able to create a vocal, vibrant community, centred around the city of Saskatoon. Second, a close examination of gay and lesbian activism in the province indicates that regardless of which party was in power, socially conservative, often religiously influenced views regarding gays and lesbians were no more uncommon in Saskatchewan than in neighbouring Alberta. While fundamentalist Christianity is assumed to have its strongest hold in the province of Alberta, there were strong pockets of such religious observance in Saskatchewan, and they found their most vocal expression during the years in which Grant Devine's Progressive Conservatives were in power (1982–1991).

While it is tempting to attribute this Christian fundamentalism to the larger proportion of prairie residents living in rural areas (by comparison with the rest of the country) it is not quite that simple, as fundamentalists come from all economic strata, and both urban and rural areas. What was different, was the way in which grassroots political activism and a strong sense of community involvement—time-tested Saskatchewan political strategies—were adapted to meet the ends of gay and lesbian community building and activism. Turning the province's small population base to their advantage, young gay activists, influenced by developments elsewhere in Canada and the United States, threw themselves into community development, coalition building, educational campaigns and outreach to rural gays and lesbians in their attempts to give gays and lesbians a public presence and a political voice in the province. In a minor, but influential way, the public support of the United Church and the Catholic Church aided the activists and the government's cause. Ultimately, in Saskatchewan gay activism was primarily an act of public education of government officials and the population, as opposed to more litigious or radical activism elsewhere. It was no coincidence that the vast majority of the key players in gay and lesbian activism were educators, or former educators, or from families with strong emphasis on education or religion (and hence of the importance of church leadership positions).

In tracing the public discourses about homosexuality in Saskatchewan, this chapter draws upon straight and gay media sources, upon documents from the early gay organizations, and upon oral histories with local activists.[2] During the 20 years under consideration, the province's gay and lesbian individuals witnessed the birth of gay organizations, ending forever the years of isolation and invisibility. Subsequent to the closeted years, one can trace a "golden age" of homosexuality, when it appeared that the community was primed for extensive growth, when governments were willing to listen, if not heed, the gay political message, and when, for the first time, there was significant, sustained, positive public discourse about homosexuality in the provincial media. One significant catalyst for that change, was the 1975 Doug Wilson case on the University of Saskatchewan campus, which provided straight Saskatchewan residents with a home-grown, non-threatening gay victim and forged a coalition of straight and gay activists, academics and supporters who sought justice on his behalf. Wilson did not win his legal battle, but in the process a gay hero was created and his charisma, and political will, served as an important stimulus for more community and political initiatives. Subsequently, in the late 1970s and early 1980s, a period of retrenchment began, motivated in part by gay and lesbian community politics, but also by the economic and political climate in the province. The recession of the early 1980s and the provincial victory of the Progressive Conservatives exacerbated the community's difficulties. Particularly in Premier Grant Devine's second term in office, the media was full of homophobic pronouncements by key government officials and the officially sanctioned fundamentalist backlash nearly extinguished the heady, optimistic liberationism of the 1970s. Although government-sanctioned homophobia ended with the election of the Roy Romanow's NDP in 1991, there were sufficient numbers of individuals and organizations, including the remaining PC MLAs, who continued to disseminate their homophobic ideas. In particular, this centred upon the political debates about the extension of human rights to gays and lesbians, an NDP promise of many years' duration.

This chapter's focus on provincial discourses of homosexuality within the framework of gay and lesbian human rights activism permits a number of conclusions about the history of gay and lesbian communities on the prairies. First, it demonstrates the importance of gay activists and their public education campaigns—both with elected government officials and with the general public. Attempts to educate straight politicians and residents about the realities of homosexual lives in Saskatchewan, particularly emphasizing the routine discrimination that could be meted out, were fundamental to changing the provincial perception of homosexuality. Prior to 1971, knowledge of homosexuality, and certainly public discourse about the Saskatchewan experience, was rare. Newspaper reports about gay and lesbian developments in North America were covered sporadically but the consistent conclusion that heterosexual readers would have formulated was that homosexuality and homosexuals lived elsewhere. Peter Millard, a former English professor at the University of Saskatchewan recalled that this local ignorance and naiveté actually served professional and middle-aged, closeted gay men quite well, as they were free to live their lives without suspicion or derision. After the advent of gay organizations in the community, this would no longer be possible and even people like Millard, who would become a very public spokesperson for gay activism, were initially discomfited.[3] The media coverage of Wilson's case demonstrated conclusively how little most people actually knew about "professed homosexuals" and equally important, demonstrated their vulnerability if they ventured out of the closet. Subsequent to Wilson's case, one can see a growth in awareness, and in some cases tolerance and acceptance. The 1980s backlash hit the community and those who thought of themselves as "progressives" particularly hard—and while many like to think of it as an anomaly, the wave of fundamentalist Christianity certainly found a small, but vocal and willing audience in the province. That the tide was turned, and that the NDP government once again embraced partial equality as its goal, was not a *fait accompli*, but the result of much hard work by activists and their supporters. However the small cadre of activists were not just engaged with politicizing straight residents, they were also in the process of building a visible queer community by creating dedicated gay space, and cultural and social events. Additionally, Saskatoon's gay and lesbian organizations served a hinterland of rural and small town gays and lesbians and thus promoted pride and awareness throughout the province. Ultimately, in 1993 the Romanow government reluctantly acted on its promises to the gay community to extend human rights legislation. The intensive media coverage of this political debate indicated how strongly socially conservative, usually fundamentalist Christian-based views, were held in the province at the same time that media polls indicated that the majority of residents, urban and rural, subscribed to the view that homosexuals should not be victims of discrimination. It is too simplistic to suggest that the impact of the gay educational and outreach campaigns was solely responsible for this shift, but it is fair to conclude that it did play a part in changing the mindset of the countryside.

Gay Life and Organizing in Saskatoon Prior to 1975

Formal gay organizations came to Saskatchewan in March 1971, when an advertisement for Saskatoon Gay Liberation was placed in the organization's column of Vancouver's alternative paper, the *Georgia Straight*. A box number was provided for respondents, and slowly a few people began to write to Gens (then Doug) Hellquist about this new organization.[4] Prior to the start of formal organizations in the city, there were, of course, bars and cruising areas within the downtown core that were known within gay male circles as likely meeting places. Two bars in particular—the Cove at the King George Hotel, and the second floor lounge at the Bessborough Hotel (a Saskatoon landmark and former CP hotel)—were popular places. The prime outdoor cruising area was Kiwanis Park, a downtown park that runs parallel with the South Saskatchewan River, from the Bessborough Hotel to the University Bridge. Additionally, there were a couple of small social circles of middle-aged gay men, some affiliated with the university, some not, which held regular house parties during the late 1960s. According to Tom Warner, a former resident of Prince Albert, it took perseverance to find these links to the underground community and once known, invitations were restricted to those who were popular, or who did not displease the organizers.[5] There was no sense of a "gay community" then but only fragmentary social circles.[6] Hellquist reported that it was after consultation and encouragement from one of his mentors, Professor Dan Nahlbach, the Head of the Drama Department at the University of Saskatchewan, that he placed the *Georgia Straight* advertisement.[7] Nahlbach was originally from Buffalo, NY, and many interview participants recalled the fabulous, sometimes outrageous, parties that he presided over at his City Park home. Nahlbach had imported what many believed was an American mode of gay socializing to the city, when he implemented a camp version of "family-style" socializing with himself as the head matriarch, Gladys Stafford, and all the younger men initiated into the group were given female names and referred to as "daughters." This role playing subsequently became a source of tension and was abandoned shortly after the formation of the gay organization, as members adopted the new gay pride and liberationist perspective, and no doubt sought independence from the social control of the older generation.[8] For his part, Hellquist recalled that he was also inspired by other North American developments, in particular, the

Stonewall Inn riots in New York City, the incipient gay rights movement in the U.S., and the establishment of private gay social clubs in Calgary and Edmonton, all of which he remembered reading about in the pages of the *Georgia Straight*.

Responses to the *Georgia Straight* ad were not numerous, but from the surviving letters one can offer a partial reconstruction of the initial participants. First, most of the respondents were Saskatoon men, primarily in their 20s, although one elderly man did write for information. A couple of letters were received from smaller towns, including North Battleford, Prince Albert and Humboldt. Most individuals were single, and although most indicated that they had never made contact with such an organization before, a few correspondents stated that they were acquainted with other groups and publications. For instance, one man wrote:

> *I have lived in Saskatoon for five years and was so surprised to pick up a copy of the* Georgia Straight *yesterday and find an address for Gay Lib in Saskatoon.... I am a member of Mattachine of New York—it keeps me in touch a little with those whose interests corresponds with mine...*[9]

The only letter in the file from a woman was similarly instructive about the terminology and cultural references of the pre-liberationist world. "Debbie" wrote:

> *As a lonely lesbian of many years, it was with great delight that I read your ad. I subscribed to the* Ladder *for a couple of years, read anything published by Ann Aldrich or anything pertaining to the so-called "twilight zone." This, however is not the same as meeting others of the third sex in a society which either refuses to recognize us or regards us with scorn.*[10]

Based on these responses, "a letter of intent was sent to every known gay person in Saskatoon (about 25) informing them of a meeting to organize the gay community. At this first meeting in October 1971 a committee was appointed to investigate the possibilities for a gay organization."[11] The result was the Zodiac Friendship Society (ZFS), an umbrella organization which was formally incorporated in March 1972. The innocuous "Age of Aquarius" name was a cautiously strategic one as the founders were uncertain about how residents of the city might react. Private parties, many held at the home of a fine arts professor, Don McNamee, were used as fundraisers to enable Zodiac to save money towards eventually establishing its own gay centre.[12]

In addition to Zodiac, there were other shorter-lived groups that operated in the early 1970s, including Saskatoon GATE (Gay Alliance Toward Equality), which was affiliated with chapters in Toronto, Vancouver, Edmonton, and Regina, as well as the Gay Students Alliance, started by University of Saskatchewan student Bruce Garman, which had ties to other university groups throughout Canada and parts of the U.S. In the fall of 1972, ZFS issued a press release indicating that at a meeting of all these organizations, they decided to work together to "bring about the total liberation of the gay community."[13] The new name of this political activist group would be Saskatoon Gay Action (SGA), and it would function as a committee of ZFS.

ZFS's membership base grew steadily. Two years later it had 60 members, and was attracting upwards of 250 people to its weekly Saturday night dances. The dances, which started in February 1972, were initially held at the Unitarian Centre, on the city's east side.[14] Unlike Regina, Calgary, Edmonton and Winnipeg, where private, members-only social clubs were established first and had no official links with political organizations, Zodiac's social club, called the Gemini Club, was the moneymaker that permitted it to fund its political and social service activities, including peer counselling, a speaker's bureau for high school and university classes, week-night drop-ins, an educational committee that wrote pamphlets, a newsletter, a library committee, and its activist group (Saskatoon Gay Action) which focussed on legal and legislative changes aimed at eradicating discrimination. While the vast majority of members and non-members enjoyed the well-attended socials and dances, only a core of activists undertook political work. Subsequent to the group's formation, weekly ads were placed in the city's newspapers (which took persistence as the papers were initially reluctant to print the word "homosexual"), and those ads drew over 200 responses in the first ten months.[15]

More representative of the larger community are the numerous letters from rural dwellers, more letters from women (although men still predominate), and a number of letters from Regina residents, frustrated with the lack of similar organizations in their community. For whatever reason, Regina was not as well served by gay organizations, and over the course of the time that the Zodiac and later the Gay Community Centre would be front and centre in Saskatoon, Regina would be host to a number of campus groups, including GATE Regina, and the University of Saskatchewan Homophile Association (Regina Campus). The city also had a private members' club, called the Odyssey Club, which was not formally affiliated with gay activism. The few extant letters from Regina organizations indicate that they were aware of the gulf between the two cities. In 1972 a member of GATE Regina wrote:

> the primary purpose of the group is to look at the existing conditions in Regina and to take the necessary positive steps required to make the "gay scene" more gay. You may be aware that our northern brothers and sisters in Saskatoon have been more energetic in community planning than ourselves.[16]

Subsequently, much of Regina's lesbian and gay community energy went into maintaining their social club. To date, interviews also indicate that Regina was a far less welcoming city than Saskatoon.[17]

By all accounts, prior to the massive public attention accorded the Wilson case in 1975, the Gay Community Centre of Saskatoon had made a series of significant social and political accomplishments. Politically, its public education campaigns were well underway. In 1972, Saskatoon Gay Action met with ten different groups, as well as giving a television interview to "inform the public of the truth about gay people."[18] It ran weekly advertisements in the local newspapers, advertising the group and significantly increasing the numbers of people who were aware of gay activity. In August 1973, Saskatoon Gay Action's Bruce Garman wrote to city council to request that the city proclaim the week of August 19–26 Gay Pride Week, stating "this week is set apart by Canada's gay citizens to demonstrate their pride in their sexuality and their desire to be allowed to live their lives without the fear of discrimination and oppression."[19] City council declined, and in the newspaper account, Alderman Penner was quoted as saying "I think there are certain matters that are subject to the privacy of the individual, that don't need any proclamation or public statement made about them."[20] In November 1974, SGA brought the American lesbian couple, Del Martin and Phyllis Lyons, to the University of Saskatchewan campus to speak about their role as the founders of the Daughters of Bilitis. The visit of Martin and Lyons was widely covered in both the *Star Phoenix*, and *The Sheaf*, the university newspaper.

With respect to more formalized political work towards changing the legal status of homosexuals, SGA demanded that the government include protections for "gay human rights." On February 24, 1973, Hellquist and Garman had a successful meeting with the Board of the Human Rights Association which requested that they write a brief about the nature of gay discrimination in the province.[21] Later that year, SGA met with Attorney General Roy Romanow's executive assistant, to present the completed brief which the newsletter reported, "received a very positive reception" with Romanow's assistant noting both that "recommended changes were long overdue" and that Romanow, himself, "felt positive" about the brief.[22] The brief was also favourably received by the Saskatchewan Human Rights Commission which formally recommended to Romanow that homosexuals should be protected from discrimination.[23] The ease with which SGA was able to meet, and seemingly convince government and public officials, led them to publish this human rights update in their newsletter:

> SGA expects the legislation covering gay human rights will definitely be presented at the next session of the legislature, in February of 1974. If the legislation is passed, it will be the first of its kind in Canada, and perhaps first in North America.[24]

After a meeting between Romanow and Peter Millard, president of the Gay Community Centre of Saskatoon, in the fall of 1974, it became apparent that the NDP were not going to revise the code, as they had promised. Partly because of that back-tracking, the members of the SGA decided to send questionnaires to all candidates in the June 1975 provincial election, polling them on their stand with respect to gay human rights legislation. Although few of the questionnaires were ultimately returned, it was the intention of SGA to publicize, in a paid advertisement in the *Star Phoenix*, the candidates' responses. The newspaper refused, citing concerns about whether the candidates had "given authorization to use their names publicly."[25] SGA issued a statement, claiming that the *Star Phoenix*'s actions were "just one more instance in which the press discriminates against gay people and refuses to allow free access to the press which is a right that is supposed to be guaranteed in our country." To publicize the discrimination a small group of activists picketed the newspaper's offices. Curiously, although the paper was reluctant to publish the viewpoints of political candidates, they were not adverse to running a prominent, front-page photograph of Saskatoon's first public gay demonstration. Front and centre in the photo was a individual soon to make headlines across the province—neophyte activist Doug Wilson.

However, before moving on to a discussion of Wilson's situation it is important to convey a sense of the social and community-building goals of the ZFS. Parallel to its political and educational activities, ZFS was also making advancements on its work towards building an active gay and lesbian community in the city. The weekly dances held at the Unitarian Centre were extremely successful, and attracted a diverse crowd of men, and a few women. Thanks to the admission and liquor sales, within a year the group was financially secure enough to look for permanent quarters. On March 17, 1973, the renamed Gay Community Centre opened its own offices on the second floor of a main downtown street, at 124A 2nd Avenue North. The Centre was "the first gay organization in Canada to be established in a city the size of Saskatoon."[26] At the time, the only other city in Canada that had a gay community centre was Toronto. In 1973, Ed Jackson, a member of the *Body Politic* collective visited Saskatoon, and described the crowd at an evening dance as "convivial," with members ranging in age from "16 to 71, the latter being a friendly Ukrainian gentleman who faithfully supports and attends every dance and drop-in because he can remember those lonely years when he knew only one other gay person in Saskatoon."[27] Interviews indicate that women did attend these dances, but they were in the minority compared with gay males. The Centre housed a library, phoneline, offered counselling, and held both dances, drop-in nights, and coffee houses. Fortuitously, they were across the hall from the Saskatoon Women's Centre, and this permitted much interchange of ideas and dialogue between feminist activists and gay activists. Up to this point, the activist wing of ZFS had been almost exclusively male, with a smaller group of gay women. This exposure to feminists, both heterosexual and lesbian, was an important development for two reasons. First, it gave the gay men a crash course in gender politics, which, naturally, had some important applications for their gay struggle. Second, it brought a handful of vocal feminist lesbians into regular contact and work with the Saskatoon Gay Community Centre.

The Doug Wilson Case, 1975–76

It was in this context, one of substantial gains in community awareness, growing gay pride and publicity, and a sense of optimism about the future of gay liberation that the Doug Wilson case would unfold on the University of Saskatchewan campus in Saskatoon. What follows below is not an exhaustive account, but a summary of events within the framework of the extension of human rights coverage.[28] Briefly, then, in the fall of 1975 Doug Wilson was a master's student in the Department of Educational Foundations. Originally from the small town of Meadow Lake, four hours northwest of Saskatoon, Wilson had already completed an undergraduate degree in Education at the University of Saskatchewan. He taught for two years in the small, northwestern town of Makwa, before he returned to the university to embark on a graduate degree. In his mid-20s at the time of the controversy, Wilson had been out in the community for less than a year, but he had disclosed his sexual orientation to his family and a few close friends. Wilson was a new member of SGA, and had participated in the *Star Phoenix* picket in June 1975. So, it was not terribly surprising that when he returned to classes that fall, he would attempt to restart a gay group on campus. Fatefully, he placed a small advertisement in *The Sheaf*, which read: "Anyone interested in participating in a campus gay organization. Contact Doug Wilson, Box 203 College of Education."[29] All of the people interviewed indicated that Wilson's ad was not calculated to inflame the administrators, but an innocent mistake in which he did not realize that using his campus mailing address would prove controversial. My informants believed that Wilson had mistakenly assumed that developments off campus, and throughout the rest of North America, would be mirrored and embraced on campus.

Immediately, the ads were brought to the attention of the dean of the College of Education, Dr. J.B. Kirkpatrick. In the fall of 1975, Dean Kirkpatrick was one year away from retirement, and at the end of a 20-year tenure as dean of the College of Education. Dean Kirkpatrick had overseen the Saskatoon Normal School's transformation into the College of Education, and its formal move to campus, and some have indicated that this left Kirkpatrick ever cautious about the College's reputation, particularly as reflected by the city's school boards.[30] A former champion athlete from the city of Saskatoon who held graduate degrees in physical education and teaching at Columbia University Teacher's College, Kirkpatrick was, by all accounts, an old-school administrator whose decisions were, he believed, final. Within days of the publication of the first two advertisements, Kirkpatrick had a closed-door meeting with Wilson where he informed him that his public identification with the gay movement was, in Kirkpatrick's assessment, very damaging to the college's relationship with the Saskatoon school boards. The punishment meted out by the dean was that Wilson was removed from the list of graduate students who were responsible for supervising the in-classroom practicums of student teachers. Wilson was not fired from his job as a sessional lecturer in the College nor was the completion of his degree in question. However, the dean's unilateral decision to abruptly remove Wilson from the supervisor's list, an honour bestowed only on the most academically accomplished students, and an action which overrode the decision of Wilson's department, was a very obvious reprimand. The dean did not help his cause when, in interviews with *The Sheaf*, Kirkpatrick said his decision was "a personal, moral judgement that had nothing to do with Wilson's abilities."[31]

Further compounding the situation, the university's president, Dr. R.W. Begg, a former army officer and cancer researcher who was in his first year as president, fully supported Kirkpatrick's "managerial decision." In a press conference called to "clarify" the situation Dr. Begg did everything but, and succeeded in inflaming public opinion. Begg candidly told the reporters that "public identification of Mr. Wilson with the gay movement could create a 'disaster' if he were allowed to supervise teachers in schools" because it would compromise Wilson's abilities to do his job, affect the students, and most importantly, potentially damage the relationship between the school boards and the university, although he offered no further explanations of how this might occur. To those who questioned why someone with Wilson's record would have been treated in such a manner, Begg offered the opinion that "the decision … to prevent a known homosexual from supervising practice teachers in the city schools is compatible with concepts of civil rights and human rights" and warned that "if damage has been done to Wilson, it is not the fault of the dean of Education but the fault of those who are publicizing it."[32] Like Kirkpatrick, Begg believed that administrative decisions, much like military orders, were to be followed, not questioned, and hence Wilson's decision to challenge them was, in his analysis, the reason for Wilson's grief.

Almost immediately after the Wilson situation became public knowledge on campus, thanks to front page articles in the student newspaper, both the Educational Students' Union and the University of Saskatchewan Students' Union passed motions demanding his reinstatement. Wilson's department also reaffirmed its decision to place him on the supervision list. Finally, and most critically, the Committee to Defend Doug Wilson was created. This group was a coalition of straight and gay academics, students, and activists, including Pat Atkinson, Skip Kutz, Neil Richards, Gens Hellquist, Deb Hopkins, Norman Zepp, Judy Varga, Mel McCoriston, Kate McCoriston, Bill Slights, Richard Nordahl, and Peter Millard.[33] This committee would be instrumental in organizing the opposition to Wilson's treatment, and for their savvy use of campus, local and eventually national media in their attempt to reverse the Dean's decision. Ultimately, the Committee to Defend Doug Wilson presided over a series of meetings, organized a petition and letter-writing campaign and was successful in getting the Saskatchewan Human Rights Commission to investigate Wilson's treatment. The decision of the Saskatchewan Human Rights Commission to investigate Wilson's treatment was a Canadian landmark, because previously no other provincial human rights commission had accepted a gay rights case. When attempts to negotiate a settlement failed, the commission informed the university that it would launch a formal inquiry.

Notably, Wilson's case was also groundbreaking provincially because it was the first time that positive, public discussions about homosexuality and the treatment of homosexuals were openly discussed and received such extensive provincial media attention. Provincially, coverage of the Wilson situation was followed by newspapers and television news programs, and it was the topic of discussion on radio phone-in shows, cable television programs, and subsequently, of course, with the general public. But this was not just a Saskatchewan story. Wilson's case received extensive national media coverage when the story was picked up by the Canadian Press service and carried in papers across the country. Wilson was also interviewed for a segment on *W5*, CTV's newsmagazine program. Begg and Wilson were both interviewed by Barbara Frum on her national CBC radio program *As It Happens*.

On campus that fall *The Sheaf* continued to print update articles; it published a special four-page insert about homosexuality, and consistently published letters from students, staff, and faculty, on both sides of the controversy. At the faculty level, debate was often highly charged, and the issue had gone all the way to University Council before discussion was tabled while a committee was established to report on the issue of sexual discrimination.[34] The Special Council Committee Concerning Discrimination on Sexual Orientation (usually referred to by the shorter name, the Schmeiser Commission, for its chairman, law professor Doug Schmeiser) was charged with the task of studying the issue and inviting input from all colleges on whether or not to formalize a policy for dealing with future situations. Behind the scenes, the university lawyers were in the process of requesting an injunction to halt the Saskatchewan Human Rights Commission inquiry. It was the university's legal position that the Commission had overstepped its bounds since sexual orientation was not enumerated in the provincial code. For its part, the Committee to Defend Wilson kept up its pressure. It circulated a petition with its demands that Wilson be reinstated, that he receive an apology from the administration, and that the university adopt a non-discrimination policy. The petition eventually had 4,500 signatures from across the country. Equally important, the Committee was able to make significant connections with other labour, political, women's and social groups, to increase its support base. This was a model that the Zodiac Friendship Society had adopted, and would be followed in subsequent activism surrounding the extension of human rights coverage. For example, when the Committee to Defend Wilson organized a picket of fall convocation, in addition to members of the Gay Community Centre, it was joined by diverse group of representatives, including "the Women's Centre, The Saskatoon Alliance Against Racism, Men's Liberation, Campus Organizations, [and the] Saskatchewan Association of Human Rights."[35]

Regardless of the coalition of activist groups and individuals, and in spite of all the letters that President Begg received, imploring him to reverse his decision on the Wilson case, the outcome of the case was less successful than the Committee and its supporters might have hoped. In January 1976, the University's lawyer, Robert McKercher, QC, successfully argued that the Commission had overstepped its bounds because Wilson's discrimination was not based on his "sex" as the Commission claimed, but upon his "sexual orientation" which was not a ground open to the Commission at that time. Justice J. Johnson agreed, and thus the inquiry was prohibited. The victory came on campus, where the Schmeiser Commission Report was tabled in late January 1976. In general the report recommended no discrimination on the grounds of sexual orientation on campus although the original version included an escape clause that would have allowed administrators in certain colleges to exercise discretion, particularly when it involved relations with off-campus organizations. This was a blatant attempt to allow the College of Education, in particular, to continue with its policies. The report's recommendations were vigourously debated in a March council meeting; eventually the anti-discrimination side won, and the offending clause was removed. For Wilson this was a symbolic victory since it was always clear that whatever the decision it would not retroactively apply to his case.

The Committee's hard work to publicize the basic issues of the case, and explain why and how Wilson's situation was merely a symbol of a much larger problem of gay discrimination in Saskatchewan, had been very effective in getting its message out to the populace. The Committee was organized, focussed, and tireless in the way it provided educational information to the press, the campus groups, concerned individuals, and the Schmeiser Commission. For his part, of course, Wilson's personality, character, and identity were key to making this such a compelling situation. Here was a gay activist that most residents of Saskatchewan could relate to—he had been raised in a rural area, to farming parents; he was a hard-working, talented university student; he was also photogenic, energetic and determined to be treated decently. A better poster candidate for such a cause could not have been found. Wilson devoted significant energy to politicizing the cause—travelling across the country to attend demonstrations and to speak, personally serving as a contact person for many other closeted gays who sought advice from the only gay person they "knew," and ultimately becoming an important volunteer activist and organizer in the community and the province.

Once one delves into archival correspondence about Wilson, his case, and gay organizations in which he was involved, it is immediately apparent what resonance the case had with people. Many people wrote to Wilson, and he, in turn, kept up an active correspondence. Many rural gays, and a few lesbians, came to see him as a role model for gay pride and perseverance. In many of these cases one can chart the development of the writers from anxious people, struggling to accept their sexual orientation to, a number of years and/or letters later, their prideful acceptance of who they were. Some of them were effortlessly writing about gay activism, or interested in gay and lesbian events, engaged in the political debates (if not active participants given their small town and rural locations), and some adopted Wilson's favourite gay liberationist signature, "in gay love and pride." One such individual, a 68-year-old retired schoolteacher from Nipawin, indicated that he had been gay since his teenage years but had never, to that date, been involved with a gay organization. He followed the Wilson case, listened to Wilson on the radio, and in one letter wrote:

> I shall be most interested in the doings at the centre [Saskatoon Gay Community Centre]. This "in closet" living for gay people must not continue any longer. I am indeed pleased that efforts are being made to change this. We need more with the fortitude of Doug Wilson.[36]

One can never know how many were inspired by Wilson's actions, or by the hard work of some of the key committee representatives who often acted as media spokesmen, primarily Millard and Hellquist. Here, in a 1976 letter to Hellquist, a gay farmer from Wartime, describes the case's impact on his life:

> I meant to write and tell you before that I saw you on TV when you were interviewed in connection with Doug Wilson. I was proud of you. You came across very good on TV and created a good image. I think that the more gays who come out of the closet and create a good image, the better off we will be.[37]

With time, of course, comes a more nuanced perspective on Wilson's impact. Longtime activist, organizer, and gay historian Tom Warner reflected that

> he [Wilson] did really good, groundbreaking stuff but at the same time there has been a whole mythology that has been created around him.... . When his case gained publicity it was probably the first time that a lot of gays and lesbians on the prairies saw anything positive on television and in the newspapers, positive in the sense that people were fighting back, they were speaking out in public situations.

As Warner himself has discovered, "a lot of people that I have come across since have said for them that was the first thing they ever saw about the movement, about its objectives, in terms of the mainstream stuff and it was a really eye-opening experience for them."[38] Wilson's impact was important, and for many he would always personify gay pride and activism, but Wilson was not the Saskatchewan gay movement. Without the groundwork laid by the Zodiac Friendship Society, and later the Gay Community Centre, and the Committee to Defend Doug Wilson, the case would not have been as prominent, nor as successful in educating the public. Furthermore, in the years afterwards, Wilson's leadership played a key role within the community, but, again, he was part of various collectives and organizations.

Human Rights Activism, 1976–82

The Wilson case stimulated considerable interest in the extension of human rights protection to gays and lesbians because it conclusively demonstrated that omission of sexual orientation in the code prevented the Saskatchewan Human Rights Commission from investigating the discriminatory practices undertaken at the College of Education. Wilson left the MEd program in the spring of 1976, deducing, no doubt, that the future of a "publicly" gay teacher in the province would be a difficult if not impossible.[39] Unemployed, and holding a series of part-time jobs, including office cleaning to pay his rent, Wilson used his status as one of the best known gays in the province to advance gay interests by acting, first, as the president of the Saskatoon Gay Centre. The wide publicity about the case also stimulated interest in other stories of gay discrimination and of ongoing work for human rights advocacy. For instance, in November 1976, in a *Sheaf* article called "Protection for Gay People" the views of the minister responsible were described unflatteringly:

> in a bear pit session before a meeting of a Saskatchewan Association on Human Rights, Mr. Romanow, the cabinet minister responsible for Human Rights legislation stated that we should move slowly in some areas of Human Rights as there may be a backlash.[40]

Wilson became involved in the Saskatchewan Association on Human Rights, chairing a sub-committee on sexual orientation. In March 1977, he was one of the organizers of what was billed as "the largest gay rights demonstration ever held on the Prairies," when 125 protestors chanting "gay rights now" and "talk is cheap, we want action now" delivered a brief to the Legislature demanding the extension of human rights coverage, and presented the government with the latest brief on the topic.[41] Later that fall, Wilson was elected to the Board of Directors of the Saskatchewan Association on Human Rights. Through this voluntary, non-governmental organization, Wilson was able to initiate important public education about gay and lesbian issues, including to "assemble an information kit on gays to be distributed throughout the province to guidance counsellors, school and public libraries; and finally to produce a half-hour video tape on gay rights for broadcast on public television."[42] Eventually, Wilson would become the executive director of this organization, a move that recognized his work on human rights issues and served to legitimize his message.

Given an expansion in his minority rights focus, and broadening his perspective to include provincial goals, it was natural that Wilson began discussions with other groups about the formation of a provincial coalition. In discussions in Regina in December 1977, a decision was made to launch a provincial group focussed upon gay activism and education. The goals of the Saskatchewan Gay Coalition (SGC) were to effect "political, social and educational action to ensure full human rights for all gay men and lesbians in Saskatchewan."[43] The assembled group included representatives from Regina's Gay Community Centre, in addition to individuals active in a variety of Saskatoon groups, including the Gay Community Centre, the Gay Academic Union, the Lesbian Caucus of Saskatoon's Women's Liberation and Gay Alliance of Youth. The Coalition aimed to be non-sexist, and "in recognition of the common oppression of women and gays the SGC" also "included among its goals, support for feminist issues of concern to all women."[44] Joining Wilson on the Coalition were Susan Langers, Kay Bierwiler, Wiesia Kolansinka, Terry Nelson and Marg Taylor.

One of the goals of SGC that made it quite distinctive was its outreach to rural and small town gays and lesbians, via meetings with members of the coalition, in addition to membership in the newsletter, alternatively called *Gay Saskatchewan* or *Grassroots*. Run on a shoestring budget, with an editorial collective of half a dozen individuals, *Gay Saskatchewan* went from a few dozen members/subscribers in 1978 to over 2,100 shortly before its demise in 1981. Although *Gay Saskatchewan* had readers across Canada and in many of the midwestern United States, it was primarily about Saskatchewan. Additionally, Wilson was part of the group who started Metamorphosis, an annual lesbian and gay cultural celebration, held each Thanksgiving weekend. This event drew upwards of 200 people from across the region for entertainment, art, dances, a demonstration and march, coffee houses, and a feast. According to reports in the *Body Politic*, "one woman from Toronto described Metamorphosis as the best cultural festival she had attended. 'There was a tremendous strengthening of people, culture and community over the weekend'."[45] This venue for cultural and community celebration provided SGC with a platform to politicize those within the gay community as well as residents of the city. Over 50 gays and lesbians marched through downtown Saskatoon, from the Gay Community Centre offices to City Hall where a rally was held. This "parade" was given prominent coverage in the local newspaper, complete with a photograph of the activists, whose chant "out of the closet, into the streets, gay liberation now" drew the attention of "Saturday morning shoppers."[46] Wilson reportedly admonished the marchers about the upcoming provincial election, and encouraged them to find out where their candidates stood on prohibiting discrimination on the basis of sexual orientation. "Politicians are afraid. It's a contentious issue," Wilson said, but in his summation to the reporter he stressed how "events like Metamorphosis give confidence to the gay community."[47]

Political and cultural developments within Saskatoon and the province were not the only contemporary discussions of homosexual rights in the country. In December 1977, the province of Quebec had quietly added sexual orientation to its human rights code. As well, the federal government was exploring a proposal for a charter of rights and freedoms. Gordon Fairweather, the chairman of the Canadian Human Rights Commission, received national media coverage when he urged that federal legislators amend the charter to "protect citizens against discrimination on the basis of marital status, sexual orientation, and physical handicap."[48] Similarly, coverage of the first gay case to make it to the Supreme Court docket, GATE (Vancouver) vs. the *Vancouver Sun*, due to be heard in October 1978, all fostered a climate in which rights talk were receiving media coverage.

Throughout the 1970s, as members of Saskatoon's gay community and later the SGC were publicly lobbying provincial MLAs, there was a covert campaign within the NDP to get a resolution on human rights coverage for sexual orientation discussed on the convention floor. Should such proposed legislation pass at the convention, it would form part of the recommended policies awaiting the following legislative sessions. Both straight and gay media indicated that the debate about sexual orientation, held in November 1978 at the provincial NDP convention, was controversial. Reports in the *Star Phoenix* and the Regina *Leader Post* indicated that a "call for the Saskatchewan government to enact a law prohibiting discrimination on the basis of sexual orientation highlighted the final day" of the convention, yet a "counted show of hands vote" indicated that a majority approved a resolution "asking for amendments to human rights legislation forbidding discrimination on the basis of age, marital status, sexual orientation or handicap."[49] These media reports quoted unnamed representatives who feared that "broadcasting" such "private acts" was worrisome, or who openly speculated about the impact of gay teachers. One of the vocal supporters was Saskatoon-Nutana delegate Skip Kutz (a former member of the Committee to Defend Doug Wilson) whose strong support for the resolution urged the convention delegates to "note that the issue is a moral one and when one group in society is allowed to be discriminated against, 'you can't tell people in Saskatchewan that progress has been made in human rights'."[50]

Gay press coverage was more detailed. It indicated that members of both the NDP and SGC were instrumental in this development. Neil Richards and Michael Gordon, both members of SGC and delegates at the convention, also spoke in favour of the motion. A spokesperson for SGC said, "It took five years of intensive lobbying to do this, and it's important to realize that the debate was carried by straight supporters."[51] Passage was important, but opponents, including Consumer Affairs minister Ed Whelan, were quick to note that "entrenching homosexual rights would create problems for school boards concerned about their influence on children."[52]

Similarly, in Premier Blakeney's final address to the convention, he noted that "balancing rights" between "the rights of the minority groups to be free from discrimination" against the "rights of groups like school boards to be able to employ teachers who meet the standards the board set" would be a challenge, and indicated that it would "require 'a good deal of thought to see what the appropriate role of government is'."[53] So, while open discussion and majority support of the resolution were important, an astute political observer could detect wavering support for the resolution from the start.

Immediately thereafter, many lengthy condemnatory letters were published in the urban and rural papers on the issue. Most were from concerned parents and churchmen, most notably the Reverend Henry Friesen, of Renaissance, who felt compelled to "register our distress and to express our strongest opposition to the implications of the resolution." Most took biblically conservative positions, and almost all of them drew scarifying pictures of the gay teacher in the classroom, such as the following representative excerpt from Friesen. He noted that if the legislation passed it "would make it necessary for parents to send their children into classrooms presided over by a teacher who could be a homosexual and teach this sin as a normal way of life. That would in essence create the same problem as a teacher teaching his pupils how to rob a bank!"[54] While most of these letters appeared to come from concerned individuals there were some clear indications within the SGC and from NDP insiders, that the religious right had begun a letter writing campaign to provincial politicians. John Cooper and Maureen Semchuk alerted students, via the University of Regina newspaper *The Carillon*, that "if the majority of the population disapproves of discrimination but do not make their views known, the vocal fundamentalist minority may carry the day."[55] A small group of determined activists, including Neil Richards and Peter Millard, often took it upon themselves to respond with their own editorial letters, refuting the ignorance and bigotry with established fact.

In January 1979, the SGC presented a brief to all MLAs entitled "Lesbians and Gay Men—A Minority Without Rights," which once again put forward the case for human rights protection for sexual orientation. The next month, three members of SGC met with the Attorney General, Roy Romanow, for the first time since 1974. During that meeting, as reported in the *Body Politic*, Romanow "refused to indicate whether or not government was considering an amendment, but urged the SGC to continue pressuring both government and opposition caucuses."[46] Furthermore, during the meeting Romanow indicated to the delegates that there had been hot debate in caucus over the issue, and that there was a "possibility human rights coverage for gays might exclude teachers and childcare workers."[47] SGC indicated that they would not support such a move. A week later, a flippant comment from Brian Currie, president of the Saskatoon Gay Community Centre, about the likelihood of a gay NDP cabinet minister, directed the government's focus away from human rights extensions and onto the defensive, to refute Currie's assertion. In his defense, Currie claimed that he had merely been using statistical averages when he speculated about the sexual orientation of an NDP cabinet minister. However, this incident exposed the views of politicians on both sides of the debate. Dick Collver, leader of the PC opposition, demanded that Premier Blakeney answer the charge, citing his concerns that such a minister would be prone to blackmail, and furthermore that the allegation damaged the integrity of government. Reports indicated that Blakeney responded quickly, demanding that the "contemptible" comments be made outside the Legislature where the laws of slander applied.[58] Striving for levity, Romanow, the Attorney General, reportedly quipped, "have you tested your boys?"[59] Ultimately, in statements to the press, Romanow indicated that the government balked at extending human rights coverage for two reasons, first because he did not "feel the public is ready for such legislation," was based upon the "numerous letters from persons condemning any such move" which the government received.[60] This was done in spite of strong support from Ken Norman, a former University of Saskatchewan law professor, and the Director of the Saskatchewan Human Rights Commission who indicated that "the commission favoured legislation protecting homosexuals in all walks of life, including the teaching profession."[61] Secondly, Romanow and others mused openly to reporters that they did not want to give the impression that they were protecting one of their own cabinet ministers after the media brouhaha over the Currie accusation. Responses to the failure of the sexual orientation clause in the code were mixed. Publicly, the Progressive Conservatives cheered. Leader Dick Collver boasted "that his repetition of allegations of homosexuality in the provincial cabinet early this session raised such a fervour."[62] Angered and betrayed the gay community staged a protest demonstration which drew 70 people to the steps of the Legislature.[63] NDP stalwarts were also bitter, particularly at the way the convention decision had been ignored by the party in their policy formulation.[64]

Subsequently, in a retrospective analysis of his government's deliberations, Blakeney described politics as "the art of the possible" and quite simply, the NDP gauged that the majority of Saskatchewan residents were not prepared to embrace equity rights for homosexuals.[65]

The Devine Years

Subsequent to the Human Rights Code revision in 1979, it was obvious to many gay activists that there would be little reason to continue the lobbying, because the government would not be touching the legislation for a few years. In April 1982, the NDP were decisively removed from office, when 54.1% of the province voted for the Progressive Conservatives, and Grant Devine's party won 55 out of 64 seats in the Legislature.[66] This marked a sharp right turn for the province, as the Devine government implemented its neo-liberal, free-market policies. Particularly hard hit were social services and the provincial civil service. Between 1982 and 1991, those with activist inclinations felt that they were under siege—from dramatic budget cuts, the gutting of the civil service, and the ideological perspective that denigrated big government and government "handouts."[67] With respect to human rights issues, there was little cause for optimism as the Tories made it clear that they believed "government was accountable to the majority of the people in Saskatchewan" and not to "special interests" including homosexuals.[68] This contrasts sharply with federal politics, where 1982 marked the entrenchment of the Canadian Charter of Rights and Freedoms. Although Section 15, the section of the Charter dedicated to equality rights, did not explicitly include gays and lesbians, nevertheless when it took effect in 1985 it played a critical role in stimulating and advancing gay and lesbian rights in the country.[69]

After the October 1986 election, where the NDP received a slightly higher percentage of the popular vote (45.06% to 44.8% for the Tories) and the PC majority was reduced to 38 elected members, the cleavages between the right-wing "family values" discourse and minority viewpoints would be more pronounced.[70] One of the reasons, beyond the reduced majority, was a split within the electorate between rural and urban voters. All the rural ridings remained solidly Tory whereas a number of the urban ridings returned to NDP control. This marked the beginning of a distinctive electoral divide between rural and urban voters, and it encouraged the Tories to govern with a view to the perceived values of their rural base. Others, including Peter Millard, regarded the harsher, right-wing views displayed in the PCs' second term as a specific means by which minority groups were targeted, as a way to distract people from the government's fiscal record and increasingly problematic decisions.[71] In summary, the Devine years were characterized by annually increasing provincial deficits, recession, brutal cuts to the provincial civil service and to social service agencies, and in the final term, by an astonishing degree of government-sanctioned homophobia issued, primarily, from the Premier's office, and from the office of the Social Services minister, Grant Schmidt.

The official pronouncements of Grant Schmidt, a former small town lawyer from Melville, consistently sparked controversy. Schmidt frequently, and explicitly, called homosexuality a "deviant lifestyle," one which he regarded as incompatible with various forms of employment ("employers should have the right not to hire thieves, just like they should have the right not to hire homosexuals"), or with Christian ideals.[72] For his efforts to prevent homosexuals from adopting children (because they are "unstable"), Schmidt was recognized by a right-wing Christian organization, the Committee to Protect the Family, with their 1987 Pro Family Award.[73] Similarly, at the PC convention in November, the *Star Phoenix* reported that Schmidt was complimented by the rank and file for what they called his "plain spoken views."[74] Later that year, newspaper reports of the launch of an activist group called the Coalition for Human Equality, demanded Schmidt's removal because of his "homophobic comments." Peter Millard, their initial spokesman, noted that "groups are afraid to speak out against the government for fear of having their already meek funding slashed even more."[75]

While the comments of Schmidt drew the ire of progressive activists of all types, given Premier Devine's own comments about homosexuals, there was little likelihood that Schmidt would be removed from Cabinet. In March of 1988, in response to Svend Robinson's much-publicized announcement that he was gay, Devine felt compelled to offer his thoughts on the issue and his comments made the front page of the Regina and Saskatoon newspapers. Devine stated that he, as a devout Christian, felt "you love the sinner but you hate the sin," but he also indicated that "like bank robbers," he said, "he would still feel compassion towards them and would commend them from having the courage to come forwards but would not encourage that lifestyle as fashionable because it is wrong."[76] When an NDP MLA criticized Devine's comments in the Legislature, "a few Conservative backbenchers waved limp wrists at him and asked him when he was going to make his announcement."[77] Claiming that the government wishes "to discourage [homosexuals] but we do not wish to persecute them," Schmidt further explained how he wished to assist them "'to overcome these practices which I believe are not normal and not moral' and he compared them to 'drunkards, slanderers and swindlers'," while reinforcing his belief that they "should not be exposed to children for fear of setting a bad example."[78] If all the "off the cuff" comments in the Legislature and in press scrums were not enough to demonstrate the government's homophobic views, the fact that ultra-right-wing psychologist Paul Cameron, of the Family Research Institute, was invited to meet the Tory caucus while on a speaking tour of Saskatchewan (a tour sponsored by Gay Caswell, a former PC MLA and head of a pro-life group called Victorious Women of Canada) exemplified the beliefs of key governmental members.[79] Prominent press coverage of Cameron's outrageous views of the links between homosexuality and crime (which buttressed earlier comments by Schmidt and Devine) made headlines across the province, and were featured on the evening news.

Space does not permit a full accounting of the comments by Schmidt and Devine, but suffice to say that their officially sanctioned homophobia had two primary results in Saskatchewan—either to mobilize the brave few to political action, or, much more commonly, to give credence to discriminatory actions that encouraged other, smaller acts of homophobia, and drove many gays and lesbians back into the closet, fearful at the thought of economic or personal ramifications should their orientation become known. Additionally, depending on their involvement in gay or lesbian events, they also had reason to fear being targeted by right-wing religious or political organizations. Two examples of such must suffice. For instance, in 1989 an International Women's Day Dance, scheduled to be held in St. Joseph's Parish Hall in Saskatoon, was cancelled when Bernadette Mysko, executive director for Alliance for Life (an anti-abortion group), saw the flyer, and "notified the church immediately" because "the dance is known to be for lesbians."[80] Similarly, Regina Mayor Doug Archer, and Councillor Gay Helmsing, both requested an emergency meeting to attempt to withdraw their positive votes for the declaration of a gay pride weekend in June 1989, because the negative responses from residents convinced them that the "city is just not prepared to accept something like this at this time."[81] The ways in which Devine and Schmidt invoked their status in government, and their Christian beliefs, gave the views credence. At the same time that such hateful views were openly espoused by politicians and the general public alike, the watchdog agency charged with protecting minority rights, the Saskatchewan Human Rights Commission, saw its funding cut by 25%. Similarly, the Saskatchewan Association on Human Rights, a volunteer group which had been the recipient of government funding for over 15 years, was informed in May 1987 that henceforth it would be ineligible for government grants.[82]

One could go on about the rhetoric of the Devine years, but suffice to say that the impact on Saskatchewan's gay and lesbian community was profound. Combined with unemployment, massive cuts to social service sectors (a large employer of gays and lesbians), and massive cuts to progressive organizations of many stripes, it led to a besieged view of queer life in the province. In 1993, Hellquist reported "I think quite frankly during the nine years of Devine government the community went for cover"; as a result Pride Week was not celebrated for 10 years.[83] The foundation of groups like CHE were few and far between, and even they struggled to find people confident enough to risk their livelihood or their organization's funding line. Witness and government critic, Peter Millard recalled:

> I was present at a meeting called to found a group protesting the government's human rights policies, when it was virtually impossible to find a female spokesperson. No fewer than six women who were approached refused on the grounds that they were

connected with an organization that depended on public funding. They were scared at what might happen to these funds if they took a public stand. One woman employed by a federal agency finally agreed to consult her supervisor on the matter. Without a moment's hesitation the supervisor told her that if she became identified with the protest group, funding for the agency would be seriously endangered. What was more, if she ever left her job she could give up any hope of finding another government position.[84]

Prominent government homophobia, combined with right-wing economics which severely restricted funds to human rights, social service and progressive government and non-governmental groups resulted in a decade of fear, retrenchment and backlash. That many political commentators noted the ways in which the politics of hate and intolerance were mustered to distract residents from other substantial difficulties within the Devine government makes their public ideologies more repugnant. Don McNamee, a founder and key force behind the Coalition for Human Equality, was sent this letter from an NDP MLA:

members of the government appear to have adopted gay bashing as a political strategy. I suspect that they are hoping that this will divert attention from their record in other areas, and that by inciting hatred they can divide people in this province.[85]

Importantly, although the Tories believed that the countryside was solidly behind their anti-gay statements, McNamee's correspondence indicated that CHE had a small network of rural supporters. Letters exchanged with Edmonton's Gay and Lesbian Awareness (GALA), in which strategies were shared between the groups, spoke explicitly of the requirement to undertake rural outreach in Saskatchewan. For instance, in 1991, McNamee wrote:

The attached letter to the Prince Albert group is an example of our lobbying to small centres in Saskatchewan, what with the coming election. We feel the need to do it here, because we do not have the population density ... we deal with people from Swift Current, Val Marie, Weyburn, Yorkton, etc. They all have pockets of 12, 15 sometimes even 20 or 25, and they very often seek help from us.[86]

The Final Push, 1991–93

The 1991 return of the NDP was a cause for considerable optimism. One of the reasons was that in 1990, at its annual convention, the party passed a resolution vowing that it would revise the human rights code once elected. Similarly, letters from a number of NDP MLAs in Saskatoon to CHE during the last years of the Devine government indicated their firm commitment to the inclusion of sexual orientation in those revisions, as well as their willingness to speak forcefully to the issue within caucus. Hopes for a quick revision were quickly dashed, largely due to the province's fiscal situation, but also, no doubt, to continuing concerns about the rural ridings and rural residents' responses to such a change. Extant records of the CHE, and its driving force, Don McNamee, indicated that CHE's lobbying campaign was working overtime—provincially and federally—in the late 1980s and early 1990s. He, and a small group of supporters, organized fundraising dances and socials that paid for postage and printing costs to produce a series of papers, educational campaigns, and postcard mailings to both the federal PCs and the provincial NDP. The group followed the newspapers and provincial media avidly, and frequently wrote letters to the papers, and to individual columnists to critique their positions, or to educate them to the realities of the gay existence. Initially, CHE had a Regina affiliate, but when that group decided to join the national gay political group, EGALE, the Saskatoon core ran the provincial campaigns. CHE was also in contact with other gay political groups in the region, particularly GALA in Edmonton, attempting to assist them in their demands for recognition of sexual orientation as a definable clause in the Alberta Human Rights legislation. In addition to their letter-writing campaigns, and the regular educational material sent to provincial MLAs, CHE organized "several rallies, theatre functions (such as the Devine Comedy) and meetings of concerned citizens from all walks of life and political awareness."[87]

Strategically, there were differences between the ways in which earlier attempts, via Zodiac or Saskatchewan Gay Coalition had attempted to demand gay liberation in contrast to CHE's political approach—to demand equity. While vocal and insistent that they wanted to achieve equal rights for the province's gays and lesbians, they always sought to offer responses that stressed the inequities between heterosexuals and homosexuals in terms of employment, medical, and governmental rights, while downplaying sexuality. For instance in 1990, McNamee wrote:

> You are correct in stating that the fight is on the basis of Human rights. Yes, the heteros can walk hand in hand, and they talk openly about their CHOSEN partner, they can rent or buy housing freely (within their budget) without fear or bigotry. They can share spousal benefits given in employment contracts, they can obtain government benefits for the aged, etc. Members of the lesbian and gay community cannot. We cannot get the same tax breaks, dental programmes, health care benefits, housing or employment opportunities. The fight is NOT ABOUT SEX—IT IS ABOUT HUMAN PRIDE!!![88]

This more middle-class, rights-based vision was not the same as the earlier liberationist views, but it is debatable whether this was calculated strategy or represented true political beliefs. A handful of CHE letters and papers hint at tensions in the community between those who supported the earlier, broader, liberationist goals and those narrower ones. They also indicate that regardless of the message, the CHE group was determined to maintain a very respectable tone and appearance when in contact with politicians and media, again believing that this approach would pay dividends. For instance, in 1991, McNamee wrote "we hope that Gay Pride does NOT GO COUNTER PRODUCTIVE—they want to be abrasive—on election day or before."[89]

Outwardly supportive of plans to amend the code to include protection for homosexuals in the areas of employment and accommodations, the letters McNamee received from NDP MLAs hint that there were debates and tension behind the scenes as the party grappled, once again, with the "politics of the possible." With Devine retired, and most of his crew gone (11 of whom would ultimately be tried or convicted of fraud), the Tory party's defenders of the anti-gay rhetoric were weakened.[90] Seemingly overnight, a new, religiously based organization, Coalition in Support of the Family, led by Dale Hasnett, "a father of three," and "teacher in a small, church-run school in Leader" stepped into the breach.[91] Hasnett vowed to get enough signatures on a petition to challenge the NDP government's plans to include protection for homosexuals. Citing primarily biblical and medical literature (particularly gruesomely distorted notions of gay sexual behaviour, resultant illness, and the spectre of AIDS), Hasnett's ads, press conferences, and publications sparked the flame of homophobia, primarily in the rural areas where the Coalition targeted its promotions. While Coalition on the Family was the chief ringleader, it was supported in its efforts by other anti-abortion organizations, and by individuals such as the Reverend Dick Hetherington, a retired United Church minister, who bought paid advertising space in local papers to publish his view of the "sodomites." Sometimes, utilizing the ethos of "free speech," members of the media applauded the "courage" of people like Hetherington while disingenuously offering "equal time" for gays and lesbians to state their perspective.[92] Given the widespread coverage of this material, and the often earnest interviews and articles devoted to profiling leaders of the "family values" crusade, it gave Hasnett, Hetherington, and others free publicity and legitimacy. And, in striking parallels with the pro-choice versus anti-abortion debates and discourse, the "family values" adherents shrewdly positioned themselves so that they took the moral high ground, while forcing gays and lesbians onto the defensive to respond to their "claims."

However, by 1992 and 1993 a number of factors coalesced to give public support to the coalition of groups advocating gay and lesbian rights. First, Carole Greschner, the Chief Commissioner of the Saskatchewan Human Rights Commission, published her "personal viewpoint" in a number of urban and rural papers. This short essay, quickly dealt with the erroneous beliefs that the government planned to give "special rights" to gays and lesbians, and bluntly informed readers that

> for many years the Saskatchewan Human Rights Commission has called upon government to amend the Saskatchewan Human Rights Code to prohibit discrimination against lesbians and gays in housing, employment, services and other areas. Lesbians and gays have endured prejudice, hatred and exclusion for too long. Six provinces and one territory already include lesbians and gays within their human rights legislation.[93]

She quickly explained that Saskatchewan was following the lead of other provinces, and essentially bringing its Code into alignment with developments elsewhere. Importantly, Greschner drew parallels between protections already accorded religious diversity and those proposed for homosexuals, shrewdly deflecting the argument that the government was enshrining rights for a group who had made "lifestyle choices" as opposed to the many innate characteristics (race, gender) already covered by the code. Equally important were Gallup polls that indicated majority support for such initiatives. One influential poll, given the timing, was the Angus Reid-Southam News poll released in February 1993, which recorded that 52% of Albertans and 55% of Saskatchewan and Manitoba residents "believed that gays and lesbians should be protected from discrimination."[94] Residents of Quebec, the province with the longest recognition for such human rights protection, had the highest support level at 75%.[95]

While "family values" opponents made much of their religious faith, those supporters of human rights for gays and lesbians seldom evoked religious concepts. That changed in 1993, with two key interventions by the United Church and the Catholic Church. The United Church had been a consistent supporter of the demands for human rights protection for homosexuals for many years, but in 1993 it took the unusual step of placing prominent ads in the Regina and Saskatoon papers which read, in part:

The United Church Saskatchewan Conference supports Bill 38. God calls us to stand in solidarity with gay and lesbian people—the especially oppressed and marginalized of today—The time for justice is always now![96]

Placed to encourage the NDP government to pass the bill in the current session, and not delay further, this was an important gesture. Of course, the United Church had been through its own internal debates and decisions about, first, gay and lesbian members, and then, more divisively, gay and lesbian clergy, and was on record with a strong, progressive stand in favour of inclusion. Far more surprising, and virtually unheard of elsewhere, was the implicit support given by the Roman Catholic Dioceses of Saskatchewan. It made the front-page headline of the *Star Phoenix* when it was announced, in late March, that a letter would be read from the Saskatchewan Roman Catholic Bishops to parishioners at the next Sunday mass. In the letter the bishops claimed that they wanted to "contribute to this debate [on human rights] by restating some of the traditional teachings of the Catholic Church," including the view that any sexual activity outside of marriage was immoral. Nor did they veer from the Church's policy that homosexual activity was immoral, and contrary to the teachings of the Church. However, explicitly, they wrote:

> *The Roman Catholic Church teaches that all human beings should be treated equally... A new Universal Catholic Catechism states: "A significant number of men and women exhibit basic homosexual tendencies. They do not choose their homosexual condition, which is a trial for most of them. They must be accepted with respect, compassion and sensitivity. Every mark of unjust discrimination toward them is to be avoided."[97]*

While not straying from Catholic teaching on homosexuality, nevertheless in the context of the public debates surrounding Bill 38, this letter was widely interpreted as supportive of the NDP government's initiative.

All of these groups and individual statements of support, gave the NDP the moral fibre and public opinion required to introduce Bill 38 in March 1993. Justice Minister Bob Mitchell indicated that "we've had long discussion of it, going back two years, and during that time caucus has united behind the bill to a very large degree."[98] Despite the precedents elsewhere, Saskatchewan's first foray into human rights extensions for lesbians and gays was limited to forbidding discriminatory employment practices or access to housing/rental accommodations. Throughout the course of the multiple readings of the legislation, it was made clear that there would be exceptions for people renting suites in their homes, and there were ongoing discussions about whether or not professions dealing with children (teaching, childcare, etc.) should be excluded from the coverage. Ultimately, provisions to exempt school boards or daycares from the legislation were not included, but in one of the many public news conferences called by Mitchell to reassure those members of the public fearful of "special rights" or "homosexual curriculum," it was made perfectly clear that the government was not supportive of changes to adoption laws, definitions of spouses or common-law partners, pensions, or the ultimate issue, a redefinition of marriage. While it would not say so explicitly, the government's approach to the legislation was to keep it as narrowly defined as possible, so as to prevent further public backlash. Similarly, it consistently reinforced the fact that changes in the rest of Canada had been the precipitating factors for the Saskatchewan government's action. The "victory" on June 22, 1993, of the passage of the Bill 38 with a 31–10 vote (NDP members and the lone Liberal, leader Lynda Haverstock voted in favour with Tories opposed), could not be construed as a resounding demonstration of equity. This assessment was captured in an important column by Randy Burton, the *Star Phoenix*'s political columnist, who wrote:

> *Bit by painful bit, Saskatchewan is dragging itself into the modern world... . In actual fact, this amendment is going to do very little except provide legal recourse to victims of blatant discrimination... . But what the human rights amendment will do is force people to think about the issue. If it's no longer acceptable to discriminate in employment and housing, maybe it's unacceptable everywhere else, too. It will also send the message that the world really is changing, even on the island of Saskatchewan.*[99]

Asked for his contemporary assessment of the Saskatchewan campaign, Gens Hellquist bluntly offered his opinion that given politicians' fear of making tough decisions, the human rights achievement was only possible once other successful court cases (both federally and in other provinces, notably Ontario) set the standard which, ultimately, even Saskatchewan had to follow.[100]

Conclusion

In the over 20 years that Saskatchewan residents were exposed to public discourses and educational campaigns about the homosexual population of the province, it was clear that a number of factors were in play. First, initially, gay and lesbian activists sought to "come out" to the media, to dispel the ignorance and invisibility of gay lives in the province's larger cities, particularly Saskatoon. In a series of advertisements, and later newspaper accounts of the opening of the Gay Community Centre, or of the Doug Wilson case, it became clear that homosexuality was not just a foreign phenomenon, not just something that happened in Vancouver or Toronto. It was part of the fabric of the province of Saskatchewan, a fact that would eventually lead to public support for human rights protection for gays and lesbians.

One of the key catalysts for the campaign for human rights extension was the Doug Wilson case. Wilson's mistreatment at the hands of the administration, and the obvious connection between his dismissal from supervising student teachers and his formation of a gay campus organization, politicized people about the discrimination and homophobia gays and lesbians routinely encountered. Shrewdly, the Committee to Defend Doug Wilson realized that in a community and province of this size, a coalition of activists—gay and straight, feminist, working-class, and labour groups— was necessary to create a critical mass of supporters. That grassroots coalition strategy, one common to the province in which cooperative movements and community building are well known laid important groundwork for future advocacy. Equally important, the case launched Wilson's gay activist career, a career that resulted in the creation of a number of innovative groups in the province before eventually taking him to Toronto, where he ran as the first openly gay federal election candidate in 1988. The diagnosis of AIDS forced him to withdraw part way through the campaign. He died in 1992. Wilson's determination to reach out to small town and rural gays and lesbians was a slow process, but it produced a vocal minority who were prepared to support, even in very minor ways through fundraising or letter writing, initiatives like SGC's demands for human rights coverage, or CHE's demands for coverage in 1992–93.

Equally interesting, an examination of the stages by which gays and lesbians in Saskatchewan achieved their first human rights coverage demonstrates that discourse of Bible belt fundamentalism, so strongly identified with Alberta, was also a compelling force in Saskatchewan. The province was home to a number of fundamentalist groups, and had a number of prominent Christians holding office, including Premier Devine, and Social Services minister Grant Schmidt. Their statements, and the legitimacy provided by prominent print and television coverage, gave these viewpoints—that gays and lesbians were criminal, diseased, and, immoral—considerable credence. Where elsewhere I have argued that the city of Saskatoon has been a relatively moderate, accepting place for gays and lesbians, that was not the case for the province as a whole. Gay and lesbian life in rural areas, small towns, or reserves was often impossibly tough and it is from those locales that most queers migrated into the larger provincial centres, particularly Saskatoon which had a reputation as gay and lesbian friendly.[101] Regina also had a sizeable gay and lesbian community but they remained far more cautious than Saskatoon, and seldom mustered more than social organizations, while Saskatoon had a wide range of activity.[102]

Finally, the fight for human rights extension involved countless volunteers, donors, and community members who participated in fundraising events and socials, who took the time to write letters, to speak out in public, to talk with their politicians. But, given the community's small size, and the stress and strain that open gay activism caused, this was not a role everyone felt comfortable assuming. It is not surprising that those who played key roles—Peter Millard and Neil Richards—had secure jobs on campus; and that Don McNamee became such a vocal spokesman only after retirement. The two key leaders of the gay and lesbian community, Gens Hellquist and Doug Wilson, were both exceptions, fiercely determined men whose desire for justice meant sacrificing the comfortable life of secure professional employment. What is striking is the role played by educators—and that, no doubt, sculpted Saskatchewan activism into a sustained public education campaign. If not educators, all of the individuals involved came from families with strong educational emphases or ironically, from strongly religious families where service and church participation stressed leadership. As native sons and daughters, they were cognizant of the way that successful Saskatchewan activists worked—via coalitions (because of the small population base); the value placed on cooperation and community; of the need to undertake outreach with the rural areas; of the importance of perseverance and tenacity in the face of an unrelenting climate; and of a tendency of the province's residents to identify with the underdog (another factor that made Wilson's case so compelling). They couched their educational campaigns in ways with which the general public could identify, and tended to eschew radicalism. It would be incorrect to impute that this represented the true political perspective of these activists and supporters; instead, it was strategic. Ultimately, an examination of Saskatchewan's gay activists' 20-plus year struggle to achieve equity demonstrates the importance of regional perspectives in our understanding of queer activism and history.

Notes

This paper is part of a larger, SSHRC-funded study entitled *Prairie Fairies: Gay and Lesbian Community Formation, 1945–1980*. I have benefited from discussions with colleagues in the Department of History, University of Saskatchewan, as well as the generosity of my oral informants. In particular, I wish to thank Gens Hellquist, Neil Richards, Richard Nordahl and Tom Warner for their perceptive comments.

1. Three of the most recent works in this area are: Tom Warner, *Never Going Back: A History of Queer Activism in Canada* (Toronto: University of Toronto Press, 2002); Miriam Smith, *Lesbian and Gay Rights in Canada: Social Movements and Equality Seeking, 1971–1995* (Toronto: University of Toronto Press, 1999); David Rayside, *On the Fringe: Gays and Lesbians in Politics* (Cornell University Press, 1998). Warner's important new book provides a summary of national developments, including some discussion of Wilson's case and impact, but given the space constraints imposed by a national focus prevents sustained commentary. The field of Canadian history of sexuality and activism continues to expand, but with the exception of Karen Dubinsky's *Improper Advances: Rape and Heterosexual Conflict in Ontario, 1880–1929* (Chicago: University of Chicago Press, 1993), most studies concentrate primarily on southern Ontario, Toronto, Vancouver and Montreal; for instance, see Gary Kinsman, *The Regulation of Desire: Homo and Hetero Sexualities* (Montreal: Black Rose Books, 1996); Becki Ross, *The House That Jill Built: A Lesbian Nation in Formation* (Toronto: University of Toronto Press, 1995); Mary Louise Adams, *The Trouble with Normal: Postwar Youth and the Making of Heterosexuality* (Toronto: University of Toronto Press, 1997); Karen Dubinsky, *The Second Greatest Disappointment: Honeymooning and Tourism at Niagara Falls* (Toronto, 1999); Steven Maynard, "'Horrible Temptations': Sex, Men, and Working Class Male Youth in Urban Ontario, 1890–1935," *Canadian Historical Review* 78 (June 1997): 191–235; Ross Higgins, "A Sense of Belonging: Pre-liberation Space, Symbolics and Leadership in Gay Montreal" (PhD dissertation, McGill University, 1997); Marney McDiarmid, "From Mouth to Mouth: An Oral History of Lesbians and Gays in Kingston from World War II to 1980" (MA thesis, Queen's University, 1999); Dawn Elizabeth Johnston, "Sites of Resistance, Sites of Strength: The Construction and Experience of Queer Space in Calgary" (MA thesis, University of Calgary, 1999); and Noelle Lucas, "Womanspace: Building a Lesbian Community in Edmonton Alberta, 1970–1990" (MA thesis, University of Saskatchewan, 2002). For studies particularly devoted to the west, or to rural Canada, please see: Terry Chapman, "'An Oscar Wilde Type': The Abominable Crime of Buggery in Western Canada, 1890–1920" *Criminal Justice History* 4 (1983): 97–118; Terry Chapman, "Sex Crimes in Western Canada, 1890–1920" (Ph.D Dissertation, University of Alberta, 1984); Terry Chapman, "Male Homosexuality: Legal Restraints and Social Attitudes in Western Canada, 1890–1920" in Louis A. Knafla (ed.), *Law and Justice in a New Land: Essays in Western Canadian Legal History* (Toronto: Carswell, 1986), 267–92; Lyle Dick, "Heterohegemonic Discourse and Homosexual Acts: The Case of Saskatchewan in the Settlement Era." Paper presented at the Sex and State History Conference, Toronto, July 1985. For a contemporary account of gay rural life, see Michael Riordan's *Out Our Way: Gay and Lesbian Life in the Country* (Toronto: Between the Lines, 1996).

2. I am indebted to Neil Richards for collecting gay organizational, media, literary, and cultural materials for over 30 years, and his generous decision to donate this material to the Saskatchewan Archives Board, Saskatoon office. The Neil Richards Collection is an extremely rich, well-organized archive of Saskatchewan, prairie, and less frequently North American gay and lesbian materials from the late 1960s through to the present. I wish to thank Neil for allowing unrestricted access to these materials. Additionally, I was fortunate to be given access to the GALA records at the City of Edmonton Archives, and to the smaller number of fonds held at the University of Saskatchewan Archives, the Glenbow Archives, the Women's Movement Archives in Ottawa, and the Red Deer Museum's collection of contemporary gay and lesbian oral histories.

3. Peter Millard, "Or Words to that Effect" (unpublished memoir), 212. My thanks to executor Norm Zepp and the P. Millard Estate for granting access to this autobiography.

4. Gens Hellquist, Saskatoon, interview with author, December 17, 2002.

5. Tom Warner, Toronto, interview with author, March 8, 2003.

6. Saskatchewan Archives Board (SAB) Neil Richards Papers (NR) S-A821 IV.19 Correspondence, 1971–1982, File 2/8, Letter from Doug (Gens) Hellquist, Secretary, Zodiac Friendship Society in response to a request for information from "A sociology student," Winnipeg, MB, February 19, 1974. By the terms of my agreement with the SAB, I was granted full access to all the restricted documents in the Neil Richards collection with the understanding that I would not identify by name any individuals who had not openly disclosed their affiliation with the gay organizations and/or orientation (i.e. were identified in printed, public, materials).

7. Hellquist interview.

8. Both Hellquist and Warner mentioned the so-called "Stafford" family in their interviews. This became a source of friction after the establishment of the Gemini Club, as participants, including Hellquist and Peter Millard, would write in the Zodiac Newsletter about their determination to relegate the female names, "family" structure, and no doubt, control of the elders, to history and adopt more positive, gay male identities that did not rely on sex-role stereotyping. SAB NR II.213 Zodiac Friendship Society, 1971–1973; Doug Hellquist, "Commentary," *Club Gemini News* 1, no. 5 (May 1972): 2: "It is time that gay people stopped playing roles and started acting like responsible adults then maybe the rest of society would find it easier to accept us as equals and gay people wanting to come out would not be so turned off by the gay scene."

9. SAB NR A821 IV.20 Correspondence, 1971–1982 (File 1 of 2), Letter from "Gary" to Saskatoon Gay Lib, dated July 8, 1971.

10. Ibid., Letter from "Debbie" to Zodiac, dated November 1972.

11. SAB A821 IV.19 Correspondence, 1971–1982, File 2 of 8, Letter from Hellquist to "A sociology student," Winnipeg, MB, February 19, 1974.

12. University of Saskatchewan Archives (USA), Don McNamee Fonds, MG 141 B.I.22 Personal: "Don McNamee Dies" *Perceptions* 12, no. 5 (July 27, 1994): 12.

13. SAB NR A821 IV.19 Correspondence, 1971–1982, File 1 of 8; ZFS Press Release, October 19, 1972.

14. Ibid.

15. Ibid., 1971–1982, File 2 of 8 "Zodiac Friendship Society Form Letter," dated February 24, 1973.

16. Ibid., File 1 of 8, Letter from GATE Regina to Gay Community Centre, Saskatoon, dated February 7, 1972.

17. At the time of writing this paper, oral interviews are still ongoing, and so these conclusions about Regina's community are preliminary.

18. SAB NR A 595 II.213 Zodiac Friendship Society, 1971–1973; Doug Hellquist, "Editorial," *Zodiac Friendship Society News* 2, no. 1 (January 1973): 1.

19. Saskatoon Won't be Gay," *Star Phoenix*, August 14, 1973, p. 4.

20. Ibid.

21. SAB NR A 595 II.213 Zodiac Friendship Society, 1971–1973, "News," *Zodiac Friendship Society News* 2, no. 3 (March 1973): 3.

22. Ibid., "SGA News," *Zodiac Friendship Club News* 2, no. 9 (September 1973): 1.

23. "Rights Commission Decides Priorities," *Star Phoenix*, August 25, 1973.

24. SAB NR A 595 II.213 Zodiac Friendship Society, "News," *Zodiac Friendship Society News* 2, no. 3 (March 1973): 3.

25. Vern Greenshields, "Gay Community Protests Ad Decision," *Star Phoenix*, June 1975.

26. SAB NR A 821 IV.29 General Meeting Minutes, Doug Hellquist, "President's Report," 1974.

27. SAB NR A 821 IV.40 Newspaper Clippings, Ed Jackson, "Saskatoon Gay Action: Progress in a Prairie City," *The Body Politic* (1973): 23.

28. For a more extensive analysis of the Doug Wilson case, please see: V.J. Korinek, "The Most Openly Gay Person for at Least a Thousand Miles: Doug Wilson and the Politicization of a Province, 1975–1983," *Canadian Historical Review* (December 2003).

29. University of Saskatchewan, *The Sheaf* 66, no. 18 (September, 19, 1975): 2.

30. I thank my colleagues, Jim Miller and Mike Hayden, for this insight into University of Saskatchewan history, and Kirkpatrick's mindset.

31. Don Thompson, "College Dean Discriminates," *The Sheaf*, no. 66, 21 (September 30, 1975): 1.

32. Jim Duggleby, "Begg Supports Decision to Limit Homosexual Teacher," *Star Phoenix*, October 1, 1975, p. 3; J. Varga, "Begg Outlines Administration Stand," *The Sheaf* (October 3, 1975): 2.

33. While a number of people came and went from the committee throughout the term, these individuals represented the core group. Fittingly, their work was recognized in 2003 when they were awarded the University of Saskatchewan Student Union Award, the Doug Wilson Award, which recognizes gay and lesbian leadership on campus. For more details see "Doug Wilson Award," *Perceptions* 21, no. 3 (April 16, 2003): 19.

34. An interview with Richard Nordahl, a retired professor of political studies at the University of Saskatchewan, indicated what a tense time it was for faculty, particularly gay faculty. Richard Nordahl interview with author, Toronto, January 2003.

35. SAB Doug Wilson Papers (DW), A 810 File 2 The Committee to Defend Doug Wilson; "Announcement of Convocation Rally, October 25, 1975"; undated.

36. SAB NR Collection, A 821 IV.20 Correspondence, 1971–1982, File 2 of 2, "Letter from 'Retired teacher,' Nipawin, SK to Doug Wilson, undated but presumably from 1975–76."

37. Ibid., "Letter from 'Farmer,' Wartime, SK to Doug (Gens) Hellquist, dated September 8, 1976."

38. Warner, interview with author, March 8, 2003.

39. In my interview with G. Hellquist, he indicated that Wilson's decision to abandon his graduate degree and teaching career was a point of tension between them, and with other committee members. Speaking for himself, Hellquist believed that after all of the hard work the Committee to Defend Doug Wilson had performed, that Wilson should have stayed the course and worked to advance the rights of gay teachers. Interestingly, an annual College of Education Conference, entitled "Breaking the Silence," which aims to publicize the challenges faced by gay and lesbian students, teachers, and parents in and with the province's school districts, has not yet had an openly gay teacher appear to address the assembly.

40. "Protection for Gay People," *The Sheaf* (November 15, 1976): 8.

41. "Gays Stage Protest," *Leader Post*, March 14, 1977, p. 4.

42. "Human Rights Group to Push Gay Cause," *Body Politic* 42 (April 1978): 6.

43. "New Groups Formed: Saskatchewan Gay Coalition," *Body Politic* (February 1978): 13.

44. Ibid.

45. Robin Hardy, "Prairie Festival Soars to Success," *Body Politic* (November 1978): 9.

46. Eva Schacherl, "Parade Featured at Four-day Gay Convention," *Star Phoenix*, October 10, 1978, p. 4.

47. Ibid.

48. "Big Holes Seen in Charter of Human Rights," *Leader Post*, September 8, 1978, p. 5.

49. "Sexual Orientation Law Topic of Debate," *Leader Post*, November 20, 1978, p. 3.

50. Marsha Erb, "NDP Supports Homosexual Rights," *Star Phoenix*, November 20, 1978, p. 27.

51. "NDP Votes to Change Code, Protection for Gays on the Way," *Body Politic* (December 1978): 10.

52. Ibid.

53. Marsha Erb, "Blakeny Stresses Federal Involvement," *Star Phoenix*, November 20, 1978, p. 3.

54. Letter from the Rev. Henry Friesen, Chairman, Renaissance Saskatchewan, Moose Jaw to Editor," *Swift Current Sun*, December 7, 1978, p. 4.

55. John Cooper and Maureen Semchuk, "Protection for Homosexuals Urged in Human Rights Legislation," *The Carillon* 20, no. 15 (February 1, 1979): 3.

56. "Attorney General Urges Group to Continue Pressure" *Body Politic* 51 (March/April 1979): 13.

57. Ibid.

58. "Premier Attacks Collver Rumor of Gay Minister," *Globe and Mail*, March 1, 1979, p. 9.

59. Rudy Lukko, "Gay Spokesman Just Assumes One Minister is Homosexual," *Leader Post*, February 28, 1979, p. 14.

60. Larry Johnsrude, "Gays Claimed not Protected," *Star Phoenix*, April 23, 1979, p. 6.

61. Ibid.

62. "Homosexuals not Included in Addition to Rights Code," *Leader Post*, April 21, 1979, p. 8.

63. "NDP Backs Down: No Rights in Saskatchewan," *Body Politic* (June 1979): 16.

64. Don McRae and Hilary Jones, "Sexual Orientation Exclusion Ignores Convention Direction," *The Commonwealth*, May 2, 1979, p. 13.

65. Allan E. Blakeney, "Premiers and Cabinets in Saskatchewan: One Premier's View," in Howard A. Leeson (ed.), *Saskatchewan Politics: Into the 21st Century* (Regina: Canadian Plains Research Center, 2001), 93.

66. Jocelyne Praud and Sarah McQuarrie, "The Saskatchewan CCF-NDP from the Regina Manifesto to the Romanow Years," in Leeson, *Saskatchewan Politics*, 153.

67. Space does not permit a detailed discussion of the now infamous Devine government's corruption or corrosive effect on the province's debt level, civil service, or community services. Those interested would do well to consult, Janice MacKinnon, *Minding the Public Purse* (Kingston: McGill-Queen's, 2003), Lesley Biggs and Mark Stobbe (eds.), *Devine Rule in Saskatchewan: A Decade of Hope and Hardship* (Saskatoon: Fifth House, 1991), and Lorne A. Brown, Joseph K. Roberts and John W. Warnock, *Saskatchewan Politics from Left to Right '44 to '99* (Regina: Hinterland Publications, 1999).

68. Murray Mandryk, "Human Rights Group not Optimistic About Winning Tory Cabinet Support," *Leader Post*, November 19, 1985, p. A4.

69. For more information about the role of the Charter in gay and lesbian rights, see Miriam Smith, *Lesbian and Gay Rights in Canada: Social Movements and Equality Seeking, 1971–1995* (Toronto: University of Toronto Press, 1999).

70. Brown, et al., *Saskatchewan Politics from Left to Right*, 39.

71. Peter Millard, "Human Rights and the PC Government," in Biggs and Stobbe, *Devine Rule in Saskatchewan*, 33–48.

72. Earl Fowler, "Employers Entitled to Reject Gays, Schmidt Claims," *Star Phoenix*, October 31, 1987, A1.

73. "Homosexuals in Saskatchewan Can't Adopt Children Says Schmidt," *Prince Albert Daily Herald*, October 30, 1987, p. 13.

74. "Schmidt Big Hit With PCs," *Star Phoenix*, November 16, 1987, p. A10.

75. Heather MacDonald, "Schmidt's Critics Fear Retribution," *Star Phoenix*, November 3, 1987, n.p.; Richard Sandhurst, "Group Calls for Schmidt's Ouster," *The Sheaf*, November 5 1987, p, 1.

76. Vern Greenshields, "Devine Critical of Robinson's Homosexual Lifestyle," *Star Phoenix*, March 2, 1988, p. A1.

77. "Gays, Crime Comparison 'Despicable'," *Star Phoenix*, March 25, 1988, p. A6.

78. Randy Burton, "NDP is Trying to Take Over United Church: Schmidt," *Star Phoenix*, April 7, 1988, p. A3.

79. Millard, "Human Rights and the P.C. Government," 39–40.

80. Jim Burgoyne, "Coalition Denies Lesbianism Reason Dance Cancelled," *Star Phoenix*, March 4, 1989, p. A3.

81. For a sense of this event, see Therese Macdonald, "Council Backs Lesbian/Gay Proclamation," *Leader Post*, June 20, 1989, p. A3; "Regina Fights Over Gay Proclamation," *Prince Albert Daily Herald*, June 24, 1989, p. 2; Therese Macdonald, "Gay Proclamation Survives," *Leader Post*, June 24, 1989, p. A1.

82. Millard, "Human Rights and the P.C. Government," 41.

83. Jo Lynn Sheane, "Gay Pride Week First in Decade," *Star Phoenix*, June 23, 1993, p. A6.

84. Millard, "Human Rights and the P.C. Government," 45–46.

85. USA, MG 141 Don McNamee Fonds, B. Coalition for Human Equality I. Correspondence and Administration, File 5 Correspondence 1989–1993, 6 folders (1/6), "Letter from NDP MLA to Don McNamee," dated April 14, 1988.

86. Ibid., B.I. 4/6, "Letter from Don McNamee to Maureen Irwin, GALA, Edmonton," dated April 5, 1991.

87. Ibid., B.I.5 1/6, "Letter from Don McNamee to Elaine McCoy, Minister of Labour, Alberta," dated May 25, 1989.

88. Ibid., B.I.5 3/6, "Letter from Don McNamee to Dale Eisler, *Star Phoenix*," July 16, 1990.

89. Ibid., B.I.5 4/6, "Letter from Don McNamee to Maureen Irwin, GALA, Edmonton," April 5, 1991.

90. Kevin Wishlow, "Rethinking the Polarization Thesis: The Formation and Growth of the Saskatchewan Party, 1997–2001," in Leeson, *Saskatchewan Politics*, 172.

91. Don Current, "Grassroots Coalition is Determined," *Leader Post*, May 22, 1993, p. A8.

92. For an example of such an essay, see Warren Goulding, "Gay Community Lacks Hetherington's Courage," *Friday Edition*, December 17, 1993, p. 2.

93. Donna Greschner, "Amendments Important Step Towards Equality," *Melfort Journal*, February 16, 1993, p. 5.

94. Stephen Bindman, "Most Back Gay, Lesbian Rights," *Calgary Herald*, February 6, 1993, p. A1.

95. Ibid.

96. United Church Saskatchewan Conference advertisement, *Leader Post*, June 12, 1993, p. A11.

97. "Dear Catholic People of Saskatchewan," *Prairie Messenger* 70, no. 36 (April 5, 1993): 3.

98. Mark Wyatt, "Rights Code Changes Protect Homosexuals," *Leader Post*, March 18, 1993, p. A5.

99. Randy Burton, "Saskatchewan Plays Catch Up in Protecting Gays," *Star Phoenix*, May 6, 1993, p. A4.

100. Gens Hellquist, interview with author, Saskatoon, May 1, 2003.

101. Sporadically, there were print media articles about what it was like to be gay or lesbian in small-town Saskatchewan, or what it was like to an Aboriginal gay or, worse, to be an Aboriginal PWA. The conclusions were grim. For examples of this genre, see: Ted Wyman, "It's Tough to be Gay in Moose Jaw," *Moose Jaw Times Herald*, June 11, 1993, p. 3; Nicole Adams, "Daring to Deal With AIDs: Reality Comes Home to the Reserve," *Prince Albert Daily Herald*, October 4, 1993, p. 9.

102. This perplexing question defies simple answers, although many have speculated it is the large civil service presence in Regina. I hope that interviews in Regina will yield more comprehensive information on the differences between the two cities.

10

Queer Youth and Strange Representations in the Province of the "Severely Normal":
ALBERTA IN THE 1990S[1]

Gloria Filax

> *When I think of gays I don't think of sex. I think of people like W.H. Auden,*
> *Tchaikovsky, James Dean, Shakespeare, Virginia Woolf. I think of intelligence and*
> *accomplishment. Why do others insist on thinking of sex when they think about*
> *us? Do they want sex with us? Is that their problem?* (Oscar, 1998)

THE 1990S IN THE PROVINCE OF ALBERTA WERE MARKED BY ACTIVE, provincial government contestation of the legal rights of queer[2] citizens, juxtaposed with expanding lesbian and gay rights at the level of the federal government. The adoption of the Charter of Rights and Freedoms in 1982 made Canada into a more hybrid legal culture with an American-type constitutionally entrenched bill of rights (Stychin, 1995). Provincial human rights codes were to be realigned with the new federal charter, but a grey area relating to protections for sexual minority Canadians allowed for exclusion within both federal and provincial codes. A series of court challenges taken to the Supreme Court of Canada resulted in outcomes, which read inclusion of protections for gays and lesbians into the existing Charter (Yogis et al., 1996).

In Alberta, the struggle over human rights protections for lesbians and gays is one of a series of struggles produced by the contradictions between interdependence and autonomy of the regional-provincial government in relation to Canadian federalism.[3] This struggle is, as well, a struggle over what constitutes a proper, normal Alberta identity and who rightfully belongs within the Alberta community/mosaic. The province of Alberta remains unique in the Canadian mosaic of ten provinces and three territories for its continued refusal to realign its human rights code or to extend human rights protections by reading homosexuality as a protected category into the provincial human rights code.[4] Alberta Premier Ralph Klein has referred to Alberta as the province of the "severely normal."[5] As will become clear, severely normal Albertans are those Albertans who count as good, natural, and valued citizens; they are rugged individuals who are right-wing Christians; they are white, heterosexual, adult, in a stringent gender hierarchy, which produces all women as less worthy. This severely normal hierarchy produces a potent brew of sexism, misogyny, able-bodiedness, ethnocentrism, and racism, all of which saturate the homophobic and heterosexist context of Alberta as well.

It is in the context of "the severely normal" Albertan that the *Alberta Report* (hereafter *AR*), a weekly magazine with wide distribution in the province in the 1990s,[6] was able to constitute and maintain the challenge to sexual minority rights in the 1990s. The *AR* was widely distributed to libraries, schools, banks, profession-al offices, often free of charge. It contained on a weekly basis[7] sensational accounts of "homosexuals" and "homosexuality" that influenced and informed thinking, dis-cussions, and government actions and policy in relation to queer Albertans. Ironically, the *AR* contained the most complete and comprehensive coverage of sexual minori-ty issues in the province. Unlike the silence and indifference of mainstream media, the *AR* took seriously the existence of sexual minority peoples. Paying attention to this magazine provides a unique understanding of both mainstream and queer Alberta culture and politics during this time. It also provides a context for the lives of queer youth. While curriculum, pedagogy, policy, and practice related to issues for queer and questioning youth were mostly absent in Alberta schools, the *AR*, with its regular accounting of "homosexuality," was available in schools and often used as a teaching tool. Paying attention to this magazine is central to investigations of the lives of queer and questioning youth in Alberta schools.

The *AR* is remarkably the most complete and comprehensive public coverage of queer issues in Alberta during the 1990s. However, as reflected in the comments from queer youth that introduce and conclude this paper, queer youth in Alberta were not consumed by the moral panic about homosexuality fostered and generated by the *AR* in the context of the Alberta government's contestation of human rights protections for lesbians and gays.

The *Alberta Report*: Marshalling the Struggle

To celebrate the first 25 years of publication, the editors-operators of the *AR* pro-duced a special edition on January 11, 1999, summarizing the past quarter-century. The following quote tells part of this story:

> *We learned one other lesson in the latter 1980s, as we started branching out with other editions, first* Western *and then* B.C. Report. *Instead of reverting to clear con-servatism on the social issues of the day, we began to drift, subtly, into what could be called "lifestyle" coverage. That is, we gradually lost our interest in the deeper and more difficult questions posed by* sex, family, school, and faith. *There was a rea-son for this drift.* Back in the 1970s, weirdo things like radical feminism and gay rights could be dismissed, at least in Alberta, as an amusing madness. *But by the late-1980s they couldn't. They had become rooted in public policy everywhere, underlying social programs, court rulings, and school curriculum ... well, values-neutral is not just gutless, it is dull,* and circulation was slipping anyway. (Byfield, *AR*, January 11, 1999, p. 19, author's emphasis)

Keeping their eye on a formula for fiscal success, those in charge of the *AR* deter-mined that their 1980s approach did not sell magazines and that the 1990s would reverse this trend. The following is a summary of the issues *AR* took on in the 1990s:

In 1990 we got back on course. We challenged the feminist sacred cow on campus ("Women's Studies–academics or propaganda?," January 7, 1991), nut-case environmentalism ("Father Earth," May 11, 1992), the global thrust for what are deceptively promoted as "children's rights" (The Pied Piper of Ottawa," August 8, 1994), poisonous but powerful liberal currents in the churches ("See No Evil," July 8, 1996), and Ottawa's continuing abdication of responsibility for Indian justice ("Canada's Mythical Holocaust," January 26, 1998). We once again adopted causes: gun owners' rights, removal of abortion from medicare, direct democracy and taxpayer activism. We attacked as provocatively as we could the fatuous and sinister new acceptance of the gay lifestyle; it reached its apogee with our Aug. 16, 1993, cover "Can Gays be Cured?" ... *but the theme which re-emerged in our pages in the '90s which dwarfs all others in significance is that of the family.* (Byfield, *AR*, January 11, 1999, p. 19, author's emphasis)

Issues such as feminism, environmentalism, Aboriginal rights, along with homosexuality are interrelated because, according to the *AR*, they are threats to their concept of the family. According to the *AR*, "the good" is exemplified by white, Euro-Western descendants who are progressive yet traditional, natural yet highly cultured, and who are ordained by God to live within a traditional family, with "man" as dominant over the planet and all other life forms on it. The *AR* family is heterosexual and nuclear; that is, it is a father-led family with two parents of "opposite" sexes as well as children who are assumed heterosexual. This is a family that, "left to itself ... very naturally resumes its ageless pattern: father-led, mother-inspired and child-centred" (Byfield, *AR*, January 11, 1999, p. 20). This family form, according to the *AR*, has existed timelessly across the history of "mankind" but is now increasingly under threat as it has been "invaded, plundered and demoralized over the last generation" (Byfield, *AR*, January 11, 1999, p. 20). Queer people, reduced in the *AR* to "homosexuals," posed a particularly nasty threat to the viability of this family structure.

Kissing n' Telling in Banff, Alberta, November 1992

In November of 1992, the Walter Phillips Gallery, part of the Banff Centre for the Arts, hosted a 90-minute performance, *True Inversions*, as part of its three-month-long celebration entitled, "Much Sense: Erotics and Life." This work by Vancouver's Kiss & Tell consisted of a film and live talk performance that included a visual and oral exploration of lesbian sexual practices. While lesbian sex is often conflated with gay male sex or erased by "what do lesbians do in bed?," rhetoric, evasion or effacement of lesbian sex was not possible with *True Inversions*. Graphic black-and-white photographs of the Kiss & Tell collective members, stories, vignettes, and mini-plays, all made lesbian sex public.

Taking note of this public display of lesbian sex and dedicated to boosting flagging readership with "gutsy and lively" reporting, *AR* sent reporter Rick Bell to cover the performance and investigate funding for "the latest in subsidized "alienation" and lesbian porn" (December 7, 1992, p. 33). Bell revealed that the Banff Centre was provincially funded with $4.5 million from John Gogo's Department of Advanced Education while the Walter Phillips Gallery was specifically granted $15,000 from the Department of Culture and Multiculturalism headed by Doug Main. Kiss & Tell was funded by the Canada Council, a federal agency involved in funding the arts.

Culture and Multiculturalism minister Doug Main responded with a letter to the editor of *AR* which was published on December 21, 1992. Main admonished the *AR* for their "slavish devotion to point-making at the expense of good journalism" (*AR*, p. 4). He was especially offended that the story and cartoon made the suggestion that he was personally responsible for, supportive of, and even proud to be involved with *True Inversions*. Main accused the *AR* of being ignorant of facts, especially the fact that "the minister of culture is not the arbiter of taste in Alberta" but is rather responsible for the provision of infrastructural support that allows for artistic expression within the province. Departmental support for the arts, according to Main, ought not to be confused with his personal support for a specific work, in this case the work of Kiss & Tell. Main finished his long letter with the following statement:

> By the way, I think the event and its line-up of performances was disgusting. I wasn't asked to provide any special specific funding for this event. If I had been asked I would have said "No!" (*AR*, December 21, 1992, p. 4)

Link Byfield responded to Main's letter with an editorial in which he stated that if "Mr. Main wasn't responsible for subsidizing those Banff lesbians, then who was?" (*AR*, December 21, 1992, p. 2). Byfield's editorial referred to *True Inversions* as a performance by a "troupe of foul-mouthed, sex-obsessed Vancouver lesbian activists." Further he admonished Main with, "if Mr. Main says he isn't responsible for making us pay women to masturbate in public, then who does he think is?" (*AR*, December 21, 1992, p. 2). Speculating as to what Main might say if he properly shouldered the responsibility of his portfolio, Byfield wrote:

> Please be advised that as minister responsible for cultural subsidies I am accountable to the voters and taxpayers of Alberta for what you do. When we take their money we owe them the courtesy of respecting common norms of decency and religious tolerance. (*AR*, December 21, 1992, p. 4)

Byfield both misrepresented lesbian sexuality as "masturbation" as well as misunderstood the role of government funding in relation to the arts. He did not, however, misunderstand the seriousness of bringing "homosexual" issues into the public realm and the consequences of making government members squirm at being implicated in such a "scandal."

The panic engendered by the *AR* coverage of Kiss & Tell continued elsewhere in the province and into the new year. In the words of Kiss & Tell member Susan Stewart, the "offshoot of the *Alberta Report* article was a syndicated story that appeared in at least twenty little community papers sprinkled throughout Alberta, Manitoba, and environs" (Kiss & Tell, 1993, p. 72). Kevin Avram focussed more intensively on taxpayer dollars. Three headlines making use of Avram's story are from the *Hanna Herald* of Hanna, Alberta, "Government Coffers are Never Empty for 'Art'" (January 20, 1993); the *Watson Witness* of Canora, Saskatchewan, "Even Lesbianism is Government Funded" (January 6, 1993); and the *West-Central Crossroads* of Kindersley, Saskatchewan, "Tax Dollars Funding Smut" (January 6, 1993). Adding to the mix, the deputy premier of Alberta, Ken Kowalski, pronounced, "I most definitely do not endorse this. It's totally inappropriate," as reported on January 15, 1993, in the *Edmonton Sun* under a title stating that the performance was "god-awful" (p. 24). Like Avram, Kowalski did not actually see the performance. Kowalski went further with his negative judgement of Kiss & Tell, however. The *AR* reported that Mr. Kowalski asked Advanced Education minister Jack Ady to speak to institutions such as the Banff Centre and "tell them such shows are not acceptable if the public is footing the bill" (*AR*, February 1, 1993, p. 43).

Pejoratives such as "unacceptable," "disgusting," "spectacle," "lesbian porn," "foul-mouthed," "sex-obsessed," "sacrilegious obscenities," "women masturbating in public," "perversion," and so on were juxtaposed with demands to respect common norms of decency and religious tolerance. As well, a new twist was introduced to this proliferation with Main's reference to "special specific" in relation to homosexuality. This phrase worked its way into another statement by Ady and then became part of the cant from Community Development minister Dianne Mirosh, who railed against "special rights for homosexuals" in her battle to prevent inclusion of lesbian and gay rights in Alberta's human rights protections.

An effect that the *AR* did not likely intend was its publicity for the work of Kiss & Tell and the positive effects this had for breaking silence regarding lesbianism and lesbian sexuality. The discursive formation of a "homosexual" group had almost completely been about sexual minority men, usually white males. This effacement of lesbians was disrupted in Alberta with the *AR*'s reporting on *True Inversions*.

Special Treatment for Winning Albertans: k.d. lang

The *AR* was not writing in a cultural or political vacuum but had widespread support from within the elected government. Statements and actions by provincially elected politicians functioned side by side with the *AR* in the production of homophobic and heterosexist discourse. Even if individual Albertans did not subscribe to or read the numerous free copies of *AR* that were in circulation, it would be difficult to ignore homophobic statements and actions of politicians as these were reported in mainstream radio, television, and print media.

Another such occasion occurred in the midst of the "gay rights as special rights" skirmish. In January 1993, national attention focussed on k.d. lang, an out lesbian and Albertan from the town of Consort. Lang had won numerous previous music awards and was a recipient of two Canadian Juno awards, one for album of the year and one for female vocalist of year. When Albertans such as lang gain widespread recognition for outstanding achievements or performances, the Alberta government publicly announces and sends congratulations from the Legislative Assembly. Public lauding of k.d. lang as an outstanding Albertan, as based on already established criteria through previous such announcements, was refused by the provincial government ("Political Correctness," *AR*, February 8, 1993, p. 29).

In 1993, 1994, and 1995, the onslaught of articles against human rights for lesbians and gays in the *AR* proliferated as support for the *AR* by many elected politicians continued. The case of Delwin Vriend made its way through various levels of the legal system.[8] The federal Tories had fallen from power, along with their proposed changes for inclusion of sexual orientation as a protected category in the Canadian Human Rights Act (CHRA), and Chretien's Liberals were in charge of the Canadian state. Within this framework, the *AR* marshalled a different argument in its war on "homosexuality" and flagging readership. In a story entitled "Special Rights for Sodomites," reporter Champion wrote that "Canada's human rights czar makes a last plea to legitimize the homosexual lifestyle" (*AR*, April 8, 1996, p. 25). This article was partially in response to the last annual report produced by Human Rights Chief Commissioner Max Yalden before his retirement. Yalden found that Ottawa was complicit in widespread intolerance towards lesbians and gays for failing to add sexual orientation to the CHRA. Further, Yalden roundly condemned critics, like those in Alberta, for stating that inclusion of sexual orientation amounted to special rights.

Intensifications: The Calgary Board of Education

Unsurprisingly to the *AR*, feminists, considered to be part of a pro-gay cabal, were busy assaulting the natural family at United Nations' conferences ("The Ugly Canadian," *AR*, July 1, 1996, cover), and even Disney and the Catholic Church were identified as pro-gay in the *AR* battle against queer Albertans ("The Mouse Trap," *AR*, July 22, 1996, cover; "See No Evil," *AR*, July 8, 1996, cover). Disney had become a huge threat with its extension of spousal benefits to homosexual employees, such that "the Southern Baptist Convention's annual meeting in June, 13,000 delegates representing some 16 million members voted to threaten a boycott against Disney for 'promoting homosexuality'" ("Verburg," *AR*, July 22, 1996, p. 26). The Catholic Church, unlike the Baptists or the church of *AR*'s Byfields, had permitted a cover-up of homosexuality that was rampant in its flock ("See No Evil," *AR*, July 8, 1996, cover). But, according to the *AR*, the sinister threat of homosexuality was poised to strike closer to home in Alberta as the gay agenda prepared to hit Alberta schools.

On June 11, 1996, the Calgary Board of Education (CBE) heard a "Report on Counselling Support for Homosexual Youth Safety" and adopted a series of motions towards developing an information package for safety of sexual minority youth in its school district. Pat Boyle, advisor on gender issues for CBE, was part of a committee that developed an action plan for consideration by the superintendents' council. The recommendations adopted by CBE, in principle, were startling because they contrasted so starkly with the wasteland of positive initiatives for queer youth in Alberta schools. The willingness of CBE to include all staff, in particular teachers, was testimony to its interest in the well-being of all its constituent members and went beyond the Alberta Teachers' Association initiatives, protection of students, in the new millennium. The backlash that ensued effectively placed the action plan in a defensive position in which every action and purchase in support of lesbian and gay youth came under intense public scrutiny.

The February 25, 1997, meeting was the showdown for final approval of the "Guidelines for the Implementation of the Action Plan on Gay/Lesbian/Bisexual Youth and Staff Safety." Calling this meeting a showdown cannot begin to capture the cacophony of events leading up to, and the shrill tone of, this meeting. In their "Fighting Back" column, for example, the *AR* lent support to the resistance to the action plan with the following call:

> *February 12 all concerned Calgary Public School Board parents and taxpayers are asked to attend a public meeting at 7:30 p.m. at the Calgary Convention Centre, Macleod Salon D - 120 - 9 Avenue SE. The purpose of the meeting is to discuss the school board's Action Plan to adopt a policy on "Homosexual Youth Safety." The board has had very little input from parents regarding this policy (see story, page 32). Come and be informed of the effects and ramifications, and give your input. Call 403-288-5332 or 403-239-8765 for further information.* ("Fighting Back," February 10, 1997, p. 39)

Churches affiliated with the *AR* organized gatherings throughout the city. At these meetings, parents were provided with testimonials from a "recovering homosexual" with graphic details of his "deadly" gay sexual practices, generalized to all other homosexuals, along with the message that if he could beat such a depraved lifestyle so could anyone. Other information about the "depravity" of homosexuality was made available as well. Parents and other concerned types were warned to attend the February board meeting and make their voices heard, or else the gay agenda would take over their schools, recruiting and preying on their children:

> *In late August, over 100 Christians from 16 churches met at the Centre Street Church in Calgary, to discuss a recent public school board resolution to legitimize homosexuality in the curriculum. These parents decided to form a Calgary chapter of Citizens United for Responsible Education (CURE), a Toronto-based network founded in 1992.* (Woodard, September 16, 1997, p. 32)

Reading the minutes for the "regular meeting of the Board" renders the chaotic and acrimonious struggle that ensued into a dry-sounding event, something it most definitely was not (Boyle, 1997, personal communication). The meeting was packed by concerned citizens and police were in attendance in case things got completely out of hand. Mitchell wrote for the *Globe and Mail* that "by all accounts, it was a noisy meeting" (March 7, 1997, p. A2). Shouting and screaming made it difficult for the board to proceed with business. In spite of the resistance, the motion to adopt the action plan passed unanimously.

In the weeks that followed, attempts to intimidate board members and staff required that all visitors pass into the CBE building through a security point. I was one such visitor. Boyle was particularly singled out because she was a "gender consultant" and therefore an automatic enemy (CURE founder Butler quoted in Woodard, *AR*, September 16, 1996, p. 32). Phone calls to the CBE, and especially to Boyle, were screened because of the numbers of hate calls received. Boyle reported that friends of hers who attended meetings in the Calgary area organized by opponents said she was vilified so completely that her friends were aghast at what was claimed about her and became worried about her safety and well-being. Similar verbal attacks were made against other CBE members during meetings by religious fundamentalists. The *AR* assisted the cause by reproducing an excerpt made to the CBE on September 14, 1996, by concerned parent and medical doctor, Dr. L. Macphail, listing the deadliness of "the lifestyle," thus adding a further fright factor to CURE's resistances to the action plan (Macphail, October 14, 1996, p. 33).

Fear of the queer predator taking innocent children and youth was turned into a fear of the predator "nanny" state, operating in the interests of a powerful homosexual lobby. The provision of a safety action plan that would also include counselling for queer youth produced both a tacit recognition that queer youth might be in their midst and fears that the state was taking children from their parents. Organizing against state education was thus marshalled in this latest battle against homosexuality (Woodard, *AR*, October 14, 1996, p. 32). Crites, head of Parents' Choice Association, opined, "Whose kids are they anyway? We know what's best for our kids" (Mitchell, March 7, 1997, p. A2). Concerned parents were represented as those who resisted the action plan and managed the sexuality of their offspring through intimidation, psychotherapy, and ostracism. Those, especially feminists like many of the CBE members, who supported queer rights were by definition anti-family.

Whereas the *AR* cast the struggle over the action plan as an issue about "homosexual" content in the curriculum, the action plan was based on tenets of the Canadian Charter of Rights and Human Rights Act. Both the Charter and Human Rights Act are concerned with obligations of public institutions like schools to all their constituent members, including queer youth and teachers. As Boyle stated, "We have a legal obligation to make sure students are safe in our schools" (Mitchell, March 7, 1997, p. A2). Yet pressure on the CBE continued long after the plan had passed, making change difficult if not, at times, impossible. For example, with the inclusion of lesbian and gay materials into libraries there came a call for book banning by Tom Crites and his group, a call agreed to by school board Chief Superintendent Donna Michaels (Mitchell and Laghi, *Edmonton Journal*, November 20, 1997, p. A1).

Fembos, Devils, and Angels in Alberta

Feminists, animal rights activists, and environmentalists had become as exceptionally powerful as the "vociferous homosexual rights lobby" (Frey, *AR*, December 21, 1992, p. 9). At least two feature-length articles in the *AR* were devoted to the takeover of the University of Alberta by radical, postmodernist, deconstructionist feminists, also known as power feminists (Verburg, *AR*, September 30, 1996, pp. 32–37; Craig, *AR*, October 7, 1996, pp. 32–33). Professors were quoted decrying the demise of their profession and universities more generally due to power feminists who, for these academics, were linked to queer politics. According to retired professor Solomon, "a student can now graduate without taking courses which a decade ago were core subjects ... you can take all your material in some very strange areas" (as quoted in Verburg, *AR*, September 30, 1996). Elsewhere in the same article, the *AR* reported that

> [o]ne English course on gender and sexuality is reportedly taught by a male professor who once came to class dressed like a woman. In fact, cross-dressing is a theme in a handful of courses. Other courses focus on curious issues such as "fatal women," "queer communities," "diseases of the blood," and "the liabilities of childbearing." Over 20 undergraduate and graduate courses in English deal with explicitly feminist and homosexual themes, with titles such as "Feminist Cultural Materialism," and "Post Modernism and Queer Praxis." A course on Chaucer explores how "queer theory" can help postmodern readers "engage with the 'tacitly unfinished' status of the inherited premodern text." Observes one English professor: "We are now reputed as one of the leading schools in queer theory in North America." (Verburg, September 30, 1996, p. 34, emphasis in original)

Professors, such as self-appointed feminist-watcher Morton of the University of Calgary, were quoted lamenting the powerful feminist lobby and the law (Champion, September 30, 1996, p. 24), while in yet another article young female judges were blamed for fast-tracking in a way that discriminates against their male colleagues (Champion, September 30, 1996, p. 24). In an article entitled "'Especially' No White Males," University of British Columbia professor Resnick claimed that hiring practices indicate to white males that, "We legally can't rule you out, but this is who we're interested in" (Hiebert, *AR*, September 30, 1996, p. 34). Not only were feminists taking over, University of Alberta's Craig blamed feminists and other "postmodern ideologues" for the demise of good teaching (*AR*, October 6, 1996, p. 32).

No less than president and vice-chancellor Roderick Fraser (*AR*, October 21, 1996, p. 3) and Henry Marshall Tory chair Isabel Grundy (*AR*, October 28, 1996, p. 3) wrote in response to these articles, thus making apparent that academic readership of the *AR* included others employed at universities besides right-wing ideologues like Craig and Morton.

The attack on the traditional family was far reaching; from homosexual porn as art, to Disney and the Catholic Church, and now the universities. It was clear to the *AR* that a battle against western civilization itself was being waged:

> Collectively the feminists adhere to a "post-modern" ideology that rejects the intellectual and cultural heritage of Western civilization. (Verburg, *AR*, September 30, 1996, p. 32)

Meanwhile, the powerful gay lobby was blamed for the tainted blood scandal of the Red Cross. According to the *AR*, senior administrators at the Red Cross were so afraid of this powerful group and its advocates that they made poor management decisions, with deadly repercussions for their clients (Champion, September 23, 1996, pp. 23–24). Even though "no one really knows how many homosexuals there are" (Avram, *AR*, November 25, 1996, p. 26), there were still enough in Canada who were powerful enough to bring down the Canadian blood system.

As the *AR* wrote retrospectively on January 11, 1999, it targeted the homosexual agenda in the 1990s because it wanted gutsy reporting to boost flagging readership (Byfield, p. 18). Scapegoating an already vilified group and casting it as powerful and threatening was bound to create sensation and boost readership by feeding human angst over a quickly changing world as well as frighten queer and questioning youth about their adult counterparts.

While the *AR* admonished queers to stay private, two lesbians were outed in a highly public way (Verburg, September 30, 1996, p. 33), and a spectral figure, the pedophile, began to emerge as the preoccupation of the magazine. Within this widening theatre of war, the play *Angels in America* came to the province.

The cover of October 7, 1996, openly declared this war with the caption, "Controversy rages over the arrival of a play that casts AIDS-afflicted homosexuals as martyrs in the war against Western civilization," juxtaposed with the words *Angels in Alberta* and a replica of the poster for the production in Calgary. In short, the *AR* thought *Angels* to be thoroughly disgusting:

> *The devil in disguise: Angels in America, which opened in Alberta last month, is the most celebrated play of recent memory. In Alberta, however, it has been one of the most reviled. Its admirers see it as a moving depiction of the pain suffered by AIDS victims. But it has at its core a revolutionary hatred for restraint of any kind. While its critics demand an end to government sponsorship of such productions, others propose a more radical solution: empowering audiences to take back the theatres.* ("The Devil in Disguise," *AR*, October 7, 1996, p. 1)

A flurry of editorials and articles appeared in Edmonton and Calgary spearheaded by *Calgary Herald*'s Peter Stockland. The *AR* indicated that Stockland accused *Angels* of "obscenity, anti-religious hatred, and of being a demonstration of the urgent need to overhaul the province's arts funding process" (Grace, *AR*, October 7, 1996, p. 36). The *AR* also reported a survey conducted by another newspaper, the *Sun*, which surveyed Alberta MLAs for their opinions on *Angels in America* (Grace,

October 7, 1996, p. 36). MLAs Lorne Taylor, Jon Havelock, Heather Forsyth, Judy Gordon, and Ron Hierath called for the Alberta Foundation for the Arts to withdraw funding to Alberta Theatre projects. The producer-director of *Angels* condemned those who were hyper-critical of a play they had not seen. Havelock reversed his opinion after seeing the play. Minister of Community Development Shirley McClellan, in a statement from her office, "'[was] not inclined to set herself up as judge and jury'" on any AFA funded project" (Grace, *AR*, October 7, 1996, p. 37). As reported in the *AR*, the *Calgary Herald*'s Stockland "was saddened" that an unintended effect of the controversy was to boost ticket sales (Grace, October 7, 1996, p. 36). While the review by reporter Grace was itself somewhat subdued for *AR* standards writing on homosexuality, the theme of a war on Western civilization spread, gaining a new theatre—heaven:

> [Angels] *is an artistic failure but it bears a powerful revolutionary message. While it elevates the belief current in the "AIDS community": that victims of the disease are holy martyrs, homosexuals, and AIDS victims are only one division of Mr. Kushner's vaster army: one that seeks to destroy the very concepts of the law—on earth and in heaven.* (Grace, October 7, 1996, p. 34)

In yet another article in the same edition, the Marquis de Sade as well as "radical deconstructionist" Michel Foucault and structuralist Roland Barthes were provided as evidence of the folly of multiculturalism. These multicultural intellectuals were progenitors and therefore promoters of the "AIDS cult" in which the "object is to break down the moral barriers erected against perversity, not for the sake of the perverse, but to destroy the civilization those barriers protect" (Grace, *AR*, October 7, 1996, p. 39). The link between multiculturalism and homosexuality was forged on the notion that traditional Western culture was under extreme threat from hordes of people who did not belong in Alberta. Deadly, infected, and contaminating homosexual bodies was the metaphor that tied all the threatening bodies together.

In keeping with the theme of the demise and death of Western civilization, the following week the *AR* linked the "hipness" of baldness as a "sign of aging, death, debilitation, illness" with homosexuality in "an instance of mass culture devouring 'alternative' forbidden fruit" ("Naked," *AR*, October 14, 1996, cover; Cosh, October 14, 1996, pp. 26–29). The bald head of "radical deconstructionist" Foucault was pictured alongside the bald heads of other famous and less-famous folk, all implicated with homosexuality and, in the slippery slope of the death of the traditional family, Western civilization, law and order, and heaven.

Predatory Pedophiles Enter the War

While the homosexual agenda, according to the *AR*, continued to assault western civilization, the heavens, and traditional families, Promise Keepers, an organization of like-minded men were bringing salvation to the "rubble of a destroyed Western civilization" by "espousing a high-powered combination of Christianity, commitment to—and leadership of—wife and children, sexual purity, and fellowship with other men" (O'Neill with Hiebert, *AR*, December 2, 1996, p. 36). Heterosexual masculinity would save the world in the way the *AR* wanted the world to be. Women, especially those unattached to men and with children, continued to be a large threat.

AR writers had uncovered that single mothers, young ones especially, were devastating to traditional family values (Woodard, December 9, 1996, p. 38), while

Aboriginal peoples were busy trying to get more than their fair share of land (Parker, December 9, 1996, p. 8). Ethnic minorities in Alberta who supported the "right" were on the rise. This was fine by the *AR*, because even though they weren't really Albertan, they were at least politically astute (Sillars, December 16, 1996, pp. 13–14). The *AR* discovered that the conspiracy against western men and boys was worse than "no white men need apply." More than any other social group, white males were bashed and lived in an overtly hostile world, created by radical, powerful and power-hungry feminists, linked, of course, to the strident homosexual lobby (Sillars, *AR*, February 3, 1997, p. 28; Cosh, *AR*, January 6, 1997, p. 41).

These assaults were manifest in phobias against a "triune male-referenced God" and worse, were also perpetrated by other males seduced by the feminist agenda, like United Church theologian Chris Levan of Edmonton. Male-bashing was also evidenced in domestic abuse legislation, which worked against fathers (Sillars, *AR*, February 3, 1997, p. 28). Classrooms were hostile for males as well with "whacking around" as the most common discipline used against male students from kindergarten to Grade 12 (Cosh, *AR*, January 6, 1997, p. 41).

Lesbians in sport also constituted an attack on traditional heterosexual masculinity as these women had "characteristics traditionally taken as male: strength, speed, endurance and aggressiveness" (Sillars, *AR*, January 20, 1997, p. 33). Another special feature exposing the assault on males included a cover with a butch-femme couple entwined in each others' arms and facing into the shadows, with the following headline: "From Dyke to Diva"; lesbianism "has become a sexy and sophisticated refuge for women who have given up on men" ("From Dyke to Diva," *AR*, May 12, 1997, cover).

Further evidence of the spread of male-bashing was found in popular culture, which gave television viewers the sitcom *Ellen*, starring a lesbian character played by lesbian actor Ellen Degeneres (Woodard, *AR*, May 12, 1997, p. 28). Meanwhile "sodomy was salubrious" for gay men because "celibate homos were shown to be five times likelier to attempt suicide than sexually active homos" and therefore "f—— as if your life depends on it" (Grace, *AR*, January 27, 1997, p. 15). Strangely, this *AR* imperative was the healthy response for all homosexuals—even lesbians—even as the *AR* was unclear as to whether lesbians can really have sex without males and heterosexual "f——ing."

Other dangers loomed. Normal Christians were terrified by witches on the Queen Charlotte Islands (Skelly, *AR*, November 11, 1996, pp. 42–43) and devil-worshipping diesel dykes skulked in Calgary (Sillars, *AR*, March 17, 1997, pp. 24–25). Most of the province had become unsafe, as had most of the country. Vancouver was a modern-day Sodom and Gomorrah rife with "prostitution, pornography, and perversion" (Brunet, *AR*, March 10, 1997, pp. 16–19), while right-thinking Lethbridge, Alberta, knew how to limit moral pollution of the sort that had taken over Vancouver (Sillars, *AR*, March 10, 1997, p. 19). Vancouver MP Svend Robinson was especially vile for supporting the "normalizing of buggery" through the lowering of age of consent from 18 to 14 (Woodard, *AR*, March 17, 1997, p. 38), while even Preston Manning was "recruiting" in that same Sodom-like city (Power, *AR*, February 3, 1997, p. 9), giving the religious right further pause in their support for him and the Reform party. Orphans in Newfoundland had been abused by priests, making them gay, and now they were further victimized because they had AIDS (Champion, *AR*, December 23, 1996, p. 40), while Protestant, pedophile priests were responsible for the "wash-out" lives of boys now grown men (Woodard, *AR*, February 3, 1997, p. 36). As for sexual abuse of women and female children, the *AR* felt these were exaggerated or false-memories of vindictive females, and if they did happen were not really incidences of victimization or lives made difficult by men (Sillars, *AR*, February 3, 1997, p. 28).

Predatory Museums in Red Deer

According to the *AR*, new gun control legislation constituted yet another form of male-bashing. Society was becoming "more urbanized, feminized and eco-neurotic" (Sillars, *AR*, September 8, 1997, p. 28). Moreover, according to the *AR*, the right of traditional families to own their children was being undermined. This interference by outsiders included medical ethicists who called into question the necessity of circumcising male infants (Sillars, *AR*, November 17, 1997, pp. 34–35). Given that gays were suspect males to the *AR*, it was not surprising that "gays felt they had been cheated" by the removal of their foreskins (Sillars, *AR*, November 17, 1997, p. 34). A further assault on masculinity was manifest in fathers' rights being ignored as mothers were busy abducting children (Sillars, *AR*, November 17, 1997, p. 32).

As if this were not bad enough, toys could no longer be counted on to either produce gender appropriate behaviours or reveal those who were deviant:

> [P]opular new dolls range from disabled to the depraved... The doll world is becoming not only multicultural, but more raunchy... Big Dyke Barbie shows off her pierced nose, while Hooker Barbie wears a negligee and carries a condom. Drag Queen Barbie is actually Barbie companion Malibu Ken acting out in wig and gown. (Sheremeta, *AR*, July 7, 1997, p. 42)

Single mother Kari Simpson emerged as a spokesperson for the traditional family. Simpson was credible to the *AR* because she claimed to be victimized by a society that treated men unfairly. She was "forthright, even discussing the ordeal [of being a single parent and woman on her own] at her rallies" (Cunningham, *AR*, November 24, 1997, p. 34). In one such confessional moment, according to the *AR*, Simpson indicated that

> Her husband went through a painful personal period and decided he needed to find himself. She says such behaviour is symptomatic of a society that has devalued the role of fathers. While he remains uninvolved with his children, Mrs. Simpson is hopeful that he will once again assume his responsibilities. (Cunningham, November 24, 1997, p. 35)

In August 1997, the provincial government was "caught" funding a project to gather reminiscences from local gay men and lesbians in Red Deer. A mini moral panic erupted and continued for the month with letters and articles in local newspapers, statements made by provincial and federal politicians, as well as attracting national media attention. MLA Stockwell Day opened fire by declaring that "a museum … was not the appropriate place to champion the cause of gay rights" (Frum, *The Financial Post*, August 26, 1997, p. 17). Frum paraphrased Day's concerns that "the people of Red Deer would be offended by this use of public money and a public facility—especially since one of the missions of this facility is the education of the young" (August 26, 1997, p. 17). Day stated further that the grant "legitimizes a lifestyle choice that doesn't deserve this kind of attention" (McNair, *Edmonton Journal*, August 25, 1997, p. A7).

Day and fellow Red Deer MLA Victor Doerksen demanded, on behalf of their constituents, that the museum return the money and that Community Development minister Shirley McClellan cancel the grant ("Treasurer Wants Gay Study Grant Money Returned," *Edmonton Journal*, August 16, 1997, p. A1). Both claimed further that "the gay-history project offends the city's traditional values" (Goyette, *Edmonton Journal*, August 20, 1997, p. A14). MP for Yellowhead, Cliff Breitkreuz, declared, "As you know, only 30 years ago it [homosexuality] was in the Criminal Code, and people were prosecuted if they were caught sodomizing. ... it is strange to go from one extreme to another in such a short time" (McNair, *Edmonton Journal*, August 25, 1997, p. A7). No one pressed Breitkreuz on why he thought people telling their stories was the same as sodomy.

An *Edmonton Journal* editorial indicated that "gay Albertans pay taxes, vote, even buy lottery tickets" and charged Day with "catering to some narrow-minded constituents and his own prejudices" and "gay-bashing" ("Stockwell Day goes gay-bashing again," August 19, 1997, p. A12). Day responded in a letter to the editor accusing the *Edmonton Journal* of name-calling in its descriptions of his actions (August 25, 1997, p. A9). Letter writer Mathew Martin wrote in resistance to Day and his supporters with the following:

> Surely Day would not suggest that, simply because more people in our province reject than accept fundamental Christianity (whence Day draws his homophobia), muse-ums should therefore discontinue presenting the role Christianity has played in Alberta's history ... it smells like fear bred by superstition. Fear that Alberta is not made in Stockwell Day's Sunday-school image. Fear that the Red Deer museum might show that this small segment of our population, which Day prefers to think of exclusively as a statistic, are people who live, love, hurt, get angry, have jobs and live with oppression the best they can. Fear that, consequently, the Klein govern-ment's roles in maintaining a climate of fear and hostility around gays and lesbians will become visible and unacceptable. (*Edmonton Journal*, August 19, 1997, p. A13)

Community Development minister McClellan again declined to recall the grant money, and it became public that the project had begun three years previous. Premier Ralph Klein backed Day, Doerksen, and McClellan in a public relations coup that left him looking like someone trying to balance everyone's interests (Sadava, *Edmonton Journal*, August 26, 1997, p. A6). As Goyette insightfully wrote in her *Edmonton Journal* editorial, "Klein chooses to kowtow to bigots. To borrow a chilling Stockwellian phrase, he 'legitimizes a lifestyle choice that doesn't deserve this kind of attention'" (August 20, 1997, p. A14).

Meanwhile the time for the Supreme Court of Canada to hear the Vriend case loomed ever closer and the battle waged by the *AR* against homosexuality increased commensurately. Link Byfield of the *AR* offered the following sarcastic comment about the Red Deer and District Museum:

> [E]nough of this, Alberta, leave the poor Red Deer and District Museum alone. The institution fell haplessly into controversy last month by getting a $10,000 provincial grant to document the experience of homosexuals, past and present, in central

> *Alberta. It will be titled "Furtive Frontier Frolics" or "What I did in Red Deer Before*
> *I Moved to Vancouver," or something like that. (AR, September 8, 1997, p. 2)*

The *AR*, however, did not intend to leave the issue alone. If the Red Deer museum was going to go forward with such a project, Byfield wanted to offer his advice as to what it should include as well as offer more provocative titles for exhibits:

> *Suppose it wanted to demonstrate the evils of homosexuality, and all the compulsive*
> *and revolting things homosexuals do with urine and feces, and explain in graphs and*
> *diagrams why they carry such an astonishing array of intestinal parasites and vene-*
> *real diseases. Would she [McClellan] grant that too? Would we have fun-loving*
> *"Homo on the Range" in Red Deer, but up in Lacombe "The Perils of Perversion"—*
> *both sponsored and endorsed by the Alberta government? ... If Wild Pansies of Red*
> *Deer catches the public fancy, fine. (AR, September 8, 1997, p. 2)*

Contrary to the *AR*'s account of a unified "whole whimping, cavilling, sneaking, gutless Cabinet Not Responsible," widespread dissent among government members including Cabinet members had grown over the Red Deer grant (Byfield, September 8, 1997, p. 2). Moreover, given the government's opposition to including sexual orientation in the Individual Rights Protection Act, it was disingenuous of the *AR* to suggest that "homosexuality" was sponsored and endorsed by the Alberta government. A consequence of the attention given to the Red Deer and District Museum history project was a boost in visitors to both Red Deer and the museum.

Predatory Parents

Throughout 1997, another issue regarding sexual minorities in Alberta was percolating. Ms. T, a foster parent, made public the new ban on "non-traditional" families fostering children and youth, as directed by Social Services minister Stockwell Day. Beginning in 1996 the government, under the auspices of Day, had been tinkering with ideas such as the "natural family" (Goyette, *Edmonton Journal*, March 18, 1997, p. A14). The *Edmonton Journal* reported on a January 13, 1997, letter from Day to an advocacy group that represented foster parents in which he wrote:

> *In those instances where non-traditional families have had children placed with them*
> *in the past, we will not be placing more children in these homes ... however the chil-*
> *dren currently in these homes will not be removed. (Gillis, March 18, 1997, p. A6)*

Day did not specify a definition of non-traditional families, but it became clear that Ms. T, a "mother of several birth children and foster mother to over 70 foster children" over a 17-year period, was not in a traditional family any longer when she was denied foster children in January 1997. Ms. T decided to contest the decision through the government's appeal process, arguing that "it's discriminating on the basis of sexual orientation and denying children access to potentially stable foster homes" (Gillis, *Edmonton Journal*, March 21, 1997, p. A6).

Yet another home-grown moral panic was underway in Alberta. Once again, letters to the editor and editorials jammed both daily papers in Calgary and Edmonton. Deploying evasion tactics when pressed on the issue Bob Scott, responding on behalf of Family and Social Services Department, stated, "There's no department policy ... we just try to place children in the most appropriate environment" (MacKinnon, *Edmonton Journal*, July 15, 1997, p. B1). Given this statement, it is difficult to know on what grounds Ms. T was disallowed foster children.

The assistant deputy minister for children's services wrote in a memo that the

Alberta government "will not place a child in a family living in a non-traditional arrangement or with a single person when it is known within the community that they are a practising gay or lesbian" and, further, that the director of child welfare should act "as a prudent parent reflecting the values of Albertans" (MacKinnon, *Edmonton Journal*, July 15, 1997, p. B1). Which Albertans and what values were being reflected was not clear. No one said why until the new minister came on board.

In an astonishing admission made on July 16, 1997, new Social Services minister Lyle Oberg stated that the reason for "disallowing gays and lesbians from being foster parents" was "discrimination" (Arnold, *Edmonton Journal*, July 16, 1997, p. A1). Since gay and lesbian communities had indicated that they were discriminated against, Oberg ostensibly did not want to subject children in their care to this discrimination. He failed to note that his government's policy of special treatment for sexual minorities was one of the constitutive marks of that persecution. Instead of continuing discrimination by refusing foster children to capable foster parents who happened to be lesbian or gay, Oberg might have considered how the government could reduce discriminatory acts. Mark Lisac noted in his July 17, 1997, article in the *Edmonton Journal* that the "suggestive link of sexual orientation to child molesting takes us into the rough territory of slanderous bullying" and was part of the "perverse govn't bias still lurking in the closet" (July 17, 1997, p. A10).

In his *Edmonton Journal* commentary of July 25, 1997, Peter Menzies wrote that "if gays, lesbians want kids, let them make their own" (p. A17). Menzies, like so many others, did not seem to realize that many lesbians and gays do have children and that heterosexual parents "make" queer children and youth. Entering the discursive panic on July 25, Premier Ralph Klein restated that "his government has no policy on whether gays and lesbians can take care of foster children" (Arnold, *Edmonton Journal*, July 25, 1997, p. A6). Later he advised that the Tories would debate gay fostering (Arnold, *Edmonton Journal*, September 24, 1997, p. B5) but it was unclear when or where this would take place. Meanwhile, Senator Jean Forest indicated that Alberta discrimination against Alberta gays and lesbians might aptly be called "Alberta's Double Disadvantage" (*Edmonton Journal*, July 28, 1997, p. A7).

The *AR* argued against Ms. T with "only heterosexual union[s] [were] blessed by the Bible" (Bell, *Edmonton Journal*, September 22, 1997, p. A11) and reiterated its cant that "the gay lifestyle contains tremendous health risks and instability." This conflation of gay and lesbian even in the face of an explicitly lesbian public moral panic was typical of *AR* reporting (Notdorft, *Edmonton Journal*, October 6, 1997, p. A13). Former Social Services minister Connie Osterman agreed with Day and Oberg when she opined that "by and large males and females are very different, and we need that difference, and children need to understand how grown-ups make that difference work" (Daniel, *Edmonton Journal*, April 7, 1997, p. 9). "Normal" was linked, explicitly and implicitly, to natural, family, traditional, heterosexual, and gender difference throughout the *AR*'s coverage (Daniel, *AR*, April 7, 1997, p. 9; Torrance, *AR*, August 11, 1997, p. 13).

On September 18, 1997, Ms. T submitted a report to Oberg that contained a compilation of research on foster parents. This was in response to an earlier report submitted on July 11, 1997, by some of the *AR*'s favourite "experts" on homosexuality, M. Genius, of the National Foundation for Family Research and Education, and

Claudio Violato, professor at the University of Calgary. The July report cited the work of Paul Cameron of the Family Research Institute in Washington, DC. Cameron's work was deleted with an "X" in the copy I have but it is not clear that Oberg's copy had Cameron's work "X-ed" out ("A Critical Review of Literature on Homosexual Parenting," July 11, 1997). The *Edmonton Journal* reported that:

> *Cameron was expelled from the American Psychological Association in 1983 for vio-*
> *lating the association's code of ethics. Both the American and Canadian psycholog-*
> *ical associations and the American Sociological Association have censured Cameron*
> *for "consistently misinterpreting and misrepresenting research on sexuality, homo-*
> *sexuality, and lesbianism ... further Dr. John Service, executive director of the*
> *Canadian Psychological Association, said the association would have "serious con-*
> *cerns" if members cited Cameron as a legitimate researcher.* (Rusnell, October 18,
> 1997, p. B4)

In spite of the evidence offered in Ms. T's report, Oberg refused to alter his position and instead reiterated what he said earlier (Johnsrude, *Edmonton Journal*, October 3, 1997, p. B7). The Ms. T debate and moral panic continued into 1998.

The *AR* did a special feature on Ms. T. with a cover page entitled "Opening the Door to Gay Parents" on August 11, 1997. The cover, like its shadowy predecessors, "Dyke to Diva (May 12, 1997) and "Hockey Coach Predator" (January 20, 1997), featured a shadowy pair of gay men facing forward yet lurking in a doorway. They are entwined with one another while their free arms are extended out, offering an invitation to a small child who is in the forefront of the picture. The child is poised in hesitation at the threshold, uncertain as to whether he/she should enter. The *AR* represented the two adults as male even though the foster parent that had brought this issue to the public eye was Ms. T. Since lesbian predators do not have the same cultural capital as do gay men, *AR*'s conflation of lesbians with gay occurred yet again. With the words, "Klein approves homosexual foster families while the hard-liners in his caucus run for cover," the *AR* assigned blame to both the Premier and homosexuals ("Opening the Doors," August 11, 1997, cover). Inside, the caption "silence of the lambs" greeted the reader alongside a mini copy of the cover ("Silence of the Lambs," August 11, 1997, p. 1). Invoking both the Bible and a popular film, the message suggested that children were going to slaughter in this latest homosexual war against traditional families in Alberta.

Further, the *AR* was disappointed and even "mystified" by Oberg's remarks, which they thought offered support to claims of discrimination made by "homosexuals" (Torrance, August 11, 1997, p. 10). Attempting to put the government on the defensive, the *AR* sent a fax to fourteen Conservative MLAs and ministers, followed by three phone calls asking for the Klein government to state as policy that it refused foster children to homosexuals. Only one MLA, Ron Hierath, responded yet refused to criticize the Premier (Torrance, August 11, 1997, p. 11). Increasing the pressure, the *AR* sent another fax to the rest of the Conservative caucus. Again there was very little response. Searching for dissent, the *AR* found Paul Nathanson, a "homosexual," who worried "about the possibility of children being harmed by some homosexuals, primarily lesbians, who have an ideological framework that might prevent them from presenting an unbiased attitude towards the other sex" (Torrance, August 11, 1997, p. 14). The fact that most "homosexuals" were born and raised by straight parents, that many were already parents, and that some were children and youth, seemed to escape everyone.

On April 16, 1998, a Court of Queen's Bench justice ruled that the media could publish Ms. T's name, thus breaking her anonymity, a measure she had chosen in order to protect the identity of the foster child in her care. On April 20, 1998, the *AR* along with other media, released Ms. T's name and the town she lived in, publicly outing her. Given their 1993 (Byfield, June 14, 1993, p. 52) and 1997 (Owen, January 6, 1997, p. 28) stand on keeping sexual orientation a private matter, this contradiction revealed the punitive ways in which the *AR* was willing to treat sexual minorities. In her "Open Letter to an Albertan Named Ms. T," in which she refused to out Ms. T, *Edmonton Journal* writer Linda Goyette summarized this treatment by the *AR* as indicating "bigotry is a chosen lifestyle" (April 8, 1998, p. A14). An effect of this bigotry was that foster children were denied the care of one excellent foster parent, Ms. T, for the years 1997 and 1998.

Predatory Teachers, Supreme Judgements, and a Seismic Moral Panic

Christian youth, even older ones, are particularly at risk to the perils of homosexuality or so *AR* representations of the *Vriend* case would have us believe. The *Vriend* case is the signatory case to understanding representations as well as experiences of homophobia and heterosexism in Alberta during this time.

In his Court of Appeal judgement against Vriend on February 23, 1996, the Honourable Mr. Justice McClung, stated the following:

> Beyond that, I say nothing as well of the respondent's answer to the appellant's concerns that the term "sexual orientation" is limited to "traditional" homosexual practices shared by consenting adults, and its IRPA inclusion would never be raised as a permissive shield sheltering other practices, both heterosexual and homosexual, commonly regarded as deviance in both communities. It is pointless to deny that the Dahmer, Bernardo and Clifford Robert Olsen prosecutions have recently heightened public concern about violently aberrant sexual configurations and how they find expression against their victims. (McClung, JC, as quoted in *Vriend*, 1996, p. 22)

The association of Delwin Vriend with three men known for horrific crimes of murder was an epistemic assault to Vriend as well as to other sexual minorities in Alberta. On November 17, 1997, the *AR* did a special feature on Vriend entitled "Winners & Losers" (cover). The caption underneath stated, "Why do Canada's courts invent charter rights for gays and not for babies?," inserted between a picture of Vriend and his partner and a classic picture of a fetus. With this cover Vriend became the quintessential homosexual predator in a twist of *AR* il/logic, as the unborn, not just children and youth, are turned into prey and therefore unsafe. Inside the magazine, articles included, "The chosen and the choosers: once again the Supreme Court embraces gays and abandons babies"; "From perverse to macabre"; "When Vriend wins, so does Graham James"; "The slavery-abortion parallel"; and "A Supreme display of judicial prejudice."

Given the negative national attention to Alberta during the Supreme Court hearing of *Vriend*, the *AR* had work to do in its war against "homosexuality" in advance of the Supreme Court's announcement of its decision. On December 15, 1997, the *AR* featured an advertisement entitled, "Gay 101 in Our Schools?" addressed to concerned Christians, asking if they knew what their children were being taught about homosexuality in schools and whether their children knew how to protect themselves (*AR*, inside back cover). A wide-eyed little girl stares out at readers and unknown dangers in order to raise parental fears. For a small donation readers were offered membership in the Christian Heritage Party of Canada as well as a book entitled *Homosexuality and the Politics of Truth*. February 9, 1998, found a similar ad, entitled "Guess Why Trouble-makers Like Delwin Vriend Always Win in Court?," this time asking for support for Alberta Federation for Women United For Families, headed by Hermina Dykxhoorn (p. 21). Dykxhoorn's family federation needed help with their cause "against easy divorce, permissive sex-ed, radical gender feminism, the normalization of homosexuality and any other issue that threatens families" and asked for donations as well ("Guess Why Trouble-makers...," p. 21).

On January 19, 1998, the *AR* featured an article about "judicial activism," with concerns from a stern-looking provincial Justice minister Jon Havelock. The *AR* fretted over appointments made in backrooms with input from "an array of feminist, aboriginal, Jewish, gay and criminal-rights activists" (Woodard, January 19, 1998, p. 10). The problem of judicial activism, according to Havelock and *AR*, was that the Supreme Court was made up of the wrong kind of person.

Havelock was concerned about the upcoming Vriend decision and he worried "about what may happen, if they [Alberta government] do not" invoke the notwithstanding clause (Woodard, *AR*, January 19, 1998, p. 14). The *AR* spelled out the remedy for its readership if the Supreme Court ruled in favour of Vriend. The remedy was to pressure MLAs to invoke Section 33 of the Charter, the notwithstanding clause. Not only would this remove the threat of Vriend, the individual homosexual who stood in for all homosexuals, but, according to Reform MP Jason Kenney and endorsed by the *AR*, invoking the notwithstanding clause "will have begun the recovery of democracy" as well (Woodard, January 19, 1998, p. 14). Provincial Treasurer Stockwell Day indicated that the province might use the notwithstanding clause (Jeffs, *Edmonton Journal*, March 31, 1998, p. A1) and Klein mused that the Supreme Court decision could have a financial impact on the Alberta government (Jeffs and Johnsrude, *Edmonton Journal*, April 1, 1998, p. A6). Both these warnings implied that the Alberta government had a strong sense it was going to lose at the Supreme Court.

On April 2, 1998, in a stunning eight to one decision, the Supreme Court of Canada ruled in favour of Vriend and against the Province of Alberta. Alberta's human rights law was ruled unconstitutional. This ruling effectively changed the province's human rights laws to prohibit discrimination on the basis of sexual orientation:

> This is clearly an example of a distinction which demeans the individual and strengthens and perpetuates the view that gays and lesbians are less worthy of protection as individuals in Canada's society. The potential harm to the dignity and perceived worth of gay and lesbian individuals constitutes a particularly cruel form of discrimination. (Mr. Justice Peter Cory in *Vriend vs Alberta*, 102, p. 30/47)

> The Supreme Court of Canada has rebuked the Alberta government for evading its democratic duty to prevent discrimination against all Albertans, including gays and lesbians. In a unanimous decision released Thursday, the court ruled that legal protections must immediately be made available to the province's homosexual community. It ended a seven-year battle by concluding that sexual orientation must be

> "read in," or assumed to be part of, the Individual's Rights Protection Act as a prohibited ground of discrimination ... the deliberate exclusion was not an oversight. The denial of equal rights reinforces stereotypes that gays and lesbians are less deserving and less worthy, he [Cory] said. It "sends a strong and sinister message... It could well be said that it is tantamount to condoning or even encouraging discrimination against lesbians and gay men. (Ovenden, Edmonton Journal, April 3, 1998, p. A3)

> [G]iven these considerations and the context here, it is my opinion that the failure to extend protection to homosexuals under the IRPA can be seen as a form of government action that is tantamount to approving ongoing discrimination against homosexuals. Thus, in this case, legislative silence results in the drawing of a distinction. (Hunt, JA, in Vriend vs. Alberta, p. 17/47)

The Supreme Court clearly stated that the Alberta government's action was that of state produced and sanctioned discrimination and that in fact, provincial "silence" on the part of elected representatives resulted in the drawing of distinction, or special status. Victory for queer Albertans was short-lived however, as Premier Ralph Klein decided to wait a week while he consulted with his caucus, who were to hear from their constituents, whether to invoke the notwithstanding clause.

The week became open season for homophobic diatribes against Albertans who were queer. The proliferation of hate was the culmination of years of government resistance working together with organized anti-gay lobbies including the Canada Family Action Coalition headed by Roy Beyer, Calgary's Parents Rights Association, Medicine Hat Citizens' Impact Coalition, Alberta Pro-Life, Alberta Federation of Women United for the Family led by Hermina Dykxhoorn, feminist watcher and University of Calgary professor Ted Morton and his tiny Alberta Civil Society Association, and, of course, the AR (Woodard, AR, April 20, 1998, p. 13). Beyer cited fears that "the ruling could be used to protect polygamy, bestiality and pedophilia" and local Alberta Federation of Women United for the Family president Cory Morcos stated that "accepting the ruling will erode family values." Both called for Albertans to flood MLA offices with demands to invoke the notwithstanding clause (Jeffs, Edmonton Journal, April 3, 1998, p. A3).

Elected representatives made public statements as well. For example, Lac La Biche-St. Paul MLA Paul Langevin said, "People know where I stand on the gay rights issue, I believe it's a moral issue and I'm not prepared to support gay rights this time" (Johnsrude, Edmonton Journal, April 3, 1998, p. A9). Environment minister Ty Lund said, "My constituency is very, very upset that unelected judges are telling elected politicians what to do" and added that his constituents believed in law and order (Pedersen, Edmonton Journal, April 5, 1998, p. A1).

The moral panic in the wake of Vriend went beyond even the Premier's wildest imaginings. He referred to the volume of hate as "appalling faxes and phone calls" along with form and handwritten letters which "quite frankly make[s] your stomach churn" (Johnsrude, Edmonton Journal, April 8, 1998, p. A20). Thousands of calls and letters went into the Premier's office and to MLAs. Opponents of the ruling launched a newspaper and television ad campaign which argued that inclusion of sexual orientation would promote homosexuality and weaken the family. Talk show hosts entertained the spewing of hate from anyone with an opinion:

"I don't want to see them, I don't want to smell them, I don't want anything to do with them," the caller said of gays, the disgust palatable in his voice. (Geiger, April 12, 1998, *Edmonton Journal*, F4)

A week later, Klein, flanked by Cabinet ministers McClellan and Havelock, declared that the province would *not* invoke the notwithstanding clause. They would, however, place "fences" against gay rights outside of housing and employment issues. An advertisement entitled "Facts About Alberta's Human Rights Laws and the *Vriend* Decision" was placed by the government of Alberta in all daily newspapers around the province in an attempt to explain the limitedness of the decision and, hopefully, allay fears ("Facts About Alberta's Human Rights Laws," *Edmonton Journal*, April 15, 1998, p. A7).

The *AR* relentlessly objected that Albertans were opposed to the Premier's position, as if queer Albertans were not Albertans. April 20, 1998, found a special report and cover entitled "Ralph's New Friends" featuring Delwin Vriend and his partner smiling in front of the Legislative Building in Edmonton. Rural Albertans were said to be particularly upset. Annie Smith of Gwynne, Alberta, wrote in response, "It infuriates me to know that as a rural constituent, religious fundamentalists and the Alberta Federation of Women United for the Family presume to speak on my behalf. They most certainly do not represent my beliefs" (*Edmonton Journal*, April 19, 1998, p. A15).

The *AR* trotted out one of their by now stock arguments that homosexuals are really "a rich, educated, unpersecuted elite" who have tremendous political influence out of proportion with actual numbers (Woodard, April 20, 1998, p. 13). Elsewhere, concerned citizens like Mrs. Dykxhoorn, representing Alberta Federation of Women United for the Family, insisted that "the Supreme Court's decision in *Vriend* does represent an unprecedented use of raw judicial power, both in a 'social engineering' sense—attempting to remake the moral order of society—and also in a strictly legal and constitutional sense—'legislating from the bench'" (Woodard, *AR*, April 20, 1998, p. 15). The *AR* suggested further that Havelock was set up by Rod Love, aide to Klein, when Havelock attempted to use the "notwithstanding clause" earlier in March to restrict payments to Albertans who were wrongfully sterilized on behalf of the government (Woodard, April 20, 1998, p. 14). Given the public outcry against Havelock in his earlier attempt to invoke the "notwithstanding clause," it was unlikely, according to the *AR*, that he would oppose Klein's decision not to invoke the "notwithstanding clause" in *Vriend*.

In the same *AR* issue, April 20, 1998, there was another call for donations and action, this time from Roy Beyer's Canada Family Action Coalition (CFAC). The advertisement entitled "It's Not Too Late!—If Vriend Wins … Who Loses?" stated that "the natural family, the fabric of our society, will be seriously undermined" (p. 36). The ad disingenuously charged that Vriend was fired for violating the college's policy regarding sex outside of marriage. CFAC, like Alberta Federation of Women United for the Family, continued to deny that queer people like Vriend came from families much like their own.

Elsewhere, *AR* patriarch, founder, and president Ted Byfield denounced Klein's decision to not invoke the "notwithstanding clause" in *Vriend* as "probably his most grievous decision ever" (April 20, 1998, p. 44):

> *Why is this issue so divisive? I think it's because this particular activity, among males anyway, revolts and offends many people. The spectacle of men coupling, while certainly absurd and the subject of snickers and jokes from the Greeks onward, many also find repulsive. They see it as a perversion of nature, like garbage in a river of toxic blight on a forest, as something unnatural, something not intended to be.* (Byfield, April 20, 1998, p. 44)

Significantly, April 20 was the same issue in which Ms. T was outed by the *AR*.

May 4, 1998, found yet another advertisement in the *AR* by CFAC, this time for a "public rally for the family" in which Kari Simpson was to advise concerned Albertans about "the Vriend decision: what it means—what we must do" (Public Rally, p. 32). The list of potential dangers included threats to education, children and youth, the traditional family, as well as gay adoption, gay public exhibitionism, and even the curtailment of traditional free speech. The next page contained a petition sponsored by CFAC calling on Premier Klein to use the "notwithstanding clause" (Public Rally, May 4, 1998, p. 33). In the same issue, the *AR*'s token queer voice, John Mckellar of Homosexuals Opposed to Pride Extremism (HOPE) declared his group as pro-civilization and anti-special rights for gays (Woodard, May 4, 1998, p. 14).

In an August 13, 1998, interview with *Outlooks*, a Calgary magazine for Alberta's queer communities, Klein made the following statement: "What matters most to me is whether or not somebody is a good person. Are they hard-working? Honest? Sincere? Responsible? Are they good and decent human beings? Those are the important things" as reported in the *Edmonton Journal* (Arnold, August 13, 1998, p. A5). It is unlikely that Klein had a sudden epiphany in the wake of the Supreme Court ruling in *Vriend*. If he had done the right thing much earlier he would have saved thousands of taxpayer dollars spent on a series of legal battles in the service of a minority group of religious fundamentalists who wanted special rights for themselves in the province. While waiting for others to take responsibility and do the right thing, Klein aided and abetted the *AR* and its supporters in their war against homosexuality.

Will the Real Predators Please Stand Up?

In its battle against homosexuality, specifically with respect to human rights protection and funding for cultural projects related to queer Albertans, but also against the right of queer people to exist in peace and harmony or at all within the province of Alberta, the *AR* and its supporters were exposed as the real predators. They preyed on people's fears and anxieties. With their vitriol and hate, editors and writers for the *AR* preyed on the vulnerability of questioning or queer youth, who were confronted with the magazine on a regular basis in their schools. *AR* owners and writers were obsessed with sex, especially the sex lives of other people, and more particularly queer sex. Ironically, in its mission to completely eliminate a group of people from public consciousness, it made this group more public, "educating" "severely normal" Albertans but also questioning and queer youth that queer Albertans exist and that they were engaged in a range of public activities:

> *This is like a gender war, kind of thing, but this is also a war about orientation.* (Virginia, 1998)

> *I demanded that my library carry* The Advocate, *for balance, if they were going to carry the* Alberta Report *and all its fucking shit ... but the librarian said she could not do that but would not tell me why.* (Oscar, 1998)

Notes

1. This paper is a small part of a larger project working with queer youth in Edmonton and Calgary, which I began in 1995.

2. I use queer and sexual minority interchangeably and cautiously to stand in for those who may self-describe variously as lesbian, gay, transgender, transsexual, bisexual, Two-Spirit, questioning or that which lies outside what counts as normal, natural, and universal in relation to sexual practices. When I use the word homosexual this signals common useage at the time as well as the psychiatrization of same sex desires.

3. The National Energy Program under Prime Minister Pierre Trudeau was viewed by Alberta as a tax grab of Alberta's oil revenues. A book outlining this struggle is Paul Bunner (ed.), *Lougheed & the War with Ottawa: 1971–1981* (Edmonton: United Western Communications, 2003). More recently, changes to Alberta Health Care under current Premier Ralph Klein have given rise to threats to and cutting off of federal transfer payments to fund provincial health care. Alberta resistance to ratification of the Kyoto Accord this past year (2003), refusal to endorse the UN Rights of the Child, and continued opposition to federal gun registry legislation are other examples of provincial-federal tensions.

4. With federal government initiatives to expand the legal definition of marriage to same sex partners, Alberta politicians have publicly announced that Alberta may invoke the notwithstanding clause as a way of opting out of legalizing same sex marriage. Legal experts note this is not possible since the federal government has jurisdiction over and is therefore responsible for legal definition and regulation of marriage. In response, the province will refuse to provide licenses to gays and lesbians seeking to marry within the province. Elsewhere, the provinces of Ontario and BC have performed numerous same sex marriages. Within queer communities the idea of marriage remains a contentious issue but in the face of offensive homophobic discourses across the country but especially vitriolic in Alberta, most community members have been compelled to support the cause.

5. "Severely normal" was coined first in relation to the disruption of "normal" students by the integration of special needs students in public schools as reported in *AR*. Premier Ralph Klein demonstrated his awareness of this phrase and pushed it into wider spread public use by naming right-wing, conservative, and often fundamental Christian Albertans as "severely normal." As recently as May 20, 2003, the *Edmonton Journal*'s Paula Simons writes about Klein's "imaginary, prototypical, 'severely normal' Albertans" as the template against which Klein supposedly tests social thinking (pp. B1–2).

6. The *Alberta Report*, which became the *Report*, "ended its 30-year run as a fervent voice for conservatism in Alberta and the West on Monday, finally shutting down operations after years of financial troubles" (Markusoff, June 24, 2003, p. A6).

7. In my retrieval of articles related to homosexuality I excavated at least three items per *AR* weekly news magazine. All are similar in content. The articles included here are a very small part of a much larger research project.

8. In 1988, Delwin Vriend held a permanent, full-time position as a lab instructor at King's College, Edmonton, Alberta. In 1990, when asked by the college president, Vriend disclosed he was gay. In January 1991, the college adopted a position statement on homosexuality and Vriend was asked to voluntarily resign. When he refused, Vriend was fired. Vriend attempted to file a complaint of wrongful dismissal with the Alberta Human Rights Commission and was told the commission could not act on his complaint because sexual orientation was not included in the Individual's Rights Protection Act. On November 27, 1993, Vriend took his case to the Court of Queen's Bench and on April 13, 1994, Justice Anne Russell ruled that Alberta's human rights law was inconsistent with the Charter of Rights and Freedoms and the provincial act must include sexual orientation. On May 5, 1994, the Alberta government decided to appeal, and on February 23, 1996, the Court of Appeal of Alberta ruled in favour of the government in a decision by

Justice John McClung. On May 6, 1996, Vriend decided to appeal to the Supreme Court of Canada, which agreed to hear the case. On November 4, 1997, the Supreme Court hearings began. The Supreme Court heard from seventeen interveners, including religious and civil liberties groups. On April 2, 1998, the Supreme Court ruled that Alberta's human rights law was unconstitutional and must protect people from discrimination based on their sexual orientation, thus effectively changing Alberta's human rights code.

References

Primary Documents

Alberta Report (1990–98); *Edmonton Journal* (1990–98); *Calgary Herald* (1990–98).

Secondary References

Adams, M. 1997. *The Trouble With Normal: Postwar Youth and the Making of Heterosexuality.* Toronto: University of Toronto Press.

Dumas, J. 1998. "V Day." In 10th Anniversary, "Extreme Alberta," *Other Voices* (Spring): 23–38.

Epstein, D. and R. Johnson. 1998. *Schooling Sexualities.* Bristol, PA: Open University Press.

Foucault, M. 1980. *Power/Knowledge: Selected Interviews and Other Writings 1972–1977.* New York: Pantheon.

Kinsmen, G. 1996. *The Regulation of Desire: Homo and Hetero Sexualities.* Montreal: Black Rose.

Kiss & Tell. 1994. *Her Tongue on My Theory.* Vancouver: Press Gang Publishers.

MacDougall, B. 2000. *Queer Judgments.* Toronto: University of Toronto Press.

Sears, J. and W. Williams (eds.). 1997. *Overcoming Heterosexism and Homophobia.* New York: Columbia University Press.

Sedgwick, E.K. 1990. *Epistemology of the Closet.* Los Angeles: University of California Press.

Stychin, C. 1995. *Law's Desire: Sexuality and the Limits of Justice.* London and New York: Routledge.

Vriend v. Alberta. [1994] 6 WWR 414 (Alta.QB); appeal allowed (1996) 132 DLR (4th) 595 (Alta. CA); reversed (1998), 156 DLR (4th) 385 (SCC).

Warner, M. 1994. "Introduction" in M. Warner (ed.), *Fear of a Queer Planet: Queer Politics and Social Theory.* Minneapolis: University of Minnesota Press.

Yogis, J., R. Duplak and J.R. Trainor. 1996. *Sexual Orientation and Canadian Law: An Assessment of the Law Affecting Lesbian and Gay Persons.* Toronto: Emond Montgomery Publications Limited.

λ

11

Christian Opposition
to Homosexuality

Donald Cochrane

If we fight with any weapon other than rational argument, we will have given our adversaries the greatest victory that they could possibly win, that of debasing our humanity. But if we face the issue with good moral arguments ... there is reason to believe that we can prevail over prejudice, both in the courts and in the larger society of which we are a part. (Martha Nussbaum, 1999)

The content and rhetoric of the official teaching are simply repeated whenever a serious challenge seems put to it. The findings, however tentative, of exegetes, psychologists, sociologists, moral philosophers, and theologians and the experience of gays and lesbians and their families seem to have no impact whatsoever. (Jon Nilson, 2001)

Society loses much of its rationality when it comes to homosexuality and children. (Bruce MacDougall, 1998)

ORGANIZED RELIGION CONTINUES TO BE A POWERFUL FACTOR in society's evaluation of behaviour. Even those who have expressly abandoned religion often remain deeply influenced by the teachings of the very institution they have rejected. Rueda points out that "religion provides the strongest category by which human acts are evaluated—the virtuous/sinful continuum" and that "there is no question that religious institutions have freely applied ... the category of sinful when analyzing homosexual behaviour." He concludes that "religious belief is probably the single most important factor in the near-universal rejection of homosexual behaviour."[1]

With few exceptions, religious institutions in Canada remain the one major social force that openly supports discrimination against gay and lesbian citizens.[2] In the last 20 years, provincial governments have passed progressive human rights legislation favourable to gays and lesbians,[3] Parliament has extended protection to them,[4] and courts have rendered judgments that have advanced their interests.[5] But most Christian religious organizations continue to advocate a politics of exclusion and intolerance.

Some of them restrict their attention to issues of "internal politics," such as whether to ordain gay and lesbian applicants for the ministry or bless same-sex unions.[6] Others are also concerned with broader social issues—opposing initiatives that would allow gay and lesbian people to enter civil marriages, adopt children, obtain spousal benefits, and so on. In the first category, we can place Anglicans,[7] Baptists,[8] Lutherans,[9] Presbyterians,[10] and Methodists (in the United States).[11] The Roman Catholic Church has been the most active player in the second category,[12] though in the United States, the Southern Baptist Convention would be a contender for this dubious distinction.[13]

Alongside specifically religious institutions, lobby groups have formed to influence legislators to preserve traditional concepts of the family and to regulate desire. Though such organizations may appear secular, scratching beneath the surface reveals that they have close ties to traditional religion.[14]

How central are gay and lesbian issues to right-wing political movements? I suspect they are at the core. For traditionalists, it was bad enough that feminists made serious inroads into the social structure—whether in family configurations, economic organizations, or religious institutions—but that gays and lesbians should press for similar rights and opportunities is more than most can bear. The issue is essentially one about change, privilege, and power. Esterberg and Longhofer put it this way:

> The issue of homosexuality is central to this coalition. In the view of the traditionalists, the increased visibility of lesbians, gays, and bisexuals and campaigns for gay/lesbian/bisexual rights represent the final assault on morality, the family, the economic order, the strength of the nation, and the masculinist conceptions of gender that sustain these institutions. ... In these activists' eyes, the gains of the women's movement and the gay and lesbian rights movement were a clear sign of the need for action.[15]

Many religious organizations have vigorously opposed initiatives intended to guarantee equal rights and privileges to gays and lesbians. The suffering that this denial of basic rights has caused[16] warrants a closer look at the arguments used to defend this position. The principle that initiates this inquiry is simply the presumption that people should be treated equally unless there are relevant differences that would justify differential treatment. What beliefs do those who would exclude gays and lesbians have and how valid are they? Even if valid within a particular religious discourse, should they be given any authority to determine or influence laws and practices for society as a whole? The grounds typically given fall into the three categories: scriptural and theological, psychological, and prudential. I argue that each of these fails to justify the intervention of these religious organizations and lobby groups into the political process.

The Basic Tenets

It is wise to refer to the "tenets" of the evangelical Protestant position on homosexuality, rather than its "system." Its spokespersons assert beliefs, but they do not present them in any systematic way or subject them to rigorous standards of argument. They address a lay audience for whom the niceties of distinctions, inference, and evidence are not a high priority. They appear as proselytizers seeking converts, not educators promoting understanding.[17] By contrast, the Roman Catholic Church does present its views in a systematic way.[18] Through a series of missives,[19] buttressed by the sophisticated work of a number of moral theologians,[20] it does seek to advance argument and promote understanding.

The most basic tenet of the religious right[21] is that homosexual activity is always immoral, even sinful. Without that foundation, the rest of the edifice cannot be constructed. What are the basic religious propositions needed to support this basic tenet? There are four:

(1) There is a God who cares about the temporal lives and eternal souls of all people—about 6.4 billion at last count. Because He[22] is a caring God, He intervenes in human history: He commands, punishes, and rewards in this world and the next, enters into covenants, demands obedience, entertains petitions (prayers), has a Divine Plan for all persons, and has sent His only son not to judge the world but to save it.[23]

(2) He reveals His nature and His will through divinely inspired Scriptures. His pronouncements, whether given directly (as we are told they were communicated through Moses to the Ancient Israelites) or prompted by the Holy Spirit (as in the case of the Apostle Paul to the Early Christians), are definitive, clear, and unchanging.

(3) Through the Old and New Testament, God has revealed unequivocally that homosexuality is an abomination, interpreted either as a sin or a spiritual or mental sickness.

(4) Faced with the presence of gays and lesbians in our midst and their demands for an inclusive society, the churches must respond in a way that accords with their view of Scriptural authority. For the Catholic hierarchy, gays and lesbians must remain chaste; for evangelicals, parents are assured that there are strategies that will reduce the likelihood that their children will become homosexuals, and should this fate befall them, there is reparative therapy to cure them from their sickness.

The sources for the belief that homosexuality is always immoral are threefold: scriptural and theological, psychological, and prudential. However, the latter two act only in an auxiliary capacity. If you are persuaded by the first, you will find additional comfort in the latter two. If the first fails, the walls of Jericho will crumble. If all three fail as justifications for the moral judgments right wingers make—as I think they do—we might speculate about other kinds of explanations for the attitudes they hold. We could ask whether their "reasons" might be rationalizations for some psychological phenomena that exist just below the surface of their own psyches.

Scriptural and Theological Bases for Moral Disapproval

First, proponents must believe in the existence of God. For atheists and agnostics, their argument has no traction. Second, the nature of the divine needed to anchor the argument is very particular. Only a God who has a personal relationship with believers will suit the purpose. Deists and pantheists would not be impressed. If these two theological premises are not accepted, the rest of the argument falters.

But according to the religious right, God determines what is morally good and bad. He possesses a Divine Plan for us that, fortunately, is fully recorded in the Holy Word. Believers claim to have detailed knowledge of God's plan for us, including our sexuality. Specifically, His approval of human sexual relationships is limited to the union of man and woman in marriage (Genesis 1:27–28; 2:18, 23–24). Sin has warped our perspective of healthy sexuality (2 Peter 2:2–3a; 3:3). Homosexuality is a symptom of our fallen state. The good news is that God's power can bring healing and restoration (Romans 1:18–32). Once healed and restored, gay and lesbian people can enter into heterosexual relationships and, only then, experience the joys of marriage and family.[24]

Problems for members of the religious right break out over their interpretation of Scripture. Their literal understanding of Biblical texts has been subjected to much hermeneutical questioning and argument. To what extent are the selected texts composed with specific cultural or historical contexts in mind?[25] How seriously is the "sin" of homosexual sexuality taken in Old and New Testament passages when compared to others that are considered?[26] Are the texts that are so often cited even about homosexuality?[27] Given that our Western conception—and so our understanding—of homosexuality began to dawn on us only about 150 years ago, could anything in the Scriptures be particularly relevant?[28]

One example will suffice to illustrate the difficulty the religious right has in maintaining its position. In order to hold an absolute moral standard, it must reject any attempt to loosen the stringency of its literalist biblical interpretation. This allows its proponents to claim moral certainty on the issue—that is, that homosexual activity is always an abomination before God and so always a moral transgression. But to generate this conclusion, it must hold that all similar biblical injunctions must be treated in the same manner. The need for consistency lands right wingers with commitments they would rather not have. They criticize liberal Christians for selecting just the passages that promote liberal outcomes and ignoring "inconvenient" texts. However, they engage in the very same practice.

Leviticus 20:13 is often cited to provide moral leverage for condemning homosexuality: "If a man has sexual relations with another man, they have done a disgusting thing, and both shall be put to death. They are responsible for their own death."[29] Members of the religious right appropriate the first half of the first sentence, but they dance gingerly around the second and the last sentence that assigns blame.[30] The chapter begins "The Lord told Moses to say to the people of Israel..." There is no reason for fundamentalists to believe that the command to impose the death penalty is anything other than the Word of God. But if the death penalty prescription is not mandatory, why should the proscription against homosexual relations be considered absolute—unless one has resorted to picking and choosing parts of texts to suit a predetermined view? If the Bible is taken as the final and definitive statement of God's wishes, much vigilante activity is called for.[31]

Alternative Bases for Moral Disapproval

Biblical underpinnings are not convincing to everyone, so other grounds are brought to bear. If sinfulness cannot be proven, perhaps mental illness can. Until 1973, "Homosexuality" could be found as a category of mental disorder in the *Diagnostic and Statistical Manual* (*DSM*) of the American Psychiatric Association (APA). Until that time, the religiously conservative could claim support from psychiatrists and psychologists. But then an APA committee reviewed the scientific literature and consulted with experts in the field. They concluded that "for a mental condition to be considered a psychiatric disorder, it should either regularly cause emotional distress or regularly be associated with clinically significant impairment of social function-ing."[33] Homosexuality in and of itself did not meet either of these criteria. Arguably, gay and lesbian people experience mental illness—perhaps even to a greater degree than heterosexuals—not because they are intrinsically disordered but because of the hostile social environment in which they live. In December 1973, the APA's Board of Trustees deleted homosexuality from its official categorization of mental disor-ders.[34] Officially, then, gay and lesbian people are not mentally ill simply by virtue of being homosexual.[35]

However, the Protestant evangelical and Catholic churches continue to claim that gay and lesbian people suffer from a "disorder."[36] In their own accounts, they do not provide a definition of the kind of disorder they have in mind, and they do not argue for the criteria that would help us identify cases that would count from those that would not. "Disorder" necessarily carries negative connotations and so operates as a prejudicial label in their writing. Because of its semi-clinical overtones, the word appears to justify a bias that one may already have against gay and lesbian people. It certainly does not encourage rational consideration. This "disorder," then, is of a theological kind, the origins of which are metaphysical at best. Apart from using the same word as was once used by mental health practitioners, this concept bears no substantial similarity in meaning to the one once employed in the fields of psychi-atry and psychology, and so these advocates commit what is known in philosophy as the "fallacy of equivocation."[37]

We are left to ask why the APA has not added a new category—"Homophobia"—to its diagnostic list. If "homophobia" can reasonably be defined as "the irrational fear or hatred of gays and lesbians," it would seem to have all the characteristics needed to be a suitable entry, for it designates an irrational attitude that can and does result in violent and anti-social behaviour.[38] Interestingly, George Weinberg, who coined the word "homophobia" in 1969, begins his *Society and the Healthy Homosexual* with this forceful claim: "I would never consider a patient healthy unless he had overcome his prejudice against homosexuality."

Notwithstanding narrowly and arbitrarily interpreted scriptural references, and the influential APA 1973 decision that undermined the force of mental-health argu-ments, the religious right still points to dire consequences of accepting gays and les-bians as fully equal persons for individuals, families, societies, and the whole of Western civilization. For example, in a "Focus on the Family" essay, Don Schmierer claims that homosexuality "involves physical, emotional, and spiritual dangers, such as decreased life expectancy, disease, and high suicide rates."[39] As part of its man-date, the Culture and Family Institute claims that "the homosexual activist move-ment and other forces ... threaten to undermine marriage, family, and religious freedom."[40] In an apocalyptic moment, Pat Robertson told viewers of his TV pro-gram, "The 700 Club," that "the Apostle Paul made it abundantly clear in the Book of Romans that the acceptance of homosexuality is the last step in the decline of Gentile civilization."[41]

The first position rests on a confusion of causes. If it is shown empirically that gays and lesbians have a lower life expectancy and higher suicide rate than similar hetero-sexual populations, it is reasonable to assess the contribution made to this unhappy state of affairs by the very toxic social atmosphere that Schmierer's religiosity promotes.[42] Sexual diseases are rampant in heterosexual as well as in homosexual communities and for many of the same reasons. They can also be ameliorated by some of the same means. Expanding marriage to include same-sex couples would be one such measure. Far from undermining marriage and the family, it would strengthen the institution and increase social stability. Finally, extending human rights to gays and lesbians would hardly diminish religious freedom, though it might rein in some bigotry.[43]

The Problem of Choice

To defend its position, the religious right needs to take a stand on the origins of homosexuality. Despite acknowledging that the scientific evidence is not conclusive, evangelical fundamentalists insist that gays and lesbians in some sense "choose" their "lifestyle." Gays and lesbians, thus, can be held accountable for their orientation. As their "preference" is unnatural and abnormal, they have an obligation to make every effort to become heterosexual.

If gays and lesbians are to be held accountable for their orientation and activity that might flow from it, some degree of freedom of choice must be available to them. Even if it were possible, it hardly seems likely that many people would choose to be gay or lesbian. As Posner puts it so pointedly:

> Given the personal and social disadvantages to which homosexuality subjects a person in our society, the idea that millions of young men and women have chosen it or will choose it in the same fashion in which they might choose a career or a place to live or a political party or even a religious faith seems preposterous.[44]

Both Catholics and Protestant fundamentalists concede that the scientific evidence on the origins of homosexuality is not conclusive. As early as 1976, the Roman Catholic Church thought it could reasonably distinguish between

> homosexuals whose tendency comes from a false education, from a lack of normal sexual development, from habit, from bad example, or from other similar causes, and is transitory or at least not incurable; and homosexuals who are definitively such because of some kind of innate instinct or a pathological constitution judged to be incurable.[45]

The Church did not speculate on the proportions of gays and lesbians that might fall into each category, but it was prepared to contemplate the possibility that some—perhaps most or all—homosexuals are such by virtue of some biological factor. The Church further concedes that reparative therapy is not an option for some. It hastens to add that, in spite of this biological determinism, the sexual acts of homosexuals are "intrinsically disordered and can in no case be approved of."[46] If some gays and lesbians cannot be said to have chosen their orientation, it is within their power to control their actions:

> What, then, are homosexual persons to do who seek to follow the Lord? Fundamentally, they are called to enact the will of God in their life by joining whatever sufferings and difficulties they experience in virtue of their condition to the sacrifice of the Lord's Cross. That Cross, for the believer, is a fruitful sacrifice since from that death come life and redemption. ... It is, in effect, none other than the teaching of Paul the Apostle to the Galatians when he says that... "You cannot belong to Christ unless you crucify all self-indulgent passions and desire..." (5:24). Christians who are homosexual are called, as all of us are, to a chaste life.[47]

CHRISTIAN OPPOSITION TO HOMOSEXUALITY - CHAPTER ELEVEN λ

Protestant fundamentalists bring a touch of American pragmatism to the issue. Though they also acknowledge that the scientific evidence is inconclusive,[48] they proceed nevertheless as if one's sexuality is quite malleable—at least, the sexuality of homosexuals. No one is beyond the reach of salvation. Indeed, they hold out the promise that homosexuality can be prevented with proper parenting[49]; if that fails, gays and lesbians can always be "fixed" by reparative therapy.[50]

Catholics and others who allow for cases of biological determinism, combined with a strong version of the Creator story, create for themselves a minor theological problem. Can God really have created people who in their essential nature are an abomination? Is He without blame for the apparent curse He has inflicted on some of His children? What a strange God! Those who believe that homosexuality is created by parental influences, poor models, gender ambiguity, and the like evade this dilemma.[51] Responsibility, then, falls on social conditions and individual choice. As Esterberg and Longhofer point out:

> In a perverse twist, [these] religious rightists end up (unintentionally) as standard bearers for a constructionist view of sexuality, while many lesbian and gay activists then take up an essentialist position.[52]

Actually, the picture is probably a little more complicated than this. The Protestant right takes a pragmatic, constructionist position on strategic grounds—that is, it permits them to believe that "conversion" to heterosexuality is possible. Should a "gay gene" ever be found, they would be the first to line up on the biological side of the debate and begin counselling gays and lesbians to undergo medical gene manipulation. Sexual-orientation salvation is the goal by whatever means.

There is something in the religious right's antipathy to homosexuality that is reminiscent of pre-Newtonian beliefs about motion. For Aristotle, bodies at rest were regarded as in a natural state. What needed explanation was motion: all instances of motion had to have a "mover." By contrast, Newton postulated two natural states for bodies—motion and rest. When a body that had been moving on a flat surface slowed and came to rest, friction was invoked to account for the change. Were there no friction, the body would never come to rest. Similarly, the religious right believes that only heterosexuality is natural and so it is homosexuality that needs to be explained. But if we postulate that the two states are natural,[53] then neither needs to be explained. Outside of the extraordinary theological apparatus they employ, no one would see the need to change. We need a Newtonian revolution in our thinking about sexuality.

The Inanity of "Lifestyle" Talk

Those on the religious right like to characterize gays and lesbians as having a "lifestyle," rather than a sexual orientation. This helps them maintain the illusion that gays and lesbians have made a choice on a par with deciding to decorate their homes with furnishings from IKEA. To refer to gays and lesbians possessing a lifestyle trivializes central portions of their identity and their relationships. To see how flaccid this word is in this context, take up this challenge: offer a complete description of a heterosexual lifestyle. This is not a difficult assignment; it is an impossible one. The stupidity of using "lifestyle" in this context is immediately revealed. The comedian, George Carlin, offers wise counsel:

> *And you will not hear me referring to anyone's lifestyle. If you want to know what a moronic word "lifestyle" is, all you have to do is realize that in a technical sense Attila the Hun had an active, outdoor lifestyle.*[54]

The second use of the word is much nastier: "lifestyle" acts covertly as a euphemism for sexual activity that members of the religious right would rather not talk about in "polite" society. It suggests that the lives of homosexuals revolve around the pursuit of promiscuous sexual encounters. There are two issues here. First, promiscuity "is not a result of an individual's sexual orientation, but a reflection of an individual's values, beliefs, and personal standards."[55] Second, those on the religious right purport to be appalled by the nature of homosexual sexual activity. But simply to argue "I find 'X' disgusting, therefore 'X' is morally bad" is to commit what is referred to in philosophical ethics as the "is-ought" fallacy—in this case, to argue directly from a psychological state of mind to a moral conclusion.[56] One can be disgusted by something and the reaction need have no moral content. However, it might be worth inquiring whether one's sense of being repelled does have some kind of moral basis. One rightfully recoils at the thought of Auschwitz because what was done on that site was morally horrific, but the place is not the site of immoral events *because* one is repelled. That is, the moral judgment is logically prior to the attitude of disgust that is simply the appropriate emotional response. Kolnai sums up this point neatly:

> *It is certainly true that disgust does not attain normative certainty, as does contempt. Rather, it manifests an intimate intermingling with extra-ethical emotions of taste. In general, it can only serve as a signpost towards a subsequent ethical judgement, and cannot be its immediate determining factor.*[57]

Disgust is more a matter of taste than morals and does not provide us with a reliable moral compass. As to the matter at hand, Quinton reminds us that:

> *In general, full-blooded sexual activity of any kind is not aesthetically suitable for close inspection. Heterosexuals and homosexuals alike adopt ridiculous positions, emit hoarse, inarticulate cries, [and] twist their faces absurdly in the culminating phase of their relations.*[58]

Talk about "lifestyle" should be banished from this discourse as totally unhelpful.

Accounting for Vehemence

What can account for the vehemence of the religious right in condemning homosexuality? After all, other "biblical sins" do not result in calls for such harsh treatment. Boswell observes:

> *The very same books that are thought to condemn homosexual acts condemn hypocrisy in the most strident terms and on greater authority*[59]*; and yet Western society did not create any social taboos against hypocrisy, did not claim that hypocrites were "unnatural," did not segregate them into an oppressed minority, did not enact laws punishing their sin by castration or death.*[60]

Something more than Scriptural authority is needed to explain the repressive behaviour of European and North American states throughout their histories, or as Boswell puts it, "biblical strictures have been employed with great selectivity by all Christian states, and in a historical context what determines the selection is clearly the crucial issue."[61]

The underlying causes of homophobia are little understood. Relatively speaking, they have been subject to very little theoretical and empirical scrutiny.[62] Yet, for many Christians, contemplating homosexuality is a psychic volcano always threatening to explode. Farley speculates that

> the vehemence of the negative judgements that continue to be made regarding homosexual activity and relationships. ... [has] the power of an unreasoned taboo, lodged in and reinforcing a kind of unreflective repulsion that must be addressed if we are to move forward politically on these issues.[63]

I suspect there are deep and pervasive sociological and psychological causes of homophobia.[64] While evangelical Protestants and their Roman Catholic cousins hardly possess a monopoly on them, they are able to offer a degree of respectability to those who feel a need for it.[65] We know that acquiring a homophobic attitude is a learned process. Young people pick it up on school playgrounds, in classrooms, from coaches and teachers, in Bible classes, and on the internet. Homophobia is in the very air they breathe. Efforts in schools to inoculate them against the contagion are vigorously opposed by parent and church groups. Add to this a psychological dimension (that admittedly is little understood) and is it any wonder that a new, deeply homophobic generation arises? This is fertile ground for the predatory religious right to promote its bigoted agenda.

Notes

1. Rueda, (1982), 243.
2. Of course there are exceptions to this generalization—notably, the United Church of Canada, the Society of Friends, and the Unitarian Church. In general, the more theologically liberal a religious community is, the more liberal it will be on gay and lesbian issues. I have restricted this chapter to evangelical Protestant and Roman Catholic churches partly because they have been the most active and vociferous on the issue of homosexuality and partly to keep the length of the chapter manageable. For an excellent survey of the positions of different religions, see Marilyn Bennett Alexander (1998).
3. All provinces now have "sexual orientation" written into their human rights codes so that gays and lesbians are legally protected from discrimination.
4. In a recent example, the Senate gave final reading on April 28, 2004 to Bill 250 that expanded the definition of "identifiable group" to include sexual orientation in the hate propaganda provisions of the Criminal Code (s. 318). It was given royal assent by the Governor General on April 29, 2004 and went into effect immediately. The bill had been opposed earlier in the House of Commons by the Canadian Alliance and a smattering of Conservatives and Liberals. Outside pressure groups that opposed the bill included Focus on the Family (Canada), The Evangelical Fellowship of Canada, Canada Family Action Coalition, and the Canadian Conference of Catholic Bishops.
5. Among the more important cases heard by the Supreme Court of Canada are *Haig* v. *Canada* (1992), 16 C.H.R.R. D/226 (Ont. CA); *Egan* v. *Canada* [1995] 2 S.C.R. 513; *Moore* v. *Canada* (Treasury Board) (1996), 25 C.H.R.R. D/351 (Can. Trib.); *Vriend* v. *Alberta* [1998], 1 S.C.R. 493; *Little Sisters Book and Art Emporium* v. *Canada (Minister of Justice)* [2000], 2 S.C.R. 1120; and *Chamberlain* v. *Surrey School District No. 36* [2002] 4 S.C.R. 710. The narrow split

decision in *Canada (Attorney General)* v. *Mossop* was only a temporary setback. The Parliamentary Research Branch (PRB) of Canada's Library of Parliament has prepared a valuable survey of legal cases and government legislation entitled "Sexual Orientation and Legal Rights" (2003) which is available at <http://www.parl.gc.ca/information/library/PRBpubs/921-e.htm>.

6. Most Christian churches in North America forbid the ordination of gay and lesbian clergy. However, according to Andy Lang, managing editor of the United Church of Christ's "United Church News–Online Edition," some 24 Protestant churches in Continental Europe permit ordination. See his June 2002 "Global Trend: World's Oldest Protestant Churches Now Ordain Gays and Lesbians" at <http://www.ucc.org/ucnews/jun02/trend.htm>.

7. See the Anglican Church's press release of October 30, 1997 entitled "Human Sexuality: A Statement by the Anglican Bishops of Canada—1997." The church recalled its statement of 1979 in which it rejected "the blessing of homosexual unions" and permitted the ordination of gay and lesbian clergy, provided they inform their bishop of their sexual orientation and promise to abstain from all homosexual acts. The church continued to study the question of homosexuality in the larger context of human sexuality; the tone of its 1997 statement is conciliatory and the church remained open to continued dialogue while it searched for wider consensus. However, it retained its original position on holy matrimony and on the ordination of gay and lesbian clerics. Consensus clearly had not been reached by June 2001 when the New Westminster diocese's governing body, the synod, voted 63% in favour of blessing gay and lesbian unions. The decision caught the attention of Archbishop Carey ("Gay Unions a Threat to Church, Leader Warns," *Globe and Mail*, May 30, 2003, p. A8) and some other communions, especially that of Nigeria. See also the uproar over the ordination of Bishop Gene Robinson in New Hampshire on March 7, 2004, the first openly gay bishop in all of Christendom, and the failed attempt by the Bishop of Oxford in June 2003 to install Dr. Jeffrey John as Bishop of Reading. More recently, the Anglican Church of Canada voted to delay a decision on whether to permit the blessing of same-sex marriage and called, instead, for a two-year study on whether same-sex rituals are "a matter of doctrine" (Canadian Press, June 3, 2004).

8. For example, at its 2004 Assembly, the Baptist Convention of Ontario and Quebec relied on a 1988 resolution that stated that "homosexual behaviour is unacceptable in the sight of God, since it is contrary to Scriptural principles of morality and family life." It then passed a recommendation urging its members "to oppose all efforts by any court or legislative body to validate or legalize same-sex marriages."

9. Both the Lutheran Church–Canada and the Evangelical Lutheran Church of Canada rely on 1993 convention resolutions on homosexuality. In the first case, the church declared that "homosexuality is a distortion of God's intention for the human race, and homosexual thoughts, desires, words, and deeds are contrary to God's will"; in the second, the church reaffirmed its bishops' statement that "a self-declared and practicing homosexual person is not to be approved for ordination and, if already ordained, is not to be recommended for call."

10. In 1997, the General Assembly of the Presbyterian Church in Canada passed Overture No. 15, which asked a special committee on sexual orientation "to clarify the limits of the role that homosexual and lesbian people play within The Presbyterian Church in Canada" (*A&P* p. 503). Six years later, the committee submitted its final report to the 129th General Assembly (2003). The report was referred to other committees. A recommendation to encourage congregations and sessions to use the study guide, *Listening … Understanding Human Sexuality*, was defeated. The denomination will not be making significant changes any time soon. Presumably, the formation of the subcommittee arose out of the acrimonious debate in the 1996 General Assembly over the efforts by the congregation of St. Andrews Presbyterian Church in Lachine, Quebec, to ordain Darryl MacDonald, the first openly gay candidate for ministry in the church's history. See "Church Struggles With Gay Ordination" and "Presbyterians Reject Congregation's Bid to Hire Gay Minister," *Globe and Mail*, May 13 and June 11, 1996 respectively.

11. See reports of the 2004 United Methodist Church General Conference in which the church reaffirmed its stand that it "does not condone the practice of homosexuality and considers the practice incompatible with Christian teachings" and that "avowed practicing homosexuals are not

to be accepted as candidates, ordained as ministers, or appointed to serve in the United Methodist Church." For a very useful summary of struggles within Protestant denominations in the United States, see Cadge (2002).

12. The Church has been active in attempting to influence the political process. See, for example, "Presentation by the Canadian Conference of Catholic Bishops (CCCB) to the House of Commons Standing Committee on Justice and Human Rights on the Discussion Paper Marriage and Legal Recognition of Same-Sex Unions" (February 13, 2003); "Letter from the CCCB, President Bishop Jacques Berthelet, C.S.V., to Prime Minister Jean Chretien Regarding Marriage and Same-Sex Unions" (June 19, 2003); and "CCCB Statement on the Tabling of Draft Legislation by the Federal Government Regarding Marriage" (July 17, 2003). See also the attempts of Bishop Fred Henry of Calgary to bully the Prime Minister by suggesting that he "risks burning in hell if he makes same-sex marriage legal in Canada" ("Chrétien's 'Morally Grave' Error," *Globe and Mail*, July 31, 2003). Meanwhile, in the United States, the Catholic Church was making similar moves. On September 10, 2003 the Administrative Committee of the U.S. Conference of Catholic Bishops released a statement entitled "Promote, Preserve, Protect Marriage," calling for a constitutional amendment to protect "the unique social and legal status of marriage." The Church thus lined up with Republican President George Bush, though quite possibly for different reasons. Speaking from the Roosevelt Room in the White House on February 24, 2004, President Bush warned, "If we are to prevent the meaning of marriage from being changed forever [by activist judges], our nation must enact a constitutional amendment to protect marriage in America."

13. At its June meetings, the Southern Baptist Convention's anti-gay and anti-lesbian resolutions are almost an annual event: "On Same-Sex Marriage" (2003), "On the Judicial Oppression of the Boy Scouts of America" (2000), "On the Threat of New Age Globalism" (2000), "Resolution on President Clinton's Gay and Lesbian Pride Month Proclamation" (1999), "Resolution on the President's Executive Order on Homosexual Federal Employees" (1998), "Resolution on Domestic Partner Benefits" (1997), "Resolution on Homosexual Marriage" (1996), "Resolution on Disney Company Policy" (1996), "Resolution on Homosexuality, Military Service, and Civil Rights" (1993), "Resolution on Support of the Boy Scouts of America" (1992), "Resolution on the Use of Government Funds to Encourage Immoral Sexual Behavior" (1991), "Resolution on the White House Conference on the Family" (1980), "Resolutions on Homosexuality" (1988, 1985, 1980, and 1977), "Resolution on Human Rights and Certain Misapplications" (1977), "Resolution on Religious Liberty and Employment Practices" (1977).

14. For example, Rev. Donald Wildmon, Chairman and Founder of the American Family Association (AFA) claims that "the Bush administration is opening its arms to homosexual activists who have been working diligently to overthrow the traditional views of Western civiliza- tion regarding human sexuality, marriage, and family. The AFA would never support the policies of a political party that embraced the homosexual movement. Period." (April 16, 2001, AFA Press Release) The President of the American Center for Law and Justice is also the founder of the "700 Club" and the Christian Coalition. The ACLJ's director, Jay Sekulow, is quoted as ask- ing, "Can you imagine, that in public schools of America today, students are being taught that homosexual conduct, which in many states is still deemed illegal, is not only a viable alternative lifestyle, but is actually equal to heterosexual relationships?" (January 2, 1997, *Danbury News- Times*) The founders of the Alliance Defense Fund include Bill Bright, founder of Campus Crusade for Christ, Larry Burkett, founder of Christian Financial Concepts, Rev. James Dobson, founder of Focus on the Family, Rev. D. James Kennedy, founder of Coral Ridge Ministries, Marlin Maddoux, President of International Christian Media, and Rev. Don Wildmon, founder of the AFA. They claim that one of the two issues that unite the founders is "their work against ... gays and lesbians. They are particularly tireless in attacking any and every attempt by gays and lesbians to have families, domestic partnership or civil unions, or be protected from discrimina- tion in employment or housing." The founder and chairman of the Traditional Values Coalition and an aide to Pat Robertson in 1987, Rev. Louis Sheldon, fears that "[a]s homosexuals continue to make inroads into public schools, more children will be molested and indoctrinated into the

world of homosexuality. Many of them will die in that world" (In "Homosexuals Recruit Public School Children." Special report, Volume 18, Number 11, n.d.).

The three most active lobby groups in Canada are the Canada Family Action Coalition (CFAC), Focus on the Family–Canada, and REAL (Realistic, Equal, Active for Life) Women of Canada. CFAC's co-founder and executive director has a diversified background as a family and addictions counsellor, dean of a Bible college, and associate pastor. The organization's president, Dr. Charles McVety, is president of Canada Christian College in Toronto. CFAC was founded in early 1997 "with a vision to see Judeo-Christian moral principles restored in Canada." Its policies and statements are to be "founded upon the Bible." Focus on the Family–Canada, an off-shoot of the American organization, has been running radio spots and display ads in 26 Canadian newspapers promoting the view that marriage means the union of a man and woman. The ad copy reads "Traditional marriage–if you believe in it, protect it." According to Derek Rogusky, the group's vice-president for family policy and director of research, the campaign had cost about $600,000 by the third week of the 2004 federal election campaign (Jeff Sallot, *Globe and Mail*, May 19, 2004, p. A6). REAL Women are active in the courts and the election campaigns in attempts to ensure that elected MPs support the traditional definition of marriage. To this end, on July 7, 2003, they announced their intention to apply for Leave to Appeal to the Supreme Court of Canada from the Ontario Court of Appeal's decision on same-sex marriage. One question in their survey for candidates in the 2004 election reads: "If elected, would you support Parliament invoking Section 33 of the Charter of Rights, the notwithstanding clause, to preserve and protect the definition of marriage as the union of one man and one woman?" Clearly, the correct answer from their point of view is "yes." For an interesting discussion of these groups, see Herman (1994).

15. Kristen Esterberg and Jeffery Longhofer, "Researching the Radical Right: Responses to Anti-Lesbian/Gay Initiatives," 184.

16. For a chilling historical account of how gay and lesbian people have been treated throughout the history of Western civilization, see Crompton (2003). For an overview of the stigma, prejudice, and violence directed against gays and lesbians in the United States at present, see Herek, 1991.

17. See, for example, "It is easier to nauseate than educate," uttered by Tony Marco, co-founder of Colorado for Family Values on his group's publicity tactics for getting the state's anti-gay amendment passed. This quotation was published in "The Freedom Watch," *The Citizens Project Newsletter* 2, no. 2 (April–May 1993) and reproduced in *The Gay Almanac* (1996).

18. However one assesses the Roman Catholic position on homosexuality in the end, one can say that its proponents strive for higher levels of rational coherence. Sidney Callahan (2001, p. 202) claims correctly, I believe, that "[t]he interlocking assumptions and fundamental presuppositions that undergird current Roman Catholic teaching on sexuality are a tightly wrapped package…" though she concludes in the final analysis, "they are not rationally convincing, morally helpful, or theologically adequate."

19. In the last quarter of a century, the Church has set out its views on homosexuality in four major documents: (1) *Personae Humana-Declaration on Certain Questions Concerning Sexual Ethics* (1976); (2) *Letter to the Bishops of the Catholic Church on the Pastoral Care of Homosexual Persons* (1986); (3) *Some Considerations Concerning the Response to Legislative Proposals on the Non-Discrimination of Homosexual Persons* (1992); and (4) *Considerations Regarding Proposals to Give Recognition to Unions between Homosexual Persons* (2003).

20. In particular, see the work of John Finnis, Robert P. George, Germain Grisez, and William E. May. Challenging criticisms have been mounted by Stephen Macedo, Charles E. Curran, Mark Strasser, and Judith Plaskow.

21. No one term completely captures the many differences among the religious institutions and agencies discussed in this chapter. Where these are significant, I point them out. Churches vary in the way they promulgate their version of the faith: for example, Presbyterians vote on motions at their annual general assemblies; the Vatican publishes authoritative letters to its bishops;

evangelical Protestants are activists who make constant use of television and the internet. But despite these rather superficial differences, they all subscribe to the four tenets I have postulated. For convenience, I refer to these conservative religious institutions and agencies as the "religious right."

22. In these circles, God is always referred to in the masculine form.

23. "For God so loved the world, that He gave His only begotten Son, that whosoever believeth in Him should not perish, but have everlasting life." *The Holy Bible* (1953), John 3:16.

24. The Focus on the Family website offers links to Exodus International, "a coalition of Christian ministries that offers support to those seeking to overcome homosexuality" and the National Association for Research and Therapy of Homosexuality (NARTH) that claims to be "an organization of nearly 700 professionals who treat homosexuality." This website also displays the story of Anne and John Paulk, the poster couple for reparative therapy, who through the services of Exodus International claim to have overcome their homosexuality and eventually married. ("In 1982, Anne Paulk gave her life to Jesus Christ and began trying to leave lesbianism behind. This quest for answers led her to Exodus International in 1988...") They are the joint authors of *Love Won Out: How God's Love Helped Two People Leave Homosexuality and Find Each Other* (1999).

25. White, 2001, pp. 134–149; Malina, 2001, pp. 152ff; D'Angelo, 2001, p. 193.

26. Boswell, 1980, p. 7; Nilson, 2001, p. 64, pp. 66–67; D'Angelo, p.178.

27. Wink, 1999, pp. 33–49; Nilson, 2001, p. 81; Grippo, 1988, pp. 33–39.

28. Wink, 1999, p. 36; Hanigan, 1988, pp. 40–41; and Di Vito, 2001.

29. *Good News Bible*, Leviticus 20:13. Interestingly, the "companion piece," found in Leviticus 18:22, is satisfied to remark simply that "God hates that." The death penalty is not mentioned.

30. For example, in response to *Listening … Understanding Human Sexuality*, a study guide produced by The Presbyterian Church in Canada's General Assembly Special Committee on Sexual Orientation, the minister of St. Andrews Church, Moncton, New Brunswick, conveniently interpreted the recommendation for the death penalty metaphorically: "Asked if it wasn't 'extreme' to quote Leviticus 20:13 which prescribes death for men having sex with each other, Rev. Martin Kreplin said the verse indicates the seriousness with which God takes the matter of homosexuality" (*The Presbyterian Record*, June 2003)! Cp. Wink, 1999, p. 35.

31. The Biblical literalist has to come to grips with a long list of offences for which the God of the Old Testament seeks the death penalty. In Leviticus alone, death is prescribed for parents who offer their children to "Molech" (Leviticus 20.2), for cursing your mother or father (Leviticus 2:11), for incest with your mother, mother-in-law, or daughter-in-law (Leviticus 20:11–12), for bestiality (Leviticus 20:16–16), and for anyone who "consults the spirits of the dead" (Leviticus 20:27).

32. Malina (2001, fn. 7, pp. 172–73) demonstrates that in one place or another in the Old Testament "the death penalty attaches to all of the Ten Commandments; the one exception is coveting (i.e., stealing). The Book of Deuteronomy contains some of the more extreme recommendations to be found in the Bible. Moses was obliged to convey to the Israelites all that the Lord had commanded him to tell them. Among the examples is this one: If you have a son who is stubborn and rebellious, who wastes money and is a drunkard, and who will not obey you though you punish him, you are to take him to the leaders of your town where he is to stand trial. If found guilty, 'the men of the city are to stone him to death'." (Deuteronomy 21:18–21). In another passage (Deuteronomy 25: 11–12), "if two men are fighting, and the wife of one of them intervenes by grabbing the genitals of her husband's adversary, you are to show her no mercy, and cut off her hand."

33. American Psychiatric Association, 1996.

34. The American Psychological Association followed suit in 1975 as did the American Medical Association: "AMA policy is unequivocal—discrimination based on sexual orientation is improper and unacceptable by any part of the federation of medicine" (American Medical Association, Reports of Board of Trustees, Annual Meeting of the House of Delegates, June 1993). As to how homosexuality came to be classified as an illness in the first place, see Vern Bullough (1974).

35. For a survey of relevant research, see Crawford and Zamboni (2001) and, in particular, their judgment on the Cameron and Cameron studies (p. 242).

36. See "Dr. Dobson's Study" at <http://www.family.org/docstudy/newsletters/a021043.cfm>: "What do we know about this disorder? Well, first, it is a disorder, despite the denials of the American Psychiatric Association." Dobson, who heads Focus on the Family, charges that the APA succumbed to "great political pressure from gays and lesbians"—some of whom, he exclaims as if surprised, are psychiatrists! The language emanating from the Vatican is especially aggressive. In its "On the Pastoral Care of Homosexual Persons" (1986), homosexual actions are described as "intrinsically disordered," and the tendency towards these actions is judged "an intrinsic moral evil." Practicing homosexuals are "exclude[d] from the People of God" and in need of a "conversion from evil." What is required of them is to "crucify all [their] self-indulgent passions and desires," to "carry the cross," and to lead a chaste life.

37. The fallacy of equivocation is committed when someone uses the same word in different meanings in an argument, in such a way that the argument would be correct only if the word actually meant the same each time around.

38. In a 1969 study, the American psychologist George Weinberg was the first to use the word "homophobia." He employed it again in his *Society and the Healthy Homosexual* (1972) where he defined it as "the fear expressed by heterosexuals of being in the presence of homosexuals, and the loathing that [some] homosexual persons have for themselves." The latter part of the definition refers to "internalized homophobia." For an extended discussion of homophobia, see Martin Kantor (1998). For definitions of homophobia, see Coleman (1995), 134; Kosnik et al. (1977), 270, n. 146; Posner (1992), 292; Berube (1990), 264; and Hopkins (1998), 172ff.

39. Quoted from the Focus on the Family website at
<http://www.family.org/fofmag/pp/a0024031.cfm>

40. Quoted from the Culture and Family Institute website at
<http://cultureandfamily.org/about/>

41. Thomas B. Edsall, *The Washington Post* (June 10, 1998). Patty Silverman, a Christian Broadcasting Network spokeswoman, confirmed the accuracy of the transcript of Robertson's text for Edsall and supplied a page from Robertson's *Answers to 200 of Life's Most Probing Questions* in which he wrote: "The Bible says that because of certain abominations such as homosexuality, a land shall vomit out its inhabitants... . From a biblical standpoint, the rise of homosexuality is a sign that a society is in the last stages of decay."

42. For a brief summary of recent research, see Tori and DeAngelis, "New Data on Lesbian, Gay and Bisexual Mental Health: New Findings Overturn Previous Beliefs," *Monitor on Psychology* 33, no. 2 (February 2002) (available at <http://www.apa.org/monitor/feb02/lgtoc.html>). The pioneering work was done by Evelyn Hooker in "The Adjustment of the Male Overt Homosexual," *Journal of Projective Techniques* 21 (1957): 18–31. For more recent, extended discussions, see J. Gonsiorek (1991) and J.S. Bohan (1996).

43. The most extreme example would be the utterances and antics of Rev. Fred ("God hates fags") Phelps, minister of Westboro Baptist Church in Topeka, Kansas.

44. Posner (1992), 296–97.

45. Sacred Congregation for the Doctrine of the Faith, *Personae Humana–Declaration on Certain Questions Concerning Sexual Ethics, Origins* 5 (1976), viii.

46. Ibid.

47. Congregation for the Doctrine of the Faith, "Letter to the Bishops of the Catholic Church on the Pastoral Care of Homosexual Persons" (1986), 12.

48. "No one can say definitely what causes a person to be homosexual. We have to acknowledge that there could be inheritable tendencies ... in some individuals. There is no proof of such influence to this point, but we can't rule it out in specific cases... . While homosexuality and lesbianism [*sic*] are not exclusively induced by heredity, it is important to emphasize that it often occurs in those who did not choose it." Dr. James Dobson, "Website of Focus on the Family," <http://www.family.org/docstudy>.

49. Elsewhere, Dobson does claim to know what causes a man to be attracted to the same sex: "Chapter 9 of my latest book, *Bringing Up Boys* (2001) provides a definitive explanation, I believe, regarding the origins of homosexuality." He then quotes at length from Joseph Nicolosi who in Dobson's estimation is "the foremost authority on the prevention and treatment of homosexuality today." Nicolosi (2002) believes the role of the father in his son's development into heterosexual masculinity is [...] critical ("Mothers make boys. Fathers make men."). Nicolosi claims that there is "a high correlation between feminine behavior in boyhood and adult homosexuality." Thus, "the boy's father has his part to do. He needs to mirror and affirm his son's maleness. He can play rough-and-tumble games with his son, in ways that are decidedly different from the games he would play with a little girl. He can help his son learn to throw and catch a ball. He can teach him to pound a square wooden peg into a square hole in a pegboard. He can even take his son into the shower, where the boy cannot help but notice that Dad has a penis, just like his, only bigger." All quotations are taken from <http://www.family.org/docstudy>.

50. See, for example, Joseph Nicolosi (1991). Dr. Nicolosi is also president of the National Association for Research and Therapy of Homosexuality (NARTH) which is based in Encino, California. See also Exodus International at <http://www.exodusintl.org>.

51. "God is infinitely just. I don't believe he would speak of homosexuality in the Scriptures as an abominable sin and list it among the most despicable of human behaviors if men and women bore no responsibility for engaging in it (see Corinthians 6:9–10). That is not how He does his business." Dr. James Dobson, "A Website of Focus on the Family"
<http://www.family.org/docstudy>.

52. Esterberg and Longhofer (1998), 194. For extended discussions of the essentialist and constructivist positions, see Davison (1991) and Stein (1999), as well as Haldeman (1999) who claims that "[e]ssentialism is the very cornerstone by which LGB people have defined and protected themselves" (p. 58).

53. This is much oversimplified, but it is sufficient to make the point about the religious right. Human sexuality is much more variegated than is represented by postulating simply two orientations.

54. Carlin, 1990.

55. *What We Wish We Had Known* (2001), 18.

56. To fill out the syllogism, one would have to provide a major premise—something like, "Everything I find disgusting is morally wrong" or "Everything anyone finds disgusting is morally wrong." While these premises would ensure logical validity, they create very serious problems for moral argument. See also, Posner (1992), 300ff. Quinton (1998), 252, rightly regards the "argument from disgust" as the "argument of last resort."

57. Kolnai (2004), 83.

58. Quinton (1998), 253.

59. For the texts Boswell would refer to, see the Old Testament: Job 8:13; 13:16; 15:34; 17:8; 20:5; 27:8; 34:30; 36:13–14; Psalms 35:16; Proverbs 11:9; Isaiah 10:6; 32:6; 33:14; and Jeremiah 23:15; and the New Testament: Matthew 6:2, 5, 16; 7:3–5; 15:7–9; 16:3; 22:15,18; 23:13–33; 24:50–51; Mark 7:6–13; Luke 6:41–42; 11:44; 12:56; 13:15; I Timothy 4:2; James 3:17–18; and I Peter 2:1–2.

60. Boswell (1980), 7.

61. Ibid.

62. Compare, for example, the almost endless studies that have been conducted on gays and lesbians with those conducted on their oppressors. Why this is so would be an interesting study in the sociology of knowledge.

63. Farley (1998), 102.

64. For a useful, if brief, exploration of some starting places, see Hopkins, 1998.

65. See Rueda (1982), 242 ff.

References

Alexander, Marilyn Bennett. 1998. "Religion and Spirituality." In Neil Schlager (ed.), *Gay and Lesbian Almanac*. New York: St. James Press.

American Psychiatric Association. 1996. "Gay and Lesbian Issues—Background and Ordering Information." Available at <http://www.psych.org/public_info/homose~1.cfm

Berube, Allan. 1990. *Coming Out Under Fire: The History of Gay Men and Women in World War Two*. New York: The Free Press.

Bohan, Janis S. 1996. *Psychology and Sexual Orientation: Coming to Terms*. New York: Routledge.

Bohan, Janis S. and Glenda M. Russell. 1999. *Conversations about Psychology and Sexual Orientation*. New York: New York University Press.

Boswell, John. 1980. *Christianity, Social Tolerance, and Homosexuality: Gay People in Western Europe from the Beginning of the Christian Era to the Fourteenth Century*. Chicago: University of Chicago Press.

Bullough, Vern. 1974. "Homosexuality and the Medical Model." *Journal of Homosexuality* 1, no. 1: 99–110.

Cadge, Wendy. 2002. "Vital Conflicts: The Mainline Denominations Debate Homosexuality." In Robert Wuthnow and John H. Evans (eds.), *The Quiet Hand of God: Faith-based Activism and the Public Role of Mainline Protestantism*. Berkeley, CA: University of California Press.

Callahan, Sidney. 2001. "Homosexuality, Moral Theology, and Scientific Evidence." In Patricia Beattie Jung with Joseph Andrew Coray (eds.), *Sexual Diversity and Catholicism*. Collegeville, MN: The Liturgical Press.

Carlin, George. 1990. *Parental Advisory: Explicit Lyrics*. Audio CD. Atlantic.

Coleman, Gerald D. 1995. *Homosexuality: Catholic Teaching and Pastoral Practice*. New York: Paulist Press.

Crawford, Isaiah and Brian D. Zamboni. 2001. "Informing the Debate on Homosexuality." In Patricia Beattie Jung with Joseph Andrew Coray (eds.), *Sexual Diversity and Catholicism*. Collegeville, MN: The Liturgical Press.

Crompton, Louis. 2003. *Homosexuality & Civilization*. Cambridge, MA: Belknap Press of Harvard University Press.

D'Angelo, Mary Rose. 2001. "Perfect Fear Casteth Out Love: Reading, Citing, and Rape." In Patricia Beattie Jung with Joseph Andrew Coray (eds.), *Sexual Diversity and Catholicism*. Collegeville, MN: The Liturgical Press.

Davison, Gerard C. 1991. "Constructionism and Morality in Therapy for Homosexuality." In John Gonsiorek and James D. Weinrich (eds.), *Homosexuality: Research Implications for Public Policy*. Newbury Park, CA: Sage Publications.

Di Vito, Robert A. 2001. "Questions about the Construction of (Homo)sexuality: Same-Sex Relations in the Hebrew Bible." In Patricia Beattie Jung with Joseph Andrew Coray (eds.), *Sexual Diversity and Catholicism*. Collegeville, MN: The Liturgical Press.

Dobson, James. 2001. *Bringing Up Boys: Practical Advice and Encouragement for Those Shaping the Next Generation of Men*. Carol Stream, IL: Tyndale House Publishers.

Esterberg, Kristen and Jeffery Longhofer. 1998. "Researching the Radical Right: Responses to Anti-Lesbian/Gay Initiatives." In Janice L. Ristock and Catherine G. Taylor (eds.), *Inside the Academy and Out: Lesbian/Gay/Queer Studies and Social Action*. Toronto: University of Toronto Press.

Farley, Margaret. 1998. "Response to James Hannigan and Charles Curran." In Saul Olyan and Martha Nussbaum (eds.), *Sexual Orientation and Human Rights in American Religious Discourse*. New York and Oxford: Oxford University Press.

Gay Almanac. 1996. Compiled by the National Museum and Archive of Lesbian and Gay History: A Program of the Lesbian and Gay Community Services Center (New York). New York: Berkley Books.

Gonsiorek, John. 1991. "The Empirical Basis for the Demise of the Illness Model of Homosexuality." In John Gonsiorek and James D. Weinrich (eds.), *Homosexuality: Research Implications for Public Policy*. Newbury Park, CA: Sage Publications.

Good News Bible. 1984. Toronto: Canadian Bible Society.

Grippo, Dan. 1988. "The Vatican Can Slight Scripture for Its Purpose." In Jeannine Gramick and Pat Furey (eds.), *The Vatican and Homosexuality*. New York: Crossroad.

Haldeman, Douglas. 1999. "The Best of Both Worlds: Essentialism, Social Constructivism, and Clinical Practice." In Janis S. Bohan and Glenda M. Russell (eds.), *Conversations about Psychology and Sexual Orientation*. New York: New York University Press.

Hanigan, James P. 1988. *Homosexuality: The Test Case for Christian Sexual Ethics*. New York: Paulist Press.

Herek, Gregory M. 1991. "Stigma, Prejudice, and Violence against Lesbians and Gay Men." In John Gonsiorek and James D. Weinrich (eds.), *Homosexuality: Research Implications for Public Policy*. Newbury Park, CA: Sage Publications.

Herman, Didi. 1994. "Normalcy on the Defensive: New Christian Right Sexual Politics." In Didi Herman, *Rights of Passage: Struggles for Lesbian and Gay Legal Equality*. Toronto: University of Toronto Press.

Holy Bible. 1953. King James Version. New York: Thomas Nelson.

Hopkins, Patrick D. 1998. "Gender Treachery: Homophobia, Masculinity, and Threatened Identities." In Naomi Zack, Laurie Shrage and Crispin Sartwell (eds.), *Race, Class, Gender, and Sexuality: The Big Questions*. Malden, MA: Blackwell Publishers.

Hunt, Mary E. 2001. "Catholic Lesbian Feminist Theology." In Patricia B. Jung and Joseph A Coray (eds.), *Sexual Diversity and Catholicism: Toward the Development of a Moral Theology*. Collegeville, MN: The Liturgical Press.

Kantor, Martin. 1998. *Homophobia: Description, Development, and Dynamics of Gay Bashing*. Westport, CT: Praeger.

Kolnai, Aurel. 2004. *On Disgust*. Barry Smith and Carolyn Korsmeyer (eds). Chicago: Open Court.

Kosnik, Anthony et al. 1977. *Human Sexuality: New Directions in American Catholic Thought*. New York: Paulist Press.

MacDougall, Bruce. 1998. "Silence in the Classroom: Limits on Homosexual Expression and Visibility in Education and the Privileging of Homophobic Religious Ideology," *Saskatchewan Law Review* 41: 61 (at note 166).

Malina, Bruce J. 2001. "The New Testament and Homosexuality." In Patricia B. Jung and Joseph A Coray (eds.), *Sexual Diversity and Catholicism: Toward the Development of a Moral Theology*. Collegeville, MN: The Liturgical Press.

Nicolosi, Joseph. 1991. *Reparative Therapy of Male Homosexuality*. Northvale, NJ: Jason Aronson, Inc.

Nicolosi, Joseph and Linda Ames. 2002. *A Parent's Guide to Preventing Homosexuality*. Downers Grove, IL: InterVarsity Press.

Nilson, Jon. 2001. "The Church and Homosexuality: A Longerian Approach." In Patricia B. Jung and Joseph A Coray (eds.), *Sexual Diversity and Catholicism: Toward the Development of a Moral Theology*. Collegeville, MN: The Liturgical Press.

Nussbaum, Martha. 1999. *Sex and Social Justice*. New York: Oxford University Press.

Olyan, Saul and Martha Nussbaum (eds.). 1998. *Sexual Orientation and Human Rights in American Religious Discourse*. New York: Oxford University Press.

Paulk, Anne and John. 1999. *Love Won Out: How God's Love Helped Two People Leave Homosexuality and Find Each Other*. Carol Stream, IL: Tyndale House Publishers.

Posner, Richard A. 1992. *Sex and Reason*. Cambridge, MA: Harvard University Press.

Quinton, Anthony. 1998. "Homosexuality." In Anthony Quinton, *From Wodehouse to Wittgenstein: Essays*. New York: St. Martin's Press.

Rueda, Enrique. 1982. *The Homosexual Network: Private Lives and Public Policy*. Old Greenwich, CT: The Devin Adair Company.

Stein, Edward. 1999. "Essentialism and Constructionism about Sexual Orientation" and "Sexual Orientation and Choice." In Edward Stein, *The Mismeasure of Desire: The Science, Theory, and Ethics of Sexual Orientation*. New York: Oxford University Press.

Triana, Cristina L.H. 2001. "Papal Ideals, Marital Realities: One View from the Ground." In Patricia Beattie Jung with Joseph Andrew Coray (eds.), *Sexual Diversity and Catholicism*. Collegeville, MN: The Liturgical Press.

Weinberg, George H. 1972. *Society and the Healthy Homosexual*. New York, St. Martin's Press.

White, Leland. 2001. "Romans 1:26–27: The Claim that Homosexuality is Unnatural." In Patricia Beattie Jung with Joseph Andrew Coray (eds.), *Sexual Diversity and Catholicism*. Collegeville, MN: The Liturgical Press.

What We Wish We Had Known. Prepared by the First Tuesday Group, The Presbyterian Church Mt. Kisco, New York. Available at <http://www.mkpc.org/Blue_Book_2001.pdf>.

Wink, Walter. 1999. "Homosexuality and the Bible." In Walter Wink (ed.), *Homosexuality and Christian Faith*. Minneapolis, MN: Fortress Press.

12

A Queer Reading of the Swift Current Hockey Scandal Through Representations of Family Dysfunction and Youth Innocence

Debra Shogan

IN THIS CHAPTER, I FIRST READ OR INTERPRET NEWSPAPER representations of Swift Current as a dysfunctional family created by a story about sexual abuse that highlights notions of complicity, duplicity, and innocence. Next, in order to confound and confront these representations, I intervene with my own experiences as a queer youth who lived in Swift Current in the 1950s and 1960s, during which time I was often enamoured by adults who were my mentors. By interjecting some of my experiences, I hope to disrupt the story of Swift Current as a dysfunctional family, as well as open up notions of authority, the innocence of youth, and sexual abuse to other possibilities. I offer my experiences not to assert the truth of these things, but to make a deconstructive move by applying a different or "queer" reading of a set of meanings to Swift Current and the relationships of the people who live and have lived there.

In his provocative book, *Erotic Innocence*, James Kincaid (1998) explores why certain stories and not others are generated about sexual abuse of children and youth. It is not, as Kincaid emphasizes, that sexual abuse of children and youth is unreal. Rather, what we understand as the reality of abuse is informed by cultural stories about youth innocence and youth sexuality. Central to these stories is the idea that sexual abuse of children and youth is "a clearly defined, discernible, marginal activity engaged in by others who can be (along with their acts) identified and punished, maybe even eliminated altogether" (Kincaid, 1998, p. 232).

The clearly defined "reality" of sexual abuse that is of interest to me in this chapter is the story of sexual abuse in dysfunctional families, in which family members are thought to assume particular, definable roles that contribute to the abuse. I am interested in how representations by the popular media of the sexual abuse scandal involving Graham James, former coach of the Swift Current Broncos Junior Hockey team, relied on dominant cultural stories about the definability of sexual abuse, the innocence of children and youth, and about sexual abuse in dysfunctional families.[1] I focus on how newspaper accounts constructed meaning about the events, people, and place associated with the scandal and how these accounts were based on a pervasive cultural narrative that gave "form to ... our ways of seeing children, sexuality, and transgression" (Kincaid, 1998, p. 5). Demonstrating how the media represented the scandal is not intended as a denial of events that took place in Swift Current. Rather, it is an attempt to make apparent how these representations made sense in the context of stories which render all young people as innocent and naïve, and which portrays sexual abuse as completely understandable within dysfunctional families.

Graham James began his coaching career in Manitoba in the late 1970s and by the beginning of the 1980s he had become a Junior A hockey coach. He first encountered Sheldon Kennedy at a hockey school in 1982 when Kennedy was 13 years old. In 1984, Graham James recruited Kennedy to his Winnipeg team and, when this team was moved to Moose Jaw, James arranged to have Kennedy move with him. According to Kennedy, James began sexual contact with him not long after his arrival in Winnipeg. While in Moose Jaw, the expectation that Kennedy would go to James's apartment every Tuesday and Thursday began and continued until Kennedy was 19 years old.

James was dismissed from the Moose Jaw team for suspected improprieties that were only revealed once the abuse story broke. He moved Kennedy with him to Winnipeg for a short time and then in 1986 he became the head coach of the Swift Current Broncos. He ensured that Kennedy joined him there. In 1986, a bus accident killed four of the Bronco players and James was credited with helping the surviving players through the ordeal (Robinson, 1998, p. 160). In 1989, the Swift Current Broncos won the Memorial Cup with the most successful record ever in the Canadian Junior Hockey League. Sheldon Kennedy had outstanding seasons both in 1988 and in 1989 and was named to the national junior team in 1988.

Kennedy was drafted by the Detroit Red Wings in 1989 and acquired a reputation as someone emotionally out of control. He was convicted of reckless driving and charged with drug possession, and he was traded a number of times. Meanwhile in Swift Current, James continued his success as a winning coach and his popularity as a colourful personality. However, at the end of the 1993–94 season, James's contract was not renewed. He subsequently appeared in Calgary where he became part-owner, general manager, and head coach of the Calgary Hitmen (Robinson, 1998, p. 164). In 1997, while playing for the Boston Bruins, Kennedy went public with his story.

In 1997, Graham James was sentenced to three-and-a-half years in prison. He was released from prison in July 2000 and, to the consternation of the Canadian Hockey Association and of many in the sporting public, James became a coach with the Spanish national team.

News media across North America became interested in Swift Current once the story broke that Graham James had been charged with assaulting junior hockey players and particularly when Sheldon Kennedy, by then an NHL player, came forward to talk publicly about what had happened.

The Globe and Mail, for example, described Swift Current this way:

> *To understand why the James affair has hit Swift Current so hard, you first need to understand how small the city is and how big the sport.*
>
> *Swift Current is the sort of place where people are excited that Tommy Hunter is coming this month to perform... It's the sort of place where people are still known by what church they belong to, where you could drive down the fiendishly cold main street last week and see a whole row of cars left running and unlocked*
>
> *... In such a climate, those who play for the Broncos are local heroes who stand a chance of living the Canadian dream of playing in the NHL, feted guests of honour at fowl suppers, and community leaders with a stature far beyond their years.*
> (Mitchell, January 14, 1997, p. A6)

Swift Current was also described by the media as angry and betrayed (Brownridge, January 4, 1997, p. A2) and as a town of deep shame (Gillis, January 12, 1997, p. A1). This small prairie city was reduced simultaneously to a city of perversion and bucolic innocence: a place with "its heart broken, its shoulders slumping, every bone in its body aching as it searches within itself for answers" (Drinnan, January 9, 1997, p. B1). As I explain, these contradictory representations can coexist within narratives about sexual abuse in dysfunctional families.

Referring to writing about her experiences with the diagnosis and medical treatment of breast cancer, Eve Sedgwick indicates that "it's hard not to think of this ... experience as ... an adventure in applied deconstruction" (1993, p. 12). Sedgwick's experiences with the medicalization of breast cancer called into question neatly packaged oppositions between safety and danger, fear and hope, past and future, thought and act, the natural and the technological, and, in doing so, disrupted precise definitions of identity, gender, and sexuality (Sedgwick, 1993, pp. 12, 13). Likewise, recounting some of my experiences of sexuality as a youth living in Swift Current, including my pursuit of my coach, has the potential to call into question oppositions between innocence and dysfunction, the normal and the perverted, and insiders and outsiders and, in doing so, disrupt the tidy stories told about sexual abuse of innocent youth in dysfunctional families. I intend the intervention of my experiences as a queer reading, where queer suggests that "meanings ... can be at loose ends with each other" (Sedgwick, 1993, p. 6). In turn, I hope to show that lives of young people exceed representations of them as innocent and gullible, while also showing that the sexual lives of young people are not so easily captured in the few roles available from stories about dysfunction.

Dysfunctional Swift Current and Stories of Sexual Abuse

Experts in psychology, social work, and other human sciences have had a prominent role in producing a story about sexual abuse in dysfunctional families that has become familiar in this culture (see Rush, 1980; Miller, 1983; Armstrong, 1984; Crewsdon, 1988; La Fontaine, 1990). This is a story of sexual abuse in a "family system gone wrong [where] each family member own[s] a piece of the problem" (Dinsmore, 1997, p. 15). According to Gilmartin (1994), family pathology is not regarded as an "idiosyncratic behavior of a single member of that unit; rather, the family system is implicated as causing and perpetuating whatever problem that exists" (p. 82). Family members are all implicated in the abuse as victims, perpetrators, gullible innocents, or complicit third parties (Butler, 1985).

Official city information sources and outside media represent Swift Current as valuing families. The city website, for example, indicates:

> Swift Current is a city of families and friends. Our continuing efforts to maintain a high quality of life and opportunity for our neighbours is only rivalled by our desire to welcome new families to Swift Current and make new friends. (Swift Current, 2001)

Swift Current not only values family, it *is* a family, according to some. For example, Joe Arling, a hotel owner and member of the board of directors of the Broncos was reported in 1997 to say:

> This is a community with very strong morals and beliefs. It has very strong family values and in a way, it's a family itself. To me, what Graham did was a violation of trust and position, just like priests and teachers have abused their positions. Hockey just happened to be the venue, in this case. But like anywhere, there'll be significant hurt here. No one would have expected it to happen in this community. (Quoted in Gillis, January 11, 1997, p. H2)

As I have said, newspaper reporters' attempt to understand what happened in Swift Current was cast in terms of the familiar cultural story about sexual abuse in dysfunctional families. People in Swift Current were represented as recognizing the dysfunction of the community:

> One thing's certain, this farming, railway and oil community—a well-spring of dedicated, sometimes brilliant hockey players—will never feel the same about itself. Or its and Canada's favourite game. (Gillis, January 14, 1997, p. A2)

As a dysfunctional family, Swift Current was represented as complicit in the sexual abuse of the junior hockey players who lived there. In some accounts, James was cast as a member of this dysfunctional family (Swift Current) that made possible the abuse of Kennedy and other junior hockey players:

> while preying on boys for his confessed sexual gratification, James could not operate alone. He had help and lots of it. Passive, blind, hopelessly naive help from those who most trusted the junior hockey coach: parents, billets, league and team administrators, and teammates. (Ormsby, January 4, 1997, p. D3)

Many reporters and some residents of the city were reported to have thought it was impossible that no one knew that the sexual abuse was happening in Swift Current. Two residents of the Saskatchewan city were quoted as saying:

> I just can't imagine how somebody could live with these players and not try to figure out why they were spending so much time with the coach.

> What do you mean nobody knew? I'm sure people knew, but they just didn't do anything. (Quoted in Gillis, January 12, 1997, p. A4)

Another account went so far as to surmise that the team organization refused therapy for team players after the tragic bus accident in 1986 left four players dead, because they were afraid that "the terrible truth about James' sexual shenanigans [would] surface" (McConachie, January 15, 1997, p. B1). In these representations, Swift Current assumed the role of the mother within the dysfunctional family: the "invisible third partner, 'colluding' in the sexual interaction between the abuser and the child or abandoning the child to the abuser" (see Butler, 1985, pp. 102, 113). It is assumed in this conventional story about sexual abuse that abuse would not have occurred if the mother, in this case Swift Current, had not created a particular emotional climate through "commission and omission" (Butler, 1985, p. 114).

Central to the story of sexual abuse in dysfunctional families is the gullibility of at least some family members. Reporters represented Swift Current as innocently caught up in and bewildered by the events:

> Meanwhile, the citizens of Swift Current will never understand how or why all of them came to be victims, too. But that's what happens when sexual abuse, society's dirty little secret, rears its ugly head in your community. There are good people in Swift Current, good people, salt-of-the-earth people, who are torturing themselves, trying to understand what it is that went on behind closed doors in their community and why they weren't able to recognize the signs. (Drinnan, January 9, 1997, p. B1)

The trainer of the Broncos was reported to say, "I've been lying awake every night thinking, Did I miss something? Were there signs I didn't see? But there just weren't any hints" (quoted in Gillis, January 14, 1997, p. A2).

The cultural story of sexual abuse in dysfunctional families includes accounts of loyalty of members to the abuser (see esp. Butler, 1985, p. 121). The loyalty of certain Swift Current residents to James was central to some media depictions. When faced with the allegations about James, team president John Rittinger was reported to have said: "the Graham I know was always a pleasant, humorous fellow. It's impossible for me to believe that a man of his intelligence would get involved in something like this. I couldn't be more devastated by this if Graham had died. I couldn't feel worse by this if it was my own family" (quoted in Todd, January 4, 1997, p. G2). There were many letters of support submitted at James's trial by former players and administrators of the Broncos' organization (Robinson, 1998, p. 168). This loyalty to James was interpreted as just another indication of the dysfunction of the city.

Gilmartin indicates that social-psychological explanations of sexual abuse of children in families "keeps the focus on individual families as the problem and ignores the societal power imbalances which many families mimic" (1994, p. 87). Much of the reporting about the James case, while differing about whether Swift Current was complicit, innocent, or both, nevertheless represented this place as an aberration among Canadian cities. Administrators of hockey governing bodies were also keen to make the point that what had happened in Swift Current was not representative of hockey culture. Hockey authorities were quick to represent the James case as an isolated incident and not reflective of junior hockey (see Todd, January 4, 1997, p. G2). However, accounts such as Laura Robinson's (1998) in, *Crossing the Line: Violence and Sexual Assault in Canada's National Sport* document how abuse of and by hockey players may be central to hockey culture. Robinson argues that abuse in hockey is institutionalised and that abuse takes many forms including pressure on young players to excel and conform, hazing rituals, and sexual abuse.

A common representation by the media of the James affair was that James duped Swift Current by fooling residents with his charm and knowledge of hockey:

> This was a man of contradictions... James was a pillar of the community. He was a role model. He was on the Broncos' bus that ugly night 10 years ago and he helped the community mend its broken heart, the same heart he would smash to smithereens. He picked that team up by the skatelaces and took it to a Memorial Cup championship just three years later. It was a miracle that put Swift Current on the map. Now it turns out he was the devil in disguise. (Drinnan, January 9, 1997, p. B1)

In this representation, James is not one of the family. He is an outsider, described by one of the players' billets as "an import to the community" (quoted in Gillis, January 14, 1997, A2). The mayor of the city at the time also distanced the community from James by indicating that "this is an isolated event by perhaps a deranged person. Certainly, it doesn't reflect the community" (quoted in Vanstone, January 11, 1997, p. A1).

While, for the most part, the mainstream media did not link the charges of abuse to James's homosexuality, they did portray him as "a very private man, rarely seen socially" (Brownridge, January 4, 1997, p. A1). The *Alberta Report*, a right-wing, Christian fundamentalist newsweekly accused other media of downplaying James's homosexuality and ignoring what they portrayed as "the known link between homosexuality and pedophilia" (Sillars, January 20, 1997, p. 34). Albert Howlett, a Broncos supporter, shared the indignation: "You pretty near have to put him down near the lowest class of person you can be. What he did with those boys was terrible" (quoted in Vanstone, January 11, 1997, p. A1).

Many in the city were reported to have known about James's homosexuality, with the effect that reporters did not take seriously the representation of the city by one of its citizens as a naïve, small Bible-belt town (Mitchell, January 14, 1997, p. A6). A former Broncos director was reported to say that:

> There were rumors about Graham's sexual orientation, but never any suggestion he was sexually abusing players... Innuendo, suspicion and rumour was all there was, and until someone comes forward, there's really nothing you can do. If you decided to end a coaching contract on something like that, human rights would be all over you. (Quoted in Gillis, January 14, 1997, p. A2)

In another report, the following was attributed to the director: "Some of the club's inner circle suspected that Mr. James was a homosexual but they were broad-minded enough not to assume that a gay man also had a taste for the youths under his control" (Mitchell, January 14, 1997, p. A6). That the "homophobic world of junior hockey" (Todd, January 4, 1997, p. G2) would be so open to homosexuality stretched the limits of credulity for most reporters. One asked rhetorically

> Could it be that as long as you're winning and developing NHL stars, people look the other way? Could it be that James would have been found out long ago if he was a losing coach? (Todd, January 4, 1997, p. G2)

A flurry of articles identifying other "homosexual" coaches who had been "known" to prey on players (see Houston and Campbell, January 9, 1997, p. A1; Spector, January 9, 1997, p. A1; Stock and Crowley, January 7, 1997, p. A1) belied the representation of James as an exception. Many of these coaches were dead and not in a position to defend themselves. Most attention was paid to Brian Shaw, former coach, general manager and owner of the Edmonton Oil Kings and Portland Winter Hawks. The *Edmonton Journal* also carried a front-page story with pictures about Peter Spear, who died in 1988, and who allegedly abused at least one of his players (Spector, January 9, 1997, p. A1). None of these accounts of homosexuality in hockey, including the disingenuous reference to looking the other way, acknowledged what many of the reporters must have regularly witnessed: the homoeroticism of the locker room. As Brian Pronger indicates, "locker rooms are places where orthodox men like to hang around naked, talking and joking with each other" (1992,

p. 76). In response to the revelation that James regularly showered with his players after practices, Western Hockey League coach, Mike Babcock, reported that in the aftermath of the scandal, he and his assistant coaches had talked about whether they should continue to shower with players when the team was on the road ("Stars," January 22, 1997, p. E2). If there were indications of James's sexual interest in Broncos players, they may have been indistinguishable from homoerotic interactions taken for granted on male sporting teams.

The story about sexual abuse in families and family-like settings is not able to account for homoerotic behavior on male athletic teams, nor can it contain Kennedy or James's understanding of what happened between them. When asked about his willingness to go to where James was coaching after the first sexual encounter, Kennedy responded, "Well yeah ... I was scared sh__less... I knew right after, but there was nothing I could do because I wanted to play" ("Player," January 7, 1997, p. D10). Jimmy Devellano, who drafted Kennedy from Swift Current, was one of many people surprised by Kennedy's accusations because, according to Devellano, Kennedy "always talked about Graham so sincerely" (Simmons, January 8, 1997, p. B1). A former Broncos vice-president said he was told that James was "doing it" with Kennedy. "I figured that if they were doing it, they were doing it with consent" (quoted in Vanstone, January 11, 1997, p. A5). Kennedy later said that he believed that James was in love with him. He also indicated that James knew what he was doing and "he should have known that it wasn't accepted, because I had mentioned many times that I hated it" (Board, January 7, 1997, p. D1). Kennedy said that he could not tell anybody because "I was so scared to come out and admit it happened to me. I was scared to say I was with another man" ("Learning," January 7, 1997, p. A2). James commented after his trial that he realized that Kennedy was not comfortable with the sex but he tolerated it because, "he legitimately cared. Not about THAT [the sex] obviously. He cared. He knew I was lonely and you know, that sort of registered as desperation" (Spector, January 9, 1997, p. D6). When asked in an interview from prison whether he realized that what he was doing was wrong, James responded:

> When you're attracted to somebody, you're blinded, and you try to justify things, and you figure if you can do enough for somebody then somehow that makes up for it. ("Caring," January 7, 1997, p. K2)

> I suppose you don't think these things ... will be brought out into the general public. It's like anybody's sex life, it goes out in the general public [and] it doesn't look too flattering. ("James," January 8, 1997, p. E2)

Irrespective of the homoeroticism of the locker room or what James or Kennedy had to say, media representations of Swift Current and the people who lived there sustained an understanding of sexual abuse consistent with conventional stories of abuse in dysfunctional families. This is a story of youth innocence, collusion, duplicity, and gullibility. Swift Current and the events that took place there are open for other readings.

Another Reading of Swift Current

As it turns out, many of the places in which the events that implicated James and Kennedy occurred were places I had inhabited under different conditions, 20 years earlier. During high school, I lived in a house on Jubilee Drive in the northeast side of the city. This house was later sold to a couple who billeted Broncos players through the 1990s. Kennedy was one of these players.

Kennedy would have left the side door into the car park every Tuesday and Thursday evening to go to Graham James's house. Was his room the southeast bedroom where I had spent so much time as a 15-year-old thinking about my first girlfriend? This girlfriend was 18, and under today's laws would be considered an adult. As I found out later, she was two-timing me with her female college coach.

Many reporters have wondered how the people of Swift Current, especially those billeting players, could not have known that a player was sexually involved with the coach. They surmised that people must have known or were too simple or naïve to have guessed. I often went to my basketball coach's apartment, usually unannounced, hoping to seduce her. I was oblivious to whether the neighbours knew. My coach's careful closing of the curtains upon my arrival was reason for me to be hopeful of what might happen but, as I think about it now, she was likely very aware that some would think that a player should not be in her coach's home unsupervised at night. Only she and I were aware that the 17-year-old girl was pursuing the 25-year-old coach. Applied to me, the story of innocence and dysfunction would have shrunk a "smart and active older adolescent ... into a child, a generic essence-of-child" (Kincaid, 1998, p. 31).

My mother did not ask me questions about spending time with my coach. Instead, my mother often helped me buy chocolate bars for her. Nor did she have much to say about the black eye my coach accidentally gave me when we were wrestling in the locker room. This black eye would have been very difficult for my coach to explain if someone had chosen to cast my relationship with her as inappropriate. In some accounts, James was accused of threatening Kennedy with a gun. James had this to say about the gun:

> There was a gun in a sense of a Cluseau-Kato type thing. He'd chase me until I could find something to stop him, and vice versa. Then we'd laugh about it. That's all there was to it. (Spector, January 9, 1997, p. D6)

Was my mother complicit in my sexual encounters with girls my own age? Was she implicated in my active pursuit of a young woman in authority who, arguably, in sexual terms was more innocent than I was? My mother told me much later that she did not have the language to broach my sexuality with me. According to the familiar story, this inability to talk about what may have appeared as an unusual relationship with my coach is evidence of the dysfunction of my family. As the titles of books telling this story reflect, silence is considered to be central to dysfunction (Butler, 1985; Miller, 1983; Rush, 1980). I had a sense, then, however, that by helping me buy small presents for my coach, my mother was communicating her tacit approval of me.

Agonizing about what the adults should or should not have known or done cannot account for the complications of people's lives. For example, the couple who began billeting Broncos players, including Kennedy, did so after losing two of their sons in a tragic vehicle accident. How and if this tragic event affected the decisions that were made in relation to the boys in their care cannot be captured by implying that they somehow colluded in what was later understood as Kennedy's abuse. They may have been unable to make explicit what was later construed as a terrible abuse of authority by a coach whose "victim" left his home twice a week, every week, for four years to visit the coach.

Swift Current cannot be captured by stories about dysfunction and innocence, nor can the relationships between the adults and youth who live and have lived there. Many of my memories of living as a child and teenager in Swift Current reproduce this as a time and place marked by innocence, exuberance, creativity, and fun. But I know that these memories make sense to me in contrast to the heaviness that often accompanies adulthood. With little effort, however, I can also remember the stranger in the car who persisted in trying to give me a ride home when I was five; the woman who did some sewing for my mother who was found dead in the Swift Current creek; the rape of one of my sister's friends; the way the kids at school treated the children of one family because they were poor and Arab and lived in the valley; the man who turned out to be a woman who drove the "honey wagon" (the name given for the horse-drawn wagon that carried the sewage from the outdoor toilets used by the people in the valley); children throwing rocks at the man with cerebral palsy who dared to try to walk in his neighbourhood; what I now understand to be the racism that invaded the speech of the adults around me; or the awesome wrath of one of my teachers when I was 10 because I persisted in playing hockey with the boys.

Years later, my mother apologized for not doing something more to ease what she thought must have been a horrible time for me living in Swift Current. But it was not a horrible time. Rather it was then and there that I found other girls like me and we engaged in sexual lives not remotely imagined in representations of Swift Current as a quaint, quiet family town or as a dysfunctional city complicit in the sexual abuse of its young people. Still, I am surprised at the apparent casualness to homosexuality expressed by at least some in the community during the James scandal. In the 1960s, I would have sworn that, except for those of us engaged in these thrilling subterranean practices, no one had a clue that people did these things.

At least some people did know about these practices when I lived there, including my mother, as did some during the time James and Kennedy were living in Swift Current. Yet, dominant cultural stories about families, sexuality, relationships, and youth innocence still circulate, making it difficult to understand events, people, and places in anything but the terms of these stories. What has changed, however, is that queer stories are being told about the relationships between people that occurred in these places.[2] These queer stories situate dysfunction not in individuals or places but in a cultural story that simplifies complicated lives. The dysfunction of the cultural story is that it permits only two main roles, "monster and victim … along with supporting parts for police, judges, juries, therapists, parents, friends, journalists, and lawyers" (Kincaid, 1998, p. 30).

I want to emphasize that I am not saying that my experiences in Swift Current prove somehow that Kennedy was not traumatized by the sexual encounters he had with James. Rather, I want to show that the stories about dysfunctional families and the innocence of youth are too simple to capture the complexity of relationships, events, and people. In their simplicity, they have the effect of fixing what we can know about a place, people who live there, and events in a way that is "intolerant and relentless" (Kincaid, 1998, p. 30). A queer reading renders a little less tidy the meaning of the people and events of Swift Current and in so doing allows another look at dysfunction and youth innocence.

Notes

1. Parts of this paper were previously published under the title, "Queering Pervert City," *torquere* 4–5 (2002–2003): 110–24.
2. I want to thank James McNinch for helping me with this point.

References

Armstrong, L. 1984. *Home Front: Notes from the Family War Zone*. New York: McGraw-Hill.

Board, M. 1997. "Kennedy Describes His Life as a Lonely Hell." *Gazette* (Montreal), January 7, D1.

Brownridge, D. 1997. "A Feeling of Betrayal." *Leader-Post* (Regina), January 4, A1.

Brownridge, D. 1997. "Assault Charges Stun Swift Current." *Star-Phoenix* (Saskatoon), January 4, A2.

Butler, S. 1985. *Conspiracy of Silence*. Volcano, CA: Volcano.

"Caring Coach Tells His Story." 1997. *Edmonton Sun*, January 12, 12.

Crewsdon, J. 1988. *By Silence Betrayed: Sexual Abuse of Children in America*. New York: Little Brown & Co.

Dinsmore, C. 1991. *From Surviving to Thriving: Incest, Feminism, and Recovery*. New York: State University of New York Press.

Drinnan, G. 1997. "Swift Current Tries to Heal Its Wounds." *Leader-Post*, January 9, B1.

Gillis, C. 1997. "Hockeytown, Canada Searches Its Soul." *Edmonton Journal*, January 11, H1–H2.

——. 1997. "Sex Assaults Shock Prairie Town." *Gazette*, January 12, A1, A4.

——. 1997. "James Incident Steals City of Its Innocence." *Star-Phoenix*, January 14, A2.

Gilmartin, P. 1994. *Rape, Incest, and Child Sexual Abuse*. New York: Garland.

Houston, W. and N. Campbell. 1997. "Ex-WHL Boss Abused Players." *Globe and Mail*, January 9, A1.

"James Says He Feels Betrayed by Kennedy." 199. *Vancouver Sun*, January 8, E2.

Kincaid, J.R. 1998. *Erotic Innocence: The Culture of Child Molesting*. Durham: Duke University Press.

LaFontaine, J. 1990. *Child Sexual Abuse*. Cambridge, UK: Polity Press.

"Learning to Live Again." 1997. *Leader-Post*, January 7, A1, A12.

McConachie, D. 1997. "Independent Investigation Needed by WHL." *Star-Phoenix*, January 15, B1.

Miller, A. 1983. *Thou Shalt Not Be Aware*. New York: Farrar, Straus & Giroux.

Mitchell, A. 1997. "Swift Current's Hockey Pride Left in Tatters." *Globe and Mail*, January 14, A6.

Ormsby, M. 1997. "Be Vigilant to Protect Vulnerable Youngsters." *Toronto Star*, January 4, D3.

"Player's Self-esteem Sank After Years of Abuse." 1997. *Vancouver Sun*, January 7, D10.

Pronger, B. 1992. *The Arena of Masculinity: Sports, Homosexuality and the Meaning of Sex*. Toronto: University of Toronto Press.

Robinson, L. 1998. *Crossing the Line: Violence and Sexual Assault in Canada's National Sport*. Toronto: McClelland and Stewart.

Rush, F. 1980. *The Best Kept Secret: Sexual Abuse of Children*. Englewood Cliffs, NJ: Prentice-Hall.

Scott, J. 1992. "Experience." In J. Butler and J. Scott (eds.), *Feminists Theorize the Political*. New York: Routledge.

Sedgwick, E.K. 1993. *Tendencies*. Durham: Duke University Press.

Sillars, L. 1997. "Hockey Pays the Price for Gay Tolerance." *Alberta Report*, January 20, 30–34.

Simmons, S. 1997. "Many Tried to Help a Troubled Kennedy." *Star-Phoenix*, January 8, B1.

Stock, C. and N. Cowley. 1997. "The Saddest Power Play." *Edmonton Journal*, January 7, A12.

Spector, M. 1997. "Scars That Last a Lifetime." *Edmonton Journal*, January 9, A1, A9.

——. 1997. "Kennedy Disclosure a Betrayal: James." *Star-Phoenix*, January 9, D6.

"Stars Looking to Shine Over Hockey Scandal." 1997. *Leader-Post*, January 22, E2.

Swift Current Community Information. (2001, December 1). *http://www.city.swift-current.sk.ca/info/index/htm*.

Todd, J. 1997. "Junior Hockey Looks Other Way." *Gazette*, January 4, G2.

Vanstone, R. 1997. "Shadow Over a Hockey Town." *Leader-Post*, January 11, A1.

13

Teaching Tolerance, Mirroring Diversity, Understanding Difference:
THE EFFECT AND IMPLICATIONS OF THE *CHAMBERLAIN* CASE

Bruce MacDougall & Paul T. Clarke

Introduction

One of the most important cases on education administration is the recent Supreme Court of Canada case of *Chamberlain* v *Board of Trustees of School District No. 36 (Surrey)*.[1] The case dealt with issues related to education law and constitutional law, though on the latter issue little was said explicitly. In this chapter, we look first at what the court decided in terms of administrative law. On its face the Chamberlain decision is primarily concerned with administrative law issues. But we then examine the constitutional issues that were germane to the case and were largely left unconsidered. They are important issues to consider because they are in fact at the heart of the case that went to the court. These issues raise important questions about the meaning of equality and the way in which conflict between fulfilling constitutional guarantees (in this case, for religion and sexual orientation) can be resolved. Furthermore, although the majority of the court did not rely on the Canadian Charter of Rights and Freedoms[2] in its formal analysis, the Charter values of accommodation, tolerance and respect for diversity (as reflected in s. 15, for example) loom large in the background of the majority approach. In the final part of the chapter, we consider the implications of the case for the various stakeholders in our public schools.

Facts

The *Chamberlain* case arose out of the provisions of the BC School Act which says:

> *76(1) All schools must be conducted on strictly secular and non-sectarian principles.*
>
> *(2) The highest morality must be inculcated, but no religion, dogma or creed is to be taught in a school or Provincial school.*[3]

A resolution, referred to as the "Three Books Resolution," was passed by the Board of Trustees of the Surrey School District on April 24, 1997, indicating that the Board did not approve the use of three books depicting children with same-sex parents as "Recommended Learning Resources."[4] The issue arose against a background of considerable public acrimony and religious fervour in Surrey. The petitioners, led by Mr. Chamberlain, a primary school teacher, applied under the Judicial Review Procedure Act[5] for an order quashing the "Three Books Resolution" and another on the basis that that (and another) resolution infringed the School Act and the Charter. The Chambers judge quashed the "Three Books Resolution" as being contrary to the above provisions of the School Act.[6] She found as a fact that those who argued in favour of and voted for the resolution were significantly influenced by religious considerations, specifically opposed to homosexual conduct, and that this was contrary to s. 76(1) which forbade the school board from implementing a decision made on religious views.[7] That decision was overturned by a unanimous BC Court of Appeal which held that the "Three Books Resolution" was consistent with the School Act and within the jurisdiction of the Surrey School Board. That decision in turn was overturned by a majority of the Supreme Court of Canada.

Issues

McLachlin CJ wrote the main judgment for the majority.[8] As she saw it, there were two grounds of appeal:

> a) the board acted outside its mandate under the School Act

> b) the resolution violated the Charter.

She found that the Board's decision was to be set aside on the first ground. She did not, therefore, at least explicitly, deal with the Charter. This is unfortunate because the dissenting judge did deal rather extensively with this area, even though he was of the view that the constitutional issues had not been fully argued. The leading judgment thus leaves largely unexamined the important question of the intersection between constitutional protection of religion and of sexual orientation. While it is understandable why McLachlin CJ took this approach, it is still disheartening because the issues in the case essentially arose because of this intersection. Significantly too, this conflict arose in an education context where such clashes of priorities might be expected to arise in the future.

Even so, the case is important for what it says about the education system. It is one of only a handful of cases from the Supreme Court of Canada dealing with education administration and how rights issues play out in the education context. Not surprisingly, schools and, to a lesser extent, colleges and universities are the subject of a constant political attention at different levels. They are institutions that many have almost daily contact with, often through their children. Because of the acceptance of their pivotal role in inculcating societal norms[9] and ideas they are naturally going to be subject to political change in a democracy where personalities and parties change on a regular basis. Other institutions that once had more of a direct role in determining the standards of society now attempt to retain such a role through influencing educational policy. Sometimes this role is retained through separate institutions. As was evident in Chamberlain, however, even in public school systems, religious bodies and individuals sometimes seek to extend their influence to cover all students in the school and various aspects of education administration. If achieved, this would be a most insidious form of religious control in that a school that is pur-portedly public and secular would be subjecting its students to tuition that is heavi-ly religiously constrained, though presented as not being so.

The courts, on the other hand, have historically shown little inclination to get involved in educational issues and have seldom been invited to do so.[10] This has been attributed to the high costs and the delay in getting a final decision,[11] but it could also be attributed to an historical notion that such matters do not "belong" in court.[12] This is not for lack of any jurisdiction by the courts to act. As *Chamberlain* conclusively decided, actions by schools or school boards are state actions that are subject to Charter scrutiny. Courts cannot, however, simply intrude into an area of social or political life unless there is a complainant before the court, but there will be no com-plainant if the court is perceived to be uninterested in certain types of complainants or in certain types of cases. The judiciary has not created much of a comfortable envi-ronment for these education issues to be dealt with. In part this is because students, especially elementary and high school students, are not significant in the judicial imag-ination.[13] They are seen as little more than appendages of their parents. And some courts and judges are prone to take a dismissive view of the legitimacy of intervention of teachers, interest groups and so on, in such litigation. Even the dissenting judge, Gonthier J, in *Chamberlain* wondered whether the claimants in *Chamberlain* were the appropriate parties to bring the claim because they were not directly affected.[14]

What can courts do to ensure fairness in education, perhaps particularly when issues arise involving the interests of a minority group such as gays and lesbians? We will argue that their role will be primarily to review decisions by educational institu-tions that run counter to the inclusive-accommodative ideal that Canadian courts have adopted in the context of issues having a constitutional/rights aspect. Courts can ensure protections for teachers and students who are homosexual or who are "suspected" of being so. Courts can be more flexible on issues of standing and understand the difficulties that a gay or lesbian student will have in personally bringing a rights claim before the court. Courts can ensure that the guarantee of non-discrimination in s. 15 of the Charter is treated as a factor to be considered whenever the court is asked to resolve a legal dispute, whether that case is squarely a "s. 15 case" or not. These imperatives raise aspects of both administrative law and constitutional law, and that is how the Supreme Court of Canada framed the issues in *Chamberlain*.

Administrative Law

McLachlin CJ gave an important boost to the idea that education decisions, made by a school board, are subject to judicial review. This approach is important because it represents a change in the standoffish approach courts have taken in the past, noted above. McLachlin CJ said:

> *My colleague, Gonthier J., and I, while differing in the result, agree on many points in this appeal: that the Board's decision is subject to review by the courts; that the appropriate standard of review is reasonableness; that, as an elected representative body, the Board is accountable to its local community; that its decisions about which books to approve as supplementary learning resources may reflect the concerns of particular parents and the distinct needs of the local community; and finally, that the requirement of secularism laid out in s. 76 does not prevent religious concerns*

> from being among those matters of local and parental concern that influence educa-
> tional policy.[15]

McLachlin CJ made clear that when reviewing the decision of a body such as a school board, courts are to use a "functional and pragmatic" approach to review.[16] Furthermore, in a case such as *Chamberlain*, McLachlin CJ thought the appropriate standard within that "functional and pragmatic" approach is "reasonableness."[17] McLachlin CJ was of the view that a court ought to ensure a proper degree of deference to a board's decisions, but, importantly, she added that because a case like *Chamberlain* involved a human rights dimension, there could be less deference. The court is well placed, she said, to resolve human rights issues. Rights law and constitutional law generally in Canada would have benefitted greatly from her fuller exposition on this point. She did say, however, that different types of human rights issues do "play out differently."[18] So, the extent to which deference is lessened by the presence of a human rights issue "will vary from case to case." The relevant question, she said, should always be "whether the courts have an expertise equal to or better than that of the board, relative to the particular human rights issue that is faced." She said that the nature of the problem in *Chamberlain* negated the suggestion that the courts should accord high deference to the Board's decision. She said:

> This is not simply a case of the Board balancing different interests in the communi-
> ty. This is a case requiring the Board to determine how to accommodate the concerns
> of some members of the community in the context of a broader program of tolerance
> and respect for diversity. This question attracts court supervision and militates in
> favour of a stricter standard.[19]

To a certain extent, however, McLachlin CJ attributed this extended ability of courts to interfere in the board's decision to legislative intent. She said: "These goals, touching on fundamental human rights and constitutional values, suggest the legislature intended a relatively robust level of court supervision."[20] Worryingly, perhaps, the implication might be that a legislature could equally direct that such decisions could be insulated from court review. It is, however, just as arguable that McLachlin CJ was suggesting that equality interests should be robustly protected in any context by the Charter, but unfortunately she did not feel the need to elaborate more on this point. It is, therefore, unclear to what extent it would be permissible for the legislature to eliminate court supervision of a board's decision, or to what extent a legislature could authorise decisions made by such boards or others based on religious values. For example, s. 264(c) of the Ontario Education Act says that it is the "duty" of a teacher "to inculcate by precept and example respect for religion and the principles of Judaeo-Christian morality."[21] As we will elaborate in the next section on the constitutional issues, we are of the view that the legislature would be acting in an unconstitutional way if it provided, in its legislation governing schools, that religious views could somehow trump other constitutional values.

In the context of the particular legislation in BC, however, the legislature stipulated that board decisions had to be based on strict secularism and non-discrimination. At the core of the case, therefore, is the meaning of secularism and how that gets implemented by an administrative body like a school board. McLachlin CJ structured her approach to this matter as follows: (1) the meaning of the Act's insistence on strict secularism; (2) the role of the Board as representative of the community; and (3) the role of parents in choosing materials for classroom use.[22] Because of the legislative base for its authority and the School Act's "insistence on secularism and non-discrimination," McLachlin CJ was of the view that a school board could act only within relatively narrow confines. She said:

> ... school boards possess only those powers their statute confers on them. ... [They] must act in a strictly secular manner. It must foster an atmosphere of tolerance and respect. It must not allow itself to be dominated by one religious or moral point of view, but must respect a diversity of views. It must adhere to the processes set out by the Act, which for approval of supplementary materials include acting according to a general regulation and considering the learning objectives of the provincial curriculum.[23]

If the board is under legislative constraints in terms of how it can make decisions, what of other participants in the education process, particularly parents? Can the existence of an important role for parents mean a school can in practice be administered or a curriculum taught in a way that would be impermissible for a school board itself to mandate? Gonthier J stressed the decisive role of parents in the education of children, thus jeopardising the interests of inclusion and accommodation of minorities if such interests run contrary to the beliefs of parents. He said that in educating children, parents play the primary role and the state the secondary.[24] Parents, he said, "have the right to bring up and educate children in line with their conscientious beliefs."[25] McLachlin CJ agreed that there is an important role for parents in school administration. However, she said that, according to the BC legislation, the involvement of parents in the stage of selecting materials to be used in a particular class, could come only after materials have been approved for general use by the Board.[26] Thus the parental action could only be exercised within some of the confines as that exercised by the board. If this were the end of the constraints on parental action, however, parents might still act in a way so as to exclude content important to certain minorities but rejected by influential parents. So, it was important for McLachlin CJ's reasons that she cautioned that although parental involvement was important, it cannot come at the expense of respect for the values and practices of all members of the school community. She said:

> The requirement of secularism in s. 76 of the School Act, the emphasis on tolerance in the Preamble, and the insistence of the curriculum on increasing awareness of a broad array of family types, all show, in my view, that parental concerns must be accommodated in a way that respects diversity. Parental views, however important, cannot override the imperative placed upon the British Columbia public schools to mirror the diversity of the community and teach tolerance and understanding of difference.[27]

Her views in this context could be reconfigured so as to make the argument that a board cannot delegate to get away from legislative imperatives imposed on it. But the issue still arises, however, as to whether legislation could withstand constitutional scrutiny if it were drafted so as to allow parents a far greater role at, say, the early stages of curriculum development. Or, could the legislature simply surrender control of important areas of education and education administration to entities such as parents' groups so as to avoid constitutional, particularly Charter, requirements that would constrain the government? That is an issue for the next section of the chapter.

On the administrative law points, and applying the standard of reasonableness she had earlier concluded was appropriate to test the decision of the School Board,

McLachlin CJ said that in this case there had been a series of errors.[28] The Board's first error had been to violate the principles of secularism and tolerance in s. 76 of the School Act. Instead of proceeding on the basis of respect for all types of families, the Superintendent and the Board had proceeded "on an exclusionary philosophy." They had acted on the concern of certain parents about the morality of same-sex relationships, without considering the interest of same-sex parented families and the children who belong to them in receiving equal recognition and respect in the school system. The Board could not reject books simply because certain parents found the relationships depicted in them controversial or objectionable. This approach to inclusion was rooted in the legislative mandate, but as we will argue in the next section, it should be seen as a manifestation of a more general constitutional principle.

The Board's second error had been to depart from the regulation it had made pursuant to Ministerial Order as to how decisions on supplementary resources should be made. The Board's regulation recognized the existence of diverse communities within the School District and the Board's duty to approach the needs of each with respect and tolerance. Contrary to this requirement, the Board had given no consideration to the needs of children of same-sex parented families and instead based its decision on the views of a particular group who were opposed to any depiction of same-sex relationships in K-1 school materials. This "particular group's" views were based on religious ideas of intolerance towards gays and lesbians.

According to McLachlin CJ, the Board's third error was to have applied the wrong criteria. The Board either ignored or mistook the requirements of the School Act and the learning outcomes of the curriculum. The curriculum stated that children at the K-1 level should be able to discuss their family models, whatever these may be, and that all children should be made aware of the diversity of family models that exist in our society. The Board had not considered this objective. Indeed, as McLachlin CJ pointed out, the Superintendent, whose views appear to have guided the Board, had taken the view that unless the curriculum expressly required that same-sex parented families should be discussed, the Board need not inquire into the relevance or suitability of the books as learning resources. This pre-emptive action, preventing even a discussion of the books, was an erroneous interpretation of the School Act and the Ministerial Orders, as well as of the Board's own general regulation on selection criteria.

Constitutional Law

The *Chamberlain* case raises issues of the meaning of the constitutional equality guarantees for gays and lesbians and how they can be preserved when opposed by claims for constitutional protection for religious expression. The case also raises the question of how a court should respond if education legislation did not impose strictly secular requirements, thus allowing religion-grounded values to preclude inclusion and participation in educational matters by minorities out of favour with the particular religion. These issues raised by *Chamberlain* were not conclusively addressed. McLachlin CJ did not need to go into the constitutional arguments behind the case in much detail. Nor would it have been appropriate given the limited treatment of those issues at the courts below. However, she did make some important inferential comments in the constitutional context and some extrapolation from what she did say is probably legitimate. Gonthier J too was aware of the limits of the Charter arguments in this case, though he felt less constraint in making points about the Charter.

Chamberlain is one of a series of recent Canadian cases where tension is evident between constitutional protection for equality and for religious expression.[29] The facts of the case raise the question of what equality means and the extent to which it can be constrained by religious views. In the context of the cases on sexual orientation, the jurisprudence in the past decade or so has tended towards a sharpening of focus in the tension between the goal of sexual orientation equality and certain religious views. Though those religious views can hardly be said to have changed, the legal and social position of gays and lesbians has changed. Opposition to equality for homosexuals and homosexuality could, before the 1990s, be characterised as just a "traditional" values approach without any particular religious connotation, much as incest or bigamy might still be seen.[30] However, as litigation and legislation have moved Canadian law to a fuller conception of equality for gays and lesbians, the religious underpinning of the remaining barriers to equality have become clear.[31] Thus, in the marriage cases, for example, the arguments against allowing same-sex marriage are essentially religious in nature.[32] In the Hall case, where a Catholic high school graduate was told not to bring his same-sex date to the prom, the religious nature of the opposition to equality is readily apparent.[33] In *Chamberlain*, the opposition to books on homosexuality was religion-based.

The conflict with constitutional religion guarantees might be thought to represent a formidable barrier to the further extension of the ideal of equality for gays and lesbians or for other minority sexualities. In fact, it can be argued that this situation in fact represents an advance for gay and lesbian equality precisely because it underlines the *religious* nature of the anti-homosexual rhetoric. A court, to give credence to such arguments, must, as Gonthier J did in *Chamberlain*, directly side with particular exclusionary religious arguments that trump the more general constitutional value which is equality. Furthermore, the court challenges to traditional legal views on sexuality affect the religious position in that that position must be particularised for the court, rendering it no longer monolithic. It becomes apparent that there is an indeterminate quality to the character of much religious teaching, especially on sexuality issues, even within a given denomination.[34] Those who argue for the "religious" position in many cases will have difficulty saying just what that religious position is. On the other hand, the equality position will usually be straightforward.

Many of the recent cases, including *Chamberlain*, can be assessed or repositioned as part of a legal discourse about the meaning and content of equality. The Supreme Court of Canada has stressed again and again the importance of the equality guarantee in s. 15 of the Charter. In *Law*,[35] Iacobucci J said:

> It may be said that the purpose of s. 15(1) is to prevent the violation of essential human dignity and freedom through the imposition of disadvantage, stereotyping, or political or social prejudice, and to promote a society in which all persons enjoy equal recognition at law as human beings or as members of Canadian society, equally capable and equally deserving of concern, respect and consideration.[36]

The Supreme Court of Canada and other courts have breathed life into the equality section of the Charter. Equality is to be widely construed and limited only with great hesitation. While the *Law* case and other cases at the Supreme Court of Canada[37] have dealt with s. 15 by defining discrimination, setting out the purpose of s. 15 or giving a legal test for whether s. 15 is breached, they have not actually expressly considered or described the *contents* of equality. One of us has argued elsewhere that in order for there to be *real* legal equality for the members of a given group, the state must show towards the members of the particular group compassion, condonation and celebration.[38] Absent any one of those elements and the members of the group might have partial equality but not complete legal equality.

Compassion is the bare principle that the members of the group should not be discriminated against just because of their membership in the group. That point is widely conceded to gays and lesbians.[39] Condonation is the involvement or the engagement by the state (or some other authority) with the members of the group not just to protect them from discrimination but to offer them something of some benefit. Condonation implicates the state in the activities of the members of the group. The state is not just a defender of the *existence* of the members of the group in a way it is with compassion, but the state actually fosters the *activities* of the members of the group in some way. It can do this without necessarily approving of or blessing the members of the group or their activities. Some religions have had difficulty (to say the least) with expansion of this aspect of equality even to gays and lesbians. Any involvement by the state, implicating it in gays and lesbians doing something (like forming relationships or adopting children), is frowned upon.[40] The particular religion might defend *being* homosexual (compassion) but not doing homosexual things (condonation).[41]

The third field of discourse about equality, and the one where in Canada most legal controversies with respect to homosexuality now arise, is in the context of celebration. Here, the state does not just tolerate or facilitate the members of a particular group as in compassion or condonation, it also celebrates them. They are treated in a positive way. The "benefits" at this level are not so much tangible as symbolic or supportive, in the sense of fostering the members of the *group* and encouraging the group's fluorishing as an integrated and *valued* part of the society. There have been judicial statements recognising the importance of symbolic issues in the equality context. For example, in *Halpern*, LaForme J said:

> There are distinct and profound benefits in marriage, which as I noted previously are not satisfied merely by providing equivalent economic benefits, rights and obligations through some other means. Simply put, such alternative methods do not have the same meaning or significance as access to them by right of entry to a basic social and cultural institution.[42]

The issues raised in *Chamberlain*, while having some aspect of condonation, are probably best characterised as issues relating to the celebration of homosexuality. McLachlin CJ's views, especially in her critique of the reasonableness of the school board's decision, fit in the celebration of equality idea that places such emphasis on the symbolic importance of being included in a positive way. Gays and lesbians can hardly be celebrated, and therefore hardly be treated as equals, if books about them are deliberately excluded from schools.

The *Chamberlain* case, therefore, can be seen as very much part of a continuing legal discourse on the content and meaning of equality for gays and lesbians. But how do constitutional imperatives relating to equality fit in a context where other individuals or groups argue that facilitating that equality intrudes on their constitutional rights? Elsewhere, one of us has suggested that there is a proper constituional backdrop against which these issues should be considered. There is a general consensus that an appropriate Canadian approach in rights cases is to be as inclusive and as accommodative as possible.[43] An inclusive approach is one which is receptive to those who are different from the majority. It accepts difference and does not have a single model person as the ideal but is open to including as many different backgrounds or characteristics as possible. An accommodative approach resolves disputes by preferring compromise and accommodation instead of resorting to conflict which will result in a winner and a loser. It comprehends all individuals and groups and does not engage in a practice of having a dominant group make concessions to a minority group. If such approaches are available, whatever their flaws, when minority groups other than homosexuals or when equality issues other than homosexuality are being considered in either a legal or a political context, then there is no reason for a regression to traditional religious standards or prejudices when it is homosexuals or homosexuality which is being considered. The judiciary must not automatically rely on "moral and ethical" or "religious" values about homosexuals and homosexuality which may well have changed or no longer be appropriate. The inclusiveness and accommodation that characterise the Canadian ideal must apply to homosexuals just as it does to individuals of various religious, ethnic or racial groups.

In the context of the inclusive-accommodative ideal, what is a court to do, then, when it is faced with a situation where respecting religious views generates a different resolution from respecting the right to freedom from discrimination on the basis of sexual orientation? The answer is clear; that which includes and accommodates prevails. When a religious organisation or a person with strong, proselytising religious views enters into a public arena in any way, such as education, the organisation or the person must expect to operate in the public arena by respecting the social ideals of inclusion and accommodation, just as a gay business person, whatever his personal beliefs, must not discriminate on the basis of race, sex, religion, and so on.[44]

The requirement for inclusion and accommodation, even in the context of protecting sexual orientation rights which upset certain religious sensibilities, does not set up a hierarchy of bases of discrimination—one triumphing over another. In fact it is meant to be quite the opposite. It is consistent with what Lamer CJC has said in *Dagenais* v CBC:

> *A hierarchical approach to rights, which places some over others, must be avoided, both when interpreting the Charter and when developing the common law. When the protected rights of two individuals come into conflict, as can occur in the case of publication bans, Charter principles require a balance to be achieved that fully respects the importance of both sets of rights.*[45]

Inclusion and accommodation for homosexuals does not mean that religion is being excluded and refused accommodation. Religious ideology simply should not be used to determine what people who may not be of that religion can do or how they should lead their lives or what they should teach or be taught. Religious freedom should not prevail over freedom of sexual orientation, just because religious freedom has been recognised for a longer time and because religious ideas have infused the common law. Recognising true equality for homosexuality does not impair religious freedom. Le Bel J made the point:

> The powers of trustees to make policy decisions reflecting their beliefs or those of parents do not extend as far as their personal freedom of religion and conscience, but it does not follow that their decisions may not be influenced by religious convictions. What s. 76 rules out is policy based on beliefs that are intolerant of others. It is of little import whether those beliefs are religious, moral or philosophical.[46]

The majority's views in *Chamberlain* can be seen as another affirmation of the inclusive-accommodative ideal and that issues involving homosexual equality and secular ideals are to be tested against this inclusive-accommodative standard, even when opposed by religious values or interests. How did McLachlin CJ recognise the need for inclusion and accommodation? She said: "The School Act's emphasis on secularism reflects the fact that Canada is a diverse and multicultural society, bound together by the values of accommodation, tolerance and respect for diversity."[47] McLachlin CJ recognised that inclusion and accommodation are essential to the smooth operation of a society such as Canada's, anywhere, but especially in a multicultural area such as Surrey. She said: "if the school is to function in an atmosphere of tolerance and respect, in accordance with s. 76, the view that a certain lawful way of living is morally questionable cannot become the basis of school policy."[48]

What does this need to accommodate mean in practice in the context of Board decisions? McLachlin CJ said:

> In summary, the Act's requirement of strict secularism means that the Board must conduct its deliberations on all matters, including the approval of supplementary resources, in a manner that respects the views of all members of the school community. It cannot prefer the religious views of some people in its district to the views of other segments of the community. Nor can it appeal to views that deny the equal validity of the lawful lifestyles of some in the school community. The Board must act in a way that promotes respect and tolerance for all the diverse groups that it represents and serves.[49]

McLachlin CJ criticised the decisions of the Superintendant and the Board about the materials being controversial. Such an approach was contrary to this need to accommodate and include. Furthermore, as McLachlin CJ said, part of the education system's role is to encourage and instill just these particular ideals of inclusion and accommodation even if they run counter to parents' religious views. Part of the manifestation of inclusion at the school level will involve exposing students to celebration of those groups, ideas, and so on that their parents, for whatever reason, including religion, do not celebrate. As McLachlin CJ said: "Learning about tolerance is therefore learning that other people's entitlement to respect from us does not depend on whether their views accord with our own. Children cannot learn this unless they are exposed to views that differ from those they are taught at home."[50]

It is important as well that the issues about equality not be circumvented by characterising a particular case, such as that in *Chamberlain*, as not about equality. In *Chamberlain*, Gonthier J fell into this trap by adopting the religious characterisation of homosexuality as a morality issue rather than an equality issue:

> The moral status of same-sex relationships is controversial: to say otherwise is to ignore the reality of competing beliefs which led to this case. This moral debate, however, is clearly distinct from the very clear proposition that no persons are to be

discriminated against on the basis of sexual orientation. The appellants, using the courts, seek to make this controversial moral issue uncontroversial by saying that s. 15 and "Charter values" are required to eradicate moral beliefs, because the hypothesis is that possible future acts of discrimination are likely to emanate from such beliefs.[51]

He continued:

The respondent's reading of local parental concern is that the books portray same-sex parents as being on a moral par with heterosexual parents, i.e., there are many kinds of relationships that are out there, and none is better or worse than the others. This is a moral message, and a moral message of some concern to these parents since they disapprove of same-sex relationships. This view is concerned about the moral equating of homosexual parents with heterosexual parents, which is implicit in the identification, in all three of the books, of homosexual "Moms" and "Dads." The message which caused concern, in the words of one parent's affidavit, is that: "Mommies and Daddies are seen as good things in the eyes of my children and therefore the lifestyles of the Mommies and Daddies in the stories must be acceptable..."[52]

Such an approach undermines the idea of equality rights as disconnected from freedom of expression. It turns equality rights issues (at least with respect to homosexuality) into religious/morality debates. Gonthier J in *Chamberlain* (as did the majority in *TWU*)[53] seemed largely prepared to accept this approach in the context of homosexual rights. Would the response be the same if issues of women's equality or racial equality were redesignated as just "rooted in differing faith conceptions"? There are, for example, strong "religious/moral" views on (that is, against) things like Jewish integration, women's equality, mixed marriages and so on. It would be astonishing, however, to see those issues treated by the courts in such a fashion as homosexual equality was by Gonthier J and some judges in past cases. The fact that homosexual issues can be so treated, however, shows that homosexuality still has some way to go to achieve the equality of equality protection that some other grounds of difference enjoy. Homosexual equality is, contrary to what some judges appear to believe, *especially* in need of Charter protection and vigilance from the courts.

LeBel J picked up on this double standard and marginalisation of homosexual equality. He said:

The incompatibility of the views expressed in the affidavits with the principles of secularism and non-sectarianism would perhaps be even more apparent if the parents had objected to the portrayal of families of a particular religious background— Muslim families, for example. No doubt the practices of Muslims are contrary to the teachings of some other religions; indeed, their beliefs are deeply opposed to those of some other religions. But Christian or Hindu parents could not object (unless they renounced any claim that their objections were non-sectarian) to the mere presence of a Muslim family in a story book, or the mere intimation that happy, likeable Muslim families exist, on the basis that Muslims do and believe some things with which they do not agree, or that encountering these stories might bring children face to face with the reality that not everyone shares their parents' beliefs. Parents who raised such objections would demonstrate their outright rejection of the principles of pluralism and tolerance enshrined in the School Act and, indeed, at the very heart of the Canadian society in which young schoolchildren are learning to participate.[54]

Implications for Educational Stakeholders

From an educational perspective, the potential implications of this judgment for Canadian educators and those with an interest in our public schools are far reaching and involve various stakeholders. These include: provincial ministries of education, boards of education, teacher professional organizations, administrators, teachers, students and parents. By virtue of its decision in *Chamberlain*, the Supreme Court of Canada has extended an invitation to the various actors to exercise curricular leadership, by working individually and in concert with one another, to promote an inclusive and accepting environment for gays and lesbians in our public schools.

Provincial and Local Leadership

At the *provincial* and *local* levels, ministries or departments of education and local school boards should revisit their curriculum. They will soon realize that there exists a void when it comes to the availability of gay- and lesbian-friendly curricular materials. In the vast majority of cases, these materials simply do not exist within the confines of the traditional curriculum. In *Chamberlain*, the provincial ministry refused an earlier request from Mr. Chamberlain to place the three banned books on its list of core materials for the province's Kindergarten-Grade 1 students studying the contemporary family. Hence, provincial and local authorities should work to create appropriate curricular materials, which reflect the lives and experiences of gay and lesbian Canadians. In the *Chamberlain* case, the Supreme Court of Canada referred to the gender equity outline, which forms part of the British Columbia provincial curriculum. This document specifies that: "Gender equitable education involves the inclusion of the experiences, perceptions, and perspectives of girls and women, as well as boys and men, in all aspects of education." We suggest that provincial ministries create a similar document and approach related to sexual orientation. Hence, an inclusive approach would likewise reflect the *experiences, perceptions*, and *perspectives* of gays and lesbians in our society.

Ministries and boards should also look at the distinction between *core* and *supplementary* materials. The Supreme Court of Canada highlighted this distinction in *Chamberlain*. Core materials go to the heart of the curriculum and are required to be used in every classroom. Supplementary materials, however, do not carry the same weight. They are not mandatory and their inclusion in the classroom remains at the discretion of individual teachers. These materials provide a range of resources available to teachers who may (or may not) choose to use them to enrich the learning experiences of students. In *Chamberlain*, Mr. Chamberlain tried unsuccessfully to have the three books classified, not as core or required materials but simply as supplementary. Even if the Surrey school board had approved all three books as supplementary materials, teachers would have been neither obliged nor strongly encouraged to use them. Instead, teachers could have used the materials to meet the needs of the particular children in their classroom. Yet, by banning the books altogether, the Supreme Court of Canada noted:

> [W]ithout the Board's approval of these or equivalent materials, teachers who have students from same-sex parented families might be left without resources to assist them in having their particular families discussed and understood.[55]

Nonetheless, approval of the three books as supplementary materials, had it occurred, would not have been the end of the matter. A true commitment to equality will require integration of gay- and lesbian-friendly materials as part of the provincial core curriculum. Otherwise, problems of legitimacy and consistency arise if some teachers have the option of including (and excluding) materials on the basis of personal preference and individual whim. How can we take issues of human rights for gays and lesbians seriously if we study these questions under the rubric of supplementary (read secondary, incidental) materials?

The use of supplementary materials in these circumstances is also problematic because it may lead to a patchwork or ad hoc approach to the treatment of gay and lesbian issues at the school board level. Since local boards (at least in British Columbia) control the use of supplementary materials, some might choose to include gay and lesbian friendly materials in the curriculum while other boards might refuse to incorporate them.[56] Provincial leadership is the answer to this conundrum. If provinces, through their respective ministries of education, are serious about their commitment to ensuring equality for gays and lesbians in our public schools, they will mandate core provincial curriculum, which reflects, and values, the reality and experiences of gays and lesbians in our society.

Teacher Professional Organizations

Teacher professional organizations also have a pivotal leadership role to assume in advancing and protecting the educational and curricular interests of gays and lesbians in our schools. This leadership, in fact, has been forthcoming and is illustrated, by way of example, in the work of the teaching profession in British Columbia and Saskatchewan.

In *TWU v. British Columbia College of Teachers*,[57] the College refused to accredit Trinity Western University's (TWU) teacher education program. Students attending TWU were required to sign a community waiver stating that they would refrain from biblically condemned practices including homosexuality. The College felt that this requirement ran afoul of human rights legislation and might foster discriminatory attitudes among teacher graduates from TWU who planned to work in the province's public schools where they would be in contact with gay and lesbian students. The College thus argued that it was protecting the public interest by opposing TWU's application for accreditation.

The Supreme Court of Canada ultimately forced the College to accede to TWU's request. Uppermost in its mind, the court highlighted the fact that the College could adduce no evidence that TWU education graduates discriminated (or would discriminate) against gay and lesbian students in the public schools.[58] This approach, while privileging religious belief, fails to address the underlying discriminatory attitudes which flow from TWU's community waiver. These attitudes, which are the source of all homophobic acts, seriously undermine the notion of gay and lesbian equality. The College recognized this and took what it deemed proactive measures to counter the harmful and hurtful stereotypes reflected in the TWU waiver. In this way, the College exercised leadership by standing up for the rights and interests of gay and lesbian students in the public schools of British Columbia.

On another front, the College has also taken action to counter homophobia in the schools. In April of 2003,[59] it suspended Chris Kempling from teaching for one month after finding him guilty of conduct unbecoming a member of the College. Mr. Kempling, an evangelical lay preacher, wrote to his local paper expressing the following views: "Many health professionals, including myself, believe homosexuality to be the result of abnormal psychosocial influences." He also wrote: "The majority of religions consider [gay] behaviour to be immoral." Even though Mr. Kempling did not express his opinions in the classroom or on school property, the College ruled that his antihomosexual letters were incompatible with "his role as a teacher in a school system that must function in an environment of tolerance and understanding." In addition, the College noted: "His actions disclose a failure to uphold values that are fundamental to the education system and Canadian society, values that include sexual equality and respect for persons of differing sexual orientation."[60] The College's decision to discipline Mr. Kempling for homophobic remarks expressed outside the school reflects a concern for the informal curricular influences that teachers can have on students and the school community. The College recognizes that what a teacher says outside the classroom can be just as relevant and powerful as what s/he says in the classroom.[61]

The Saskatchewan Teachers' Federation (STF) is also striving to eliminate homophobia in the province's schools. The STF prepared *Safe Schools: Breaking the Silence on Sexual Difference* in 2002. This publication, available to the province's teachers and schools, examines attitudes and beliefs about sexual identity as well as the facts and myths relating to homosexuality. It also reflects the experiences of teachers and students who have encountered homophobia in Saskatchewan schools. The document then goes on to address a host of critical questions. These include: What can be done to support LGBT students in Saskatchewan classrooms and schools? How do I handle LGBT issues in the classroom? What should I do to deal with harassment? Why is stopping homophobia important? The STF has also been an active participant in the annual "Breaking the Silence" conference, which is hosted by the College of Education at the University of Saskatchewan.[62] This provincial conference examines issues related to gays and lesbians in Saskatchewan schools. From a curricular perspective, and under the aegis of this event, the STF also aims to make available to educators appropriate resources and strategies to help make Saskatchewan schools a safe and caring place for gays and lesbians.[63]

In-School Administrators

School administrators can show curricular leadership by embracing the ideals of inclusion and accommodation at the school level. Principals and vice-principals can do this in various ways. They can support LGBT students and teachers by guaranteeing that they are free from harassment in a safe and caring environment. This teaches students and others about the informal curriculum, namely, what is and is not acceptable in terms of appropriate behaviour. School administrators can also support teachers and students who wish to examine LGBT issues in the curricular context in an appropriate and professional manner. This entails ensuring that suitable gay- and lesbian-friendly curricula are available in the school and that opportunities for discussion of these materials in the classroom are permitted and encouraged. Finally, principals and vice-principals can stand up to political pressures from those few, yet irate and intolerant parents and community members who wish to keep gay and lesbian friendly curricular materials out of the schools. By creating a safe curricular space, they say no to homophobic attitudes and assist in legitimizing the place of gays and lesbians in our schools.

Teachers

Teachers are arguably the most important advocates of an inclusive curriculum. Their contact with students is immediate, ongoing, and inescapable. Hence, their potential impact on student beliefs and attitudes is significant. As educators, they can exercise their academic or professional freedom to call into question heterosexist curricular materials and include, where appropriate, gay- and lesbian-friendly curricular materials in their teaching. As role models, teachers have the potential to shape the informal curriculum by fostering positive and healthy attitudes about sexuality, including homosexuality.

Academic Freedom

One of the co-authors has argued in some detail elsewhere that public school teachers should be entitled to some measure of academic freedom.[64] As *professionals* who exercise some measure of independent judgment and as *educators* who must prepare our students for citizenship and competition in local and global markets, teachers need some degree of academic and professional freedom to do their jobs. This freedom covers to some extent both *what* is taught and, to a much greater extent, *how* it is taught. It makes possible the teaching of critical thinking, by developing the necessary skills and dispositions, which is a central goal of a liberal education.[65]

In the initial statement of claim, Mr. Chamberlain argued that the Surrey School Board's book banning resolution violated his academic freedom and constitutionally protected right to free speech. Yet, the Supreme Court of Canada did not expressly address these issues in its decision. Nonetheless, the case arguably buttresses the claim that public school teachers should have some degree of professional autonomy to do their job. After all, Mr. Chamberlain wanted to introduce the three books to his K–1 students because he believed the existing curriculum silenced the family reality of an entire sexual minority. Hence, he used his academic freedom in a responsible way to challenge a heterosexist curriculum that excluded the perspectives and experiences of a minority group. In this way, he sought to promote an inclusive study of the family, which valued the lives and contributions of gays and lesbians. In retrospect, this challenge to an underinclusive curriculum, and subsequently to the School Board's resolution to ban the three books, was possible because Mr. Chamberlain decided to exercise his academic freedom as a professional and caring teacher.

This is not to suggest that academic freedom is a license which allows teachers to do whatever they want in the classroom. On the contrary, valid and legitimate restrictions exist which can, and do, limit the curricular speech and academic freedom of teachers. The American courts have identified a number of *bona fide* pedagogical concerns or interests, which may justify limiting the curricular expression of teachers.[66] The critical ones may be summarised as follows: the "fair and objective presentation of materials" concern; the "appropriateness of the materials" concern; the "general control of the curriculum" concern; and the "material and substantial disruption" concern. It is likely that Canadian adjudicators will adopt these pedagogical rationales to restrict teachers' academic freedom.[67] Each concern will be briefly examined to explain why the Surrey School Board's refusal to allow the three books in the classroom did not constitute a justifiable infringement on Mr. Chamberlain's academic freedom.

Under the first concern, educators are required to present (controversial) materials in a fair and balanced manner. They cannot indoctrinate students or undermine critical thinking by presenting a single perspective or one side of the story. In *Chamberlain*, the Supreme Court of Canada noted that the Kindergarten and Grade 1 curriculum required that students learn about families in the modern context. The variety of these family models is extensive. As the court noted:

> *The children attending B.C.'s public schools come from many different types of families—"traditional" families parented by both biological parents; "single-parent" families, parented by either a man or a woman; families with step-parents; families with adopted children; foster families; interracial families; families with parents of different religious or cultural heritages; families in which siblings or members of the extended family live together; and same-sex parented families.*[68]

The three books that Mr. Chamberlain proposed to use, as supplementary materials, do not indoctrinate or undermine critical thinking. They do not demonize heterosexual families or other kinds of families. The books simply reflect the social reality of many gays and lesbians who choose to live as legally functioning families (like other families) that care for and love their own. Hence, the books accurately reflect a variation, or another possibility of, what constitutes a family. Arguably, they promote critical thinking and tolerance by exposing children, unfamiliar with same-sex parented families, to a different type of family model.

As for the second concern, teachers must use materials which are appropriate given the age and maturity of their students. The Board felt that five- and six-year-olds were too young to be introduced to books depicting families with same-sex parents. The Court refuted this claim, noting that the curriculum itself designated the topic as age appropriate by indicating that all types of families found in the community should be discussed by K–1 students, including same-sex parented families. Furthermore, the books did not raise issues of sexuality and sexual practices.[69]

Lastly, the Supreme Court of Canada refuted arguments to ban the books based on fears of "cognitive dissonance." Certain parents believed that the message of the books, conveyed to their children while in school, would conflict with their beliefs and values shared at home.[70] The court acknowledged that the materials might raise questions. It noted, however, that these questions might still arise, regardless of the books, given the existence of same-sex parented families in the K–1 parent population and in the broader world in which the K–1 children lived. More significantly, the court highlighted the importance of exposing children to some cognitive dissonance as a means of teaching them about tolerance.[71] Mr. Chamberlain's proposed use of the three books met the criterion of appropriateness.

With respect to the third concern, school boards have a legitimate interest in controlling the curriculum. They want to ensure that teachers will use methods and materials that are current, accurate, relevant, and of demonstrated pedagogical value. This control, in turn, facilitates the promotion of legitimate educational goals. In essence, general curricular control prevents teachers from teaching whatever they want using whatever methods they deem appropriate.

In *Chamberlain*, the teacher never attempted to arrogate unto himself control of the curriculum. Rather, he sought Board approval before using the three books in class. The curriculum required that Mr. Chamberlain teach his Kindergarten and Grade 1 students about diverse family structures, with gay and lesbian families being but one example of this familial diversity. Hence, he was working squarely within the confines of the mandated curriculum when he proposed to use the three books. In contradistinction, the Surrey School Board's curricular control of the banned materials could not be justified. As the Supreme Court of Canada observed:

> What the Superintendent and the Board did not consider is as telling as what they did consider. The Superintendent's statement does not refer to the absence of restriction on the curriculum's direction to discuss different family types. It does not refer to the emphasis in the School Act and curriculum on tolerance, respect, inclusion and understanding of social and family diversity. And it does not refer to the secular nature of the public school system and its mandate to provide a nurturing and validating learning experience for all children, regardless of the types of families they come from.[72]

In essence, Mr. Chamberlain used his academic freedom to challenge heterosexist and underinclusive curriculum. This freedom should protect teachers who use gay and lesbian-friendly material provided they, like all teachers using all materials, do not usurp curricular control from their employing board.

Under the fourth concern, teachers' academic or professional freedom may be limited when the exercise of that freedom leads to a "material and substantial" disruption of the educational process.[73] Boards of education retain basic control over the day-to-day administration of their schools. Under provincial school legislation, Canadian public teachers must "maintain good order and proper discipline." Good classroom management facilitates teaching and learning. These activities cannot occur where chaos abounds. Hence, a public school teacher who promoted torture as a valid means of student discipline might expect a tidal wave of protest from students and parents which could lead to a material and substantial disruption of the learning environment. A restriction on this teacher's academic freedom would be justified for obvious pedagogical and moral reasons.

This test can be problematic, however, because its exclusive focus on consequences may not always be related to legitimate pedagogical concerns. In *Chamberlain*, opposition to the three books originated primarily in the religious beliefs of certain parents and community leaders. They oppose homosexuality because they believe it is wrong and immoral. Yet, no evidence was led to suggest that the three books' content, or their prescribed use, ran afoul of sound pedagogical principles. Here, the uproar by a vocal few (and subsequent ban of the three books) was based on improper considerations.

In *Chamberlain*, the Supreme Court of Canada ruled that the School Board was not entitled to reject the books simply because certain parents found the relationship depicted in them controversial or objectionable. The high court stated that parental involvement in education could not undermine support for diversity and tolerance of different family types, including gay and lesbian families. The use of appropriate gay and lesbian friendly curriculum in our public schools cannot be banned, for mere political reasons, under the guise of the "material and substantial" disruption test.

To recap, some measure of academic freedom for public school teachers is necessary to protect their use of gay- and lesbian-friendly curricular materials. This freedom, however, is not a license to do whatever one pleases. Canadian adjudicators will probably use legal principles articulated by American courts to restrict academic freedom on all teacher speech, including curricular speech about gay and lesbian issues. Hence, teachers using gay- and lesbian-friendly curricula must present the materials in a fair and objective manner, consider the appropriateness of the materials given the age and maturity of the students, respect the employer's general right to control the curriculum, and avoid creating a material and substantial disruption related to valid pedagogical concerns.

The reasoning of the Supreme Court of Canada lends strong support to the contention that Mr. Chamberlain exercised his academic freedom in a responsible and professional manner when he attempted to seek approval for the three books. The books did not indoctrinate students and were age appropriate given the demands of the curriculum to teach students about different types of family units. Furthermore, Mr. Chamberlain did not arrogate curricular control unto himself by seeking Board permission to use the books. Finally, no material and substantial disruption occurred that could be linked to legitimate pedagogical concerns. In fact, most parents of students in Mr. Chamberlain's class supported his use of the books. Only a few, for religious reasons, opposed the texts.

Given the *Chamberlain* decision, teachers should now feel emboldened to use gay- and lesbian-friendly curricular materials where appropriate to do so. A strong case in favour of academic freedom supports this exercise of professional autonomy. Restrictions on the use of these materials, as for all teaching materials, must be governed by professionalism, relevance and sound pedagogical principles. Mr. Chamberlain's curricular leadership needs to be emulated. By challenging under-inclusive and heterosexist curricula, teachers open up new spaces and possibilities for gays and lesbians in our schools. This is consistent with the creation of a safe and accommodative environment, which respects the dignity of all sexual minorities in the school context.

Role Modeling

Some degree of academic freedom should allow teachers to talk about gay and lesbian issues within the confines of the official curriculum. When teachers are allowed and encouraged to use gay- and lesbian- friendly materials in our public schools, certain gay and lesbian teachers (if they so choose) may feel confident and willing to personalize the curriculum by disclosing their own sexual orientation to students in professional and appropriate ways. A gay teacher may place a picture of his partner on his classroom desk. A lesbian teacher may authorize the public and congratulatory announcement, in school, of the birth or adoption of a child to the teacher and her partner.

In these ways, gay and lesbian educators have a unique opportunity to serve as appropriate role models for both gay and lesbian and straight students.[74] First, if a gay or lesbian teacher decides to "come out" at an appropriate time and in an appropriate manner, and is allowed to do so, the importance of the act cannot be ignored. The message is clear. Being homosexual is legitimate and acceptable in an inclusive and caring school community. Gay and lesbian students may feel less isolated.

Potentially, they will have a person in a position of trust and authority with whom they can identify. Should the gay or lesbian students voluntarily choose to speak with the teacher or another person, such as a school counsellor, they may feel more inclined to follow this course of action knowing that they are not alone.

Second, gay and lesbian teachers who are "out," and happy and comfortable with their decision, may also act as role models for heterosexual students. They may challenge the destructive myths that homosexuality is immoral and that gays and lesbians are monsters, child molesters and recruiters. In *Re Assiniboine*, arbitrator Gabbert noted that the lesbian teacher who wanted to disclose her sexual orientation argued "that by personalizing this issue she would be much more effective at countering the stereotyping that was typical of the heterosexual majority of her students."[75] Gay and lesbian educators may help heterosexual students overcome irrational fears and (intentional and unintentional) prejudices about gays and lesbians. They may also educate some straight students who are simply unaware of the struggles and discrimination confronting gays and lesbians in today's society. By being who they are, gay and lesbian educators can legitimize homosexuality as an acceptable and healthy state of being.[76]

Implications for Students and Parents

The *Chamberlain* decision has important implications for students and parents. The use of gay- and lesbian-friendly materials allows gay and lesbian students to recognize themselves, in a public and open way, in the curriculum. The symbolic value of the state's official imprimatur cannot be underestimated. It helps validate and legitimize the worth of this sexual minority as a group deserving of equal respect and consideration. This act of validation and legitimacy says that it is okay to be gay or lesbian, just as it is okay to be straight. It makes no moral judgments related to one's sexual orientation. It accepts people for who they are, not for what some people would want them to be. This inclusive approach will help establish a safe school environment for gay and lesbian students. When these students no longer have to hide their sexual orientation, for fear of physical beatings, shame or rejection, they will be able to take their rightful and respectful places within a caring and compassionate public school system.

When our schools allow gay and lesbian students to celebrate who they are, just as they allow straight students to celebrate who they are, then we will have created an inclusive and accommodative environment for all students irrespective of sexual orientation. We should not forget that students look to teachers and administrators as role models to exemplify ways of acting and being in the world. In this sense, as persons in positions of trust and authority, educators have the potential to influence the attitudes and behaviours of their students. When teachers and administrators show a caring and respectful attitude towards all students, including gay and lesbian students, students will take their cues accordingly. Students will rise to the occasion when they are expected to exemplify conduct, which is tolerant, just and fair. We, as adults, can also learn from our children and our students. Younger children, in particular, have a propensity to see things as they are and to accept things the way they are. As Justice MacKenzie of the Court of Appeal in *Chamberlain* noted:

> The irony of all this was that the battle was ostensibly over the means of conveying
> the value of loving and caring family relationships, whatever their form. It is hard

to resist the thought that K–1 children may have a better appreciation of that value than any of the contending adults. Alternative family arrangements must now be a fact of life for virtually every child in public schools in Surrey either as a result of personal circumstances or the circumstances of friends and classmates well-known to them. K–1 children for the most part are too young to form critical normative judgments. They simply accept the variety around them as fact and welcome all the love and care they receive.[77]

Like students, parents have a right to an inclusive curriculum. Hence, gay and lesbian parents can expect a school system which values diversity and equality by reflecting their lives and experiences in the curriculum. When this occurs, gay and lesbian parents are more likely to have greater confidence in their schools because their perspective and voice will be included. In the *Chamberlain* case, most parents (including straight parents) supported the use of the three books. This is not to say that certain parents will not object to the use of gay- and lesbian-friendly curricula in our public schools. For obvious reasons, we cannot force or coerce parents to adopt views with which they disagree. Freedom of conscience and religion must be protected and these parents must be entitled to their opinions even if we think that they are wrong. In this sense, we acknowledge that religion plays an important part in our society and culture and shapes the values and beliefs that people hold.

By the same token, the Supreme Court of Canada has made it abundantly clear that religious belief which runs afoul of the Charter and its equality guarantees cannot be the basis of public policy for our public and secular schools. In other words, religious intolerance of gays and lesbians can never be justified as a basis on which to discriminate against this sexual minority in the school context. Using biblical passages, or other sacred texts, to keep gay- and lesbian-friendly curricula out of our schools is no longer acceptable. Gays and lesbians belong in our public schools and they are entitled to see themselves in the school curriculum.

How should we treat parents who do not want their children exposed to gay- and lesbian-friendly curricular materials? On one hand, parents who object to these materials can be accommodated. Their children could be exempted from studying or reading books about same-sex parented families on the basis that these books offend their religious beliefs. Their children can be offered alternative curricular resources. On the other hand, to suggest that some curricular materials (i.e. gay- and lesbian-friendly materials) are less worthy than others for study and consideration naturally causes concern for those who wish to create a truly inclusive and accommodative school environment. As a matter of principle, this approach is problematic because it tends to marginalize and discriminate on the basis of sexual orientation. As a matter of practice, would school boards accommodate parents who objected (for religious reasons) to books for K–1 students, which depicted interracial families? If they would not, then why should sexual orientation be treated any differently than race? If we are serious about our commitment to equality, and to protecting the rights and interests of gays and lesbians in our public and secular schools, then the case for allowing curricular exemptions to objecting parents cannot be sustained.

A Coda

In December of 2002, the Supreme Court of Canada handed down its decision in the *Chamberlain* case. While it struck down the School Board resolution banning the three books, it did not force the School Board to accept the use of the texts as supplementary materials. Rather, it remanded the matter back to the Board so the Board could reconsider Mr. Chamberlain's request in accordance with the legal principles enunciated in the judgment. Most notably, the requirement of secularity in British Columbia's School Act had to be respected. Hence, religious justification as a basis for excluding the three books was no longer acceptable. The Supreme Court of Canada recognized, however, that the Surrey Board is not obliged to approve every supplementary resource with which it is presented. As the Court declared:

> It can reject supplementary materials—even supplementary materials that are relevant to the curriculum—if it does so on valid grounds, such as excessive level of difficulty, discriminatory content, inaccuracy, ineffectiveness, or availability of other materials to achieve the same goals. Had the Board proceeded as required by the Act, the curriculum and its own general regulation, its decision might have been unassailable. The difficulty is that the Board did not do so here.[78]

Seizing on this part of the judgment, the Surrey school board finally made a decision on June 12, 2003. Once again, it decided to ban the books. This time, however, it stayed clear of religious arguments as a justification to ban the books, preferring to adopt other reasons to keep the stories from young children. As reported in the *Globe and Mail*,[79] reasons for excluding the texts included bad grammar, confusing scenarios and unfair depictions of authority figures. More specifically, board chairwoman Mary Polak criticized the uneven spelling in *Asha's Mums*, noting it used the U.S. way to spell "favorite," dropping the "u" in one sentence then reverted to the Canadian way in another section. She also noted that in the same book, the first page starts in the present tense, then reverts to the past tense: "This type of error is terribly confusing for an emergent reader."

Another trustee noted that the illustrations in *Asha's Mums* did not properly match the text. In one part of the story, Asha indicates that she put on her favourite red sweat suit. The accompanying black and white illustration shows her in a white shirt. Some trustees also took exception to the manner in which same-sex families broached the issue of tolerance. By way of example, Ms. Polak maintained that the main characters in *Asha's Mums* tried to persuade people who did not agree with same-sex families to abandon their beliefs. She said that this is not what tolerance is about. The reasons offered to exclude the books were frivolous, unbelievably nitpicky, and simply disheartening. One could argue that this was but another smokescreen to hide the homophobia raging at the Board level. The decision arguably did not respect the letter or spirit of the law as reflected in the Supreme Court of Canada's decision. As Mr. Chamberlain opined, no book in the curriculum could have withstood the kind of scrutiny the three books were subjected to.

This fortunately was not the end of the matter. Within a few weeks of the Board's June 12 decision, a committee of parents, trustees, teachers and administrators from the Surrey School Board approved two books with same-gender family content for the K–1 level.[80] The books are *Who's in a Family* by Robert Skutch and *ABC: A Family Alphabet* Book by Bobbie Combs.[81] This committee will now forward its recommandations to the Surrey Superintendent of Schools who is expected to approve the two books as district recommended learning resources. The Surrey Teachers' Association and Surrey parents have submitted additional resources on same gender and heterosexual families for consideration by district staff and/or this committee in the fall. Committee members have been assured that this will be an ongoing process of review in the 2003–04 school year.

Conclusion

It is important to remember that law and education are normative forces that can be used to help combat homophobia. They are similar to the extent that both of these social institutions help shape and mould human conduct. Each is concerned with inculcating values and norms, which govern human behaviour. From a normative perspective, judges and educators share a common concern—the just and fair treatment of all people including minorities such as gays and lesbians. Yet, law and education serve distinctive functions and purposes. Hence, their roles are not always identical. In the context of fighting homophobia, the courts have a twofold purpose. First, they further our understanding of the ideals of inclusion and accommodation as reflected in human rights legislation and the Charter. Second, they attempt to uphold those ideals in legal decisions so as to prevent discrimination against gays and lesbians on the basis of their sexual orientation. Yet, the courts must always wait until somebody brings the issue of homophobia before them prior to acting. They do not adjudicate in a vacuum. In this sense, their role is a *reactive* one.

Educators, on the other hand, are called upon to enlighten their students about the truths and myths surrounding sexual orientation. They educate by challenging the erroneous, stereotypical and harmful attitudes that others hold about gays and lesbians. They seek to dispel the irrational and hurtful beliefs that undergird homophobia. In this sense, their role can be seen as being *proactive*. Ideally, educators want to prevent students and others from holding discriminatory opinions and attitudes (whether intentional or unintentional), which must come prior to, and are the source of, all discriminatory action.

In the *Chamberlain* case, the forces of law and education (reflected respectively in the decision of the majority of the Supreme Court of Canada and the commitment of Mr. Chamberlain and his supporters) have come together to advance significantly the rights and interests of the gay and lesbian constituency in Canada's public school system. As a result of this convergence, we hope that our schools will be inspired to take new bold steps to ensure that the ideals of openness, inclusion and celebration are extended to all, including gay and lesbian stakeholders, in our educational community.

Notes

1. *Chamberlain v Board of Trustees of School District No. 36 (Surrey)* 2002 SCC 86 [*Chamberlain*].
2. Canadian Charter of Rights and Freedoms, Part I of the Constitution Act, 1982, being Schedule B to the Canada Act, 1982 (U.K.) 1982, c. 11.
3. School Act RSBC 1996, c. 412.
4. The Board issued no prohibition on the three books being available as library resources. The difference between a recommended learning resource and a library resource seemed to be that the former "is relevant to the learning outcomes and content of the course or courses" whereas the

latter is intended to be merely "appropriate for the curriculum." (*Chamberlain v Surrey School District No. 36*, 2000 BCCA 519 [*Chamberlain (CA)*], para 53) The three books are: *Asha's Mums* (1990) by R. Elwin and M. Paules, *Belinda's Bouquet* (1991) by L. Newman, and *One Dad, Two Dads, Brown Dad, Blue Dads* (1994) by J. Valentine. In *Asha's Mums*, the young Asha has a problem when she decides to go on a school outing with her classmates. She needs written authorization from her mother and father before she can go on the trip. Asha, however, has two mothers. Her parents visit the school and explain their family situation, which solves the problem. In *Belinda's Bouquet*, the school bus driver calls the young Belinda fat. Hurt by this comment, she recovers her self-esteem after being reassured by one of the two mothers of a school friend. And in *One Dad, Two Dads, Brown Dad, Blue Dads*, a young white girl asks a young black boy a series of questions about his two dads who have blue skin. These questions probe whether the dads work, cough and eat cookies. There is no mention of sex or sexuality in any of the three books.

5. Judicial Review Procedure Act, RSBC 1996, c. 241.

6. *Chamberlain v Surrey School District No. 36*, [1998] BCJ No. 2923 (QL) (BCSC) [*Chamberlain (SC)*], para. 94.

7. Furthermore she concluded that this interpretation was consistent with the guarantee of religious freedom expressed in the Charter.

8. The other judges who agreed with McLachlin CJ were Justices L'Heureux-Dubé, Iacobucci, Major, Binnie and Arbour. LeBel J wrote separate concurring reasons and Gonthier J, Bastarache J concurring, dissented.

9. See Bruce MacDougall, *Queer Judgments: Homosexuality, Expression and the Courts in Canada* (Toronto: University of Toronto Press, 2000), ch. 3, "Silence in the Courts"; Michael Manley-Casimir, "Teaching as a Normative Enterprise," *Education and Law Journal* 5 (1993): 1; Stephen Arons, "Constitutional Litigation and Education Reform: Canada's Opportunity," ch. 8 in Michael E. Manley-Casimir and Terri A. Sussel (eds.), *Courts in the Classroom: Education and the Charter of Rights and Freedoms* (Calgary: Detselig, 1986), 153.

10. For treatments of education and the law, see Douglas A. Schmeiser and Roderick J. Wood, "Student Rights under the Charter," *Saskatchewan Law Review* 49 (1984): 49; A. Wayne MacKay, *Education Law in Canada* (Toronto: Emond-Montgomery, 1984). For a treatment of how disputes between teachers and school boards are resolved, see Stuart Piddocke, "Settling Disputes between School Boards and Teachers: A Review of Formal Procedures and Some Provincial Variations," *Education and Law Journal* 5 (1993): 23.

11. A. Wayne MacKay, *Education Law in Canada*, 29.

12. See ibid., passim. See also David Givan, "The Ross Decision and Control in Professional Employment," *University of New Brunswick Law Journal* 41 (1992): 333.

13. See A. Wayne MacKay, "The Canadian Charter of Rights and Freedoms: A Springboard to Students' Rights," *Windsor Yearbook of Access to Justice* 4 (1984): 174.

14. *Chamberlain*, para. 124–25.

15. Ibid., para. 3.

16. Ibid., para. 4.

17. Gonthier J, dissenting about much in the case, did agree that this was the proper standard of review.

18. *Chamberlain*, para. 11.

19. Ibid., para. 13.

20. Ibid., para. 14.

21. Education Act, RSO 1990 c. E.2. Likewise, s. 54(e) of the Nova Scotia Education Act said until recently that it was the "duty" of a teacher in a public school to "encourage the pupils by precept and example a respect for religion and the principles of Christian morality..." Education Act, RSNS 1989, c. 136.

22. *Chamberlain*, para. 17.

23. Ibid., para. 28.

24. Ibid., para. 102.

25. Ibid., para. 107.

26. Ibid., para. 32.

27. Ibid., para. 33.

28. Ibid., para. 58–61.

29 The constitutional arguments the authors set out in this section of the chapter are largely a synthesis of portions of the arguments made by one of us in the following: Bruce MacDougall, *Queer Judgments*, note 9; Bruce MacDougall, "The Separation of Church and Date: Destabilizing Traditional Religion-Based Legal Norms on Sexuality," *University of British Columbia Law Review* 36 (2003): 1; Bruce MacDougall, "A Respectful Distance: Appellate Courts Consider Religious Motivation of Public Figures in Homosexual Equality Discourse—The Cases of *Chamberlain* and *Trinity Western University*," *University of British Columbia Law Review* 35 (2002): 511; Bruce MacDougall, "The Celebration of Same-Sex Marriage," *Ottawa Law Review* 32 (2000-01): 235.

30. E.g., *Re Attorney-General of Canada v Mossop* (1990), 71 DLR (4th) 661 (FCA), per Marceau JA at 673-4; *R. v Duvuvier, Kowalchuk and Hollingsworth* (1990), 75 OR (2d) 203 (HCJ). See Bruce MacDougall, *Queer Judgments*, ch. 2. The situation changed with a series of cases beginning with: *Veysey v Correctional Service of Canada* (1990), 43 Admin. LR 316 (FCA); *Knodel v BC (Medical Services Commission)* (1991), 58 BCLR (2d) 356 (SC).

31. Note: There have been religious intervenors in many of the gay and lesbian cases: *Egan v Canada*, [1995] 2 SCR 513; *Vriend v Alberta*, [1998] 1 SCR 493; *M v H*, [1999] 2 SCR 3; *Trinity Western University v BC College of Teachers*, [2001] 1 SCR 772 ["TWU"]; *Barbeau v BC (Att. Gen.)*, 2003 BCCA 251; and of course *Chamberlain*. And note especially para. 25 of *Egan* where La Forest J approved the concept of family offered by counsel for the "Inter-Faith Coalition on Marriage and the Family."

32. See *Barbeau*; *Halpern v Canada (Attorney General)*, [2003] OJ No. 2268 (QL) (CA); *Halpern v Canada (Attorney General)*, [2002] OJ No. 2714 (QL) (SCJ); *Hendricks c Québec (Proc. gén)*, [2002] JQ no. 3816 (QL) (Sup. Ct. Que.). As one of us said in "The Celebration of Same-Sex Marriage": "One of the difficulties in changing the definition of marriage is that it is an institution that, for many people, still carries with it strong *religious* connotations which argue against its opening up to same-sex couples. Not surprisingly, those who argue against any admission of same-sex couples to marriage tend to have conservative religious connections." Despite claims to the contrary there are no arguments against same-sex marriages that are not essentially religious in nature. The arguments from tradition, definition and morality are, in fact, all religiously rooted.

33. See MacDougall, "The Separation of Church and Date."

34. This was evident in *Hall* in the conflicting evidence of the Roman Catholic church teachings. *Hall v Powers*, [2002] OJ No. 1803 (QL) (SCJ). What would a court make of the current Anglican teaching on homosexuality given the active debate in that church about the blessing of same-sex unions? E.g. Michael Valpy, "Anglican Rift Looms Over Same-sex Unions," *Globe and Mail*, June 12, 2002, pp. A1 and A6. And, see the conflicting religious views on marriage detailed by Blair J in *Halpern* (SCJ). Of course, this is not just a problem for religions in Canada. See, e.g., Ingrid Lund-Andersen, "The Danish Registered Partnership Act, 1989: Has the Act Meant a Change in Attitudes?," ch. 21 of Robert Wintemute and Mads Andenæs (eds.), *Legal Recognition of Same-Sex Partnerships: A Study of National, European and International Law* (Oxford: Hart Publ., 2001).

35. *Law v Canada (Minister of Employment and Immigration)*, [1999] 1 SCR 497.

36. Ibid., para. 51.

37. See those cases cited in *Law*.

38. MacDougall, "The Celebration of Same-Sex Marriage," esp. 252–60.

39. *Hall*, para. 23; and see *Hendricks* (SCJ), para. 27.

40. See Bruce MacDougall, "A Respectful Distance," 532–33.

41. In *Hall*, the school principal denied permission to Hall to bring his date to the prom because, he reasoned, "this would be seen as … condonation of conduct which is contrary to Catholic church teachings" (para. 4). In at least the principal's mind, homosexuals merited equality no further than the level of compassion.

42. *Halpern* (SCJ), para. 376.

43. See MacDougall, *Queer Judgments*, 129–35.

44. See *Jones* v *The Queen* (1986), 31 DLR (4th) 569 (SCC); *Zylberberg* v *Sudbury (Board of Education)* (1988), 52 DLR (4th) 577 (Ont. CA). On this case, see Carol A. Stephenson, "Religious Exercises and Instruction in Ontario Public Schools," *University of Toronto Faculty of Law Review* 49 (1991): 82. See also *Russow* v *British Columbia (Attorney-General)* (1989), 62 DLR (4th) 98 (BCSC).

45. *Dagenais* v *CBC*, [1994] 3 SCR 835.

46. *Chamberlain*, para. 210.

47. Ibid., para. 21.

48. Ibid., para. 20.

49. Ibid., para. 25. The use by McLachlin CJ of the term "lawful lifestyles of some" is somewhat strange. This term has been used to diminish homosexual sexual orientation as a sort of caprice, on par with a choice of décor or degree of house clutter.

50. *Chamberlain*, para. 66.

51. Ibid., para. 150.

52. Ibid., para. 172.

53. *TWU* (see note 31).

54. *Chamberlain*, para. 214.

55. Ibid., para. 35.

56. This in fact has been the approach in British Columbia.

57. *TWU*.

58. One can only shudder, in the curricular context, when one thinks of the reaction a gay or lesbian student must have upon learning that his or her teacher is a TWU graduate. See Bruce MacDougall, "A Respectful Distance."

59. See "Teacher Suspended for Antigay Letters: Evangelical Christian Expressed Views in Local Newspaper; Not in Classroom," *Globe and Mail*, April 23, 2003, p. A2.

60. Mr. Kempling has indicated that he will fight the suspension in the courts. He maintains that his freedom of religion and freedom of expression allow him to hold and to express his antigay views in the public eye. It is worth noting that the BCCT took strong disciplinary action against Mr. Kempling while his employer appears to have been silently watching on the sidelines to see how things unfold.

61. See *Ross* v *New Brunswick School District No. 13* [1996] 1 S.C.R. 825 for a similar situation involving racist speech by a teacher.

62. See website: http//:www.usask.ca/education/edfdt/breaksilence.htm

63. At the university level, the Faculty of Education (Professor James McNinch) at the University of Regina has just offered (May 2003) the undergraduate class "Schooling and Sexual Difference." The course description states: "This course will provide the rationale, background, and strategies for understanding sexual identity and the social constructs of inclusivity and difference in our schools. This course will examine the pedagogical and curricular implications for all educators of lesbian, gay, transsexual and two-spirited, and bi-sexual (LGTB) students and teachers in our schools." In the statement of rationale, we read: "LGTB students and teachers are the last minority group to be tolerated, accepted, understood, appreciated, and officially recognized in our school systems. This course will encourage students to clarify their own understanding of sexual identity. Ignorance of and discrimination directed against approximately

5–10% of the school population continues because of this silence and lack of recognition. This course seeks to redress this injustice." At the University of Saskatchewan, the College of Education (Professor Don Cochrane) has offered a similar course since 1996.

64. See Paul Clarke, "Canadian Public School Teachers and Free Speech: An Employment Law Analysis," *Education and Law Journal* 9, no. 1 (1998): 43–96. Canadian courts have yet to rule specifically on this issue.

65. If we wish to promote critical thinking as a fundamental educational goal in our public schools, the argument for some degree of academic freedom becomes compelling. This freedom allows teachers (in the early grades) to initiate students into the art of asking intelligent questions and (in the later years) to challenge received wisdom and conventional thinking in responsible and thoughtful ways. The realization of academic freedom must, of necessity, invoke some measure of free speech. If teachers are not free to communicate ideas and exchange opinions through open discourse, academic freedom is nothing but an empty conceptual shell. Consequently, academic freedom lives through academic speech. In *R. v Keegstra*, [1990] 3 SCR 697, McLachlin J of the Supreme Court of Canada stated that the constitutionally protected right to free speech, under s.2(b) of the Charter, is the "pivotal freedom on which all others depend" (p. 79). She also outlined three theoretical rationales frequently cited to justify free speech. First, freedom of expression is valuable because it leads to the discovery of truth. Second, free speech promotes the free exchange of ideas essential to democracy and the efficient functioning of democratic institutions. Third, free speech is important because it protects autonomy and makes possible individual self-fulfilment. These three justifications for free speech are equally applicable to an understanding and defence of academic freedom. Hence, the Charter may enhance teachers' academic freedom when the exercise of that freedom advances the core values associated with free speech.

66. We borrow from the American experience because of a dearth of case law in Canada. See Paul Clarke, "Canadian Public School Teachers and Free Speech: A Constitutional Law Analysis," *Education and Law Journal* 9 no. 3 (1998): 315–82.

67. Ibid.

68. *Chamberlain*, para. 20.

69. Justice Saunders found this to be the case at the trial level.

70. The claim to "cognitive dissonance" was nothing more than a smokescreen for disguised homophobia. This wanting to shut down questions, which students may ask, is also disquieting because it is fundamentally anti-intellectual. Students should be encouraged to ask questions about other types of families because this is the natural and curious thing to do. Confronting students with difference and helping them make sense of the difference is at the heart of a vibrant and healthy education system.

71. *Chamberlain*, para. 66.

72. Ibid., para. 49. The Court also rejected the Surrey School Board's claim that the three books did not have to be used as supplementary materials because they were not expressly authorized by the Board or by the provincial ministry of education.

73. More specifically, in *Tinker v Des Moines Independent Community School District* (1969), 393 U.S. 503, the United States Supreme Court stated that school authorities may restrict student speech if the speech "would materially and substantially interfere with the requirements of appropriate discipline in the operation of the school" (p. 509). The same test has been applied to teachers.

74. This is reflected in arbitrator Gabbert's comments in *Re: Assiniboine South School Division No. 3 and M.T.S.* (1997), 64 L.A.C. (4th) 155, when he criticised the school board's non-disclosure policies on sexual orientation for failing to "take seriously the positive impact for both the self-esteem of gay students and the growth of tolerance among non-gay students that Ms M'Lot's revelation would contribute" (p. 199). The lesbian teacher, Ms. M'Lot, appealed unsuccessfully the non-disclosure policy to the Court of Appeal. The Supreme Court of Canada denied leave to appeal.

75. *Re: Assiniboine*, p. 187.

76. One's sexual orientation is not determinative of one's success as a role model. Homosexual, like heterosexual, educators can be good or bad exemplars. An appropriate role model is judged by the quality and strength of his or her moral character and not on the basis of his or her sexual orientation.

77. *Chamberlain (CA)*, para 58.

78. Ibid., para. 70.

79. See Jane Armstrong, "B.C. Board Finds New Basis to Ban Books," *Globe and Mail*, June 14, 2003, p. A9.

80. See, "New Books on Same-sex Families Approved," *Globe and Mail*, June 27, 2003, p. A7.

81. Mr. Skutch's book depicts many different family units including single-parent families, lesbian and gay families, mixed-race families, and families with divorced parents and grandparents. Ms. Combs' book shows children and parents engaging in usual family activities. All the families in her book are headed by gay or lesbian parents.

Part III
Implications for Practice

Playing by the Rules:

BUILDING A RATIONALE TO OFFER A COURSE ON SCHOOLING AND SEXUAL IDENTITIES IN A FACULTY OF EDUCATION

James McNinch

Introduction

> *In imagining possibilities, we act as prophets of our own existence.*
>
> Paul Ricoeur

This chapter shares the rationale I constructed so that a course on sexual identities and schooling would be approved as an elective in the Faculty of Education at the University of Regina, Saskatchewan. It is also a story of my own changing identity as an advocate for such curricular change in 2001–2002. The rationale appeals to several foundational assumptions found in most teacher preparation programs: a largely feminist-driven concern for equity and social justice, and small "l" liberalism reflected in the concepts of ethics, citizenship and an ideology of inclusiveness. Further, I suggest these foundational arguments contribute effectively and appropriately to the construction of the identity of teachers and teacher educators on the basis of notions of authenticity, integrity and narrativity. In reading this, imagine being part of an ongoing discussion about the connection of LGBT (lesbian, gay, bisexual, and transsexual and two-spirited) issues to broader foundational issues of change in society, in the helping professions generally, and in education specifically.

Setting

The Saskatchewan setting for a course on sexual identities and schooling is important to understand. Sixty percent of the population lives in rural or small communities with populations of less than 10,000. In this province, women routinely gravitate after supper to the kitchen to do the dishes and talk children and gardens, while the men retire to the porch or the living room to talk crops and hockey. Sex, money, religion, and politics are regarded as inappropriate topics. The false binary of such gender roles in a family environment is problematic for more people than just gays and lesbians. But this is a province where the cooperative movement was born of pragmatism not altruism. You didn't help your neighbour because of what was once known quaintly as "brotherly love." Waves of immigration to the prairies meant that neighbours were often "different"—in their language, in their culture, in their faith. As a relative of mine once put it, "they ate funny food, wore strange clothes, smelled of garlic and you couldn't understand anything they said and so you didn't trust them." You helped neighbours like this only because you knew in your bones that your own survival ultimately might depend on it. Even those of us who live in Saskatchewan cities come from rural backgrounds typified by such experience.

Importantly, for both urban and rural citizens, the tension between difference and sameness, particularly drawn along lines of race and ancestry, is part of the Saskatchewan culture. While southern Saskatchewan spawned socialism and univer-sal health care, only one generation separates us from European immigrant ancestors for whom marriage outside one's faith, race, or class was considered heretical. Spinsters and bachelors, even when they lived with members of the same sex, were assumed to be "queer ducks" perhaps, but they were not assumed to have a sexual identity. "Doing gender" hasn't changed much in this milieu: yes, girls can play hock-ey and boys can take ballet, but in a small town the boy better not play with Barbie dolls or the girl with Tonka trucks or something will be deemed to be "wrong." Since the Depression, this is a province that annually exports many of its high school and university graduates; the gay and lesbian ones have been the first to leave for larger, more cosmopolitan (and anonymous) centres such as Vancouver, Calgary and Toronto.

Despite huge advances in the rights and visibility of LGBTs in the last two decades of the 20th century, the creation of an imagined community of discourse, specifically a course for undergraduate education students called "Schooling and Sexual Identities," was something that some members of the Faculty of Education regarded as necessary or long overdue as we entered the 21st century. The hurt, the fear, the anguish of sexual difference, the silence, the masking, and the isolation have left deep scars on LGBTs in the social and cultural environment of the prairies, which is often as harsh and contradictory as its inhospitable climate.

While Gay and Lesbian Studies in the Arts and Humanities have been regarded on many campuses across North America and Europe as a legitimate cross-disciplinary fields of inquiry since the 1980s, schools and faculties of Education have seldom been included in that cross-fertilization. To the credit of the Women's Studies pro-gram at the University of Regina, it offers a number of its own courses and cross-listed ones from other departments, which address gender formation and human sexuality, but none deal with a specific educational context or with LGBT issues. One such cross-listed course, the Faculty of Education's "Women and Education 308," is an exploration of feminist perspectives of educational issues. LGBT issues in education were not being served directly by any of these complementary objec-tives. Once the Women's Studies coordinator reviewed the initial proposal for the LGBT education course, she accepted it as a cross-listed course, provided that some seats were reserved for students from other faculties besides Education. This chap-ter, then, shares the rationales to have such a course approved as an elective in our Faculty of Education.[1]

The Course: Sexual Minorities in Schools

Course Description

This course provides the rationale, background, and strategies for understanding sexual identities and the social constructions of inclusivity and difference in schools. The course will examine the pedagogical and curricular implications (for all educators) of LGBT students and teachers in our schools.

Statement of Rationale

LGBT students and teachers are the last minority group to be tolerated, accepted, understood, appreciated, and officially recognized in our school systems. This course will encourage students to clarify their own understanding of sexual identity. The course will address ignorance of and discrimination directed against sexual minorities in schools. Because of this silence and lack of recognition, sexual minority students do not find the same support that heterosexual students do. This course seeks to explore and redress this injustice.

Course Intentions

First, symbolically, such a course would serve as a flagship, signalling to our Saskatchewan educational partners and to all our students that sexual identity issues were important in pre-service teacher preparation. This would be an active way of declaring that homophobia in the province was as unacceptable as racism, and was something that we, as a faculty, were committed to eradicating. Second, on an individual level, the course would serve as a safe place for all students to discuss the formation of their sexual identity and its relation to their formation as teachers with ethical and pedagogical responsibilities to their students. I hypothesized this to be particularly so for the LGBT students in training who deserve an emotionally and intellectually safe environment in which to explore these issues, particularly if deciding whether or not to open the door of the closet to become a publicly queer teacher.

Course Objectives

The objectives of the course are to understand theory and to transform practice. Students, therefore, are invited to:

- understand the interwoven social, cultural, and personal and interpersonal components of sexual identity formation;
- become familiar with the social, biological and historical construction of homosexuality, including the constructs of sin, pathology, and preference;
- appreciate the implications of heterosexual privilege with respect to the positionality of sexual and other minorities;
- acquire a vocabulary for examining myths and stereotypes, and common elements of various forms of oppression, including "outing" and "closeting";
- analyze various models of identity development in LGBT youth and adults;
- be better prepared (then) to create a safer and more inclusive school environment and develop appropriate classroom and counselling strategies and a stronger, more confident view of their sexual identity as part of their teacher identity.

Course Topics

Topics that will be explored in the course range from religion and spirituality to media representations of gender to instructional strategies. They include:

- sexism, heterosexism, and homophobia;
- the pedagogical implications of heterosexual privilege;
- the social, biological, and historical construction of homosexuality;
- the personal development of an individual's sexual identity;
- cross-cultural understandings of homosexuality, including two-spirited people;
- religion, spirituality and homosexuality;
- equity, diversity and inclusivity;
- justice and the law;
- how the media constructs gender and sexuality;
- activism and support in and out of the classroom;
- strategies, lessons, and resources (both for working with LGTB students and for fighting homophobia).

Promoting the Gay Agenda

With key support from the associate dean and three female colleagues who offered critical advice as we conceptualized the course, I was able to imagine that it was my duty to dispel the negative connotation that such a course would be promoting a "gay agenda." In light of religious and political opposition to "gay rights," it came as a revelation that I actually *was* promoting a gay agenda, at least according to what Liberal member of Parliament Tom Wappel (2000) calls "the radical homosexual movement":

> When you go home tonight, go to your dictionaries and look up the words "homophobia" and "homophobic." Unless you have a 1999 edition of one or two "new wave" dictionaries, you will not find these words. Why not? Because they did not even exist until 1994 when they were invented by the radical homosexual movement as a tactic to marginalize and embarrass those, like me, who do not agree with their agenda. What is this agenda? It is to force everyone, not just to tolerate homosexuality, but to actively accept and embrace it as normal, and to teach our children that it is normal, so as to permit homosexual marriage, adoption and benefits. They want to make it illegal to say anything negative about the practice, even if you, as a matter of religion, believe it to be abnormal and sinful. The activists are well on their way to the successful completion of their agenda.

Such opposition made me aware that one of the implicit fundamentals of teacher preparation is the division between behaviour and identity. To underline the inconsistency between behavior and identity and between word and deed, in the curriculum of our Faculty and of our provincial Department of Education (now, Saskatchewan Learning), I pointed to curricular claims to celebrate and affirm the diversity of the K–12 student population while studiously ignoring LGBT issues. In other words, I demonstrated the privileging of heterosexual relations in teacher education, closeting the issue of sexual diversity behind walls of silence and what Brown (2000), in referring to Sedgwick's work (1990), called "knowing by not knowing" an "open secret"' because "meaning is generated on absence as well as just presence" (pp. 13–14). I had to critique the passive/aggressive resistance of homophobic bourgeois primness that constitutes heteronormativity.

I could do this by pointing to the province's teachers' federation, the professional and self-regulating body which was producing two documents on envisioning schools as safe places by supporting sexual difference for students and teachers, while we in preservice education buried our heads in the sand. I pointed out that an esteemed colleague, Donald Cochrane, at the University of Saskatchewan in Saskatoon, had pioneered a foundations course on Gay and Lesbian Issues in Education and had been running an annual conference for five years in order to "break the silence." I pointed to a similar course at York University, a new one proposed at OISE, and modules on the subject in the Faculty of Education at the University of Alberta to contextualize our "provincialism."

Perhaps most importantly, and again on the advice of three wise women in the faculty, I formed an advisory committee from the community—students, educators, and "elders" from LGBT circles to affirm and share in this creation of an imagined community. Although the advisory committee seldom met as a group, each member was adamant that if the university was not going to be part of the solution, it was then definitely part of the problem of perpetuating homophobia. We could quote ACT UP's widely publicized AIDS education program: "silence equals death!" (Silversides, 2003). This stage in the development of the course was crucial in confirming the appropriateness of and need for the course by tying it to the community at large.

One implication of this silent masking is the social construction of a closet for queer students when they apply for pre-service teacher education programs. Ironically, gays and lesbians are required to do "hetero drag" and pretend that the teacher identity they don—which supports diversity and inclusivity and social justice for the marginalized and disadvantaged (aka "youth at risk")—is for the projected "other," and not for themselves. We are, in effect, asking LGBT students to replicate a school system which had already helped to oppress them because their model of the "at risk" student is still based on the 19th century charity and residential school model of "lady bountiful" extending her (expensively gloved) hand to the less fortunate.

Another implication of silence is the danger of plain ignorance: we permit pre-service teachers to enter the schools without exploring LGBT issues, many thinking homosexuality is a "new thing," a "lifestyle choice," and not "natural."[2] The only mention of homosexuality in the Saskatchewan curriculum is in one sentence in the Grade 9 Health curriculum—a sentence which also includes the word AIDS. As a result, novice teachers are ill prepared to combat bullying or sexual harassment, much less to offer a safe, encouraging place for LGBT students to flourish. In our society, where eros and the erotic have been denied space in the classroom, as bell hooks (1994) pointed out, and where Western thought has "unsexed the mind" (Alexander, 1997, p. 339), "sexual citizenship ... is privatized, deradicalized, de-eroticized and *confined* in all senses of the word: kept in place, policed, limited" (Bell and Binnie, 2000, p. 3), particularly by institutions such as schools.

How then to challenge the power and privilege of homophobic resistance to the supposedly gay agenda? Almost 25 years ago, Adrienne Rich (cited in Richardson, 2000) spoke of the damage caused by the "institutionalization of heterosexuality, imposed, managed, organized, [and] propagandized" (p. 22). What follows describes in some detail the strands of the rationale for a course on schooling and sexual identities that would challenge the normative hegemony of heterosexism.

Equity and Social Justice

Given the faculty's purported allegiance to equity and social justice, this was the safest and most logical place to start. Our faculty has a long tradition of integrating theory and practice to "serve the needs of all children of the province." We strive to "prepare teachers to address both equity and excellence" (*Faculty of Education Response to the Task Force and Public Dialogue on the Role of the School Final Report*, 2001, p. 7). The educational partnership in Saskatchewan needs to exercise "moral courage" (p. 8) "by further developing ... the pathway ... [and] value and practice inclusion, dialogue and consensus if a shared vision is to be realized" (p. 9).

Within the equity and social justice model, which has always identified students with all sorts of special needs, I could play to the emotions, cite statistics about the vulnerability of LGBT kids to be "at risk"—the runaways, the drop-outs, the drug and alcohol abuse, the STD and HIV health risks of promiscuity, the suicides, the dilemmas for parents and families of queer youth, and the dilemmas for straight youth with LGBT parents. At its worst, this approach appeals to the "mother superior" model of teacher education—"Trust in me, my child, I know what is good for you and a LGBT course will be good for you." But, at its best, this approach appeals to the educator as nurturer and to the maternal instincts of early childhood and elementary educators. I quoted a Saskatchewan mother's words used by the Saskatchewan Teachers' Federation (2002) in their document:

> Imagine what it might have been if from childhood he'd [my son] known the words for how he was different and that that difference was fine—just a normal variation of human sexuality. Imagine if he had gone to schools where homophobia wasn't tolerated, where teachers and support staff were openly supportive of all diversity, where anti-homophobia education was a part of the curriculum, where openly gay teachers were free to be the wonderful role models that they are. (Preface)

In other words, imagining a LGBT course would be the kind, humane, equitable and socially responsible thing to do. For the Faculty of Education, at the University of Regina, this is what education has been about; a course on LGBT would be part of a respected child-centred pedagogical tradition.

Ethical Persuasion and Old-Time Religion

A second argument appeals to individual faculty members' sense of ethics. Closely related to the equity and social justice framework are issues of "personal authenticity and integrity." The work of Parker Palmer (1998) proved invaluable in drawing connections between each individual and his or her own fears and sense of "other." Personally, I was greatly inspired and strengthened by Palmer on my own path to advocating for this imagined discourse, and I was able to share my experience of "coming out" with colleagues.

Palmer (1998) challenges teachers, "To teach authentically one must no longer avoid the threat of a live encounter" (p. 37), meaning we must not hide ourselves from others. Palmer argues persuasively that to continue to be of service to their students, educators must confront their fears—fears of others, fear of our own ignorance, fear of self. Palmer encourages isolated teachers to live "divided no more, teaching from a 'heart of hope' (p. 163) to form "communities of congruence" (p. 172) for mutual support and a shared vision. In workshops, Palmer's facilitators ask teachers to reflect metaphysically on their condition:

What questions are you living at this stage of your life? Are there other questions you would like to be living? Can you say that you have or had an experience of community? What has been healthy and unhealthy about that connection to community? What does it mean to be "in community with one's self?" What do you fear in exposing your inner life? (Livsey, 1999, pp. 16–22)

Palmer (1998) encourages us to reflect on our own experience and ask our own questions. Some of mine are: What is the relationship between identity and integrity? How have gendered teaching roles affected my definition of self? How do I move beyond "performativity" ("doing gender" and "doing teacher") that may distance me from my students and from myself? What are the pedagogical implications of being an out-gay professor?[3]

Ethical arguments based on authenticity and integrity are persuasive and effective in a faculty of education because many faculty members have understood issues through their connection to organized religion. In southern Saskatchewan this means particular denominations of Christianity: United, Lutheran, Anglican, Catholic and Evangelical, each with its own struggle to come to terms with homosexual desire and same-sex relationships. Faculty members are more likely to be active members of a church than of a political party. As a Quaker, Palmer took church-based morality out of the pulpit and expressed it as a values-based eco-humanistic and liberation theology which broadens its appeal to those working for social justice in education and other fields of community development. Palmer has been inspired particularly by the peaceful, but not passive, resolution of the civil rights movement in the United States and uses it as a model for how individuals can reach out to others, build community, and effect change. The connections to the gay liberation movement are obvious and significant.

Paying Homage to the Feminist Diaspora

Feminism has made the most significant contribution to the foundational studies of LGBT issues in education and to queer studies as an academic stream. A rationale that builds on feminist liberationist theory dates back to Germaine Greer and Gloria Steinem in the 1970s and continues with the critical theory of radical lesbians and queer theorists such as Butler (1990). Such a strand of the rationale need not be concerned with the dialogues/diatribes between heterosexual feminism and political lesbianism. All feminists appreciate the relationship between the private and the public and, perhaps most crucially, that the personal *is* political. Feminists have long conceptualized, largely from their own experience, how definitions of masculinity and femininity are socially constructed and how they play themselves "out" in this world. Because of this, I could make a fundamental link through Palmer and Friere's liberationist pedagogy to feminism which understands that the personal is political and is also pedagogical.

What theoretical shift did I expect "hetero feminist" colleagues to make along this continuum? The arguments of equity and social justice and antiracist education were already theirs. The shift moved into the realm of sex. The identity politics of social and cultural citizenship had to be extended to sexual citizenship. For me, a telling example from the 1960s points to the most significant change in this field in the last 30 years. Trudeau's famous edict that the state had "no (damn) business in the bedrooms of the nation" was revolutionary in its day. However, we now see with hindsight that, in privileging privacy and separating intimacy from the public arena, society was closeting sexuality in general, and privileging heterosexual normativity in the public sphere, particularly in North America where the female body has been used to sell everything from tractors to depilitators. It is a commonplace in feminist thinking that the duality between private and public has served to embed sexist views of women as property and as sexual objects. Feminist liberation movements created a new sense of authorship, often raucous and conflicted, but always genuine in understanding that the personal is more than "private." One only has to see how issues such as definitions of work, both paid and unpaid, prostitution, pornography, rape laws, and spousal abuse are personal issues that are critical matters of concern in public discourse. Feminists, like the civil rights activists before them, well understood that the power to change society depends very much on who controls the discourse—both the media and the message. They could now understand how LGBTs were walking a similar path, "doing" or being forced to "do gender" (Butler's phrase), every day of their lives. As Richardson (2000) concludes, "Being queer is not about a right to privacy, it's about the freedom to be public" (p. 48).

Appealing to the substantive ontologies and epistemologies of feminism and their connection to LGBT issues proved to be one of the most salient arguments in providing a rationale to faculty for a course on sexual identities. I was able to defer to long-time feminists by acknowledging how they had, both in theory and in practice, paved the way for the gay liberation movement. I appealed to these women's sense of themselves as both maternal and intellectual nurturers. Feminists in the faculty had helped me to imagine a discourse on sexual minorities in the 21st century because they had imagined a new discourse for themselves in the last three decades of the 20th century. "The classroom remains the most radical space of possibility ... we can know beyond the boundaries of what is acceptable ... so that we can create new visions" (hooks, 1994, p. 12).

Other Important "isms"—From Alienation to Zen

Feminism, however, was not the only movement to impact on academics and educators in the 1960s and 1970s. Other epistemologies provided both historical context and rationale for the elevation of queer studies and LGBT discourse and continue to be an animating spirit for LGBT definitions of identity formation and a vocabulary of both the inner and the outer world.

First, there is Hegel and Marx (and later the Frankfurt School of the 1950s and 1960s, including Benjamin and Althusser) to whom we owe our understanding of the dialectic, of the class wars, of structural issues such as asymmetrical power relationships, of the importance of knowing who owns the means of production and distribution, and the objectification of individuals and the reification of ideas and making fetishes of objects in a capitalist system. The LGBT rhetoric of oppression stems from this tradition.

Then, from Freud, Jung, and post-Freudian theory, in psychoanalysis, we have an understanding of self, of instincts, inner worlds, psychic realities, what Lacan went on to define as "the imaginary register" (cited in Zaretsky, 1994, p. 202). At its healthiest, this imaginary register of spirit, sense, and sex is integrative and celebrative; at its worst, it is fragmented, bitchy, neurotic and narcissistic. Jung helped Westerners see the masculine and feminine in us all. Indeed "analysis" of the "self" on the psychologist's couch, and hypothesizing the influence of the mother and the father on identity formation, did much to initiate contemporary debates between constructivists and essentialists. From institutional and clinical practice to self-help and self-improvement movements, the field of psychology did much to both repress and liberate individual LGTB people in the last century and problematize the relationship between the body and the mind. By the beginning of the 20th century, the field of psychology had pathologized homosexuality, but then went on to depathologize it by the end of the century, although the concept of "gender identity disorder" continues to confuse the issues.[4] In addition, a queer orientation connects, too, with the European existentialist tradition and the American Beat generation of the 1950s. LGBTs have inherited and have lived, I argue, a profound understanding of the "outsider," of alienation, of reification, of the self-consciousness involved in ontological exercises such as defining self and creating meaning and choosing to act. "Coming out" is still conceptualized, like suicide or sex, as the ultimate existential experience.

From this rich intellectual heritage, we have been able to understand identity formation as part of the dialectic between an inner circle (self, family, and kinship) and the outer (the world of commerce, business, trade, and industry). Postmodernists, certainly Foucault, would be the first to acknowledge that Marxists, Freudians, and Existentialists have been the primary contributors to our understanding of struggles against forms of ethical, racial, social, and religious domination and forms of exploitation that separate us from the means of production, that make commodities and consumers of us all and the stances we make to protect ourselves. Issues such as sexual identity and sexual orientation relate to larger themes, beyond the constriction of names and label:

> [In Zen] *fundamentally not one thing exists ... one no longer feels that he is an ego, except by definition. He sees that his ego is his personal or social role, a somewhat arbitrary selection of experiences with which he has been taught to identify himself. (Why, for example, do we say "I think" but not "I am beating my heart"?). Having seen this, he continues to play his social role without being taken in by it... He plays it cool.* (Watts cited in Charters, 1992, p. 610)

Small "l" Liberalism and Citizenship

But ethics, equity and social justice perspectives stem from a much longer tradition —that of small "l" liberalism and its focus on citizenship. For colleagues who teach social studies methods courses and educational foundation courses this is familiar territory. I was able to pitch my appeal to their understanding of the construct of rights and responsibilities defined by nation states, an understanding that constitutes so much of the history-based curriculum in schools. Often official histories are couched in this language of liberalism, which tends to assume perpetual progress rather than simply constant change. Histories purport to show how high-born men (always men) of goodwill have exercised their responsibility not to be brutish to the labouring classes, dumb animals, small children, women or racial "others." The official history of the Commonwealth reads something like that.

The work of the British sociologist T.H. Marshall after World War II was seminal in summarizing how the movement in western Europe to expand civil and legal rights in the 18th century (e.g., the right to own property and the right to representation in the courts) preceded the expansion, in the 19th century, of political rights (such as freedom of speech and the right to vote). These rights were eventually extended (i.e., given over, but not without a struggle) first to men without property, then to women, and finally to colonized, and other "visible" and "minority" groups such as First Peoples. Then, in the 20th century, "rights" were expanded to include social and civil rights—the right to work, the right to access health care, the right to an education, the right to freedom from want or misery. The most recent of these rights gained have been in the areas of human rights legislation and the right to freedom from discrimination on a variety of grounds, the last ground identified as "sexual orientation." The United Nations, while an incredibly dense bureaucratic system, continues to embody this liberal idealism around the world. In March 2004, for example, 53 nations met in Geneva to discuss, argue, vote and then publicly declare whether sexual orientation and gender identity are human rights or not. (The vote was ultimately postponed because of opposition from Muslim countries.) This history of the extension of rights to various distinct groups is a powerful liberal argument for equality for LGBTs.

When Western leaders invoke "human rights," when they want to trade with countries with quite different histories from our own, they draw on this liberal tradition. When lawyers appear before the Supreme Court of Canada and invoke the Charter of Rights and Freedoms to argue for social and economic benefits to same-sex couples, it is this tradition they invoke. ("Let gays and lesbians marry and suffer like the rest of us" quips Joe Arvay, a noted human rights lawyer.) Clearly, this liberalism can be a powerful ally in imagining the inclusion of LGBT issues in education. This is the liberalism of "moral outrage" that causes "right-minded" and politically "correct" people to save whales, hug trees, preserve old buildings, make pariahs of smokers, and shudder to think about circumcision of women in Africa and child-labour in India, and urge political leaders to sign the Kyoto accord. This same sensibility is a combination of what the 19th century French understood as *sentiment* and what the British public school class still calls "fair play." It can and has been extended to "accommodate" disadvantaged and purportedly "invisible" groups: people with learning disabilities and sexual minorities, for example. The other side of this liberal argument is a more conservative one that tries to demonstrate the "advantage" of LGBTs and therefore the lack of any need for "special rights," much less tolerance or even "accommodation" under the law.

Like acknowledging our indebtedness to feminism, appreciating the impact of liberalism on the extension of rights to LGBT citizens is significant because, in the Western world today, socialization, primarily through education, has replaced property owning as the determiner of citizenship. If you are not incarcerated for being a criminal or if you are not mentally ill and medicated to live in a group home or on the streets, in other words, if schooling has successfully socialized you to citizenship, you can join a health club, vote, recycle, pay taxes, rotate your tires every 10,000 km, have a mortgage, and deal with your parents' dying and death. In other words, you will have been encouraged by multiple complex factors, dictated by self-interest and the good of all, to *"play by the rules"* (including marrying and having children). Therefore, to deny gay and lesbian students and teachers their identity is to deny them full rights of citizenship. According to this liberal argument, the impact on professional practice is profound because it implies an obligation to include. Imagining this community is imagining a fairer, more inclusive community.

The Post-colonial Experience—Building a Queer Nation

Being able to extend this liberal argument to the realm of cultural citizenship is one of the most relevant rationales for a course on sexual identities and schooling. Cultural citizenship has strong appeal to educators working in postcolonial fields of multicultural, antiracist, and First Peoples' education. These areas have quite different stances regarding identity. I am aware of and agree with the critique of the "mere pluralism" of multiculturalism, which can lead to assimilation and loss of identity, leaving behind only token symbols of heritage. But think of the cultural concept of *nation* espoused by the *separatistes* of the francophone communities (and their maligned, but apparently necessary, language police). Think, too, of First Nations' peoples struggle to preserve their languages and deal nation-to-nation with the provincial and federal governments in renegotiating treaty rights.

The LGBT community has borrowed heavily from this field of thought and action over the last 20 years. Thanks to the work of Pakulski (1997) and others on cultural citizenship, we can now talk about how LGBTs, as the Haida, or Micmac, or Québécois, or the Bosnians or Palestinians, have rights as individuals and as distinct groups. Instead of marginality and invisibility, as cultural citizens we are entitled to "symbolic presence and visibility." We can, for example, raise the rainbow and pink triangle flags at City Hall to launch "gay pride" week. Instead of stigmatization as sinful sodomites, we are entitled as cultural citizens to "endignifying representation." Thus, a dozen gay and lesbian choirs from across Canada congregate to sing and celebrate their history, their struggles, their difference. Instead of assimilation as closeted, and hence harmless, citizens, we are entitled to "the right to the propagation of our own identity" (Richardson, 2000, pp. 73–75). This was acknowledged, for example, in 2001, when the Saskatchewan Arts Board publicly funded openly gay composer David McIntyre to write the music and lyrics to a song cycle of the coming out and other stories of gay and lesbian choir members. It is clear that LGBT "claims for legitimacy or recognition are [much] more than claims for tolerance" (Calhoun, 1994, p. 25). Thus, the acknowledgement of queer culture and identities is about imagining and then creating a more vibrant, self-supporting, and sustaining community.

One critique of acknowledging and even celebrating difference is that it leads to the fragmentation of society into a series of special-interest and lobby groups in which the whole is no longer greater than the sum of its parts. Often this critique is fed by a nostalgia for a "simpler," more "straight"-forward time, constructed by self-deception. This line of thinking feeds more conservative arguments about core values (often a code for specific religiously fundamentalist and narrowly defined family values) being negated in a nation that has lost its vision and purpose. Nevertheless, postcolonial thought provides crucial insights into the use and abuse of power in the construction of and discourse around the formation of identity of individuals and groups. Most importantly, perhaps, it helps to contextualize "white privilege" in most queer discourse. This strand helps us to connect the movement for rights of citizenship to LGTB people in the postcolonial tradition and to remind us that any nation, however defined, is composed of a complex diversity of unique individuals.

Foucault's Postmodern Antidote to the Ken Doll

Gay and lesbian educators have always been drawn to what is now referred to in provincial departments of education as "diversity education" because of its critique of power relationships, its egalitarianism, its romanticism, its inclusivity. There is a promise of hugs and hot cocoa in diversity education that suggests no one need be excluded; indeed, we might dare to celebrate our differences together. At the very least, the diversity stance of cultural citizenship prepares us to tackle a more problematic position—that of sexual citizenship. It is more challenging to traverse this larger gap than the smallerer one defined by the liberalism of social and political citizenship.

Sexual citizenship and the shaping of desire are at the heart of what defines LGBT difference. Foucault's (1979) influence on postmodernist thinking is crucial here. Again, feminists mapped this terrain, particularly around issues of sexual reproduction and sexual freedom and expression, but issues of domination and subservience and age of consent have been central to the transgressive quality of LGBT identity. Foucault has been instrumental in creating a theoretical stance that enables pedagogical and curricular development around queer issues.

This will prove to be substantive work if only to reduce misperceptions and stereotypes perpetuated in families and schools and churches about what constitutes perversion and who determines the continuum between wellness and pathology and between normality and abnormality. For example, even realistically imagined communities can be skewed by media representation. On Pride TV we see 20-year-old giggling gay men playing the dating game or guessing the sexual orientation of some cute guy. Flip to the Home and Garden channel and you will see homosexual men of a certain age (like me) portrayed as a bunch of Martha Stewart wannabes. This is the sanitization of the queer image—an imagined community where everybody is part of a monogamous couple, loves to shop for tasteful bric-a-brac, and dies for that perfect pair of shoes and the hunky boyfriend; in fact, this is just another form of doing drag.

My neighbours are comfortable with this image of my same-sex partner and I because it is ultimately nonthreatening to their heternormativity; in fact, it pays homage to it because, by sprinkling a bit of fairy dust around, we "do domesticity" (cook, clean, garden, arrange flowers and interior decorate) better than they do. This is the classic imitative role of the oppressed to become what oppresses you. The "domesticated" gay who no longer frequents the clubs and the bath-houses is the clean, safe, and homogenized version of homosexuality created for middle America where the morality of capitalism elevates our status and worth as consumers with taste and cash to spend. If we are indeed "born to shop," then we are part of any good capitalist's imagined community. I live this life contradictorily; it is part of being *un nouveau bourgeois*, rising like so many in the field of education from the rural agrarian and working class to the urban middle class. Drawing on Nietzsche's definition of historical sense, Champagne (1995) warns clearly of the danger of this sanitizing process; it produces an imagined past, "monumental celebrations of the gay spirit" (p. 136) and "antiquarian homosexualities" (p. 137), as well as a future reduced to "the fictive" (p. 141) and "dilettantish displays of queer pride" (p. 139).

But through Foucault (1979), we are able to see history as a story of the struggles against forms of subjectification by which I take him to mean, as in homophobia, the internalization of the objectification of the oppressed. Thus, "if we overthrow structures, discourse, and power strategies," according to Foucault, there is no "true" or essential identity waiting to be liberated. Identity then is not something whose assertion leads to liberation, but rather something we need to be liberated from (Zaretsky cited in Calhoun, 1994, p. 210).

This speaks directly to LGBT students and teachers alike who have shrouded a silence, constructed of externalized and internalized fear, around their sexuality. Foucault (1979), Butler (1990), and many others urge us to throw away hetero drag, but also to discard the clichés of homo drag as well. The imagined community dwells beyond the confines of what others think we should be. Proposing a course on LGBT issues is also about extending and defining the geography of space for gays, how space is "materialized" in the culture beyond the stereotypes of the bars and bath-houses, far away from the West End of Vancouver or Church Street in Toronto. Many, like Brown (2000), understand that transforming "space to place" is another, braver performance of the scripts of gender and sexuality (pp. 142–43). Until now this is a script that LGBT teachers have had to discard or mask in the schools. Imagine providing all prospective teachers in their pre-service education with some direction and cues for this daunting "role."

> A naked lunch is natural to us,
> We eat reality sandwiches.
> But allegories are so much lettuce.
> Don't hide the madness.
>   (Ginsberg, cited in Charters, 1992, p. 101)

Narrativity—Telling a Tall Tale

The field of teacher preparation, particularly the professional studies area which concerns itself with teacher identity, has many advocates and practitioners of narrativity, as well as champions of the qualitative and action research that has been done to legitimize the concept that "social life is itself *storied* and that narrative is an *ontological condition of social life*" (Somers and Gibson cited in Calhoun, 1994, p. 38). Over the last decade, we have learned that "people are guided to act in certain ways, and not others, on the basis of the projections, expectations, and memories derived from a multiplicity but ultimately limited repertoire of available social, public and cultural narratives" (p. 38).[5]

Somers and Gibson (cited in Calhoun, 1994) usefully outline the interconnected spirals between four dimensions of narrativity: ontological, public, conceptual, and metanarrativity (pp. 61–64). Clearly much work has been and can still be done in seeing the dialectic playing out between these narrative layers in the lives of queer students and teachers. Over the past two decades, we have been ready to narrate/create/re-create ourselves to ourselves and for others. Testaments of the personal journey and the structuring and collecting of interviews have proven to be powerful ways of knowing the subjectivity of a "queer" reality.

However, we need to explicate what the relationship is between the first level, the personal ontological narrative, and the second, the public level of narrativity. For example, who are we, as a condition for knowing what to do and not do as closeted queer teachers? Further, how do the public narratives articulated by churches and schools about behaviour and identity inform or deform this ontology? "Love the sinner, hate the sin" urges the Church. Speaking to the Durham Catholic School Board about Marc Hall's request to bring his boyfriend to the high school prom, a priest attempted to explain that square dancing is nonsexual but slow dancing is. (He had obviously never seen the cowboy's square dance at the Calgary Gay Rodeo.) Catholic school boards reflect the conflicted nature of their interpretation of sexual orientation: for example, a teacher would never be fired simply because she was lesbian but, if she exhibited a "gay lifestyle" by openly living with and loving another woman, she could be. Pre-service teachers need to understand the distinction between sexual identity, sexual behaviour, and sexual orientation.

A young man recently asked me: "Should I identify my sexual orientation when applying to a teacher education program?" After all, there is a section on the form used at the University of Regina by the Faculty of Education that asks the applicant to describe "circumstances related to the principles of equity and inclusion which might warrant special consideration for the applicant's acceptance to the program." Is this an invitation to disclose and be welcomed as "special"? Would a queer narrative be read by the selection committee as a reason for accepting or rejecting a student? Sexual orientation "doesn't matter," only when it is presumed to be heterosexual and homosexuality is masked. In applying to a teacher education program it is still probably best to leave the sexual identity baggage at home since teacher education programs have implicitly adopted the US military's position: "don't ask; don't tell."

To explore another example, we might ask what the impact is of conceptual narratives such as agency, self-efficacy, intentionality, essentialism, constructionism and historicism on identity formation and the positionality of self and others? How do the larger-than-life themes and mythic characters, that is, the metanarratives, play out in the lives of LGTBs? These metanarratives include us even if we are not there: religious fundamentalism, the decline of the West, the Fall of the Roman Empire, the tragedy of AIDS, the rise of Islam, the triumph of good, the triumph of evil, John Wayne, Luke Skywalker, Princess Lea, Ken and Barbie, Jeff Stryker, Mae West! Circles enclose again when we attribute, at least from Machiavelli on, that certain individuals and certain groups often have control over which narratives predominate and which particularly become the official ones. Who is accepted and who is shunned, who is celebrated and who is reviled, who is forgiven and who is punished; the answer to these questions will depend in large part on the distribution of power.

The Naughty Bits—What Needs to be Said

The critically transgressive nature of some aspects of queer sexual culture and its sexual citizens is probably the most problematic area to broach in a Faculty of Education. Educators are more comfortable with a slapstick, goofy, a-sexual Jack of *Three's Company* than the spectre of a character as darkly comic as *Myra Breckinridge*. Nevertheless, it is important to understand how difference formulates or "queers" a construct of criticism. One of the foundational issues here is how the dialectic of marginality—the constant flux between the outsider and the establishment—serves to define both. Foucault (1979), for example, draws attention to how queer practices, some of which he calls "the technologies of self "—of bondage, submission and debasement of the self in body piercing, tattooing and genital shaving—once on the margins of what was regarded as "deviant" have now become part of the heterosexual mainstream. Some argue that infliction by the self on the self and the creation of a "nonidentity" have become symbols of the postmodern stance against dominance (Champagne, 1995, p. 60). The semiotic symbolism of such signs can confuse and disturb teacher educators who see them as an affront to their own value system and to the values transmitted in teacher education. Thus, a broader understanding of the complexity involved in defining deviance is a foundational aspect of the imagined discourse envisioned.

Through specific sexual practice, queer culture also offers a strong critique of romanticism that rubs against the grain of teacher preparation programs. The anonymity of sex in bath-house and movie theatre settings, for example, as well as the lack of tenderness in much gay pornography, serve to celebrate bodily instinct, need, and desire rather than the more "civil" ideas about romance, love, commitment, and monogamy. Perhaps even more unsettling to those transmitting values through teacher education is gay pornography's explicit denunciation of the hetero feminist argument that eroticism is about mutuality while pornography is about domination. Gay pornography often involves consensual sado-masochism. So this side of sexuality can be disturbing, regardless of people's own sexual identity, behaviour, or orientation. The fundamental problem is that teacher education programs do not know what to do with people who "flaunt" or "indulge" their sexuality—homo or hetero—or even those who simply identify their homosexuality, and who thus don't conform to heteronormative behaviour or what is coded as "family values."

But this "darker side" does need to be talked about. There are more complex issues to come to terms with; several examples will illustrate this point. Indeed some would go so far as to argue that the lack of "difficult" issues in teacher education programs is one reason teachers are ill-prepared to deal with the many real "difficulties" they will inevitably encounter in the classroom. Teachers need to understand the failure of sexual education programs of all kinds to reduce the incidents of teenage pregnancy or stem the rise of sexually transmitted diseases in Canada. Teachers need to understand the influence and various interpretations of pornography as well as the debates about the limits of freedom of expression in light of the ongoing harassment of the Little Sisters' Bookstore by Canada Customs. They need to know that the statistics on runaway street kids and teen suicide point to a majority who have faced a lack of acceptance or a fear of a lack of acceptance of their sexual identity (Bagley and Tremblay, 2001; Leslie, Stein and Rotheram-Borus, 2002). They need to know that violent hate crimes are committed against sexually different minorities more than any other protected minority category. They need to know how to situate the arguments surrounding the Surrey School Board's fear of the representation of same-sex families in such children's books as *One Dad, Two Dads* and *Asha's Mums*, and the fight with gay and lesbian parents and teachers and the Supreme Court ruling against the school board. They need to understand the arguments Queen's Counsel, Joe Arvay, made on behalf of the teachers who wish to acknowledge with their kindergarten students that there are many different kinds of families. Teachers need to understand the implications of the hate-mongering of fringe fundamentalist Christians who quote God in Leviticus saying, "sodomites must be killed" and reconcile this with their own implicit or explicit religious and/or spiritual beliefs. Teachers need to be conversant with the implications of the decision of the Durham Catholic School Board not to allow Marc Hall to attend his high school prom with his boyfriend and the subsequent provincial court reversal of that decision. Teachers should be familiar with the story of Graham James, the hockey coach accused and banished as a pedophile of Sheldon Kennedy, then a junior hockey player. Merely in terms of information, teachers need to understand what it means to be a "lip-stick lesbian," or a "bear," or the difference between transsexual and transgendered. These broader issues here include understanding such things as age of consent, asymmetrical power relations, the role of the media, and internalized homophobia.

The brutal rape and murder of Pamela George, a Native "prostitute," by Alex Ternowetsky and Steven Kummerfield, young white, middle-class Regina men, raised many disturbing issues. In addition to the overt misogyny and racism of the act, serious questions about the justice system still linger as Razack's (2000) analysis shows. But neither Razack nor attribution by the Crown in the case ever suggested a "queer" theory: Alex and Steven were best buddies; even in their drunkenness they could not express their homoerotic desire for each other directly. Details from the trial indicate "she [Pamela] ultimately agreed to perform oral sex and all three remained in the front seat of the car while this was in progress" (p. 115). A queer interpretation suggests the only way the young men could express their repressed sexual longing for each other was to degrade Pamela George's body into an object and use a "squaw" between them to mask their passion for each other. The last gruesome step was to bludgeon her for their wrong-doing and leave her to die.

This is not the imagined community we would wish to live in, but it is an important aspect of the nature of the discourse we would wish to explore. Teachers in training, for their own and their students' sake, need to understand the issues at stake here, if we are ever going to prevent the racism, the bullying, and the homophobia rampant in our schools and society. For everyone's sake, we must act to imagine teacher education where educators create theoretical and practical frameworks which encourage students to frankly and thoroughly discuss and understand sexuality including sexual identity, sexual behaviour and sexual orientation, and the implications of this understanding for the classroom.

Guilt and Shame (My Own Journey)

Prompted by allies and a constituency to represent, rather than just construct the rationales for a course on sexual minorities, I reflect now that I had to create, in narrative tradition, a dragon to slay or, as it turned out, a windmill to flail at. That "monster," fashioned unconsciously on Arendt's (1994) "banality of evil," goes something like this: Within the culture of teacher education, gentility is a mask with a cute button nose turned-up in distaste for anything sexual. Queerness is suppressed in the name of good taste and appropriateness.

It is ironic, however, that I seemed compelled to demonize perceived resistance in the same way that the religious opposition has demonized "the gay agenda." Adversarial thrust and parry occur behind shells of rhetorical armour, while real people hide underneath. You can appreciate that this was not the imagined community of LGBT discourse I had envisioned.

Penultimately, the case for a course on sexual identity would rest not on any one ethical, epistemological, ontological or even ideological rationale or critique. It was embarrassing for me as an educator and as an out gay man to see how little we (I) do to prepare teachers to tackle these issues in the classroom. We (I) do nothing to make them brave and to imagine communities of respect for all. I was embarrassed that popular culture misinforms the public about homosexuality in situation comedies and media advertisements, yet we will not break the silence in our curriculum.

I was ashamed of myself. This is not an act of revolutionary proportions; it is not an act of bravery. I am not brave. No, it is the likes of Marc Hall—just a 17-year-old kid —who is brave. All we educators might be able to do to save face in the profession and in society is to play catch-up before being left completely behind.

We know that when a politician like Joe Clark, albeit desperate for votes and open-ly courting the gay constituency to contrast with the Alliance Party, rides in a convert-ible at the head of the Gay Pride Parade in Calgary, as he did three years ago, that the time has surely come for teacher education programs to include sexual citizenship in the curriculum. We know we are already guiltily running behind the bandwagon try-ing to catch up when the courts and legislatures in BC, Quebec, Ontario and Yukon pass or uphold laws recognizing the "civil union" of same-sex couples and their legal right to adopt children. As society changes and as equity is achieved step by step, what role and obligation do we have as educators? We must provide, as the curriculum writ-ers say, the appropriate "windows and mirrors," and set them at the right size and height so that we might engage all our students in critiques of the discourse of con-demnation and tolerance and help them to engage in a discourse of understanding and celebration of LGBT students and teachers, and ultimately themselves.

Conclusion: Timing and Expediency

Postscript: the story of building a rationale for a course on schooling and sexual minorities ends not with a bang but a whimper. Luttwack (cited in Champagne, 1995) insists "the logic of strategy is not linear but paradoxical. If you want to suc-ceed in it, you should do the wrong thing, not the right thing" (p. xxxviii). The stalling and passive resistance that I fashioned into the dragon turned out to be little more than a paper tiger. Perhaps I had merely projected my own guilt, shame, and apprehensions about moving forward on this topic onto the faculty as a whole. Except for a well-attended seminar that I gave, there was little dialogue, or contro-versy. Those with the strongest reservations, perhaps those who live by the faith of their churches, were the most silent, but I interpreted this as a sign of their profes-sionalism, and a sign of respect for difference that they would expect me to extend to them. Many new allies came on board. A colleague revising a textbook for second-ary teacher preparation asked for appropriate references on inclusion of gay and les-bian issues. In the end, the associate dean, always a champion of social justice issues, saw an administrative way to break the impasse. In planning class offerings, a gap appeared in the Spring/Summer semester of 2003. Those who usually teach the Women in Education course regularly offered at that time would be away on sabbat-ical and there was a need for someone to teach a social justice course. A course of Schooling and Sexual Identities could fill the gap.

Hall (cited in Champagne, 1995) has argued that in the intersection of multiple discourses and identities, "no identity is ever commensurate with the multiple and fractured experience of the subject" (p. 61). In addition, as Weeks (1985) points out, identities are "provisional, ever precarious, dependent upon, and constantly challenged by, an unstable relation of unconscious forces, changing social and person-al meanings, and historical contingencies" (p. 186). The poet, Rilke, expresses simi-lar sentiments more elegantly: "Be patient toward all that is unsolved in your heart and try to love … and live the questions themselves" (cited in Palmer, 1998, p. 86).

In this imagined community of discourse, teacher educators can relegate to the past the closeting of these issues and our "passing" invisibly as something we are not. The future is much more "straight" forward. Our self-creation is never on grounds freely chosen, but we are able now to take the next step in teacher education to reconcile teacher behaviour and identity with that of lesbian, gay, bisexual, transsexual and two-spirited behaviour and identity. Breaking the curricular silence in teacher education is but the first chapter in this exciting story.

Notes

1. A course proposal was submitted in May 2001. A brief summary of the need for and the rationales of such a course were presented to faculty at a noon-hour seminar in March 2002. Earlier forms of this paper were shared at conferences of the Canadian Society for the Study of Higher Education and the Canadian Lesbian and Gay Studies Association in May 2002. It was finally agreed to offer this course for the first time in the Spring session in May 2003.
2. This became evident to me while doing workshops on the topic of sexual identities and sexual orientation with pre-internship students in the secondary education program.
3. So I could share the path I had walked, thanks to Palmer. Cynically too, or perhaps just humorously, I could even posit myself as an "organic intellectual" operating within the paradigm of emancipatory research. "I was one of those gay guys so I must know 'from the heart' what I was talking about." I could also admonish those who would not confront their fears by quoting Rumi, a favourite Persian poet of Palmer's: "If you are here unfaithfully with us/You're causing terrible damage" (Palmer, 1998, p. 189).
4. This rich and conflicting history of psychology speaks particularly to educational psychologists who understand the need for a LGBT course, if only to reinforce their own teachings in the complex field of human development and theories of motivation and learning.
5. As a teacher of English literature and composition, as well as teacher education, I am always happy and sometimes bemused when various disciplines "discover" narrative and the key dimensions of time, space, and relationality. Cultures of Indigenous Peoples have always relied on narrative to define and sustain their existence. Now that fields such as education and sociology have discovered the narrative in research, they are sure to discover its elements of plot, setting, character and theme!

References

Alexander, T.M. 1997. "Eros and Understanding: Gadamer's Aesthetic Ontology of the Community." Pp. 322–45 in *The Philosophy of Hans-Georg Gadamer*, edited by L. Hahn. Chicago: Open Court.

Arendt, H. 1994. *Eichmann in Jerusalem: A Report on the Banality of Evil*. New York: Penguin.

Bagley, C. and P. Tremblay. 2000. "Elevated Rates of Suicidal Behavior in Gay, Lesbian and Bisexual Youth." *Crisis* 21, no. 3: 111–17. Review at: <http://www.virtualcity.com/youthsuicide/#New%20Papers>

Bell, D. and J. Binnie. 2000. *The Sexual Citizen: Queer Politics and Beyond*. Cambridge: Polity Press.

Brown, M. 2000. *Closet Space: Geographies of Metaphor from the Body to the Globe*. London: Routledge.

Butler, J. 1990. *Gender Trouble*. London: Routledge.

Calhoun, C. (ed.). 1994. *Social Theory and the Politics of Identity*. Cambridge, MA: Blackwell.

Champagne, J. 1995. *The Ethics of Marginality: A New Approach to Gay Studies*. Minneapolis: University of Minnesota Press.

Charters, A. (ed.). 1992. *The Portable Beat Reader*. New York: Penguin.

Foucault, M. 1979. *The History of Sexuality, Volume One*. London: Allen Lane.

hooks, b. 1994. *Teaching to Transgress: Education as the Practice of Freedom*. New York: Routledge.

Leslie, M.B., J.A. Stein and M.J. Rotheram-Borus. 2002. "Sex-specific Predictors of Suicidality Among Runaway Youth." *Journal of Clinical Child and Adolescent Psychology* 31, no. 1: 27–40. At <http://www.virtualcity.com/youthsuicide/street.htm>

Livsey, R. 1999. *The Courage to Teach: A Guide for Reflection and Renewal*. San Francisco: Jossey-Bass.

Marshall, T.H. 1950. *Citizenship and Social Class and Other Essays*. Cambridge, MA: Cambridge University Press.

——. 1964. *Sociology at the Crossroads: Class, Citizenship and Social Development*. New York: Doubleday.

McIntyre, D.L. 2002. "'I Could Not Speak My Heart.' Watershed Stories: Songs of Gay and Lesbian Experience." Unpublished.

Pakulski, J. 1997. "Cultural Citizenship." *Citizenship Studies* 1, no. 1: 73–76.

Palmer, P.J. 1998. *The Courage to Teach: Exploring the Inner Landscape of a Teacher's Life*. San Francisco: Jossey-Bass.

Razack, S. 2000. "Gendered Racial Violence and Spatialized Justice: The Murder of Pamela George." *Canadian Journal of Law and Society/Revue canadienne droit et société* 15, no. 2: 91–130.

Richardson, D. 2000. *Rethinking Sexuality*. London: Sage.

Saskatchewan Teachers' Federation. 2002. *Equity in Education: Supporting Lesbian, Gay, Bisexual, Two-spirit and Transgender Students in Saskatchewan Schools*. Saskatoon: Saskatchewan Professional Development Unit.

Sedgwick, E. 1990. *Epistemology of the Closet*. Berkeley, CA: University of California Press.

Silversides, A. 2003. *AIDS Activist: Michael Lynch and the Politics of Community*. Toronto: Between the Lines.

Somers, M.R. and G.D. Gibson. 1994. "Reclaiming the Epistemological 'Other': Narrative and the Social Construction of Identity. In *Social Theory and the Politics of Identity*, edited by C. Calhoun. Cambridge, MA: Blackwell.

University of Regina. 2001. *Faculty of Education Response to the Task Force and Public Dialogue on the Role of the School Final Report*. Regina: Faculty of Education, University of Regina.

Wappel, T. 2000. "Being a Christian in Politics." Originally published in the *Theological Digest & Outlook* (March). churchalivecanada.org/ accessed June 3. 2004.

Weeks, J. 1985. *Sexuality and Its Discontents*. London: Routledge.

Zaretsky, E. 1994. Identity Theory, Identity Politics: Psychoanalysis, Marxism, Post-structuralism." In *Social Theory and the Politics of Identity*, edited by C. Calhoun. Cambridge, MA: Blackwell.

λ

Disrupting Binaries of Self and Other:

ANTI-HOMOPHOBIC PEDAGOGIES FOR STUDENT TEACHERS

Carol Schick

15

I N A DISCUSSION ABOUT PROBLEMATIC ISSUES OF A SOCIAL NATURE, one frequently hears that public schools need to be doing something about whatever has been designated as the problem. This solution of "more education" is quickly raised as the answer to a host of issues, from not knowing how to apply for a line of credit to not showing proper respect for authority figures. There are many ideas and detailed prescriptions about what should be taught in schools. From my perspective, one would be hard pressed to find a more important way to spend school time than to consider what it means to treat each person with dignity and respect. While this worthy aim is not amenable to a simple answer or method, we can begin by recognizing that a solution may be discomforting to what we can allow ourselves to know. We can prepare to be unsettled about who we have come to know ourselves and others to be.

Students I teach are enrolled in an undergraduate program that will qualify them to become public school teachers in secondary and elementary schools. I teach a course to pre-service teachers that addresses issues of inequality and oppression in Canadian society. The course examines the social construction of identities shaped by gender, race, social class, sexual orientation, able-bodiedness, language, religion and ethnicity. We look closely at how power relations produce inequalities and meanings attached to "difference." One mistaken assumption for courses like this is that schools are sites for learning about *equality*, as if inequality occurred elsewhere and had only to be corrected when it showed up at schools. One frequently hears justice issues taken up as a matter of individual tolerance or fairness, with teacher advocacy seen as something akin to charity or extra-curricular work. The focus is usually placed on individuals or their cultures, or on groups which are disadvantaged by limited and discreet acts of discrimination. Discrimination is enacted both individually and through cultural practices of the schools. At a more foundational level, discrimination is an effect of the very thinking about what will be considered "normal" thought and behaviour. Systemic and personal disadvantage can be observed in and produced through interpersonal exchanges including language. It is a mistake to think that inequality is caused simply by individual acts and remedied by refraining from doing the same. Instead, I try to point out that in spite of the many fine things that can take place in schools, they are also sites for the production of inequality, oppression and injustice that is socially and culturally authorized. Inequality is produced in many overt ways in schools including through the curriculum, how the curriculum is taught and who does the teaching.

Discourses of inequality construct and touch the lives of all students and teachers and not only those who are on the receiving end of overt discrimination. In this chapter, I describe my approach to teaching about the construction of oppression in education, particularly with respect to homophobia. Participating in anti-homophobic discourses and other types of anti-oppressive education is an opportunity for teaching and learning about more equitable social relations in our schools. In this particular program, the course I teach is one of the few opportunities to speak directly about issues of social inequality as they affect education.

In this chapter about anti-oppressive teaching, I describe some of the considerations and dilemmas I bring to how anti-homophobic education can be done at all given the limitations of time and resources—including the limitations of my own knowledge. Perhaps one of the greatest challenges to disrupting and refusing homophobia in schools is at once the banality and yet the exceptional nature of anti-oppressive education in this era of popular culture, in which the other is well known and lives next door or maybe under the same roof; indeed, "we" may very well be "the other." There is an unfortunate assumption that problems of inequality such as homophobia, racism and sexism have already been solved, or are soon to be solved by positive feelings of personal empowerment. If outbreaks of discrimination do occur, they are the result of a few "bad apples." Examples of inequality that were once tolerated by an older generation are no longer acceptable. It is simply not cool to discriminate.

Students who plan to be teachers already assume that they are well intended and will, therefore, treat all students equitably—knowing that it is neither professional nor contemporary to be racist, sexist or homophobic, at least not overtly so. While they are preparing to be at least tolerant of "otherness" or "difference," they also need to learn how they have already been "schooled"—through processes of formal education—in the construction of racism, sexism, homophobia and other forms of oppression.

It is worth considering how anti-homophobic education, which requires more than good will, can be done at all given the invisibility of the issues for most students and the fact that anti-oppressive education of any kind does not provide easy answers. I will describe some of the practical and theoretical dilemmas that frame my teaching in this area of anti-oppressive education, which must deal with partial and open-ended answers and not a little resistance. Anti-homophobic teaching involves the difficult task of re-examining "normalcy" at the same time as it challenges and de-familiarizes a notion of self and others. This involves a different kind of pedagogy and not one that simply says "do this instead of that." My attempts to disrupt marginality in education settings must consider the mixed potential for refusal as well as reification of oppressive school norms. Regrettably, this pedagogy has the potential to make things worse without making them better. This chapter is most definitely not a blueprint, but more a series of considerations about how one might think through, and with the issue named as homophobia. I am not describing "how to" teach in an anti-homophobic manner as I think such instruction misses the point about the nature of the problem. Asking questions such as who holds the "problem of homophobia" and what counts as a solution seem appropriate for a pedagogy that disrupts, refuses and challenges oppression in schools.

Student Teachers and Homophobia: Confounding the Subject

Anti-oppressive education involves teaching and learning that work against various forms of oppression. This education takes into account the complexities of interlocking identifications as they are played out through hierarchies of social class, race, gender, sexual orientation and so forth. One of the problems in a course that teaches anti-oppressive education is that there is far too much to be considered in a single course about any of these important areas of inequality; on the other hand, there are some similarities and theoretical constructs that help us understand the systemic nature of oppression when we look across the issues of socially constructed identities. It is important to recognize that identifications are not simply "given" or "fixed" or "chosen." Identifications are understood for the way their meanings are socially constructed through discourses of unequal power relations. In spite of the popular mantra that suggests we are singular and self-made, identifications are produced through sets of multifaceted relations that are multiple, interlocking and shifting. Identities are never separate—such as only female or working-class or straight or mentally challenged. No one is completely defined by a single identification and no one ever goes without also having a gender, race and social class, even if one's racial or sexual identification seems to go unnoticed at a particular moment or in a particular context.

The interlocking nature of identity construction can be illustrated in the admonition that one "act like a lady," an expression made familiar to me when I was young. Parents of that era were not only attending to their girls' particular gender formation; they were also instructing girls in the social expectations of what it meant to be white, straight and from a particular social class. The term "lady" is not only about gender but also about the other identifications implied by default; that is, the identities "white" lady and "straight" lady were already assumed within the category "lady." Similarly, the category "teacher" generally suggests the categories white, straight, and middle-class whether or not this is individually true of the people who identify as or aspire to be teachers. Further, in all aspects of school curriculum, "student" is mostly assumed to be "straight" student. Students I teach are invited to examine the categories of "student" and "teacher" that are freighted with layers of social implications, such as the question of who can be a teacher or how students "should" grow and develop. They realize that their identifications are not simply labels but rather performative practices that they have negotiated through their own desires and responses to social expectations.

What does it mean to teach in one very short course about the construction of oppression in education, particularly with respect to homophobia? First, my own social position as a white, straight, middle-aged woman both limits what I can say, at the same time that it affords certain opportunities. It is ironic that in areas of social justice—when talking about inequality, being seen as "objective" and believable can often coincide with being less informed. Among some audiences, even though my understanding of the effects of homophobia is second-hand, my speaking against homophobia will not be seen as "self-interested," but perhaps "unbiased." This is similar to the way that white people are sometimes called upon to verify a charge of racism made by a person of colour, or the way a man will be able to decide whether or not a situation is sexist. What I say in my courses comes directly from how I am informed about and positioned as a straight woman with respect to GLBT issues. From my stand as a feminist and anti-racist educator, I recognize that my knowledge is both ongoing and partial.

Second, students learn that anti-oppressive education is mainly about their own lives as future teachers and their interactions with those they teach. Students bring various layers of understanding and experience to the course, and naturally, some are gay, lesbian, bisexual, transgendered or an intersexed minority. Some students have been informed by religious teachings that condemn homosexuality and insist that heterosexuality is the only natural possibility. Most are very interested in the opportunity to talk and learn about sexual orientation because it is one of the "loud silences" that almost never gets discussed, even though teachers deal with its consequences daily. On topics of discrimination and inequality, students learn that ending discrimination will not happen once and for all through a course in "tolerance" or prejudice management. Instead, ending discrimination is a process of uncovering one's own involvement with oppression, a process that is lifelong. This is not an entirely comfortable course for students or for me as we begin the difficult task of both learning and "unlearning." However, I maintain that it is neither possible nor perhaps even desirable to avoid personal discomfort when learning about the effects of discrimination such as homophobia, especially given that discriminatory practices are serious matters that can ruin one's life chances and even cause death.

One other conceptual hurdle in teaching about equality of sexual orientation in schools is the notion of objectivity and the assumption that one must teach "both sides." This is, of course, an absurd notion if one considers that the other side of "equality" is "inequality"—as if the latter deserves equal opportunity. On the topic of sexual orientation, what is generally meant by "both sides" is whether homosexuality is "right or wrong." This is akin to asking whether being a racial minority or a woman or a person from the working-class is "right or wrong." In socially and religiously conservative areas, such as where I teach, the rightness or wrongness of homosexuality still lingers not too far in the background of student consciousness. Therefore, I acknowledge at the outset that while the matter of sexual orientation is a religious question for some people, our classroom discussions will not be based on the rightness or wrongness of homosexuality or assumptions about its morality based on religious teaching. As religion is not my area of expertise, it is doubtful that I would easily be able to dissuade students from their beliefs that have taken a lifetime of instruction to accumulate. We agree to respect each other's religious views, even though we may disagree, noting that people of the same faith community may hold contrasting positions. We recognize that it is quite possible to belong to any of the world religions and to be gay- and lesbian-positive and that it is particular interpretations of religious understanding that see homosexuality as wrong. I commend the students to their own faith communities to carry out these debates. Furthermore, people often hold conflicting views within their own hearts and minds regarding religion and homosexuality and may need time to sort things through. However, I challenge students to consider the negative effects that religious teachings have had on the lives of sexual minorities. The phrase that a truly religious person will "love the sinner" seems exceedingly sanctimonious given the overtly negative stand towards homosexuality by some faith communities. While religious teaching might be opposed to overt violence against homosexuals, religious leaders should look to the violence that is done in their names by the irreligious. Surely faith groups must bear some responsibility for virulent homophobia that is carried out in society when intolerance of homosexuality is enshrined in religious doctrine.

Dilemmas of What (Not) to Teach About Homophobia

Regardless of religious beliefs or personal prejudices, students know that as future teachers they are obliged to address the needs of sexual minorities in schools. This obligation is no indication that straight teachers will be sympathetic to or know how to support or become conscious of the anxieties of GLBT students. But beginning teachers are informed that sexual orientation is read into the Canadian Charter of Rights and Freedoms, and that consequently, sexual minorities are legally protected from discrimination; pedagogically, teachers know they must abide by a code of ethics in which they are expected to provide an education for all their students. The emphasis of the course, therefore, is on homophobia, simply defined here as the many ways in which people are oppressed on the basis of sexual orientation. We study how homophobia affects and constructs identities of both insider and outsider within society and schools—in short, how homophobia affects everyone, some in ways more devastating than others. One of the most important aims of the course is to encourage future teachers to recognize their own homophobia and see how it contributes to the marginalization of GLBT students. They are invited to find ways of openly supporting all diversity including anti-homophobic education as part of the curriculum.

Students arrive with a variety of knowledge ranging from personal experience to uninformed and harmful stereotypes. Even if they have not been aware of it, students have already met and will continue to meet gay, lesbian, bisexual and transgendered people. It is likely that they have had GLBT teachers and even now have closeted friends and relatives. In their careers as teachers, they will certainly meet GLBT students, colleagues, administrators and parents of students. Pre-service students need to understand the implications of homophobia in schools because, at a minimum, they will encounter GLBT persons in every aspect of schooling. While most students arrive with partial and/or distorted ideas about homosexuality accumulated from their own school experiences, most students have not had an opportunity to exchange information and ask questions in an open forum. Therefore, it is necessary to provide some basic information that would qualify, in Kumashiro's (2000) terms, as education *about* the "other."

In a short exercise, I ask students to name the fears they might have regarding homosexuality and thus take the opportunity to dispel some of their most commonplace and virulent misconceptions and myths. For example, we state directly that homosexuality is not a choice but an orientation.[1] We affirm that child molesting is far more likely to be committed by a straight person than by a sexual minority; straight people cannot be "converted" to being homosexual and vice versa; homosexuality is not a recent phenomenon; it is found across time, cultures and species. This fairly instrumental teaching method attempts to provide information against the harm done by partial and misleading knowledge; this format of learning *about* the other is the way students expect to engage this topic.

When I consider the range of issues and the limited time available, I realize how my choices of what to teach could be seen as tokenism. A visit to any database on homosexuality and schooling will produce pages of topics including queer theory, histories of sexual orientation, psychoanalysis and desire, prejudice and intolerance, the everyday experiences of GLBT people in schools, queer literature, coming out stories, the social construction of heteronormativity, as well as positive steps that schools should take to support all diversity. For basic facts and practical considerations that student teachers need to know, there are armloads of books, articles, videos, information packages, support groups and workshops available to anyone who looks for them. There are many practical ideas about how to construct a supportive classroom environment, what to say to students who come out, how to advocate for more professional training. All of this learning *about* homosexuality and GLBT people is important. However, this approach about "what to do" runs the risk of impressing on students that homosexuality is an exception, something to be included on top of an already full curriculum, or treated as a special event. Kumishiro says that if education *about* the other is the only form students receive, the information eventually trivializes the lives and experiences of the other. Even if information sessions are "successful," the approach cannot avoid rendering complex lives as something to be understood, creating voyeurs of straight students and reinforcing a social and intellectual division of "us" and "them." Focusing on problematic situations for GLBT students has the potential of reinforcing the notion that a GLBT student's status as a sexual minority is something for which the student must be consoled. Beginning teachers may miss the point that it is not homosexuality, but rather homophobia that is the problem, and that while GLBT students may need support and encouragement against the negative social consequences of homophobia in schools, GLBT students do not have to accept condolences for who they are.

Information sessions, as helpful as they might be on one level, eventually foreclose on what can be thought or what has already been excluded by the nature of this approach. What remains is the dominant narrative that summarizes "the" GLBT experience. The shifting nature of identity construction further complicates the assumption that one will know "what is best" for marginalized students or even more questionable, that one will know "who they are." Will students want private support or public recognition? Who will be included? How can victims of bullying be supported whether or not they are GLBT students? Where is the space for "questioning" students? Which support group will racial minority GLBT students attend? This informational approach of learning *about* the other has the potential to increase the marginalization of GLBT students and teachers because it does little to disrupt the notion of what is considered "normal." Focusing on the "other" may create empathy, but ultimately it "maintains the centrality and normalcy of the self" (Kumashiro, 2000, p. 45). In this process, the status of an oppressed minority is set up as an exception whose highest expectation is to secure rights and respect, all the while remaining outside of "how we do things." The effect producing empathy for minorities may be laudable, empathy is not a panacea for prejudice, nor an alternative to human rights (Kumashiro, 2000).

I have described some of the conceptual and practical pitfalls of organizing anti-oppressive learning that reinforces stereotypes of the other. Attempts simply to "understand" or learn about the other do not transform the process "by which the Other is differentiated from and subordinated to the 'norm'" (Kumashiro, 2000, p. 35). What remain in place are false binaries between legitimate and alternative ways of being. What is required is a pedagogy that is critical of binaries that construct marginality and privilege and the social structures that legitimize and maintain them. Such a pedagogy does not reference an individualized, "other-centred" discourse, but takes into account the social and cultural assumptions that produce the identities of all students. A critical pedagogy disrupts the notion that social privilege is naturally occurring; it questions whether "normalcy" and entitlement are possible without the construction of deviance and material disadvantage. Anti-oppressive education that critiques the privileging of certain identities and their "common sense" status may have its drawbacks. However, it significantly moves education forward by rejecting the notion that marginality is only the problem of minorities in which teachers may participate as well-intended, but uninvolved helpers. A critical approach maintains that homosexuality affects teachers' own lives in various ways. Most particularly, if they are straight, they likely benefit from unspoken heterosexual privilege. They also have an investment in not noticing that homophobia disciplines the assumptions of what it means to be male or female. Although homophobia affects the lives of GLBT people in the school system in the most serious ways, the identities of straight people are also implicated in and produced through its effects. The next section describes an approach that complicates binaries and "common sense" privileging of heteronormativity.

Getting Personal About Privilege

Like race privilege, heterosexual privilege is an unearned, often taken-for-granted way of living that is assumed to be superior and also normal. People who experience heterosexual privilege may be well aware that GLBT people experience discrimination. But they do not realize that being straight affords them protection and opportunities that are not similarly extended to members of the GLBT community. Peggy McIntosh (1998) writes about the effects of white privilege, saying "In proportion as my [white] racial group was being made confident, comfortable, and oblivious, other groups were likely being made inconfident, uncomfortable, and alienated" (p. 168). Like being white, being straight mostly goes unnoticed by people who experience its unearned protection. Being unaware of one's privilege is indeed one of its markers. Unearned heterosexual privilege also protects straight people from an awareness that what is considered "normal" is only possible through the marginalization of other lives. Heterosexual privilege obscures the fact that homophobia is not simply someone else's problem in which straight educators may participate as innocent helpers. Homophobia and unearned advantage for straight people implicates them whether they approve of their unearned entitlement or not.

I introduce students to the concept of "heteronormativity": the notion that heterosexuality is the only "natural" orientation. Another useful concept is "heterosexism," which is the belief in the inherent superiority of heterosexuality as a sexual orientation. These two concepts of heteronormativity and heterosexism are played out daily in schools by constructing a privileged social space for straight students and teachers that depends on the negative construction of homosexuality. Heteronormativity as well as homophobia affect straight educators in ways that are not necessarily obvious to them. Discrimination and the social construction of marginalized identities not only restrict straight educators from fully identifying with or acting in solidarity with GLBT students; the effects of heteronormativity and homophobia also discipline one's gender assignment by producing social assumptions of "acceptable" masculine and feminine behaviour and identities. I briefly defined homophobia above as "the many ways in which people are oppressed on the basis of sexual orientation." A more expansive definition comes from Audre Lourde's *Sister Outsider* (1984). She says that homophobia is "the fear of feelings of love for members of one's own sex and therefore the hatred of those feelings in others." Lourde's definition sheds light on one of the most commonplace effects of homophobia: the efforts to enforce compulsory heterosexuality and the construction of gendered identifications as distinct and separate.

The idea of interlocking oppressions mentioned above is useful here in illustrating that homophobia depends on aspects of sexism that consider the categories of sex and gender as "fixed" or "given." These categories are taken as binary opposites and not socially constructed or open to the constant negotiation that is part of their performance. Constructed notions of gender and sex help us understand that these categories are not simple, biological identifications. Rather, their meanings are socially produced through the effects of power relations. The identifications of masculine/feminine, male/female are not distinct but must be made to seem so for the support of a patriarchal system of male superiority.

The supposed "naturalness" of male dominance and female subordination depends on two notions. First, that all men are more or less alike and that women are mostly all alike. Second, as gender roles are "fixed," men and women are decidedly unlike each other, or so goes the assumption. This so-called gender divide, however, is not found in everyday experiences where men and women have much in common and there is a wide range of how masculinity and femininity are performed. Unfortunately, a great deal of effort goes into constraining the roles of masculinity and femininity and reinforcing differences between men and women, even where no differences exist. It is at this point that sexism and homophobia interlock most clearly. The emphasis on distinct masculine and feminine roles in schools is part of a patriarchal system that can only claim masculine superiority and privilege if masculinity can illustrate and maintain entitlement over and a distinction from femininity.

One way that male students are "schooled" in their performance is through repudiation of the feminine in such things as dress, interests, attitude, and stature. The male who fails at his gender assignment risks the greatest punishment. A failed male can be taunted with either sexist or homophobic remarks; he can be charged with being either a sissy or a fag. Both taunts are meant to inflict harm in their implication "not dominant," "not-male." Males are taught from an early age that being associated with the feminine is cause for shame. I once overheard a teacher shouting encouragement to her very young students while they were running a race. She encouraged the boys by saying, "Don't let the girls beat you." In so doing she signaled to both boys and girls that it is shameful and unnatural for boys to lose to girls. She also signaled the expectation of male superiority and the naturalness of a second-place finish for girls. Patriarchy needs a gender divide because failing to distinguish between men and women might mean less respect for men, that is, if they are treated with the same respect that women receive.

This discussion of sexism and male/female difference may seem as if I am changing the subject from sexual orientation to gender oppression. Obviously, the former topic has not been exhausted in any way. However, the construction and performance of gendered identities is integrally linked to sexual orientation in schools. Heterosexism, homophobia and sexism "discipline" and regulate the performance of masculinity and femininity through the notion of compulsory heterosexuality. Pointing out the connections between these interlocking oppressions is useful in my teaching, considering the sexual orientation of most of my students. Even though students may be interested, they don't see what this really has to do with them. They are prepared, after all, to be tolerant. Because most student teachers are straight, they will always be challenged—as am I—to see how they are affected by heterosexual privilege. We will always be suspect in our attention to homophobia from which we receive unearned advantage. The anonymous author of "'Miss is a Lesbian': The Experience of a White Lesbian Teacher in a Boys' School" (1989) has much to say on this topic. She describes the lack of support coming from colleagues in her fight against sexism and homophobia among the school's boys. Her colleagues mean to be sympathetic but don't really see how the boys' homophobic behaviour affects them. She states: "It is always the burden of the homosexual teacher to identify and explain and point to all solutions. Is it possible for a person who defines her/himself as heterosexual to be angry about compulsory heterosexuality?" In that heterosexuality is a conditioning process performed to the advantage of some and not others, all teachers have an investment in exploring these interlocking oppressions of homophobia and sexism. Students have more potential to understand the repression against same-sex loving when they reflect on how it has powerfully restricted and informed their own gender performance.

I don't wish to exaggerate the connections between interlocking oppressions or to collapse their differences. While they have areas of common influence, it would be a mistake to suggest that homophobia is subsumed in sexism or vice versa. However, it is helpful for student teachers to see that as schooling reinforces hegemonic masculinity it also limits notions of acceptable male performance. The narrow prescription, including opposite-sex relations and hyper-masculine activity, is a prescription that few males can fulfill—even if they choose to do so. What is useful about making these connections is that as gendered identities can be understood as more than the binary opposite of something else, norms of sexual orientation also become more fluid. Here is potential for creating doubts, spaces and gaps that permit uncertain identities, inchoate desires and knowledge in process. Here are possibilities for students changing how they see themselves.

Risking Heteronormativity

The assumption that all students will "naturally" form opposite-sex attractions is perhaps taken as the greatest indicator of sexual identification. Strict designations about what it means to be male or female and the social sanctions against "ambiguous" gender assignment reinforce "compulsory heterosexuality." The fear of loving a same-sex person or, even less demonstrably, of not performing the socially acknowledged roles of a "real" male or female has consequences for GLBT people who cannot or do not care to hide their orientation. There is a great deal of effort that goes into performing a straight gender role because of the negative consequences of homophobic reactions. Davison (2000) says that it is the heterosexual performance that is the most studied and carefully prepared. "Appearing straight" is the real performance that takes place in schools. Heterosexuality is a learned performance to rival any homosexual display or "drag."

Heteronormative displays of masculinity and femininity are rigidly produced through violence, harassment, name-calling, silent disapproval, ostracism, and the many ways that devalue human beings. Homophobia is constantly displayed throughout education institutions in the way it "disciplines" or polices the assignment of gender roles. In this way homophobia constrains (or straightens) the lives of all who are affected by school cultures. Through the everyday actions in the institution, hegemonic heterosexuality becomes normalized. There is plenty of subtle and outright coercion, that Davison calls "social terrorism by peers," to guide males and females to their "proper" gender performances (such as acting "like a lady"). Male and female students who do not uphold their gender roles in socially acceptable ways will be "disciplined" by peers and adults. Masculinity and femininity are not mere identifications in schools. The expectations for how they will be embodied, performed and controlled are on regular display in every high school hallway: "Thus high school becomes a strong filter for hegemonic gender patterns" (Davison, 2000, p. 46). The coercion of which Davison speaks is born from both anger and fear—that if gender performances are not upheld as distinctly separate and if gender roles are blurred—then there can be no claim to male superiority over women.

Curricular materials privilege heterosexuality as moral and as a common sense expectation for human interaction. Heterosexual display is performed and legitimated in classrooms, hallways and special functions throughout the school including whom you may take to the prom without getting a court order. Overt displays of heterosexual sex may be considered excessive, but not unnatural. At the same time, even the mildest representation or display of homosexual identity can provoke the accusation that one is "flaunting it." Support for queer students requires, at a minimum, more than a response to symptoms or the achievement of tepid tolerance, which is really a form of resignation and disgust. Schools have a responsibility to disrupt their routine privileging of particular kinds of student identities while marginalizing others.

Homophobia and hegemonic gender roles have the potential to be reinforced throughout curricular practices unless teachers see how their own performances as gendered subjectivities uphold heteronormativity and sexism. As ever, the best teaching is by example and openness: How are teachers performing what it means to be masculine and feminine? Male teachers whose authority depends on masculine bravura are modeling exclusionary forms of control available only through aggression and dominance. Female teachers who refer to homophobic taunts merely as bad manners or as "words we don't use here" are shirking their responsibilities and missing an opportunity to speak directly about issues of justice and homophobia. Teachers might examine their gendered performances and ask what their teaching makes possible and what is makes impossible. How far does the education they offer students go to interrupt the repetition of privilege? What opportunities do teachers give students, especially boys, to take responsibility for and love each other? What are the examples of family that can be considered normal? How open is the teacher to students not "outing" themselves? School personnel continually produce both normalcy and deviance through what is taught, what can be talked about, and what must remain silent.

An outcome of the course is that we all learn the ways that heterosexuality, as a compulsory orientation, constructs school curricula inside and outside the classroom. Whether or not one identifies as gay or lesbian or bisexual or straight, all identities as teachers and students have been shaped by the discourses that homophobia authorizes. Given that heteronormativity is enforced in schools in physical and often violent ways, beginning teachers need to consider whether they will be the allies of all students whose schooling is compromised by homophobia.

Conclusion

Deborah Britzman (1995), an educational theorist who writes brilliantly on many topics including queer pedagogy, invites readers to consider something that sounds like a contradiction in terms. She suggests that in the realm of education theory, we consider what cannot be thought. She asks: What it is that resists being considered? In particular, what cannot be thought about schooling, knowledge and pedagogy and why is this thinking resisted? One possibility is to ask how discrimination against sexual minorities is most often considered (if at all) as a one-off topic and not as a structuring system for educational thinking throughout the curriculum. How do the assumed "naturalness" of heterosexuality and the hegemony of schooling processes construct the "rightness or wrongness" of homosexuality, in spite of inclusive and compensatory initiatives?

It is clear to me that my teaching about homophobia is limited by my own sexual orientation and the limits of what I can bear to know (Felman, 1987). What I share with my students is partial knowledge and an unconscious refusal to think beyond the "common sense" discourses of normalcy. For teaching and learning in anti-oppressive education, we need to aim beyond the limits of inclusion and exclusion that structure lives of school personnel on all sides of an unnatural divide. I propose to include more disruptive knowledge, less security of "results," more unsettled and unsettling questions. Through destabilizing some of the certainties about who students and teachers can consider themselves to be, we begin to imagine "different possibilities for teaching and learning" (Kumashiro, 2001, p. 11).

Note

1. Although straight people sometimes believe that they have chosen to be heterosexual, one's sexual orientation is not something that can be chosen, demanded or outlawed (in Canada). The range of sexual desire is rich, broad, complex and something to be discovered. The notion of choice implies that there are better or worse, natural or unnatural expressions of identity. The misconception follows that there is a distinct "lifestyle" to accompany and encompass either gay or straight lives.

References

Britzman, D. 1995. "Is There a Queer Pedagogy? Or, Stop Reading Straight." *Educational Theory* 45, no. 2: 151–65.

Davison, K. 2000. "Masculinities, Sexualities and the Student Body: 'Sorting' Gender Identities in School." In Carl James (ed.), *Experiencing Difference*. Halifax: Fernwood.

Felman, S. 1987. *Jacques Lacan and the Adventure of Insight: Psychoanalysis in Contemporary Culture*. Cambridge: Harvard University Press.

Kumashiro, K. 2001. "'Posts': Perspectives on Anti-oppressive Education in Social Studies, English, Mathematics, and Science Classrooms." *Educational Researcher* 30, no. 3: 3–12.

——. 2000. "Toward a Theory of Anti-oppressive Education." *Review of Educational Research* 70: 25–53.

McIntosh, P. 1989. "'Miss is a Lesbian': The Experience of a White Lesbian Teacher in a Boys' School." In H. DeLyon and F.W. Migniuolo (eds.), *Women Teachers: Issues and Experiences*. Milton Keynes: Open University Press.

——. 1998. "White Privilege: Unpacking the Invisible Knapsack." In Paula S. Rothenberg (ed.), *Race, Class, and Gender in the United States: An Integrated Study*. New York: St. Martin's Press.

16

Performing and Culture:
HOMOPHOBIA IN CANADIAN THEATRE

Wes D. Pearce

> *If he came out, his career would be over—he would not be given the parts that he's given right now. So does he want to be an artist more than he wants to be honest? I think he does. And I can't blame him, because I know if he came out, that would be it for the career he loves.*
>
> Cher (Wieder, p. 78)

Introduction

In 2001, Jeff Perrotti and Kim Westheimer published a book entitled *When the Drama Club is Not Enough: Lessons from the Safe Schools Program for Gay and Lesbian Students*, chronicling the development of the Massachusetts Safe Schools Program. I was interested in the book, not so much because of its content, but because its title, *When the Drama Club is Not Enough*, assumes and reinforces numerous cultural assumptions made about gay students, drama departments and theatre in general. All of these assumptions need to be reexamined. Drawing on personal interviews, published personal accounts, theoretical and research literature as well as my own story, this chapter will first examine the historical and cultural assumptions and mythology that surround professional theatre. Such an examination is imperative because much of what we do in theatre departments and theatre schools is a continuation of the attitudes and experiences encountered in the professional world. Having established this larger historical/cultural context, I will then focus this discussion on examining the systemic hetero-normativity/homophobia that dominates the thinking, development and curricula of most Canadian university theatre programs. Although the ultimate goal of this chapter is to suggest coordinated strategies for making the classroom a better (and hopefully safer) space for queer students, it is also my hope to initiate a critical (re)examination of the cultural assumptions/stereotypes of who performs theatre.

Homophobia in the Theatre

In *Culture Clash: The Making of Gay Sensibility*, Michael Bronski argues that although "common perception saw Broadway, and hence the theater in general, as a port of safety for homosexuals, the reality was quite different" (p. 111). In the introduction to *Passing Performances*, Fergus (Tad) Currie (past executive member of Actor's Equity and chair of Theatre at Illinois State University) elaborates on Bronski's theme:

> *Actors afraid to reveal their sexual identity for fear of losing employment; actors who, having "come out" were at best tolerated, and in the worst cases made to feel like second-class citizens; producers who, for a variety of reasons including their own homophobia refused to hire openly gay or lesbian actors.... . Many gays and lesbians in the entertainment industry forced to remain in the closet, thus robbing them not only of their identity but also placing them under pressures that are counterproductive to a creative life.*

Historically, it has been assumed that large numbers of "sodomites" and "sexual deviants" were involved in the production of theatre. Ben Jonson's[1] *Poetaster* (1601) is one of the earliest examples of a cultural text stating the "unstatable." In this play, Ovid Sr. (a father) is horrified that Ovid Jr. (his son) desires to become a "playwright":

> *What? shall I have*
> *my Son a Stager now? an Enghle for Players? a Gull?*
> *a Rook? a Shot-clog? to make Suppers, and be laught*
> *at? Publius, I will set thee on the Funeral Pile first.*
> (1.2.22–24)

This early example, I would argue, suggests that for (at least) the past 400 years the public has assumed that the theatre is full of sexual deviants, and yet this same general public is extremely uneasy about the reality of gay artists in theatre. Nicholas de Jongh links this modern tension between "homosexuality and the theater to the Puritans, who demonized ... the actor's body in public performance, linking it to prostitution and the worst of all carnal sins, sodomy" (p. 5). Such homophobic thinking has led to continual assumptions, held by both scientists and laypersons about the contamination of "acts"[2] (Case, p. vii). This homophobic posturing is often presented under the guise of scientific fact, as in Martin Hoffman's *The Gay World: Male Homosexuality and the Social Creation of Evil*:

> *I have also observed that homosexuals are particularly attracted to professional careers in the arts, especially in the performing arts, and a number of other writers have noted that there seems to be an unusual percentage of homosexuals that have taken up acting as a profession.* (p. 72)

Similarly, in 1987 Richard Green's book, *The "Sissy Boy Syndrome" and the Development of Homosexuality*, noted that, "It is commonly accepted that many homosexuals are found in the entertainment field, as in the acting profession ... [still] ... there is no adequate survey to verify this belief" (p. 256). In spite of this lack of hard data, it remains a fact that many of the theatre-going public still believe gay men dominate the theatre and yet at the same time they wish it wasn't so.[3] It is within this context that I position this chapter. As a gay man who teaches costume design and works extensively in the professional theatre I became curious about how this cultural stereotype/expectation was influencing the experience(s) queer students often encounter (or don't encounter) when studying theatre.

Despite theatre's unstable history it has preserved itself (in some form or another) since the days of ancient Greece. Since the rise of the Elizabethan theatre, Western society has become conflicted between what it expects (that there are gay men in theatre) and what happens when society finds that what it expects is true (that there are, in fact, gay men in theatre). Shawn Mitchell,* a gay (if not publicly out) student who has just finished his MA in drama education, comments that "a notion that has haunted me is one my parents mentioned earlier on, that a friend of theirs, when I was a child, told them not to get me involved in theatre as there were a lot of gays there. I guess that is somewhat telling, as is the fact I remember their saying it so vividly." Further, it is important to realize that this general unease, expressed by Shawn's parents' friend, is not simply held by cultural critics or the "uninformed masses" but manifests itself in theatrical practice. In a recent conversation, Allen McInnis (currently the Artistic Director for Toronto's Lorraine Kimsa Theatre for Young People) mentioned that

> some years ago, I couldn't get an audition to play the title role of Hosanna in a production in Victoria … I heard … that the director had said openly that he wasn't auditioning gay actors. He didn't want to make the audience uncomfortable by hiring an obviously [openly?] gay man to play the part of a [n obvious] gay man!!! I laugh when I think of it but, you know, I think there are some directors out there who would still feel the same way.

In the winter of 2001, Scott Burke (then artistic director of Ship's Company Theatre and currently artistic director of Theatre New Brunswick) was asked to direct a production of *Kilt* for Neptune Theatre's second stage. He told me that while the production was a success and sold out for the run, it was also the only play of the second stage season to feature a gay love story and the only play of the series to be given a substantially shorter run. Burke remarked, only half jokingly, that while he was glad that Neptune produced the play, the fact that the theatre felt the need to limit the amount of "gay time" in the schedule underscored some homophobic fears about the production and Neptune's subscription base.

Taken to an extreme this lurking homophobia can lead to the systemic silencing of queer voices. Even if one argues that theatre seems a protective place for queer artists, it is still not a place where queer issues are necessarily dealt with in an honest manner. The experiences of gay men are seldom the subject of serious discourse (and the experiences of lesbians are dealt with less often): our experiences end up as gossipy disclosure in dreary biographies of late, great closeted British or American stage legends,[4] or worse, our experiences are simply ignored because it is assumed that a straight audience has nothing to learn from us. Attempting to rectify this situation can still be a risky proposition. For instance, "When [*Angels in America*] was staged at Alberta Theatre Projects … a few MLAs tried to pull government funding from [the theatre company] because of their production of a gay play…" (Barnard, p. B4). The production raised such controversy that no corporate sponsor could be found for the Pulitzer Prize winning dramas. Instead, ATP turned to individuals in order to underwrite the $50,000 sponsorship needed to mount both productions

(Bennett, p. 171). In discussing the necessity and merits of producing *Angels in America*, Bob White, current artistic director of ATP,[5] argued that "It became important, as a gay man, to produce this play in Calgary and I had to make that clear to the Board."[6] The board eventually supported the creative efforts of the artistic team and White comments that the hysteria around the production became so acute that the all the members of the ATP board were implicated in the conservative backlash around *Angels*. Suddenly, straight board members were "contaminated" by being associated with this production and were being challenged by the larger community as to what they were doing with "that gay theatre."

I myself have had an occasional moment that underscores the odd reality of the theatrical environment. While working on a production of *Cruel Tears* for Regina's Globe Theatre, I was cautioned that I might have to "butch up" one of the male leads because he was gay. In the end, I did nothing beyond what was drawn in the original sketch and the actor/character still appeared more "masculine" than anyone else on stage. It was an odd comment that seemed to suggest that gender identity was intimately connected with sexual orientation, and odder still coming, as it did, from a director who is the most politically and artistically supportive straight ally with whom I have ever worked.

Based on my own experience and other evidence as presented above, I would argue that the latent homophobia within the professional theatre is exacerbated by a certain cultural anxiety about gender identity or, more specifically, what is understood as masculine.[7] I would argue that much of the homophobia found in theatre (both professionally and in theatre schools) emerges as a response from heterosexual men who feel they have to prove that their "masculinity" is not in question. It could be argued that heterosexual men who work in theatre often feel the need to repeatedly demonstrate that they are straight, that they are not part of the "gay theatre mafia" and that they share no part of this cultural assumption of gay men and theatre.[8]

Given the value that society places on heteronormativity, "passing for straight" is seen by many gay men as being an important part of their identity and, unfortunately, important to maintaining their careers: "If however your career depended on any kind of a romantic image, whether as an actor or as a pop star, the danger of alienating audiences was still too real and, amazingly, remains so to this day, more than 100 years after the death of [Oscar] Wilde" (Morley, p. 43). The desire to be seen as "a man" or to "pass" as "a man" or as "masculine" as opposed to "a fag" can put enormous pressures on individuals, not simply preventing them from being totally engaged in their work as artists but forcing them to make further compromises with their lives. Shawn Mitchell admits that as a result of staying closeted in his professional and academic life, he often passes for straight. However, the cost of his successful passing has been his inability to ever be "completely engaged in any role." It is not my intention to create the impression that theatre is rife with homophobia because many queer artists have found, in professional performance and theatre, a freedom that would be denied them in many other careers. The evidence, however, suggests professional theatre (and the entertainment world at large) is not, and has never been, a bastion where gay artists can take for granted that their identity is safe.

Isolation and Silence in University Theatre Departments

Just as the world of theatre is not a stress-free haven for gay artists, neither is the environment of theatre schools one of unconditional welcome for gay students. Stories (both personal and published) highlighting incidents of homophobia within the academe are not isolated, nor are they products of the "hysterical" mind; rather, they are supported by studies demonstrating that university and college environments are not necessarily the tolerant establishments we have long been led to believe they are.[9] Just as the university campus is a reflection of the larger society and all the good and bad contained within it, so too is a university theatre department a reflection of the societal and professional prejudices found outside its walls. Inevitably the attitudes of the professional world of theatre are reflected in the attitudes and choices of theatre departments given that so many theatre faculty members also work in the professional world.

Unlike students of 30 or 40 years ago, the majority of students today are not afraid to tell their parents that they are majoring in theatre,[10] and most parental concerns have to do with long-term financial stability rather than concerns that their sons will be "turned" (or at least considered) gay. This, however, is not to say that queer students are not troubled, provoked and scared by their individual processes of coming out. Queer students often arrive with greater social/peer expectations about life in a theatre department than do their straight counterparts. It is in this area that I believe theatre departments are not doing enough to support queer students. I have often heard stories of queer students who register in theatre classes hoping to find "their people."[11] Sadly, what queer students still questioning their sexual identity often find is a hetero-centrist environment that isn't as welcoming as they imagined. In order to gather information to write this chapter, I had the opportunity to talk to a number of theatre professionals who remarked that when they were attending theatre they were the only out students in their classes (often even the program). Many talked about how difficult that was, especially when some of them had chosen to study theatre assuming that they would find a lot of support with their peers. Stephen Franklin, now a fundraiser in Calgary, notes that while attending Ryerson in the late 1970s he was often isolated because he was gay:

> There's the assumption that everyone in theatre is gay. Often guys that were unsure of their sexuality tended to avoid me in order to avoid being labeled gay. To be labeled gay or even have a gay friend would confirm those fears or suspicions of family and friends.

Many aspects of gay culture and the lives of queer students have changed since Franklin was a student, but my own relatively recent experiences continue to demonstrate that "out" students can expect little inherent support from theatre school.

I attended the Theatre Department at the University of Regina during the early 1990s and found myself to be the only openly gay student in a student body of approximately 60. This in itself was not a problem, but it was compounded by the fact that there was very little queer representation in the plays I was studying. In addition, these scripts were not being given any queer analysis in class discussions, nor was there much queer(ed) representation as part of our production season.[12] In a similar manner there were no queer characters or queer issues visible on the stage of the Globe Theatre (Regina's only professional theatre). The end result of all these incidents was that I felt a very real sense of isolation. My expectations when I went to do my Master of Fine Arts at the University of Calgary were higher than for my undergrad years. I assumed there would be a larger community of gay students and that gay issues (or at least gender issues) would form a greater part of the curriculum. My experience, in fact, was quite different. Out of 20 grad students, I was the only one who was openly gay. There were gay faculty members in the department but they did not seem interested in incorporating gay work into their classes/productions; with the exception of Genet's *The Balcony* and Churchill's *Cloud Nine*, I did not see myself reflected in the department.

Clearly, the sense of isolation and the overwhelming "sounds of silence" that I experienced can negatively affect a student's academic career. In a discussion I had with Robert Wallace, this isolation confirms his belief that the face of homophobia in the contemporary academe is indifference. Homophobia within theatre schools becomes more visible and possibly even more harmful when the assumptions of a theatre department culture are no longer simply negligent but rather are practiced as "unofficial" policy. Dick Scanlan (co-author of the book for the 2002 musical *Thoroughly Modern Millie* "studied drama at Carnegie Mellon University until he was kicked out for not showing sufficient 'professional promise'—code words, he says, for being too feminine" (Meers, 54–55). Although Scanlan's experience may be an extreme case, it highlights a tension that exists between theatre departments and their gay students, which is similar to the tension that exists between the larger academic theatre population[13] and the queer faculty who teach and conduct research in such departments.

I am not arguing that theatre departments are necessarily hostile. Most theatre departments offer a modicum of safety for gay students. Illustrating this point Allen MacInnis recalls that

> at university in the mid-70s, I was openly gay. I was a drama student in the Faculty of Education at the University of Alberta (Edmonton) and, despite being headed toward becoming a teacher, I expected respect and tolerance for being a gay man. On the whole, I felt I received it, but I was very aware of feeling unsafe outside the Drama Department and the Drama section of the Education faculty.

Yet, even in the relative safety of a theatre department, systemic and latent homophobia is almost always present and is damaging to queer students. When I asked Shawn Mitchell why he had chosen to remain closeted, even at the expense of his art, he suggested that it was because "of not wanting a label," adding that in his experience, openly gay students often avoided one another. His responses lead me to suspect that the lack of role models and positive, in-class experiences and representations of "self" lead queer students to develop an internalized homophobia that manifests itself in a pattern of avoidance, forcing queer students to be defensive and reactive. Theatre departments and individual faculty members are often unaware of their students' expectations. The result of this ignorance for queer students can be an uncomfortable silence, similar to that which greeted gay theatre students 40 years ago. This silence is illustrated by the experience of Kevin Daniels,* who received his BA (Drama) in 2002 from a university in a large Western Canadian city. In commenting on his recent education, he noted that the problem was not that gay plays were not studied. To him the problem was that it often felt like "the gay play" was being taught like it was part of a laundry list of minority voices that had to be taught before getting back to the "dead, white guys." To Daniels, the problem was the lack of other support: queer scenes were not used in class, queer plays were not produced on the main stage, and there was little queer presence in critical or cultural readings.

This indifference towards queer voices and queer texts (intentional or not) places the burden of responsibility squarely on the shoulders of gay and lesbian academics within the "system." In discussing his experiences as a student Christopher Grignard stated that "the gay subject matter question is usually emphasized or brought in by gay academics." It becomes important for me and other queer educators to be a presence within the institution and to begin to undo those years of heteronormativity to which queer students (and faculty) have been subjected. Doubtless there be will resistance to this from straight and gay faculty:

> Many heterosexual teachers may feel, "Why make such an issue of my sexuality? It's nobody's business." Yet their wedding rings and casual remarks about a "husband" or "wife," in the classroom and out, suggest that sexuality in America [and Canada] is everybody's business, that institutionalized heterosexuality constantly makes an issue of sexuality. [And what's worse] To protect themselves, some tightly [and I would argue not so tightly] closeted teachers censor their own syllabi and discussions—to the point of presenting inaccurate and homophobic information about the course material studied. (Pobo, pp. 1–2)

I am arguing that "out" faculty members must bring themselves and their lives into the classroom situation in order to offer balance and "othered" images for students to see. We often forget that (like it or not) the understanding among students is that "being a professor at a major college or university means being able to share your life experiences and knowledge with students—not only to educate them in your academic area but also to benefit them as people, to help them live their lives" (Verraros). I would add that putting ourselves and our stories into the classroom is important in trying the naturalize the academe. The bigger challenges, however, for those of us teaching in theatre departments are the issues of curriculum development, representation(s) in the production season and the development of safe and productive teaching spaces outside of the traditional classroom.

Curriculum Development and Queer Content

In a celebratory article written just before the dawn of the 21st century, playwright David Drake wrote:

> Calling up the 20th century's most significant playwrights would be a much easier task if one only had to pinpoint straight guys. Eugene O'Neill, Arthur Miller, Neil Simon, Rodgers and Hammerstein. David Mamet. Blackout. Curtain. The End. (p. 56)

In his short article he asks, "Where would politics, war, religion, marriage and love, valour and compassion have been without the homosexual playwright?" He then goes on to answer his own question by naming over 40 homosexual playwrights who have given shape, substance and a voice to contemporary theatre. Edward Albee, Tennessee Williams, Stephen Sondheim, Harvey Fierstein, Lanford Wilson, Tony Kushner, Noel Coward, Terrence McNally, Jean Genet, Tim Miller, Larry Kramer and William Inge are included on his list; many more voices (women, non-American, coloured) also come to mind. Such celebrations are necessary. Theatre students need to be repeatedly introduced to the fact that homosexual/gay/queer artists are a tangible and valuable part of historic and contemporary theatre. The more frequent these interventions/celebrations become the less easy it becomes for hostile students to dismiss the queer experience:

> *Vexed and elusive as it is, [the naming of historical same-sex desire] is vital ... because of the highly influential and complex ways historical icons shape the self-conceptions of people across the social spectrum, both in their own time and now. The ramifications are both personal and political. While those of us who identify as gay and lesbian have always projected fantasies of desire and identification onto puta-tively heterosexual stars, it can be immensely validating, not to mention arousing, to know that these fantasies are not pure projection, that, in the face of our continuing degradation, widely worshiped icons were at least in some measure like us. For those who identify as straight, evidence of the role of same-sex sexual desire in star per-formers' careers can be profoundly disorienting. Certainly it increases awareness of the constructed, contingent, and shifting nature of all sexualities, including their own.* (Schanke, pp. 8–9)

Clearly identifying and naming our history becomes the pedagogical equivalent of the ACT UP chant: "We're Here, We're Queer, Get Used To It!"

If we (as queer educators) don't "name names" as it were, we run the risk of abandoning all of our students to an oppressive and damaging silence. Stephen Heatley (now a member of the theatre at the University of British Columbia) recalled being a "not-out undergrad [and] picking up a copy of *Fortune and Men's Eyes* and being absolutely riveted by it. In fact, I was so enthralled reading it in the library that I missed an entire class. Finally there were characters that were not being represented on stage. It was very affirming (even if they were all in jail) and made a huge impact on me." I don't think the importance of introducing all of our students to gay texts can be overstated. As Heatley makes clear, queer students recognizing themselves in a play becomes an extremely liberating and important moment in their development as citizens with healthy self identities. Loutzenheiser argues that "If gay, lesbian and bisexual issues are not discussed in the curriculum, the only repre-sentations that gay and heterosexual students alike have are the extremes that the media often chooses to portray" (p. 61). Even with today's online and web savvy stu-dents, being exposed to writers, situations and characters that move beyond chat room discussions is important and necessary to fostering a more complete under-standing of "who I am."

Introducing gay and lesbian drama (or naming playwrights) into the classroom is, in and of itself, a political act. Robert Wallace makes a similar assertion in the intro-duction to *Making, Out* when he writes that "all the writers in this book, by publicly declaring they are gay, contribute as much to the social sense of 'gayness' as to the gay characters they create" (p. 12). In terms of curriculum development, this nam-ing helps to shift the focus of the class away from the traditional hetero-normative centre:

> *A lecture, or an entire course, on gay and lesbian drama tells students that issues of sexual difference are important in society. To discuss plays labeled as Gay and Lesbian Drama, asserts that sexual identities distinct from the mainstream popula-tion exist and that such plays (and such identities) merit study.* (Abel, p. 32)

Similarly, by "failing to recognize the existence of gay men, lesbians and bisexuals [through curriculum development], schools participate in naming heterosexuality as 'normal'... The assumption of heterosexuality is a lens through which assumptions are formed…" (Loutzenheiser, p. 60). Certainly, theatre departments have to do more than just serve the needs of the queer students who are involved in a department; however, ignoring (or not understanding) the cultural/personal expectation(s) that queer students often have about theatre programs is extremely disadvantageous. Wallace notes that several years ago York University made a conscious decision to focus on racial identity, with the end result that issues around gender or sexual identity were "more or less ignored." He comments that often the "gestures made are little more than nods of tokenism, which allow students to see these things [sexual/gender diversity] as exceptions rather than the norm." Hopefully by introducing my students to mainstream drama that is queer I can help to make diversity the norm rather than the exception.

Important, too, is the understanding that "for too long the canon has represented the ideology of the ruling class … [and that by] including all people in the canon gives all people a sense of possibility, of future, of the likelihood of success" (Gaard, p. 32). While I would like to think that our heterosexual colleagues might present a queer voice in the classroom it seems self-defeating to expect them to do all the work for our students (and for us). In a costume design class that I regularly teach, three out of the four scripts that I use have overt gay content (or characters): *Hosanna* by Michel Tremblay, *The Orphan Muses* by Michel Marc Bouchard, and *Grace* by Michael L. MacLennan. Any thoughts I had about having too many "gay plays" on my syllabi were quickly removed when I noticed that, with the exception of *The Laramie Project*, none of my colleagues were using any plays with overt gay/queer content. Incorporating queer texts into the curriculum can be as simple as teaching Christopher Marlowe's *Edward II* rather than Marlowe's *Dr. Faustus*, or by introducing the biography of Tennessee Williams and the subsequent queer reading of *A Streetcar Named Desire* into class discussions. Pedagogical approaches to teaching drama within the classroom have changed, making this easier than ever. Wallace talks of the void he found in his classes where "I was studying work by gay authors [like Tennessee Williams] but no one was ever discussing biography." He comments wryly that "no one would think about let alone talk about" the possibility of the gay perspective. Bronski forcefully argues the importance of students understanding the entire historical context surrounding a particular script or a particular playwright. It is important for all theatre students to know that "to write about his own gay experience, Williams realized that he had to make it as palatable to his audience as possible" (p. 114). The fact that Williams claimed "I am Blanche Dubois" in no way diminishes one of the greatest characters ever written for the stage, and may in fact give students greater insight into the character and the play. Supporting gay students in a meaningful way often requires more than teaching canonical plays such as *Fortune and Men's Eyes* or *Lilies or the Revival of a Romantic Drama*. However, the forefronting of queer work is an important starting point and helps to underscore the necessity that queer identity, queer perspectives and queer thought be introduced into the general curriculum the way that issues of gender or race have been.

Productions and Queer Representation

In theatre departments, perhaps more than in any other area of the academe, the spaces outside of the traditional classrooms are profoundly important areas of both teaching and learning. Classes focused on intense scene studies, rehearsals and productions, and other aspects of theatre programs present opportunities for either the development or the negation of a gay student's identity. The most obvious, important and public arena of learning within a theatre department happens (almost always) within the production schedule where classroom lessons are practically applied and where the department's identity is most visible. The production experience is invaluable for all students and yet continues to be an area where homophobic activity is bound to run rampant. Christopher Grignard, now a graduate student at the University of Alberta, commented that during a production of *The Three Sisters* at the University of East Anglia, he was "put off by the masculinity that accumulated when all the straight male actors [got together]." He added that during the University of Alberta's 2002 production of *Lysistrata* he again "experienced the masculine overdrive that [was] rampant when the straight guy actors got together with their giant phalluses. There was the playing around with 'gayness' that always sickens me. Straight guys joking around sexually with other straight guys is fun for them."[14] It is possible that this playing around is the result of students being uncomfortable with their own sexuality; such "play" is homophobic and damaging to gay students, regardless of where it occurs.

I have commented throughout this chapter about not "seeing myself" in the main stage productions of the universities I have attended, and how isolating this can be. The production season, being the public profile of the university (and theatre department), is emblematic of the institution it represents, and the absence of queer characters, queer plays and queer playwrights says much about the department and the university it is attached to. Thus it is to counteract the scarceness of queer representations in productions at the University of Regina that I use a lot of queer drama in my classes. Although the arguments for not doing a "gay play" are many, I think they can be reduced to a general uneasiness felt by heterosexual faculty about exploring an unfamiliar world. Or is it a more deeply felt conviction that "the gay canon," despite the immense talent mentioned by Drake, is somehow inferior to the "real canon"? The absence of queer themes and queer characters may also reflect a usually unspoken concern for "audience satisfaction." Abel writes that "few activities will make a general audience squirm more than watching two men of the same sex kissing passionately on stage" (p. 37). Whatever the reasons, the absence of queer plays and characters in the production schedule of most theatre departments reinforces a feeling with queer students that they are "other"—someone whose story isn't worth telling or, worse, someone to be "feared, odd, [and] fundamentally different" (Loutzenheiser, p. 59). As well, it reinforces the unwritten code that for some reason it is okay for a gay student to be forced to play straight throughout his college years but yet unreasonable for a straight student to be asked to play gay for a classroom project (or if the role is accepted that this is somehow a brave act, requiring lots of "courage").

The reasons why gay/lesbian faculty members (myself included) do not fight harder to have plays with gay content produced may have something to do with the fact that controversy is easier to avoid. Despite a very long list of great works in the queer canon, there is still the fear that a "gay play" will be controversial. In addition queer faculty typically enjoy a minority voice within a department and can easily be voted down.[15] Furthermore, there is a fear, based on the experiences of several universities (and even a professional company like Alberta Theatre Projects) that presenting a play like *Corpus Christi* or *Angels in America* will be seen by students, the university administration, or the larger community as teaching "pro-gay propaganda." Fear of being accused of teaching "gay propaganda" can be a serious concern for educators. Shawn Mitchell mentions that "as a director, I have been in situations where I know a youth is gay and I eggshell walk a bit as I do not want to be seen as swaying this [student]." This fear of being seen as teaching "gay propaganda" is, I feel, an ongoing threat to the academic freedom of many teachers and institutions, in the face of efforts to silence gay theatre. In 1989 a production of Larry Kramer's *The Normal Heart* at Southwest Missouri State University was marred by controversy and violence by upset students and residents (Abel, p. 37). In 2001, certain residents of Fort Wayne who were upset with the upcoming Indiana University production of Terrence McNally's *Corpus Christi* took Purdue University–Fort Wayne to court. A federal appeals court eventually ruled that the production could proceed as scheduled (*The Advocate*, 2001). These acrimonious stories are further evidence that queer faculty cannot rely on our colleagues to tell our stories.

Scene Studies and Explorations of Queer Identities

It is important for educators "to be aware of sexual difference and [to be] sensitive to the problems which students face in coming to terms with their sexuality" (Abel, p. 40). All educators must be made aware of the real dangers and abuse to which many of their students are subject on a daily basis.[16] Given this climate of hostility, it is critically important that those of us privileged to be openly "out" theatre educators ensure that our queer students feel they can be who they really are in our "classroom" spaces. These students deserve our trust and support because "the gay teacher knows how it feels to be given inaccurate information about issues that are crucial to his or her identity, to be told not to ask certain questions or read certain texts, and how it feels to be isolated from one's peers" (Waldo, p. 28). MA student, Christopher Grignard observed that an unhealthy or toxic environment in a production space can be very destructive, and BA graduate Kevin Daniels stated that he felt isolated because his scene study work was always based on characters in a heterosexual world. More specifically Abel writes:

> Scene work, scripted or improvisational, provides an ideal tool to explore the complex social issues which surround the formation of sexual identity. A class can use a variety of exercises to explore how socially reinforced behavioral patterns create sexual identities and how an audience learns to read sexual identities. ... Doing scene study work on sexual identity in a closed classroom is relatively "safe." (pp. 36–37)

This statement underscores yet again the importance for those of us who are inside theatre schools to make curriculum choices that allow for multiple worlds to be explored.

Bradley Smith,* who was entering grad school as I was finishing my thesis, and who then returned for some years to teach at his alma mater (a smaller university in Western Canada), commented that returning as possibly the only openly gay member of the entire faculty was a bit daunting. Upon returning, Smith told me that he didn't want to be pigeonholed as "a gay director." He also felt unprepared when he became a magnet for gay students in a variety of disciplines who were seeking advice and support. Students, he added, are often desperate to have someone to talk to, despite the fact that gay students appear have more peer support and resources at their disposal than in his own undergraduate days. As educators, it is important for us to create teaching environments where we do not self-censor or force our students to do the same. This is not what Smith found in the drama department; here there were gay students feeling that they had no place to go or no place to express themselves. In this relatively small university and community, it is easy to see how the silences in curriculum and representation would be "interpreted by students as confirmation that homosexuality is shameful and bad; otherwise it would be acceptable to bring up as part of the school's curriculum" (Loutzenheiser, p. 61). Smith's solution was not to direct radical gay plays as part of the production season but to develop his scene study class into a "safe space" for students to explore in a way and in a space where they would not be picked on, intimidated or humiliated. As well, he introduced plays with gay characters and situations (like *Grace* and *For Whom the Southern Bell Tolls*) into all his other classes, thus encouraging all students to access this material in a non-threatening manner. His scene study class became a safe place because he simply allowed it to become so, not because he forced it to become a gay space (as part of the "gay agenda"). In Smith's last year at the school, 10 out of 12 students chose to do work that had queer content although few (if any) of them identified as gay. He commented that other faculty in the department were surprised to see so much queer content in final productions. Most of the faculty had assumed that teaching a queer play (or two) in class was all they needed to do in order to have "this gay thing covered."

Wallace echoes much of these concerns and insights when discussing a course on performing gender which he developed and taught for York University:

> *The first time I taught it, every gay student in the department took it and it was very supportive. A few students came out and I had four "bois" from the Village that talked very openly about everything and the work in* The Playground *[the end of semester presentation[was very gay and quite queer.* The Playground *was received well by students and most, but not all, of the faculty was supportive.*

The second year Wallace offered the class it was smaller and the students were more reserved and closeted. By the end of the class, however, more students came out than in the previous year. In the third year, Wallace mentioned the he had "one student who was out but very quiet and careful about it and yet, he wrote, performed and directed the most gay piece in [the three years of] *The Playground*, which was autobiographical and very brave." Wallace concludes that the course demonstrated the necessity for students to be given the opportunity to experiment and play in a safe environment. Furthermore, he argues that the fact that the students and the course are not getting any systemic support from the department, faculty or other students only makes the queer students who register in the course feel marginalized even in a city where (at least off campus) they can and are proudly out. Except for the encouragement they were getting from Wallace himself, the students (mainly men) who were already confident in their gayness were not finding peer or faculty support for what they were doing. Wallace commends the students who "had to do it all themselves. No one is giving them the resources or providing a role model or legitimizing their voices." I consider this lack of support very ironical: since the opportunity to "legitimize a voice" is what most gay students who enter a university—more specifically, a theatre department—are looking for and expecting to find.

Queer Faculty Supporting Queer Students

Legitimizing the voices of queer students in the academe is an ongoing fight. Despite outside projections of what is going on within theatre departments, the fact remains that queer students do not automatically find a "place at the table," and often only do so when established "out" faculty create the necessary environment. In writing this chapter, my concerns are not about catering to a particular interest group but rather ensuring that queer students not be disadvantaged by a particular curriculum or mindset—especially a mindset that assumes that "the theatre" takes care of gay people. Anecdotal and research evidence seems to indicate that in a majority of theatre departments this is not true. The problems that most first-year (or possibly even all undergraduate) students experience are further complicated for queer students when the positive academic environment they expected to find is not there. Certainly, I think that there are areas of the academe outside of theatre departments that are much more homophobic and possibly even dangerous for queer persons. However, the evidence presented in this chapter seems to suggest the importance that queer faculty have in terms of supporting queer students (and their studies). It becomes our responsibility to understand our students' expectations and then respond to these expectations in meaningful ways. I have argued in this chapter that by making positive changes in curricula, including representations of queerness in productions and ensuring the use of scene study spaces as safe spaces, queer faculty and our straight colleagues can go a long way to ensuring that the expectations of our queer students are met with lived and positive experiences.

Notes

* At the request of some of the interviewees, names have been changed.

1. Historically, Jonson himself would have been considered socially (if not sexually) deviant by most people of his time, for the theatre, like musical practices, was "an agent of moral ambiguity always in danger of bestowing deviant status upon its practitioners." (Brett, p. 11)

2. In this instance, Sue Ellen Case is referring not only to actors, acting, and dramatized action, but also to all cultural practices which assume or contain some aspect of a performative nature (dance, music, theatre, performance art, etc.).

3. The historic posturing over the role of deviants in the theatre is not necessarily related to the sins of the homosexual sodomite, but it is important to remember that even someone like the very heterosexual Molière was denied burial rites by the church and was eventually given a proper burial only when Louis XIV intervened. Such negativity towards the theatre found renewed vigour and took an extremely homophobic tone in the aftermath of the Oscar Wilde trials. These often unfounded homophobic attacks have continued throughout the 20th century and have often been led by a number of cultural critics based in London and New York City.

   Recently Doug Arrell published an article in the *Journal of Dramatic Theory and Criticism* entitled "Homophobic Criticism and Its Disguises: The Case of Stanley Kauffmann," which chronicles the role that Kauffmann played in maintaining the anti-gay tone of criticism in the major papers of New York City (pp. 95–110). And in *Something for the Boys*, John Clum argues that this homophobia continues, making special note of Mark Steyn's 1997 book *Broadway Babies Say Goodnight: Musicals Then and Now*, and attacking the tone and content of Steyn's chapter entitled "'The Fags', in which [he] addresses the issue of gay influence on the theater and gay reception of musicals, pointing out that 'The Broadway musical encompassed everything except the one subject its creators were specially expert in'" (p. 2). Steyn's comments seem of another age and are more in keeping with the notorious work of Kauffmann and other homophobic critics, proving that cultural homophobia is alive and well at the end of the 20th century.

4. What I am arguing here is not meant to denigrate new and important work such as *Passing Performances: Queer Readings of Leading Players in American Theatre History*, in which the editors argue "that knowledge of the role of same-sex sexual desire in historical figures' theatrical careers is central to understanding their contributions and essential to writing a fuller and more accurate account of history and the changing current attitudes. Indeed, not to write this history is to be complicit in what has been called 'inning,' the perpetuation of systematic denials that foster the climate of shame and risk surrounding same-sex eroticism within and without the theatre." Rather I am opposed to, or bored by, the "sensation" revelations usually made in un-authorized biographies that part with such secrets in the hope that "reputations of cherished icons will be tarnished and the value of their art negated" (Schanke, p. 3).

5. During the 1994–95 season in which *Angels in America* was produced Bob White was an artistic associate of ATP, director of *Millennium Approaches*, and co-director of *Perestroika*.

6. He adds that the discussions around *Angels* raised further issues with the board; for example, domestic partner benefits [specifically same-sex benefits] had languished behind other contract negotiations. While unable to explain specifically why such apathy is accepted when dealing with these benefit discussions within a theatre context, he argues that the "tenuousness of artistic appointments often leads to a 'don't rock the boat' mentality" and adds that post-*Angels*, the benefits package has been changed.

7. If gender is unstable, as argued by Judith Butler and many others, a heterosexual actor may find his identity questioned insofar as his "passing" may be too good, leading to the rejection or exclusion of others. Accepting Peter Nardi's argument surrounding a spectrum of masculinities rather than "the more intimidating phrase of masculinity" (p. 7) still does not negate all of the tension that surrounds men who work in theatre. The nature of the continual problems surrounding gender assumptions and gender realities has had profound and devastating effects upon the cultural society of which gay artists are a part.

8. "It is interesting that when plays with gay protagonists have been produced on Broadway, the program often made clear that the author was married and had fathered children" (Curtin, p. 327). Susan Bennett wryly comments on this when referencing Elissa Barnard's preview piece about Neptune Theatre's production of *Angels in America*: "While on one hand, she quotes Peter Hutt's criticism of the real Roy Cohn and his refusal in a *60 Minutes* interview to admit to either homosexuality or AIDS, she is also at pains to point out that Hutt will celebrate finishing his run as Kushner's Roy Cohn with a Caribbean holiday 'with his wife, who'll come to see him in *Angels*, and his two daughters, who won't'" (pp. 169–70). The necessity to prove oneself "as a man" as opposed to the effeminate stereotype is a difficult challenge for most heterosexual and, I would argue, homosexual men in theatre, resulting in a number of diverse yet related responses. Again the tone of Barnard's article clearly tries to prove that the actors in Kushner's play are not gay, and in fact she allows both Pettle (playing Louis) and Hutt (playing Roy Cohn) to do everything they can to remove any doubt as to their sexuality, virility and masculinity from the reader's/viewer's mind. This is the argument often made against gay actors coming out—that once the audience knows that a "leading man" is gay, they would be unable to accept him in the part of a straight man. Again the hypocrisy of this seems apparent. This confusion around gender leads to homophobic bullying, internalized homophobia, and very curious solutions as men try to define "the self" against this expectation.

9. In a study of college freshmen, D'Augelli and Rose (1990) reported that 30% of those sampled preferred a college environment without any homosexuals. Abbott and Liddell (1996) reported that "lesbigay students experience more alienation from the campus environment than their heterosexual peers" (p. 51) and Hinrichs and Rosenberg demonstrated that "those [on college or university campuses] with more traditional sex-role attitudes have more negative attitudes

toward homosexuality than those with less traditional attitudes" (p. 78). Further anecdotal evidence seems to support Wallace's claim that "the benign face of homophobia in the contemporary academe is indifference." I might further suggest that this indifference is further complicated by the systemic heteronormativity that permeates the academy, the professional theatre and the larger day-to-day world in which we find ourselves.

10. Robert Wallace, one of the pioneers of queer theory in Canada and more specifically in analyzing and critically examining the intersection of queer theory/theatre, has been at the forefront of gay theatre and theatre in the academe for about 30 years. He remarks that when he was entering university in the pre-Stonewall years of the early 1960s, he was interested in studying theatre but ended up being an English/Creative Writing major. In fact, he had to lie to his parents about taking a theatre course: "Theatre was associated with fags and by taking a theatre course I would confirm their worst fears."

11. I find it interesting that in Bennett's article she mentions that in the same preview article for the Neptune production of *Angels in America*, we are informed that Jordan Pettle (who was playing Louis) "got into acting in high school because acting, rather than sport (his apparent first choice) made it easier to meet girls" (p. 170).

12. During my three years in the department there was a stereotypically "butch-dyke" sister as part of the "kooky" family in the murder mystery *Tomb with a View*, and the gay character in *Shadowbox*.

13. Perhaps this tension is also evident in the fact that until 1991, the Association for Theatre in Higher Education (ATHE) didn't have a Gay and Lesbian Theatre division—long after many academic organizations in other fields. Was this tardiness the result of straight academics within ATHE not wanting to acknowledge the gay and lesbian presence within the larger organization for fear of being contaminated with the "queer theatre brush"?

14. Aristophanes's play tells the comic story of a group of Athenian women who withhold sex from their warrior husbands in order to end a war. Generally the production is designed with the warrior husbands wearing outlandishly grotesque phalluses that serve to emphasis the sexual frustration of the warrior husband and his growing desire for sexual release.

15. Robert Wallace mentions that he is the gay presence at Glendon College (an affiliate at York University). He adds that at York University there is no tenured gay or lesbian on staff in the drama department; however, "a few out people have taught in the program [as sessionals, etc.], thus bringing a developing gay sensibility to the department." In Vancouver, Stephen Heatley comments: "I am certainly the only gay faculty member in theatre at the University of British Columbia. At least there are two of you at the University of Regina." Given the gay populations of all three cities (Toronto, Vancouver and Regina), this is extremely ironic. Many gay faculty teaching in theatre departments across the country would concur with Wallace when he comments that in terms of department policy, there "is no thought about queerness through pedagogy and a dearth of queer materials made available to students."

16. Other reports have surveyed LGBT students concerning their experiences of harassment and violence. For example, on one large campus D'Augelli found that 77% of a sample of lesbian and gay undergraduates had been verbally abused because of their sexual orientation, 27% had been threatened with physical violence, and 3% had been punched, hit, kicked or beaten. In another study it was reported that 27 of 37 graduate students surveyed had concealed their sexual orientation from a faculty member because of fears of harassment or unequal treatment (Waldo, p. 745).

References

Abbott, Elizabeth and Debora L. Liddell. 1996. "Alienation of Students: Does Sexual Orientation Matter?" *College Student Affairs Journal* 16, no. 1 (Fall): 45–55.

Abel, Sam. 1994. "Gay and Lesbian Studies and the Theatre Curriculum." *Theatre Topics* 4, no. 1 (March): 31–44.

Arrell, Doug. 2002. "Homophobic Criticism and Its Disguises: The Case of Stanley Kauffman." *Journal of Dramatic Theory and Criticism* (Spring): 95–110.

Barnard, Elissa. 1995. "Angels Among Us." *Halifax Chronicle-Herald*, February 6, B1+.

Bennett, Susan. 1996. "Only in Alberta? Angels in America and Canada." *Theatre Research in Canada/Recherches Théâtrales au Canada* 17, no. 2 (Fall): 160–74.

Brett, Philip. 1994. "Masculinity, Essentialism, and the Closet." Pp. 9–26 in *Queering the Pitch: The New Gay and Lesbian Musicology*, edited by Philip Brett, Elizabeth Wood and Gary C. Thomas. New York: Routledge Press.

Bronski, Michael. 1984. *Culture Clash: The Making of Gay Sensibility*. Boston: South End Press.

Burke, Scott. 2002. Personal interview, February 29.

Butler, Judith. 1990. "Performative Acts and Gender Constitution: An Essay in Phenomenology and Feminist Theory." Pp. 270–82 in *Performing Feminisms: Feminist Critical Theory and Theatre*, edited by Sue-Ellen Case. Baltimore: The John Hopkins University Press.

Case, Sue-Ellen, Philip Brett and Susan Leigh Foster. 1995. "Introduction" in *Cruising the Performative*, edited by Sue-Ellen Case, Philip Brett and Susan Leigh Foster. Indianapolis: Indiana University Press.

Clum, John. 1999. *Something for the Boys: Musical Theatre and Gay Culture*. New York: St. Martin's Press.

Curtin, Kaier. 1987. *"We Can Always Call Them Bulgarians": The Emergence of Lesbians and Gay Men on the American Stage*. Boston: Alyson Publications.

Daniels, Kevin*. 2002. Personal interview, May 29.

Drake, David. 1999. "Look Back in Wonder." *Genre* 76 (December).

Dyer, Richard. 2002. *The Culture of Queers*. New York: Routledge Press.

Epstein, Jeffery. 2002. "Let Them Eat Cake." *Out* (June): 92–99.

Gaard, Greta. 1992. "Opening Up the Canon: The Importance of Teaching Lesbian and Gay Literatures." *Feminist Teacher* 6, no. 3 (Winter): 30–33.

Greene, Richard. 1987. *The "Sissy Boy Syndrome" and the Development of Homosexuality*. New Haven: Yale University Press.

Grignard, Christopher. 2003. "Re: Response for Paper." E-mail to the author, March 17.

Heatley, Stephen. 2003. "Re: Response for Paper." E-mail to the author, January 10.

Hinrichs, Donald W. and Pamela J. Rosenberg. 2002. "Attitudes Toward Gay, Lesbian and Bisexual Persons Among Heterosexual Liberal Arts College Students." *Journal of Homosexuality* 43, no. 1: 61–84.

Hoffman, Martin. 1968. *The Gay World: Male Homosexuality and the Social Creation of Evil*. New York: Basic Books.

De Jongh, Nicholas. 1992. *Not in Front of the Audience: Homosexuality on Stage*. New York: Routledge Press.

Jonson, Ben. 1995. *Poetaster*, edited by Tom Cain. Manchester: Manchester University Press.

Loutzenheiser, Lisa W. 1996. "How Schools Play "'Smear the Queer'." *Feminist Teacher* 10, no. 2 (Winter): 59–64.

McInnis, Allen. 2002. Letter to the author, January 26.

Meers, Erik. 2002. "Passion Play." *The Advocate* (April 30).

Mitchell, Shawn*. 2003. "Re: Response for Paper." E-mail to the author, June 25.

Morley, Sheridan. 2001. "Theatrical Double Standards (Homosexuality in the Theater)." *Spectator* (May 5): 43.

Perrotti, Jeff and Kim Westheimer. 2001. *When the Drama Club is Not Enough: Lessons from the Safe Schools Program for Gay and Lesbian Students*. Boston: Beacon Press.

Pobo, Kenneth. 1999. "The Gay/Lesbian Teacher As Role Model." *The Humanist* 59, no. 1 (March): 26–29.

Schanke, Robert A. and Kim Marra (eds.). 1998. *Passing Performances: Queer Readings of Leading Players in American Theater History*. Ann Arbor: University of Michigan Press.

Sinfield, Alan. 1999. *Out on Stage: Lesbian and Gay Theatre in the Twentieth Century*. New Haven: Yale University Press.

Smith, Bradley*. 2003. Personal interview, March 1.

Unkown. 2001. "Court Denies Appeal Against *Corpus Christi*." *The Advocate Online* (August 9). http://www.advocate.com/new_news.asp?id=331&sd=08/09/01

Unkown. 2002. "Openly Gay Student Deleted from School Brochure." *The Advocate Online* (April 20). http://www.advocate.com/new_news.asp?id=3997&sd=04/20/02-04/22/02

Verraros, Jim. 2003. "First Person: My Favorite Teacher." *The Advocate Online* (June 19). http://www.advocate.com/html/stories/892/892_verraros.asp

Waldo, Craig R. 1998. "Out on Campus: Sexual Orientation and Academic Climate in a University Context." *American Journal of Community Psychology* 26 (October): 745–57.

Wallace, Robert. 1992. "Introduction" in *Making Out: Plays by Gay Men*. Toronto: Coach House Press.

———. 2003. Personal interview, July 23.

White, Bob. 2002. Personal interview, February 27.

Wieder, Judy. 2002. "Cher Shares." *Out* (May): 50–58, 72–78.

17

Operation "Special":
INTERROGATING THE QUEER PRODUCTION
OF EVERYDAY MYTHS IN SPECIAL EDUCATION

Scott Anthony Thompson

Introduction

It is interesting to have chosen a career, as I have, where everything is "special." The education is special, the students are special, the services to support the students are special; indeed, some schools and community centres are special, the cases are special, the awards and recognition are special, the equipment and apparatus are special —even the Olympics are special (see Wolfensberger 1995). One is not a teacher or an educator, but a *special* education teacher or a *special* educator. As a community-based caregiver, complete strangers would walk up to me (while I was accompanying a special person), and without the slightest hesitation declare, "You need to be a special person to do that kind of work." Everything is so special; in fact, I wonder whether a rather clever and incessant kind of *special* branding campaign has occurred without my notice. I continue to look for the *special* label—you know, the serendipitous placement of *special* in the latest teen adventure movie, on cereal boxes (Eat this kids, it will make you special!), on vitamins, or on towels of star athletic team-players who need them to repetitively wipe down their sweat during break-away television interviews.

And, if my career field with such market branding is not *special*—well, then it is simply *exceptional*. Many presumably well-meaning, non-special, non-exceptional people fail to recognize that a large part of what makes supporting people with special needs/disabilities/exceptionalities challenging is the material manifestation of such pitying and condescending attitudes. The job is often made more challenging when such individuals wish to identify as LGTTB (lesbian, gay, transgender, two-spirited, bisexual) in some way. It is the interrogation of the production of these myths[1]—these discursive and queerly fictive spaces—that are at the heart of this analysis. By *queerly fictive spaces*, I mean to underscore how and why these myths operate and/or appear as they do; I query the implied authority of the everyday status quo. *The production of fictive spaces* is to be read as probing the taken for granted assumptions around everyday experiences of LGTTB people with developmental disabilities—fictive spaces (or myths) that special educators[2] and parents must daily combat, acquiesce and/or propagate.

Purpose

Enforcing the "hidden curriculum" within schools may be considered to be the enactment of at least two significant institutional and rubricated myths of interest here; namely ableism and heteronormativity.[3] Ableism is the performed privilege of the able-bodied and in particular over those labelled as "disabled"; hetero-normativity attempts to make explicit the insistence of heterosexuality within the *normal*. Taken together, ableism and heternormativity variously produce within schools and communities certain kinds of acceptable people with special needs (see Brantlinger 1988, 1992). Of course, able-bodied/heteronormative myths are rife within most educational and community contexts (see especially McRuer and Wilkerson, 2003); however, they appear to act most fervently and saliently within special education. Normalizing forces are often bound up in noble, ameliorative, special educational efforts—efforts that appear so virtuous that they almost belie ideology. When students with developmental disabilities attempt to fashion identities *counter* to these acceptable (and often able-bodied) notions of what it means to have a special need (i.e. *queer* identities), then these disabling myths, such as the interminable child, the helpless invalid, the eternal innocent, etc., are (most apparently) enacted.[4] Arguably, less apparent is the production of disabling and heteronormative myths within environments of students and teachers who are the *most* able, the *most* intelligent, the *most* exceptional, and—I dare say—the most special.

To uncover how special education produces (read: constrains) LGTTB people with developmental disabilities, I present six queerly fictive spaces; namely: queerness is invisible and non-existent; contagious; entails recruitment; is reducible to observable micro-behaviours; is worse than any incarnation of heterosexuality; and is anti-Christian. When taken together, these fictive spaces constitute a complex and mythic bricolage. Originally from the French, the word *bricolage* refers to a construction comprised of any materials simply lying about; a mythic bricolage, then attempts to capture the "apparent" rationality and "innocent" spontaneity of these disabling and heteronormative fictive spaces. Within this *mythic bricolage*, at times these disabling/heteronormative spaces operate as tautologies, expressing both interdependence and interchangeablility. At other times they operate incompatibly— almost contradictorily. My hope is to facilitate narrative resonance of how these myths work "on the ground" through detailed vignettes culled from special education, the context with which I am most familiar, to those environments of yours, the reader.[5]

Community-Based Educators

I interviewed seven community-based caregivers as part of the data collection for *Disabling Sexualities* (Thompson 2003). All caregivers worked in either the Western US or Western Canada. Four caregivers directly supported gay/bi men with developmental disabilities. At the time of the interviews, Will was a care aide running a licensed residence for people with developmental disabilities out of his home. Felicia provided a similar service from her home, a respite service on weekends only. Judy, Jenn and Mitch[6] were sex education/support group counsellors, among other jobs they did to support these folks.

Judy facilitated a group entitled Smart Dating, a sex education, support and counselling group for people of any sexual orientation with developmental disabilities. Jenn performed two jobs and hence provided two perspectives useful to this project. First, she was a Sexual Health Educator for the Sunnyhill Sexual Resource Network (SSRN) a non-profit government agency set up to provide parents, caregivers and people with developmental disabilities access to information on healthy sexuality and sexual abuse prevention. In this capacity, Jenn traveled throughout British Columbia delivering workshops, and meeting many different people. Jenn left SSRN to take up the position of Youth Coordinator at The Centre: A Place for Lesbian, Gay, Bisexual, Transgender People and Their Allies. Part of this job involved counselling LGTTB youth in the GAB (Gay and Bisexual) group, and occasionally youths with a developmental disability would attend the group. Mitch founded A Safe Place, a group exclusively for gay/bi men with developmental disabilities (and/or men who have sex with other men).

The Deployment of Special Forces:
Queerly Invoked Myths and Their Effects

Queerly discursive practices like heteronormativity and ableism may propagate through and constitute implausible fictions, but their effects are real. Part of the efficiency of these myths lies within their frequent alignment within natural, common sense and taken-for-granted views—albeit often inaccurate—of developmental disability and queerness. There is a necessary plausibility. The intention here is to interrogate such naturalness by examining several queerly fictive spaces, the by-lines of which are listed here:

- Queer Un/knowing
- Queer ConsCRIPtion
- Queer Contagion
- Queer Lessons ... or Behaviour Management 101
- Queerly Straight Heterosexuality
- In the Name of the Queer Father

Queer Un/knowing

As the now famous mantra of ACT-UP, SILENCE=DEATH, echoes through the historic halls of public queer activism (DeLuca, 1999), its lessons and impact remain salient for LGTTB people with developmental disabilities. If ignorance is not apart from knowledge, but rather an emotionally charged and constructed part of knowledge (Britzman 1995), if it takes effort *not* to know, then perhaps it requires a special kind of pedagogy to silence, to produce ignorance of and for homo/sexualized identities of students with developmental disabilities:

> Service workers have balked at actively supporting people in "ordinary" sexual roles, because beneath the rhetoric workers suspect that these "ordinary" roles are off limits. What is valued for others is greeted with fear, hostility and disapproval by members of the public when it is people with learning disabilities who want to engage in

> *sexual activities. Indeed part of the eugenic agenda is still alive and well in that services are supposed to act as a container and regulator of the sexual behaviour of people with learning disabilities.* (Brown, 1994, p. 129)

For example, as Jenn delivered workshops on healthy sexuality to large groups of caregivers supporting people with developmental disabilities, rarely did a workshop participant ever broach homosexualities as a topic. However, once assemblies were broken down

> *In small groups, where people are sharing stories and you get to know more about them, you hear a little bit more. [Workshop participants] say things like "In my 20 years experience that [homosexuality; queerness] has never been an issue" [Jenn's emphasis].*

Interesting the use of the word "*that.*" What is in, what is implied in that "*that?*" It may be difficult to believe that over a 20-year span supporting people with developmental disabilities, one has never had to deal with *that* "issue." Since Jenn reported that she heard this comment somewhat frequently, perhaps it signals, at the very least, a discomfort on the part of some caregivers. Or, perhaps such situations may be characterized as active denial, active unknowing, and thereby active silencing of same-sex expression among people with developmental disabilities. At the Wellness Disability Initiative of the BC Coalition of People with Disabilities, Shelley states that caregivers do not request, nor have they ever requested resources for same-sex partners:

> *Shelley: I have never had that question, and I have never seen any indication of that in the files that it has been a question. And that doesn't surprise me given that the whole issue of sexuality in general is not usually discussed. ... I've not even had any really in-depth questions or discussions with caregivers and professionals. And that's not to say that they wouldn't feel comfortable with, just that it is not happening right now.*
>
> *S. Anthony: Questions about sexuality?*
>
> *Shelley: About sexuality in general.*

Apparently, sexuality does not "come up"—even in discussions about ... well, sexuality. An important reason for a lack of discussion around LGTTB people with developmental disabilities may be due in part by another queerly fictive construction; perhaps the oldest fiction in the book of perversion, that of conscription.

Queer ConsCRIPtion[7]

Sedgwick (1993) offers a powerful critique, in the article "How to Bring Up Your Kids Gay," of the medical apparatus and its continual pathology of queer identity into castigated behaviours. As Sedgwick unpacks the practices behind the "new and improved" term *gender identity disorder* directed primarily at effeminate boys, she argues that though the terms and the definitions change, their impact does not: "It's always open season on gay kids" (Sedgwick, 1993 p. 69). For example, science does not typically fund research projects with the aim of generating queerness:

> *If I had ever, in any medium, seen any researcher or popularizer refer even once to any supposed gay-producing circumstance as the* proper *hormone balance, or the* conducive *endocrine environment, for gay generation, I would be less chilled by the breezes of all this technological confidence. As things are, a medicalized dream of the*

> *prevention of gay bodies seems to be the less visible, far more respectable underside*
> *of the AIDS-fueled public dream of their extirpation.* (Sedgwick 1990, p. 43)

Queerly fictive spaces are not so different within education than in medicine. Producing prime queerness through curriculum and instruction remains an underfunded research agenda within education generally. Having said that, some educators see our role as preventing, precluding and prohibiting "gayness"; since LGTTB educators teach and easily transmit "it"—a Gestaltian pedagogy, that is, merely being around educators who identify as LGTTB will inevitably produce the (dreaded) "Ah ha! I'm queer!" epiphany.

The myth of conscription is quite salient for LGTTB special educators, since students with developmental disabilities are often constructed as immature, child-like and forever incapable of being informed (Ellis 1992, Jenkinson 1993, Turnbull, Ellis, Boggs, Brooks and Biklen 1981, Wolfensberger 1972), and therefore extremely vulnerable to such indoctrination. So, to discuss homosexuality is promote it: "No, it's not appropriate for me as a teacher to encourage one sexual orientation over another," was a comment that Jenn heard more than once during her career at SSRN. Perhaps not unsurprisingly, the more "challenged" a person with a developmental disability is, the more valence this fiction carries. The more "disabled" a person is or appears, for example, if s/he communicates in unconventional and unusual ways, the more caregivers may be inclined to be charged with consCRIPtion. Judy from Smart Dating elucidates:

> *Well, a number of years ago, I was involved with a young man with a significant disability. He didn't really use words to communicate. He writes things down ... he is not a verbal communicator. He was a gay man, and I worked with connecting him up to a support worker, who was gay, but their relationship was not sexual, obviously. It was to do things together, and to connect up in the community, because exactly what you are saying, it is not sexual. [It] is a way of being, and to have that be OK, and to get some support for who he was. And coincidentally, that same support worker was doing a men's sexuality group with me. And the man [with a disability] was a part of that group as well. And it was, it became a little bit of the incident, actually, because the man with disabilities started to say some things that he learned in the group. This is not unusual, but because he was saying the support worker, who was gay, and he talked about it with other support [workers], with other staff people, there was a lot of misunderstanding—about what this young man was saying. ... I had to write this long letter saying that's not what's going on. There's nothing sexual, he said these things because there was this group going on and it was not unusual for people to talk... And he ended up, he didn't continue coming to the sexuality group, because it was too dangerous for the support worker. Because I didn't want any—nor did he—any kind of allegations that were going on there, they were unfounded completely! ... I believe that [the allegation] was picked up, because of people's misunderstandings about that issue. And the fact that that even happened, that there was a contract with the Ministry for the man who is identified as being gay, to be a support worker for a man who has developmental disability. That was a major thing for that to happen, and it has gone by the boards. It is not happening anymore. And it was never clearly stated, why it stopped, but it just didn't; it wasn't accepted.*

Not only did this support worker face unspoken yet powerful charges that he was *making* the individual gay, but the worker was tacitly accused of being sexual with the individual. As Judy emphatically notes, nothing happened—except, of course, another incarnation of the queer production of a pernicious fiction about caregivers, and notably about LGTTB caregivers.

Supporting/validating *any* sexual identity for individuals with developmental disabilities may be seen as literally making individuals be sexual (and probably uncontrollably so), as opposed to seeing sexuality as part of the human condition. Therefore, or so the argument goes, supporting homo/sexuality not only makes people sexual, not only produces sexuality, but—wait for it—makes them [homo]sexual. And, so the argument goes further, queerness can *only* be taught by one who is queer; "takes one to teach one."

Perhaps strangely, I argue that for some LGTTB caregivers these two fictive spaces—supporting sexuality as producing sex and supporting homo/sexuality is producing homo/sexuals—do not necessarily operate in tandem. One myth can operate without the other. Consider the following example. Will is an openly gay caregiver who supports Kenneth, another openly gay man, but who is labelled with a developmental disability:

> S. Anthony: *You know some people might say you are promoting homosexuality. Did you ever fear that?*
>
> Will: *No, I never felt that, though I can understand what you're talking about. Kenneth himself was always self-identified. And who he portrayed, he always portrayed that he was more capable. It could be more that people afterwards would go, "Do you think that's right?" And I would say, "Well that's him and [he is] making his choices. He has a right to do that."*

Since Kenneth presents as gay, and this seems to be accepted at least in some circles, what is questioned "afterwards?" Presumably, people accept Kenneth's cultural identity—that of queerness; what may be up for grabs, then, is Kenneth's sexual life. Kenneth may be seen as a de-sexualized homosexual, and therefore, an acceptable homosexual with a developmental disability. What is at stake for some caregivers may be a pull to support LGTTB *cultural* identities for students with developmental disabilities without supporting the messiness of sexuality. Contrarily, there is evidence that some men with developmental disabilities have sex with other men, for example, and choose not to identify as gay/bi (Thompson, D. 1994). Community special educators in such scenarios are faced with supporting safer-sex practices, for example, without necessarily imputing a gay/bi cultural identification.

Given all of this, educators often find clearing up misconceptions emotionally difficult. While delivering workshops on healthy sexuality for SSRN, Jenn experienced anxiety and apprehension when attempting to confront caregivers' homophobic attitudes. She wrestled with how much to "let go" and how much to challenge. Conscriptive myths operated to inhibit open dialogue among some of the participants and herself in the workshops on healthy sexuality. The consequences were not mythic, they were real:

> I mean when you're about to go to 40 parents in the gym… And a parent says, "You know my kid may have masturbated in public but at least they are not homosexual." And everybody there goes "Ha, ha, ha"; they laugh. And then you realise that was very intimidating. I mean I really struggled with how much I didn't want to let it go, but at the same time I have a personal fear of everything from—is this going to give my agency bad name if I take this up? Am I going to be safe walking to my

car at the end of the night? Like, because thinking I might say something about this, are they immediately going to jump to "she's gay?" Which as I said never really happened but there was always the fear. (Pause) Particularly when you're dealing with people who were just so smug in the fact, you know, "Well of course it's wrong to be gay." You know? I struggled with that. So I would say something like, "If your child was gay I'm sure you would deal with that just as well as you're dealing with this now." And if there was fall-out from that, I never pushed it anymore because I just did not want to. And I certainly never said: "Well I'm bisexual, is that a problem for you?" It probably wouldn't be the most effective way to deal with it anyway. But the reason I stayed away from doing that was of this fear, this personal fear.

Queer Contagion

Using such logic, if queerness can be taught, then so too can it be caught. The myths of queer conscription and queer contagion are intimately related, since queerness is emphatically facile to teach—and most especially by queer caregivers—so is it alarmingly easy to contract. In the following story, Alisa from SSRN explains how this queer fiction is propagated by a caregiver. The caregiver acts in ways in which it appears, *quite literally*, that s/he believes s/he will be defiled or "queerified" through touching a "client" who "is" LGTTB:

[If] a person with developmental disability [is] depending upon that community of people that I have discussed—[which] may not necessarily be pro-sex—what message are you teaching them? You're teaching them to suppress their feelings, suppress their emotions, suppress their need for intimacy, and hide. That is not OK—and that it's different. And they will feel [this] from their caregiver. I have been told that in direct conversation with two men with developmental disabilities that identify; one as bisexual and one as gay. They don't understand the subtle social cues, but they're picking up that something is different about them. And their caregiver doesn't really feel good about touching them, or even shaking hands.

Queer Lessons or Behaviour Management 101

One way to avoid teaching or catching queerness is to train straightness (see for example RuPaul's convincing portrayal of a straight-making counsellor/football coach in the film *But I'm a Cheerleader: A Comedy of Sexual Dysfunction*, 2002). Indeed, some argue that [hetero]sexuality is not so much taught as vigorously enforced and monitored (see Brown, 1994). In the field of special education as in others, compulsory heterosexuality becomes enacted in various ways. A common heterosexist pedagogy here improperly invokes the language and techniques of behaviour management. Instead of conceptualizing relationships as part of the human spirit, for special people (i.e., for people with developmental disabilities), relationships may become operationalized behaviours. Hence, relationships are subject to task analyses—sets of observable tasks broken down into their most minute and most mundane detail in order to be "trained." From this perspective queerness is not a cultural or personal identity, but rather

homosexuality may be a socially isolating behaviour pattern, *rather than a widely accepted and integrating* behaviour pattern. *The strongly negative response voiced by many in America should be remembered when increased community interaction is being sought for persons with mental retardation.* (Emphasis added; Edwards and Elkins 1988, p. 67)

Since, queerness is a "mere"

> learned behaviour pattern *that is very confusing to persons with mental retardation who are struggling to learn more commonly accepted social-sexual interaction[;] therefore, homosexuality is neither encouraged nor taught as an alternative lifestyle, by either author, to persons with mental retardation* (emphasis added, Edwards & Elkins 1988, p. 67).

The myth operating here is that if homo/sexuality is a set of learned behaviour patterns, then so too is heterosexuality, and surely we must teach the correct models.

Sex education researchers and clinicians in the 1980s and into the 1990s have strongly argued against such relational reductionism (see especially Kempton & Kahn, 1991). However, some theorists note the incessant residue of such dehumanizing belief systems. Interestingly here, such reductionist residue is often lined up with heterosexism. Brown says it this way:

> *In reviewing contemporary writing about sexuality ... the reduction of sex to a biological imperative is challenged. In learning disability services, however, the notion lives on that sexual behaviour is natural and sufficiently pre-programmed to ensure that if impediments are removed people with learning disabilities will be able to enjoy heterosexual relationships. Sex education for people with learning disabilities tends to have focused on biological rather than social issues and to have assumed a heterosexist preference and a familial context for all relationships even where neither seems applicable to the person's current or foreseeable future.* (Brown 1994, p. 131)

Regardless of how sex education researchers attempt to combat such queerly fictive spaces within their own theories, within their own discipline, the mutation of human intimate relationships into correct sets of behaviours may still occur in certain group homes, and residential placements, as Alisa attests:

> *Alisa: I've had caregivers, the caregivers that are calling in (pause) not because; generally speaking and unfortunately, they're not calling to support their client's choice of sexual orientation. But in a response to a situation that has occurred... And they're [caregivers] looking to do behaviour modification ... to teach them correct appropriate sexual behaviour [Alisa's emphasis], were the words that I have been told.*
>
> *Scott: Which is?*
>
> *Alisa: Heterosexuality. That's a quote!*

Queerly Straight Heterosexuality

However queerly or oddly one may perform the straight-man, often any degree of heterosexuality is categorically superior to hints of LGTTB identification for people with developmental disabilities. This statement is not as trite as it appears. Scotti, Slack, Bowman and Morris (1996; see also Scotti, Ujcich, Nangle, Weigle, Ellis, Kirk, Vittiberga, Giacoletti and Carr-Nangle 1996) developed the perceptions of a sexuality "scale" (i.e. observations and evaluations of the sexualities of persons who have a developmental disability from the perspective of the able-bodied), where the authors concluded that

> *a number of studies have consistently found that the staff members of residential facilities only condone less sexually explicit behaviours, such as hand-holding, kissing and masturbation, and do not approve of behaviours such as intercourse or oral sex.* (Scotti et al. 1996a, p. 250)

This "toleration continuum," from least to most explicit sexual behaviour, breaks down, not surprisingly, for *any* same-sex behaviour: "One interesting finding is that the participants found that… prolonged [heterosexual] kissing in public to be just as unacceptable as … [any, presumably private] same gender activity" (p. 260). Jenn's experience bears this out:

> It was not an unusual thing, and I think I'd heard this two or three times, just because it struck me in such a personal way. Where I would be out in the community in a workshop with parents or service providers who would say, "You know I have a client who is sexually aggressive towards other clients, or is masturbating in public all the time." And then say "Oh well, I can deal with that, you know at least they're not gay." That kind of comment would come up, and trying to never let it escape without comment. But also knowing that I didn't want to make a bigger deal out of it … then [pause] because you have your own fear, when you are queer and in the field, of being accused of pushing your own agenda, right? But I had to tell them that that was not OK.

Compulsory heterosexuality may operate so forcefully that any straight behaviours—even violent heterosexual acts—are more "tolerable" than, for example, consensual same-sex expressions in the context of a loving partnership between two people with developmental disabilities. Notice too, when Jenn says "when you are queer and in the field, of being accused of pushing your own agenda," that compulsory heterosexuality can work in tandem with the fictive spaces of conscription and contagion, such that mentioning queer issues in public is akin to breeding them, sometimes creating an unsafe environment for LGTTB educators. And perhaps nowhere are educators who support LGTTB with developmental disabilities more vulnerable than within the church.

In the Queer Name of the Father

Whatever personal beliefs about queer people those who identify as Christian (or as members of other religious systems) hold, the church's impact on queer folks is undeniable. Some historians claim that significant roots of homophobia lie squarely within Christianity (Fone, 2000). Indeed these impacts continue to occur in Canada:

> As [Canadian] gays and lesbians celebrated federal legislation that would allow same-sex marriages, some Roman Catholic parishioners were getting a different message at Sunday services. On orders from the Vatican, the Catholic Church started outlining the church's opposition to the draft bill unveiled last month. At St. Michael's Cathedral in Toronto, church officials handed out pamphlets explaining Vatican guidelines that warn it is immoral to support same-sex unions. The Vatican launched a global campaign against same-sex marriage July 31 urging Roman Catholic politicians and others to oppose all legal efforts to sanctify homosexual unions. Its 12-page decree warned Catholic politicians that they have a moral duty to keep same-sex unions from being legalized. "Marriage is holy, while homosexual acts go against the natural moral law," the document reads. (www.cbc.ca, August 2003)

And recently in Regina, Saskatchewan, Larry Spencer, a Canadian Alliance MP and one-time Baptist pastor, stated his belief that there is a "homosexual conspiracy." According to reports:

> a conspiracy to seduce and recruit young boys in playgrounds and locker rooms and that there is also an infiltration into the North American judiciary, schools, religious

community and entertainment industry by homosexuals... Spencer then said that practising homosexuals like New Democratic MP Svend Robinson, could transform themselves into heterosexuals with proper training, comparing the procedure to long-distance running or weight-lifting. (www.sask.cbc.ca, November 2003)

It should not be surprising then that LGTTB educators from *Disabling Sexualities* had to wade through some of the everyday manifestations of these religious ideologies, especially if caregivers were *known* to support LGTTB persons with developmental disabilities. Mitch, a co-facilitator of A Safe Place for gay/bi men with a developmental disability, presents as extremely articulate and unflappable—an almost imposing professional in the field. Yet he was forced to endure a co-worker's "strong values":

> *There was this woman who [I] was working with and she had always been nice to me and I had always known she had extremely strong values. Several times, you know, beyond the times that I told her I was gay and in a relationship, she would make a comment about a single woman in the office [who] would be wonderful for me, which I would find kind of offensive. ... And we were sort of skirting each other as staff. And when she heard about this group [A Safe Place] I was doing, I was really nervous. I was really concerned she was going to have some negative attitudes.*

Mitch's colleague would speak condescendingly to him about A Safe Place. She would say,

> *things like, you know "I hope you're teaching them to be safe." And sometimes I know these people are coming from a position that is not necessarily pro-gay at all. People who I know that identify themselves as Christians could think homosexuality is wrong. ... [So], I've encountered it [homophobia, heterosexism, heteronormativity] in my own work, [although it's not] the worst I've encountered. I can say that I've encountered a huge amount of negativity [but] I'm pretty well regarded in my office. People know that I am knowledgeable, and know that I can back up what I am saying, and read the rules or regulations that require them not to do that.*

Able-bodied educators have some means to battle such attitudes; often times, LGTTB people with developmental disabilities do not have support resources to deal with such enshrined myths. Alternatively, some people with severe developmental disabilities may be unaware of how their identity is being constructed by those around them. For example, Felicia, a respite caregiver who supported Lester, a man with a severe developmental disability, recalled an incident where Lester was labelled "gay" by staff in reports within his former institution. Another respite provider, Samantha, was upset about this situation:

> *Felicia: My understanding is that there were direct caregivers filling out reports, and that's where that [the "gay" label] came from was the reports. Now his life skills worker, who then became his proprietary care-provider, was very upset over this because she was Catholic.*
>
> *S. Anthony: So she ... this is [Samantha]?*
>
> *Felicia: This is [Samantha], and she refused [to discuss] that he could possibly be gay and I believe even wrote a report back saying that this was unfair treatment.*
>
> *S. Anthony: Unfair, because she felt it was attributing, (pause) what did she feel?*
>
> *Felicia: Well, my understanding was that her belief [was that] people [who] were gay were the devil.*

Calls to Action

The purpose of this chapter has been to illustrate the complexities between and among each of these six fictive spaces, and how they operate within the specialness of the everyday. Taken together these queerly fictive practices create idealized norms for students with developmental disabilities: namely non-sexual persons (at best) or marginally heterosexual (if necessary). I end here with calls to action, appeals to be heard and voiced within education generally—appeals which implore more questions than answers. I begin with educators.

Everyday Advocacy

As educators, we cannot passively sit on the sidelines; we cannot produce LGTTB ignorances; we cannot unknow—the costs are too great for LGTTB students (Gibson, 1989; Levine and Beeler, 1997). They need front-line advocates, everyday advocacy. In order to combat these myths we need to position ourselves as supporters in the everyday: in classrooms, school hallways, and cafeterias. Returning to the data from *Disabling Sexualities* for a moment, Jenn provides her perspective on both the responsibility and personal development required to be an advocate for LGTTB students with developmental disabilities:

> *Anybody who is willing to accept this person's self-identification [as someone] who is gay, or any of those terms [is an advocate for LGTTB persons with developmental disabilities]. Without trying to find an excuse for it, or reason for it. Like, "Oh there's just not enough opportunity for opposite-sex activities." Anybody who is willing to take that seriously is a helper, anybody who's not afraid to push somebody in one direction or another. Somebody who's not afraid of something like, "Well maybe it's [that] they're not gay [and] I'll make them gay," because they take them to a gay event. So people that are dealing with their own s*** are able to support [LGTTB] people with developmental disabilities.*

Educators need to work through the myths of the queerness of un/knowing, contagion, recruitment, heterosexualities, religion, and micro-managing of relations

> *in order to effectively support LGTTB students. And here's the thing: everyday advocacy call us to "deal with their own stuff"... In this sense, the work of everyday advocacy is not a special field, special skill... In fact, there is nothing special about it; it is as plain as a late slip, a teacher's room coffee fund, or the predictable annual chocolate-covered almond fund-raiser. We are all everyday advocates.*

And what of our teaching practices? Is there a queer pedagogy[8] (Britzman 1995; Bryson and de Castell 1993; Quinlivan and Town 1999), and, if so, how do we implement and evaluate such instructional strategies within our local contexts here on the prairies?

These questions raise still more questions, such as what are the responsibilities of school boards and teacher education programs to support pre-service and in-service teachers to confront their own homophobia, to help teachers work through these thorny and often internalized heteronormative fictive spaces. Of course, these calls to action need to be much broader than educators' everyday advocacy; school boards, teacher federations and teacher education programs must play significant roles in ameliorating the effects of these six queerly fictive spaces. I consider here only two key areas: curriculum and policy.

A Queer Curriculum

There is a call to explore what appears as an obvious relatedness between compulsory heterosexuality, imploring and demanding straightness, and curriculum. In some ways the curriculum may be considered the ultimate producer of LGTTB ignorance, often reflecting a monolithic straightness through its chosen characters and frequently anonymous authors. Sedgwick queries:

> Has there ever been a gay Socrates? Has there ever been a gay Shakespeare? Has there ever been a gay Proust? Does the Pope wear a dress? If these questions startle, it is not least as tautologies. A short answer, though a very incomplete one, might be that not only have there been a gay Socrates, Shakespeare, and Proust, but that their names are Socrates, Shakespeare, and Proust. (1990, p. 52)

Can Shakespeare be gay in small-town Saskatchewan? How can queerness even be introduced, and—if accomplished—how do such introductions within curriculum diffuse some of the drag of heterosexuality? Perhaps we may begin with Tadei (2002), the librarian who compiled a multi-grade bibliography of LGTTB-friendly resources, which may be included within Saskatchewan school libraries. In true prairie fashion, Tadei attempted to include only those resources that were of modest cost. There are other notable efforts within the prairies, such as the annual conference, "Breaking the Silence: Gays and Lesbians in our Schools" at the University of Saskatchewan, and "AGAPE: A Sex-and-Gender Differences and Schooling Focus Group" in the Faculty of Education, University of Alberta. "Schooling and Sexual Identities," a course on LGTTB issues is now an elective part of the curriculum at the University of Regina.

Athanases (1996) explored several diversities within a language arts curriculum, including race, religious affiliation, ability, gender, and sexual orientation. Weekly, students read short stories and novels on each topic in the sequence. The story "Dear Anita," by a gay Catholic, was read last, so that students could understand how various differences are marginalized through society. Therefore, students developed empathy more easily for those who are queer. McNinch, Thompson and Totten (2004) have explored youths' attitudes to homophobia and sexual orientation in a Regina high school Humanities 10 classroom. Many theorists have pondered how to make visible queerness within or as curriculum. There seems to be some consensus that queerness needs to be throughout curriculum, and not confined to a queer day, for example. But, again, how that could be approached within the local prairie context needs to be further explored.

Additionally, with respect to curricular issues, research needs to be conducted to evaluate how initiatives such as School[PLUS] (2002, and Tymchak 2001) may impact the visibility of queerness and ameliorate heteronormative effects within Saskatchewan schools. School[PLUS] may be thought of as a kind of meta-curriculum— a call to organize educational, social, medical and judicial services within the province of Saskatchewan, such that schools become the hub of these activities for children and youth.

The Role of Policy

The role of policy within education is as complex as education itself. Does policy reflect or produce or define best educational practice? Or all three? Can policy offer us any hope to ameliorate the effects of these disabling and heteronormative myths? Roe (1994) proposes a rather innovative methodology—*narrative policy analysis*— in which he attempts to elucidate the politics and power relations within policy. Many questions are raised. What does policy look like if read as narrative? Who are the protagonists? Who are the antagonists? Who are the supporting characters? What access to power does each have? Do the policy authors define the roles? If the antagonist and protagonist roles were reversed, would policy look different? For example, if people with disabilities constructed guidelines for their caregivers, would personal care policies be different?

If adolescents who identify as queer within local schools were to participate in constructing a school district's policy in the areas of anti-discrimination, anti-bullying and anti-harassment, what would education look like? Would it be consistent with the Saskatchewan Teachers' Federation's *Safe Schools: Breaking the Silence on Sexual Difference* (2002)? Would "sexual orientation" as a specific category be named within such policies developed for particular school boards regardless of religious or other affiliation? Would such policy facilitate a local Marc Hall (Smith 2002) to attend a high school prom with a same-sex partner?

Conclusion

Living in Saskatchewan, as I do, I am often teased about the vast horizontal, which presents as the landscape. As a relative of mine once emphatically replied to such a characterization, "the prairies are most definitely not flat, they undulate!" I have come to appreciate the special-ness of the golden undulations. And in a certain sense that is our task in supporting LGTTB students—not to straighten them out so they lie flat, but to learn how to appreciate and value queerness as it is presented to us. I can learn to be special; I can support others who are special—so long as I am able to queerly ripple along.

Notes

Correspondence concerning this article should be addressed to S. Anthony Thompson, Faculty of Education, University of Regina, 3737 Wascana Parkway, Regina, Saskatchewan, Canada, S4S 0A2. Preparation of this article was supported in part by Social Sciences and Humanities Research Council of Canada (SSHRC) Grant No. 752-98-1744 and by Start-up Research Funds, Faculty of Education, University of Regina. My thanks to Dr. Kathleen O'Reilly-Scanlon and Dr. James McNinch for thoughtful edits to this paper; however, I take full responsibility for the content.

1. The word "myth" has been variously invoked when discussing the plight of people with developmental disabilities in North American contexts (see Wolfensberger 1972 for a classic example). Although some myths are positive, others are destructive—such myths are the subject of this chapter.

2. The term *special educator* is used here broadly to include teachers within school systems but also community-based personnel, such as social workers, life-skills workers, behaviour therapists, etc.

3. Of course, homophobia, the hatred of LGTTB persons, and heterosexism, the privileging of heterosexual relations and identities, also figure significantly into the production of such myths.

4. The words *most apparently* are bracketed and used here to highlight the contention that disabling myths are always at work, but sometimes only when one attempts to resist them does their impact seem real.

5. The key participants in the project *Disabling Sexualities* were self-identified gay/bisexual men with developmental disabilities; two of whom identified as First Nations men (two-spirited individuals). I interviewed key participants' caregivers. One caregiver, Jenn, did talk about supporting lesbians with developmental disabilities as well as one person who identified as transgender. Therefore, this analysis does include perspectives around supporting each of the complex identities represented by LGTTB.

The data for these queerly fictive productions is based upon exploratory identity work of gay and bisexual (gay/bi) men with developmental disabilities from across Western Canada and the US, as well as their community-based caregivers (Thompson, 1998, 2002; Thompson, Bryson & deCastell 2001). Although students with developmental disabilities necessarily negotiate through disabling and homophobic myths, the focus here is upon educators' navigation through these queerly fictive spaces. I take this emphasis to underscore the vital role educators have in promoting healthy sexuality for all students. Next, then, is an introduction to the community-based educators.

6. Will, Felicia, Mitch and Judy are pseudonyms, so chosen since each caregiver directly supported one of the gay/bi men with developmental disabilities in *Disabling Sexualities*. Caregiver pseudonyms help preserve the anonymity and confidentiality of these key participants. Alisa, Jenn and Shelley did not directly support a key participant and chose not to use a pseudonym.

Although Judy, Jenn and Mitch are now primarily in administrative and counselling positions, each of these community-based educators has substantial experience directly supporting people with developmental disabilities one-to-one in the community. Shelley and Alisa, the two remaining professionals, often interacted with people with developmental disabilities and their caregivers, although they do not directly support such individuals. Shelley was the coordinator of the Wellness and Disability Initiative (WDI) of the British Columbia Coalition of People with Disabilities (BCCPD) and Alisa was the Library Technician; in some ways, I describe her as an informal intake worker at SSRN.

7. The term "consCRIPtion" is meant to be read seriously and respectfully. I hope to invoke the referent "crip," from "crip[ple]"—a word reclaimed by a recent movement of people with physical disabilities, much like "queer" has been reclaimed by some LGTTB persons.

8. Not surprisingly there are varying views on what constitutes a queer pedagogy. Some queer pedagogical researchers tend to teach and to structure learning environments in such a way as to shift the power imbalance from heterosexualities to qu<e>eries within classrooms, or attempt to value all sexualities equally; thus ostensibly making identity itself a moot category.

References

Athanases, S.Z. 1996. "A Gay-themed Lesson in an Ethnic Literature Curriculum: Tenth Graders' Responses to 'Dear Anita'." *Harvard Educational Review, Special issue: Lesbian, Gay Bisexual and Transgender People and Education* 66, no. 2: 231–57.

Babbit, J. (director). 2002. *But I'm a Cheerleader: A Comedy of Sexual Dysfunction*. Lions Gate Films: A Lions Gate Entertainment Company Retrieved from:

http://www.lionsgatefilms.com/dnm/profile.html?pid=IN-T-00807. Accessed October 8, 2003.

Brantlinger, E. 1992. "Sexuality Education in the Secondary Special Education Curriculum: Teachers' Perceptions and Concerns." *Teacher Education and Special Education* 15, no. 1: 32–40.

Brantlinger, E. 1988. "Teacher's Perceptions of the Sexuality of Their Secondary Students With Mild Retardation." *Education and Training in Mental Retardation* 23: 24–27.

Britzman, D. 1995. "Is There a Queer Pedagogy? Or, Stop Reading Straight." *Educational Theory* 45, no. 2: 151–65.

Brown, H. 1994. "'An Ordinary Sexual Life?': A Review of the Normalisation Principle as It Applies to the Sexual Options of People with Learning Disabilities." *Disability & Society* 9, no. 1: 123–43.

Bryson, M. and S. de Castell. 1993. "Queer Pedagogy: Praxis Makes Im/perfect." *Canadian Journal of Education* 18, no. 3: 285–305.

DeLuca, K.M. 1999. "Unruly Arguments: The Body Rhetoric of Earth First!, ACT UP, and Queer Nation." *Argumentation and Advocacy* 36: 9–21.

Edwards, J.P. and T.E. Elkins. 1988. *Just Between Us: A Social Sexual Guide for Parents and Professionals With Concerns for Persons With Developmental Disabilities.* Portland, OR: Ednick Communications.

Ellis, J.W. 1992. "Decisions by and for People With Mental Retardation: Balancing Considerations of Autonomy and Protection." *Villanova Law Review* 371779–1809.

Erlandson, C. 2002. *Safe Schools: Breaking the Silence on Sexual Difference.* Saskatoon, Saskatchewan: Saskatchewan Teachers' Federation, Saskatchewan Professional Development Unit.

Fone, B. 2000. *Homophobia: A History.* New York: Picador USA.

Gibson, P. 1989. "Gay Male and Lesbian Youth Suicide." In G. Remafedi (ed.), *Death by Denial: Studies of Suicide in Gay and Lesbian Teenagers.* Boston: Alyson Publications, pp. 15–69.

Jenkinson, J. 1993. "Who Shall Decide? The Relevance of Theory and Research to Decision-making by People With an Intellectual Disability." *Disability, Handicap & Society* 8: 361–75.

Kempton, W. and E. Kahn. 1991. "Sexuality and People with Intellectual Disabilities: A Historical Perspective." *Sexuality and Disability* 9, no. 2: 93–111.

Levine, L. and L. Beeler. 1997. "Sexual Orientation and Youth Suicide." Presented at the Third Bi-Regional Adolescent Suicide Prevention Conference in Breckenridge, Colorado, September 21–23.

McNinch, J., S.A. Thompson and M. Totten. 2004. "Que(e)rying Inclusive Practice: Exploring and Challenging Homophobia in Curricula and Schools." A Research Project in process funded by the Dr. Stirling McDowell Foundation for Research into Teaching.

McRuer, R. and A.L. Wilkerson (eds.). 2003. "Desiring Disability: Queer Theory Meets Disability Studies. [Special issue] *A Journal of Lesbian and Gay Studies* 9: 1–2.

No author. 2003 (August). "Church Takes Same-Sex Warning to the Pulpit." Retrieved January 26, 2004, from http://www.cbc.ca/storyview/CBC/2003/08/03/samesex_030803

No author. 2003 (November). "Regina MP Canned Over Comments on Gays. Retrieved January 26, 2004, from http://sask.cbc.ca/regional/servlet/View?filename=spencer031127

No author. 2002. "Working Together Toward SchoolPLUS: Parent and Community Partnerships in Education. Handbook." Saskatchewan Learning: Policy and Planning Unit. Retrieved on January 27, 2004 from

http://www.sasked.gov.sk.ca/k/pecs/spip/docs/roleofsch/may2002prnthndbook.pdf

Quinlivan, K. and S. Town. 1999. "Queer Pedagogy, Educational Practice and Lesbian and Gay Youth." *Qualitative Studies in Education* 12, no. 5: 509–24.

Roe, E. 1994. *Narrative Policy Analysis.* Durham, NC: Duke University Press.

Sedgwick, E. 1990. *Epistemology of the Closet.* Berkeley: University of California.

———. 1993. "How to Bring Up Your Kids Gay." In M. Warner (ed.), *Fear of a Queer Planet: Queer Politics and Social Theory.* Minneapolis: University of Minnesota Press, 69–81.

Scotti, J., B. Slack, R. Bowman and T. Morris. 1996. "College Student Attitudes Concerning the Sexuality of Persons With Mental Retardation: Development of the Perceptions of Sexuality Scale." *Sexuality and Disability* 14, no. 4: 249–63.

Scotti, J., K. Ujcich, D. Nangle, K. Weigle, J. Ellis, K. Kirk, G. Vittiberga, A. Giacoletti and R. Carr-Nangle. 1996. "Evaluation of an HIV/AIDS Education Program for Family-based Foster-care Providers." *Mental Retardation* 34, no. 7: 75–82.

Smith, G. 2002. "Gay Teen Wins Prom Fight." *Globe and Mail*, May 11, pp. A1, A10.

Tadei, K. 2002. "It's OK to Have This Book in Your Public School Library. Gay, Lesbian, Bisexual, Transgender and Two-spirited People: A Bibliography of Resources." Research Project #74 Dr. Stirling McDowell Foundation for Research into Teaching. Retrieved January 27, 2004 from http://www.mcdowellfoundation.ca/main_mcdowell/projects/research_rep/project_74.pdf

Thompson, D. 1994. "The Sexual Experiences of Men with Learning Disabilities Having Sex With Men: Issues for HIV Prevention." *Sexuality and Disability* 12: 221–42.

Thompson, S.A. 1998. "Queer Abilities: A Queerly-abled Analysis of Persons With Developmental Disabilities Who Self-identify as Gay, Lesbian, Bisexual or Transgendered." In L. Muzzin (ed.), *Reflecting Social Life: Analysis and Interpretation in Qualitative Research. Proceedings of Qualitatives '98*. Toronto, Canada [on computer disc].

——. 2002. "Disabling Sexualities: An Exploratory Multiple Case Study of Self-identified Gay and Bisexual Men With Developmental Disabilities." Ph.D. dissertation, University of British Columbia.

——. 2003. "Subversive Political Praxis: Supporting Choice, Power and Control for People With Developmental Disabilities." *Disability & Society* 18, no. 6: 719–35.

Thompson, S.A., M. Bryson and S. deCastell. 2001. "Prospects for Identity Formation for Lesbian, Gay or Bisexual Persons With Developmental Disabilities." *International Journal of Disability, Development and Education* 48, no. 1: 53–65.

Turnbull, R., J. Ellis, E. Boggs, P. Brooks and D. Biklen. 1981. *The Least Restrictive Alternative: Principles and Practices*. Washington, DC: American Association on Mental Deficiency.

Tymchak, M. and the Saskatchewan Instructional Development & Research Unit (SIDRU). 2001. *The Role of the School: SchoolPlus: A Vision for Children and Youth. Toward a New School, Community and Human Service Partnership in Saskatchewan*. Regina, Saskatchewan: Final Report to the Minister of Education Government of Saskatchewan.

Wolfensberger, W. 1972. *Normalisation: The Principle of Normalisation in Human Services*. Toronto: National Institute on Mental Retardation.

——. 1995. "Of 'Normalisation,' Lifestyles, the Special Olympics, Deinstitutionalization, Mainstreaming, Integration, and Cabbages and Kings." *Mental Retardation* 33, no. 2: 128–31.

18

Engaging Sex-and-Gender Differences:

EDUCATIONAL AND CULTURAL CHANGE INITIATIVES IN ALBERTA

André P. Grace & Kristopher Wells

Without the existence of supportive classroom environments, homosexual and bisexual students will be forced to remain invisible and reluctant to approach their teachers. They will be victims of identity erasure, forced into ... a spiral of silence in which lesbians and gays modify their behaviour to avoid the impact of prejudice.

Madame Justice L'Heureux-Dubé, Dissenting Opinion,
BCCT v. Trinity Western University [2001], at para. 91

Introduction

Historically, LGBTQ (lesbian, gay, bisexual, transgender, and queer) students and teachers have been variously disenfranchised, defiled, and dismissed in schools (Epstein & Johnson, 1998; Grace & Benson, 2000; Grace & Wells, 2001; Jennings, 1994; Quinlivan & Town, 1999). Yet schools are supposedly inclusive institutions that exist to meet the needs and assist the growth and development of *every* student. They are also teachers' workplaces where teachers ought to be supported personally and professionally so that they can be happy, safe, secure, and productive citizen workers. However, in its resource guide designed to help teachers address hetero-sexism and homophobia in elementary schools, the Surrey Teachers' Association of the British Columbia Teachers' Federation unequivocally states, "Schools remain one of the last bastions of tolerated hatred toward GLBT [gay, lesbian, bisexual, and transgender] people" (STA, 2000, p. 2). The Association emphasizes that schools must "truly care about ALL of our students and families" (STA, 2000, p. 2). We would add teachers as a third crucial interest group to this statement of care, noting that *all* teachers must include LGBTQ teachers who experience tremendous pressure as they try to balance work (being a secure and productive teacher) with life (being a safe and content LGBTQ person). Schools, indeed all sectors of education including school-district management, school boards, school trustees, and provincial/territorial departments of education have an obligation to eradicate tolerated hatred toward LGBTQ persons in school settings. This obligation is clearly mandated by Section 15 of the Canadian Charter of Rights and Freedoms, which provides LGBTQ persons and citizens with constitutional protection against discrimination on the ground of sexual orientation (DJC, 1982/2002). It is also mandated in the statement of purpose of the Canadian Human Rights Act, which categorically prohibits discrimination against LGBTQ persons and citizens (DJC, 2001):

> The purpose of this Act is to extend the laws in Canada to give effect ... to the principle that all individuals should have an opportunity equal with other individuals to make for themselves the lives that they are able and wish to have and to have their needs accommodated, consistent with their duties and obligations as members of society, without being hindered in or prevented from doing so by discriminatory practices based on race, national or ethnic origin, colour, religion, age, sex, sexual orientation, marital status, family status, disability or conviction for an offense for which a pardon has been granted. (p. 1)

The perennial marginalization of LGBTQ students and teachers in school settings replicates the historical sociocultural positioning of these individuals as sex-and-gender outlaws (Tierney, 1997). The price of such constructed discriminatory notoriety is often physical and emotional abuse and battery by unthinking, unfeeling homophobes who are far less sanctioned within the heteronormative institutional confines of education than the LGBTQ individuals they hurt. In the face of this intolerance and despite it, LGBTQ students and teachers have become more visible and vocal in demanding their rights to full citizenship and participation. They are working to resist, deconstruct, and transform their fugitive identity constructions so that they can fully be, become, and belong in schools and other sociocultural settings. As gay men and as educators of educators, we feel an obligation to assist LGBTQ students and teachers and non-LGBTQ allies in this important sociocultural and political work.

In this chapter we discuss our ongoing educational and cultural initiatives in Alberta to profile LGBTQ issues of equity, social justice, safety, and inclusion in education and the larger culture and society. These initiatives are caught up in our larger concerns with education for citizenship, building communities of dialogue and difference, and engaging in inclusive educational and cultural practices to promote human and civil rights. In our work we engage in an inclusive public pedagogy that is about accepting and accommodating LGBTQ persons. We characterize this pedagogy as a project in LGBTQ networking and, as facilitators and participants in this project, we aim to contest and disrupt sociocultural dynamics where ignorance leads to fear, and fear leads to symbolic and real violence against LGBTQ persons in schools and other sociocultural sites in the community. Thus we emphasize the importance of *seeing and knowing sex-and-gender differences* since simply getting to know an LGBTQ person can make a positive difference (Grace, 2001).

We begin by describing two educational initiatives that are integral to our inclusive public pedagogical project to make Queerness—being, believing, desiring, becoming, belonging, and acting LGBTQ—visible and known in education. First, we talk about our work with the Alberta Teachers' Association's Safe and Caring Schools

Project (SACS). We overview our efforts to provide teachers with knowledge and resources designed to help them address heterosexism and homophobia in schools. Then we explore our work with AGAPE, which is an LGBTQ focus group in the Faculty of Education, University of Alberta that considers issues in relation to sex-and-gender differences and education and culture. We recount our efforts to meet the personal and professional needs expressed by LGBTQ and allied undergraduate and graduate students, faculty, and staff as well as practicing teachers in the greater Edmonton area. We talk about our use of inclusive activities and resources to help educators build educational practices that counter heterosexism and homophobia. We also overview our use of resource-based lectures and workshops to bring AGAPE's inclusive message to pre-service teacher education in core courses including (1) ethics and school law and (2) classroom management.

Next we describe two community initiatives in which we participate to make Queerness visible and known in our heterosexualizing culture and heteronormative society. First, we talk about our work with the Diversity Conferences of Alberta Society (DCAS), which is a community group that engages in public pedagogical work to counter homophobia and prejudice in the culturally conservative province of Alberta. We profile DCAS colleagues as a diverse group of cultural workers whose members represent an array of religious and nonreligious positions as well as sex-and-gender differences. We discuss DCAS's educational and sociocultural efforts to provide opportunities for people to engage in learning as liberation and affirmation. Then we highlight our work with Youth Understanding Youth (YUY), which is a self-supporting social/support group for LGBTQ and questioning youth (aged 25 and under) in the greater Edmonton area. We provide an overview of sociocultural strategies that YUY uses to provide informal learning for LGBTQ and questioning youth. We consider how YUY strives to create a safe environment in which youth can explore and express their needs and interests in an atmosphere where they can expect to be supported and respected as persons with unique characteristics and capacities.

We end this chapter with a concluding perspective that speaks to the importance of this public pedagogical and cultural work in Canadian culture and society. We assert that such work is still vital because significant LGBTQ-positive changes in our laws and legislation have yet to translate fully into sociocultural changes that reflect the complete accommodation of LGBTQ persons and citizens. As a postscript we offer two poems which capture the intensity of the struggle of engaging in queer advocacy "teaching in the fray."

Educational Initiatives to Recognize, Respect, and Honour LGBTQ Persons in Education in Alberta

So what can teacher-educators do in everyday teaching and in other educational endeavors to increase LGBTQ visibility and understanding? How might teacher-educators working in schools as public spaces advance LGBTQ struggles for the rights and privileges of full citizenship? These questions are difficult to answer because they are linked to struggles for increased LGBTQ human and civil rights that are social, moral, and political in nature. In the sociocultural fray of education, Charter-guaranteed individual rights are increasingly pitted against constitutional rights such as freedom of religion. Since *all* these rights are core rights defying hierarchical categorization in Canadian democracy, judges who arbitrate conflicts around them find themselves engaged in a complex, value-driven decision-making process. Acknowledging these difficulties that situate our work in a dangerous sociopolitical and moral intersection, let us overview two ways in which we intersect the personal and the professional in our LGBTQ work in pre-service teacher education and in-service teacher development.

Alberta Teachers' Association's Safe and Caring Schools Project (SACS)

In 1991 Delwin Vriend, an "out" gay educator at King's University College, a Christian college in Edmonton, was dismissed on the pretext that his sexual orientation violated that institution's religious policy. Vriend courageously took his discrimination case through a lengthy judicial process, and the Supreme Court of Canada handed down its long-awaited decision in Vriend on April 2, 1998 (Grace, 2003; Saunders, 2002). The decision was in the educator's favor in his legal challenge to have sexual orientation read into the then-existing Alberta Individual's Rights Protection Act.[1] The Court's ruling was in keeping with equality provisions in Section 15(1) of the federal Charter in which sexual orientation, as a protected category of person, is considered analogous to other personal characteristics listed there. In the wake of this decision, the Alberta Teachers' Association (ATA) recommended an amendment to its Code of Professional Conduct that would require teachers to teach in a manner that respects a person's sexual orientation. This amendment was overwhelmingly passed at the 1999 Annual Representative Assembly. Kris describes what happened subsequently:

> I met with members of the ATA several times in the months following the Vriend decision to discuss the most effective way that the ATA could assist teachers in meeting their new professional responsibilities to create safe, caring, and inclusive school environments for LGBTQ students. There were two substantial challenges. The first was to make teachers aware of the change, and the second was to develop the necessary resources to help teachers live out this change in their classrooms and schools.

> To help address these challenges we made an important connection with the newly formed ATA Safe and Caring Schools (SACS) Project. The mandate of this project is to develop proactive violence prevention programs, resources, and strategies that are designed to assist schools in developing human rights' cultures that promote responsible citizenship, peace, and non-violence. As a newly appointed member of the steering committee for the SACS Project, I was invited to present a workshop for junior and senior high school teachers and counselors who were receiving training on how to integrate violence-prevention concepts and principles into their classroom teaching. During this anti-homophobia workshop I asked teachers to reflect on a series of key questions that were designed to encourage them to assess their individual, school, and community attitudes, values, and beliefs. After each teacher engaged in personal reflection, we did group work to identify factors that help or hinder Alberta's teachers in addressing homophobia and heterosexism. The teachers' responses are compiled in the following lists of bullets:

> Addressing Homophobia and Heterosexism: Factors That Help

> • Media coverage
> • Education on LGBTQ topics
> • Community supports/programs
> • Professional development on LGBTQ topics

- *Model appropriate behaviour*
- *Supportive existing laws/legislation*
- *Factual research*
- *Stories/testimonials/guest speakers*
- *Guidance/counseling*
- *Inclusive school vision*
- *Questioning what the purpose of schooling is*
- *Discussion to help create safe and caring schools*
- *Dispelling myths*
- *Address underlying issues (i.e. bullying)*
- *Enforcing inclusive policies*
- *Teacher beliefs that support inclusive schools*
- *Minimizing "hallway" behaviour*
- *The SACS program*
- *Role play (Drama)*

Addressing Homophobia and Heterosexism: Factors That Hinder

- *Conservative religion/faith perspectives*
- *Teacher beliefs/reluctance to address the issues*
- *Student hostility/attitudes*
- *Fear of LGBTQ differences*
- *Community hostility/climate*
- *Lack of knowledge and understanding*
- *School board policy that forbids discussion of LGBTQ issues*
- *Discomfort in addressing any issues of sexuality*
- *Fears associated with threats to masculinity/developing identity at puberty*
- *Presumed heterosexuality*
- *Gay image/activism … gay pride in your face*
- *Avoidance/pretend it doesn't exist*
- *"Red neck" mentality/prejudice*
- *Confusion over sex vs. sexuality*
- *Controversial nature of subject*
- *Morality and values issue*
- *Sexual ambiguity*
- *Parental attitudes*

As teachers engaged in a group discussion of what they perceived to be existing barriers in discussing issues related to sex-and-gender differences, they shared various insights. One teacher stated, "I believe there is a fear or lack of understanding. … There doesn't seem to be an appropriate avenue for addressing questions and concerns." Another teacher asserted, "Homophobia derives from ignorance and possibly fear. It also comes from ignorance at home." In discussing ways to overcome these barriers one teacher suggested, "The starting point should be to engage in more discussion with people, opening the door for people to say what they think and feel. I would anticipate that there is both fear and resistance in staff, students, and parents."

From this beginning, my work in teacher development around LGBTQ issues and inclusive pedagogy continues. Most recently I have developed three complementary educational workshops to promote and sustain professional development learning communities that address sex-and-gender differences. They are contained in a resource entitled Building Safe and Caring Classrooms, Schools, and Communities for Lesbian, Gay, Bisexual and Transgender Students: Professional Development Workshops for Alberta Teachers (Wells, 2003). The workshops have been field-

tested at several teachers' conventions in Alberta, and they were highlighted in a featured session at the 2003 National Safe and Caring Schools and Communities Conference in Halifax, Nova Scotia.

As part of its encompassing work, the ATA's Safe and Caring Schools Project strives to help teachers, parents, and other interest groups to understand and address sex-and-gender differences in their classrooms, schools, and communities. Two recent initiatives are ATA milestones. First, SACS, in partnership with Edmonton's Orlando Books Collective, has created a resource guide for teachers entitled "Safe and Caring Schools for Lesbian and Gay Youth: A Guide for Teachers" (ATA & OBC, 2002). This guidebook is the ATA's first substantial resource designed to help teachers develop an inclusive practice that recognizes and accommodates the educational needs and concerns of LGBTQ students in Alberta schools. Second, the ATA has developed a Sexual Orientation and Gender Identity Educational Website.[2] This cyber-resource complements and expands on information in the guidebook, providing Alberta teachers with current information, research, resources, and community-based contacts to assist them to meet the needs of LGBTQ students and teachers (Wells, 2002).

Another milestone event in LGBTQ-inclusive education has recently occurred at the national level. The Canadian Teachers' Federation (CTF), in partnership with the Elementary Teachers' Federation of Ontario (ETFO), has published its first comprehensive LGBTQ educational resource manual entitled *Seeing the Rainbow: Teachers Talk About Bisexual, Gay, Lesbian, Transgender, and Two-Spirited Realities* (CTF & ETFO, 2003). This important document is focused on providing information and resources to build democratic and inclusive classroom communities in which LGBTQ persons and issues are acknowledged and accommodated. *Seeing the Rainbow* is divided into three key sections that feature important background information, teacher narratives, and essential resources for further inquiry. The information section provides a rich compilation of definitions and lesson plans that can help educators address health, safety, legal, and educational concerns in work on sex-and-gender differences in their classrooms and schools. The second section features teachers' personal narratives that provide both a testament to the significant work ongoing in Canadian schools and a challenge to engage in the important work that remains to be done. The third section outlines international, national, and provincial resource agencies, books, and videos that are designed to provide teachers with additional sources of information and support.

These educational initiatives for democratic education and social justice exemplify the significant work provincially and nationally to make Canada's classrooms safer and more inclusive places, where the dignity and integrity of all students and teachers is recognized, respected, and honoured.

AGAPE: A Sex-and-Gender Differences and Schooling Focus Group

AGAPE is located in the Faculty of Education, University of Alberta, which is home to over 3,000 undergraduate and graduate students from all regions of Canada plus an array of other countries. This focus group exists to provide a forum for students, faculty, staff, and community members to take up issues of sex-and-gender differences in relation to access and accommodation in educational and other sociocultural contexts. André describes AGAPE's purposes and functions:

During the 2000–01 academic year, I initiated (with the support of the Faculty of Education at the University of Alberta) a new focus group called AGAPE, which considers issues in relation to sex-and-gender differences and schooling. AGAPE, as Martin Luther King, Jr. understood it, stands for "disinterested love. ... AGAPE does not begin by discriminating between worthy and unworthy people, or any qualities people possess. It begins by loving others for their sakes. ... It springs from the need of the other person" (cited in Tierney, 1993, p. 23). From this inclusive perspective, our group is designed to focus on the personal and professional needs that LGBTQ undergraduate and graduate students, faculty, and staff have. Straight allies are also welcome. In addition, we have advertised our presence in the greater Edmonton community, inviting teachers working in K–12 schools and other interested community members to participate with us.

AGAPE members have worked to build an on-campus LGBTQ resource base that is useful to pre-service and practicing teachers and community members. In our biweekly meetings we

• *share and discuss narratives of schooling;*
• *use forms of LGBTQ popular culture including LGBTQ-themed music, films, and magazines as resources to help us build teaching practices that counter heterosexism and homophobia;*
• *take up issues in relation to job searches and schools as workplaces;*
• *engage in role plays and other forms of drama as pedagogy to explore LGBTQ issues and concerns in relation to schooling;*
• *examine policies and practices in schools, districts, and provincial teachers' associations/federations across Canada;*
• *examine materials from various Safe and Caring Schools Initiatives/Coalitions in Canada and the United States;*
• *deliberate with invited presenters including LGBTQ researchers and activists as well as community groups like PFLAG (Parents, Families, and Friends of Lesbians and Gays); and*
• *provide a space to network and socialize in a safe, supportive setting.*

As well, each November AGAPE members host a one-day conference using the theme "Sex-and-Gender Differences in Education and Culture." The conference provides an opportunity for educational interest groups from local, provincial, and national jurisdictions to come together to dialogue and share resources. It also provides an opportunity for them to assess changes, progress, and possibilities regarding inclusivity for LGBTQ students and teachers in Canadian education.

Let me overview a typical academic year's activities. We began 2001–02 by reviewing a variety of resources on antigay violence in schools as a way to focus concerns on the safety and security of LGBTQ youth. On October 11th we celebrated National Coming Out Day in Canada with events that included hosting an LGBTQ Curriculum/Resource Fair in the main-floor cafeteria of our Education North Building. Over the course of several meetings, we viewed and discussed new LGBTQ educational videos, several produced by the National Film Board of Canada, that explore such issues as LGBTQ teen suicide, LGBTQ parents/straight schools, and homophobic language.[3] At the request of graduate students engaged in research with LGBTQ youth less than 18 years of age, we organized a session with invited educational researchers to discuss the issue of the ethical implications of research involving LGBTQ youth.[4] Early in the New Year, we provided input into the development of the ATA's "Sexual Orientation and Gender Identity Website." Next, using the document A Resource for an Inclusive Community: A Teacher's Guide for and

about Persons with Same Sex Attractions *(ACSTA, 2001), AGAPE members inves-*
tigated Roman Catholic initiatives to address the needs of LGBTQ youth in educa-
tional settings in Calgary. We also explored school/LGBTQ community relations,
inviting a member from the Gay and Lesbian Community Center of Edmonton to
speak with us about community-based forms of LGBTQ education that, among other
things, challenge the lack of LGBTQ content in formalized schooling.

AGAPE has been growing slowly but surely since its inception nearly two years ago.
While an increasing number of faculty, staff, graduate students, and teachers from
the community attend our meetings regularly, sadly it is rare for an undergraduate
education student to attend. Sometimes an undergrad will email me or drop by my
office for an impromptu chat. When I ask them about attending AGAPE, they raise
concerns about being seen entering or leaving the meeting room. I have changed ven-
ues to a more obscure location, but still undergrads stay away. They tell me they
worry about being outed or, if straight, being labeled LGBTQ, and how such profil-
ing would affect getting a job and being safe and secure.

In addition to our work with AGAPE, we engage in other initiatives that promote
various educational and safety/security interests of LGBTQ students and teachers.
We consider these initiatives to be important interventions that help to make
LGBTQ persons and issues visible in teacher education as a field of study and practice. However, as "resist-stances" practiced in the face of systemic and structural
barriers, we know we have much work to do to fulfill Queer theory's desire to bring
an illimitable array of LGBTQ differences and positionalities openly and freely into
educational space. This is because education remains a conservative space, a space
where it is preferable to integrate or assimilate difference—when difference is
attended to at all—rather than to let difference be or to honour it. We are reminded of this every time a third or fourth year undergraduate education student uses one
of our workshops as an opportunity to declare, "This is the first time in my program
that an instructor has brought up the issue of sexual orientation."

We now overview two initiatives that are parts of core courses in our teacher education program:

Educational Policy Studies 410–Ethics and School Law: I have included a module
on sex-and-gender differences and schooling in a core course I teach that introduces
undergraduate students to ethics and school law. Using this module, pre-service
teachers study sexual orientation as a category of person in relation to the Canadian
Charter of Rights and Freedoms; other federal legislation; provincial/ territorial
human rights codes; provincial/territorial education acts; and teacher
association/federation documents focused on professional code of conduct and teach-
ers' rights, responsibilities, and liabilities. They also analyze case studies focused on
sex-and-gender differences and schooling in relation to contemporary challenges in
the Canadian courts. As well, this module also involves a focus on information and
resources available to assist teachers learn about issues of sex-and-gender differ-
ences so they might meet educational and sociocultural needs of LGBTQ youth.

Educational Policy Studies 310–Managing the Learning Environment: Each term we
develop and deliver workshops for pre-service teachers registered in all sections of a
core teaching methods course connected to their practice teaching. We invite col-
leagues and members of PFLAG and other community groups to help us deliver these
workshops to about 400 undergraduates a year. The workshops focus on addressing
issues of sex-and-gender differences in school settings, building a resource base, and
networking with the larger community. In addition to inviting guest speakers, we use

video clips, narrative vignettes and poetry, and resource handouts to focus discussions around sex-and-gender differences, homophobia, violence, and schooling. The workshops also include a discussion on guidelines for developing an inclusive curriculum and bias-free teaching materials. They also highlight initiatives like Safe and Caring Schools, which operate to promote the educational interests of LGBTQ and other students for whom schools can be unsafe places.

With each of these educational initiatives, we promote the educational and security interests of LGBTQ students and teachers, and we focus on the responsible, caring, and respectful treatment of LGBTQ persons in education and culture. This is our way to connect the personal and the professional.

Cultural Initiatives to Recognize, Respect, and Honour LGBTQ Persons in Alberta

So what can teacher-educators and other citizens do in the community to increase LGBTQ visibility and advance the LGBTQ struggle to obtain the rights and privileges of full citizenship? What are some possible ways to bring issues of LGBTQ access and accommodation to the fore in culture and society? It is important to take up these questions, especially because changes in Canadian law and legislation enhancing LGBTQ human and civil rights have been slow to translate into broader cultural changes. What is written down in judgments and statutes is still not lived out to the extent that LGBTQ persons can engage fully in life, learning, and work. Here we describe two community initiatives in which we participate with other LGBTQ persons and straight allies to help counteract the lived reality of exclusion and violence that remains all too pervasive in so many LGBTQ lives.

The Diversity Conferences of Alberta Society

The Diversity Conferences of Alberta Society (DCAS) was incorporated in 1998 to continue the spiritual and cultural work that Reverend Bert and Evelyn Frey, now retired from pastoral work with the United Church of Canada, had begun to address homophobia and prejudice in the predominantly conservative province of Alberta (DCAS, 2001). DCAS is a diverse group of cultural workers whose members reflect an array of sex-and-gender differences that cannot be reduced to simplistic male/female and homo/heterosexual dichotomous classifications. The group also reflects an array of religious positions, including Judaism, Islam, Wicca, and Christianity; some members have no religious affiliation. DCAS provides space and place for

• *LGBTQ youth and adults who want to deliberate issues of sexuality and spirituality,*
• *non-LGBTQ youth and adults who seek constructive dialogue with LGBTQ persons so they can build communities that affirm and accommodate spiritual and sexual differences,*
• *professionals who counsel people around sex-and-gender differences,*
• *people with LGBTQ family members and friends, and*
• *paid and volunteer workers in social justice and helping organizations (DCAS, 2001).*

As it works to meet the needs of this diverse public, DCAS provides educational and other sociocultural opportunities for people "to learn, to question, to celebrate, to liberate, to integrate, and to affirm" (DCAS, 2001, p.1). André describes his work with DCAS:

I began my work with DCAS in Fall 1999 when I moved to Edmonton to work in educational policy studies at the University of Alberta. As a member of the Board of Directors, I engage in cultural work where I speak and take steps to help other persons (a) deliberate issues of sexuality and spirituality, and (b) engage in social and cultural education so that, one day, LGBTQ persons will experience the rights and privileges of full personhood and citizenship. For example, in coordinating action groups for the 2002 DCAS Spring Conference, I worked with other group members to highlight intersections of sex-and-gender differences with other relationships of power including race, ethnicity, class, ability, and age. For example, to focus on age as a relationship of power, we developed workshops to enable older LGBTQ persons to deal with issues of sexuality and spirituality in relation to aging in a youth-oriented LGBTQ culture that too often demeans and isolates older persons. We also worked to develop workshops to enable LGBTQ and questioning youth to engage issues of sexuality and spirituality, and the challenges, risks, liabilities, and possibilities associated with "coming out" in faith, educational, familial, and other communities.

Youth Understanding Youth

Youth Understanding Youth (YUY) is Edmonton's community-based social/support group for LGBTQ and questioning youth as well as allied non-LGBTQ youth under the age of 25. YUY's mandate is to develop a self-supporting volunteer group that strives to create a safe environment in which youth can explore and express their needs in an atmosphere where they can expect to be supported and respected for their contributions and unique individual differences (YUY, 2003). The youth group serves as an example of an informal learning community that seeks to empower LGBTQ youth by accounting for the educational absences and constructed silences that surround their sex-and-gender differences in many formal educational environments.

YUY operates by developing a curriculum based on the lived and learned experiences of its membership. Every two months youth group members hold a planning meeting to discuss and coordinate activities and events for the upcoming weeks. This educational project is designed around five focus areas that follow one another sequentially from week to week. Discussion Nights provide members with opportunities to explore contemporary issues that impact their daily lives and experiences. For example, discussions have focused on safer sex practices and drug and alcohol use/abuse. There have also been LGBTQ history nights where members share readings and discuss pivotal events like Stonewall and the "Hidden Holocaust." Activity Nights enable youth group members to participate in safe events that occur in a supervised and non-threatening environment. These activities often include events like beach volleyball, bowling, and picnics. Sharing our Stories Night creates a space for youth group members to take centre stage and share their stories about coming out and coming to terms as LGBTQ youth in Alberta. For many youth this is the first time that they have had the opportunity to share their personal narratives in spaces where they can receive unconditional support and encouragement. Movie Night focuses on viewing and discussing contemporary LGBTQ-themed movies such as *Headwig and the Angry Inch* or the recent documentary *Prom Fight*, which highlighted the story of Canadian teen Marc Hall and his fight to take his boyfriend to his high school prom. Movie night provides an important social and cultural space where youth group members have the opportunity to view and discuss films that they cannot safely watch at home or school. Fringe Night is considered a special night at the youth group where members are invited to share their special talents with the group. In the past YUY members have read poetry, and shared artwork, music, and dance that they have created. Each of these five rotating focus areas serves as an important component in building an LGBTQ public pedagogy for social justice. This pedagogy strives to disturb the dominant heteronormative educational and cultural discourse that serves to keep LGBTQ persons and issues in the social, political, and educational closet (Grace & Wells, 2001).

In his current research Kris has conducted a study of LGBTQ youth involvement in informal education under the auspices of YUY. He shares some of their stories:

> Jamie, a 21-year old lesbian, told me how her involvement with YUY helped her to develop a renewed sense of hope and possibility for the future:
>
>> Words can't even describe it! I came in [to YUY] not being in a good place. I came out of nowhere really. I suppose that a lot of the people that come to the group come out of nowhere. That's how it is. [One day] you are in hiding, and then you're not. All of the sudden there was this possibility. Being gay wasn't just a word; it was a possibility. There were friends, and dances, and debates to be had, and books to be read. It changed everything. It was the difference between I can't get out of bed in the morning, to I'm so excited I can't go to sleep. A huge difference!
>
> Jordana, a 19-year-old lesbian of colour, who was cast out of her home when she came out, reflects on the importance of YUY in helping her to rebuild her life:
>
>> YUY is awesome because I have made a lot of good friends. I always look forward to coming to the group. It's something really good to do. Just knowing that there are other kids who are walking the same path as you gives you so much self-esteem and support to want to be strong. When you know that you are not the only one, somehow it makes you stronger.
>>
>> The facilitators at YUY have retreats for us and sometimes they share their life stories. It's good to see positive role models because, as a lesbian or gay youth, our role models usually end up being on TV or on shows like Queer as Folk or in pornographic movies. I think it is awesome to have good role models here. [The facilitators] all have good jobs, which is not what I've been told by other people who say that if you are gay you will not have a good life and you'll be alone, but these people aren't. All of them have houses and they have their lives together. It's awesome to see older adults. We don't meet these people in gay bars. The gay bars are not usually the places in which [youth] learn life lessons. I really like it here.
>
> Kevin, a 17-year-old male, describes how YUY has served as an important social and cultural space in his community:
>
>> I was surprised and relieved that there were other gay people like me out there. I knew there were others, but to actually see them is a lot different than to just know. I went regularly for quite a while, and I built a friendship group that worked well for me. I finally had a place to hang out with people that were like myself. They were people that I could relate to, people I could have fun with. [YUY is a place] where you don't have to worry about looking at someone the wrong way, or saying the wrong thing. You could just let it all hang out. You could just be yourself.

As these narratives reflect, youth's learning is not limited to formal educational settings. Important learning also occurs in the safety and security of LGBTQ community groups. When formal educational environments fail to meet the needs of LGBTQ youth, some of them "are fortunate enough to find the strength and fortitude to continue educating themselves and each other in spaces they craft and tenaciously hold onto, often against great odds" (Weis and Fine, 2001, p. 498). Learning communities such as YUY "serve to sculpt real and imaginary corners for peace, solace, communion, social critique, personal and collective work. These are spaces of deep, sustained community-based educative work" (Weis and Fine, 2001, p. 498). In these educative spaces LGBTQ youth confront, deconstruct, resist, and redefine identity-limiting stereotypes and discourses that often provide "harsh humiliating public representations of their race, ethnicity, gender, class, and sexuality" (Weis and Fine, 2001, p. 498). It is in these informal learning communities that LGBTQ youth can begin to transgress social, cultural, and educational boundaries in an effort to re-imagine new possibilities for personal and social growth and development.

Concluding Perspective

In contemporary culture, schools are agitating sites where violences are perpetrated against many historically disenfranchised groups. Sadly, in the language of hate used to aggravate these violences, the words "fag" and "gay" are used as umbrella slurs to name and express xenophobia. Xenophobia is a hatred of all differences including LGBTQ differences. When one student calls another student a fag, he or she might mean that the person being verbally assaulted is LGBTQ, or they might mean that the person is undesirably different from them in some other way. When one student tells another that his shirt is gay, it means that there is something wrong with the shirt and it shouldn't be worn in public. Two things are clear about the use of the words "fag" or "gay" in these contexts. First, in a local sociocultural context, it is meant to be an insult and a deprecation of the person or object so labeled. Second, in a broader sociocultural context, it is a failure to live out the tenets of the Charter in sociocultural practices in schools.

There are many ways in which LGBTQ (or those perceived to be LGBTQ) students are harassed or violated in schools. In *Understanding Anti-Gay Harassment and Violence in Schools*, a report on the five-year anti-violence research project of the Safe Schools Coalition of Washington State (1999), there is an all-too-familiar summary of violences perpetrated against LGBTQ students. These violences, which are sometimes sporadic and sometimes relentless, include verbal harassment, offensive jokes, insulting gestures, public humiliation, threats, bullying, physical assaults, and rapes. This sad and sick state of affairs demands that teacher-educators work diligently to expose, confront, and sanction perpetrators of these violences. Of course, the list of perpetrators is not limited to heterosexist and homophobic students. There are heterosexist and homophobic school administrators and teachers who also commit violences against young LGBTQ (or perceived to be LGBTQ) persons. These violences take form in anti-LGBTQ comments and actions, and in failures to intervene when students engage in verbal or other forms of anti-LGBTQ assault. Heterosexist and homophobic parents, school district personnel, and other "community" members can also be added to the list of perpetrators. Their collective efforts are designed to shape classrooms as heteronormative cultural sites. In doing so they commit a range of violences, which are perhaps all the more insidious when they are caught up in a melding of the moral and the political that is prevalent in the larger culture and society (Grace, 2001). These violences include calls for the removal of library books that depict same-sex parents, calls for the removal of openly LGBTQ teachers from classroom practice, calls to ban attempts to establish gay-straight student alliance clubs in schools, and moves to ignore or dismiss the gravity and pervasiveness of LGBTQ teen suicides.

Unless teacher-educators become cultural workers who intervene to build what Tierney (1993) calls communities of difference in education and the larger culture and society, notions like cultural democracy will remain confined to the critical discourse of the academic page. As gay men and as educators of educators, we feel compelled to act. Each of us takes it as his duty and obligation to be a presence, a voice, a writer, an actor, an advocate, a deliberator, and an agent in the political and pedagogical task of building inclusionary and transformative educational environments. In doing so, we develop and share resources that teacher-educators and other cultural workers can use to develop their own inclusive educational and cultural practices. For us, engaging in these LGBTQ educational and cultural initiatives is part of our sociocultural and political work to enhance awareness and accommodation for LGBTQ persons in everyday life, learning, and work. As inclusive educators, this engagement is part of our efforts to help revise pedagogical relations that maintain exclusionary institutional structures and relationships of power. It involves critical questioning of dominant cultural boundaries and societal comfort levels, and it involves contestation of classroom environments, texts, methods, languages, and educational theories that erase LGBTQ persons. For us, it also involves living *out*, unapologetic lives in the intersection of the personal and the professional. In composite, this educational and cultural work comprises an act of opposition. As a process it is friction-ridden, aiming to contest stereotyping of nonconformist being/acting as it troubles engrained perceptions of the normal and acceptable (hooks, 1994). Simultaneously, it is an act of bracing LGBTQ differences and positions, and a process of accommodating and honouring them. Engaging in this work is living out an ethics of care and engaging a public pedagogy of respect. It is taking inclusive laws and legislation into everyday life, learning, and work in Canadian culture and society.

Postscript: Teaching in the Fray of Sex-and-Gender Differences

Kris: The poem "We are Their Greatest Fear" emerged from an interview that I conducted with Khym, a teacher who participated in a violence prevention workshop that I presented to train facilitators. The workshop was held under the auspices of the Alberta Teachers' Association's Safe and Caring Schools Project. During this session I engaged junior and senior high school teachers in an activity that explored factors that help or hinder Alberta teachers in addressing homophobia and heterosexism in their schools, classrooms, and community environments. After the workshop I asked for volunteers to meet with me to discuss their experiences further. Khym responded, and he and I had a long conversation about his experiences as an "out" gay male educator in southern Alberta.

Khym is a teacher and learning team facilitator for Palliser Regional Schools. He has a Master's degree focusing on school/organizational culture and change, and he is involved in facilitating professional learning opportunities to address bullying and safe schools issues. The following found poem highlights some of Khym's experiences describing his life-and-work reality.

We are Their Greatest Fear

Khym Goslin and Kris Wells

The word was out that I was gay
I am very open at work
I make my presence known

Southern Alberta is Alliance country
a gay pride flag hangs on our flagpole
most have no clue
doorbell rings
other gays and lesbians appreciate the openness

Kids have asked
the answer is really irrelevant
Would I ask a straight person that question?
What is the real question?

We work for kids
we fight for kids
everything else becomes irrelevant

Two ex-students
spray paint
Goslin is gay

I arrive at 7:30 AM
the janitor is there
scrubbing off my name
he grumbles…
"Damn kids have no respect"
a personal sign of his protection
I am touched by his concern

Many feel less confident about being out than I am
homophobia is a real issue
degrading names
slurs
scribbles on notebooks
off colour jokes
bullying
all unchallenged

Teachers hear
"Johnny you are such a queer"
they walk away
fearing to make any comment
"Johnny you are such a nigger"

they stop
and correct the behaviour

Gays and lesbians are invisible

Beaten and killed like Matthew Shepard
outrageous numbers of nameless
men and women
die each year

I would like to share with teachers
some of the
Hurt
Pain
Death
that gay and lesbian kids have experienced

The only thing that stopped me
was my fear
I have begun to move away from being afraid
I am comfortable about being open
I am prepared to challenge fellow administrators
I don't shy away from kids
I clearly state my values

Today
after 28 years of living with my partner
both teaching for the same school division
recognized as a gay couple
respected for our ability
beyond our sexuality
very little stops us

But what a price to have had to pay
years of being closeted
years of over achievement
years of giving hours and hours away to community service
just to feel that nothing really needs to stop us
from sharing the message

Was it worth it?
You bet
I would rather not do it again
I wish that others will not have to repeat it
but if that is what it takes to say
I made a difference to that student
to that teacher
so be it

It is important to be a visible role model
helping to take back the language of hatred
helping to take back the power of intimidation
standing up for human rights

It must piss some people off
to know that we can continue to live a good life
with fine friends
supported by loved ones
knowing that we are their greatest fear

Having taught in junior and senior high-school classrooms for 15 years, I can relate to Khym's experiences of homophobia and violence in school settings. I remember the devastation of moments when I was the object of verbal homophobic slurs and hateful graffiti. I know what it is like to lose my breath in fear. For example, I remember gasping for air the day I found pornographic pictures of naked men stuffed behind the wiper blade of my car windshield. I know the trauma of trying to balance a professional life marked by workaholism—as a gay man I felt that I had to work harder, faster—with a personal life marked by a closeted, unhappy existence in the Catholic schools where I worked.

I deeply admire "out" LGBTQ teachers who are change agents and cultural workers. However, whether we are out or closeted, we all should strive to be teachers with capacity, teachers who focus on diversity and make a difference, teachers who are there for every student. Indeed all teachers—LGBTQ and non-LGBTQ—should have such mindful character since they have a professional and ethical responsibility to be there for all students in their care. My poem "Will You Be the Teacher?" asks teachers to consider this responsibility. Yes, a Code of Professional Conduct might require you *the teacher* to take responsibility. *However, won't you do it just because it's the right thing to do?* After all, if you work in a publicly funded institution, then all students lie within the parameters of what should be your inclusive, ethical practice. Such a practice includes LGBTQ students, students with LGBTQ parents, *every* student!

Will You Be the Teacher?

André P. Grace

Joan brought her two moms to school today
It was *Meet the Parents Day* in her grade two class
And for Joan it was another kind of *Pride Day*

When her teacher asked her to introduce her parents
Joan beamed
She was very proud
You could see the light in her eyes
She just loved her moms

Joan was lucky this year
She had a teacher who cared
She had a teacher who didn't judge

Joan had her turn to talk about her parents
Just like all the other kids
In her grade two class
Kids who thought her mom the firefighter was cool
Even when some of their parents winced

Will the light stay in Joan's eyes next year?
Will you be the teacher who keeps it there?
Will you be the teacher who comforts her when she starts to notice the winces?

And what about that day when Joan is in grade seven
And her parents come to *Sports Day*
Only to be called "Dykes!"
Only to be demeaned
By a pack of cruel boys

Will you be the teacher who takes the boys to task?
Will you be the teacher who grasps the teachable moment?
Or will you ignore their slurs
Teaching those boys that homophobia is ok
Teaching Joan that she and her family don't really matter

Notes

1. The current legislation providing Albertans with protection of their human rights is entitled the Human Rights, Citizenship and Multiculturalism Act. While sexual orientation is not explicitly stated in the Act, the Government of Alberta has agreed to *read in* sexual orientation as a protected ground in light of the Vriend decision (AHRCC, 2001).

2. The ATA provided Kris with an Inclusive Communities Grant from its Diversity, Equity, and Human Rights Committee to develop this Website. The site is available online at http://www.teachers.ab.ca/diversity/Sexual_Orientation/Index.htm

3. Two new educational videos produced by the Canadian National Film Board (NFB) have been well received by AGAPE members and students in workshops. The NFB (2001) provides this description of the video *In Other Words* (27 min.), which is suggested for students in grade seven and up. "Homophobic language is a common verbal put-down among young people, but many adults feel uncomfortable responding to it. *In Other Words* is a tool for teachers, counsellors and youth groups who want to explore homophobic language heard in schools and other youth hangouts" (p. 32). Of *Sticks and Stones* (17 min.) the NFB (2001) says, "With today's diversity of families, more kids are being raised by same-sex parents—something which can cause problems for children. *Sticks and Stones* features children aged 8 to 12 talking about their experiences with name-calling and bullying in the schoolyard, along with short animated sequences about the history of derogatory slang" (p. 59).

4. As invited researchers spoke with AGAPE members about ethical implications of research involving LGBTQ youth, topics deliberated included protecting LGBTQ youth from harm, and anonymity and confidentiality issues when working with LGBTQ youth. There was considerable discussion of the issue of obtaining informed parental consent when involving LGBTQ youth less than 18 years of age in research initiatives. Our university's ethics policy requires informed parental consent when any young person less than 18 years of age is involved as a research participant. Questions AGAPE members raised included:
When an LGBTQ youth less than 18 years of age is living in a safe house because parents/guardians had kicked him or her out of the house for disclosing his or her Queerness, what adult signs for such a youth who might wish to participate in a research project? When an LGBTQ youth less than 18 years of age is closeted at home, is such a young person best excluded from a research initiative since to attempt to meet the ethical requirement of informed

parental consent can place that youth at risk in the home place? Everyone struggled to find answers to these questions, and discussed the possibility of change. One researcher provided a precedent for change whereby the Faculty approved changes in ethical protocol so graduate students could attend to specific cultural requirements when conducting research in Aboriginal communities. However, the questions raised by AGAPE members indicate a need to rethink ethical requirements when it comes to research that could put LGBTQ youth at risk.

References

Alberta Human Rights and Citizenship Commission (AHRCC). 2001. *Protected Areas and Grounds Under the Human Rights, Citizenship and Multiculturalism Act.* [Online.] Available: http://www.albertahumanrights.ab.ca/publications/Info_Protect_Areas_ Grounds%20Oct01.asp

Alberta Catholic School Trustees' Association (ACSTA). 2001. *A Resource for an Inclusive Community: A Teacher's Guide for and about Persons With Same Sex Attractions.* Calgary, AB: Author.

Alberta Teachers' Association and the Orlando Books Collective (ATA & OBC). 2002. *Safe and Caring Schools for Lesbian and Gay Youth: A Guide for Teachers.* Edmonton, AB: Authors.

British Columbia College of Teachers v. Trinity Western University, [2001] S.C.C. 31. File No: 27168. Retrieved May 31, 2001 from

http://www.lexum.umontreal.ca /csc-scc/en/rec/texte/trinity.en.txt

Canadian Teachers' Federation & The Elementary Teachers' Federation of Ontario (CTF & ETFO). 2003. *Seeing the Rainbow: Teachers Talk About Bisexual, Gay, Lesbian, Transgender and Two-spirited Realities.* Ottawa, ON: Authors.

Department of Justice, Canada (DJC). 1982/2002. Canadian Charter of Rights and Freedoms. [Online.] Available: http://laws.justice.gc.ca/en/charter/const_en.html

Department of Justice, Canada (DJC). 2001. Canadian Human Rights Act. [Online]. Available: http://laws.justice.gc.ca/en/H-6/26172.html

Diversity Conferences of Alberta (DCAS). 2001. *DCAS Mission Statement.* [Brochure]. Edmonton, AB: Author.

Epstein, D. and R. Johnson (eds.). 1998. *Schooling Sexualities.* Bristol, PA: Open University Press.

Grace, A.P. 2001. "Using LGBTQ Cultural Studies to Transgress Adult Educational Space." In V. Sheared and P.A. Sissel (eds.), *Making Space: Merging Theory and Practice in Adult Education.* Westport, CN: Bergin & Garvey.

———. 2003. *Citizen Queer: Mediating Welfare and Work in Education and Culture.* Proceedings of the 44th Annual US National Adult Education Research Conference, San Francisco State University, San Francisco, CA.

Grace, A.P. and F.J. Benson. 2000. "Using Autobiographical Queer Life Narratives of Teachers to Connect Personal, Political and Pedagogical Spaces." *International Journal of Inclusive Education* 4, no. 2: 89–109.

Grace, A.P. and K. Wells. 2001. "Getting an Education in Edmonton, Alberta: The Case of Queer Youth." *Torquere, Journal of the Canadian Lesbian and Gay Studies Association* 3.

hooks, b. 1994. *Teaching to Transgress: Education as the Practice of Freedom.* New York: Routledge.

Jennings, K. (ed.). 1994. *One Teacher in 10: Gay and Lesbian Educators Tell Their Stories.* Boston: Alyson Publications.

National Film Board of Canada (NFB). 200). *Looking at Canada: NFB Resource Catalogue 2001–2002.* Montreal, QC: Author.

Quinlivan, K. and S. Town. 1999. "LGBTQ Pedagogy, Educational Practice and Lesbian and Gay Youth." *Qualitative Studies in Education* 12, no. 5: 509–24.

Safe Schools WA. 1999. "Understanding Anti-gay Harassment and Violence in Schools: A Report on the Five Year Anti-violence Research Project of the Safe Schools Coalition of Washington State" [Online]. Available: http://www.safeschools-wa.org/ss5find1.html

Saunders, P. 2002. "The Charter at 20." [Online]. Available:
http://cbc.ca/news/ features/constitution/

Surrey Teachers' Association (STA). 2000. *"Moving Beyond Silence:" Addressing Homophobia in Elementary Schools*. Surrey, BC: Author.

Tierney, W.G. 1993. *Building Communities of Difference*. Toronto: OISE Press.

———. 1997. *Academic Outlaws: LGBTQ Theory and Cultural Studies in the Academy*. Thousand Oaks, CA: Sage Publications.

Weis, L. and M. Fine. 2001. "Extraordinary Conversations in Public Schools." *Qualitative Studies in Education* 14, no. 4: 497–523.

Wells, K. 2003. *Building Safe and Caring Classrooms, Schools, and Communities for Lesbian, Gay, Bisexual and Transgender Students: Professional Development Workshops for Alberta Teachers*. Edmonton, AB: Alberta Teachers' Association.

———. 2002. *Sexual Orientation and Gender Identity. A Professional Development Website for Alberta Teachers*. Edmonton, AB: Alberta Teachers' Association. [Online.] Available: http://www.teachers.ab.ca/diversity/Sexual_Orientation/Index.htm

Youth Understanding Youth (YUY). [Brochure]. 2003. YUY's *Philosophy and Mission Statement*. Edmonton, AB: Author.

19

From Naïveté to Advocacy:
STUDENT-TEACHERS REFLECT ON A COURSE ON SCHOOLING AND SEXUAL IDENTITIES

James McNinch

Introduction

Chapter 14 in this volume articulates the reasons why a course on schooling and sexual identity is a necessary part of the pre-service education of student-teachers. This chapter reports qualitatively on the "results" of teaching such a course for the first time in the spring of 2003 at the University of Regina. This chapter outlines the responses and reactions of students to the course as it was structured.[1]

I owe an enormous debt of gratitude to the students of this first course. Their openness and willingness to share with others their own understanding and growth is really what this chapter is all about. The voices in this chapter are theirs; I am but the recorder and organizer of the comments and thoughts of 34 student-teachers. I am proud to dedicate this chapter to all of them.[2]

While the primary purpose of this chapter is to share the feelings and thoughts of pre-service teachers on the topic of schooling and sexual identities, the secondary purpose is a form of pedagogical enquiry into my own practice. I am assuming that any evaluation of a class rests, in the end, on criteria that determine and assess how much students have actually learned. This chapter, then, is also about tracking student learning, in response to specific structures (the course objectives, the content, the format, and the assignments) as much as it is about describing students' engagement in a particular curriculum.

The rationale for the course was grounded partially in queer theory generally, but more specifically within the liberal critique of exclusionary education that privileges some and silences others, and a more obvious feminist critique of gendered and sexualized behaviour being determined by much of the practice in schools. It was my hope for a student learning outcome that, in Van Manem's (1991) phrase, students would understand "the meaning of pedagogical thoughtfulness."

In reference to the assignments I gave the class, I have organized the work of the students into four somewhat arbitrary stages of development: (1) ignorance and misconceptions; (2) sensitivity and awareness; (3) apprehension—complexity, ambiguity; and (4) advocacy and action. The comments of the students come from a number of sources, but are found primarily in the responses to specific questions on specific assignments.

It will become apparent to the reader of this chapter that students soon become empowered by learning a new language, in this case a language of social justice. This is an exciting aspect of teaching, familiar to all teachers who introduce new concepts to students. Empowerment occurs with students whether we are sounding out words phonetically, or measuring the truth of geometric equations, showing them how a cheque book is balanced, or uncovering historical details of the North-West Resistance. In each case, if we introduce students to a new language and they are able to understand the world with a more sophisticated understanding of how and why it works the way it does, then in turn, new knowledge, skills, and attitudes prepare them to act. There is no guarantee students will act or that social justice will be achieved, but new knowledge is a necessary pre-condition of pedagogical and curricular change and action. Heterosexual teachers, much like the parents of queer kids, have to "come out" as an ally of equity for LGBT students in schools if they are going to practice inclusive education.

Pre-service Education Students

Students in both our elementary and secondary programs, as well as the smaller Arts Education program, are required to take an Education Foundations course at the 300 level in order to graduate. Other courses students might opt for include multicultural education, women and education, moral education, or the philosophy or sociology of education. For a number of administrative reasons, the choices available to students are limited, particularly in the spring/summer session courses that start in May and run in various three- and six-week blocks between May and August.

Few students signed up for this course only because of the subject matter; most took it because it fit their academic, work, and personal schedules. Some took it to ease their load in the fall term, others because it allowed them to intern in the fall and finish their degree by Christmas. Only one student, a young man in the Faculty of Arts who hoped to transfer to the Faculty of Education, was openly gay. There were only two other males in the class: a Catholic city boy in the Arts Education program, and a Protestant farm kid who was majoring in Health and Physical Education. The rest of the class was composed of 31 women in their third or fourth year of the program, about equally divided between the elementary and the secondary program. Many students were quite young, in their early twenties if they had entered university directly from high school, although at least a third of the class was older. In other words, the students did not start this course with a vested interest in schooling and sexual identities, although many professed a strong interest in the topic, and a waiting list longer than the number of students able to enrol in the course confirmed at least a healthy curiosity in the course content.

The Course Structure and Objectives

I organized the course around two theoretical issues relating to the constructions of identity: concepts of difference and positionality, and understandings of gender and sexual formations. The more practical considerations related to building an understanding of the roles and responsibilities of teachers and their relation to curriculum and schools. In other words, the course asked pre-service teachers to think about the complex topics of gendered and sexual identities and what might they do as a result of this thinking.

The five major objectives of the course were to:

- *understand the interwoven social, cultural, and personal and interpersonal components of sexual identity formation;*
- *become familiar with the social, biological, and historical construction of homosexuality, including the constructs of sin, pathology, and preference;*
- *appreciate the implications of heterosexual privilege with respect to the positionality of sexual minorities;*
- *acquire a vocabulary for examining myths and stereotypes, and common elements of various forms of oppression, including outing and "closeting"; and*
- *analyze various models of identity development in LGBT youth.*

(See Chapter 14 for a full description of the objectives and theoretical rationale for the course).

The Assignments

How Do We Know What We Think We Know About Gendered and Sexual Identities?

Sharing with students my own journey to become an out-gay educator, I asked them to explore their own past by answering four specific questions. The first was, "When were you aware that you were, for whatever reason, different from other people, or that some other person or people were different from you?" I asked students to reflect on the nature of difference and to look at the power relationships in this difference.

From there, I asked students to write about their first awareness of their own gendered and sexual identity and to explore their comfort level with the topic of sexuality in general. The next step was to ask them about their understanding of sexual difference. What did they know about homosexuality and where did this knowledge come from, and what was the influence of personal experience, peers, friends, parents, the church, and the media in informing them? I also asked them to identify and make distinctions between values and knowledge in this discussion.

Finally, I asked them to remember the role teachers and schools in general played, both formally and informally, in their development of any understanding of sexual difference. I also asked them if they knew any gay or lesbian students or teachers when they were in school.

Gendered and Sexual Identities in the Media

The second assignment built on what the memory work had dredged up. The assumption to test was that various forms of popular media shape and mirror reality. I asked students to look at artifacts about sexual difference from the press, film, television, and the Internet. I asked them to come to terms with the projection of the sexuality defined or portrayed and the explicit and implicit values of the discourse. I asked them a series of questions: What is regarded or assumed to be "normal" or natural and what is regarded as "abnormal"? How are female and male sexuality constructed and how are masculinity and femininity constructed? Is it possible, in Judith Butler's famous phrase, to see gender and sexuality as "performances"? I also asked them to "pretend" to the positionality of their parents or grandparents in interpreting the artifact to measure any degree of generational dissonance. This assignment required them to make a poster about their artifact and to explain it to the class.

Reading Responses

The third assignment was actually an ongoing reflective journal entry of their responses to the 13 articles and textbooks for the course. I focussed their entries by asking three questions: "Can you state the writer's main point or thesis in a short paragraph and explain the effectiveness of the author in making his or her point? What have you learned about the topic of sexuality and sexual difference? What implications are there for schooling and for your teaching?" I asked students to participate in weekly "jig-saw" exercises of their readings to promote articulation and clarification and ownership of the material. These journal entries became the basis for the final reflective exercise. Based on the five major objectives for the course, I required the students to gauge their own learning and to answer the questions: "In what way are you better prepared to make schools affirming and inclusive spaces for all students?" and "What else do you need to know and do and what kinds of further support would you require to continue this work?"

Curriculum: What Does It Look Like? What Does It Sound Like?

The final assignment of the course asked students to turn theory into practice. I asked students to critique some element of the elementary or secondary curriculum and to find a way to integrate sexual difference into the curriculum in an age-appropriate way by finding resources and building a lesson. Two alternatives to this assignment were to explore a community group that supports or criticizes sexual difference or to interview someone about their sexual formation and identity. All the students chose to do the lesson plan, in part because the alternatives appeared to be more time-consuming.

Starting Positions: Apprehension, Ignorance and Misconceptions

Many students were apprehensive about this course simply because it was new and there was no reference point from previous students. Mini-workshops on the topics of sexual harassment and homophobia in various professional studies courses had not been comprehensive. Although she "needed" to take this course in May so she could get married in the summer before starting her four-month internship in the schools, Lindsay "was a little afraid, perhaps of the unknown (what I now know is called xenophobia). I wasn't sure what we were going to cover in class or just what exactly I was supposed to say or do in class."[3] This was a common starting position: not exactly defensive, but unsure of the "appropriate" stance in relation to the "other."

Jill was even more specific: "When I initially registered for this class I had a different idea of what the topic was. I would tell other people that this class was going to teach me to be able to 'deal with' gay and lesbian people in schools." In musing on the role of culture, Jenny noted "the media had caused me to think that homosexuals were outcasts and different enough that they couldn't fit it." Connie, the first to admit her naïveté, stated simply: "I just never thought about this topic and how it might relate to my teaching." Eugenie, a mature woman with grown kids who had "been around the block" as she described it, had no idea of the extent of "the negativity toward allowing even the simplest basic rights to LGBT individuals and couples." Angela, in acknowledging that she had gay and lesbian friends, admitted she "was still apprehensive about the topic of sexual difference and schooling."

Anonymously, one of the students wrote at the beginning of the class about the very real taboos that exist in school systems around this topic. "I know that when someone hears about a teacher or a counsellor being gay, they are shocked and surprised ... [and think] how can a person be like 'that' and be employed in the position of a role model!"

The first assignment on difference and identity stirred up many memories and prompted much animated discussion. Not surprisingly, but nonetheless disheartening, most understandings of "difference" for these Saskatchewan students came from the naming of race and ancestry in a culture of oppression. One student remembered wondering why another little girl with black on her skin would not wash it off. For another, this meant her mother not allowing her to have a sleep-over with a friend "because she's Native."[4] For another, it was the eeriness of the abysmal poverty of urban Natives that confirmed a difference reinforced by words, remembered from their past, like "squaw" and "breed." It became quickly apparent to students that we come to know what it means to be "normal" by naming and "dealing with" what is regarded as aberrant. April, for example, remembered a cousin her own age, maybe six, who had to wear a diaper and was severely spanked when he peed his pants. As a child, she understood she was simply someone he was not, and did not want to be.

Students informed me that memories of sexuality in childhood often stem from a construct of guilt and repression. Gillian remembers, following a sex-education class in Grade 6, stealthily looking up words like *vagina* and *intercourse* in the dictionary. Deadra will never forget a classic realignment with the norms that were new to her when she was admonished for not colouring "properly," and her family urging her, "Why don't you just try to fit in?"

This need to colour and fit "between the lines" is critical to the formation of gendered behaviour as well. Many women in the class talked of their pre-pubescent "crushes on the cute, popular boys," and clinging to the crush as if their identity depended on it being affirmed by their peers. As many others, like Daina, spoke of her friends in Grade 3 "who couldn't stop talking about some boy or other," at recess, in the lunch room, passing notes in class. "In order to fit in, I convinced myself I liked him as well." Students began to appreciate how hetero-normativity is, among other things, a socialized behaviour.

The socialization of hetero-normativity becomes more complicated and even more rigid in adolescence. Some students remembered sex education classes in Grade 9 with mannequins to show prostate and breast cancer, but the teacher too embarrassed to talk about intercourse or reproduction except to warn against sexually transmitted diseases. Sexuality as a pathology is the construct in which the dread of the malignancy of sexual difference flourishes. Fear denies pleasure and desire: "you'd better be on something so you don't screw up your future," one student remembers her mother insisting without any sense of irony or the double entendre. Students remember the active, gossipy speculation about "who is or isn't gay," the use of the label to brand shy and unpopular kids, of guys "you just knew were gay," and peers who would name and mis-educate other students about who was "obviously a fag" in order to draw attention to themselves as somehow knowledgeable in this arena.

Lindsay shared a wonderful story about pulling into a gas station in the family vehicle when she was about 11 and being unable to take her eyes off a beautiful young woman, and then for the rest of the road trip worrying and wondering, "does this mean I'm a lesbian?" Students readily agreed that sexual identity formation is a confusing process, that children need to know that same-sex attraction is part of adolescent development, and the intimacy of friendship does not necessarily imply sexual attraction. Incrementally, then, the next step would be able to say, as does one of the girls in the film, *Bend It Like Beckham* (2002), to her mother, "and even if I was [a lesbian], it's not *that* big a deal, you know."

Janet remembers a sleep-over, at about the same age, when she woke up cuddled against another girl and feeling "ashamed and afraid to think I was weird." Such trauma polices and binds our gendered sexuality. Games like "spin the bottle," during middle years, tend to confirm what is natural: "I like boys!" But Chris remembers playing the game in Grade 6 and hoping that kissing girls would "make me straight," while at the same time thinking "I would like to kiss the boy sitting across from me."

Many students talked or wrote about their liberal parents and definitions of "normal" that were more inclusive than the previous excerpts may indicate. Some students spoke of sisters, aunts, uncles, cousins or family friends who were known to be gay or lesbian and the varying degrees with which this was accepted.

However, even tolerance presumes to judge. Listen to Sharri: "We just found out the [United Church] minister we hired is lesbian and everyone is saying we wouldn't have hired her if we knew, and why does she have to mention it like she's proud of it?"

Sexuality and Sexual Difference: "I'm Talking 'bout a Small Town!"

Janet captures best the essence of the ambiguous and problematic position in which she finds herself: a pre-service teacher from rural Saskatchewan who will soon marry and return to a farm and to a school in a small town:

> I think we are very "in the closet" in that many schools do not address issues such as these and that may have to do with being such a rural province. I talk from experience ... coming from a small town to the "big city," I had no idea that homosexuality was so "out there." Until I came to university, I knew no one that was gay or lesbian, at least not anyone who said, in fear of rejection from the community.

Britzman (1998) speaks about the need, in anti-oppressive education, for students to "un-learn" what they thought they knew, but it is also true that students need to re-evaluate what exactly they didn't know and why they didn't know it. Students began to ask themselves this when reflecting on the small towns they came from where everyone's story is "the same."[5]

Most startlingly to me, the out-gay professor, was a sentiment shared by many of the younger students and expressed succinctly by Erin. "Before this class I thought homosexuality was a 'new thing' and that it had nothing to do with biology or history." We discussed this idea at some length in class. Almost all the students shared the belief that same-sex bonding and other same-sex behaviour was limited to humans because they had never been taught about the sexual diversity found in Nature. Similarly, while the women in the class understood and shared stories of their infatuations and obsessions over "cute" boys when they were in the primary grades, the idea that some pre-pubescent children could be attracted to members of the same sex had simply not occurred to them because of the "official" privileging of the story of compulsory heterosexuality.

Many students seemed to believe that homosexuality had something to do with sexual liberation. Perhaps because adolescence is a period of sexual exploration and experimentation, many stated that is why they could believe that same-sex relationships were a "preference," part of a smorgasbord running the sexual gamut, a fashionable choice in a liberated age. Might we understand this, somewhat patronizingly, by acknowledging that each generation believes (or is allowed to believe) that they and they alone have invented or at least discovered sex for the first time? This is the ultimate confusion between an individual's and a society's construction of gendered sexual identity as Overall (2004) points out. In other words, the misconceptions or assumptions about sexuality that each generation owns and positions lead to the construction of a default, non-judgemental, and oh-so-liberal position: "to each his or her own" (as student Carson articulated) that implies that sexuality is "merely" about choice.

It was clear, too, from student responses to media representations of same-sex desire, that the inclination to understand sexual orientation as a sexual "preference" stemmed from the concept of "lifestyle choices." Thus young people see the "right" to tattoos and body piercings, as well as whom one chooses to sleep with, as "cool" acts of "free-will" or choice, rather than two separate issues: individuals caught between self-expression and the world of "fashion," and the more fundamental issue of same-sex desire.

Echoing many women in the course, Stacey, another rural woman from a farm family with strong Christian values, was explicit in charting her own understanding of choice and preference over the course: "I personally thought homosexuality was a choice but now I see it is not." However, it is clear that in making this "move," Stacey is still uncomfortable and confuses sexual orientation with choosing to be out. She asks: "Why would someone 'choose' all these myths and stereotypes to be against them when they could be easily more accepted into society?" This understanding of difference does not eliminate the presumed borders of the closet.

Autumn, a pre-service secondary social studies teacher, and someone who was able to speak eloquently about what she called "the important social issues," reflected that although she had never regarded herself as homophobic, she also had never thought she had "a duty to speak-up and ensure inclusiveness for sexual minorities."

Jill came to class assuming somehow that the only people who chose to be out were gay activists with a political and personal agenda. At the end of class she reflected on her own white privilege:

> This assumption seems silly now, but it just never occurred to me that people might be scared to speak out. I now see how scary it would be to be a minority when you have to defend yourself or hide yourself everyday.

Sharmayn, a light-skinned woman of Métis ancestry, was quite aware of issues of inequity and social justice and shared a story of the shock produced in acquaintances who meet her husband and children for the first time because they "look like Indians." Yet even she confessed: "I can honestly say that the thought of any of my students being LGBT never even entered my mind, and here I thought I was fully prepared to go into a classroom and teach to the diverse needs of all my students." This provided an opportunity to discuss the complications coming from multiple and interlocking identities of race, sex, class, religion, and sexual-orientation (Razack, 2002). Even interrupted and interrogated by the assignments, many of the students' sense of self seemed, in comparison, to be quite uncomplicated.

Gender, Sex, and Sexual Orientation

The course invited students to speculate on their own gendered and sexual identity. Gillian recalls her reaction to the course's first assignment:

> When I had to discuss at what age I realized I was straight, or when I started liking boys, I felt ridiculous! It appeared so natural and normal to me that I could not remember a "starting point." I recognized how stupid I felt and how angry I was at having to answer such a question!

Sharri, a poised and well-groomed woman and a strong Catholic with young children, laughed when she shared with the class what she had written: "I never thought about it [sexual orientation] but I've made assumptions that people are simply heterosexual and of course you don't have to come out if you're straight!" Janet agreed: "I never really thought about why I came to be heterosexual or why I chose my life the way I did. I may never have thought much about it because it was so accepted and expected by society." Queer theory makes much of the clarity and insight provided by a queer perspective: acute understandings of difference stem from disengaging oneself from the heteronormative assumptions that "work" for the majority. This is probably one of the most important points about learning about gendered and sexual difference that the class identified.

For Cliff, an artist and a dreamer, and one of the class's "token straight guys," as he jokingly came to call himself, the first assignment caused him to reflect that

> I just never realized our entire social structure is geared towards sex, but only heterosexual sex. ... even though I have been bombarded with messages about how a "real" man should act and feel and want. I have lived my life trying to live up to these fantastic standards of masculinity.

Not unexpectedly, then, assumptions about what is "normal" and what is "natural" permeated the discourse of the class discussions. As Joella pointed out, "The most significant myth addressed for me was that homosexuality is a choice. By putting it in the context of identity formation, I was able to see that sexual orientation for homosexuals is no different or less important than it is for me as a heterosexual." Students came to understand that "choice" is not about one's sexual orientation but about why and how a person chooses to perform and behave in public. As the course instructor, I think that this comprehension formed the *raison d'être* of the entire class.

Growth: Awareness, Understanding, Empathy, Ambiguity

Perhaps the biggest stumbling block to connecting sexuality to gender identity was a growing realization by the students that the curriculum is not just silent on the issue of homosexuality, it is silent on sexuality in general, except for some heterosexist assumptions about same-sex dating and love. Health curricula, targeted, often too late, at 15- and 16-year-olds, tend to fall into three camps: clinical emphasis on anatomy and "parts," planned parenthood initiatives that direct students to the prevention of pregnancy and the avoidance of sexually transmitted diseases, and religiously informed modules which stress complete abstinence from sexual behaviour. The disjuncture between the actual sexual behaviour of adolescents and the omission of sexuality from the school curriculum has been well documented (Ponton, 2001).

Compounding this problem is an apparent discrepancy between the opinions of teenagers and adults about what constitutes sexual behaviour in the first place. Yet anyone who has spent any time in high schools knows that schools are locations of much sexual or sexualized behaviour—as young people struggle to achieve their own understanding of sexual development, self-expression, and identity formation.

I must admit it came as a surprise to me, a child of the 1950s and 1960s, that high schools are still seriously conflicted spaces that perpetuate gendered identity and privilege heterosexual "winners" and disparage "othered losers." Students wrote about such cultural practices as "Slave Day" and "Mardi Gras" and the crowning of Kings and Queens in elaborate and complicated popularity contests which often reward individuals who have sold the most raffle tickets. These are elements of schooling that I assumed had died when I left high school 40 years ago. Such practices make implicit assumptions about what appropriate sexuality is. It is embodied in the high school quarterback (the cutest and smartest of the team) and the prettiest cheerleader (who has learned to get all her homework done by whatever means and never kisses and tells). These stereotypes represent a certain received and replicated kind of class sophistication and propriety. Such individuals are, in this construct, allowed to "get engaged" in Grade 12, and send a coded message about what is normal, expected, and approved (even if a chorus of adults wring their hands and worry about diminished options for higher education and opportunities to enter the middle class). Students confirmed that this romantic ideal is still privileged as an embodiment of healthy sexuality and serves to implicitly police deviance from this norm. It is in this gendered cultural construct that gay and lesbian students struggle to achieve their own understanding of sexual development, self-expression, and identity formation.

All students, regardless of their sexual orientation, are disadvantaged in such a milieu where homosexuality is mentioned only once in the official Saskatchewan K–12 curriculum, in the same sentence with the acronym AIDS. This silence is further conflicted with other constructs of reality in the popular media: the young gay couple on the Canadian television program, *Degrassi*, have just done a lovely job of decorating the gym for the prom in the theme of "Ali Baba and the Forty Thieves."

Contrast such happy fantasy in popular culture with reports that female adolescents do not regard "giving blow-jobs as engaging in sex" (Morris, 2004). Then there is the testimony of a young man in a workshop on sexual identity who attests that "at home watching TV with his parents, if a hot sex scene comes on TV," his embarrassed discomfort is so high that he still has to leave the room on the pretext of needing a drink of water. His classmate echoes an age-old comment of adolescents: "I'm convinced that my parents never have sex and that I'm adopted or the result of immaculate conception." This common disjuncture between the generations continues to create a serious disruption in beginning to understand sexuality, both hetero and homo, as deep-seated desire, not a lifestyle choice.

Important First Steps: Cognition and Self-Awareness

The reading by Jennifer Harding (1998) on essentialism and constructivism in gendering identity caused Sara to reflect: "Our context decides how we are going to 'perform' who we are. I now see how much of 'us' is constructed through the context in which we live." This is an important first step: it is possible for students to understand the relationship between essentialism and constructivism and Tammy went on to write about the construction of the "other" as "wrong." It was very clear to me, however, that it was students articulating an understanding of the complicated formation of their *own* gendered sexuality, not that of others, that helped them to *own* the knowledge of how, as Britzman (1998) says, "the production of deviancy is intimately tied to the very possibility of normalcy."

Educators know that little learning is purely cognitive; the affective domain is never isolated. In other words, knowledge and information can lead to a change in values and beliefs. While this may seem obvious, many students in the class suggested a causal link between cognition and understanding which in turn can lead to action and advocacy. As one student summarized:

> My heterosexual privilege blinded me to the lack of representations of sexual differences. Now I am conscious of gendered language and the roles I have associated with each gender. I am more conscious of my own biases and stereotypes, and I am more comfortable discussing sexual differences and confronting my friends and family about their biases. Moreover, I am conscious of the lack of representation of sexual minorities in the curriculum.

Sharri, a woman who talked of her early years as a girl who played sports better than most of the boys, had made this comment near the beginning of the class. But even Janelle, a mature married woman with kids of her own, and a strongly formulated sense of herself that included a highly developed sense of propriety, concluded at the end of the course: "Everyday I would tell my Aunt and Uncle about 'what I had learned in class.' This was always a great conversation starter. I feel that I now really look at people differently and I can *almost* [my italics] empathize." One can only imagine the conversations, but the important point is that students were actually talking about the topic of sexual difference, even if it is never really possible to understand what it is like to be part of a minority, particularly a sexual minority.

The empowerment of a new viewpoint and a new rhetoric can be a heady experience to a new recruit with a new mission and moral purpose. Sharmayn captures this when she says:

> I have knowledge and awareness now of heterosexual privilege in our society, and it angers me. I have been in many debates with my friends and family since this course started and I am mystified and irritated at their ignorance and intolerance to sexual diversity.

This new positionality on the topic is both liberating and disquieting. Many students contrasted the energy and freedom they found in this foundations classroom with the vulnerability and defensiveness many of them experienced outside this safe environment.

Social Constructivism and Identity Formation

The readings helped students to understand that schools are not value-neutral and that the position of teacher is a complex one interwoven with the values, beliefs and assumptions he or she consciously and unconsciously carries to each child in the classroom. Kumashiro (2000) speaks of the need for "disruptive knowledge" to challenge oppression. Nicole said: "Both implicit and explicit forms of homophobia are factors which have positioned homosexuals in oppression, with schools being one of the perpetrators of this oppression." Cliff added: "This course has opened my eyes to the destructive power of heteronormative assumptions." Students were able, in light of readings from Bruce Bagemihl's important work, *Biological Exuberance: Animal Homosexuality and Natural Diversity* (1999), Colin Spencer's *Homosexuality: A History* (1995), and Martin Cannon's "The Regulation of First Nations Sexuality" (1998) to conclude with Autumn that "these articles showed me that homosexuality is a natural phenomenon existing throughout time and throughout Nature. In [Aboriginal cultures] it was colonialism and Christianity that changed this from natural to sin." April concluded her critique of the readings by saying:

> This class has helped me understand that the current situation is a construction, one built on a history of social constructions about homosexuality. This means that we can work towards a new and more inclusive social construction.

With this newfound knowledge and perspective, how did these pre-service teachers begin to reformulate their own identities and responsibilities? On the course evaluation form one student wrote: "If I hadn't taken this particular course, I would have finished seven years of university education without every having homosexuality explicitly discussed in class." Another student asked how it was that she could have taken three multicultural classes and three Indian Studies courses and never heard of the gender role assignment inherent in the Indian Act or the gift of transgendered and two-spiritedness in traditional Aboriginal cultures.

For some, having acquired a new vocabulary and world view, it was now a question of being obliged to speak. Closets are not just for the sexually oppressed. Advocates have to stand up and be clear about what they believe and what they want to do. Cari was able to articulate the double bind of silence: "I learned it is as though not speaking out is to not accept oneself, which is worse than not being accepted by others." Anonymously, one student summarized: "The ideal of being oneself is easy to espouse when that self is an accepted social norm!" Another said simply: "[Now I know] homophobia is a learned behaviour produced by social pressures to conform to norms."

How Far Will Empathy Take Us?

Endowed with all sorts of privilege associated with race, class, and status as a university teacher, I embodied only one narrow view of what homosexuality looks and sounds like. More significantly, however, from the gay and lesbian guest speakers, both adults and youth, as well as various images from films, students were able to put a face and voice to the abstraction of homosexuality. Listening to the lived stories, it was hard for students to ignore the human reality of gay and lesbian identity. April wrote: "I didn't realize that the fear of sexist and homophobic abuse from other students prevented certain individuals from exploring or putting their best efforts into activities." Students heard dramatic stories of the tension and anxiety inherent in being closeted and the fear of being "outed" and how difficult the construct of same-sex relationships can be in such a position. Gay university students, lesbian moms, and gay Christians came to tell their stories and students were able to empathize. "I now understand some of the pain and struggles LGBT students have to face," said Connie, a young woman who admitted at the beginning that she had simply never even considered this issue before. Another student concluded: "I have learned that LGBT people are not monsters or freaks. I have met some wonderful people lately who just happen to be gay: normal folks living regular lives." Gillian, who admitted to being "prejudiced" at the beginning, described, perhaps somewhat self-servingly but nonetheless sincerely, at the end of the course this sense of personal transformation (if only it was this easy!):

> It was nice to be able to admit to my faults and make amends so I could move on as a new and better person who believed in the good of people rather than judging them by their sexual orientation.

Even though empathy is a powerful tool to effect change, I felt it was important for my students to understand that fundamental structural changes are necessary in schools, regardless of empathy. Fonow and Marty (1992) talk about "relocating responsibility for homophobic attitudes" (p. 164); however, revisionist attitudes and intent don't necessarily lead to clarity of purpose or action.

Complications, Ambiguity, Real Concerns

After exposure to and explorations of complicated issues in sexual identity, do preservice teachers know enough, have enough confidence, and believe strongly enough that they can make a difference? Being thoughtful and reflective sometimes precludes action. The old adage, about being part of the problem if you are not part of the solution, was a rather hackneyed card for me to play, but it did "force" or at least encourage students to speculate about their role in the schools. One student wrote: "Waiting until the children are aware of their own sexuality is too late. After all, how can homosexual children be aware of what they are if they do not know what it means to be gay?" On the other hand, the responsibility extends to those who are already aware: "I also learned that many children know from a young age that they are homosexual."

Victoria bravely articulated the idealistic and unproven position of most of the students when she said: "I want to be pro-active, not re-active, and educate the students and staff about sexual difference to ensure that everyone can be who they are and feel safe to do so. Students need to feel safe before they can start to learn and grow." As the instructor of the course, my question continues to be: "Does such a new position end up being simply the politically correct posturing of white privilege?"

Autumn, always the champion of social justice, stated: "I have a duty to be more than just accepting. I need to break the silence." But Cliff countered: "One teacher who does work in a Catholic system has said to me—'you just don't go there!'" Tammy, a very quiet student, mused: "Would I get fired if I used supportive material?" Sharmayn, always the cautious realist, suggested: "I don't think we can do this without the support and approval of the parents." Carson added: "I am confident about working with students and parents, but I have concerns about a lack of support from administration."

Importantly, students began to appreciate that teaching is more than just a relationship between students and teacher. If nothing else, students came to appreciate that it is not just individuals who make a difference. All the "differences" have already been constructed before student-teachers appear on the scene with their earnest and noble zeal to change the world. Some frustrated finger-pointing and blaming by students, near the end of the course, reflected their discomfort, not with the complications of gender and sexuality and sexual difference, but with the confusion and ambiguity inherent in this topic in the public setting of the classroom. This paralleled a growing realization that as teachers they are caught in a complex web of value-laden power relations with little "control" of their own sense of influence or agency. Gillian, an articulate well-travelled pre-service high-school science teacher, was honest enough to understand that she alone could not change the world, and was left feeling the burden of such responsibility:

> I am worried about repercussions from parents and school boards. I am still uncomfortable about discussing this controversial topic in my class. I know and believe it to be an important issue, however I don't know how to best support my students without receiving my own personal backlash. I am nervous in case a student does come out or reach out for my support. I am not sure what I could say or do to better their position…. I am worried about taking a position of trust which they have placed in me and failing. Letting down a student is a very scary thought.

The "problem" is a conundrum: some of the students' growing awareness was that the topic of sexuality in schools is still very problematic and, by extension, the topic of sexual orientation is a tainted taboo capable of infecting those who are in contact with it. As a result, despite sea changes in government policy and legislation, and public attitudes towards homosexuality and same-sex relationships, the issue of sexual orientation remains, perhaps because these students have not yet spent much time in the schools, both visceral and theoretical at the same time. Without enough classroom experience to ground them, apprehension is the reality they feel and resistance is the reality they imagine.

Sex Versus Love in the Name of Identity

Another weakness inherent in offering a course on sexual orientation to pre-service teachers is the danger of sanitizing sexual orientation and perhaps, according to some queer theorists (like Champagne, 1995, for example), diminishing the radicalness of the queerly different stance represented by same-sex desire. Like many of the students in the class, finding their own way through sexual difference, Autumn grabbed at an "easy out," or at least something relatively uncomplicated and already sanctioned by schools and curriculum: "As the lesbian couple who came to speak to us said, 'It's not about sex, it's about love'."

Undoubtedly love is the hook that allows everyone to buy into inclusive education. Educators can only win on the field of sexual difference and the politics of sex by retreating from the issue of same-sex desire. We even concede a stalemate on the field of anti-oppressive education if we simply allow that two people can have a relationship defined not by desire but by "love." In the debate about same-sex marriage, for example, this is the safely and appropriately liberal default. We aren't asking about the private sexual practices of same-sex couples any more than we query the sexual practice of heterosexual couples. We simply acknowledge that their desire to be with one another is ultimately not about sex but about romance. I asked the class to consider if this issue is more than just about having same-sex statuettes on top of the wedding cake?

Students grappled throughout the course with how "popular" culture, generally meant to include the media, but to which I would add the discourse in the hallways and classrooms of our schools, depicts, shapes, and polices the formation of our gendered and sexual identities. The course afforded Chris, the one openly gay young man in the class, to reflect on the objectification of his own reality in gay magazines like *Out*, *Instinct*, and *The Advocate*. He saw all the "hot bodies" and "soft porn" as a put-down and refutation of his own reality. He spoke eloquently of the period of his own coming out—"exiting a straight identity" and attempting to forge a gay one—only to find no reflection of himself in the discourse of the schools (simply a silenced absence). Turning to the media he found only images in magazines of a certain kind of buff and hairless physicality, and on TV stereotypes of a kind of "cute" vacuous-ness, or bitchiness, in such programs as *Queer Eye for the Straight Guy* and *Will and Grace*, or gay characters who are not different because they "act straight" as in *Dawson's Creek*. Chris's position is an alienated one—unable to relate to or identify with the physical or emotional portraits of who he was supposed to "be." Through Chris's analysis of his untenable position, straight students in the class were able to appreciate stereotyping in a new way:

> The media assignment caused me to look internally. The magazines I looked at are intended for a gay audience. So what makes us want to see these kinds of [explicitly sexualized] ads?

Chris argued that "naked beautiful bodies" reduce his identity, diminish his own sense of agency, and can "confuse and hurt children's development." Chris asked, "If young people, gay or straight, do not fit with what they see in the media to be the norm, what are we doing to their minds?" Queer theory, on the other hand, challenges this wholesomeness as a perversion that polices rather than indulges the passion of same-sex desire.

Empathy and understanding for Chris's position from the rest of the class occurred because, of course, many of the women in the class already understood how highly idealized images of the female body have been used and reduced to sell products. Chris's look at the same issue from the vantage point of his "othered" queerness, helped them to understand that the issue of a perceived "gay lifestyle" is as much an effective marketing ploy of our consumer society as it is a misunderstanding and misrepresentation of gender and sexuality. Angella, already in tune with the issues as a social studies major, commented: "Students need to see positive, creative, contributing LGBT role models (from today and from history) rather than sexual caricatures from the media."

Coming to Terms With the Body

It is not such a great distance from the pages of such magazines as *Out* and television episodes of *Oz* or *Queer as Folk* to the locker rooms and gymnasiums of our schools. In a puritan and prurient society, physical education classes make everyone vulnerable because, unlike the traditional classroom, they focus intently on the body. Gard's article, "What do We do in Physical Education?" (2001) provoked one student to write: "As a phys ed major, I learned that phys ed is a space to 'practice' being boys or girls: to be cool, sporty, 'jockey,' and [most of all] straight." Admitting that she always hated gym, another student added: "I have developed an understanding of why physical education, with its emphasis on competition and comparisons, can be detrimental to many children." Another concluded: "I learned that physical education can be one of the worst places for homophobic abuse and the domination of heterosexist privilege." Even Connie, always slow to admit that any "issues" were complicated, including her own lack of a "sexual identity," finally said: "I looked at the implications for my teaching. Now I understand, for example, how a phys-ed class is an ideal place for homophobic bullying and reinforcing heterosexism."

Chris, "our" only gay student (and I use this possessive pronoun deliberately), tried to articulate his sense of "otherness," despite the inclusive climate in the classroom. It seemed to me that other students exhibited a warm and open attitude towards him. He made friends with one young woman whose cousin routinely does drag at the local gay club. However, Chris also felt the need to resist what he interpreted as a maternal or patronizing stance of some of the students:

> I believe there are still a few people in this class who believe homosexuals should just be happy with what we have. I don't think they are trying to be mean; I think they simply do not realize some of their privileges when it comes to social freedoms.

Tara realized that identity is not a static concept:

> Even though this assignment is complete, I am still struggling with it. I am still unsure of my own sexual identity and it continues to develop, but as it does, I am now aware of social constructs and how I may have been influenced.

Reconciling the Body with Christ

In opposition to the "other," Michelle, struggling to reconcile "new knowledge" with her conservatively religious background, honestly expressed her lack of understanding:

> I still don't really understand the concept of positionality. I understand that when you have privilege over other minorities it means that [you] are looked upon as part of the norm and that you can receive more benefits than say someone of a different race. But I'm not sure how that works in regards to sexual minorities because most people can't tell.

Stacey, a business education major from rural Saskatchewan with a strong religious background, was sceptical throughout the course. At the end she tried this stance on for size:

> I still don't believe that I am as understanding of the topic to fully stand up against people that are against homosexuality, but I do feel that the argument to treat all as equals in the schools is powerful. I now feel more comfortable putting myself in situations where students may be teasing and name-calling and I can stop that behaviour. Such a small step ... but this can lead to bigger and better things.

The collision between an unquestioned identity formulated in the past and grounded in religion, on the one hand, and the introduction of a broader construct of spirituality, caused a certain degree of stress; as the instructor I interpreted this as a positive signal indicative of learning. Even Tara, from a liberal family and an "accepting" church, said: "The class made me question my religion. I see my religion as more of a family tradition than a spirituality I chose. Now I am questioning exactly how I feel towards my religion. This is something I need to do to have a strong sense of self which [in turn] is something I need as a teacher." Erin agreed: "This class also made me examine my beliefs about religion and my views on some of the constructions out there. This has made me a more creative and critical thinker." My own late father, brought up in an Irish Protestant household, regarded education as the tool with which to fight what he saw as the narrow-minded bigotry and ignorance of all religions, would have concurred. Lindsay, ever the pragmatist and someone not appreciative of ambiguity, tried to "juggle the balls" in this way: "Even though I am a Christian and hold many Christian morals, values, and beliefs, I don't possess a dislike in any way for homosexual people... If we don't stand up for LGBT students, then who will?" At least in such thinking, we find a personalized interpretation of the Catholic and other churches' adage "to love the sinner even if we hate the sin." If this is more than just tolerance, political correctness, or empathy, perhaps we can take some satisfaction in this new positionality.

What Does It Look Like? What Does It Sound Like?
Integration of Sexual Difference into Classroom Lessons

Pragmatists would argue that the "lesson plan assignment" was the most important part of the course. Space does not permit a full discussion of this exercise, but several representative pieces may serve as examples. My objective here was not necessarily for students to "queer the curriculum" by disrupting or displacing heterosexuality; rather I wanted my students to simply practice inclusivity (see D'Augelli and Patterson, 1995, and Connelly, 1999) by broadening the view of sexuality, in the most liberal of ways, to include same-sex constructs.

The invisibility of LGBT students, curiously, becomes the lack of a problem. "So what's the problem?" or "So what do *they* want anyway?" is a common stance in school staff rooms where the response, "Well, we don't have any gay students (or First Nations or Métis students, or Muslim students or any particular minority group) in our schools," becomes a rationale for passive resistance to change and inclusion. LGBT students can only become "other" if they out themselves or others out them. In the same way that the popular TV show, *Seinfeld*, purported to "be about nothing," the official school curriculum is disingenuously posited as "neutral" and disengaged from reality. At least *Seinfeld* built and played to the irony: "nothing" is actually "everything." In schools, on the other hand, "no problem," visible or not, becomes a curious sign of success.

I introduced students to the commonplaces of curriculum as a series of "windows and mirrors," a concept none of them claimed to have ever been introduced to. Style (1996) suggests curriculum is like a window opening onto the reality of the world, and like a mirror providing reflections back to students of who they think they are. These windows and mirrors must be at the right "height," that is, they must be, from a developmental perspective, "age appropriate" so that students can see through the windows and into the mirrors when they are ready. Kumashiro (2000) suggests that curricular innovation can go beyond merely "educating about or for the other" (p. 25) and can critique social privilege and cause students (and ultimately society) to change.

Many of the pre-service teachers in elementary education chose to replicate what I had modelled by using picture and storybooks with themes about children in same-sex families. Most of these resources reinforce the adage: "What makes a family?

LOVE makes a family!" These books tend to be about "the other" (providing a window to other realities such as same-sex families), but also intended "for" the other, that is students who come from "different" families. American resources include single-parent families and intergenerational and interracial families as part of the "field" in which one might also find same-sex families. Most of the pre-service teachers students argued that such resources could also be used effectively as "mirrors," reflecting back to the children in their classes a view of themselves that was clearly valued and included. Difference here is not just accommodated or acknowledged as "special"; it is integrated and "normalized" for the sake of all the children in the class. In the same vein, much adolescent literature, concerned with the impact of a gay or lesbian youth "coming out," such as Diana Wieler's resilient and still very current *Bad Boy* (1989), is both "for and about" the "other," since its primary audience is heterosexual adolescents who are provided with cues to a range of emotional responses to this topic.[6]

What Makes a Family?

Gillian took the curricular emphasis on family and adapted it into an already established kinesthetic activity suitable for K–3 children. In the standard lesson, children are invited to make a bracelet or necklace using coloured beads to symbolize connections and relationships. A yellow bead might stand for "dogs" and green beads stand for "cats." Similarly, other colours are assigned to siblings and parents and grandparents. Children are encouraged to select the beads for the string according to the composition of their family. The teacher invokes an understanding that difference is not better or worse, but rather that difference is normative: "How many grandmothers do you have?" "How many of you have an uncle or auntie living with you?" "Does anyone in your family use a wheelchair?" Some children might have two dogs, a cat, a brother, a sister, and one mum, while another family, Gillian stressed, might have one dog, two cats, a brother, and two dads. While this may seem painfully obvious, this thoughtful act of encouraging children to claim and reproduce their own identities is a simple act of integration with profound implications. From the innocuous and more revealing dynamics of the child's representation of family, a teacher will also learn about the children and serve to honour their background. The silence is not only broken: diversity is celebrated. Knowing the competitiveness endemic at that age, one imagines children establishing bragging rights on the premise that two dads, like two of anything, is better than one dad, based on simple addition! The two premises of such integrative movement in the curriculum, based on the principle of "windows and mirrors," are inclusion and authenticity.[7]

Jean, il aime le garcon qui s'appelle Michel

Denis, a pre-service teacher of core French, modelled this "authentic inclusiveness" in a grade nine class. His purpose in the lesson was to introduce students to gendered pronouns and the relationship between male and female names. Thus, he boldly included *"elle aime Jeanne,"* along with *"elle aime Jean,"* and *"il aime Michel"* along with *"il aime Michelle."* When students said something was wrong, he shrugged his shoulders and said *"Quoi? Expliquez s'il vous plait."* What followed was an opportunity for the teacher to point out not only that *aimer* means to like as well as to love but that same-sex attraction is certainly *"possible et normale."* The class then moved on to another grammatical point. This is important because the topic of sexual orientation does not have to be the primary learning objective of a lesson; it can be included simply at an appropriate "teachable moment," sometimes as nothing more than an aside, or an example.

Reader Responses to Disembodied Voices

Other lessons, however, were more pointed. Nicole, for a high school English class, based her lesson on the concept of disembodied voices and reader response. Using a number of gay and lesbian poets including Adrienne Rich, Audre Lorde, and Langston Hughes, as well as Shakespeare, she detached the poets' names from the poems. She then asked students to discover in the texts who was speaking and who was the object of the passion. A number of critical points already articulated in the curriculum were made: we cannot always presume that the voice in a poem is the voice of the poet; as readers we endow the voices with intent and see the objects of their desire. A literary window might also serve as one's own literary mirror. Who is "right"? The student who "reads" sexual desire as heterosexual or homosexual? How do we know? Nicole correctly assumed that most students would read themselves into the texts and then have to come to terms with difference when she revealed some of the biographical details of the poets' lives.

Media Objectification

Chris, the only non-education student in the class, was quite intimidated by the assignment to build a lesson plan. His media study, however, would fit well in any number of social studies, humanities, and English courses in studying media representations of gendered sexuality. His plan was to have students use magazines and web-site images to make two posters. One poster would present the media ideals perpetuated about youthful, sexualized perfection and the class would have to articulate the values embedded in the imagery. The second poster would represent the students as they actually perceived themselves, including what they liked to do, what was important to them, and what they believed in. Cliff hypothesized that the discrepancy between the two posters would make a powerful statement.

Class discussion suggested that if there were no discrepancy between students' understanding of media representations and their projection of their "real" self, that would make an even more powerful statement. Chris's objective, or "agenda" as he called it, was to show that sexuality sells almost everything in our society, but that it is a particular kind of heterosexuality that excludes sexual difference. This led the class to a discussion of androgyny as a recent, but fading, "fashion" that could be interpreted as signalling a blurring of rigid stereotypes of masculinity and femininity. This led to talk of Madison Avenue's rediscovery of body hair on men as the cutting-edge definition of a more masculine "metrosexual." Even if LGBT high school students might not, understandably, "come out" to their classmates after such a lesson, the pre-service teachers believed that most students might reach some consensus about the power of the media to shape and influence our ideas about who we are, who we think we are, and who we think we want to be.

Let's Do It With Numbers

Connie, the pre-service high school math teacher, was dubious about this assignment. "What," she kept asking me, "has the study of mathematics to do with sexual orientation?" I had to admit that I didn't know the answer, but I insisted that she examine the official math curriculum for a way to integrate these two disparate topics. The day before her presentation, she came to class with a smug grin on her face. "I've found a way!" she exclaimed. The Grade 12 curriculum specifies that students should be introduced to basic issues in statistics and the key concepts of validity and reliability. Connie saw a window: statistics are gathered about everything, and recently by Statistics Canada soliciting information about how many Canadians were living in "same-sex households." Connie suggested that basic knowledge about statistics could be illustrated using any topic, but that the issues of validity and reliability might be well tested by exploring the reasons that individuals might choose or not choose to declare their sexual orientation when they were filling in the census section about same sex households.

Statistics suddenly became a rich field for exploring the politics of being "out." Armed with new knowledge from the course, Connie built a series of lesson plans that would examine the principles of basic statistics and then introduce the concepts of variability and reliability around same-sex relationships. What factors, she asked, might mitigate these stats being truly reliable? What variables need to be taken into account in understanding the reported numbers? By this time Connie was conversant enough with the issues of denial and closeting to know that there would be many reasons to question the validity and reliability of self-reported same-sex households.

Other students chimed in, wondering exactly what Statistics Canada might mean by "household" in the first place. Others asked pertinent questions: if two sisters live together isn't that a same-sex household? Business education students were able to contribute to the discussion from a tax perspective: same-sex couples had the right to claim "dependency" but did that mean they would declare the same relationship to Statistics Canada? Would it be important to correlate information from the two different reporting sources? Was that even legal? Social studies students asked about "the right to privacy" surrounding tax information. In other words, the lesson was a resounding success. And again—the subject to be "taught" was not same-sex relationships, but the issues of validity and reliability as key concepts in teaching students about statistical variables. Further, statistics offered a window through which to discuss the financial implications of the federal government's position on same-sex relationships which, as the social studies majors were quick to point out, leads to an even more interesting discussion of the issues surrounding same-sex civil unions and gay marriage. The class concluded that mathematics is, indeed, a rich space for discussion of sexual orientation.

Warrior Love

Cliff, the arts education student, wanted to "push the envelope," as he put it. His lesson plan for the Drama 10 curriculum involved the concept of guided imagery: suggesting a scenario for students that allows them to viscerally involve themselves in a dramatic situation. This lesson stemmed from Cliff's own research into the cultural practices of the samurai and the same-sex relationships between seasoned and novice warriors. The situation Cliff envisaged centred on violence and abuse—someone would become the victim, and the student participants would have to ad lib themselves in and out of the scenario. Cliff guided the students into the situation—a young person, with whom the participants identify, is accused of or confronted with his or her "gayness" by a group of adolescent rowdies. Another scenario had samurai warriors practicing their martial arts and exhibiting great tenderness to one another with lines like "I know I can depend on you in battle because of our mutual love for each other." Cliff was unsure, exactly, where this would go in an improvisation exercise, but he did know that drama classes have always been spaces where adolescent boys' nervousness about "acting" and their insecurities about sexual identity quickly bubble to the surface through the joking imitation and mocking of "faggy" or effeminate mannerisms. As an arts educator, this was a space he wanted with these exercises to reconstruct in a more positive way.

Brown Dad Blue Dad

Later, in a seminar for their peers, Cliff and his colleague, Deadra, structured a lesson on a variation of the famous "blue eyes-brown eyes" experiment of Jane Elliot.[8] They asked students to pick a tile out of a box, but not to tell anyone what the colour of the tile was. There were only two tiles: red and blue. They then began a conversation for the benefit of the class that denigrated the blue tile people as biologically inferior, socially and sexually perverted and untrustworthy, and religiously immoral and to be feared for their power to conscript, contaminate and corrupt. This reconstruction of the homophobic arguments was powerful. It served, much like the innocuous children's book *One Dad, Two Dads, Brown Dad, Blue Dads* at the core of the Surrey School Board's book banning, to upset the equilibrium around "difference" and those who are "othered." The debriefing confirmed all the tenets of anti-oppressive education: those, like the blues, who are diminished and negated, directly or by innuendo, are marginalized and silenced, are unsure of their rights and are filled with resentment and a sense of injustice. The "truth" of their reality is socially constructed. Those, like the reds, who are positioned in the centre by approval, feel a sense of privilege that becomes their due, are all too ready to make a claim to innate superiority, and are convinced of their right to do so. The "truth" of their reality is also socially constructed. This powerful lesson, the class concluded, should be a foundational exercise in a curriculum that claims to strive for social justice.

Conclusion

I would suggest that these sample lessons, like the entire course in which they were situated, in "dealing" directly and indirectly with homophobia and same-sex desire and relationships, are neither radical nor subversive. If we substitute already "sanctified" equity categories—women, religious groups, visible minorities, and people with disabilities—we know that the official curriculum has already "accommodated" certain kinds of difference. Taking the bold step to include same-sex orientation is simply an act of inclusion. Through these specific assignments and the course in general, students had imagined themselves breaking the silence and opening the closet door on the last controversial issue to be addressed in our schools. They were able to point themselves in the right direction and find a way to adapt the official curriculum to include sexual difference, to create windows and mirrors so that students in K–12 classrooms can begin to understand what sexual difference looks like and what it sounds like. What is looks and sounds like is normal.

For some, the course was an extension of what they already "knew." Tamara captured the wonderful and inspiring idealism of pre-service teachers when she wrote:

"This class has reawakened the socialist in me and I was primed and ready to address [the issue of] inclusion in schools. I have realized how truly invisible homosexuality is in the schools." Cliff confirmed pre-service teachers' desire to effect change to "do good": "This class was a great beginning to my own *crusade* [my emphasis] against homophobia. The rest of the things that I need must be provided by myself, starting with courage!" Nicole, calm and reflective, concluded that she would be able to"implicitly educate both heterosexual and homosexual students that sexual diversity is natural and part of humanity." Victoria pointed to a better future: "Small steps, but maybe someday sexual difference won't need to be an issue." Angela reflected on her own experience in the schools as a pre-service teacher for three years, even though her use of the passive tense makes her less an agent of change than a supporter of it: "It bolsters my heart to know that there are changes being made. I have experienced so much cynicism among teaching staff, jokes made at a students' expense, that [it] makes me wonder why they were in the [teaching] profession at all." Cari, in response to the question, "What have we missed, what else do we need to know?" responded with a more articulate equivalent of "chill, dude": "Realistically, you've done all you could do, James. Now it is up to us to figure it out as we go. Each school has its own context, and will require its own unique handling of the situation."

What of my reflective enquiry into my own practice? The most important thing I learned in offering this course for the first time is that it is not possible to understand and accommodate sexual "difference," and all that it entails, without taking the time to explore the gendered and sexualized identity formation of all students. The class started by exploring their own experience of difference, gender and sexuality. For many this was an awkward and difficult beginning because their own privilege had been left unexamined and simply taken for granted. The tentativeness and awareness of the complications embedded in the construction of identity became a starting position to begin to understand "the other," that is, people whose sexual orientation was not the same as their own. I am also very much aware of how teaching pre-service teachers "for" and "about" difference can be reductionistic. Recently revived communications theories from the 1960s and 1970s remind us that even with the best of intentions we can never know whether or how we are affecting change. It would be naïve to suppose that knowledge leads to empathy or that empathy will lead to action in any kind of sequential or causal relationship.

Is it possible for a pre-service education class, grounded in advocacy, equity and social justice issues to "fail"? Student surveys at the end of the course indicated a very high degree of satisfaction with the course offering. But how do you measure the cognitive and affective "movement" in a class that socially conservative critics would describe as merely "advancing the gay agenda"? How do you assess the impact of the teaching? Can cynics dismiss the course as nothing but an exercise in political correctness? What does it mean when a student writes, "It is our ethical and legal obligation to attempt to stop homophobia and discrimination against LGBT students." What if students are simply mouthing the appropriate words and feeding back to me what they think I want to hear?

First, I can answer this question by saying that I came to know the genuineness and integrity of the students, and respected their capacity for critical inquiry. Secondly, they have trusted me to share the "evidence" of their writing. This chapter shows how students engaged in honest, critical and reflective practice around a difficult topic and how they learned and grew as a result. Even if it is not necessary to "queer" the curriculum at the K–12 and university level, it is necessary to re-affirm the innate idealism of pre-service teachers, and to affirm and support their rights and their responsibilities to make classrooms safe and caring and empowering places for all their students.

Notes

1. A note on the collection and use of the data. I asked all of the students to voluntarily sign a release form agreeing to allow their work, their thoughts and musings, both oral and written, to be included in my writing about the offering of this course. These forms were collected and sealed and not opened until after the class was over and the grades were assigned in order not to prejudice the assessment of any of the students. As it turned out, all of the students were happy to share their thoughts and understandings with a wider audience. An argument might even be made that this sense of a "public" audience, a sense that they were the first "guinea pigs" of what was called an "experimental" course offered for the first time, motivated students to be more forthcoming that they might be.

2. Tara Goldstein and another instructor at the the Ontario Institute for Studies in Education offered a course "Inqueeries About Education" to 11 students for the first time in May and June 2003, and offered it again in 2004 to 17 students.

3. A note on names. Though students did not request it, I have ensured that student anonymity is protected by using pseudonyms throughout this paper.

4. A note on student voice. I have standardized the voice of the students in this paper, in terms of spelling, grammar and usage. I do this for the sake of the reader and general issues of fluency. This is not, for example, the kind of historical or rhetorical article in which the intrusion of "*sic*" is necessary or appropriate. For a number of egalitarian and stylistic reasons that could be the topic of another article (but which I will not articulate here), I choose to "make standard" what students have spoken or written. For example, the student quoted here used the word "native," but I have capitalized it to "Native" to indicate a distinct group of people, rather than just the more generic meaning "of this place," which diminishes, in my opinion, the First Peoples of Canada. I have not, however, put words into the mouths of the students and where coherency is needed I have inserted square brackets, [...], to indicate my editorial intrusion or elision.

5. David McIntyre (2004) has written a song which anyone from a small town can relate to:

    I'm thinking 'bout a small town
    I'm thinking 'bout a place I loved to hate!
    Couldn't wait—to leave it behind.
    Everybody knew everybody else
    "Like a book" they said "I read ya like a book."
    Now I tell them, I think they should know,
    There's a chapter that nobody's read.
    Pokey little buildings, dusty gravel roads,
    People at their windows, lookin' down their nose
    Tell'n ya how to think and tell'n ya what to wear,
    You're livin' in a fish tank, pretendin' not to care.
    Wanna turn the page, finish the story.

6. For more resources a good starting point is K. Tadei, *"It's OK to Have This Book in Your Public School Library": Gay, Lesbian, Bisexual, Transgender and Two-spirited People: A Bibliography of Resources* (Research Project #74, Dr. Stirling McDowell Foundation for Research into Teaching. Saskatoon: Saskatchewan Teachers' Federation, 2002).

7. There are still, of course, secrets and closets not to be opened. Such an exercise does not ask that a red bead stand for an abusive mom or a green bead represent an alcoholic father.

8. The work of Jane Elliot has been documented on three educational videos: *The Angry Eye*, *In the Eye of the Storm*, and *A Class Divided*. See Bruce MacDougall and Paul Clarke's article in this volume for a full account of the fate of the books involved in the Surrey Book Ban, including *One Dad, Two Dads, Brown Dad, Blue Dads* (1994) by Johnny Valentine, illustrated by Melody Sarecky and published by Alyson Books.

References

Bagemihl, B. 1999. *Biological Exuberance: Animal Homosexuality and Natural Diversity*. London: St. Martin's Press.

Britzman, D.P. 1998. *Lost Subjects, Contested Objects: Toward a Psychoanalytic Inquiry of Learning*. Albany: State University of New York Press.

Cannon, M. 1998. "The Regulation of First Nations Sexuality." *The Canadian Journal of Native Studies* 18, no. 1: 1–18.

Champagne, J. 1995. *The Ethics of Marginality: A New Approach to Gay Studies*. Minneapolis: University of Minnesota Press.

D'Augelli, A.R. and C.J. Patterson. 1995. *Lesbian, Gay, and Bisexual Identities Over the Lifespan: Psychological Perspectives*. New York: Oxford University Press.

Fonow M. and Marty, D. 1992. "Teaching College Students about Sexual Identity from Feminist Perspectives." In J. Sears (ed.), *Sexuality and the Curriculum: The Politics and Practices of Sexuality Education*. New York: Teachers College Press.

Gard, M. 2002. "What Do We Do in Physical Education?" In R. Kassen (ed.), *Getting Ready for Benjamin: Preparing Teachers for Sexual Diversity in the Classroom*. New York: Rowman & Littlefield.

Harding, J. 1998. *Sex Acts: Practices of Femininity and Masculinity*. London: Sage Publications.

Harris, Simon. 1995. *Lesbian and Gay Issues in the English Classroom: The Importance of Being Honest*. London: Open University Press.

Kumashiro, K.K. 2000. "Toward a Theory of Anti-Oppressive Education." *Review of Educational Research* 70, no. 10: 25–53.

Morris, C. 2004. "P.E.I Baseball Prospect Found Guilty in Sordid Sex Case." Canadian Press story retrieved May 11, 2004, from *www.canoe.ca/Slam031022/mlb_can-cp.html*

Ponton, L.P. 2001. *The Sex Lives of Teenagers: Revealing the Secret World of Adolescent Boys and Girls*. New York: Dutton Publishing.

Spencer, C. 1996. *The History of Homosexuality*. London: Harcourt.

Style. E. 1996. "Curriculum as Window & Mirror." Retrieved from The Wellesley Centers for Women SEED Project on Inclusive Curriculum (Seeking Education Equity & Diversity): *www.wcwonline.org/seed/curriculum.html* (accessed April 20, 2003).

Wieler, D. 1989. *Bad Boy*. Vancouver: Douglas and McIntyre.

Index

Note: Where initials are given to describe people, follow this key: G: gay; L: lesbian; B: bisexual; T: transgender; T: two-spirit; Q: queer.

A

Abbott, Elizabeth, 268-9
ABC: A Family Alphabet, 213
Abel, Sam, 262, 264-5, 270
Abelove, Henry
    The Lesbian and Gay Studies Reader, 79, 106-7
Abinati, Abby, 52, 54, 56, 76
Aboriginal people, *see* First Nations communities
ableism, 274-5
Aboriginal communities, *see* First Nations
    communities
abuse, 22, 50, 52, 54-5, 57, 63, 66, 228, 230, 290,
    298, 304
    see also sexual abuse
Academic Outlaws: LGBTQ Theory and Cultural
    Studies in the Academy, 307
Access to Care: Exploring the Health and Well-being
    of Gay, Lesbian, Bisexual and Two-Spirit People
    in Canada, 79
Achtenberg, Roberta, 52, 57, 76
Act for the Gradual Enfranchisement of Indians,
    An, 101, 105
Act for the Protection of the Indians in Upper
    Canada from Imposition, and the Property
    Occupied or Enjoyed by Them from Trespass
    and Injury, An, 105
actors, gay and lesbian, 256-8, 261, 268
acts of survival, 59-60, 62, 64-5, 71
    from oppression, 73-5
Adam, Barry
    The Making of a Gay and Lesbian Movement,
    49, 76
Adams, M.
    Teaching for Diversity and Social Justice:
    A Sourcebook, 45, 48
Adams, Mary Louise
    The Trouble with Normal: Postwar Youth and
    the Making of Heterosexuality, 133, 161
Adams, Nicole, 137
additive model, 51, 59, 75
Adnan, E., 31, 41
adolescence, 34-6, 52-3, 58, 61
adoption by homosexuals, 130, 164, 226
adult GLB communities, 50-1, 59, 65, 67
Advocate, The, 159, 322
Ady, Jack, 142-3
AGAPE, 291, 294-5, 296, 305-6
ageism, 51, 53
Aguirre, Rick, 49
AIDS, 55, 57, 128, 131, 148, 227, 236, 268, 277,
    317
AIDS Activist: Michael Lynch and the Politics of
    Community, 227, 241

Alberta
    Aboriginal rights in, 141, 149
    anti-gay lobbies in, 157
    anti-special rights for gays, 159
    concept of family in, 141
    conservatism in, 160
    definition of marriage in, 160
    discrimination prohibited on sexual orientation,
        156-7, 160-1
    ethnocentrism in, 140, 149
    experience of homosexuals in, 151
    feminists in, 141, 145-6, 149
    gay activism in, 156
    gay discrimination in, 153-4
    gay lifestyle in, 141, 145
    gay rights issue in, 139-40, 143, 156-61, 297,
        305
    gay-bashing in, 151
    heterosexism in, 140, 143, 155
    heterosexism in schools in, 292-3, 295, 301
    homophobia in, 140, 143, 151, 155, 160
    homophobia in schools in, 292, 293, 295, 297,
        301
    homosexual rights lobby in, 142, 146-7, 149
    homosexuality in, 140-1, 144-5, 148
    homosexuality, war on, 155, 159
    house and employment issues for gays in, 158
    inclusion for LGBTQ persons, 144, 290, 292,
        294
    LGBTQ issues in, 290, 296-7
    mainstream media in, 140, 143, 150
    misogyny in, 140
    oppression of homosexuals in, 151
    queer issues in, 140, 144, 157-9
    queer people as threats to family, 141, 145
    queer rights in, 145
    queer youth in, 139-40, 144
    racism in, 140
    religious fundamentalists in, 145, 149, 151,
        158-60
    safe and caring schools in, 293, 298
    safety for LGBTQ persons, 290, 292, 297
    sexism in, 140
    sexual minorities in, 140, 155
    sexual orientation in human rights code, 128
    support of lesbian and gay youth, 144
    traditional families in, 154
    violence prevention programs in, 292, 295
Alberta Catholic School Trustees' Association
    (ACSTA)
    A Resource for an Inclusive Community:
    A Teacher's Guide for and about Persons With
    Same Sex Attractions, 296, 306

Alberta Civil Society Association, 157
Alberta Federation for Women United For Families, 156-8
Alberta Foundation for the Arts, 148
Alberta Human Rights and Citizenship Commission (AHRCC)
  Protected Areas and Grounds Under the Human Rights, Citizenship and Multiculturalism Act, 306
Alberta Human Rights, Citizenship and Multiculturalism Act, 7, 128
Alberta Human Rights Commission, 160
Alberta Individual's Rights Protection Act, 152, 157, 160, 292
Alberta Pro-Life, 157
Alberta Report (AR), 140–61, 186
Alberta Teachers' Association (ATA), 144, 290, 292, 295, 301, 305
  Safe and Caring Schools for Lesbian and Gay Youth: A Guide for Teachers, 294, 306
Alberta Theatre Projects (ATP), 148, 257-8, 264, 268
Alberta, University of, 146, 227, 260, 264, 284, 291, 294-5, 298
Albertans
  as "severely normal," 139-40, 159-60
Aldrich, Ann, 113
Alexander, T.M., 227, 240
Alexander, Marilyn Bennett, 178
Albee, Edward, 261
alliance clubs for gay/straight students, 301
Alliance Defense Fund, 173
Alliance for Life, 126
Alliance Party, see Canadian Alliance Party
Alyson Publications penpal exchange program, 69
American Center for Law and Justice, 173
American Family Association (AFA), 173
American Medical Association, 175
American Psychiatric Association, 166-7, 175-6, 178
American Psychological Association, 154, 175
American Sociological Association, 154
Ames, Linda
  A Parent's Guide to Preventing Homosexuality, 177, 179
anal sex, age of consent for, 54
And Then I Became Gay: Youth Men's Stories, 42
Andenaes, Mads
  Legal Recognition of Same-Sex Partnerships: A Study of National, European and International Law, 216
Anderson, Dennis A., 31, 35, 41, 50, 55, 63, 65, 76
Anderson, Margaret L.
  Race, Class, and Gender: An Anthology, 50-1, 60, 75-7
androgyny, 326
Angels in Alberta, 147-8
Angels in America, 147, 257-8, 265, 268-9
Anglican Church of Canada, 164, 172, 216, 229
anorexia, 16
Anthony, Gretchen, 70
anti-oppressive education, 244-6, 249, 253, 314, 328
Anzul, M.
  On Writing Qualitative Research: Living by Words, 18

Arbour J, 215
Archer, Doug, 126
  Arduous Journey: Canadian Indians and Decolonization, 106
Are We Persons Yet? Law and Sexuality in Canada, 18
Arena of Masculinity: Sports, Homosexuality and the Meaning of Sex, The, 186, 190
Arendt, H.
  Eichmann in Jerusalem: A Report on the Banality of Evil, 238, 240
Aristophanes, 269
Arling, Joe, 184
Armstrong, Jane, 219
Armstrong, L.
  Home Front: Notes from the Family War Zone, 183, 190
Arons, Stephen, 215
Arrell, Doug, 267, 270
Arvay, Joe, 232, 237
As It Happens (CBC radio), 118
Asha's Mums, 213, 215, 237
Athanases, S.Z., 284, 286
Atkinson, Pat, 117
Avram, Kevin, 142, 147
Ayim, M.
  The Gender Question in Education, 92

B
Babbit, J.
  But I'm a Cheerleader: A Comedy of Sexual Dysfunction, 286
Babcock, Mike, 187
Bad Boy, 325, 331
Bagemihl, B.
  Biological Exuberance: Animal Homosexuality and Natural Diversity, 319, 331
Bagley, C, 50, 76, 237, 240
  Suicidal Behaviors in Adolescents and Adults: Research, Taxonomy and Prevention, 76
Baker, J.M.
  How Homophobia Hurts Children: Nurturing Diversity at Home, at School, and in the Community, 7, 18
Balcony, The, 260
Banff Centre for the Arts, 141-2
Bannerji, Himani, 104, 106
Baptist Church, 164
Baptist Church (Westboro), 176
Baptist Convention (ON & Que), 172
Barale, Michele Aina
  The Lesbian and Gay Studies Reader, 79, 106-7
Barber, Jaime, 63
Barnard, Elissa, 257, 268, 270
Barthes, Roland, 148
Bass, Ellen
  Free Your Mind: The Book for Gay, Lesbian and Bisexual Youth and Their Allies, 55-6, 58-9, 62-4, 66-7, 69, 71-2, 76
Bastarche, J., 215
BC Coalition of People with Disabilities (BCCPD), 276, 286
BC Report (Western), 140
BC School Act, 193-4, 196-8, 202-3, 209, 213
BC Teachers' Federation, 289

Beal, Becky, 60, 72, 76
Becoming Gay: The Journey to Self-acceptance, 32, 42
Beeler, L., 283, 287
Begg, R.W., 117-8
    Being Homosexual: Gay Men and Their Development, 42
Belinda's Bouquet, 215
Bell, D.
    The Sexual Citizen: Queer Politics and Beyond, 227, 240
Bell, L.
    Teaching for Diversity and Social Justice: Sourcebook, 45, 48
Bell, Rick, 141, 153
Bella Coola Nation, homosexuality in, 97
Bend It Like Beckham, 314
benefits, for domestic partners, 268
Bennett, Susan, 258, 268-70
Benson, F.J., 289, 306
Benson, Kathryn Zamora, 73
berdaches, 97-100, 104-5
Bergman, Brian, 54, 76
Bernardo, Paul, 155
Berthelet, Bishop Jacques, 173
Berube, Allan
    Coming Out Under Fire: The History of Gay Men and Women in World War Two, 176, 178
Bessborough Hotel (Saskatoon), 112
Best Kept Secret: Sexual Abuse of Children, The, 183, 188, 190
bestiality, 157, 175
Beyer, Roy, 157-8
Bierwiler, Kay, 121
Biggs, Lesley
    Devine Rule in Saskatchewan: A Decade of Hope and Hardship, 136
bigotry, 123, 155, 168, 171
Biklen, D.
    The Least Restrictive Alternative: Principles and Practices, 277, 288
Biklen, S.
    Qualitative Research for Education: An Introduction to Theory and Methods, 46, 48
Bill C-138 (Canada), 75
Bill 38 (Saskatchewan), 109, 130
Billie De Frank Gay and Lesbian Community Centre, 71
Bindman, Stephen, 137
Binnie J, 215
    The Sexual Citizen: Queer Politics and Beyond, 227, 240
Biological Exuberance: Animal Homosexuality and Natural Diversity, 319, 331
Birkholz, Dan, 72-3
bisexual persons, 39, 53-4, 57, 61, 67, 70, 160, 273
bisexuality, negative social value of, 52
Blackeney, Allan E., 136
    government of, 123-4
Blair J, 216
blending, 61, 62
Blumenfeld, Warren J., 52, 56, 72, 76
    Looking at Gay and Lesbian Life, 104, 106
Board, M., 190
Boas, Franz, 97

Bodies That Matter: On the Discursive Limits of Sex," 92
body altering, 90
body piercing, 236
Body Politic collective, 115-6, 121, 123
Bogdan, R.
    Qualitative Research for Education: An Introduction to Theory and Methods, 46, 48
Boggs, E.
    The Least Restrictive Alternative: Principles and Practices, 277, 288
Bohan, Janis, S.
    Conversations about Psychology and Sexual Orientation, 178-9
    Psychology and Sexual Orientation: Coming to Terms, 176, 178
books, featuring same-sex parents, 301
    banning of, 328
Books, S.
    Invisible Children in the Society and Its Schools, 18
Bossu, Jean Bernard, 96
Boston Bruins, 182
Boswell, John, 105-6
    Christianity, Social Tolerance, and Homosexuality: Gay People in Western Europe from the Beginning of the Christian Era to the Fourteenth Century, 175, 177-8
Bouchard, Michel Marc
    The Orphan Muses, 263
Boudier, Neely, 64
Bowman, R., 287
Boxer, Andrew
    Children of Horizons: How Gay and Lesbian Teens are Leading A New Way Out of the Closet, 53, 64, 66, 77
Boyer, Debra, 53, 67, 76
Boyle, Pat, 144-6
Boys' Club, 22
Brantlinger, E., 274, 286-7
Breitkreuz, Cliff, 151
Brett, Philip, 267
    Cruising the Performative, 270
    Queering the Pitch: The New Gay and Lesbian Musicology, 270
Bright, Bill, 173
    Bringing Up Boys: Practical Advice and Encouragement for Those Shaping the Next Generation of Men, 177-8
British Columbia College of Teachers v Trinity Western University, 289, 306
British Columbia, University of, 146, 262, 269
Britzman, D.P., 82, 91, 253-4, 275, 283, 287
    Lost Subjects, Contested Objects: Toward a Psychoanalytic Inquiry of Learning, 314, 318, 331
Broadway Babies Say Goodnight: Musicals Then and Now, 267
Brock University Senate Research Ethics Board, 41
Brodribb, Somer, 96, 106
Bronski, Michael
    Culture Clash: The Making of Gay Sensibility, 256, 263, 270
Brooks, P.
    The Least Restrictive Alternative: Principles and Practices, 277, 288

Brotman, Shari
Access to Care: Exploring the Health and Well-being of Gay, Lesbian, Bisexual and Two-Spirit People in Canada, 56, 79
Brown, H., 276, 279-80, 287
Brown, Lorne A.
Saskatchewan Politics from Left to Right '44 to '99, 136
Brown, M.
Closet Space: Geographies of Metaphor from the Body to the Globe, 235, 240
Brownridge, D., 183, 186, 190
Bryson, M., 283, 286-8
buggery, normalizing of, 149
Building Communities of Difference, 307
Building Safe and Caring Classrooms, Schools, and Communities for Lesbian, Gay, Bisexual and Transgender Students, 293, 307
bull-dyke (name-calling), 84
Bullough, Vern, 175, 178
bullying, 227, 238, 248, 268, 293, 300, 302, 305, 323
anti-gay, 4, 19-20, 22, 25, 34, 36, 153
of gender ambiguous, 82, 86-7
Bunner, Paul
Lougheed & the War with Ottawa: 1971-1981, 160
Burgoyne, Jim, 137
Burke, Peter
New Perspectives on Historical Writing, 107
Burke, Phyllis
Gender Shock: Exploding the Myths of Male & Female, 82-3, 90-1
Burke, Scott, 257, 270
Burkett, Larry, 173
Burton, Randy, 131, 136-7
Bush, George, President, 173
But I'm a Cheerleader: A Comedy of Sexual Dysfunction, 279, 286
Butler, Judith, 145, 268, 270, 312
Bodies That Matter: On the Discursive Limits of "Sex," 91-2
Feminists Theorize the Political, 81, 92, 191
Gender Trouble, 229-30, 235, 241
The Psychic Life of Power, 92
Butler, S.
Conspiracy of Silence, 183-5, 188, 190
Butler-Kisber, L., 7, 18
By Silence Betrayed: Sexual Abuse of Children in America, 183, 190
Byfield, Link, 140-2, 144, 147, 151-2, 155, 158-9
Byfield, Ted, 158

C
Cabaz, R.P.
Textbook of Homosexuality and Mental Health, 42
Cadge, Wendy, 178
Cain, Tom
Poetaster, 270
Calderwood, Brent, 66, 71
Calgary Board of Education (CBE), 144-6
Calgary Convention Centre, 144
Calgary Gay Rodeo, 236
Calgary Herald, 147-8, 161

Calgary Hitmen, 182
Calgary, University of, 146, 154, 157, 260
Calhoun, C.
Social Theory and the Politics of Identity, 233, 235, 241
Callahan, Sidney, 174, 178
Cameron, Paul, 126, 154
Campbell, N., 186, 190
Campus Crusade for Christ, 173
Canada Christian College (Toronto), 174
Canada Family Action Coalition (CFAC), 157-9, 171, 174
Canadian Alliance Party, 171, 239, 281
Canadian Charter of Rights and Freedoms, 53, 122, 124, 139, 160, 174, 193, 195, 199, 203, 214-5, 247, 232, 290-1, 296, 300, 306
role in gay and lesbian rights, 136
Canadian Conference of Catholic Bishops (CCCB), 171, 173
Canadian Hockey Association, 182
Canadian Human Rights Act (CHRA), 143, 290
Canadian Human Rights Commission, 122
Canadian Lesbian and Gay Studies Association, 240
Canadian Psychological Association, 154
Canadian Teachers' Federation (CTF)
Seeing the Rainbow: Teachers Talk About Bisexual, Gay, Lesbian, Transgender and Two-spirited Realities, 294, 306
Cannon, M., 319, 331
capitalism, growth of, 102-3
capitulation, 61
Caragata, Warren, 53, 76
Carillon, The, 123
Carlin, George
Parental Advisory: Explicit Lyrics, 169, 177-8
Carnegie Mellon University, 260
Carr-Nangle, R., 280, 288
Case, Sue-Ellen
Cruising the Performative, 256, 267, 270
Performing Feminisms: Feminist Critical Theory and Theatre, 270
Catholic Children Aid Society (Ontario), 58
Catholic Church, 110, 129, 144, 147
prohibition of homosexuality, 55
sex outside of marriage prohibited, 130
Centre: A Place for Lesbian, Gay, Bisexual, Transgender People and Their Allies, The, 275
Centre Street Church (Calgary), 145
Challenging Lesbian and Gay Inequalities in Education, 77
Chamberlain v Board of Trustees of School District No. 36 (Surrey), 193, 195-6, 198-200, 202-4, 208-9, 211-5
Chamberlain, Mr., 194, 204, 207, 209-10, 213-4
Champagne, J.
The Ethics of Marginality: A New Approach to Gay Studies, 234, 236, 239, 241, 321, 331
Chandler, Kurt
Passages of Pride: True Stories and Lesbian and Gay Teenagers, 49-50, 52-3, 63-8, 70-1, 73, 76
Changing Family, The, 78
Chapman, Terry, 133
Charter of Rights and Freedoms, *see* Canadian Charter of Rights and Freedoms

Charters, A.
  The Portable Beat Reader, 231, 235, 241
Chase, C., 31, 41
  *Queer 13: Lesbian and Gay Writers Recall
    Seventh Grade*, 41-2
chastity for gays and lesbians, 165
Chauncey, George, Jr.
  *Hidden from History: Reclaiming the Gay and
    Lesbian Past*, 106
Cheyenne, homosexuality among, 97
Child Sexual Abuse, 183, 190
children, 54, 82, 150, 153, 247
*Children of Horizons: How Gay and Lesbian Teens
  are Leading a New Way Out of the Closet*, 77
Chin, J., 32, 41
Chrétien, Jean, Prime Minister, 143, 173
Christian Broadcasting Network, 176
Christian Coalition, 173
Christian Financial Concepts, 173
Christian Heritage Party of Canada, 156
Christian organizations
  as intolerant of gays, 164
  opposing equal rights for gays and lesbians, 164,
    173
  ordaining lesbians and gays, 164, 172
  preserving tradition family concept, 164
  as right-wing, 140
  and same-sex unions, 164, 172
Christianity, 297
  and homosexuality, 148
  as oppressing homosexuality, 5, 163, 172
  oppressive of GLB youth, 58
  and sexual morality, 96
*Christianity, Social Tolerance, and Homosexuality:
  Gay People in Western Europe from the
  Beginning of the Christian Era to the Fourteenth
  Century*, 175, 177-8
Churchill, Caryl
  Cloud Nine, 260
  *Citizen Queer: Mediating Welfare and Work in
    Education and Culture*, 306
Citizens United for Responsible Education
  (CURE), 145
Citizenship and Social Class and Other Essays, 241
Clandinin, D.J., 29-30, 41
  *Narrative Inquiry: Experience and Story in
    Qualitative Research*, 7, 18, 29, 41
Clark, Joe, 239
Clarke, Paul, 218
classroom communities, inclusive, 294, 301
classroom, safer space for queer students, 255, 257,
  259-61, 265-7, 318
Clinton, William Jefferson, President, 173
closet, 319
  coming out of, *see* coming out
  remaining in, 12, 34, 36, 60, 64, 74, 240, 256,
    303, 311, 314, 320, 327
  safety of, 62, 68
*Closet Space: Geographies of Metaphor from the
  Body to the Globe*, 240
Cloud Nine, 260
Clum, John
  *Something for the Boys: Musical Theatre and
    Gay Culture*, 267, 270

Coalition for Gay Rights in Ontario (CLGRO)
  *The Ontario Human Rights Omission: A Brief
    to Members of the Ontario Legislature*, 76
  *Systems Failure: A Report on the Experiences of
    Sexual Minorities in Ontario's Health-Care
    and Social-Services Systems*, 56, 76
Coalition for Human Equality (CHE), 125-8, 131
Coalition in Support of the Family, 128-9
Cochrane, Professor Don, 218, 227
Code of Professional Conduct, of ATA, 292
Cohn, Roy, 268
Coleman, Eli, 53, 67, 76
Coleman, Gerald D.
  *Homosexuality: Catholic Teaching and Pastoral
    Practice*, 176, 178
Collecting and Interpreting Qualitative Materials,
  18
Collver, Dick, 123-4
colonialism, 319
colonization, of Indians, 85, 95, 97, 100-2, 104
Colorado for Family Values, 174
Columbia University Teacher's College, 117
Columbine High School (Colorado), 19
Combs, Bobbie, 213, 219
coming out, 6-7, 11-2, 15, 17, 31-4, 40, 46, 49, 61,
  69, 71, 74, 134, 231, 233, 248, 253, 256, 266,
  298-9, 325-6
  as bisexual, 34, 37, 39
  as defiance, 60, 70
  to doctor, 56
  to families, 53-4
  to mother, 37-8, 89
  as mother of gay offspring, 47
  to oneself, 62-3
  to parents, 25, 36-7, 66, 84, 89
*Coming Out of the Classroom Closet: Gay and
  Lesbian Students, Teachers and Curricula*, 76
*Coming Out Under Fire: The History of Gay Men
  and Women in World War Two*, 176, 178
Committee to Defend Doug Wilson, 117-8, 120,
  122, 131, 135
Committee to Protect the Family, 125
Common Curriculum (Ontario), 55
common-law partners, benefits for, 130
condemnation of GLB youth, 58, 63
*Confessions of a Rock Lobster: A Story About
  Growing Up Gay*, 77
Connelly, F.M., 29-30, 41, 324
  *Narrative Inquiry: Experience and Story in
    Qualitative Research*, 7, 18, 29, 41
conscientization (Freire), 44
Conspiracy of Silence, 183-5, 188, 190
*Conversations about Psychology and Sexual
  Orientation*, 178-9
conversion, 61
Cooper, John, 123, 136
coping mechanisms, 60-2
Coral Ridge Ministries, 173
Coray, Joseph Andrew
  *Sexual Diversity and Catholicism: Toward the
    Development a Moral Theology*, 178-80
Corpus Christi, 265
Cory, Peter, Mr. Justice, 156-7
counselling services, queer-positive, 55-6

Courage to Teach: Exploring the Inner Landscape of a Teacher's Life, The, 241

Courage to Teach: A Guide for Reflection and Renewal, The, 241

Courts in the Classroom: Education and the Charter of Rights and Freedoms, 215

covering, 61

Coward, Noel, 261

Cranston, Kevin, 57, 76

Crawford, Isaiah, 176, 178

Crewsdon, J.
　By Silence Betrayed: Sexual Abuse of Children in America, 183, 190

Crichlow, Warren
　Race, Identity and Representation in Education, 106

Criminal Code of Canada, 54, 151, 171

Crites, Tom, 146

critical consciousness (re homosexuality), 43-4, 47

Crompton, Louis
　Homosexuality & Civilization, 174, 178

cross-dressing, 146

cross-gendered occupations, 101

Crossing the Line: Violence and Sexual Assault in Canada's National Sport, 182, 185, 190

Crowley, N., 186, 191

Cruel Tears, 258

Cruikshank, Margaret
　The Gay and Lesbian Liberation Movement, 49, 76
　Cruising the Performative, 270
　Culture Clash: The Making of Gay Sensibility, 256, 270

culture, dominant, 60, 72-4

Culture and Family Institute, 167, 176

culture, gay, 73

Culture of Queers, The, 270

Curran, Charles E., 174

Current, Don, 137

curriculum
　absence of sexuality in, 317
　homosexual content in, 145-6
　inclusive and authentic, 325, 328
　on sexual differences, 312, 316, 318
　in university theatre programs, 255, 260-3, 265-7

Currie, Brian, 123-4

Currie, Fergus (Tad), 256

Curtin, Kaier
　"We Can Always Call Them Bulgarians": The Emergence of Lesbians and Gay Men on the American Stage, 270

D

Dagenais v CBC, 201

D'Angelo, Mary Rose, 175, 178

Daniels, Kevin, 265

Das Gupta, Tania, 75

dating, 34, 38, 55

D'Augelli, A.R., 30-2, 34-6, 42, 268-9
　Lesbian, Gay, and Bisexual Identities Over the Lifespan: Psychological Perspectives, 42, 324, 331

Daughters of Bilitis, 114

Davison, Gerard C., 177-8

Davison, K., 252, 254

Day, Stockwell, 150-3, 156

DCAS Mission Statement, 306

de Anza, Juan Bautista, 96

de Castell, S., 283, 286-8

De Jongh, Nicholas
　Not in Front of the Audience: Homosexuality on Stage, 256, 270

Death by Denial: Studies of Suicide in Gay and Lesbian Teenagers, 48, 57, 79, 287

DeCrescenzo, Teresa
　Helping Gay and Lesbian Youth: New Policies, New Programs, New Practice, 55, 65, 76-7, 79

Dee, Tim, 68

Degeneres, Ellen, 149

Degrassi, 317

DeLuca, K.M., 275, 287

DeLyon, H.
　Women Teachers: Issues and Experiences, 254

Denzin, N.K. (ed.)
　Collecting and Interpreting Qualitative Materials, 18

Department of Indian and Northern Affairs, 102

dependency, as reason to avoid coming out, 60, 63-4, 73

depression, of queer youth, 5-6, 14-6, 31

Detroit Red Wings, 182

Devallano, Jimmy, 187

Devine Comedy, 128

Devine, Grant
　government of, 111, 124-7, 132, 136

Devine Rule in Saskatchewan: A Decade of Hope and Hardship, 136

Dewey, J.
　Experience and Education, 30, 41-2

Di Vito, Robert A., 175, 178

Diagnostic and Statistical Manual (DSM), 56, 166

Diamond, Lisa, 30

Dick, Lyle, 133

diesel dykes (name-calling), 149

different, being, 23-4

Diller, A.
　The Gender Question in Education, 92

Dinsmore, C.
　From Surviving to Thriving: Incest, Feminism, and Recovery, 183, 190

Disabling Sexualities, 274, 282-3, 286

disabilities, students with, 274-5, 277-8

disclosure
　to family, 36
　to others, 31, 34-6, 40
　at workplace, 75
　see also coming out

discrimination, 37, 100, 200
　acts of, 243, 246
　based on sexual orientation, 46-7, 54, 175, 290
　by employers, 53
　of LGBT persons, 7, 10
　protection from, 171, 247

disgust for homosexual lifestyle, 170

Disney corporation, as promoting homosexuality, 144, 147

diversity
　education, 233
　respect for, in society, 193, 196, 198, 202, 209, 212

in schools, 247-8
Diversity Conferences of Alberta (DCAS)
DCAS Mission Statement, 291, 297, 298, 306
Diversity Day, 71, 73
Diversity, Equity, and Human Rights Committee,
     305
Dobson, Rev. James, 173, 176-7
     *Bringing Up Boys: Practical Advice and
     Encouragement for Those Shaping the Next
     Generation of Men*, 177-8
Dobinson, Cheryl, 59, 77
Doerksen, Victor, 151
Doing Feminist Research, 42
domination, 50-1, 72, 95
*Domination and the Arts of Resistance: Hidden
     Transcripts*, 79
Donnelly, Peter, 60, 72, 76-7
double life, leading, 61
Doug Wilson Award, 135
Douglas, Tommy, CCF government of, 109
Downing, M.
     *On Writing Qualitative Research: Living by
     Words*, 18
drag, 235, 252
drag balls, 73
drag, as form of escape, 73
drag, hetero, 227
drag, performing in, 26
drag scene, involvement in, 74
Drake, David, 261, 264, 270
drama, gay and lesbian, 262
Drinnan, G., 183, 185, 190
drugs,
     abuse of, 50, 228, 298
     to change sexual orientation, 56
     trafficking in, 53, 67
Druke, Mary, 105-6
Dube, Eric, 30
Duberman, Martin
     *Hidden from History: Reclaiming the Gay and
     Lesbian Past*, 106
Dubinsky, Karen
     *Improper Advances: Rape and Heterosexual
     Conflict in Ontario, 1880-1929*, 133
     *The Second Greatest Disappointment:
     Honeymooning and Tourism at Niagara Falls*,
     133
Due, Linnea
     *Joining the Tribe: Growing up Gay and Lesbian
     in the 90's*, 64-9, 71-3, 77
Duff, Lyn, 65
Duggleby, Jim, 135
Dumas, J., 161
Duplak, R., 139
     *Sexual Orientation and Canadian Law: An
     Assessment of the Law: An Assessment of the
     Law Affecting Lesbian and Gay Persons*, 161
Durby, Dennis, 50, 52, 54-9, 61-2, 67, 77
Durham Catholic District School Board, 72, 237
Dyer, Richard
     The Culture of Queers, 270
dyke (name-calling), 45, 305
Dykxhoorn, Hermina, 156-8

E
East Anglia, University of, 264
Edmonton, City of, Archives, 133
Edmonton Journal, 146, 151-61, 186
Edmonton Oil Kings, 186
Edmonton Sun, 142, 147
Edsall, Thomas B., 176
education
     antiracist, 229
     exclusionary, 309
     gender-sensitive, 91
     inclusive, 310, 312, 321, 323-4
     issues, feminist perspective on, 224
     to promote human rights, 290
     see also schools; special education
Education Law in Canada, 215
educational environment, 7-8
     inclusion and accommodation of minorities,
          197–8, 201-2, 206, 212, 214
     rights issues in, 194-6
educators, *see* teachers
Edward II, 263
Edwards, J.P.
     *Just Between Us: A Social Sexual Guide for
     Parents and Professionals With Concerns for
     Persons With Developmental Disabilities*,
     279-80, 287
*Eichmann in Jerusalem: A Report on the Banality
     of Evil*, 240
electroshock treatment, to change orientation, 56
Elementary Teachers' Federation of Ontario
     (ETFO)
     *Seeing the Rainbow: Teachers Talk About
     Bisexual, Gay, Lesbian, Transgender and Two-
     spirited Realities*, 294, 306
Elkins, T.E.
     *Just Between Us: A Social Sexual Guide for
     Parents and Professionals With Concerns for
     Persons With Developmental Disabilities*,
     279-80, 287
Ellen (sitcom), 149
Elliot, Jane, 328
Ellis, C.
     *Investigating Subjectivity: Research on Lived
     Experience*, 18
Ellis, J.W., 277, 280, 287-8
     *The Least Restrictive Alternative: Principles and
     Practices*, 288
Elwin, R.
     Asha's Mums, 215
Ely, M.
     *On Writing Qualitative Research: Living by
     Words*, 7, 18
Engles, Frederic
     *The Origin of the Family, Private Property and
     the State*, 103, 106
entertrainment industry, 256, 282
Epistemology of the Closet, 161, 226, 241, 287
Epstein, Debbie, 55, 77
     *Challenging Lesbian and Gay Inequalities in
     Education*, 76-7
     Schooling Sexualities, 7, 18, 161, 289, 306
Epstein, Jeffery, 270
Equality for Gays and Lesbians Everywhere
     (EGALE), 128

Equity in Education: Supporting Lesbian, Gay, Bisexual, Two-spirit and Transgender Students in Saskatchewan Schools, 241

Erlandson, C.
  Safe Schools: Breaking the Silence on Sexual Difference, 287

Erotic Innocence: The Culture of Child Molesting, 181-2, 188-90

eroticism, 237

Erb, Marsha, 135-6

Erwin, John, 70

escaping, 74

Eshelman, J. Ross
  The Family, 51, 77

Esterberg, Kristen, 164, 169, 174, 177-8

Ethics of Marginality: A New Approach to Gay Studies, The, 241, 331

Evangelical Fellowship of Canada, 171

Evangelical Lutheran Church of Canada, 172

Evans, John H.
  The Quiet Hand of God: Faith-based Activism and the Public Role of Mainline Protestantism, 178

exclusion, politics of, 23

Exodus International, 175, 177

Experiencing Difference, 254

Experience and Education, 42

exploitation, 59

F

Faculty of Education Response to the Task Force and Public Dialogue on the Role of the School Final Report, 228, 241

fag (name-calling), 45, 250, 258, 269, 300, 314

faggot (name-calling), 4-5, 20-1, 24-6, 86-8

faggy (name-calling), 328

Fairweather, Gordon, 122

fairy (name-calling), 24

families
  assault on, 164
  diversity of, 305
  dysfunctional, 182-5, 187-9
  father-led, 141
  interracial, 212
  mistreatment of GLB youth, 52-3
  models of, 198, 207-10, 219, 237, 325
  non-traditional, 152-3
  nuclear, heterosexual, 102
  as socially enforced relationship, 52
  struggles in, 51
  traditional, 147-8, 150, 164

Family, The, 77

Family Research Institute (Wash DC), 126, 154

family values, 129, 157, 233, 237

Farley, Margaret, 171, 177-8

fathers, abusive, 65

fathers' role, in traditional family, 150

Faye, Mike, 49, 77

Fear of a Queer Planet: Queer Politics and Social Theory, 80, 161, 287

Fejes, Fred, 58, 77

Feldman, Douglas, 57, 77

Felman, S.
  Jacques Lacan and the Adventure of Insight: Psychoanalysis in Contemporary Culture, 253-4

female sexual identity disturbance, 82

femininity, 26, 87, 90, 104, 229-30, 250-2, 312, 326

feminism, 91, 156, 164, 229, 234

feminist liberation movement, 229-30

Feminists Theorize the Political, 92, 190

Ferree, Myra Marx, 51

ferren, don, 57-8, 77

fictive spaces, *see* queerly fictive spaces

Fierstein, Harvey, 72, 261

Financial Post, 150

Finding Freedom in the Classroom: A Practical Introduction to Critical Theory, 48

Fine, M., 300, 307

Finnis, John, 174

First Nations communities, 82-3, 96, 306
  and ethnocentrism, 100
  and missionaries, 97-100, 104
  and patriarchy, 100, 102-4
  and reserve system, 100, 102
  cross-gendered behaviour in, 99, 103-4
  effect of Christianity on, 319
  effect of colonialism on, 319
  erotic relationships in, 95-6, 99
  gender hierarchy in, 103
  gender relationships, 95-6, 99, 101
  heterosexual nuclear family in, 102
  homosexual behaviour in, 99, 102
  illegitimate children in, 102-3
  institutionalized domination in, 101
  "perverse" addictions among, 96
  racist sexism in, 95
  rights of, 232
  same-sex relationships in, 102, 105
  sex/gender systems, 97, 99, 101
  sexual practices of, 97, 104
  sexual roles among, 97
  sexuality of, 85, 97-100, 313
  sexuality, regulation of, 85, 102-4
  status entitlement, 101-2
  suppression of homosexual behaviours, 100
  systems of domination in, 102, 104-5
  women excluded from status, 101-2

Flaherty, M.G.
  Investigating Subjectivity: Research on Lived Experience, 18

Focus on the Family-Canada, 171, 173-7

Fone, B.
  Homophobia: A History, 281, 287

Fonow, M., 320, 331

Font, Pedro (Jesuit), 96

Forest, Jean, 153

Forsyth, Heather, 148

Fortune and Men's Eyes, 261, 263

foster parents, homosexual, 152-4

Foster, Susan Leigh
  Cruising the Performative, 270

Fowler, Earl, 136

Foucault, Michel, 148, 231, 233
  The History of Sexuality. Vol I: An Introduction, 85, 92, 98, 106, 234, 235-6, 241
  Power/Knowledge: Selected Interviews and Other Writings 1972-1977, 161

Franklin, Stephen, 259

Fraser, Roderick, 147

freak (name-calling), 4
free speech, 207, 218
Free Your Mind: The Book for Gay, Lesbian and Bisexual Youth and Their Allies, 76
Freire, Paulo, 44, 229
Frey, Evelyn, 297
Frey, Reverend Bert, 297
Fricke, Aaron, 63, 69
    Confessions of a Rock Lobster: A Story About Growing Up Gay, 77
Frideres, James S.
    Indian and Northern Affairs Canada The Indian Act Past and Present: A Manual on Registration and Entitlement Legislation, 106
    Native People in Canada: Contemporary Conflicts, 100, 106
Friend, R.A., 7, 18
Friesen, Reverend Henry, 123, 136
From Surviving to Thriving: Incest, Feminism, and Recovery, 183, 190
From Wodehouse to Wittgenstein: Essays, 177, 179
Frye, Marilyn, 50-1, 77
    The Politics of Reality, 81, 92
Frum, Barbara, 118
Furey, Pat
    The Vatican and Homosexuality, 179
Futterman, D.
    Lesbian & Gay Youth: Care & Counseling, 7, 18

G
Gaard, Greta, 263, 270
Gard, M., 331
Garman, Bruce, 113-5
Garnets, L.D., 34, 42
gay (name-calling), 45, 300
Gay Academic Union, 121
gay activism, 293, 315
gay adoption, 159
gay agenda, 226-7, 238
Gay Alliance Toward Equality (GATE), 113-4, 122, 134
Gay Alliance of Youth, 121
Gay Almanac, The, 174, 178
Gay American History, 106
gay bars, 69, 299
gay bashing, 46, 127
gay, being, 40
    definition of, 24
    identity, 30-2, 50, 61, 70, 89, 99
    as non-choice, 9, 13
    self-identification, 31-2
    traces of, 25
gay characters (in media), 322
gay characters, in plays, 21, 25
Gay Community Centre, 114-5, 120-1, 123, 131, 134
gay community, 12, 15, 26, 38, 113
gay culture, 11, 39, 73, 259
gay educators, 29, 35, 292
gay foster parents, denied foster children, 152-5
gay jokes, 47
Gay and Lesbian Almanac, 178
Gay and Lesbian Awareness (GALA) (Edmonton), 127-8

Gay and Lesbian Liberation Movement, The, 76
gay liberation movement, 229-30
gay lifestyle, 32, 34, 67, 153, 237, 322
gay magazines, 16
gay males, 5, 11, 13, 39, 54, 150
    charter rights for, 155
    domesticated, 234
    as dropouts, 55
    heterosexual dating by, 64
    playing roles, 134
    risk behaviours of, 57
    running away from families, 65
    as sex workers, 67, 70
    sexual orientation awareness of, 30, 33
    in small-town Saskatchewan, 132-3, 137
gay marriage, 26, 44, 46, 327
gay parents, 53
gay plays, 260-4, 266, 268
gay pornography, *see* pornography
gay pride, 15, 26, 32, 45, 126, 128, 233, 293, 302
Gay Pride Parade, 239
Gay Pride Week, 114, 126
gay rights, 113, 140, 143, 150, 226
Gay Saskatchewan (or *Grassroots*), 121
gay scene, 134
gay sexual practices, 141, 145
gay social clubs, 113
Gay Students Alliance, 113
gay students, closeted, 29
gay teachers, 122-3, 135
Gay Teen: Educational Practice and Theory for Lesbian, Gay, and Bisexual Adolescents, The, 41-2, 76-80
gay theatre, 257-8, 265, 267, 269
gay world, 50
Gay World: Male Homosexuality and the Social Creation of Evil, The, 256, 270
gay youth, *see* youth, gay
Gayle-Deutsch, Alisa, 75, 77
Gay/Lesbian Almanac, 106
gays and lesbians, 133, 237
    equality for, 200-5, 211, 214, 217
    as minority group in education, 195, 204-6, 212
    protections for, 139, 144
    self-esteem of, 215, 218
    as teachers, 237
    as theatre students, 259-60, 264-5, 268
    tolerance for, 197-8, 200, 202, 208-9, 211-4, 218
gay-straight alliance, at school, 10-1
Gemini Club, 113, 134
gender
    appropriate behaviours, 150
    bias, eliminating, 81
    classification system, 90, 99, 103
    conformity, 90-1
    inequalities in 91
    issues, in theatre schools, 260
    hierarchy of, 140
    masculinist conceptions of, 164
    nonconformity in, 82-3, 90-1
    normalization of, 90
    oppression based on, 243, 245
    and sexuality, 224-5, 235, 311, 315-7, 321-2, 326

variation on, 91
gender advantage, of heterosexuals, 26
gender ambiguity, 81, 91, 169
gender assignment, 250, 252
gender differences, 74, 90-1, 290-1, 293-8
gender equity, 204
gender identity, 85, 231-3, 258, 276
Gender Identity Disorder (GID) of Childhood,
    82, 85, 90
gender roles, 224, 250-2, 319
Gender Shock: Exploding the Myths of Male &
    Female, 82, 91
gender standards, 82, 91
Gender Trouble, 241
gender-crossing, 97-9
gendered behaviour, 81, 309
gendered language, 318
gendered sexuality, 314, 316, 318
gendered tasks, 100, 103-4
Genet, Jean
    The Balcony, 260
genital altering, 90, 236
Genius, M., 153
George, Robert P., 174
George, Pamela, 238, 241
Georgia Straight, 112-3
Getting Ready for Benjamin: Preparing Teachers for
    Sexual Diversity in the Classroom, 331
Giacoletti, A., 280, 288
Gibson, G.D., 235, 241
Gibson, Paul, 45, 48, 283, 287
Gillis, C., 152, 183-4, 186, 190
Gilmartin, P.
    Rape, Incest, and Child Sexual Abuse, 183,
    185, 190
Givan, David, 215
GLB communities, 52, 54, 56, 58, 60-2, 64, 69-70,
    74
GLB persons, 53-4
GLB students, 55-6
GLB youth, *see* youth, GLB
GLB-inclusive counselling, 58
GLB-inclusive curriculum, 58
GLB-positive persons, 70
GLBT issues
    in education, 246
    in performing arts, 262-3
GLBT students
    anxieties of, 247
    discriminated against, 249-50, 253
    marginalization of, 247-9
    as oppressed minority, 248-9, 252
Glenbow Archives, 133
Glendon College, 269
Globe and Mail, 145, 183, 213, 216-7
Globe Theatre, Regina, 258-9
Glsene, C., 18
Gogo, John, 141
Gonsiorek, John
    Homosexuality: Research Implications for Public
    Policy, 176, 178-9
Guiney, J.J., 29, 42
Gonthier J, 195, 197, 199, 202-3, 215
Good News Bible, 179

Goodman, Gerre
    No Turning Back: Lesbian and Gay Liberation
    for the 80's, 53, 58, 77
Gordon, Judy, 148
Gordon, Michael, 122
Goslin, Khym, 301-2, 304
Goulding, Warren, 137
Gover, Jill, 52, 77
Goyette, Linda, 151-2, 155
Grace, André P., 7, 147-8, 289-90, 294, 297, 301,
    304, 306
    Citizen Queer: Mediating Welfare and Work in
    Education and Culture, 292, 306
Grahn, Amy, 66
Gramick
    The Vatican and Homosexuality, 179
Grassroots (or *Gay Saskatchewan*), 121
Green, Robin, 58, 77
Greene, Richard
    The "Sissy Boy Syndrome" and the Development
    of Homosexuality, 256, 270
Greenshields, Vern, 134, 136
Greer, Germaine, 229
Greschner, Carole, 129
Greschner, Donna, 137
Gretchel, Michele M., 57, 65, 77
Griffin, P.
    Teaching for Diversity and Social Justice:
    A Sourcebook, 45, 48
Grignard, Christopher, 261, 264-5, 270
Grippo, Dan, 175, 179
Grisez, Germain, 174
Gross, Larry, 58, 77
Grundy, Isabel, 147
Gruneau, Richard B.
    Popular Cultures and Political Practices, 76
Guy Game, 22

H
Hahn, L.
    The Philosophy of Hans-Georg Gadamer, 240
Haldeman, Douglas, 177, 179
Hall, Marc, 72, 199, 235, 237, 239, 285, 298
Halperin, David
    The Lesbian and Gay Studies Reader, 79, 106-7
Halpern case, 200, 216
Handbook of Child and Adolescent Sexual Problems,
    90
Hanigan, James
    Homosexuality: The Test Case for Christian
    Sexual Ethics, 175, 179
Hanna Herald, 142
Hantzis, Darlene M., 58, 77
harassment, 22-3, 37, 53, 55, 63-6, 84, 87, 252
    see also sexual harassment
Harbeck, Karen, 50, 60, 77
    Coming Out of the Classroom Closet: Gay and
    Lesbian Students, Teachers and Curricula, 76
Harding, Jennifer, 318
    Sex Acts: Practices of Femininity and
    Masculinity, 331
Hardy, Robin, 135
Harris, Simon
    Lesbian and Gay Issues in the English
    Classroom: The Importance of Being Honest,
    331

Hartman, Joyce, 45, 48
Haymes, Richard, 53, 57, 67, 78
Harvey Milk High School (New York), 66
Hasnett, Dale, 128, 129
hate, at root of homophobia, 46-7
hatred of GLB youth, 58
Havelock, Jon, 148, 156, 158
Haverstock, Lynda, 131
Hayden, Mike, 135
Hayes, Evann, 73
hazing rituals, 185
Headwig and the Angry, 298
Heatley, Stephen, 262, 269-70
Helping Gay and Lesbian Youth: New Policies,
  New Programs, New Practice, 55, 76-7, 79
Hellquist, Gens (Doug), 112, 115, 117, 120, 126,
  131–5, 137
Helmsing, Gay, 126
Henderson, M.G., 34, 36, 42
Henry, Bishop Fred (Calgary), 173
Her Tongue on my Theory, 161
Herdt, Gilbert
  Children of Horizons: How Gay and Lesbian
  Teens are Leading a New Way Out of the
  Closet, 53, 64, 66, 77
Herek, Gregory, 174, 179
  Stigma and Sexual Orientation: Understanding
  Prejudice Against Lesbians, Gay Men, and
  Bisexuals, 42
Herman, Didi
  Rights of Passage: Struggles for Lesbian and
  Gay Legal Equality, 179
hermaphrodites, 96
Heron, Ann
  Two Teenagers in Twenty: Writings by Gay and
  Lesbian Youth, 53-4, 62-4, 68- 73, 77
Hershberger, S.L., 31-2, 35-6, 42
heteronormativity, 8, 81, 226, 234, 237, 248-53,
  274, 282, 290
  assumptions of, 316-7, 319
  myths of, 274
  as socialized behaviour, 291, 313
  in society, 258, 261, 269
  in theatre programs, 255, 269
heterosexism, 7, 36, 39, 51, 53, 55, 59, 66, 96,
  100, 104, 226-7, 249-51, 280, 282, 285, 323
  in schools, 72, 289, 300
  societal, 53, 55
heterosexual
  assumptions, 34, 57, 64
  behaviour, as civilized, 96, 99, 101, 104
  dating, 64
  normativity, 230, 236
  norms, refusing to comply with, 71
  relations, dominance of, 72
  relationships, for disabled people, 280
  relationships, for lesbians and gays, 166
  sex acts, 32, 61, 99, 252, 316
  socialization, 32
  through denial, 61, 63
heterosexual couples, sexual practices of, 321
heterosexual privilege, 225-6, 311, 317-8, 323
heterosexuality, 60, 71
  appearances of, 70
  compulsory, 64, 250-2, 279, 281, 284, 315

conversion to, 169
culture of, 291, 298
institutionalized, 261
as only natural state,
as presumed, 36, 50, 262,
as privilege, 249, 251
queerly straight, 275
as superior, 250, 280, 285
Hetherington, Reverend Dick, 129
Hetrick, Emery S., 50, 52-3, 61-2, 78
Hetrick Martin Institute (New York), 68
Hidden from History: Reclaiming the Gay and
  Lesbian Past, 106
hidden transcripts, 70-1
Hierath, Ron, 148, 154
Higgins, Ross, 133
Hill Collins, Patricia, 50-1, 59-60, 74-5, 78
  Race, Class, and Gender: An Anthology, 50-1,
  60, 76-7
Hinchey, Patricia
  Finding Freedom in the Classroom: A Practical
  Introduction to Critical Theory, 43, 48
Hinrichs, Donald W., 268, 270
History of Homosexuality, The, 319, 331
History of Sexuality. Vol. I: An Introduction, The,
  92, 106, 241
HIV/AIDS, see AIDS
HIV/AIDS education programs, 57
hockey coaches, homosexual, 186
hockey players, junior, sexual abuse of, 184, 186
Hoffman, Martin
  The Gay World: Male Homosexuality and the
  Social Creation of Evil, 256, 270
Holleran, A., 31, 42
Holy Bible, King James Version, 175, 179
Home Front: Notes from the Family War Zone, 183,
  190
homo (name-calling), 4
homoerotic desires, 238
homoeroticism, in locker room, 186-7
homophobia, 7, 9, 26, 33, 39, 43-4, 46-7, 55, 66,
  72-3, 91, 226-8, 234, 282, 284-5
  acts of, 205, 213
  as abuse, 54, 57, 319, 323
  attitudes of, 315, 320, 321
  causes of, 171
  in education, 43, 46, 244–53
  internalized, 31, 35, 47, 176, 260, 268
  as irrational fear or hatred, 167, 176
  as learned behaviour, 319
  and oppression, 319
  remarks of, 45, 55, 206, 305
  rooted in Christianity, 281
  as social justice issue, 45
  in schools, 289, 297, 300, 302, 304-5, 312
  in theatre, 255-9, 264
  unconscious, 43
Homophobia: Description, Development, and
  Dynamics of Gay Bashing, 176, 179
Homophobia: A History, 287
homosexual activism,
  as undermining family, 167, 173
homosexual agenda, 148
homosexual communities, 156
homosexual curriculum, 130

…sexual, de-sexualized, 278
…osexual desire, 229
…mosexual lifestyle, 125, 203
    as choice, 169, 170
homosexual men, queer image of, 234
*Homosexual Network: Private Lives and Public
    Policy, The*, 171, 177, 180
homosexual persons, 32
    adopting children, 200, 239
    and AIDS, 147-8, 150
    behaviour of, 98, 100, 163, 165-6
    as child molesters, 211
    celebration of, 200
    closeted, 257, 268
    condonation of, 200, 217
    conscription of, 276
    discrimination of, 130
    identity, contemporary, 99
    legal status of, 115
    making effort to be heterosexual, 168
    as marginalized, 328
    in occupations dealing with children, 130
    parents of, 310
    and promiscuity, 170
    rights of, 72
    as sexually deviant, 267
    as silenced, 328
    sexual diseases of, 168
    silenced, 309
    stereotyping of, 157, 199, 211
    suicide rate of, 167
    as unpersecuted elite, 158
    violence against, 247
    as workaholics, 304
    as youth predators, 155
homosexual sex acts, 32, 61, 63, 99, 155, 170
    as against natural law, 281-2
    as disgusting, 170
    as disordered, 168, 176
    in Native North American cultures, 99
    as against religion, 194, 198-9, 201
homosexual stereotypes, 311, 315, 317-8, 322
homosexual students, 232, 311
    protection for, 195, 217
homosexual teachers, 232
    as predators, 173
    as recruiters of youth, 174
    protection for, 195, 217
homosexuality, 25, 33, 45, 47, 68, 105, 151, 154,
    237
    among Aboriginal populations, 95, 99
    and biological determinism, 168-9
    as choice, 247, 253
    Christian opposition to, 163
    condemned by religions, 58, 246
    constructs of, 226
    conversion to heterosexuality, 169
    decriminalization of, 44
    denial of, 61, 64
    as deviance, 318
    as disorder, 206
    encouragement of, 59
    as equal to heterosexuality, 173
    evils of, 152
    homophobic attitude toward, 171

    images of in media, 59
    as inherited tendencies, 176
    institutionalized, 99
    intolerance of, 247
    as lifestyle choice, 129, 151, 168, 170, 227,
        315-6
    as masked, 236
    as mental illness, 56, 166-7
    as morality issue, 202, 205, 209, 211
    in Native North American cultures, 97-9, 102
    negative social value of, 52
    as non-choice, 4
    normalization of, 156
    not encouraged for persons with mental
        retardation, 280
    as orientation, 247-8
    origins of, 168, 176-7
    overcoming it, 175
    as pathology, 225, 231, 234, 311
    as perversion, 55, 148, 159, 276, 322
    as preference, 311, 315
    prejudices surrounding, 46
    prevention and treatment of, 177
    promotion of, 277
    and religion, 247
    repression of, 61, 64
    santizing of, 234
    in schools, 55
    as shameful, 266
    silence on, 55
    as sin, 44, 225, 311
    social disadvantages of, 168, 279
    stigma of, 62
    as taboo, 171
    taught in schools, 156
    tendencies of, 130
    as weakening families, 157-9
*Homosexuality: Catholic Teaching and Pastoral
    Practice*, 176, 178
Homosexuality and Christian Faith, 175, 180
Homosexuality & Civilization, 174, 178
Homosexuality and the Politics of Truth, 156
*Homosexuality: Research Implications for Public
    Policy*, 176, 178-9
*Homosexuality: The Test Case for Christian Sexual
    Ethics*, 175, 179
Homosexuals Opposed to Pride Extremism
    (HOPE), 159
Hooker, Evelyn, 176
hooks, bell
    *Teaching to Transgress: Education as the
        Practice of Freedom*, 227, 230, 241, 306
Hopkins, Deb, 117
Hopkins, Patrick D., 176-7, 179
hormone treatments, for gender ambiguity, 85
Hosanna, 263
*House That Jill Built: A Lesbian Nation in
    Formation, The*, 133
Houston, B.
    The Gender Question in Education, 92
Houston, W., 186, 190
*How Homophobia Hurts Children: Nurturing
Diversity at Home, at School, and in the
    Community*, 18
Howlett, Albert, 186

Human Rights, Citizenship and Multiculturalism Act (Alberta), 305
human rights codes, 139
    sexual orientation included, 171
human rights legislation, 54, 205, 214, 232
    for gays and lesbians, 163, 249
human rights protections (for queer persons), 7
Human Sexuality: New Directions in American Catholic Thought, 176, 179
Hunt, Mary E., 157, 179
Hunter, Joyce
    Learning to Live: Evaluating and Treating Suicidal Teens in Community Settings, 53, 55, 57-8, 64-5, 67, 69, 78
Hutt, Peter, 268
Hutter, Mark
    The Changing Family, 60, 66, 78
hustling, 67

I
Iacobucci J, 199, 215
identity erasure, 289
Illinois State University, 256
Imperial Leather Race, Gender and Sexuality in Colonial Contest, 95, 106
Improper Advances: Rape and Heterosexual Conflict in Ontario 1880-1929, 133
Inclusive Communities Grant, 305
inclusiveness, 325
Indian Act, 85, 96, 100, 102, 319
    heterosexism in, 100-2
    legitimacy defined by, 103
    as nation building, 103-4
    patriarchy in, 100-3
    as policy, 85, 100, 102
    racism in, 100-1
    status and citizenship in, 101, 103-5
Indian Acts and Amendments 1868-1975. An Indexed Collection, 107
Indian communities, status, 95, 100
Indian and Northern Affairs Canada, 105
Indian and Northern Affairs Canada The Indian Act Past and Present: A Manual on Registration and Entitlement Legislation, 106
Indiana University, 265
Indians, *see* First Nations communities
inequality in society, 51, 60, 243-4, 246
Inge, William, 261
injustice in society, 244
inning, 268
innocence, of children and youth, 181-2, 187-9
Inside the Academy and Out: Lesbian/Gay/Queer Studies and Social Action, 178
Instinct, 322
International Christian Media, 173
International Women's Day Dance, 126
Internet, 20, 68, 171, 175
    as safe place for LGBT youth, 9, 14, 37, 39
intersexed persons, as minority, 246
Interviews: An Introduction to Qualitative Research Interviewing, 41-2
intimidation, 55
Investigating Subjectivity: Research on Lived Experience, 18
invisibility of lesbians, gays, bisexuals, 164

Invisible Children in the Society and Its Schools, 18
Iroquoian Nations, matriarchy in, 105
Isay, R.A.
    Becoming Gay: The Journey to Self-acceptance, 32, 42
    Being Homosexual: Gay Men and Their Development, 31, 42
Islam, 297
isolation, 64, 89
isolation rooms, to change sexual orientation, 56

J
Jackson, Ed, 115
Jacques Lacan and the Adventure of Insight: Psychoanalysis in Contemporary Culture, 254
James, Carol
    Experiencing Difference, 254
James, Graham, 155, 181-5, 187-8
    as homosexual, 186, 189
    as pedophile, 237
Jamieson, Kathleen, 101, 106
Jenkinson, J., 277, 287
Jennings, K.
    One Teacher in 10: Gay and Lesbian Educators Tell Their Stories, 289, 306
John, Dr. Jeffrey, 172
Johnson, Derek, 65
Johnson, Justice J., 119
Johnson, Lynn, 59
Johnson, Paul, 67, 73
Johnson, Richard, 55, 77
    Schooling Sexualities, 7, 18, 161, 289, 306
Johnsrude, Larry, 136, 154, 156-7
Johnston, Dawn Elizabeth, 133
Joining the Tribe: Growing up Gay and Lesbian in the 90's, 77
Jones, Hilary, 136
Jonson, Ben
    Poetaster, 256, 267, 270
Judaism, 297
Judicial Review Procedure Act, 194, 215
Jung, Patricia Beattie, 230
    Sexual Diversity and Catholicism: Toward the Development of a Moral Theology, 178-80
Just Between Us: A Social Sexual Guide for Parents and Professionals With Concerns for Persons With Developmental Disabilities, 287

K
Kahn, E., 280, 287
Kantor, Martin
    Homophobia: Description, Development, and Dynamics of Gay Bashing, 176, 179
Kassen, R.
    Getting Ready for Benjamin: Preparing Teachers for Sexual Diversity in the Classroom, 331
Katz, Jonathan
    Gay American History, 96, 99, 106
    Gay/Lesbian Almanac, 96, 104, 106
Kauffmann, Stanley, 267-8
Kaufman, Kate
    Free Your Mind: The Book for Gay, Lesbian and Bisexual Youth and Their Allies, 55-6, 58-9, 62-4, 66-7, 69, 71-2, 76
Kempling, Chris, 205-6, 217

Kempton, W., 280, 287
Kennedy, Rev. D. James, 173
Kennedy, Sheldon, 182, 184, 187-9, 237
Kenney, Jason, 156
Khayatt, Didi, 52, 55, 64-5, 69, 72, 78
Kielwasser, Alfred P., 58-9, 78
Kilt (play), 257
Kincaid, J.R.
    *Erotic Innocence: The Culture of Child
    Molesting*, 181-2, 188-90
King George Hotel (Saskatoon), 112
King, Nancy, R., 60, 73, 75, 78
King's College, Edmonton, 160
King's University college, 292
Kinsman, Gary
    *The Regulation of Desire: Homo and Hetero
    Sexualities*, 133, 161
    The Regulation of Desire: Sexuality in Canada,
    54, 78, 96, 105-6
Kirk, K., 280, 288
Kirkness, Verna, 105-6
Kirkpatrick, J.B., 116-7, 135
Kiss & Tell, 141-3
    Her Tongue on my Theory, 161
Kiwanis Park (Saskatoon), 112
Klein, Ralph, 139, 156-60
    government of, 151, 154
Kleinerman, Shulmit, 53, 77
Knafla, Louis A.
    *Law and Justice in a New Land: Essays in
    Western Canadian Legal History*, 133
Kolansinka, Wiesia, 121
Kolnai, Aurel
    On Disgust, 170, 177, 179
Korinek, Valerie J., 135
    *Prairie Fairies: Gay and Lesbian Community
    Formation, 1945-1980*, 133
Koski, Michael J., 50, 55, 67, 79
Kosnik, Anthony
    *Human Sexuality: New Directions in American
    Catholic Thought*, 176, 179
Kowalski, Ken, 142
Kramer, Larry, 261
    The Normal Heart, 265
Kreplin, Rev. Martin, 175
Kuklin, Susan
    *Speaking Out: Teenagers Take on Race, Sex, and
    Identity*, 71-2, 78
Kumashiro, K., 247-8, 253-4, 319, 324, 331
Kummerfield, Steven, 238
Kushner, Tony, 148, 261
Kutz, Skip, 117, 122
Kutz, Stan, 55, 78
Kvale, S.
    *Interviews: An Introduction to Qualitative
    Research Interviewing*, 41-2

L
La Fontaine, J.
    Child Sexual Abuse, 183, 190
La Forest J., 216
Lacan, Jacques, 230
Ladder (publication), 113
Lafitau, Joseph Francois, 96
LaForme J., 200

Laghi, Brian, 54, 78, 146
Lahey, K.
    *Are We Persons Yet? Law and Sexuality in
    Canada*, 7, 18
Lamer CJC, 201
Lang, Andy, 172
lang, k.d., 143
Langen, Scott, 58, 78
Langers, Susan, 121
Langevin, Paul, 157
Laramie Project, The, 263
*Law and Justice in a New Land: Essays in Western
    Canadian Legal History*, 133
Law's Desire: Sexuality and the Limits of Justice,
    161
*Learning to Live: Evaluating and Treating Suicidal
    Teens in Community Settings*, 55, 57-8, 64-5,
    67, 69, 78
*Least Restrictive Alternative: Principles and
    Practices, The*, 288
LeBel J, 203, 215
Leck, Glorianne, 52, 55, 78
Leeson, Howard A.
    Saskatchewan Politics: Into the 21st Century,
    136
*Legal Recognition of Same-Sex Partnerships: A Study
    of National, European and International Law*,
    216
Lehr, Valerie, 58, 77
Lemert, Charles
    *Social Theory: The Multicultural and Classic
    Readings*, 78
Lesbian Caucus of Saskatoon's Women's Liberation,
    121
Lesbian Gay Bi Youth Line, 50, 55, 62, 65-9, 71-3,
    75, 78
*Lesbian, Gay, and Bisexual Identities Over the
    Lifespan: Psychological Perspectives*, 42, 331
*Lesbian and Gay Issues in the English Classroom:
    The Importance of Being Honest*, 331
*Lesbian and Gay Rights in Canada: Social
    Movements and Equality Seeking, 1971-1995*,
    133, 136
Lesbian and Gay Studies Reader, The, 79, 106-7
Lesbian & Gay Youth: Care & Counseling, 18
lesbian magazines, 16
lesbian persons, 5, 11. 54, 58, 61, 70, 142-3, 154
    in films, 59
    in school, 12
    in sport, as threat to men, 149
    as sex workers, 67
lesbian porn, *see* pornography
lesbian sex acts, 141, 149
lesbian youth, *see* youth, lesbian 7, 13, 17
lesbianism, 143, 149, 154, 229
Leslie, M.B., 237, 241
Levan, Chris, 149
Levine, L., 283, 287
lezzie (name-calling), 84
LGBT persons, 224, 226, 228, 234
    as alienated, 231
    as outsiders, 231
    citizen rights for, 233
    community groups of, 233
    discrimination of, 232
    tolerance and accommodation for, 232

LGBT students, 235, 239, 320
    discrimination of, 225
    equity for, 310
    fighting homophobia, 226
    harassment of, 269
    and inclusivity, 225
    invisibility of, 324
    as out, 324, 326
    supported in public schools, 206, 217
LGBT teachers, 225, 235, 239
LGBT youth, *see* youth, LGBT
LGBTQ persons
    accommodated, 291-2, 294-5, 301, 304
    community groups of, 300
    human rights of, 291, 298, 303, 313
    protected from discrimination, 290, 296-7
    stereotypes about, 300
LGBTQ students, 304, 324
    as disenfranchised, 289, 299
    as invisible, 290-1, 301, 316
    harassed, 300
    marginalization of, 290, 297, 299
    public humiliation of, 300
    violence towards, 300
LGBTQ teachers, 289, 290, 296-7, 301
    as change agents, 304
LGBTQ youth, *see* youth, LGBTQ
LGBTQ, out of the closet, 296, 301
LGTTB persons
    caregivers of, 278, 286
    educators of, 277, 281-2
    as marginalized, 284
    with disabilities, 273–6, 278–9, 280–6
L'Heureux-Dube, MJ, 215, 289
liberalism, 223, 231, 234
Liddell, Debora L., 268-9
Lilies or the Revival of a Romantic Drama, 263
Lincoln, Y.S.
    *Collecting and Interpreting Qualitative
    Materials*, 18
Lipkin, A., 32, 42
    *Understanding Homosexuality, Changing
    Schools*, 7, 18
Lisac, Mark, 153
Listening ... Understanding Human Sexuality, 172,
    175
literature, queer-positive, 56
Little Sisters' Bookstore (Vancouver), 237
*Living the Spirit: A Gay American Indian
    Anthology*, 106
Livsey, R.
    *The Courage to Teach: A Guide for Reflection
    and Renewal*, 229, 241
Longhofer, Jeffery, 164, 169, 174, 177-8
Looking at Gay and Lesbian Life, 106
Lorde, Audre, 326
Lorraine Kimsa Theatre for Youth People (Toronto),
    257
*Lost Subjects, Contested Objects: Toward a
    Psychoanalytic Inquiry of Learning*, 331
Lougheed & the War with Ottawa: 1971-1981, 160
Lourde, Audre
    Sister Outsider, 250
Loutzenheiser, Lisa W., 262-4, 266, 270
Love, Rod, 158

*Love Won Out: How God's Love Helped Two People
    Leave Homosexuality and Find Each Other*,
    175, 179
Lowenthal, M., 31, 42
Lucas, Noelle, 133
Lukko, Rudy, 136
Lund, Ty, 157
Lund-Andersen, Ingrid, 216
Lutheran Church-Canada, 164, 172, 229
lying, to hide homosexuality, 4
Lyons, Phyllis, 114
Lysistrata, 264

M
Mabry, M., 31, 42
McCarthy, Cameron
    Race, Identity and Representation in Education,
    106
McClaren, Peter, 60, 78
McClellan, Shirley, 148, 151-2, 158
McClintock, Anne
    *Imperial Leather Race, Gender and Sexuality in
    Colonial Contest*, 95, 105-6
McClung, Mr. Justice, 155, 161
McConachie, D., 184, 190
McCoriston, Kate, 117
McCoriston, Mel, 117
McDiarmid, Marney, 133
MacDonald, Darryl, 172
MacDonald, Heather, 136
Macdonald, Therese, 137
MacDougall, Bruce, 163, 179, 216-7
    *Queer Judgments: Homosexuality, Expression
    and the Courts in Canada*, 7, 18, 161, 215-6
Macedo, Stephen, 174
McGaughy, Renee, 65
MacInnis, Allen, 257, 260, 270
McIntosh, P., 249, 254
McIntyre, D.L., 241, 333
MacKay, A. Wayne
    Education Law in Canada, 215
Mckellar, John, 159
MacKenzie, Justice, 211
McKercher, Robert, 119
MacKinnon, Janice, 152-3
    Minding the Public Purse, 136
McLachlin, CJ, 194-6, 198, 200, 202, 215, 217-8
MacLennan, Michael L.
    Grace, 263
McNally, Terrence, 261, 265
    Corpus Christi, 265
McNamee, Don, 113, 127-8, 132
McNinch, Dr. James, 190, 217, 284-5, 287
Macphail, Dr. L., 145
Mcquarrie, Sarah, 136
McRae, Don, 136
McRuer, R., 274, 287
McVety, Charles, 174
Maddoux, Marlin, 173
Main, Doug, 141, 143
Major J, 215
Makin, Kirk, 54, 78
Making of a Gay and Lesbian Movement, The, 49
Making Out: Plays by Gay Men, 262, 271
*Making Space: Merging Theory and Practice in
    Adult Education*, 306

male bonding, 21
male-bashing, 149-50
Malina, Bruce J., 175, 179
Mallon, Gary, 56-7, 78
mama's boy (name-calling), 23
manliness, 22
Manning, Preston, 149
Manem, Van, 309
Mandryk, Murray, 136
Manley-Casimir, Michael, 215
    Courts in the Classroom: Education and the
    Charter of Rights and Freedoms, 215
Marckx, Sara, 71
Marco, Tony, 174
marginalization, 60, 72, 74, 244, 249
    of gender ambiguous, 84
    of LGBT persons, 7
Marlowe, Christopher
    Dr. Faustus, 263
    Edward II, 263
marriage, 130, 216
    for same-sex couples, 163, 168, 172-3, 199,
        216, 226, 281
    heterosexual, 101, 166, 174
Marshall, Henry, Tory chair, 147
Marshall, T.H., 231
    Citizenship and Social Class and Other Essays,
        241
    Sociology at the Crossroads: Class, Citizenship
        and Social Development, 241
Marra, Kim
    Passing Performances: Queer Readings of
    Leading Players in American Theater History,
    271
Martin, A. Damien, 50, 52-3, 61-2, 78
Martin, Del, 114
Martin, Mathew, 151
Martinez, Theresa A., 60, 72, 78
Marty, D., 320, 331
masculinity, 19, 26, 104, 230, 250-2, 230, 250-2,
        258, 264, 268, 293, 312, 316, 326
    assault on, 150
    crisis in, 22
    heterosexual, 148-9, 177
masking, 224, 227, 235, 238
Massachusetts Safe Schools Program, 255
masturbation, public, 142-3
Matriarchy and the Canadian Charter:
    A Discussion Paper, 106
matrix of domination model, 59, 60, 74
Mattachine (club, New York), 113
Matthew Shepard Story, The (movie), 46
May, William E., 174
Maynard, Steven, 133
media, 58-9, 62, 110, 118, 122, 230, 238
    Christian fundamentalist, 186
    coverage of LGBTQ issues, 292
    portrayal of homosexuality, 140, 226, 311-2,
        315, 317, 234, 322, 326
Medicine Hat Citizens' Impact Coalition, 157
Meers, Erik, 270
Men's Liberation, 118
mental retardation, 279
Menzies, Peter, 153
Metamorphosis (celebration), 121-2

Methodist Church, 164
Michaels, Donna, 146
Migniuolo, F.W.
    Women Teachers: Issues and Experiences, 254
Miles, Robert
    Racism, 97, 106
Millard, Peter, 111, 115, 117, 120, 123, 125-6,
    132, 134
Millennium Approaches, 268
Miller, A.
    Thou Shalt Not Be Aware, 183, 188, 190
Miller, Jim, 135
Miller, Tim, 261
Minding the Public Purse, 136
Minois, homosexuality among, 97
minority group rights, 123
minstrelization, 61
Mirosh, Dianne, 143
Mismeasure of Desire: The Science, Theory, and
    Ethics of Sexual Orientation, The, 177, 180
misogyny, 23, 238
Mitchell, Bob, 130
Mitchell, A., 183, 186, 190
Monahan, Nicki, 52, 54-6, 63, 65-6, 71, 80
morality, Judaeo-Christian, 196
Morcos, Cory, 157
Morgan, K.
    The Gender Question in Education, 92
Morley, Sheridan, 258, 270
Morris, C., 317, 331
Morris, T., 287
Morrison, R. Bruce
    Native Peoples: The Canadian Experience, 106
Morton, Ted, 147, 157
mothers, as verbally abusive, 36
"Moving Beyond Silence": Addressing
    Homosexuality in Elementary Schools, 307
Muller, Lynne, 45, 48
multiculturalism, 148, 233
Muzzin, L.
    Reflecting Social Life: Analysis and
    Interpretation in Qualitative Research, 288
Muzzonigro, Peter Gerard, 49-50, 52, 61-2, 64, 78
Mysko, Bernadette, 126

N
Nabozny, Jamie Stuart, 71-2
Nahlbach, Dan, Professor, 112
name-calling, 4, 87, 252, 305, 323
Nangle, D., 280, 288
Nardi, Peter, 268
Narrative Inquiry: Experience and Story in
    Qualitative Research, 18, 41
Narrative Policy Analysis, 287
Nathanson, Paul, 154
National Association for Research and Therapy of
    Homosexuality (NARTH), 175, 177
National Coming Out Day (Canada), 295
National Film Board of Canada, 295, 305-6
National Foundation for Family Research and
    Education, 153
National Hockey League, 183
Native North Americans, see First Nations
    communities
Native people, see First Nations communities

Native People in Canada: Contemporary Conflicts, 106
Native Peoples: The Canadian Experience, 106
Native Women's Association of Canada
  Matriarchy and the Canadian Charter: A Discussion Paper, 105-6
Neil Richards Collection, 133-4
Nelson, Terry, 121
Neptune Theatre, 257, 268-9
Never Going Back: A History of Queer Activism in Canada, 133
New Democratic Party (NDP), 109, 111, 115, 130, 282
  advocating for gays, 122, 124, 127-8, 131, 135
New Perspectives on Historical Writing, 107
Newman, Bernie Sue, 49-50, 52, 61-2, 64, 78
Newman, L.
  Belinda's Bouquet, 215
Ng, Roxana, 95, 100, 106
Nicolosi, Joseph
  A Parent's Guide to Preventing Homosexuality, 177, 179
  Reparative Therapy of Male Homosexuality, 177,   179
Nilson, Jon, 163, 175, 179
No Turning Back: Lesbian and Gay Liberation for the 80's, 77
nomadism, 100
Nordahl, Richard, 117, 133, 135
Normal Heart, The, 265
Normalisation: The Principle of Normalisation in Human Services, 288
Norman, Ken, 124
Not in Front of the Audience: Homosexuality on Stage, 256, 270
notwithstanding clause, 156-9, 174
Nova Scotia Education Act, 215
Nussbaum, Martha
  Sex and Social Justice, 163, 179
  Sexual Orientation and Human Rights in American Religious Discourse, 178-9

O
Oakley, A., 41-2
Oberg, Lyle, 153-4
O'Brien, Mary
  The Politics of Reproduction, 103, 106
obscenity laws, 54
O'Conor, Andi, 52, 55-6, 78
Odyssey Club (Saskatoon), 114
offstage, 60, 68, 70
Oikawa, Mona
  Resist! Essays Against a Homophobic Culture, 77
Olyan, Saul
  Sexual Orientation and Human Rights in American Religious Discourse, 178-9
On Disgust, 170, 179
On the Fringe: Gays and Lesbians in Politics, 133
On Writing Qualitative Research: Living by Words, 18
One Dad, Two Dads, Brown Dad, Blue Dads, 215, 237, 328, 331
One Teacher in 10: Gay and Lesbian Educators Tell Their Stories, 306

Ontario Education Act, 196
Ontario Human Rights code, 55
Ontario Human Rights Omission: A Brief to Members of the Ontario Legislature, The, 76
Ontario Institute for Studies in Education (OISE), 227
Open Lives Safe Schools: Addressing Gay and Lesbian Issues in Education, 54, 77-8, 80
oppression, 72-3, 243, 313
  age-based, 51, 59
  escaping, 65
  forms of, 245, 247, 250
  of GLB youth, 49
  of homosexuals, 319
  institutionalized, 59
  resistance to, 69-71, 74
  in schools, 245-6
  systems of, for First Nations, 96
oral sex, 238
ordination of gay and lesbian clergy, 172
O'Reilly-Scanlon, Dr. Kathleen, 285
Orientalism, 106
Origin of the Family, Private Property and the State, The, 106
Orlando Books Collective (OBC)
  Safe and Caring Schools for Lesbian and Gay Youth: A Guide for Teachers, 294, 306
Ormsby, M., 184, 190
Orphan Muses, The, 263
Osterman, Connie, 153
ostracism, 22, 58, 252
Other Young Lives II, 55, 59, 78
Out, 322
out, being, 35, 155, 159, 259, 302, 315
  fear of, 320
  see also coming out
Out Our Way: Gay and Lesbian Life in the Country, 133
Out on Stage: Lesbian and Gay Theatre in the Twentieth Century, 271
Outlooks, 159
Overcoming Heterosexism and Homophobia, 161
Oz, 322

P
Packwood, A., 40, 42
Padgug, Robert, 98, 106
Pakulski, J., 233, 241
Palmer, P.J.
  The Courage to Teach: Exploring the Inner Landscape of a Teacher's Life, 228-9, 239–41
paranoia, of homosexual, 4
Parental Advisory: Explicit Lyrics, 177-8
parents
  gay-positive, 53
  heterosexual, 153
  homosexual, 154
  responses to child's gayness, 52
  same-sex, 194, 198, 203-4, 208, 212, 219, 305
Parents' Choice Association, 145
Parents, Families, and Friends of Lesbians and Gays (PFLAG), 295-6
Parent's Guide to Preventing Homosexuality, A, 169, 177, 179
Parents' Response (Calgary), 56

Parents Rights Association (Calgary), 157
Parr, Joy, 95, 106
Passages of Pride: True Stories and Lesbian and Gay Teenagers, 50, 76
Passing Performances: Queer Readings of Leading Players in American Theater History, 256, 268, 271
passing for straight, 61, 63, 258, 268
patriarchy, 95-6 100, 251
Patterson, C.J.
    Lesbian, Gay, and Bisexual Identities Over the Lifespan: Psychological Perspectives, 42, 324, 331
Paules, M.
    Asha's Mums, 215
Paulk, Anne and John
    Love Won Out: How God's Love Helped Two People Leave Homosexuality and Find Each Other, 175, 179
pedophile priests, 150
pedophilia, 59, 147, 157, 237
    link with homosexuality, 186
penpals, 68-9
Perestroika, 268
performing arts
    dominated by homosexuals, 256-7
    portrayal of homosexuals in, 262
    queer issues dealt with, 257, 259, 263
    straight actors in, 264
Performing Feminisms: Feminist Critical Theory and Theatre, 270
Perrotti, Jeff
    When the Drama Club is Not Enough: Lessons from the Safe Schools Program for Gay and Lesbian Students, 255, 270
persons with disabilities, 273, 283
    behaviour modification for, 280
    sexual behaviour of, 276, 280-1
    silencing of same-sex expression among, 276
Petrich, Kevin, 58, 77
Pettle, Jordan, 268-9
Phelps, Rev. Fred, 176
Philosophy of Hans-Georg Gadamer, The, 240
Philosophy and Mission Statement (YUY), 307
Piddocke, Stuart, 215
Pilkington, N.W., 31-2, 35-6, 42
Pillow, W.S.
    Working the Ruins: Feminist Poststructural Theory and Methods in Research, 8, 18
Pink, S.
    Visual Ethnography: Images, Media and Representation in Research, 17-8
Plaskow, Judith, 174
Playground, The, 266
plays, gay
    characters in, 264, 268
    gay content, 265
playwrights, homosexual, 261, 264
Plummer, Ken, 50, 56, 79
Polak, Mary, 213
police, victimization of GLB youth, 54
Politics of Reality, The, 92
Politics of Reproduction, The, 106
polygamy, 157

Ponting, J. Rick
    Arduous Journey: Canadian Indians and Decolonization, 106
Ponton, L.P.
    The Sex Lives of Teenagers: Revealing the Secret World of Adolescent Boys and Girls, 317, 331
Popular Cultures and Political Practices, 76
pornography, 25, 141, 143, 230, 237, 299, 304
Portable Beat Reader, The, 241
Portland Winter Hawks, 186
Posner, Richard A.
    Sex and Reason, 176-7, 179
Power/Knowledge: Selected Interviews and Other Writings 1972-1977, 161
Prairie Fairies: Gay and Lesbian Community Formation, 1945-1980, 133
Praud, Jocelyne, 136
prejudice, against homosexuals, 46-7
Presbyterian Church in Canada, 164, 172, 174-5, 180
Presbyterian Record, The, 175
pre-service teacher education, 291-2
    see also teacher preparation
pre-service teachers and sexual identity, 319
Price, James H., 52, 55, 79
pride colors, 16
Pride Day celebrations, 70
Pride & Prejudice: Working with Lesbian, Gay and Bisexual Youth, 18, 42, 77-80
Pride TV, 234
Pride Week, *see* Gay Pride Week
private property, 103-4
privilege, of heterosexuals, 7
Progressive Conservative Party, 124-5, 154
Prom Fight, 298
prom, high school, 55, 72, 285
Promise Keepers, 148
Pronger, B.
    The Arena of Masculinity: Sports, Homosexuality and the Meaning of Sex, 186, 190
prostitution, 53, 60, 67, 74, 149, 230, 238, 256
Protected Areas and Grounds Under the Human Rights, Citizenship and Multiculturalism Act, 306
Protestant fundamentalists, 167-9, 171, 175
Psychic Life of Power, The, 92
Psychology and Sexual Orientation: Coming to Terms, 176, 178
puberty, 24, 30-2
public school teachers, *see* teachers
public schools
    book banning in, 207
    bullying in, 227
    curricular materials in, 204-7, 210-2
    eliminating homophobia in, 206-7, 213-4, 218
    gay harassment in, 206
    gay issues in, 206
    hidden curriculum in, 274
    as inclusive, 204-5, 209-12, 232, 253
    mirroring community diversity, 197, 204
    as safe places, 206-7, 210-2, 277
    sexual harassment in, 227
    sexual minorities in, 225
    social justice model for, 228-9
    see also schools

Purdue University, 265

Q

Qualitative Research for Education: An Introduction to Theory and Methods, 48
queer (name-calling), 4, 84, 302
queer activism, 49, 275
queer, being, 26, 62, 70, 230
queer conscription, 275-7, 279, 281, 286
queer contagion, 275, 279, 281, 283
queer curriculum, 284
queer discourse, 233
queer dyke (name-calling), 85
Queer Eye for the Straight Guy, 322
Queer as Folk, 322
Queer Judgments: Homosexuality, Expression and the Courts in Canada, 18, 161, 215-6
queer persons, 27
    as artists, 258
    as children, 24, 153
    communities of, 53, 59, 69, 146, 160
    exclusion of, 7, 11, 23
    guilt of, 58
    health of, 7-8
    identity as, 274, 276
    inclusion of, 7
    as predators, 145
    rights of, 72
    as students, 227, 235, 252
    as teachers, 235
queer politics, 49
queer pride, 234
queer sexual culture, 233, 237
queer theory, 248, 269, 309, 316, 321-2
Queer 13: Lesbian and Gay Writers Recall Seventh Grade, 42
Queer Words, Queer Images: Communication and the Construction of Homosexuality, 77
queer youth, see youth, queer
queer zines, 73
Queering the Pitch: The New Gay and Lesbian Musicology, 270
queerly fictive spaces, 273–5, 277, 280-1, 283-4, 286
queerness, 238, 275-6, 278-80, 283, 285, 290-1, 305
questioning youth, see youth, questioning
Quiet Hand of God: Faith-based Activism and the Public Role of Mainline Protestantism, The, 178
Quinlivan, K., 283, 287, 289, 307
Quinton, Anthony
    From Wodehouse to Wittgenstein: Essays, 177, 179

R

Race, Class, and Gender: An Anthology, 76-7
Race, Class, Gender, and Sexuality: The Big Questions, 179
Race, Class, and Gender in the United States: An Integrated Study, 254
Race, Identity and Representation in Education, 106
racial inferiority of First Nations, 96
racial oppression, 243, 245
racism, 23, 100, 189, 238, 244, 246
Racism, 106

radical feminism, 140
radical homosexual movement, 226
Rainbow Classroom, The, 55, 57, 80
rainbow flag, 13, 15
rainbow pins, 70
Ramsey, R.
    Suicidal Behaviors in Adolescents and Adults: Research, Taxonomy and Prevention, 76
rape, 82, 84-5, 90, 189, 230, 238
Rape, Incest, and Child Sexual Abuse, 183, 185, 190
Raymond, Diane
    Looking at Gay and Lesbian Life, 104, 106
Rayside, David
    On the Fringe: Gays and Lesbians in Politics, 133
Razack, S., 238, 241, 316
Re: Assiniboine South School Division No. 3 and M.T.S., 211, 218-9
Realistic, Equal, Active for Life (REAL) Women of Canada, 174
recruiting to homosexual lifestyle, 59
Red Deer and District Museum, 133, 151-2
Red Deer, lesbians and gays in, 150
Reflecting Social Life: Analysis and Interpretation in Qualitative Research, 288
Reflective Turn: Case Studies in and on Educational Practice, The, 41
Reform party, 149
Regina *Leader Post*, 122
Regina, lesbian and gay community in, 114
Regina, University of, 123, 217, 224, 228, 236, 259, 264, 269, 285, 309
    Faculty of Education Response to the Task Force and Public Dialogue on the Role of the School Final Report, 241
Regulation of Desire: Homo and Hetero Sexualities, The, 133, 161
Regulation of Desire: Sexuality in Canada, The, 78, 106
Reiter, Reyna R.
    Toward an Anthropology of Women, 106
religion, *see* religious institutions
religious freedom, 194, 201-2, 212, 215, 217
religious fundamentalism, 236
religious institutions
    on homosexuality, 171, 226, 247
    impact on sexual behaviour, 163
    influence of on wanting to be straight, 63
    not supportive of GLB youth, 58
    supporting gay and lesbian discrimination, 163, 173
    teachings informing sexual beliefs, 246-7
religious right
    bigoted agenda of, 171, 173
    condemnation of homosexuality, 165, 167, 169-70, 175-7
    favoring sexual conversion, 169, 176
    and origins of homosexuality, 168
    taking literalist biblical interpretation, 166
Remafedi, Gary, 50, 79
    Death by Denial: Studies of Suicide in Gay and Lesbian Teenagers, 48, 57, 79, 287
Renaissance Saskatchewan, 136
reparative therapy for homosexuals, 168-9

Reparative Therapy of Male Homosexuality, 177, 179
reserve system and gendered tasks, 100-1, 103
Resist! Essays Against a Homophobic Culture, 77
resistance, 49, 59
    by queer youth, 72-3, 75
    individual, 49, 60, 62, 74
    strategies for, 74-5
    to oppression, 74
Resnick, Philip, 146
Resource for an Inclusive Community: A Teacher's Guide for and about Persons With Same Sex Attractions, A, 306
Rethinking Sexuality, 241
Reynolds, Amy L., 50, 55, 67, 79
Rich, Adrienne, 95, 104, 106, 227, 326
Richards, Neil, 117, 122-3, 132-3
Richardson, D.
    Rethinking Sexuality, 227, 230, 233, 241
Richardson, L., 7, 18
Ricketts, Wendell, 52, 57, 79
Ricouer, Paul, 223
Rights of Passage: Struggles for Lesbian and Gay Legal Equality, 179
Riordan, Michael
    Out Our Way: Gay and Lesbian Life in the Country, 133
Ringer, R. Jeffrey
    Queer Words, Queer Images: Communication and the Construction of Homosexuality, 77
Ristock, Janice L.
    Inside the Academy and Out: Lesbian/Gay/Queer Studies and Social Action, 178
Rittinger, John, 185
Rivers, Ian, 52, 55, 57, 64-5, 75, 79
Roberts, Joseph K.
    Saskatchewan Politics from Left to Right '44 to '99, 136
Roberts, H.
    Doing Feminist Research, 42
Robinson, Bishop Gene, 172
Robertson, Pat, 167, 173, 176
Robinson, L.
    Crossing the Line: Violence and Sexual Assault in Canada's National Sport, 182, 185, 190
Robinson, Svend, 125, 149, 282
Roe, E.
    Narrative Policy Analysis, 285, 287
Rogusky, Derek, 174
Role of the School: SchoolPlus: A Vision for Children and Youth, The, 288
Roman Catholic Church, 164-5, 167-8, 171, 173-4, 216-7, 229, 281, 296
    in Saskatchewan, 130
Romanow, Roy
    government of, 111, 115, 120, 123-4
Roscoe, Will
    Living the Spirit: A Gay American Indian Anthology, 97, 100, 106
Rosenberg, Pamela J., 268, 270
Ross, Becki
    The House That Jill Built: A Lesbian Nation in Formation, 133
Rothenberg, Paula S.
    Race, Class, and Gender in the United States: An Integrated Study, 254

Rotheram-Borus, M.J., 237, 241
Rowe, Bill
    Access to Care: Exploring the Health and Well-being of Gay, Lesbian, Bisexual and Two-Spirit People in Canada, 56, 79
Rubin, Gayle, 52, 54, 79, 97, 106
Rueda, Enrique
    The Homosexual Network: Private Lives and Public Policy, 163, 171, 177, 180
runaway street youth, 237
Rush, F.
    The Best Kept Secret: Sexual Abuse of Children, 183, 188, 190
Russell, Justice Anne, 160
Russell, Glenda M.
    Conversations about Psychology and Sexual Orientation, 178-9
Russell, P., 31, 42
Russow v British Columbia, 217
Ryan, Bill
    Access to Care: Exploring the Health and Well-being of Gay, Lesbian, Bisexual and Two-Spirit People in Canada, 56, 79
Ryan, C.
    Lesbian & Gay Youth: Care & Counseling, 7
Ryerson University, 259

S
sado-masochism, 237
Safe and Caring Schools for Lesbian and Gay Youth: A Guide for Teachers, 306
Safe and Caring Schools Project (SACS), 290, 292-3, 295, 297, 301
Safe Place, A., 275, 282
safe schools, 301
Safe Schools: Breaking the Silence on Sexual Difference, 206, 285, 287
Safe Schools Coalition (WA), 300, 307
safe sex, 37-8, 55, 278, 298
Said, Edward
    Orientalism, 106
Sallot, Jeff, 174
Sanders, Douglas, 101, 107
Sandhurst, Richard, 136
Sarecky, Melody, 331
Sartwell, Crispin
    Race, Class, Gender, and Sexuality: The Big Questions, 179
Saunders, P., 307
same-sex attractions, 31-2, 61-3, 160, 262, 268, 314-5, 321, 325
same-sex bonding, 315
same-sex couples, 160, 321
    benefits for, 232, 268
    civil unions of, 239
same-sex dating, 72, 317
    prom, 199
same-sex families, 208-9, 212-3, 237, 324-5
same-sex kissing, on stage, 264
same-sex marriage, 321
same-sex parents, 194, 198, 203-4, 208, 212, 301, 305
same-sex relationships, 229, 320-1, 327
    morality of, 198, 202-3
same-sex sexual expression, 54-5, 61, 95-6, 98-100

consensual, 281
silencing of, 276
same-sex unions, 281
Saskatchewan
    Aboriginal PAW in, 137
    closeted gays in, 111, 119-20, 126
    coming out in, 110, 122, 131
    course on sexual identities in, 223-5, 227, 230, 284
    employment and housing for gays and lesbians in, 109, 128-31
    gay and lesbian activism in, 109-11, 114, 118-21, 124, 131-2
    gay and lesbian communities in, 109-12, 119, 122, 124, 126, 128, 132
    gay discrimination in, 111-2, 114-5, 119-20, 123, 126
    gay liberation in, 122, 128
    gay pride in, 119-20
    homophobia in, 111, 125-7, 129, 131, 225
    homosexuality in, 109-11, 114, 118, 124, 131, 225
    human rights issues in, 120-1, 123-4, 126-7, 129, 131-2
    human rights legislation for gays and lesbians, 109-11, 115, 117-8, 120, 122-4, 127-31
    isolation and invisibility of gays and lesbians in, 110, 131
    media coverage in, 111-2, 118, 126-9, 131
    organized religion in, 110-1, 129, 132, 229
    protection for in, 118-23, 126-7, 130, 132
    public education on gay issues in, 110-12, 114, 121, 131-2
    racism in, 225
    treatment of gays and lesbians in, 110-1, 118, 125-6, 128-9
Saskatchewan Archives Board (SAB), 133-4
Saskatchewan Arts Board, 233
Saskatchewan Association of Human Rights, 118, 120-1, 126
Saskatchewan Bill of Rights, 110
Saskatchewan Board of Human Rights Association, 115
Saskatchewan Christian beliefs used to discriminate against gays, 126, 132
Saskatchewan Gay Coalition (SGC), 121-3, 128, 131
Saskatchewan Human Rights Code Act, 109, 124, 129
Saskatchewan Human Rights Commission, 109, 115, 118, 120, 124, 126, 129
Saskatchewan Instructional Development & Research Unit (SIDRU)
    The Role of the School: SchoolPlus: A Vision for Children and Youth, 288
Saskatchewan Learning, 226
Saskatchewan Politics from Left to Right '44 to '99, 136
Saskatchewan Politics: Into the 21st Century, 136
Saskatchewan Teachers' Federation (STF), 206, 285
    Equity in Education: Supporting Lesbian, Gay, Bisexual, Two-spirit and Transgender Students in Saskatchewan Schools, 241
Saskatchewan, University of, 111-3, 116, 124, 133, 135, 206, 218, 227, 284

College of Education Conference, 135
Educational Students' Union, 117
gay and lesbian leadership at, 135
gay faculty at, 135
gay movement at, 116-8, 131
Student Union, 117, 135
Saskatoon
    discrimination and oppression of gays in, 114
    feminist activism in, 116
    gay and lesbian community in, 112, 115
    gay liberation in, 116
    gay pride in, 115-6, 121
Saskatoon Alliance Against Racism, 118
Saskatoon Gay Action (SGA), 113-6
Saskatoon Gay Community Centre, 116, 118, 120
Saskatoon Gay Liberation, 112
Saskatoon Women's Centre, 116, 118
Savin-Williams, R.C., 30-2, 35, 42
    And Then I Became Gay: Youth Men's Stories, 30-2, 35-6, 42
Scanlan, Dick
    Thoroughly Modern Millie, 260
Schacherl, Eva, 135
Schaecher, Robert
    Learning to Live: Evaluating and Treating Suicidal Teens in Community Settings, 55, 57-8, 64-5, 67, 69, 78
Schanke, Robert A.
    Passing Performances: Queer Readings of Leading Players in American Theater History, 262, 268, 271
Schlager, Neil
    Gay and Lesbian Almanac, 178
Schmeiser Commission, 118-9
Schmeiser, Douglas A., 118, 215
Schmidt, Grant, 125-6, 132
Schmierer, Don, 167
Schnarch, Brian, 99, 107
Schneider, Margaret S., 34, 42, 50, 52, 54-9, 61-2, 65-7, 70, 79-80
    Pride & Prejudice: Working with Lesbian, Gay and Bisexual Youth, 7, 18, 42, 77-80
Schon, D.
    The Reflective Turn: Case Studies in and on Educational Practice, 41
school boards, 290, 321
    decisions, based on secularism and non-discrimination, 195-201, 203, 217
school, coming out in, 29-30, 35, 71
    see also coming out
school curriculum
    gay stereotypes in, 249
    heterosexism in, 55, 245, 248, 252-3
    on homosexuality, 55-6
    producing inequality, 244, 253
school environment, *see* schools
schooling and sexual identity, 227, 233, 309-10, 312-3
schooling and sexual minorities, 239
Schooling Sexualities, 18, 161, 306
schools
    as bastions of GLBT hatred, 289
    as communities of difference, 55, 301
    dropping out of, 65-7
    equality of sexual orientation in, 246

faltering of, 10-1, 14
gay in, 29-30, 35
harassment at, 55-6
heterosexism in, 73, 291
homophobia in, 36, 290-1
homosexuals in, 12, 56
oppressive to gays, 34, 55, 245
safe and inclusive, 36, 45, 47, 55-6, 68, 71,
    225-6, 228
as violent sites, 23, 26, 54, 300-1, 304, 327
see also public schools
Scott, Bob, 152
Scott, James, 191
    Domination and the Arts of Resistance: Hidden
        Transcripts, 49, 51, 60, 63, 68, 70, 73-4, 79
    Feminists Theorize the Political, 92, 191
Scotti, J., 280, 287-8
Sears, J.
    Overcoming Heterosexism and Homophobia,
        161
    Sexuality and the Curriculum: The Politics and
        Practices of Sexuality Education, 331
Second Greatest Disappointment: Honeymooning
    and Tourism at Niagara Falls, The, 133
secularism, in school board decisions, 195-8, 202-3
Sedgwick, Eve K.
    Epistemology of the Closet, 161, 226, 241,
        276-7, 284, 287
    Tendencies, 82, 92, 183, 191
Seeing the Rainbow: Teachers Talk About Bisexual,
    Gay, Lesbian, Transgender and Two-spirited
    Realities, 294, 306
Sekulow, Jay, 173
self-denial, of homosexual feelings, 62-4
self-destructive thoughts, 31
self-esteem and gay identity, 32, 36, 40
self-preservation, 64
Semchuk, Maureen, 123, 136
Service, Dr. John, 154
700 Club, The, 167, 173
sex
    addiction to, 14
    desire for, 253, 326
    education in, 55, 237, 280
    expression of, 54
    selling, for survival, 67
Sex Acts: Practices of Femininity and Masculinity,
    331
sex differences, 290-1, 293-8
Sex Lives of Teenagers: Revealing the Secret World of
    Adolescent Boys and Girls, The, 331
Sex and Reason, 176-7, 179
Sex and Social Justice, 179
Sex and State History Conference (Toronto, 1985),
    133
sex work
    as control over life, 67-8
    as entry to GLB world, 70
    as escape, 74
    to explore sexuality, 67-8
sexism, 26, 226, 244, 246, 250-2
sex-role stereotyping, 134
sexual abuse
    of children and youth, 181, 185
    in dysfunctional families, 182-5, 187

prevention of, 275
silence during, 188
of women and female children, 150
    see also abuse
sexual behaviour, 32, 85, 226-7, 237-8
sexual categories, First Nations, 95
Sexual Citizen: Queer Politics and Beyond, The, 240
sexual citizenship, 227, 229, 234, 239
sexual configurations, aberrant, 155
sexual differences, 311, 325
sexual diversity, 96, 226, 318, 325
Sexual Diversity and Catholicism: Toward the
    Development of a Moral Theology, 178-80
sexual division of labour, 100, 103-4
sexual harassment, 55, 227, 312
    see also harassment
sexual identity, 33, 61, 233, 236-8, 240, 251, 320,
    323, 328
    ambiguous, 293
    formation of, 30, 63, 226, 230-1, 311-2, 314,
        316
    of GLB youth, 75
    as portrayed in plays, 262
    questioning, 259, 265
    of students with developmental disabilities, 278
    see also sexual orientation; sexuality
sexual liberation, 315
sexual minorities, 139, 143, 160
    a course on, 238-9
    as different, 237
    history of, 105
    inclusion of, 315
    positionality of, 311, 323-4
    rights of, 232
    in schools, 225, 246-8, 253, 318
    treatment of, 153, 155
sexual orientation, 16, 231-2, 236, 238, 240, 275,
    277, 284, 290, 316, 320-1, 326-7
    attempt to change, 65
    awareness of, 31, 39
    changing, 52, 56
    discrimination based on, 46-7, 54
    dismissed for, 292
    equality in, 193-4, 199-203, 206
    freedom in, 199-201, 203, 211
    and gender identity, 90, 258, 263
    as lifestyle choice, 169
    oppression based on, 45, 243, 245-7, 251
    protected by human rights legislation, 7, 54
    same-sex, 32, 35
    in schools, 246, 248, 251
    of youth, 31, 35-6, 39
    see also sexual identity; sexuality
Sexual Orientation and Canadian Law: An
    Assessment of the Law Affecting Lesbian and
    Gay Persons, 161
Sexual Orientation and Gender Identity. A
    Professional Development Website for Alberta
    Teachers, 307
Sexual Orientation and Human Rights in American
    Religious Discourse, 178-9
sexuality, 10, 55, 81-2, 98, 318
    concealed, 62-3, 69, 230
    of First Nations, 85, 97
    regulation of, 95

in schools, 321
   societal attitudes towards, 30
   under parental control, 52
   see also sexual identity; sexual orientation
Sexuality and the Curriculum: The Politics and Practices of Sexuality Education, 331
Sexuality and Its Discontents, 241
sexuality scale, 280
sexualized behaviour, 309, 317
sexually transmitted diseases, 313, 317
Shadowbox, 269
shame, avoiding, 63
Sharpe, Jim, 106-7
Shaw, Brian, 186
Sheaf, The, 114, 116-8, 120
Sheane, Jo Lynn, 137
Sheared, V.
   Making Space: Merging Theory and Practice in Adult Education, 306
Sheldon, Rev. Louis, 173
shelter services, 57
Shepard, Matthew, 8, 303
Sheridan, Peter M., 57, 79
Shields, C., 40, 42
Ship's Company Theatre, 257
showing, of gay male, 87-9
Shrage, Laurie
   Race, Class, Gender, and Sexuality: The Big Questions, 179
Signorile, Michelangelo, 49, 52-3, 56, 59, 65, 70-2, 79
Sikes, P., 40, 42
silence, 62, 246, 252, 276
   breaking the, 238, 240, 325
Sillars, Les, 56, 79, 149-50, 186, 191
Silverman, Patty, 176
Silversides, A.
   AIDS Activist: Michael Lynch and the Politics of Community, 227, 241
Simmons, S., 187, 191
Simons, Paula, 160
Simpson, Kari, 150, 159
Sinfield, Alan
   Out on Stage: Lesbian and Gay Theatre in the Twentieth Century, 271
Singerline, Hugh, 59, 79
single mothers, 148, 150
Sioux, homosexuality among, 97
Sissel, P.A.
   Making Space: Merging Theory and Practice in Adult Education, 306
sissy (name-calling), 90, 250
sissy boy (name-calling), 4
"Sissy Boy Syndrome" and the Development of Homosexuality, The, 256, 270
sissy-fag queer (name-calling), 86, 90
Sister Outsider, 250
situational homosexual, 58
60 Minutes, interview, 268
Skutch, Robert, 213, 219
Slack, B., 287
Slights, Bill, 117
Smart Dating, 275, 277
Smith, Annie, 158
Smith, G., 285, 288

Smith, Miriam
   Lesbian and Gay Rights in Canada: Social Movements and Equality Seeking, 1971-1995, 133, 135
social justice, 231, 239, 246, 294, 297, 299, 316, 320, 328
Social Sciences and Humanities Research Council of Canada (SSHRC), 285
social services, 56
Social Theory: The Multicultural and Classic Readings, 78
Social Theory and the Politics of Identity, 241
Society of Friends, 171, 229
Society and the Healthy Homosexual, 167, 176, 180
society, heterosexist institutions in, 54, 64
Sociology at the Crossroads: Class, Citizenship and Social Development, 241
sodomy, 96-100, 104, 129, 143, 149, 151, 233, 237, 256, 267
Somers, M.R., 235, 241
Something for the Boys: Musical Theatre and Gay Culture, 270
Sondheim, Stephen, 261
Southern Baptist Convention, 164, 173
Southwest Missouri State University, 265
Speaking Out: Teenagers Take on Race, Sex, and Identity, 78
Spear, Peter, 186
Special Council Committee Concerning Discrimination on Sexual Orientation, 118
special education, 274, 277
   curriculum, LGTTB issues in, 283, 284
   educators of, 285
   myths in, 273, 285-6
   see also education; schools
Spector, M., 186-8, 191
Spencer, C.
   The History of Homosexuality, 319, 331
Spencer, Larry, 281-2
spirituality and homosexuality, 226
spousal benefits, for gays and lesbians, 144, 164
SSRN, *see* Sunnyhill Sexual Resource Network
St. Andrew's Church (NB), 175
St. Andrews Presbyterian Church (Que), 172
St. Pierre, E.A.
   Working the Ruins: Feminist Poststructural heory and Methods in Research, 8, 18
Stafford, Gladys, 112
Star Phoenix, 114-6, 122, 125, 130-1
status (Indian), entitlement to, 101
Stein, Edward
   The Mismeasure of Desire: The Science, Theory, and Ethics of Sexual Orientation, 177, 180
Stein, J.A., 237, 241
Stein, T.S.
   Law's Desire: Sexuality and the Limits of Justice, 161
   Textbook of Homosexuality and Mental Health, 42
Steinem, Gloria, 229
Stephenson, Carol A., 217
stereotypes, 17, 26, 58, 62
Stewart, Susan, 142
Steyn, Mark
   Broadway Babies Say Goodnight: Musicals Then and Now, 267-8

Stigma and Sexual Orientation: Understanding Prejudice Against Lesbians, Gay Men, and Bisexuals, 42
Stobbe, Mark
  Devine Rule in Saskatchewan: A Decade of Hope and Hardship, 136
Stock, C., 186, 191
Stockland, Peter, 147-8
straight youth, *see* youth, straight
Strasser, Mark, 174
street kids, GLB, 57
Streetcar Named Desire, A, 263
stress, reduced by disclosure, 36
Strommen, Erik, F., 52, 79
student teachers, *see* teacher preparation
Stychin, C., 139
Style, E., 331
Suicidal Behaviors in Adolescents and Adults: Research, Taxonomy and Prevention, 76
suicide, 5, 16, 69, 237
  attempts, 84, 85, 90, 149
  prevention for GLB youth, 57
Sullivan, Terrence, 50, 57, 59, 61-2, 64-5, 67, 79
Sunnyhill Sexual Resource Network (SSRN), 275, 277-9, 286
Supreme Court of Canada, 7, 139, 151, 156, 161, 171, 199-200, 204, 207-10, 213-4, 218, 232, 237, 292
surgery, gender altering, 85, 90
Surrey School Board (BC), 194, 197, 198, 204, 207-10, 212-3, 218, 237, 328
Surrey Teachers' Association (STA), 214, 289
  "Moving Beyond Silence": Addressing Homosexuality in Elementary Schools, 307
survival, acts of, 49
Sussel, Terri A.
  Courts in the Classroom: Education and the Charter of Rights and Freedoms, 215
Swenson, John, 64, 68
Swift Current
  as dysfunctional family, 181, 185, 187-9
  hockey sex scandal in, 181-2, 184-5, 187-9
  media coverage of hockey scandal, 181-7
  queer youth in, 181
Swift Current Broncos Junior Hockey team, 181-4, 186-8
Systems Failure: A Report on the Experiences of Sexual Minorities in Ontario's Health-Care and Social-Services Systems, 76

T
Tadei, K., 288
tattooing, 236
Taylor, Catherine G.
Taylor, Lorne, 148
Taylor, Marg, 121
Taylor, Nancy, 52, 59, 79
  Inside the Academy and Out: Lesbian/Gay/Queer Studies and Social Action, 178
teacher education programs, *see* teacher preparation
teacher preparation, 235, 251
  curriculum for, 297-8
  LGBTQ issues in, 223, 226-7, 232, 235, 239-40, 293, 295
  programs, 223, 226-7, 236-7, 239-40, 283

sexual orientation covered in, 296, 309, 320
  see also pre-service teacher education
teacher professional organizations, 205
teachers, 155, 223, 228, 236-7, 239, 243, 291, 300-1
  academic freedom of, 207-10, 218, 247, 249, 265
  as advocates, 207-10, 214, 246, 310, 318-9
  as role models, 219, 228, 303, 322
  disclosing sexual orientation, 210-1, 218, 228-9
  gay and lesbian, 39, 210-1, 225, 227-8, 233, 249, 251
  GLB, hiding their sexual orientation, 55, 261
  out-gay, 261, 267, 311, 313
  professional development for, 56
  of special education, 274
Teaching for Diversity and Social Justice: A Sourcebook, 48
Teaching to Transgress: Education as the Practice of Freedom, 241, 306
Telljohann, Susan K., 52, 55, 79
Tendencies, 92, 183, 191
Ternowetsky, Alex, 238
Textbook of Homosexuality and Mental Health, 42
Theatre New Brunswick, 257
theatre schools
  curriculum in, 260, 265-7
  homophobia in, 259-61, 264, 267, 269
  queer faculty in, 260-2, 264-5, 267, 269
  queer students in, 263-7
  as safe for homosexuals, 256, 259-60, 262, 268
  sexual deviants in, 256, 267
  stereotypes about homosexuals in, 255-7, 268
Thomas, Gary C.
  Queering the Pitch: The New Gay and Lesbian Musicology, 270
Thompson, Don, 135, 278, 288
Thompson, S. Anthony, 284-8
  Disabling Sexualities, 274
Thoroughly Modern Millie, 260
Thou Shalt Not Be Aware, 183, 188, 190
Three Books Resolution, 193-4
Three Sisters, The, 264
Tierney, W.G.
  Academic Outlaws: LGBTQ Theory and Cultural Studies in the Academy, 290, 307
  Building Communities of Difference, 295, 301, 307
Tinker v Des Moines Independent Community School District, 218
Todd, J., 185-6, 191
tokenism, 247, 263
Tomb with a View, 269
Torch Song Trilogy, 72
Toronto Board of Education, 66
Toronto, Church Street, 235
Totten, M., 284, 287
Toward an Anthropology of Women, 106
Town, S., 283, 287, 289, 307
Trainor, J.R., 139
  Sexual Orientation and Canadian Law: An Assessment of the Law: An Assessment of the Law Affecting Lesbian and Gay Persons, 161
transgendered persons, 160, 238, 246-7, 273, 286
  in traditional Aboriginal cultures, 319
  see also youth, transgender

transsexual persons, 160, 238, 240
Travers, Robb, 50, 52, 55-9, 63, 65-6, 71, 79-80
Tremblay, Michel
  Hosanna, 263
Tremblay, P., 50, 76, 237, 240
Tremble, Bob, 53, 65, 67, 80
Triana, Cristina L.H., 180
Triangle Program (Toronto), 66
Trinity Western University (TWU), 205
  TWU v British Columbia College of Teachers, 205, 217
Trouble With Normal: Postwar Youth and the Making of Heterosexuality, The, 133, 161
Trudeau, Pierre, 44, 229
True Inversions, 141-3
Turnbull, R.
  The Least Restrictive Alternative: Principles and Practices, 277, 288
twilight zone, 113
Two Teenagers in Twenty: Writings by Gay and Lesbian Youth, 77
two-gender, one-sexuality system, 82
two-spirited people, 100, 105, 160, 226, 240, 273
  in traditional Aboriginal cultures, 319
Tymchak, M.
  The Role of the School: SchoolPlus: A Vision for Children and Youth, 284, 288

U
Ujcich, K., 280, 288
Understanding Anti-Gay Harassment and Violence in Schools, 300
Understanding Difference Differently: Sex-and-ender OUTlaws in Alberta Schools, 18
Understanding Homosexuality, Changing Schools, 18
Unitarian Centre (Saskatoon), 113, 115
Unitarian Church, 171
United Church of Canada, 44, 129-30, 149, 171-2, 229, 297, 314
  gay and lesbian clergy in, 130
  Saskatchewan Conference, 110, 130, 136
United Methodist Church, 173
  General Conference (2004), 172
Universal Catholic Catechism, 130
University of Saskatchewan Archives (USA), 133-4
University of Saskatchewan Homophile Association (Regina), 114
Unks, Gerald, 50, 54-5, 59, 65, 80
  The Gay Teen: Educational Practice and Theory for Lesbian, Gay, and Bisexual Adolescents, 41-2, 50, 76-80
Uribe, Virginia, 52, 55-6, 63, 80

V
vaginal sex, age of consent for, 54
Vancouver Sun, 122
Vancouver, West End, 235
Varga, Judy, 117, 135
Vaid, Urvashi
  Virtual Equality: The Mainstreaming of Gay and Lesbian Liberation, 49, 80
Valentine, J.
  One Dad, Two Dads, Brown Dad, Blue Dads, 215, 331

Vanstone, R., 186, 191
Vatican and Homosexuality, The, 179
Venne, Sharon Helen
  Indian Acts and Amendments 1868-1975. An Indexed Collection, 101, 105, 107
Verraros, Jim, 271
Vicinus, Martha
  Hidden from History: Reclaiming the Gay and Lesbian Past, 106
Victorious Women of Canada, 126
Vinz, R.
  On Writing Qualitative Research: Living by Words, 18
Violato, Claudio, 154
violence, 23
  on effeminate persons, 22
  escaping, 65
  on homosexuals, 36, 247, 252, 269
  at school, 64
  threats of, 25, 55
Violence Free Schools Policy (Ontario), 55
Virtual Equality: The Mainstreaming of Gay and Lesbian Liberation, 80
Visano, Livy, 75
Visual Ethnography: Images, Media and Representation in Research, 18
Vittiberga, G., 280, 288
Vriend, Delwin, 143, 155-8, 160-1, 292
  Vriend v. Alberta, 151, 155-9, 161, 292, 305

W
W5 (CTV), 118
Waldo, Craig R., 265, 269, 271
Wallace, Robert, 260, 263, 269
  Making Out: Plays by Gay Men, 262, 266, 271
Walling, Donovan R.
  Open Lives Safe Schools: Addressing Gay and Lesbian Issues in Education, 54, 59, 77-8, 80
Walter Phillips Gallery, 141
Wappel, Tom, 226, 241
Warner, Michael
  Fear of a Queer Planet: Queer Politics and Social Theory, 75, 80, 161, 287
Warner, Tom, 112, 120, 133-4
  Never Going Back: A History of Queer Activism in Canada, 133
Warnock, John W.
  Saskatchewan Politics from Left to Right '44 to '99, 136
Watson Witness, 142
"We Can Always Call Them Bulgarians": The Emergence of Lesbians and Gay Men on the American Stage, 270
Weeks, J.
  Sexuality and Its Discontents, 239, 241
Weinberg, George H.
  Society and the Healthy Homosexual, 167, 176, 180
Weinrich, James D.
  Homosexuality: Research Implications for Public Policy, 178-9
Weigle, K., 280, 288
Weis, L., 300, 307
Wellesley Centers for Women SEED Project on Inclusive Curriculum, 331

Wellness Disability Initiative (WDI), 276, 286
Wells, Kris, 289, 299, 301-2, 305-6
    Building Safe and Caring Classrooms, Schools, and Communities for Lesbian, Gay, Bisexual and Transgender Students, 293-4, 307
    Sexual Orientation and Gender Identity. A Professional Development Website for Alberta Teachers, 307
    Understanding Difference Differently: Sex-and-Gender OUTlaws in Alberta Schools, 7-8, 18
West-Central Crossroads, 142
Western (BC Report), 140
Western Hockey League, 187
Westheimer, Kim
    When the Drama Club is Not Enough: Lessons from the Safe Schools Program for Gay and Lesbian Students, 255, 270
What We Wish We Had Known, 177, 180
Whelan, Ed, 122
When the Drama Club is Not Enough: Lessons from the Safe Schools Program for Gay and Lesbian Students, 255, 270
White, Bob, 258, 268, 271
White, Leland, 175, 180
white privilege, 233, 249, 315, 320
Whitehead, Harriet, 95, 97-9, 107
Who's in a Family, 213
Wicca, 297
Wieder, Judy, 255, 271
Wieler, D.
    Bad Boy, 325, 331
Wilde, Oscar, 258, 267
Wildmon, Rev. Donald, 173
Wilkerson, A.L., 274, 287
Will and Grace, 322
Williams, Tennessee, 261
    A Streetcar Named Desire, 263
Williams, W.
    Overcoming Heterosexism and Homophobia, 161
Wilson, C. Roderick
    Native Peoples: The Canadian Experience, 106
Wilson, Doug, 115, 118-22, 132
    case of, 111, 114, 116-8, 120, 131-3, 135
Wilson, Lanford, 261
Wink, Walter
    Homosexuality and Christian Faith, 175, 180
Wintemute, Robert
    Legal Recognition of Same-Sex Partnerships: A Study of National, European and International Law, 216
Winters, Tom, 72
Wishlow, Kevin, 137
withdrawal from society, as strategy, 63
Wolf, Michelle A., 58-9, 78
Wolfensberger, W.
    Normalisation: The Principle of Normalisation in Human Services, 273, 277, 285, 288
women, 103, 148, 150,
women's movement, 164
Women's Movement Archives (Ottawa), 133
Women Teachers: Issues and Experiences, 254
Wood, Elizabeth
    Queering the Pitch: The New Gay and Lesbian Musicology, 270

Wood, Roderick J., 215
Woodward, Joe, 56, 80
Working the Ruins: Feminist Poststructural Theory and Methods in Research, 18
Wuthnow, Robert
    The Quiet Hand of God: Faith-based Activism and the Public Role of Mainline Protestantism, 178
Wyatt, Mark, 137
Wyman, Ted, 137

X
xenophobia, 300, 312

Y
Yalden, Max, 143
Yogis, J., 139
    Sexual Orientation and Canadian Law: An Assessment of the Law: An Assessment of the Law Affecting Lesbian and Gay Persons, 161
York University, 227, 263, 266, 269
Young, Kevin, 59-60, 72, 76-7
Youth Understanding Youth (YUY), 14, 291, 298-300, 307
Youth Voices, 69, 73
youth, 75
    Aboriginal, gender ambiguous, 81
    coming out of, 49
    gender nonconforming, 35
youth, bisexual, 7, 17, 52, 74-5
    as dropouts, 55
    running away from families, 65
    self-identifying, 32
youth, gay, 7, 17, 45, 49, 52, 75, 276
    abuse of, 10
    aware of same-sex attractions, 31
    career choices for, 40
    dating to prove heterosexuality, 31
    denial of, 31
    diversity of, 30
    as racial minority, 32
    self-hatred by, 31
    sexually active, 32
youth, GLB, 49, 53, 57-8, 61-2, 65, 69-70, 181
    in abusive homes, 53-4
    coping mechanisms for, 50, 60
    dropping out of school, 50
    in employment, 53, 56
    hiding sexuality, 53, 63
    inclusivity for, 57, 59
    inequality of, 51, 54
    isolation of, 58, 74
    legalized dependence of, 52
    as oppressed group, 49-51, 53, 60, 65, 72-5
    out, 53, 71
    as runaways, 50, 53, 67, 75
    as sex workers, 50, 53, 68
    as sexual minority, 31-2, 34, 36, 43, 46, 57
    suicides of, 50
    survival by, 49-51, 66, 72
    as throwaways, 53, 67
    two-spirited, 75
youth, homes of
    as homophobic sites, 36
    as safe places, 36-7

youth, lesbian, 7, 13, 17, 52, 57
    becoming pregnant, 64
    disguising sexuality, 64
    in gay bars, 69-70
youth, LGBT
    as drop-outs, 228
    as runaways, 228
    at risk, 228
    identity development of, 311
    suicide rates of, 228
youth, LGBTQ, 291, 295-7, 299-300, 305-6
    closeted, 305
    isolated in schools, 298
    self-esteem of, 299
    suicides by, 295, 301
youth, queer, 7-8, 23, 50-1, 54, 57, 59-61, 66, 69,
      147, 160, 228
    coming out, 8
    gender ambiguity in, 81
    hiding, 12
    inequality of, 52, 54
    as invisible in school, 10
    isolation of, 68, 70
    marginalized identities, 8, 52
    mistreatment by families, 52
    quality of life of, 69
    resisting oppression, 71-2, 74
    self-discovery, 16, 30, 35
    self-esteem of, 14, 32
    self-identity of, 30-1, 35, 57
    violence towards, 8
youth, questioning, 75, 147, 160, 298
youth, straight, 17, 19, 24, 30, 38
    pretending to be, 25, 64
youth, transgender, 7, 17, 75

Z
Zack, Naomi
    Race, Class, Gender, and Sexuality: The Big
      Questions, 179
Zamboni, Brian D., 176, 178
Zaretsky, E., 230, 235, 241
Zepp, Norman, 117, 134
Zodiac Friendship Society (ZFS), 113-5, 118, 120,
      128, 134

Contributors

MARTIN CANNON is Assistant Professor of Sociology at the University of Saskatchewan. He is a status Indian from the Oneida Nation (Turtle Clan) of the Six Nations Reserve, and the descendant of a woman who lost and later acquired status under the Indian Act. In July 2002, he was appointed program coordinator for the Aboriginal Peoples and Justice Program in Sociology, and has played an active role in developing with colleagues four new Indigenous Knowledge courses. His current research and methodological interests focus on Bill C-31: An Act to Amend the Indian Act, the history of patriarchal and colonial injustice, and the way this has shaped the identity of Aboriginal peoples, including those of mixed ethno-cultural heritage.

PAUL T. CLARKE is an Associate Professor of Education at the University of Regina. He teaches in the area of educational administration at both the undergraduate and graduate levels. His research focuses on the human and constitutional rights of teachers.

DONALD COCHRANE is the Head of the Department of Educational Foundations at the University of Saskatchewan. His research interests centre around the intersection of ethics and education. He teaches a graduate class entitled "Education, Wisdom, and Nature" and a fourth-year elective entitled "Gay and Lesbian Issues in Education." For eight years, he has organized the university's "Breaking the Silence: Facing Issues of Sexual Orientation and Gender Identity." He has co-edited *The Domain of Moral Education* (1979); *The Development of Moral Reasoning: Practical Approaches* (1980); and *Philosophy of Education: Canadian Perspectives* (1982); edited *So Much for the Mind: A Case Study in Provincial Curriculum Development* (1987); and co-authored *Ethics in School Counseling* (1995) with John M. Schulte.

MARY CRONIN is a professor of Education in the Faculty of Education, University Regina where she teaches graduate and undergraduate classes in Language Arts and Reading. Her principal research is in literacy with a particular focus on family literacy. She is principal author of *Aboriginal PRINTS Family Literacy Program* and is actively involved in literacy work with low-income communities.

CHERYL DOBINSON is a bisexual writer, researcher and advocate. She holds an MA in Sociology from York University where her studies focussed on women's sexuality and queer youth. Her work has been published in *The Journal of Gay, Lesbian and Bisexual Identity*; *The Journal of Homosexuality*; *Herizons*; and *Fireweed*. She is also the creator and editor of the bi women's zine "The Fence." In 2003, Cheryl completed a project on bisexual health and wellness for the Ontario Public Health Association. She volunteers as a mentor and group facilitator for Supporting Our Youth, working with lesbian, gay, bisexual, transsexual and transgendered youth in Toronto. Her other current projects include co-ordinating a peer-based high school anti-homophobia initiative, assisting with research on emotional well-being in queer mothers, and co-editing a book titled *Voices Across the Third Wave: Feminist Anti-Oppression Perspectives*.

GLORIA FILAX is currently an assistant professor in the Master of Arts in Integrated Studies at Athabasca University. Dr. Filax first broke the silence on queer issues in the Faculty of Education at the University of Alberta in the early 1990s with her ground breaking research investigating the lived experiences of sexual minority youth in Alberta. Along with Bobbie Noble and Judy Davidson, Gloria was instrumental in opening an intellectual space on the University of Alberta campus for those interested in queer theory and scholarship resulting in the Queer Academy.

JOHN GUINEY YALLOP is a gay educator who holds a Bachelor of Arts in Philosophy and Religious Studies from Memorial University and a Bachelor of Education from the University of Toronto. He also holds a Master of Education from Brock University. Since 1983 John has taught at the primary, elementary, and middle years levels. John continues to teach elementary school students and he is currently a PhD student in Educational Studies at the University of Western Ontario. His most recent writings include narratives for modules in an online course through the University of Oulu in Finland addressing sexualized and gendered violence in educational environments. John lives in Brampton, Ontario with his partner and their daughter.

MICHAEL W. HAMANN was raised in Weyburn and is now a Regina based ceramic artist. He teaches pottery and particularly likes working with Andy, a young man with Down's Syndrome. Michael and his partner, James McNinch, are founding members of Prairie Pride Chorus, Regina's GLBT choir.

DARRIN HAGEN is an Edmonton based, musician, entertainer, infamous drag queen, and community activist. His one man show, *The Edmonton Queen, not a riverboat story* was a Sterling Award winning play at the 1996 Edmonton Fridge Theatre Festival. In 1997 the script was turned into a best-selling book.

VALERIE J. KORINEK is an Associate Professor in the Department of History at the University of Saskatchewan. She is a specialist in cultural and gender history in post-Confederation Canada and teaches undergraduate and graduate courses on women's and gender history, Canadian popular culture, and the history of sexuality. Her monograph, *Roughing it in the Suburbs: Reading Chatelaine Magazine in the Fifties and Sixties*, was published by the University of Toronto Press. Presently, she is at work on a book entitled "Prairie Fairies: The history of Western Canadian Lesbian and Gay Communities, 1945-1990." A former Torontonian, Valerie has a Ph.D. from the Department of History at the University of Toronto. She now resides in Saskatoon and spends much academic and personal time exploring the historical and contemporary differences between "Central Canada" and "the West."

BRUCE MACDOUGALL is Professor of Law at the University of British Columbia. He teaches and writes inthe areas of law and sexuality and the law of obligations. His book *Queer Judgments: Homosexuality, Expression and the Courts in Canada* was published by University of Toronto Press in 2000.

JAMES MCNINCH is the director of the Teaching Development Centre at the University of Regina where he works to improve the quality of teaching in higher education. He is a former director of the Saskatchewan Urban Native Teacher Education Program. His Ph.D. is in the Sociology of Popular Culture. He is associate editor of the *Journal of Policy and Practice in Education*. He has taught high school English and Social Studies and is an Associate Professor in the Faculty of Education where he teaches Professional Studies courses and a Foundations course in Schooling and Sexual

Identities. His research interests and publications are in the field of gendered and sexualized behaviour in the classroom, formations of teaching identities, and the culture surrounding the use and abuse of student evaluations of teaching.

WES D. PEARCE is currently Associate Professor in the Theatre Department of the University of Regina. He teaches a wide variety of design and general interest courses for the department and has pioneered a number of interdisciplinary courses, most notably with the University of Regina Music Department. He has designed sets and costumes for numerous theatre productions across Western Canada including over a dozen productions at Regina's Globe Theatre. He is a member of the Associated Designers of Canada as well as sitting on the executive board's of The Canadian Lesbian and Gay Studies Association and the Association for Canadian Theatre Research.

DEBRA SHOGAN is a professor in cultural studies of sport and leisure in the Faculty of Physical Education and Recreation at the University of Alberta. Her most recent book, *The Making of High Performance Athletes, Discipline, Diversity, and Ethics* (1999) explores the disciplined cultural production of high performance athletes and the queering of this discipline by hybrid athletes. She has published widely in feminist, queer, education, and sport publications.

CAROL SCHICK is Associate Professor in the Faculty of Education at the University of Regina. She is involved in promoting anti-oppressive education in pre-service teacher education through her work as Canada Research Chair in Social Justice and Aboriginal Education. Her research includes feminist and poststructural theories of subjectivity and discourse analysis, specifically described as anti-racist and anti-homophobic. Dr. Schick uses critical race theories and whiteness studies to live and work through tensions of postcolonial education at all levels of schooling as found on the Canadian Prairies.

S. ANTHONY THOMPSON teaches in the Faculty of Education at the University of Regina where he works in the field of special/inclusive education. He completed his dissertation: *Disabling Sexualities: An Exploratory Multiple Case Study of Self-Identified Gay and Bisexual Men with Developmental Disabilities* at the University of British Columbia. In addition, S.Anthony conducted a research project with James McNinch and Marilyn Totten entitled *Que(e)rying Inclusive Practice: Exploring and Challenging Homophobia in Curricula and Schools* supported by the Stirling McDowell Foundation, and another project entitled *Teaching to School^PLUS: An Action Research Project to Create Extended Communities of Practice for Teacher Educators to Support Students with Autism and Pervasive Developmental Disorders* conducted with Jan Seitz and supported by the Saskatchewan Instructional Research and Development Unit (SIDRU).

MARILYN TOTTEN is a high school teacher and guidance counsellor currently completing her masters in educational psychology at the university of Regina. Marilyn belongs to ACES (Action Community for Education on Sexuality) in Regina and recently participated in an action research project funded by the Stirling McDowell Foundation with James McNinch and Scott Thompson regarding homophobia in secondary schools.

KRISTOPHER WELLS is a Killam doctoral scholar in the Faculty of Education, University of Alberta. Kris's research and teaching is centered on creating safe, caring, and inclusive schools for lesbian, gay, bisexual, and trans-identified students and teachers. Kris has developed numerous educational resources designed to help pre-service and practicing teachers address sex-and-gender differences in their classrooms and schools. Kris is the author of the Alberta Teachers' Association's Sexual Orientation and Gender Identity Educational Website (http://www.teachers.ab.ca/diversity/Sexual_Orientation/Index.htm). Kris's research is supported by the Social Sciences and Humanities Research Council of Canada.

All correspondence pertaining to the issues raised in this publication should be addressed to the editors:

james.mcninch@uregina.ca
mary.cronin@uregina.ca

Acknowledgements

This book would not have been completed without the help and encouragement from many others. The editors of this volume want to thank the following:

Our publisher, the Canadian Plains Research Center (CPRC) and its executive Director, Dr. David Gautier, for supporting us from the collection's initial conception to completion.

Brian Mlazgar, CPRC's Coordinator of Publications without whose encouragement and attention to detail, *"I Could Not Speak My Heart,"* would not have been completed.

David McIntyre for generously lending the title of one his songs from *"Watershed 1"* as the title of this collection.

Michael Hamann for allowing us to use his dramatic clay sculpture of a "torso without a heart" on the cover.

Doug Stewart for his untiring support and editing help.

Our funders for the symposium to launch this volume in October, 2004: the President's Conference Fund, the Humanities Research Institute, and the Faculties of Education and Social Work, all of the University of Regina.